Official American Bar Association Guide to Approved Law Schools

2000 Edition

Prepared by the Section of Legal Education and Admissions to the Bar in cooperation with the Office of the Consultant on Legal Education to the American Bar Association

Editors:

Rick L. Morgan

Kurt Snyder, Esq.

MACMILLAN • USA

Opinions expressed in this publication are not to be deemed to represent the views of the ABA or the Section unless and until adopted pursuant to their Bylaws.

2000 Edition

Macmillan General Reference
A Pearson Education Company
1633 Broadway
New York, NY 10019-6785

Macmillan Publishing books may be purchased for business or sales promotional use. For information please write: Special Markets Department, Macmillan Publishing USA, 1633 Broadway, New York, NY 10019.

Library of Congress Number: 99-60766

ISBN: 0-02-862824-1

Manufactured in the United States of America

10 9 8 7 6 5 4 3 2 1

Table of Contents

Please Read.

The information made available through this publication was collected from questionnaires completed during the Fall 1998 academic semester and submitted by American Bar Association ("ABA") approved law schools to the ABA's Consultant on Legal Education as part of the accreditation process. The completed questionnaires provided to the Consultant's Office are certified by the dean of each law school. Each certification is submitted to the Consultant's Office as an assurance that the information provided accurately reflects prevailing conditions at the law school for which the certification is given. However, the Consultant's Office conducts no audit to verify the accuracy of the information submitted by the respective institutions.

This book contains information concerning law schools that were operating as of October 1, 1998 and were approved by the ABA to confer the first degree in law. The approval status of an individual law school can change. Therefore, if you would like to confirm whether an individual law school is approved by the ABA at a specific time after October 1, you should contact the ABA directly. You can also access this information on the Section of Legal Education and Admissions to the Bar's website: **http://www.abanet.org/legaled.** For updates or corrections to this book, please visit the Section's website.

In addition to the information submitted by the respective law schools, this publication also includes material provided by various organizations with an interest in legal education. The views expressed in this book are not necessarily those of the ABA, the Section of Legal Education and Admissions to the Bar, or the Consultant's Office. Opinions expressed in this publication are not to be deemed to represent the views of the ABA or the Section unless and until adopted pursuant to their bylaws.

Thank You.

James P. White, Consultant on Legal Education to the American Bar Association, and the Consultant's Staff would like to thank the various organizations, law schools, authors, bar examiners, and volunteers without whose assistance this book would not have become a reality. In particular, we owe much gratitude to Dean Steven R. Smith, California Western School of Law and Associate Dean Peter A. Winograd, University of New Mexico School of Law for volunteering their many hours of work. Furthermore, we would like to thank the following people and organizations: Jeffrey E. Hanson, Director, Debt Management Services at the Access Group[SM]; Lindsey Holloway, student at Indiana University Purdue University Indianapolis; Bill Kennish, Micron Systems; Jenny McMahon, Esq., ABA Standing Committee on Pro Bono and Public Services; Erica Moeser, Esq., President of the National Conference of Bar Examiners; Paula A. Patton, Esq., Executive Director of the National Association for Law Placement; Kenneth A. Harshey, student at the Indiana University School of Law - Indianapolis; Philip D. Shelton, Esq., Executive Director and President of the Law School Admission Council; and David R. Stewart, Esq. of Sidley & Austin. And finally, the editors of the book, Rick L. Morgan and Kurt Snyder, Esq., would like to thank their spouses, Terrie Morgan and Debbie Snyder, for supporting them in this endeavor.

To order additional copies of this book,
please call the ABA Service Center at (800) 285-2221.

QUESTIONNAIRE COMMITTEE OF THE SECTION OF LEGAL EDUCATION AND ADMISSIONS TO THE BAR, 1998-99

Officers

STEVEN R. SMITH
Co-Chairperson
Dean and President, California Western School of Law
San Diego, California

PETER A. WINOGRAD
Co-Chairperson
Associate Dean, University of New Mexico School of Law
Albuquerque, New Mexico

Members of the Questionnaire Committee

PAUL CIRAULO
Associate Dean, St. John's University School of Law
Jamaica, New York

JOHN MAKDISI
Dean, Loyola University School of Law -- New Orleans
New Orleans, Louisiana

MARY K. KANE
Dean, University of California Hastings College of the Law
San Francisco, California

JOHN ROBERTS
Professor, DePaul University College of Law
Chicago, Illinois

Office of the Consultant on Legal Education
550 West North Street, Suite 349
Indianapolis, Indiana 46202
http://www.abanet.org/legaled

James P. White, Consultant
J. Richard Hurt, Deputy Consultant
Kurt Snyder, Assistant Consultant
Marilyn S. Shannon, Executive Administrator
Cathy A. Schrage, Executive Assistant
Rick L. Morgan, Data Specialist
Mary D. Barron, Senior Administrative Secretary
Claudia S. Fisher, Administrative Secretary
Kimberly S. Massie, Administrative Secretary
Mary L. Kronoshek, Administrative Secretary
Kelley C. Hackett, Administrative Secretary

Section of Legal Education and Admissions to the Bar
750 North Lake Shore Drive
Chicago, Illinois 60611
http://www.abanet.org/legaled

Carl A. Brambrink, Financial Liaison
Donald Quarles, Project & Meeting Assistant

COUNCIL OF THE SECTION OF LEGAL EDUCATION AND ADMISSIONS TO THE BAR, 1998-99

Officers

RANDALL T. SHEPARD
Chairperson
Chief Justice, Indiana Supreme Court
Indianapolis, Indiana

ROBERT K. WALSH
Chairperson-Elect
Dean, Wake Forest University School of Law
Winston-Salem, North Carolina

DIANE C. YU
Vice-Chairperson
Managing Counsel, Monsanto Company
St. Louis, Missouri

HARRY E. GROVES
Secretary
Professor *Emeritus*, University of North Carolina School of Law
Chapel Hill, North Carolina

BEVERLY TARPLEY
Past Chairperson
Scarborough, Tarpley & Fouts
Abilene, Texas

JOSE GARCIA-PEDROSA
Section Delegate to the House of Delegates
Ruden, McClosky, Smith, Schuster & Russell
Miami, Florida

NORMAN REDLICH
Section Delegate to the House of Delegates
Wachtell, Lipton, Rosen & Katz
New York, New York

Members of the Council

MARTHA W. BARNETT
Holland & Knight
Tallahassee, Florida

DEL BRINKMAN (Public Member)
John S. and James Knight Foundation
Miami, Florida

LAURA N. GASAWAY
Professor, University of North Carolina School of Law
Chapel Hill, North Carolina

HERMA HILL KAY
Dean, University of California School of Law - Berkeley
Berkeley, California

JOHN R. KRAMER
Professor and Former Dean, Tulane University School of Law
New Orleans, Louisiana

ELIZABETH B. LACY
Justice, Virginia Supreme Court
Richmond, Virginia

NANCY NEUMAN (Public Member)
Lewisburg, Pennsylvania

SOLOMON OLIVER, JR.
Judge, United States District Court, Northern District of Ohio
Cleveland, Ohio

GARY H. PALM
Professor, University of Chicago School of Law
Chicago, Illinois

DOROTHY S. RIDINGS (Public Member)
President, Council on Foundations
Washington, D.C.

KENYA J.H. SMITH, *Law Student Division Liaison*
Student, University of Wisconsin School of Law
Madison, Wisconsin

STEVEN R. SMITH
Dean and President, California Western School of Law
San Diego, California

E. THOMAS SULLIVAN
Dean, University of Minnesota School of Law
Minneapolis, Minnesota

DAVID G. TRAGER
Judge, United States District Court, Eastern District of New York
Brooklyn, NY

GERALD W. VANDEWALLE
Chief Justice, North Dakota Supreme Court
Bismarck, North Dakota

Liaisons:

SARA AUSTIN
Young Lawyers Division Liaison
Countess, Gilbert, and Andrews
York, Pennsylvania

WILLIAM R. RAKES
Board of Governors Liaison
Gentry, Locke, Rakes & Moore
Roanoke, Virginia

Introduction

The American Bar Association's Section of Legal Education and Admissions to the Bar, as part of the information process relating to the accreditation of American law schools, proudly presents the 2000 edition of the *Official American Bar Association Guide to Approved Law Schools*. In 1893 the ABA created its first section, the Section of Legal Education and Admissions to the Bar. The mission of the Section is "to be a creative national force in providing leadership and services to those responsible for, and those who benefit from, a sound program of legal education and bar admissions; to provide a fair, effective, and efficient accrediting system for American law schools that promotes quality legal education; and to continue to serve, through its Council, as the nationally recognized accrediting body for American law schools."

Since the adoption of the first law school accreditation Standards by the ABA in 1921, state supreme courts and other bar admitting authorities have encouraged the ABA's accreditation efforts, and the vast majority of states rely upon ABA accreditation to determine whether the law school that an applicant attended meets the educational requirements for the applicant's admission to the bar. Graduation from a law school that is not ABA approved may qualify a person to take the bar examination in the state in which the school is located, but may not qualify the person for the examination in other states.

The purpose of accreditation is not only to review a law school's compliance with the Standards, but also to provide a vehicle for sharing information relating to ongoing developments in legal education. One facet of the accreditation process is a detailed Annual Questionnaire completed by each approved school. The information from the questionnaire is utilized to prepare comparative statistics on all phases of law school operations and is used by the Accreditation Committee and Council in their accreditation review process. Careful analysis of these data serves to identify problems a school may be experiencing that call for a special visit or some other form of assistance. The analysis also identifies trends in legal education. Moreover, Standard 509 of the Standards for Approval of Law Schools, as adopted by the ABA House of Delegates in August 1996, states: "A law school shall publish basic consumer information. The information shall be published in a fair and accurate manner reflective of actual practice." This book satisfies a law school's obligation to provide basic consumer information under Standard 509.

This book is designed to provide consumers with basic information in a simple format that will facilitate comparisons between schools. Please note that applicants should not use this book as the sole source of information regarding application and admission. Rather, this book should supplement other avenues of evaluating respective schools, including making direct contact with admissions officers, professors, students, alumni or prelaw advisors. In addition to statistics on all ABA approved law schools, this book contains information intended to help individuals prepare for the rigors and costs associated with attending law school.

The ABA does not condone, approve, or sanction the use of the data contained herein to rank law schools. In fact, the ABA disapproves of any and all rankings. The official ABA view on rankings is as follows, *"No rating of law schools beyond the simple statement of their accreditation status is attempted or advocated by the American Bar Association. Qualities that make one kind of school good for one student may not be as important to another. The American Bar Association and its Section of Legal Education and Admissions to the Bar have issued disclaimers of any law school rating system. Prospective law students should consider a variety of factors in making their choice among approved schools."*

As of October 1, 1998, a total of 182 institutions are approved by the American Bar Association: 181 confer the first degree in law (the J.D. degree); the other ABA approved school is the U.S. Army Judge Advocate General's School, which offers an officer's resident graduate course, a specialized program beyond the first degree in law. One of the 181 ABA approved law schools (Widener) also has a branch campus. Five of the 181 law schools are provisionally approved: Chapman University School of Law, Texas Wesleyan University School of Law, Thomas Jefferson School of Law, University of the District of Columbia School of Law, and the Western State University College of Law. It is the position of the ABA that students at provisionally approved law schools and persons who graduate while a school is provisionally approved should be entitled to the same recognition accorded under the ABA Standards to students and graduates of fully approved law schools. However, the criteria for eligibility to take the bar examination or to otherwise qualify for bar admission are set by each state, not by the ABA or the Council for the Section of Legal Education and Admissions to the Bar.

This book contains information concerning law schools that were operating as of October 1, 1998 and were approved by the ABA to confer the first degree in law. The approval status of an individual law school can change. Therefore, if you would like to confirm whether an individual law school is approved by the ABA at a specific time after October 1, you should contact the ABA directly. You can also access this information on the Section of Legal Education and Admissions to the Bar's website: **http://www.abanet.org/legaled.** For updates or corrections to this book, please visit the Section's website.

American Bar Association Headquarters
750 North Lake Shore Drive
Chicago, Illinois 60611
(312) 988-5000
http://www.abanet.org

Chapter One

ABA's Role in the Accreditation Process

Law schools approved by the American Bar Association (ABA) provide a legal education which meets a minimum set of standards as promulgated by the ABA. The ABA Standards for Approval of Law Schools (Standards) are designed, developed, and implemented by the judiciary, practicing bar, and the professorate for the purpose of advancing the basic goal of providing a sound program of legal education. As a result, every jurisdiction in the United States has determined that graduates of ABA approved law schools are able to sit for the bar in their respective jurisdictions. Responsibility for administering the ABA's accreditation process has been placed with the Council of the Section of Legal Education and Admissions to the Bar, which is recognized by the U.S. Department of Education as the "nationally recognized accrediting agency for schools of law." The Consultant on Legal Education to the American Bar Association and his staff assist the Council in administering the accreditation process. The role that the ABA plays as the national accrediting body has enabled accreditation to become unified and national in scope, rather than fragmented with the potential for inconsistency, among the fifty states, the District of Columbia, the Commonwealth of Puerto Rico, and other territories.

Since its inception in 1878, the American Bar Association has been concerned with improving the quality of legal education throughout the country. Following numerous studies of the educational programs available in the late 1880s and early 1900s, it was determined that a national process must be developed for ensuring the quality of the education of the prospective lawyer. Consequently, in 1921, the ABA adopted a statement for minimum standards of legal education and instituted a policy of publishing a list of law schools that complied with those standards. As of October 1, 1998, a total of 182 institutions were approved by the American Bar Association: 181 confer the first degree in law (the J.D. degree); the other ABA approved school is the U.S. Army Judge Advocate General's School, which offers an officer's resident graduate course, a specialized program beyond the first degree in law. One of the 181 ABA approved law schools (Widener) also has a branch campus. Five of the 181 law schools are provisionally approved: Chapman University School of Law, Texas Wesleyan University School of Law, Thomas Jefferson School of Law, University of the District of Columbia School of Law, and the Western State University College of Law.

Since the early 1920s, the Standards, which govern the accreditation process, have evolved into a fairly comprehensive set of criteria to ensure that graduates of ABA approved law schools receive a sound education. The Section conducts an ongoing validation process to review the Standards, Interpretations, and Rules of Procedure. As part of this review process, the Standards were revised in August of 1996 and the Rules of Procedure in August of 1997.

Today, the Standards provide that the purpose of the accreditation process is not only to review a law school's compliance with the Standards, but also to provide a vehicle for sharing information relating to ongoing developments in legal education. Moreover, the process requires schools to evaluate themselves, their goals, and to determine if they are fulfilling their mission. Furthermore, the Standards require schools to seek to exceed the minimum requirements of the Standards. Ultimately, it is the hope of the ABA that the Standards will facilitate the ability of American law schools to provide a sound education that enables graduates to practice both competently and effectively.

The Need For a Centralized Accrediting Agency

In order to obtain a license to practice law, almost all law school graduates must apply for bar admission through a state board of bar examiners. Usually this board is an agency of the highest state court in the jurisdiction, but occasionally the board is connected more closely to the state's bar association. The criteria for eligibility to take the bar examination or to otherwise qualify for bar admission are set by each state, not by the Council or ABA. In order to sit for the bar examination, most states require an applicant to hold a degree from a law school that meets acceptable established educational standards. Most states, however, have chosen not to handle the daunting task of accrediting law schools throughout the United States to determine if individuals have satisfied the requisite educational qualifications. Maintaining an accreditation process is both fiscally and administratively demanding. As a result, the vast majority of bar admission authorities in the United States rely upon ABA approval to determine whether their legal education requirement for admission to the bar is satisfied. Education at an ABA approved law school meets the requirements in every jurisdiction in the United States.

The ABA accreditation process obviates any need for an individual state court to evaluate law schools throughout the United States. The Standards, with which all ABA approved schools must comply, are the minimum requirements designed, developed, and implemented for the purpose of advancing the basic goal of providing a sound program of legal education. States can rely on the ABA to administer the accreditation process because they know that the ABA requires schools to be in full compliance with the Standards to remain on the list of approved schools. As a result, the ABA, as the national accrediting body, has enabled accreditation to become unified and national in scope, rather than fragmented with the potential for inconsistency, among the fifty states, the District of Columbia, the Commonwealth of Puerto Rico, and other territories.

Thus, the benefits of a nationally recognized accrediting agency for law schools are many. States are not burdened with maintaining an accreditation process, schools are not burdened with over 50 accrediting agencies, and students can be confident that their particular school satisfies the educational requirements of every state. Above all, the profession and the public are given assurances that lawyers have completed a course of study designed to provide them with a sound education that enables them to practice competently and effectively.

The Accreditation Process

The approval process is initiated when a school files an application, and approval will be granted only after a finding that the school offers a sound program of legal education which complies with the Standards. The accreditation process involves a regularly scheduled on-site evaluation, careful analysis of self-study data, and emphasis on the steady improvement of the quality of the law school's educational program. Provisionally approved law schools are evaluated every year and fully approved schools every seven years, unless a situation arises requiring a more frequent review at an earlier time. Approval is granted or continued based upon the school's compliance with the ABA Standards. Responsibility for administering the ABA's program of accreditation has been placed with the Council of the Section of Legal Education and Admissions to the Bar, which is assisted by the Consultant on Legal Education to the American Bar Association and his staff.

A law school that has completed at least one full year of successful operation may apply for provisional approval. A law school is granted provisional approval when it establishes that it substantially complies with each of the Standards and gives assurances that it will be in full compliance with all of the Standards within three years after receiving provisional approval. A law school that has been provisionally approved for two years may be considered for full approval by the House of Delegates of the ABA upon a finding by the Council that the school fully meets each of the Standards, as interpreted by the Council. The school must insure continued compliance with the letter and the spirit of the Standards, with particular emphasis on a steady improvement in the quality of its educational program.

The ABA Standards provide that students at provisionally approved law schools and those who graduate while a school is provisionally approved are entitled to the same recognition accorded under the Standards to students and graduates of fully approved law schools.

As part of the accreditation process, each school completes a detailed Questionnaire that serves several important functions. The data from the submitted questionnaires from all the ABA approved law schools are utilized to prepare comparative statistics on all phases of law school operation. The information is also used by the Accreditation Committee and the Council in their accreditation review process. The comparative data are also distributed to approved law schools that subscribe to the law school statistical service. Careful analysis of this information may identify problems a school is experiencing that calls for a special visit or some other form of assistance. They also identify trends in legal education.

Site evaluation teams are generally composed of legal educators (including law librarians, professional skills teachers, and other persons with specialized expertise), one or more practicing lawyers or members of the judiciary, and a university administrator. The site visit itself typically takes three to four days and includes fact finding about all aspects of the school's educational program, including the curriculum, academic program, resources, and physical plant. Conferences with faculty members, members of the bench and bar, law school administrators, and students are part of the process. Site evaluation teams visit classes and review law school policies and procedures. Prior to the site visit, team members review a detailed site evaluation questionnaire, several annual questionnaires, and an institutional self-study — all prepared by representatives of the school.

Following the visit, a report of the facts ascertained in the visit is prepared and sent to the Consultant on Legal Education for transmittal to the law school and the Accreditation Committee of the Section. Upon receiving the initial report, a school is provided an opportunity to respond, correct and/or clarify any factual errors.

The Accreditation Committee is composed of members from the academic community, the judiciary, the profession, and the public. The initial decision to continue provisional or full approval of a school is made by the Accreditation Committee. However, when the granting or removal of provisional or full approval is involved, the Accreditation Committee makes a recommendation to the Council.

The Standards

The Standards are founded primarily on the fact that law schools are the gateway to the legal profession. They are minimum requirements designed, developed, and implemented for the purpose of advancing the basic goal of providing a sound program of legal education. Graduates of approved law schools can become members of the bar in all United States jurisdictions, representing all members of the public in important interests. Therefore, an approved law school must provide an opportunity for its students to study in a diverse educational environment and, in order to protect the interests of the public, law students, and the profession,it must provide an educational program that ensures that its graduates:

(1) understand their ethical responsibilities as representatives of clients, officers of the courts, and public citizens responsible for the quality and availability of justice;

(2) receive basic education through a curriculum that develops:

(i) understanding of the theory, philosophy, role, and ramifications of the law and its institutions;

(ii) skills of legal analysis, reasoning, and problem solving; oral and written communication; legal research; and other fundamental skills necessary to participate effectively in the legal profession;

(iii) understanding of the basic principles of public and private law; and

(3) understand the law as a public profession calling for performance of pro bono legal services.

The Standards have evolved since their inception into a comprehensive statement by which legal education programs may be evaluated. The Standards define the minimum criteria for acceptable legal education and training needed to qualify students to enter the practice of law. The Standards, as developed by the Council and adopted by the House of Delegates, are published and available through the ABA Service Center, which can be reached at (800) 285-2221. They are also available *via* the Section's website at **http://www.abanet.org/legaled.**

The Standards have been developed and revised through an ongoing evaluation process conducted through the participation of legal educators, practitioners, and judges. The Standards Review Committee of the Section continually reviews the Standards and makes suggestions for changes to the Council. Amendments are adopted after a process that involves advice from a variety of constituencies, with public hearings and other opportunities for interested parties to comment. In 1994, the Section, through its Standards Review Committee, undertook a total revision of the Standards and Interpretations. The Committee conducted public hearings and sought the views of members of various constituencies interested in legal education. This process culminated in a comprehensive set of revised Standards and Interpretations that was unanimously approved by the House of Delegates in August 1996. In the following year, the House of Delegates approved a set of revised Rules of Procedure.

Continuing Revision of the Standards and Rules of Procedure

In February 1996 the Council of the Section of Legal Education and Admissions to the Bar accepted a report that detailed a schedule for reviewing the Standards, Interpretations, and Rules of Procedure for the purpose of assessing their validity and reliability. That schedule provided for a seven year period of review and commenced with the 1996-97 academic year. During that initial year the Standards Review Committee made a detailed reconsideration of the Rules of Procedure and the Policies of the Council. Its proposals were discussed at public hearings, were reviewed and revised by the Council, and were ultimately adopted by the House of Delegates in August 1997. According to the plan as initially adopted, the Standards and Interpretations were then to be reviewed during the period from 1997 to 2003.

Based upon various comments and suggestions, the Standards Review Committee recommended, and the Council of the Section adopted at its December 1997 meeting, a revised schedule for the completion of the validity and reliability review of the Standards and Interpretations. The revised schedule now provides for the review of the Standards and Interpretations to be performed over a period of three years. In particular, the schedule calls for the review of Chapters 1, 2 and 8 of the Standards and Interpretations during the 1997-1998 academic year, Chapters 3 and 4 during the 1998-1999 academic year, and Chapters 5, 6 and 7 during the 1999-2000 academic year.

In accordance with the 1998-1999 portion of that plan, the Standards Review Committee held public hearings and received comments from members of the practicing bar, the judiciary, bar administrators, and the legal academy regarding Chapters 3 and 4 of the Standards and Interpretations during the past ABA calendar year. Whereas, in 1999-2000 the Standards Review Committee will hold public hearings and solicit comments regarding Chapters 5, 6, and 7. For more information about the public hearings or proposed changes to the Standards, please visit the Section's website at **http://www.abanet.org/legaled.**

Foreign Study

The ABA approves foreign study programs of ABA approved law schools and individual foreign study programs for students who are currently enrolled in ABA approved law schools. The Council has adopted Criteria for Approval of Foreign Summer Programs, Criteria for Approval of Semester Abroad Programs, Criteria for Approval of Cooperative Programs for Foreign Study, and Criteria for Approval of Individual Student Study Abroad for Academic Credit.

Students currently enrolled at an ABA approved law school who desire to receive credit toward their J.D. degree for studies in a foreign program should read carefully the applicable criteria for their course of study. Typically, these programs are only open to students who have successfully completed their first year of study in law school. Students have four options to earn credit for foreign study in an ABA approved foreign program. They may (1) enroll in an ABA approved summer program; (2) enroll in an approved semester abroad program through an ABA approved law school; (3) earn credit from the ABA approved law school they are attending by participating in its ABA approved cooperative program with a foreign institution; and (4) establish their own semester course of study with the approval of the ABA *and* the ABA approved law school they are attending. Additional information on this subject may be obtained on the Section's website at **http://www.abanet.org/legaled.**

Post J.D. Programs and Other Programs in Addition to the J.D.

The Standards require all ABA approved law schools to obtain acquiescence from the Council prior to establishing a degree in addition to its J.D. degree program. A law school may not establish a degree program in addition to its J.D. degree program unless the school is fully approved and the quality of its J.D. degree program meets the requirements of the Standards. The additional degree program may not detract from a law school's ability to maintain a sound J.D. degree program.

Chapter Two

Pro Bono Publico Legal Services

Written by the ABA Standing Committee on Pro Bono and Public Service

When society confers the privilege to practice law on an individual, he or she accepts the responsibility to promote justice and to make justice equally accessible to all people. Thus, all lawyers should aspire to render some legal services without fee or expectation of fee for the good of the public (pro bono publico). Prospective students should be mindful of this responsibility when considering law as a career and when choosing a law school and evaluate whether a particular school will supply the necessary foundation for achieving their goals relating to pro bono. Many schools offer opportunities in career-related public resources, pro bono programming or both. The ABA Standards for Approval of Law Schools require schools to provide opportunities for students to participate in pro bono activities.

The Need for Pro Bono Service

The responsibility to perform pro bono services sets the legal profession apart from other societal roles. Pro bono opportunities offered by law schools teach students that for the economically disadvantaged, the inability to obtain legal services for basic needs, can have dire consequences. Students learn firsthand that for many people, pro bono legal assistance is vital to maintaining minimum levels of basic needs such as government benefits, income, shelter, utilities, child support and physical protection. The special skills they develop during law school can significantly benefit the underprivileged. Both law students and lawyers need to place greater emphasis on their ethical responsibility to provide pro bono services, in order to bridge the rapidly growing gap between the legal needs of those who cannot afford legal services and the resources available to meet those needs.

Pro Bono Opportunities in Law School

Some law schools offer pro bono opportunities, either through established, structured programs or unsupervised, unstructured programs. Typically, the opportunities cover a wide range of areas, such as family law, children's issues, consumer fraud, AIDS-related problems, housing, immigration, taxation, environmental law, criminal defense, elder law and death penalty appeals. Pro bono service is currently mandatory in approximately 20 law schools. These schools may require a specified number of hours of public service required as condition of graduation (e.g. 20-75 hours) or they may require clinical education, including public service components. Law schools with voluntary rather than mandatory pro bono service encourage students to assist lawyers and legal aid organizations by offering incentives, such as awards at graduation or special notations on law school transcripts, or by making pro bono an important part of a school's resources.

Many law schools make financial assistance available to students participating in pro bono activities through summer fellowships and stipends, and others even offer school-year fellowships and stipends. Some law schools offer loan repayment assistance through loan forgiveness, lower interest rates, or postponed payment of law school loans incurred by law graduates entering public interest employment. To be eligible for financial assistance, law students usually must be employed by a non-profit organization, a local, state or federal government, or a law-related public interest organization. Or they must earn income below a specified salary cap. A few schools offer post-graduate awards to law students who accept public interest positions upon graduation, and some outside fellowships are available.

Benefits of Pro Bono Programs in Law School

Pro bono programs help students develop professionalism and an understanding of a lawyer's responsibility to the community. Participation facilitates student involvement in the community and increases the availability of legal services to needy populations. Students also benefit by increasing their knowledge and marketability, gaining practical experience, developing skills, enhancing their reputations and exploring alternative career opportunities.

Other Support for Pro Bono and Public Service in Law School

Other organizations also support pro bono and public service in law school, including Pro Bono Students America (PBSA), the National Association for Public Interest Law (NAPIL) and the Association of American Law Schools (AALS). And of course, the ABA itself strongly supports pro bono and public service.

ABA Model Rules of Professional Conduct Rule 6.1 Voluntary Pro Bono Publico Service

A lawyer should aspire to render at least (50) hours of pro bono publico legal services per year. In fulfilling this responsibility, the lawyer should:

(a) provide a substantial majority of the (50) hours of legal services without fee or expectation of fee to:

- (1) persons of limited means or
- (2) charitable, religious, civic, community, governmental and educational organizations in matters which are designed primarily to address the needs of persons of limited means; and

(b) provide any additional services through:

- (1) delivery of legal services at no fee or substantially reduced fee to individuals, groups or organizations seeking to secure or protect civil rights, civil liberties or public rights, or charitable, religious, civic, community, governmental and educational organizations in matters in furtherance of their organizational purposes, where the payment of standard legal fees would significantly deplete the organization's economic resources or would be otherwise inappropriate;
- (2) delivery of legal services at a substantially reduced fee to persons of limited means; or
- (3) participation in activities for improving the law, the legal system or the legal profession.

In addition, a lawyer should voluntarily contribute financial support to organizations that provide legal services to persons of limited means.

Chapter Three

Prelaw Preparation

Written by The Prelaw Committee of the ABA Section of Legal Education and Admissions to the Bar

(What follows is a statement on preparation for legal education drafted by the Prelaw Committee of the ABA Section of Legal Education and Admissions to the Bar. It addresses the course of study and skills necessary to obtain admission into law school and to be a successful lawyer.)

Students who are successful in law school, and who become accomplished attorneys or use their legal education successfully in other areas of professional life, come to their legal education from widely differing educational and experiential backgrounds. As undergraduate students, some have majored in subjects that are traditionally considered paths to law school, such as history, English, philosophy, political science, economics or business. Other successful law students, however, have focused their undergraduate studies in areas as diverse as art, music theory, computer science, engineering, nursing or education. Many law students enter law school directly from their undergraduate studies and without having had any substantial work experience. Others begin their legal education significantly later in life, and they bring to their law school education the insights and perspectives gained from those life experiences.

Thus the ABA does **not** recommend any particular group of undergraduate majors, or courses that should be taken by those wishing to prepare for legal education; developing such a list is neither possible nor desirable. The law is too multifaceted, and the human mind too adaptable, to permit such a linear approach to preparing for law school or the practice of law. Nonetheless, there are important skills and values, and significant bodies of knowledge, that can be acquired prior to law school and that will provide a sound foundation for a sophisticated legal education. This statement presents the recommendations of the American Bar Association Section of Legal Education and Admissions to the Bar concerning preparation for a good law school experience.

Prospective law students should also consult closely with the prelaw advisor at their undergraduate institution. That individual may be able to assist current students in selecting courses or professors that will particularly assist in developing the skills and knowledge foundation that is emphasized in this statement. Taking difficult courses from demanding instructors is the best generic preparation for legal education. The prelaw advisor can also assist current and former students in choosing law schools to which to apply that are appropriate in light of a prospective student's interests and credentials. Finally, prospective law students should also consult the publications and admissions personnel of the schools to which they are considering applying for any specific recommendations that individual schools may have concerning preparation for law school.

There are numerous skills and values that are essential to success in law school and to competent lawyering. There also is a large body of information that law students, and attorneys, should possess. The three or four years that a student spends in obtaining a quality legal education can and do provide much of the information that a lawyer needs. Good legal education also aids in developing the many skills and values essential to competent lawyering. Sound legal education, however, must build upon and further refine skills, values and knowledge that the student already possesses. Even though a student may well be able to acquire in law school some specific fundamental skills and knowledge that the student's pre-law school experience has not provided, the student who comes to law school lacking a broad range of basic skills and knowledge will face an extremely difficult task.

Skills and Values

The core skills and values that are essential for competent lawyering include analytic and problem-solving skills, critical reading abilities, writing skills, oral communication and listening abilities, general research skills, task organization and management skills, and the values of serving faithfully the interests of others while also promoting justice.[1] Thus, individuals who wish to prepare adequately for legal education, and for a career in law or for other professional service that involves the use of lawyering skills, should seek educational, extracurricular and life experiences that will assist them in developing those attributes.[2] Some brief comments about each of the listed skills and values follow.

Analytic and Problem-Solving Skills

Students should seek courses and other experiences that will engage them in critical thinking about important issues, that will engender in them tolerance for uncertainty, and that will give them experience in structuring and evaluating arguments for and against propositions that are susceptible to reasoned debate. Students also should seek courses and other experiences that require them to apply previously developed principles or theories to new situations, and that demand that they develop solutions to new problems. Good legal education teaches students to "think like a lawyer," but the analytic and problem-solving skills required of attorneys are not fundamentally different from those employed by other professionals. The law school experience will develop and refine those crucial skills, but one must enter law school with a reasonably well developed set of analytic and problem-solving abilities.

Critical Reading Abilities

Preparation for legal education should include substantial experience at close reading and critical analysis of complex textual material, for much of what law students and attorneys do involves careful reading and sophisticated comprehension of judicial opinions, statutes, documents, and other written materials. As with the other skills discussed in this statement, the requisite critical reading abilities may be acquired in a wide range of experiences, including the close reading of complex material in literature, political or economic theory, philosophy, or history. The particular nature of the materials examined is not crucial; what is important is that law school not be the first time that a student has been rigorously engaged in the enterprise of carefully reading and understanding, and critically analyzing, complex written material of substantial length. Potential law students should also be aware that the study and practice of law require the ability to read and assimilate large amounts of material, often in a short period of time.

Writing Skills

Those seeking to prepare for legal education should develop a high degree of skill at written communication. Language is the most important tool of a lawyer, and lawyers must learn to express themselves clearly and concisely. Legal education provides good training in writing, and particularly in the specific techniques and forms of written expression that are common in the law. Fundamental writing skills, however, should be acquired and refined before one enters law school. Those preparing for legal education should seek as many experiences as possible that will require rigorous and analytical writing, including preparing original pieces of substantial length and revising written work in response to constructive criticism.

Oral Communication and Listening Abilities

The ability to speak clearly and persuasively is another skill that is essential to success in law school and the practice of law. Lawyers also must have excellent listening skills if they are to understand their clients and others with whom they must interact daily. As with writing skills, legal education provides excellent opportunities for refining oral communication skills, and particularly for practicing the forms and techniques of oral expression that are most common in the practice of law. Before coming to law school, however, individuals should seek to develop their basic speaking and listening skills, such as by engaging in debate, making formal presentations in class, or speaking before groups in school, the community, or the workplace.

General Research Skills

Although there are many research sources and techniques that are specific to the law, an individual need not have developed any familiarity with these specific skills or materials before entering law school. However, the individual who comes to law school without ever having undertaken a project that requires significant library research and the analysis of large amounts of information obtained from that research will be at a severe disadvantage. Those wishing to prepare for legal education should select courses and seek experiences that will require them to plan a research strategy, to undertake substantial library research, and to analyze, organize and present a reasonably large amount of material. A basic ability to use a personal computer is also increasingly important for law students, both for word processing and for computerized legal research.

Task Organization and Management Skills

The study and practice of law require the ability to organize large amounts of information, to identify objectives, and to create a structure for applying that information in an efficient way in order to achieve desired results. Many law school courses, for example, are graded primarily on the basis of one examination at the end of the course, and many projects in the practice of law require the compilation of large amounts of information from a wide variety of sources, frequently over relatively brief periods of time. Thus those entering law school must be prepared to organize and assimilate large amounts of information in a manner that facilitates the recall and application of that information in an effective and efficient manner. Some of the requisite experience can be obtained through undertaking school projects that require substantial research and writing, or through the preparation of major reports for an employer, a school, or a civic organization.

Serving Others and Promoting Justice

Each member of the legal profession should be dedicated both to the objectives of serving others honestly, competently, and responsibly, and to the goals of improving fairness and the quality of justice in the legal system. Those thinking of entering this profession would be well served by having some significant experience, before coming to law school, in which they devoted substantial effort toward assisting others. Participation in public service projects or similar efforts at achieving objectives established for common purposes can be particularly helpful.

Knowledge

In addition to these fundamental skills and values, there are some basic areas of knowledge that are important to a sophisticated legal education and to the development of a competent attorney. As law becomes more pervasive in our society, an increasingly broad range of knowledge and information from other disciplines become relevant to lawyering and to any full understanding of the legal system. Some of that knowledge, particularly that most directly relevant to particular areas of the law, can be acquired in law school or when necessary for a particular project.

There are, however, generic types of knowledge that one should possess in order to have a full appreciation of the legal system in general, to understand how disputes might be resolved, to understand and apply various legal principles and standards, and to appreciate the context in which a legal problem or dispute arises. Some of the types of knowledge that are most useful, and that would most pervasively affect one's ability to derive the maximum benefit from legal education, include the following:

> A broad understanding of history, particularly American history, and the various factors (social, political,

economic, and cultural) that have influenced the development of the pluralistic society that presently exists in the United States;

A fundamental understanding of political thought and theory, and of the contemporary American political system;

A basic understanding of ethical theory and theories of justice;

A grounding in economics, particularly elementary micro-economic theory, and an understanding of the interaction between economic theory and public policy;

Some basic mathematical and financial skills, such as an understanding of basic precalculus mathematics and an ability to analyze financial data;

A basic understanding of human behavior and social interaction; and

An understanding of diverse cultures within and beyond the United States, of international institutions and issues, and of the increasing interdependence of the nations and communities within our world.

As law has become more woven into the fabric of our society, and as that society is increasingly influenced by disparate national and global forces, a broad knowledge base is essential for success in law school and for competence in the legal profession. Knowledge of specific areas of law can and will be acquired during a good legal education, but students must come to law school with much fundamental knowledge upon which legal education can build. Thus, those considering law school should focus their substantive preparation on acquiring the broad knowledge and perspectives outlined above.

Conclusion

The skills, values and knowledge discussed in this statement may be acquired in a wide variety of ways. One may take undergraduate, graduate, or even high school courses that can assist an individual in acquiring much of the requisite information, skills and perspectives. One may also gain much of this essential background through self-learning (another essential lawyering skill), by reading, in the workplace, or through various other life experiences. Moreover, it is not essential that everyone come to law school having fully developed all of the skills, values and knowledge suggested in this statement. Some of that foundation can be acquired during the initial years of law school. However, one who begins law school having already acquired most of the skills, values and knowledge listed in this statement will have a significant advantage and will be well prepared to benefit fully from a sophisticated and challenging legal education.

---

[1] These core skill and value areas are drawn, in substantial part, from the Statement of Skills and Values contained in the 1992 Report of the American Bar Association Task Force on Law Schools and the Profession, *Legal Education and Professional Development — An Educational Continuum.*

[2] People with various disabilities, such as visual or hearing limitations, have been successful in law school and in the practice of law. Persons with such disabilities, however, should be cognizant of the particular challenges that they may face in law school and in the profession.

Rating of Law Schools

No rating of law schools beyond the simple statement of their accreditation status is attempted or advocated by the American Bar Association. Qualities that make one kind of school good for one student may not be as important to another. The American Bar Association and its Section of Legal Education and Admissions to the Bar have issued disclaimers of any law school rating system. Prospective law students should consider a variety of factors in making their choice among approved schools.

Chapter Four

Admissions Process

Written by Philip D. Shelton, Executive Director and President of the Law School Admission Council (LSAC)

Law school applicants can expect the admission process to be quite competitive. Most law schools receive more than enough applications from highly qualified candidates, many of whom would be perfectly capable of completing a law school education. The dilemma for admission committees is that limited space and resources mandate the denial of admission to many of these candidates.

Your Credentials

No concrete principles exist for predicting who will perform well in school. In order to be fair, schools rely heavily upon selection criteria that bear on expected performance in law school and can be applied objectively to all candidates. Law schools consider a variety of factors in admitting their students, and no single qualification will independently guarantee acceptance or rejection. However, the two factors that usually outweigh the rest are prior academic performance and the Law School Admission Test® score.

Undergraduate performance is generally an important indicator of how someone is likely to perform in law school. Hence, many law schools look closely at college grades when considering individual applications. Course selection also can make a difference in admission evaluations. Applicants who have taken difficult or advanced courses in their undergraduate study often are evaluated in a more favorable light than students who have concentrated on easier or less advanced subjects.

Many law schools consider undergraduate-performance trends along with a student's numerical average. Thus, they may discount a slow start in a student's undergraduate career if he or she performs exceptionally well in the later school years. Similarly, admission committees may see an undergraduate's strong start followed by a mediocre finish as an indication of lesser potential to do well in law school. Candidates are advised to comment on irregular grade trends in the personal statement section of the application.

Choosing Schools

When selecting law schools to which you will apply, the general philosophy is that you should have a threefold plan: dream a little, be realistic, and be safe. Most applicants have no trouble selecting dream schools--those that are almost, but not quite, beyond their grasp--or safe schools--those for which admission is virtually certain. Applicants often have difficulty being realistic about their qualifications and their chances of being accepted at particular law schools.

Unquestionably, the number one strategic error in law school admission is a candidate's failure to evaluate realistically his or her own credentials.

Check your qualifications against the admission profile of the law schools to which you aspire with the information contained in this publication. Most schools publish statistics in this book on the GPA and LSAT 75th percentile and 25th percentile of the most recent entering class. You may use these data to help you determine where you should apply. Apply to those law schools whose student body profiles most closely match your personal profile. Those schools will be as eager to accept you as you are to be admitted.

Other Sources of Information

The school's admission office. This is a good source for general information about your chances for admission. Do not hesitate to request admission counseling. Be sure to obtain current catalogs from each law school you are considering.

Your college or university prelaw advisor. Your prelaw advisor can often provide you with reliable information about which law schools fit your personal profile. He or she may also be able to tell you which law schools have accepted students from your school in the past and provide you with an overview of the admitted students' credentials. However, you should not necessarily narrow your focus to only those law schools where others from your undergraduate school have been admitted.

School representatives and alumni. Take advantage of opportunities to talk with law school representatives and alumni. When you talk with alumni, remember that law schools sometimes change fairly quickly. Try to talk to a recent graduate or to one who is active in alumni affairs and therefore knowledgeable about the school as it is today.

School visits. You can learn a surprising amount about a school from talks with students and faculty members. Many law schools have formal programs in which a currently enrolled student will take you on a tour of the campus and answer your questions. Such a first-hand experience can be quite valuable in assessing how you would fit into the school.

Internet. The internet is a great source of information for learning more about law schools. You can visit the LSAC homepage at **http://www.LSAC.org** or you can visit the homepage for the Section of Legal Education and Admissions to the Bar at **http://www.abanet.org/legaled.**

Admission Mechanics

Many law schools operate what is known as a rolling admission process: the school evaluates applications and informs candidates of admission decisions on a continuous basis over several months, usually beginning in late fall and extending to midsummer for waiting-list admissions.

At such schools, it is especially important for you to apply at the earliest possible date. The earlier you apply, the more places the school will have available. Most schools try to make comparable decisions throughout the admission season, even those that practice rolling admission. Still, it is disadvantageous to be one of the last applicants to complete a file. Furthermore, the more decisions you receive from law schools early in the process, the better able you will be to make your own decisions, such as whether to apply to more law schools or whether to accept a particular school's offer.

The average applicant applies to four or five law schools. You should be sure to place your applications at schools representing a range of admission standards. Even if you have top qualifications, you should apply to at least one safety school where you are almost certain of being admitted. This is your insurance policy. If you apply to a safety school in November and are accepted in January or February, you may be disappointed but not panicked if you are later rejected by your top choices.

If you have strong qualifications, but you do not quite meet the competition of those currently being admitted at a particular law school, you may be placed on a waiting list for possible admission at a later date. The law school will send you a letter notifying you of its decision as early as April or as late as July.

It is up to you whether you wish to wait for a decision from a school that has put you on a waiting list or accept an offer from a school that has already accepted you. Many law schools use seat deposits to help keep track of their new classes. For example, a school may require an initial acceptance fee of $200, which is credited to your first-term tuition if you actually register at the school; if you do not register, the deposit may be forfeited or partially refunded. A school may require a larger deposit around July 1, which is also credited to tuition. If you decline the offer of admission after you have paid your deposit, a portion of the money may be refunded, depending on the date you actually decline the offer. At some schools none of the deposit may be refunded.

Where to Attend

For some people, the choice of which law school to attend is an easy one. The most outstanding students will probably be able to go anywhere, and they will select the schools they perceive to be the most prestigious or which offer a program of particular interest. Others who need to stay in a particular area, perhaps because they have a family or a job they do not want to leave, will choose nearby schools or schools with part-time programs.

However, the majority of applicants will have to weigh a variety of personal and academic factors to come up with a list of potential schools. Then, once they have a list and more than one acceptance letter, they will have to choose a school. Applicants should consider carefully the offerings of each law school before making a decision. The quality of a law school is certainly a major consideration; however, estimations of quality are very subjective. Factors such as the campus' atmosphere, the school's devotion to teaching and learning, and the applicant's enthusiasm for the school are very important. Remember that the law school is going to be your home for three or four years. Adjusting to law school and the general attitudes of a professional school is difficult enough without the additional distraction of culture shock.

All ABA approved law schools and many non-ABA approved law schools require that you take the LSAT. The test consists of five 35-minute sections of multiple-choice questions, in three different areas. A 30-minute unscored writing sample is administered at the end of the test. The LSAT is designed to measure skills considered essential for success in law school: the reading and comprehension of complex texts with accuracy and insight; the organization and management of information and the ability to draw reasonable inferences from it; the ability to reason critically; and the analysis and evaluation of the reasoning and arguments of others.

Most law school applicants familiarize themselves with test mechanics and question types, practice on sample tests, and study the information available on test-taking techniques and strategies. Though it is difficult to say when examinees are sufficiently prepared, very few people achieve their full potential without some preparation.

The most difficult admission decisions are those regarding candidates who are neither so well qualified nor so deficient as to present a clear-cut case for acceptance or rejection. These applicants constitute the majority of the applicant pool at many law schools and are the candidates that most law schools spend the bulk of their time reviewing.

Law school admission committees also consider other criteria: undergraduate course of study; graduate work, if any; college attended; improvement in grades and grade distribution; college curricular and extracurricular activities; ethnic/racial background; individual character and personality; letters of recommendation; personal statement or essay; work experience or other post undergraduate experiences; community activities; motivation to study and reasons for deciding to study law; state of residency; difficulties overcome; pre-college preparation; past accomplishments and leadership; and anything else that would distinguish you as a candidate.

(Adapted, with permission, from The Official Guide to U.S. Law Schools, Law School Admission Council, Inc. [2000].)

See the next page for more information about the LSAT, LSAC, Law Services, or LSDAS -- or contact LSAC directly.

Law School Admission Council
Box 2000
Newtown, PA 18940-0998
(215) 968-1001
http://www.LSAC.org

Law School Admission Council (LSAC)

Adapted, with permission, from* The Official Guide to U.S. Law Schools, *Law School Admission Council, Inc. (2000)

Working with LSAC

LSAC administers the LSAT and serves as a liaison for much of the communication between you and the law schools. You are expected to send your individual law school application **directly to each law school** to which you apply; however, your test scores, transcripts, and other academic information and biographical data are sent to the law schools through the Law School Data Assembly Service (LSDAS).

Comprehensive information about LSAT registration and LSDAS subscription is set forth in complete detail in the *LSAT/LSDAS Registration and Information Book*, published annually. This publication is available at no charge through LSAC or any of 3,500 national distribution sites located on undergraduate campuses (principally prelaw advising offices and career centers) and at law schools. (LSAC operators will provide a list of distribution locations nearest your zip code; call (215) 968-1001.)

You need not subscribe to the LSDAS at the same time you register for the LSAT, but doing so will simplify the process. Application deadlines for the law schools to which you apply dictate when you should subscribe to the LSDAS.

Planning Ahead for Law School Deadlines

Most law schools have a variety of application requirements and deadlines that you must meet to be considered for admission. Many of the deadlines are listed in this book. If you are applying to a number of schools, the various deadlines and requirements can be confusing. It probably will be helpful if you set up a detailed calendar that will remind you of when and what you must do to complete an application.

You will also want to be sure you can make an LSAT score available to a law school before its application deadline. In registering for the LSAT, be sure to give yourself enough time to select a convenient testing location and prepare for the actual test.

Below is a chart listing all the scheduled test administrations, including alternate dates for Saturday Sabbath observers, along with corresponding deadlines.

Basic LSAT Date and Deadline Information (1999-2000)

All scheduled administrations of the LSAT, both for regular test takers and test takers who are Saturday Sabbath observers, are listed below along with corresponding regular registration deadlines. Dates shown represent postmark deadlines for mail registrations and receipt deadlines for telephone and online registration. The basic fee for the LSAT is $88 (published test centers only).

For information on deadlines and fees for late registrations and nonpublished test centers (domestic and foreign), partial refunds, and early score reporting by telephone (TelScore), please refer to the current *LSAT/LSDAS Registration and Information Book*, or call LSAC directly at (215) 968-1001. You can also find complete registration information on their World Wide Web site at **http://www.LSAC.org.**

LSAT Test Dates

Regular	Monday June 14, 1999	Saturday October 2, 1999	Saturday December 4, 1999	Saturday February 12, 2000
Saturday Sabbath Observers		Monday October 4, 1999	Monday December 6, 1999	Monday February 14, 2000
Score Report Mailed (Approx.)	July 13, 1999	November 1, 1999	January 6, 2000	March 10, 2000
Regular Registration Deadlines (Mail, telephone, and online)				
Domestic	May 14, 1999	September 3, 1999	November 5, 1999	January 14, 2000
Foreign	May 7, 1999	August 27, 1999	October 29, 1999	January 7, 2000

Law School Forums Sponsored by LSAC

If you are considering law school, attend a Law School Forum. Free admission. No preregistration. In one place, you can talk with representatives of LSAC-member law schools from across the United States; obtain admission materials, catalogs, and financial aid information; view video programs about the law school admission process, legal education and careers, and minority perspectives on legal education; attend informational sessions on the law school admission process, financing a legal education, and issues of importance to minority applicants; and purchase LSAC publications and LSAT preparation materials. Forum hours are generally from noon to 6 P.M. on Fridays and from 10 A.M. to 4 P.M. on Saturdays, **depending on the city**. To confirm times and learn further details, call (215) 968-1001. Check the LSAC Web site at **http://www.LSAC.org**, or watch for ads in your local media preceding the event. For further information contact: Law School Forums, LSAC, Box 40, Newtown, PA 18940-0040. The locations of the Law School Forums for 1999 are listed below.

Law School Forum Locations & Dates

Atlanta, Georgia
Friday, September 24-Saturday, September 25
Grand Hyatt Atlanta
3300 Peachtree Road
Atlanta, GA

Boston, Massachusetts
Friday, October 29-Saturday, October 30
Marriott Copley Place
110 Huntington Avenue
Boston, MA

Chicago, Illinois
Friday, November 12-Saturday, November 13
Marriott Downtown
540 North Michigan Avenue
Chicago, IL

Houston, Texas
Saturday, October 23
J.W. Marriott
5150 Westheimer Road
Houston, TX

Los Angeles, California
Friday, November 5-Saturday, November 6
Los Angeles Airport Marriott
5855 West Century Blvd.
Los Angeles, CA

New York, New York
Friday, September 17-Saturday, September 18
New York Marriott World Trade Center
Three World Trade Center
New York, NY

Oakland, California (San Francisco Bay Area)
Monday, November 8
Oakland Marriott City Center
1001 Broadway
Oakland, CA

Washington, DC
Saturday, July 18
Omni Shoreham Hotel
2500 Calvert Street, N.W.
Washington, DC

Chapter Five

Finance & Debt Management*

Written by Jeffrey E. Hanson, Director, Debt Management Services, The Access Group, Box 7430, Wilmington, Delaware 19803-0430, (800) 282-1550 http://www.accessgrp.org

Introduction: Your Educational Investment

Your education is an important investment in yourself. Getting an education requires an investment of both time and money. It is the expenditure of your scarce (limited) resources now, in the hope that you will achieve your personal, professional and financial goals in the future. Achieving your goals requires careful planning, however, especially if you will be financing any portion of your educational costs.

How you pay for your education is an important decision that will impact your financial future and the lifestyle you can afford once you graduate. It also will influence how quickly you achieve your financial goals. Unless you currently have enough money in the bank to pay for school, you will need to finance your educational investment. In other words, you will be dependent on others to help you pay for your education. Just as you investigate which schools have the best programs for you, so too must you gather information about how best to finance your degree. Deciding how you finance your degree should involve you, your family and, unless your family can finance the full cost of your education, the school you want to attend.

It is important to become well-informed about your financing options as soon as possible, and to act responsibly in the financing of your education. You can thrive in the face of your educational debt if you can accomplish the following two objectives:

- understand the financial aid process and meet all application deadlines, and
- form good financial habits

This chapter is designed to assist you in learning how to achieve these objectives.

Understanding the Financial Aid Process: Questions To Ask Before Borrowing

You should get answers to the following 13 questions as you plan the financing of your education. Some of these questions are general and apply to any school you might attend; others are more specific to the programs, policies, and procedures of each school you're considering. You should evaluate these issues as you explore your financial options, regardless of where you plan to attend school.

The financial aid staff at the schools you're considering probably are your most important resource to use in answering these questions. You also can utilize publications from funding groups, such as federal and state governments, lenders, scholarship-granting organizations, and financial aid guidebooks that are available from your local bookstore. Another useful and timely source of answers to these questions is the Internet. Many schools have their own Web sites that often include information about financial aid. Contact any school you're considering, to see if it has a Web site. Many lenders and other funding organizations also have Web sites. For example, the Web site for the Access Group, Inc., is **http://www.accessgroup.org**. Finally, there are several Web sites that have been established by government agencies and other organizations to assist students with the financing of their education such as the ABA at **http://www.abanet.org/legaled**. The following two sites may be a good place to start your search: **http://www.finaid.org** and **http://www.ed.gov.**

<u>**Question #1**</u>. *What should I be doing now to prepare for meeting the cost of my education?*

There are five steps you can take now to prepare for the cost of law school. They involve conversations with your family and with the financial aid staff at the schools you are considering attending, as well as specific actions you should take.

First, determine what resources you will be able to contribute toward your educational expenses. Your resources may include contributions from your family (and spouse, if married), the funds you will have saved by the time you enroll, and any scholarship funds you are awarded by private foundations, associations, or other organizations. This will require that you discuss the cost of law school with your family (and spouse) and determine the extent to which they plan to assist you financially. You also will need to save as much money as you can before entering law school, and explore opportunities for scholarships/fellowships from private foundations, organizations, and associations, as well as federal, state, and local government agencies.

Second, contact the law schools you are interested in attending to find out the expected cost of attendance so that you can determine if you will have sufficient funds to pay for your education or if you will need to seek additional assistance through the financial aid program offered by the school(s). If you think you will need additional financial assistance from the school, you'll need to determine what assistance is offered, the required application procedures, and any applicable deadlines. You should find out how to obtain the necessary application forms and take the necessary steps to get them once they are available.

Third, make certain you don't have credit problems. You should contact one of the three national credit reporting agencies—Equifax, Experian (formerly TRW), or Trans Union Corporation—to obtain a copy of your credit report. If you think you may have credit problems, you should review your credit history with the financial aid staff at the law school you want to attend before you apply for loans. You can obtain a copy of your credit report by following the procedure described below in the section on "Good Financial Habits" (see Habit #7).

Fourth, be careful how you use your credit cards. Consumer credit is not an investment; it is simply a means of improving your standard of living on a temporary basis. Credit card debt is bad debt. Get your credit card and other consumer debts paid off as quickly as possible. You will not be able to borrow additional student loan funds to pay your credit card bills.

Fifth, plan now and prepare yourself for the financial future you want when you complete law school by getting into the good financial habits described below.

Question #2. *What are the eligibility requirements in order to get financing for my degree?*

You must satisfy all of the following criteria to participate in the federal student financial assistance programs.

- You must be enrolled at least half-time at an eligible institution pursuing a degree or certificate.
- You must be a U.S. citizen or eligible noncitizen (e.g., permanent resident).
- You cannot currently be in default on any prior federal student loans you may have borrowed nor owe a refund on a federal grant program.
- You cannot have been charged with a drug offense.

Failure to meet any of these criteria will make you ineligible to receive funding from any of the federal assistance programs. It is very important that you contact the financial aid office at the school(s) you are considering if you think you do not meet all the criteria listed above. There may be steps that can be taken to correct the problem. *If you are an international student, please note that there currently are no federal financial aid programs available to you, but there may be private loan programs. Contact the financial aid staff at the school you want to attend for more information.*

Privately guaranteed educational loan programs not only require that you satisfy the above federal criteria, they also require that you do not have credit problems. Lenders offering privately guaranteed student loans will check your credit history before approving a loan. The credit criteria that are used vary from one lender to the next. Most look primarily at your prior pattern of payment on your credit obligations. Consequently, it is a good idea that you obtain current copies of your credit report from each of the three national credit reporting agencies if you think you'll need to apply for a privately guaranteed student loan. Contact the financial aid office at the schools you are considering, once you have copies of your credit reports, if you think you have problems that might prevent you from being able to borrow a privately guaranteed loan if one will be needed. The financial aid staff may be able to offer assistance, or guide you to an agency like the Consumer Credit Counseling Service (CCCS) to help you repair your credit.

Question #3. *What financing options/programs are available to me at the school(s) I am considering attending?*

Important Disclosure: As of the printing of this material, information regarding all aid programs is correct. Please note, however, that the specific details of these programs may change at any time due to changes in government legislation/regulation.

There are three general financing options available if you cannot pay the full cost of law school from your own resources and those of your family: (1) grants/scholarships, (2) loans, and (3) work study. The sources of these funding options include federal and state governments; the school you attend; banks and other lending organizations; and private foundations, civic organizations, and other associations. Note that loans are the most common and abundant source of funding available to law students.

Grants/Scholarships

Grants and scholarships are funds you do not have to repay. Availability of these funds is limited. In some instances, a service commitment is required in order to receive funding. There are three principal sources for grant and scholarship funding: (1) government, (2) institutional, and (3) private/civic sources.

Grant and scholarship assistance from government sources (federal/state) is dependent on the availability of funding and, in the case of state programs, the state in which you reside/attend law school. Not all states offer grant/scholarship assistance to law students. You should contact the financial aid office at the school you plan to attend to inquire about the availability of federal and state grant assistance. Be advised that some of these programs require a service commitment in order to receive the funding. Service typically requires that you practice law (oftentimes in the public interest) in a particular location for a specific period of time (usually one year of service for each year of funding support) immediately following graduation and passage of the Bar.

The institution you attend may award scholarship and/or grant assistance to students who meet their eligibility requirements. These scholarships/grants typically are funded from endowments and gifts given to the school as well as from general institutional revenues. Recipients usually have to meet specific requirements, such as a strong undergraduate academic record (referred to as merit-based aid), demonstrated financial need (referred to as need-based aid), special career objectives, or a combination of these and/or other factors. In some cases, all students are considered for funding. In other cases, you may need to submit a specific application by a particular date. You should contact the school(s) you are considering, to find out if they have any special application procedures and/or deadlines you need to follow in order to be considered for an institutional grant/scholarship.

There are a number of civic organizations and other groups that provide scholarship funding to qualified law students. Many law schools have compiled a listing of programs that have funded students attending their institutions. You should contact the financial aid office at the school(s) you are considering to obtain information about these private sources of grant/scholarship funding. You also can check the Internet and local bookstores for other sources of information on scholarships and grants.

Loan Programs

There are four general types of education loans: (1) federally guaranteed loans, (2) state-sponsored loans, (3) institutionally funded loans, and (4) privately guaranteed supplemental loans offered by private lenders. All law schools participate in the federal student loan programs sponsored by the U.S. Department of Education. U.S. citizens and eligible noncitizens pursuing a degree or certificate at least half-time can participate in these programs, provided they are neither currently in default nor owe a refund to any federal student aid program from which they previously received assistance. These federally guaranteed programs are summarized below.

Federal Loan Programs

Federal Stafford Loan (Subsidized/Unsubsidized)

Federal Stafford Loans are low-cost education loans that are guaranteed by the federal government. They are available through the William D. Ford Federal Direct Loan (FDL) Program and the Federal Family Education Loan (FFEL) Program. The terms and conditions for the FDL and FFEL programs are similar. The source of loan funds, portions of the application process, and the repayment plans available to borrowers are the major differences between the two programs. The FDL Program is funded directly by the U.S. Government whereas the FFEL Program is funded by, and the loans borrowed from, commercial lenders, such as banks, credit unions, and organizations, such as the Access Group, Inc. The school you attend determines whether you borrow from the FDL or FFEL programs. If your school does not participate in the FDL Program, you will borrow your Federal Stafford Loans through the FFEL Program. The financial aid staff at the school you attend will explain the application process and differences in repayment options.

The Federal Stafford Loan is available in two forms: subsidized and unsubsidized. Both forms are low-cost loans guaranteed by the federal government. In other words, the federal government agrees to repay your lender if you fail to do so. The subsidized Federal Stafford Loan is a need-based loan in which interest is paid by the federal government (i.e., subsidized) while you are in-school, during the grace period, and during approved deferment periods. The unsubsidized Federal Stafford Loan is not based on financial need. Interest on the unsubsidized Federal Stafford Loan is NOT paid by the federal government, and therefore begins accruing as soon as the funds are disbursed. You can pay the interest when billed or allow it to accrue and capitalize (i.e., be added to the principal) while in school, during the grace period, and during approved deferment and forbearance periods. You can use the unsubsidized Federal Stafford Loan to meet financial need not covered by other sources and/or to replace an expected family contribution.

The maximum subsidized Federal Stafford Loan per year currently is $8,500 or the amount of your unmet financial need, whichever is less. The current combined annual maximum for subsidized and unsubsidized Federal Stafford Loans is $18,500, or your cost of attendance minus any other financial aid, whichever is less. Therefore, the maximum unsubsidized Federal Stafford Loan you can borrow in a given year is the difference between the combined annual maximum (typically $18,500) and your subsidized Federal Stafford Loan eligibility. The cumulative maximum is $138,500, of which no more than $65,500 can be subsidized funds. The interest rate for all Federal Stafford Loans (both subsidized and unsubsidized) is variable with a cap of 8.25%. The rate is adjusted annually on July 1.

You are charged two fees when borrowing a Federal Stafford Loan: (1) an origination fee, and (2) a guarantee fee. The origination fee is paid to the federal government and currently is three percent (3%) of the total amount borrowed. The guarantee fee is paid to the guarantee agency if borrowing from the FFEL Program and to the federal government if borrowing from the FDL Program. The amount of this fee varies depending upon the guarantor/lender, but cannot exceed one percent (1%) of the total amount borrowed. Both fees are deducted from each disbursement of your loan.

Repayment of principal is deferred on both the subsidized and unsubsidized Federal Stafford Loans so long as you are enrolled at least half time as a student pursuing a degree or certificate. Repayment of principal (and interest on the subsidized loan) begins six months after you cease to be enrolled at least half time (remember that interest on unsubsidized loans begins accruing as soon as funds are disbursed by your lender). This six-month period is called the "grace period." You should receive repayment information from your lender prior to or during the grace period. The repayment period extends from 5 to 10 years. There is no penalty for prepayment.

A deferment or forbearance may be available under certain conditions once repayment begins if you need to postpone repayment of your loan(s). A deferment is a temporary suspension of payment on your loan. Interest is subsidized during a deferment on subsidized Federal Stafford Loans. It is not subsidized on unsubsidized loans during a deferment and therefore continues to accrue. A forbearance is a temporary suspension or reduction of payment of your loan that is granted by your lender due to economic hardship. Interest continues to accrue during a forbearance regardless of loan type. You must negotiate with your lender on the type and amount of forbearance that will be granted to you. See the Federal Stafford Loan promissory note for more information on deferments and forbearance.

Alternative repayment options (including graduated repayment, income contingent repayment and income sensitive repayment) and refinancing of your loans through the federal loan consolidation program are also available. These programs reduce the amount that must be paid each month, at least temporarily, and typically are used when the borrower anticipates that he or she will be unable to pay the minimum loan amount required under the fixed monthly payment plan. Using one of these options, however, will increase the total cost of the loan because of increased finance charges accruing on the loan principal. Thus, you should analyze your situation carefully before selecting an alternative repayment plan or consolidating your loans. More information on each of these programs is available from your financial aid office and/or your lender/servicer.

Federal Perkins Loan

The Federal Perkins Loan is both a federally guaranteed and federally subsidized loan program administered by the school you are attending. Funds for this program are provided by the federal government with your school acting as the lender. The Federal Perkins Loan Program is designed to provide need-based, low-interest financial assistance to students demonstrating high financial need. The exact loan amount offered to a student depends upon the availability of funds and the amount of his or her financial need, but cannot exceed $5,000 per year. The cumulative maximum for this program is $30,000 and includes both undergraduate and graduate borrowing. Principal and interest are deferred during the in-school years. Repayment begins following a grace period of either six or nine months depending on when you received your first Federal Perkins Loan (for most students it will be nine months). The Federal Perkins Loan interest rate currently is fixed at 5.0%.

The repayment period can last up to 10 years. Deferments and forbearances are available under certain situations once you enter repayment (refer to the Federal Perkins Loan promissory note for details) if you need to postpone repayment of your loan(s). Federal Perkins Loans also can be refinanced in the Federal Loan Consolidation Program with Federal Stafford Loans you may have borrowed. It is best not to consolidate Federal Perkins Loans if you can avoid it, because the interest rate will increase significantly when they are refinanced.

State-Funded Loan Programs

Some states offer education loan programs. Eligibility for these loans may or may not be based on financial need. Information about the availability, terms, and application procedures for these loans can be obtained from the financial aid office at the school(s) you are considering attending.

Institutional Loans

Many law schools have limited institutional loan funds available for qualified students. These loans may be used in limited amounts to cover financial need not met by federal loans. In other cases, they may be used as "loans of last resort" to assist those students who have difficulty obtaining assistance from other sources. Whatever the case, it is usually up to the financial aid staff to determine who is eligible to apply for these loans. Contact the financial aid staff at the school(s) you're considering, if you are interested in obtaining information about the availability and likelihood of being awarded an institutional loan.

Privately Guaranteed Supplemental Loans

There are a number of privately guaranteed student loan programs (e.g., Law Access® Loan Program, LawLoans, GradExcel, Professional Education Plan (PEP), GradAssist Loan). These loan programs are not based on financial need and tend to have higher fees/interest rates. They are intended to supplement the other financial assistance you are receiving. The financial aid staff at the school(s) you're considering attending can provide more detailed information about the various privately guaranteed supplemental loan programs available to law students. It is important to remember that you should borrow the minimum amount necessary, and that you cannot receive financial assistance in excess of the cost of attendance determined by the financial aid office.

Federal Work-Study

The Federal Work-Study (FWS) Program provides employment for law students who have demonstrated financial need. It allows you to earn money to help pay for your educational expenses. Community service work and work related to your course of study are encouraged. Eligibility for FWS funding depends on the availability of work-study funds at the school you are attending, the policies of the school, when you apply for financial assistance, and your level of financial need. These funds may be paid on an hourly basis or you may receive a salary from the institution you are attending. You can earn only up to the amount of your total FWS award. Be advised that not all law schools have work-study funding. Contact the financial aid office at the school(s) you are considering to inquire about the availability of this program.

Question #4. *What is the purpose of financial aid, and what do I need to know about the process?*

Financial aid programs are designed to assist you and your family in financing your educational investment. You are permitted by current federal regulations to receive assistance up to the estimated cost of attendance for your degree program, as established by the financial aid office at the school you attend. It is a very bureaucratic process. You should get answers to the following ten (10) questions about the financial aid program at each school you are interested in attending before you make any final decisions about how to finance your education. The financial aid staff at each school you are considering should be able to provide the answers you need.

i. What is the philosophy of financial aid at the institution?
ii. What grant and loan resources are available to meet my financial need?
iii. Can I meet my full financial need using those resources?
iv. Will my parents be expected to provide financial informa tion and/or contribute to my educational expenses? (In other words, will I be considered financially dependent or independent in terms of receiving institutional funding?) What options will I have if my parents refuse?
v. What is the financial aid application process?
vi. How can I obtain the needed application(s)?
vii. What are the application deadlines?
viii. What is done with all the information I provide?
ix. Will my credit history affect my ability to get financial assistance?
x. What should I know about the loans I am offered?

Question #5. *How do I apply for financial assistance, and what application(s) is(are) needed?*

Applying for financial assistance is a cooperative effort including you, your family, the financial aid staff at the school you're attending, and the lender(s) from which you borrow. Financing your education with financial aid involves multiple steps and requires that you submit various application documents. As stated previously, these steps are bureaucratic and can be very frustrating (particularly if you do not complete all required application materials correctly and/or do not adhere to established deadlines).

The specific application procedures and deadlines can vary from one school to another based on the availability of institutional resources and the financial aid operation at the school you attend. The basic procedure, however, typically includes the following initial six (6) steps.

i. Contact the school(s) you are considering attending to obtain information about their application procedures, deadlines, and any application materials they supply directly to you. This should be done around the time you are applying for admission.

ii. Obtain and complete the financial aid applications that are required by the school(s) you are considering.

You will need to complete the Free Application for Federal Student Aid (FAFSA) if you are applying for federal student aid, regardless of which school you attend.

You can apply by completing and mailing the paper version of the FAFSA, by applying electronically (through your school), or by using the U.S. Department of Education's FAFSA on the Web that is available at *www.ed.gov*. You can obtain a FAFSA from any financial aid office or from the Federal Student Aid Information Center at P.O. Box 84, Washington, D.C. 20044. You also can call the Federal Student Aid Information Center at 1-800-4-FED-AID (433-3243). *Note that if you applied for federal student aid in 1998-99, you may receive a Renewal Free Application for Federal Student Aid (Renewal FAFSA) for 1999-2000. The Renewal FAFSA can be used in place of the options described above.*

Complete any supplemental application materials that are required by the school(s) you're considering (note that not all schools require supplemental application materials).

The supplemental application typically requests information not contained on the FAFSA/Renewal FAFSA and is used for the purpose of awarding institutional funds. Some schools use fee-based supplemental applications. Others use an institutional application and/or a combination of both a fee-based application and an institutional form. Whatever procedure is used, it is important to contact the financial aid office at the schools you are considering to obtain any required necessary supplemental application material(s)/instructions.

Submit a copy of your most recent federal income tax return, if instructed to do so on your SAR, and/or if required by the school(s) you are considering attending.

It is very important to complete your federal income tax return as soon as possible for the calendar year preceding the academic year for which you're applying for financial aid so that you'll have the necessary information to complete the FAFSA/Renewal FAFSA and other application materials.

iii. Review the Student Aid Report (SAR) that you receive from the federal processor once your FAFSA/Renewal FAFSA has been processed to make certain the data you provided on your application has been entered correctly.

Follow any instructions contained on the SAR. The financial aid office at the school(s) you listed on your FAFSA/Renewal FAFSA also should receive the information electronically. They will use it to determine your eligibility for federal student aid funding.

Your eligibility for assistance will be determined by the financial aid staff once all the application information has been received and reviewed. Then you will be sent a financial aid award notice/packet informing you of the assistance you are eligible to receive. It may take a number of weeks from the time you submit your application documents until you receive a financial aid award announcement/packet. Processing of your application materials (and those of all other students) can be a very time-consuming process.

iv. Respond to your financial aid award announcement and return it to the financial aid office as instructed, once you receive it.

Typically you must indicate which portions of the award you accept and which portions you reject. Then you must return a copy of your award announcement to the financial aid office. Be certain to follow any deadline dates.

Be aware that the financial aid staff has offered the most affordable financial aid package they can, based upon your financial situation, available resources, federal/state regulations, and institutional policies. Contact the financial aid office if you feel you need additional assistance.

v. Apply for any loans you need to borrow that you have been offered by the financial aid office.

You will need to complete and submit the appropriate application(s), as instructed, for any funds you wish to borrow.

In some cases, you may be able to apply for your loan(s) electronically. You should be provided with specific instructions by the financial aid office on how to complete the loan application process. Adhere to any deadline dates and borrow the minimum amount you need. Remember, every dollar you borrow must be repaid with interest. This will have an impact on your financial future.

vi. Sign the promissory note(s) for your loan(s) if not part of the original loan application, and submit them to your lender(s).

The promissory note(s) for your loan(s) may not be part of the loan application. If so, you will need to sign the promissory note(s) once the loan(s) has(have) been processed and approved. Loan funds cannot be disbursed to you until you have signed the promissory note for the loan and returned it to your lender. The promissory note is the legally binding contract between you and your lender.

Important reminders in applying for assistance:

- Complete all required forms—neatly!
- Be consistent when completing all forms.
- Answer all questions completely.
- Apply as early as possible.
- Adhere to all published deadlines.
- Keep copies of all forms.

Question #6. *When should I apply for financial assistance, and what are the application deadlines?*

Follow all deadlines established by the school(s) you're considering. Each school can provide specific deadline information. You should apply as early as possible once application materials are available. Be advised, however, that you cannot submit the federal application, i.e., FAFSA/Renewal FAFSA, before January 1 of the year in which the academic year of your enrollment will begin.

Question #7. *Will my parents be expected to provide any of their financial information and/or contribute to the cost of my education?*

The basic philosophy of the system is to provide you with an opportunity to attend the school of your choice without regard to your financial circumstances. Some schools, however, may not have the means to meet your full financial need. Many schools also have criteria that require your parents to contribute to the extent possible before institutional resources will be offered to meet a portion of your financial need. You will want to ask the financial aid staff at each school you are considering attending about the school's policy on financial independence.

Although you will be considered by the federal government to be financially independent for the purposes of receiving federal funds, you may be considered financially dependent on your parents by the law school you are attending for the purposes of receiving institutional funds, such as grants and scholarships. The institutional policy regarding financial independence typically is more stringent than the corresponding federal regulations. It may be based on one or more factors, including your age, your prior work experience, and your status on your parents' tax returns. The institutional policy is needed because there generally are insufficient school resources to fund all students adequately with grant and/or scholarship assistance. Thus, institutional dependency policies are designed to guarantee that the distribution of these scarce institutional dollars is fair and equitable.

Question #8. *What is done with the information I (and my parents) provide?*

Your "family contribution" is determined by the financial aid staff based on the financial information provided by you and your family using guidelines established by Congress and the law school. Your "financial need" is calculated as the difference between the estimated "cost of attendance" for your degree program and the "family contribution" determined by the financial aid staff. It is this "financial need" figure that will be used by the financial aid staff to determine what assistance you are eligible to receive.

Note that your financial aid information is considered confidential and will be treated as such by the financial aid staff and your lender(s). Only those individuals responsible for processing your application materials will have access to the documents you and your family submit.

Question #9. *What should I know about the assistance (e.g., grants, loans, work-study) I am offered?*

Grants/Scholarships

You should know the answers to the following questions about any grant or scholarship award you receive.

Will it be renewed automatically in subsequent years? If so, will it be renewed for the same amount or will the amount be adjusted?

If it will not be renewed automatically, can you reapply for another grant or scholarship?

Will your academic performance in law school affect the amount of your grant or scholarship award in subsequent years?

Will you be required to provide any service in order to receive the grant or scholarship? If so, what type of service will be required and when will you need to provide it?

Loans

You should know the following information about each of the loans you are offered before you actually apply for the funds.

Loan amount offered and maximum loan eligibility

You should get answers to the following questions about the loan amount you've been offered and your maximum annual and cumulative loan eligibility in the program. Have you been offered the maximum amount from the loan program or can you apply for more funds from the program if you need additional assistance later in the academic year? In borrowing the offered amount, how close will you be to your cumulative maximum in this loan program if such a maximum exists? Will you exhaust your loan eligibility in this program before you complete your degree?

Co-signer requirements, if any

Although no federal loan programs currently require you to have a co-signer or co-borrower; some state, institutional, and privately guaranteed loan programs do require that you obtain a creditworthy co-signer in order to apply for a loan. In other cases, applying with a co-signer can reduce the cost of the loan. Whatever the situation, you should determine what co-signer requirements exist, if any, and the credit approval criteria for the loan. If you do not have someone who is willing or able to serve as your co-signer, you will need to find an alternative to the loan that is offered.

Interest rate

The interest rate is the percentage rate you are charged to borrow the loan. You should know when interest begins accruing and at what rate. You also should know whether the loan has a fixed or variable rate. If the rate is variable, you should know how it is calculated, how frequently it is adjusted, if it has a cap (in other words, an upper limit) and when the rate changes.

Impact of your credit history on loan approval

You should obtain a copy of your credit report using the steps given below in Habit #7 so that you can check on the current status of your credit. If you have credit problems, you may have trouble obtaining a portion of the loan financing you need to attend school. The financial aid staff at the school(s) you are considering may be able to counsel you about alternative financing options if you have credit problems and/or on methods to repair your credit. Having a copy of your credit report will help them advise you.

Availability of alternatives

Are there alternative loan options if you cannot meet the application and/or approval requirements of the loans you've been offered? The financial aid staff at the school(s) you are considering should be able to advise you about any financing alternatives.

Repayment terms/grace period

It is very important that you understand the terms and conditions of each loan you borrow. This will allow you to make well-informed borrowing decisions. The loan application and promissory note should provide the information you need.

Deferment and forbearance options

You may need to temporarily postpone repayment of your loans once you graduate. Therefore, it is important to know the deferment and forbearance options for each loan you borrow. This information should be contained in the application materials and the promissory note.

Reputation of lender

There are a number of questions you should answer regarding the reputation of your lender before you make a final decision on which one you'll use. What is the reputation of the lender offering the loan you need to borrow? How easy is it to solve problems with the lender? How accessible is customer assistance? Does the lender provide a toll-free number and/or a Web site you can use to get help? Does the lender specialize in making loans to law students? Does the lender offer any repayment incentives that can reduce the cost of your loan(s) once you begin repaying the borrowed funds? The financial aid staff at the school(s) you are considering may be able to help you answer these questions. You should also contact each potential lender for answers to these questions. Another source of information may be currently enrolled students who are borrowing from the lender in question.

Question #10. *What can I do to reduce the amount I have to borrow, yet still attend the school of my choice?*

You should consider applying for scholarships and grants offered by private organizations, foundations, and associations. You also should discuss the financing of your education with your family to determine the extent to which they can and will help you finance your education. It also is important to evaluate the tradeoffs associated with attending school at night so that you can work during the day versus attending school full time during the day. Attending school part time at night will allow you to borrow less money, but it will take longer to complete your training. Finally, you should adopt the financial habits described below so that you can manage your personal finances responsibly and minimize your need to borrow funds.

Question #11. *What can I do once I arrive on campus to minimize what I borrow?*

Try to live *below* your means while in school. Be thrifty! The less you spend now, the more money you'll have for expenses once you graduate. Some suggestions on how to live *below* your means are given below.

- Avoid buying for "convenience."
- Live with a roommate.
- Bring your lunch to school.
- When eating out, do it cheaply.
- Dress for less—shop at secondhand and discount stores.
- Have "free fun."
- Go to matinees or rent videos.
- Buy used books.
- Don't buy a new car; keep the car you have or buy a used car if you can't use public transit.
- When going out for drinks, go to "Happy Hours."
- Refrain from using a cell phone or pager.
- Buy with cash not credit.
- Pay the full amount due on your credit card bill(s).
- Don't charge more on your credit card(s) than you know you can repay when the bill arrives.

Question #12. *What options will I have to work while obtaining my degree?*

Current ABA guidelines strongly discourage first-year law students from working during the academic year. Working in the second and third year of law school, however, is not discouraged and, in fact, is an important strategy for gaining a job once you graduate. Working five to twenty hours a week during the school year can reduce the amount you need to borrow. Five hours per week should net you at least $1,000 for the year, which means you can reduce your borrowing by $1,000. Many schools offer part-time employment that also may provide an opportunity for you to study or get valuable professional experience. Contact the Career Planning office at the school you attend for assistance in getting part-time employment.

Question #13. *What impact will the loan(s) I borrow have on me after I complete my education?*

Your education loans must be repaid. This will reduce your disposable income during repayment. Remember, you are borrowing funds now that you will repay with your future income once you graduate.

What happens if I don't repay my loan(s)?

Failure to repay your loans will prevent you from achieving your financial goals, at least in the near term. When you fail to repay your loan(s) according to the repayment schedule, your lender will follow the collection procedures required by the government/ guarantor. If your account is not brought current, your delinquency will be reported to all national credit bureaus. Defaulted loans will affect your credit rating and jeopardize your future ability to borrow funds for any purpose. You also will be liable for any collection expenses that are incurred.

How can I effectively manage my loan portfolio?

Make a file folder for all your financial records. You should keep all loan documents in one place for easy reference and maintain a cumulative record of each loan. You also can monitor your loans by using the Loan Ledger in the *Access Advisor* software that can be downloaded at no cost from the Access Group, Inc. Web site: **http://www.accessgroup.org**. No matter what record keeping system you use, remember to keep your lenders informed of any changes in your name, address and/or registration status.

What should I do if I experience difficulty repaying my loan(s)?

The most important action to take is to contact your lender quickly before you become delinquent on your loan account and/ or go into default. Your lender may be able to offer you a deferment or forbearance under certain conditions of economic hardship.

Is there a way to refinance my loan(s) if my monthly payments are not manageable?

Yes, you should contact your lender about refinancing your federal loan portfolio. You can refinance your federal loans by paying them off with a consolidation loan. There are two consolidation programs: the Federal Consolidation Loan offered by FFEL program lenders and the Federal Direct Consolidation Loan offered by the FDL program. In both cases, a consolidation loan will stretch your payments over a longer period of time and reduce your monthly installments into one monthly repayment. The total amount you will repay increases, however, because of the extended repayment period and the potentially higher interest rate.

Refinancing of supplemental loans borrowed from private lenders also may be available. Information on consolidating these loans should be available from the lenders and usually is described in the application materials for the loan. It is important to note, however, that these privately guaranteed loans cannot be consolidated with your federally guaranteed loans.

Where can I get more information?

The best place to start when looking for more information is the financial aid office at the school(s) you are considering attending. The financial aid staff consists of professionals who are trained to serve your educational financing needs. Several additional sources of useful information are listed below.

For general information about the federal student aid process/ programs, refer to the following free U.S. Department of Education publication:

The Student Guide: Financial Aid from the U.S. Dept. of Education

This publication and other general information is available on the U.S. Department of Education Web site: **http://www.ed.gov**, or can be obtained by contacting:

Federal Student Aid Information Center
P.O. Box 84
Washington, D.C. 20044
1-(800)-4-FED-AID
1-(800)-433-3243

The toll-free TDD number is: 1-(800)-730-8913

To inquire about the processing status of your *Free Application for Federal Student Aid (FAFSA)/Renewal FAFSA,* contact:

Federal Student Aid Information Center
1-(319)-337-5665

This is a toll call. Collect calls will not be accepted and you cannot inquire about the status of your FAFSA/Renewal FAFSA using the toll-free number. Also be aware that the financial aid staff will not be able to determine the status of your FAFSA/Renewal FAFSA before your application has been processed and the results have been forwarded to the school by the federal processing center.

There is a Web site on the Internet that provides useful, up-to-date information about the financial aid process. It includes additional references and resources. The name of the Web site is "FINAID: The Financial Aid Information Page." You can access it at: **http://www.finaid.org.**

Good Habits to a Sound Financial Future: "The Borrower's Dozen"

For most people, bad habits are hard to break and it is difficult to get into good habits, particularly when it comes to money. The following "Borrower's Dozen" is a listing of 13 good financial habits that should help you achieve your goals and guide you in financing your education responsibly. It's not too early to get into these habits if you haven't already done so. The longer you wait, the more difficult it will be to get into these habits. It may not be easy for you to get into these habits, but if you can, you should have greater success achieving your financial goals. Some suggestions about how you can get into these habits are also provided.

Habit #1. Identify and record your goals.

You need to identify and record your long-term personal, professional, and financial goals. You should attempt to answer the following questions as you go about setting your goals. "How do I want to use what I have learned? What do I want to accomplish in my career? Where do I want to work? How much do I hope to earn each year? Where do I want to live? What kind of lifestyle do I want? What are my hopes for a family? When do I want to retire? What kind of lifestyle do I want once I retire?"

Habit #2. Make well-informed choices about how you use your scarce resources.

The cost of your education really is up to you. How much you "spend" getting your degree is a function of the choices or decisions you make. For example, the cost of tuition depends on the school you choose, the cost of housing depends on where you choose to live, the cost of food depends on how/where/what you choose to eat, etc. Once you make a choice, you must pay the required "cost." As such, you are responsible for the choices you make. No one else can claim that responsibility — not your parents, not your friends, not your siblings, not your financial aid officer, etc. Think carefully about what you'll have to give up once you're working, in order to pay back the debt you incurred because of the choices you made as a student. Be certain you'll be willing to make the required future sacrifices before you spend your borrowed funds while in school.

Habit #3. Don't live a lifestyle you can't afford. Live below your means while in school so that you can afford the lifestyle you want once you graduate.

If you live like someone with an advanced degree while you're in school, you may have to live like a student once you graduate! Live below your means as a student; be thrifty! Remember, you must repay every dollar you borrow (plus interest) and this will reduce your disposable income (the money you use to pay for food, rent, transportation, fun, etc.) once you graduate.

Habit #4. Budget your money just as carefully as your time; get on a monthly budget and stick to it.

Your personal budget is like a road map. It tells you who you are financially, where you are currently, and where it is you want to be. Your personal budget is an important component of any financial planning you do. The key in developing your budget is to determine how much you can afford to spend each month on the various items you purchase. The best way to develop your personal budget is to use a worksheet. A number of self-help books have alternative versions of a budget worksheet. You also can use one of the available software products like *Access Advisor, Quicken,* or *Microsoft Money. Access Advisor* is an integrated debt management software package for students that can be downloaded at no cost from the Access Group, Inc. Web site: **http://www.accessgroup.org**.

How can I make my financial aid last until the end of the term?

It's hard to make money last. This is especially true if you only receive funds once every three, four, or five months. And that's exactly what happens with your financial aid funds. These funds generally are disbursed to you once each term at or near the beginning of the term. It's your responsibility to make sure that you budget them so that they last until your next disbursement. This, however, can be very difficult. It's like getting paid once a quarter by your employer. Although your financial aid funds should never be confused with earnings, they still may be the main source of money you use to pay your expenses. And, it's important to note that the Financial Aid Office may not be able to let you borrow additional funds if you run out. Thus, how can you make the funds last?

One way to make the funds last is to open a second account—a ***"Holding Account"***— where you can hold your funds until they are to be used based on your monthly budget. More specifically:

> open a savings account and deposit your financial aid refund for the term in that account,
> have the funds you've budgeted for the month transferred electronically at the beginning of each month from your "***Holding Account"*** to your checking account, and
> try to avoid getting an ATM card or checks for this savings account so that you're not tempted to draw funds from the "***Holding Account"*** ahead of your monthly budget schedule.

Habit #5. Save a little each month (even if only $5), and plan for your financial future.

Financial planners advise that it is essential to have savings. In fact, it is a general principle that you should invest 10% of your gross monthly earnings starting at the age of 21, if at the age of 65, you want to retire and have the same lifestyle in retirement that you had when you were working. You also need to have readily available funds for emergencies and other financial goals you want to achieve. Whereas it may seem unreasonable to consider saving for retirement when you're still in school, it is important to begin saving for emergencies and other short-term needs as soon as possible. There are four steps that can help you establish a successful savings program: (1) determine your savings and investment goal(s), (2) pay yourself first, (3) make it inconvenient to withdraw funds, and (4) earn as much as you can with your savings and investments without being uncomfortable with the level of financial risk.

Habit #6. Keep accurate, well-organized records of your financial activities.

You should keep copies of all documents relating to your financial activities. For example, you should retain copies of loan documents (e.g., applications, promissory notes, lender correspondence), receipts for major purchases (e.g., appliances, furniture, cars, any items with warranties), income tax returns and all the documentation used to prepare those returns (both federal and state), and your will. You also should keep a log or journal of all conversations with the lender(s) and servicer(s) of any loans you borrow. This log should include the date and time you called, the reason for the call, any expected follow-up, and the full name of the person with whom you spoke. You can maintain a notebook-style log or maintain the log on your personal computer. Whatever form you use, it may come in handy if there is a dispute about the conversation at a later date.

Habit #7. Establish and maintain a strong credit history; review your credit report annually.

Your credit report is your "financial transcript." It's comparable to your academic transcript and much more important when it comes to achieving your financial goals. Just as you are concerned about the quality and accuracy of your academic transcript, you should be concerned about the quality and accuracy of your financial transcript — i.e., your credit report. You can request a copy of your credit report by sending a written request (typed or printed) to one of the three national credit reporting agencies listed below. You also can order a copy of your credit report by phone or via the Internet. Call or visit the Web site of each agency to select the procedure that is best suited to your needs. The toll-free telephone numbers and Web site addresses of the three national credit reporting agencies are given below.

Equifax Information Service Center
(800) 997-2493
http://www.equifax.com

Experian National Consumer Assistance Center
(888) EXPERIAN— (i.e., 397-3742)
http://www.experian.com

Trans Union Corporation Consumer Disclosure Center
(800) 888-4213
http://www.transunion.com

Habit #8. Borrow the minimum amount you need to achieve your goals.

Although often it is necessary to borrow money to invest in your education, you should always borrow the minimum amount you need at the lowest possible cost. Remember, every time you borrow money, whether an education loan or from your credit card(s), you are influencing your financial future.

Habit #9. Pay the interest on unsubsidized loans when it accrues, if possible.

You can greatly reduce the amount of your educational debt when you enter repayment if you pay the interest that accrues on unsubsidized loans while you're in school, during the grace period, and during periods of eligible deferment and forbearance. Interest that accrues on unsubsidized federal and private loans during these periods will be capitalized (that is, added to the principal balance) at some point before they enter repayment. Once that interest is added to the principal, it also begins accruing interest. This can significantly increase the total principal and amount of total finance charges you will pay. Even paying just a portion of the interest as it accrues can help you achieve your financial goals more quickly. *Note that the money you use to pay the interest should not be borrowed funds; it should come from earnings, savings, gifts received from family, or some other non-loan source.*

Habit #10. Be a well-informed borrower. Not all loans are alike; know the differences and borrow wisely.

Educate yourself about the loans you borrow. The promissory note for your loan is the "contract" between you and the lender. It stipulates all the terms and conditions of a loan as well as your rights and responsibilities as a borrower. You should read any promissory note you are required to sign before you sign it and always keep a copy of each note you sign.

Habit #11. Pay your credit card balance in full each month. Charge only what you know you can repay when the bill arrives.

Also remember to pay your credit card and all other bills by the stated due dates. This is essential if you want to avoid getting into credit problems. Responsible use of credit cards can help you manage your cash flow and provide convenience when shopping. You need to be certain, however, that you understand the "ABCs" of credit cards.

> **A** credit card can be helpful in emergencies, but emergencies rarely happen at the shopping mall, so keep your cards at home!
>
> **B**uying something on sale is still spending, not saving.
>
> **C**redit card debt is not an investment, but it can reduce your ability to invest.
>
> **D**ebt from credit cards can reduce your ability to achieve your financial goals.

Habit #12. Limit the number of credit cards you have and your available credit.

Your credit rating can be affected by the number of credit cards you have. You don't need numerous credit cards while in school. You can reduce your overall credit rating if you have more than a few credit cards, even if you owe nothing on them. Creditors like to see that you have been offered credit, have it available, but do not use it.

Which card(s) should you keep? The choice is up to you. You can keep the card with the lowest limit, the card with NO annual fee, the card that provides frequent flyer miles based on usage, etc. The best choice, however, probably is the card that has the lowest limit. You only need cards with limits of $1,000 to $2,000 to have sufficient credit for those emergencies that may occur while in school. By keeping several cards with lower limits, you are less likely to build up a balance beyond what you can afford to repay in full each month.

Habit #13. Be realistic about how much money you'll earn once you graduate; don't count on any immediate financial windfalls.

You may not be offered as much money as you expect when you graduate. Educate yourself about the job market in the field you plan to pursue. Plan for the future by estimating realistically now what your budget will be once you graduate. It may not be as much, or go as far, as you expect. You can use the Out of School budget worksheet in the *Access Advisor* software that can be downloaded from the Access Group, Inc., Web site **(http://www.accessgroup.org)** or any other budgeting spreadsheet to estimate how much discretionary income you'll have for your living expenses once you graduate. Having this information will allow you to make better choices while in school, and provide a more realistic outlook of your financial future following graduation.

Summary

Your legal education is an investment in your future, and something in which you can take pride. It can be a professionally rewarding and financially enriching experience if you:

- devise your long-term financial plan;
- manage your resources in a responsible manner;
- form good financial habits;
- make cost-effective and well-informed choices about how you use your scarce resources;
- develop a budget and live within that budget;
- work with the advisors in your financial aid office to obtain the financial assistance you need and follow the directions they provide regarding your education loans;
- borrow the minimum amount needed to achieve your educational goal(s);
- repay the loan(s) you borrow;
- avoid using credit cards except in emergencies or in situations where you'll pay the full balance when the bill arrives;
- have no regrets once you graduate about spending the resources that are required to obtain your degree; and
- can afford the lifestyle you want once you graduate.

Your education is an important key to your financial future and to your success. The questions answered here provide a guide on how to make the financing of your legal education more manageable. Knowing these answers should allow you to make responsible, well-informed financial decisions.

Chapter Six

Career Outlook

Written by the National Association for Law Placement (NALP)

Just as every law school is unique in its curricular offerings and campus culture, each differs in the range of services provided for career planning and employment. However, all career services offices and the professionals who administer them have at least one thing in common — law students and graduates are their most important concern.

Career services administrators and staff know the search for employment in today's competitive legal marketplace requires a great deal of forethought, a significant investment of time, use of a variety of communication and technological tools, and development of critical job-search related skills. It is through the law school career services program that students and new professionals can acquire the tools they need to prepare for and obtain satisfying, rewarding careers as lawyers.

Programs and Activities of Career Services Offices

Law school career services offices are very important resource partners for students who take responsibility for their own careers and take the lead in their career planning and job search effort. Career services offices cannot and do not "broker" students into jobs, nor can they offer a guarantee of a job upon graduation. Instead, they provide specialized career counseling, collect and distribute vital information and resources, and offer critical skills training, while leading the efforts of the law school to establish relationships with employers. In performing these tasks, the career services office becomes a major marketing and outreach program for its law school, as well as an invaluable resource for both law students and graduates as they chart their career paths.

Career Planning, Advising and Counseling Services

Career planning and counseling services are valuable resources law students can use to enhance their job search activities. Career planning and counseling can be of great assistance if tailored to the needs of groups of students (first year, third year, part-time, etc.), as well as individual students. These services typically include an exploration of the many career options available to lawyers and a self-inventory experience to gain insight about career aspirations. Career counseling may also provide assistance in managing educational or consumer debt.

Job Search Assistance

The development of a successful job search and career plan requires law students and graduates to assume personal responsibility for charting their search and implementing a plan to undertake it. However, the law school career services office significantly aids students in that effort: it can offer training in job prospecting, networking, resume writing, and interviewing; use of informational and technological resources to learn about employers and job opportunities; job postings and resume forwarding to assist students in connecting with employers who may not recruit locally; administration of on-campus interview programs; and management of mentoring programs between law students and alumni.

Alumni Career Resources

Some law schools have the resources to offer continuing support to law school graduates — most of whom, if true to statistical data, will change jobs at least seven times during their professional careers. Law school alumni turn to their career planning offices for advice on resumes, referrals and resources, information on the hiring needs of specific employers, and access to career-related publications. Some career services programs publish newsletters especially for alumni, offer counseling services, and organize special networking or other activities.

Past Employment Experiences, Law Student and Lawyer Employment

Prior work experience may help define interest in a future career as a lawyer. Successful work experiences demonstrating capacity for learning, business acumen, and ability to interact with clients are especially relevant to that future. However, no matter what the law students or graduates did prior to law school, they are still "new lawyers" and thus their compensation as lawyers will generally be similar to that of others who accept jobs of the same type. A student's background can be advantageous, however, by attracting the interest of employers looking for a particular type of student or a special skill.

Summer Jobs During Law School

Summer offers an opportunity for many law students to gain real world experience as a paid or unpaid clerk in a law firm, government agency, public interest organization or law related business. Internships, externships, and clerkships with law firms are ways to acquire work experience as is serving as a research assistant for a member of the law faculty. Law students who hope to work for a large law firm after graduation should be aware those firms hire entry-level lawyers primarily from their summer clerk programs. Moreover, summer jobs are important opportunities for law students to establish contacts and to receive evaluation of their work product.

School Term Employment

Students may choose to work during the school term — perhaps to gain experience or financial support. In accordance with

ABA standards, full-time law students may not be employed for more than 20 hours per week by a legal employer; however, evening division students often continue the employment they had before they entered law school. These students will need to consider the relationship of their current career with law and may need to acquire legal work experience prior to graduation. This is particularly true if evening division students anticipate making a transition into law practice.

Graduates Acquire Jobs at Various Times

The search for a full-time job is a process that is dictated not only by the effort and commitment of the candidate but also by the unique recruiting practices of various types of employers. Large firms tend to be more structured and predictable than smaller firms.

Summer Clerkship May Lead to First-Year Associate Offer

Some law firms (typically the large firms which can predict their needs well in advance) interview on campus in the fall to hire students for the following summer. If a student's performance is acceptable and the hiring needs of the firm have remained consistent with the size of the summer class, the student may receive an offer for a full-time job following graduation. Students receiving such offers make a decision on whether to accept such an offer during the fall of their third year of law school. Some government agencies (typically Department of Justice and other large agencies)

Initial Employment by Type of Employer
Class of 1997 -- As of February 15, 1998
# of jobs = 31,413

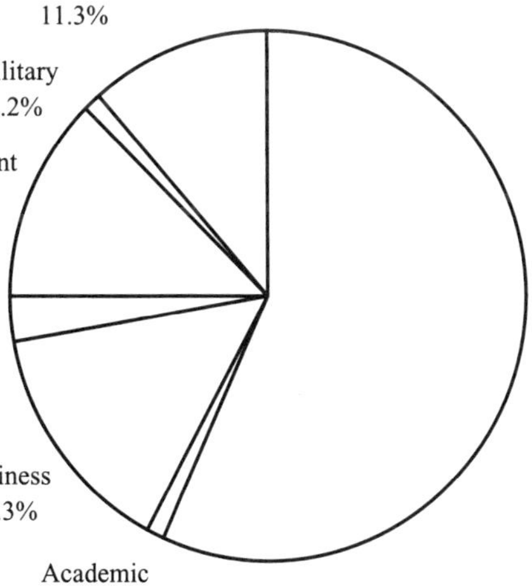

Note: Figures in this chart reflect all job types -- both legal and other. For clarity, the category for unknown employer type, representing 1.8% of jobs, is not shown.

have Honors programs which work in a similar manner, although few of those agencies actually conduct on-campus interviews.

Employers Hire in Spring From Third Year Class

Smaller private practice employers and a significant number of public interest and government agencies interview and hire third-year law students during the spring of the student's third year. This timetable enables them to predict more accurately their hiring needs and offers both employers and students an additional semester of law school for hiring/career decisions.

Judicial Clerkships are a Source of Post-Graduation Employment

Jobs as clerks for judges at the local, state or federal level provide postgraduate employment for about 12 percent of law graduates. These job offers typically encompass one or two years and provide invaluable experience in the court system. Judicial clerks balance the advantages of the clerkship experience with the delay of entering full-time practice.

Offers of Employment Occur After Graduation or Bar Passage

Many private practice employers, public interest agencies, and most government employers extend offers of employment after graduation from law school and bar passage. Thus, graduates may not acquire their first job until six to nine months after graduation. Understanding hiring practices of the broad range of legal employers enables job seekers to interpret a law school's data on employment more accurately. Law schools whose graduates are employed by a significant number of government or small firm employers will naturally have statistical data showing fewer graduates employed at graduation while schools whose graduates are employed primarily in large law firms will have statistical data that shows more graduates employed at graduation.

Principles and Standards Guide Job Offers and Responses

Both employers and students are guided in the employment process by NALP's Principles and Standards for Law Placement and Recruitment Activities. These guidelines are promulgated to ensure that students have an adequate opportunity to make decisions about offers of employment without undue pressure and that employers will receive responses from students in a timely manner. Copies of the Principles and Standards are available through each law school or by contacting NALP.

Graduates Choose Jobs According to Interests

Members of each graduating class acquire full and part-time jobs with an array of public and private, legal and nonlegal organizations. By definition, a "legal" job is a position requiring a juris doctor and requiring substantial use of legal skills and training. In contrast, "nonlegal" jobs are positions that do not require a juris doctor and may or may not make specific use of legal skills and background. Law graduates have in the past obtained legal, nonlegal, full and part-time jobs from these five general types of employers:

Private Practice — includes all positions within a law firm, including solo practitioner, associate, law clerk, paralegal and administrative or support staff.

Public Interest — includes positions funded by the Legal Services Corporation and others providing civil legal and indigent services as well as positions with nonprofit advocacy or cause-related organizations.

Government — includes all levels and branches of government, including public defender and prosecutor positions, positions with the military, and all other agencies, such as the Small Business Administration, state or local transit authorities, congressional committees, law enforcement, and social services.

Judicial Clerkship — a one- or two-year appointment clerking for a judge on the federal, state, or local level.

Business and Industry — includes positions in accounting firms, insurance companies, banking and financial institutions, corporations, companies and organizations of all sizes, such as private hospitals, retail establishments, consulting and public relations firms, political campaigns, trade associations and labor unions.

Academic — includes work as a law professor, law librarian, administrator or faculty member in higher education or other academic settings, including elementary and secondary schools.

Employment Outlook for New Lawyers

Making an informed choice to pursue a career in the law must include an examination of law school curricula, student services and admission requirements. Of equal importance is undertaking a comprehensive self-inventory on career aspirations and realistically and candidly assessing the options and prospects for employment after graduation.

The latter assessment requires a basic understanding of how the legal profession has evolved during recent years, including the changes in the ways in which law is practiced, and how the growth of the profession will affect the employment prospects and experiences of future lawyers.

The legal profession has experienced significant changes in its demographic composition during the past two decades.

Since the early 1970s the composition of what was once known as "the gentlemanly profession" has been transformed by the entry of a substantial number of women and, to a lesser degree, minorities into the nation's law schools and ultimately into the practicing bar. In 1997, 44 percent of law graduates were women, a substantial increase over the 15 percent who graduated in 1975. Minorities comprised 19 percent of the 1997 graduating class as compared to 5.4 percent of the 1975 class.

Since 1991, the percentage of graduates accepting legal positions as their first jobs has diminished from more than 84% to 78% for the Class of 1997. Private practice employment decreased from 62% in 1990 to the current rate of 55.6%.

The increased frequency with which graduates initially acquire nonlegal jobs after law school has been documented by NALP data — and anecdotal information also suggests that attorneys leaving the practice of law to pursue nonlegal entrepreneurial or business careers has increased dramatically in recent years.

Law firm structure and strategies for hiring and growth have changed in response to the market economy.

Today, approximately 350 law firms each employ more than 100 lawyers, a sharp contrast to the "less than a dozen firms in 1960" or the 47 firms doing so in 1978. Some analysts project that the number of large firms will continue to increase as a result of mergers and the competitive advantage offered by a national or international presence.

Today, legal employers carefully plan for growth and hire entry level, lateral and summer clerks accordingly. Some law firms only grow "internally" — meaning they hire only entry-level attor-

Initial Job Types
Class of 1997 -- As of February 15, 1998
# of graduates = 35,193

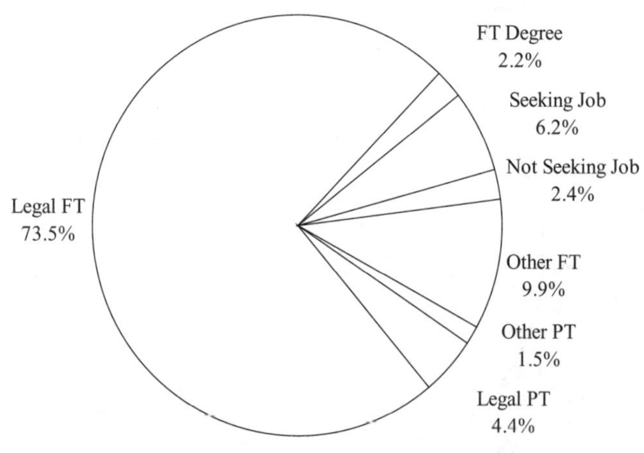

Note: Chart excludes 12 employed graduates for whom job type, e.g., legal or other, was not reported. The sum of individual percentages for job categories exceeds the overall employment rate because of rounding.

neys, monitoring and grooming them for partnership in their seventh or eighth year. This strategy precipitates the outplacement of a predictable percentage of associates each year — those who are judged not to be of partnership caliber.

Some firms grow through the expansion or creation of practice groups — a strategy that may predicate aggressive recruitment or "cherry picking" of lateral associates and experienced partners. Associates in today's legal market frequently make several lateral moves before settling into a partnership track at a firm, and partners with a substantial book of business now move from firm to firm, an occurrence rare before the 1980s.

The business operations of law firms have changed in response to client demand and the need to be profitable.

In many respects, the law profession has been forced to conduct itself as a business. Managing partners must sustain "profitability" in order to retain partners who could, ostensibly, take their talent and clientele to other firms. Recruitment and accounting practices, like attorney overhead and billables, are carefully scrutinized for cost effectiveness. Thus, to a certain extent, an attorney's success is tied to his profitability and his ability to cultivate clients.

Government and public interest hiring has declined during recent years due to budget restraints and calls for smaller and more efficient governments at the federal, state and local levels.

Law graduates who are dedicated to public service employment have generally been successful in obtaining jobs — but sometimes only because they acted in an entrepreneurial manner and utilized special grant programs to fund their jobs. Graduates of the future are likely to find that the opportunities in public service will remain somewhat limited and that median compensation is less likely to equal or exceed that for other employment.

Employment Experiences of Graduates

Women and Minorities

Data on the Class of 1997 show that fewer women entered private practice compared with men, whereas more obtained government, clerkship and public interest positions. The same was true for minorities compared to non-minorities, although the percentage of minorities obtaining clerkship positions was somewhat lower. About 47% of employed minority women obtained jobs in private practice compared with 53.8% of non-minority women. Among minority men, 51.4% obtained private practice jobs compared with 58.5% of non-minority men. Viewed from another perspective, minorities — who as a group constituted about 19% of the Class of 1997 — obtained 16% of all law firm jobs obtained by the Class of 1997.

Graduates with Disabilities

NALP data on the Class of 1997 included about 500 graduates with disabilities. Compared to non-disabled graduates, disabled graduates were more likely to be unemployed six months after graduation, and those who were employed were less likely to be employed in full-time legal positions. Less than half of the employed disabled graduates obtained jobs in private practice, while 18% obtained government jobs and 6.7% obtained public interest positions. Business and clerkships accounted for 13.1% and 8.9% of jobs, respectively. The median salary for disabled graduates was $40,000 compared to the national median for all graduates of $41,000.

Older Graduates

The median age of the Class of 1997 was 27. Compared to their counterparts age 30 or younger, those 31 or older were far less likely to be employed in a full-time legal job and far more likely to be employed in a nonlegal position. Unemployment rates were highest among graduates age 41 or older.

Jobs in business and academic settings were considerably more common among older employed graduates. While only 10.1% of employed graduates in the 20-25 age bracket acquired jobs in business and industry, about one-quarter of those age 36 or older did so.

Women age 31-35 reported median salaries of $40,000 and men age 31-35 reported median salaries of $45,000. Similarly, women age 41-45 reported median salaries of $40,000 while men in that same age bracket reported salaries of $50,000.

Geography Impacts Employment and Compensation of New Graduates

Two regions, the Mid-Atlantic and South Atlantic (U.S. Census Bureau Regions) dominated the job market for new graduates, accounting for a plurality (40%) of the jobs of the Class of 1997 for which a location was reported. The East North Central and Pacific states, each accounted for an additional 14-15% of jobs. The East South Central and Mountain states provided the fewest jobs.

Median starting salaries were generally higher and more dispersed in regions supporting more jobs. Among these large regions, the median starting salary was the highest in the Pacific states and at $50,000 it was $4,000 above the median starting salary in the Mid-Atlantic region, the one that had the most jobs.

NALP Information

Continued on Next Page

National Association for Law Placement (NALP) Charts

1997 Employment by Region

	Number of Jobs Reported in Region	Median Salary for All Jobs
New England	1,847	$40,000
Mid Atlantic	6,101	$46,000
East North Central	4,288	$40,000
West North Central	1,815	$35,000
South Atlantic	5,819	$40,000
East South Central	1,221	$37,500
West South Central	2,622	$44,000
Mountain	1,471	$37,500
Pacific	4,577	$50,000

1997 Employment by Type

	Number of Jobs Acquired	Salary Median
Academic	379	$36,000
Business / Industry	4,413	$46,000
Judicial Clerkships	3,491	$36,000
Government	4,241	$35,000
Public Interest	871	$30,000
Private Practice All Sizes	17,456	$55,000
Private Practice 2 - 10 Attorneys	5,524	$35,000
Private Practice 11 - 25 Attorneys	1,817	$42,000
Private Practice 26 - 50 Attorneys	1,161	$50,000
Private Practice 51 - 100 Attorneys	1,155	$58,000
Private Practice 101 - 250 Attorneys	1,958	$67,000
Private Practice 250 + Attorneys	2,685	$80,000

Six Year Overview

	Class of 1992	Class of 1993	Class of 1994	Class of 1995	Class of 1996	Class of 1997
Number of Graduates	39,405	39,914	39,305	39,199	39,920	40,114
Percent employed six months post-graduation	83.5%	83.4%	84.7%	86.7%	87.4%	89.2%
Percent employed in Private Practice jobs	59%	57.1%	55%	56.1%	55.7%	55.6%
Compensation Medians (All jobs)	$36,000	$36,000	$37,000	$40,000	$40,000	$41,000
Most frequently reported salaries	NA	NA	$30,000 (6.6%) $35,000 (5.4%)	$30,000 (7.4%) $35,000 (5.1%)	$30,000 (7.3%) $30,000 (5.1%)	$30,000 (6.4%) $35,000 (5.0%)

Chapter Seven

Bar Admissions

Written by Erica Moeser, President of the National Conference of Bar Examiners (NCBE)

General Information

In order to obtain a license to practice law, almost all law school graduates must apply for bar admission through a state board of bar examiners. Most often this board is an agency of the highest state court in the jurisdiction, but occasionally the board is connected more closely to the state's bar association. The criteria for eligibility to take the bar examination or to otherwise qualify for bar admission are set by each state.

Licensing involves a demonstration of worthiness in two distinct areas. The first is competence. For initial licensure, competence is ordinarily established by a showing that the applicant holds an acceptable educational credential (with rare exception, a J.D. degree) from a law school that meets educational standards, and by achieving a passing score on the bar examination.

The most common testing configuration consists of a two-day bar examination, one day of which is devoted to the Multistate Bar Examination, a standardized 200-item test covering six areas (Constitutional Law, Contracts, Criminal Law, Evidence, Real Property, and Torts). The second day of testing is typically comprised of locally crafted essays from a broader range of subject matters; however, in a growing number of states, nationally developed tests, such as the Multistate Essay Examination and the Multistate Performance Test, are used to round out the test.

In addition, almost all jurisdictions require that the applicant present an acceptable score on the Multistate Professional Responsibility Examination, which is separately administered three times each year.

The second area of inquiry by bar examiners involves the character and fitness of applicants for a law license. In this regard, bar examiners seek background information concerning each applicant that is relevant to the appropriateness of granting a professional credential. Because law is a public profession, and because the degree of harm a lawyer, once licensed, can inflict is substantial, decisions about who should be admitted to practice law are made carefully by bar examining boards.

Boards of bar examiners in most jurisdictions expect to hear from prospective candidates during the final year of law school. Bar examinations are ordinarily offered at the end of February and July, with considerably more applicants taking the summer test because it falls after graduation from law school.

Some boards offer or require law student registration at an earlier point in law school. This preliminary processing, where available, permits the board to review character and fitness issues in advance.

As state-specific information is so important (and so variable) in the lawyer-licensing process, law students should contact the board of bar examiners in the jurisdiction(s) in which they are most likely to practice law.

Using the Charts in this Book

The charts provided in this book permit prospective law school applicants to learn something about the basic requirements for bar admission in each jurisdiction and to compare the performance of recent graduates from each school on the bar examination in those jurisdictions in which the law schools' graduates took the test. Note that the information provided relates to persons who took the bar examination in the state for the first time.

This information allows the reader to consider the following questions:

— Did graduates of one law school perform as well as the graduates of other law schools? For example, if 90% of one law school's graduates who took the test as first-time-takers passed the test compared to 60% from another law school, the prospective applicant may be validly concerned about whether the admissions policies of the second school are sufficiently selective, or whether the second school offers an education that will reasonably assure success on a licensing examination after three years of study.

— How does the passing percentage for first-time-takers at a law school compare with the overall pass rate for first-time-takers in the state? For example, while a law school with a passing percentage of 75% may be doing relatively well in a jurisdiction with an overall pass rate of 60%, a 75% pass rate may be of some concern in a jurisdiction in which the overall pass rate is 93%.

Of course, there are many reasons why one law school may outperform another in the long- or the short-run, and bar performance alone should not be used as the sole measure of assessing law school quality. Because each state's bar examining board sets its own passing score on the bar examination, comparisons of the passing percentages for law schools across state lines may not be as useful to prospective applicants.

In any event, the material appearing with regard to bar admissions offers needed insight into the performance of each law school's graduates. As it is necessary to obtain a license in order to practice law, applicants are better equipped to make application and attendance decisions when armed with bar passage information.

If you would like additional information relating to bar admissions about a specific state, please contact the appropriate authority in that state. For your convenience, this chapter contains contact information for the state board of bar examiners in each state. Also, you may want to visit the websites for NCBE and the ABA at **http://www.ncbex.org** and at **http://www.abanet.org/legaled.**

BAR ADMISSIONS

	Generally, is graduation from an ABA approved law school required?*	Bar Passage Rates					
		% of First Time Takers Passing - Summer 1996	% of First Time Takers Passing - Winter 1997	% of First Time Takers Passing - Combined Summer 1996 Winter 1997	% of First Time Takers Passing - Summer 1997	% of First Time Takers Passing - Winter 1998	% of First Time Takers Passing - Combined Summer 1997 Winter 1998
Alabama	YES	78%	66%	74%	80%	68%	76%
Alaska	YES	83%	67%	77%	76%	70%	74%
Arizona	YES	83%	81%	82%	84%	72%	80%
Arkansas	YES	84%	77%	82%	74%	77%	75%
California	NO	69%	62%	67%	75%	57%	71%
Colorado	YES	89%	82%	87%	83%	77%	81%
Connecticut	NO	84%	84%	84%	85%	81%	84%
Delaware	YES	NA	No Test	NA	62%	NA	62%
Florida	YES	84%	85%	84%	84%	82%	83%
Georgia	YES	88%	76%	83%	86%	74%	83%
Hawaii	YES	76%	57%	70%	81%	NA	81%
Idaho	YES	81%	68%	76%	75%	76%	75%
Illinois	YES	86%	84%	86%	87%	80%	85%
Indiana	YES	78%	88%	80%	93%	92%	93%
Iowa	YES	78%	80%	78%	86%	83%	85%
Kansas	YES	87%	93%	90%	87%	87%	87%
Kentucky	YES	84%	82%	83%	65%	86%	70%
Louisiana	YES	69%	54%	66%	62%	54%	61%
Maine	NO	81%	84%	82%	63%	83%	69%
Maryland	YES	76%	79%	76%	69%	83%	72%
Massachusetts	YES	83%	76%	81%	84%	72%	82%
Michigan	YES	84%	86%	85%	89%	79%	86%
Minnesota	YES	92%	84%	91%	93%	77%	90%
Mississippi	YES	94%	84%	91%	93%	82%	90%
Missouri	YES	83%	81%	82%	86%	81%	85%
Montana	YES	94%	No Test	94%	91%	90%	91%

* Graduation from a state-approved law school which is not ABA approved may qualify a person to take the bar examination in the state in which the school is located, but may not qualify the person for the examination in other states. You may wish to contact the bar admission authorities in the state(s) in which you intend to practice for more information on whether graduation from a law school that is not approved will qualify you to take the bar examination in that state. Please note that many jurisdictions have exceptions to the general rule. For example, many jurisdictions will allow individuals who did not graduate from an ABA approved law school to sit for the bar exam if they have been admitted to practice law in another state for a set amount of years. The state of Alabama allows graduates of non-ABA approved schools to sit for the bar exam if the schools are located in the state of Alabama. Connecticut will allow graduates of law schools approved by the Connecticut Bar Examiner Committee to sit for the bar exam.

BAR ADMISSIONS

	Generally, is graduation from an ABA approved law school required?*	Bar Passage Rates					
		% of First Time Takers Passing - Summer 1996	% of First Time Takers Passing - Winter 1997	% of First Time Takers Passing - Combined Summer 1996 Winter 1997	% of First Time Takers Passing - Summer 1997	% of First Time Takers Passing - Winter 1998	% of First Time Takers Passing - Combined Summer 1997 Winter 1998
Nebraska	YES	97%	87%	95%	88%	73%	87%
Nevada	YES	69%	No Test	69%	67%	No Test	67%
New Hampshire	YES	77%	77%	77%	77%	71%	75%
New Jersey	YES	78%	68%	77%	77%	No Test	77%
New Mexico	YES	89%	94%	91%	94%	92%	93%
New York	YES	78%	67%	77%	78%	65%	76%
North Carolina	YES	81%	76%	80%	85%	73%	82%
North Dakota	YES	85%	No Test	85%	85%	0%	85%
Ohio	YES	90%	89%	90%	79%	75%	78%
Oklahoma	YES	84%	88%	85%	81%	87%	82%
Oregon	YES	77%	74%	77%	74%	68%	72%
Pennsylvania	YES	75%	76%	75%	81%	73%	79%
Rhode Island	YES	67%	88%	72%	61%	69%	64%
South Carolina	YES	90%	82%	88%	86%	75%	84%
South Dakota	YES	86%	88%	86%	90%	82%	89%
Tennessee	YES	81%	72%	79%	81%	76%	80%
Texas	YES	84%	81%	84%	83%	73%	81%
Utah	YES	92%	95%	93%	93%	92%	93%
Vermont	YES	88%	67%	79%	80%	86%	82%
Virginia	YES	80%	66%	77%	76%	68%	75%
Washington	YES	73%	82%	76%	73%	83%	76%
West Virginia	YES	80%	64%	79%	85%	67%	84%
Wisconsin	NO	93%	90%	92%	86%	86%	86%
Wyoming	NO	76%	75%	76%	78%	69%	74%
District of Columbia	NO	78%	83%	79%	75%	61%	72%
Puerto Rico	YES	71%	53%	68%	63%	53%	61%

* Graduation from a state-approved law school which is not ABA approved may qualify a person to take the bar examination in the state in which the school is located, but may not qualify the person for the examination in other states. You may wish to contact the bar admission authorities in the state(s) in which you intend to practice for more information on whether graduation from a law school that is not approved will qualify you to take the bar examination in that state. Please note that many jurisdictions have exceptions to the general rule. For example, many jurisdictions will allow individuals who did not graduate from an ABA approved law school to sit for the bar exam if they have been admitted to practice law in another state for a set amount of years. The state of Alabama allows graduates of non-ABA approved schools to sit for the bar exam if the schools are located in the state of Alabama. Connecticut will allow graduates of law schools approved by the Connecticut Bar Examiner Committee to sit for the bar exam.

STATE BAR EXAMINERS

ALABAMA
Board of Bar Examiners
Alabama State Bar
P.O. Box 671
Montgomery, AL 36101
TEL: 205/269-1515

ALASKA
Committee of Law Examiners
Alaska Bar Association
P.O. Box 100279
Anchorage, AK 99510-0279
TEL: 907/272-7469
www.alaskabar.org

ARIZONA
Committee on Examinations
and Character and Fitness
111 W. Monroe
Phoenix, AZ 85003-1742
TEL: 602/340-7295

ARKANSAS
State Board of Law Examiners
2400 Justice Building
625 Marshall
Little Rock, AR 72201
TEL: 501/374-1855
www.state.ar.us/supremecourt

CALIFORNIA
The State Bar of California
Office of Admissions
555 Franklin Street
San Francisco, CA 94102
TEL: 415/561-8303
www.calbar.org

COLORADO
Supreme Court
Board of Law Examiners
600 17th St., Ste. 520-S
Denver, CO 80202
TEL: 303/893-8096

CONNECTICUT
Connecticut Bar Examining
Committee
287 Main Street
East Hartford, CT 06118-1885
TEL: 860/568-3450

DELAWARE
Board of Bar Examiners for
the State of Delaware
200 W. Ninth St., Ste. 300-B
Wilmington, DE 19801
TEL: 302/577-7038

DIST. OF COLUMBIA
Director of Admissions
D.C. Court of Appeals
Room 4200
500 Indiana Avenue, N.W.
Washington, DC 20001
TEL: 202/879-2710
www.dcbar.org/about/admit.html

FLORIDA
Florida Board of Bar Examiners
1891 Eider Court
Tallahassee, FL 32399-1750
TEL: 904/487-1292
www.barexam.org/florida

GEORGIA
Supreme Court of Georgia
Office of Bar Admissions
P.O. Box 38466
Atlanta, GA 30334-0466
TEL: 404/656-3490
www2.state.ga.us/Courts/bar/barhome.htm

GUAM
Board of Law Examiners
Supreme Court of Guam
Suite 300, Guam Judicial Cntr.
120 West O'Brien Drive
Hagatna, Guam 96910
TEL: 671/475-3180

HAWAII
Supreme Court of Hawai'i
Ali'i lani Hale
417 South King Street
Honolulu, HI 96813-2912
TEL: 808/539-4919, 4977

IDAHO
Admissions Administrator
Idaho State Bar
PO Box 895
525 West Jefferson
Boise, ID 83701
TEL: 208/334-4500
www.state.id.us/isb

ILLINOIS
Illinois Board of Admissions
to the Bar
430 First of America Center
Springfield, IL 62701
TEL: 217/522-5917

INDIANA
Indiana State Board of
Law Examiners
National City Center
Suite 1070, South Tower
115 W. Washington St., #1070
Indianapolis, IN 46204-3417
TEL: 317/232-2552

IOWA
Clerk
Supreme Court of Iowa
State Capitol Building
Des Moines, IA 50319
TEL: 515/281-5911

KANSAS
Kansas Board of Law
Examiners
Kansas Judicial Center
301 S. West 10th Ave., Rm.374
Topeka, KS 66612-1507
TEL: 785/296-8410
www.lawlib.wuacc.edu/kscases/kscases.htm

KENTUCKY
Kentucky Board of Bar
Examiners
1510 Newtown Pike, Suite X
Lexington, KY 40511
TEL: 606/246-2381
www.cris.com/~kbbe/

LOUISIANA
Louisiana Committee on
Bar Admissions
601 St. Charles Avenue
New Orleans, LA 70130
TEL: 504/566-1600
www.lsba.org

MAINE
Maine Board of Bar Examiners
P.O. Box 30
Augusta, ME 04332-0030
TEL: 207/623-2464

MARYLAND
State Board of Law Examiners
People's Resource Center
100 Community Pl., Rm. 1210
Crownsville, MD 21032-2026
TEL: 410/514-7044

MASSACHUSETTS
Massachusetts Board of Bar
Examiners
77 Franklin Street
Boston, MA 02110
TEL: 617/482-4466, 4467

MICHIGAN
Michigan Board of Law
Examiners
200 Washington Square North
P.O. Box 30104
Lansing, MI 48909
TEL: 517/334-6992

MINNESOTA
Minnesota State Board of
Law Examiners
Minnesota Judicial Center
25 Constitution Avenue
Suite 110
St. Paul, MN 55155
TEL: 612/297-1800
www.courts.state.mn.us/blexam/bleintro.html

MISSISSIPPI
Mississippi Board of
Bar Admissions
P.O. Box 1449
Jackson, MS 39215-1449
TEL: 601/354-6055
www.mssc.state.ms.us

MISSOURI
Missouri State Board of
Law Examiners
P.O. Box 150
Jefferson City, MO 65102
TEL: 573/751-4144
www.osca.state.mo.us

MONTANA
Board of Bar Examiners
Room 315, Justice Building
215 North Sanders
Helena, MT 59620
TEL: 406/444-2621

NEBRASKA
Nebraska State Bar Commission
635 South 14th Street
P.O. Box 81809
Lincoln, NE 68501
TEL: 402/475-7091
www.nebar.com

NEVADA
State Bar of Nevada
201 Las Vegas Blvd. South
Suite 200
Las Vegas, NV 89101
TEL: 702/382-2200
www.nvbar.org/admissions

NEW HAMPSHIRE
Clerk of the Supreme Court
Supreme Court Building
Concord, NH 03301
TEL: 603/271-2646
www.state.nh.us/courts/supreme.htm

NEW JERSEY
New Jersey Board of Bar Examiners
P.O. Box 973
Trenton, NJ 08625-0973
TEL: 609/984-7785
www.state.nj.us/judiciary/bar_admissions/home.htm

NEW MEXICO
New Mexico State Board of Bar Examiners
9420 Indian School Rd. NE
Albuquerque, NM 87112
TEL: 505/271-9706
www.nmexam.org

NEW YORK
New York State Board of Law Examiners
7 Executive Centre Drive
Albany, NY 12203
TEL: 518/452-8700
www.nybarexam.org

NORTH CAROLINA
Board of Bar Examiners
P.O. Box 2946
208 Fayetteville Street
Raleigh, NC 27602
TEL: 919/828-4886

NORTH DAKOTA
State Bar Board
1st Floor, Judicial Wing
600 East Boulevard Avenue
Bismarck, ND 58505-0530
TEL: 701/328-4201
www.court.state.nd.us

NORTHERN MARIANA ISLANDS
Supreme Court of the Commonwealth of the Northern Mariana Islands
P.O. Box 2165
Saipan, MP 96950
TEL: 670/234-5175, 5176, 5177

OHIO
Ohio Board of Bar Examiners
State Office Tower
30 East Broad Street, 2nd Floor
Columbus, OH 43215-3414
TEL: 614/466-1541
www.sconet.ohio.gov

OKLAHOMA
Oklahoma Board of Bar Examiners
P.O. Box 53036
Oklahoma City, OK 73152
TEL: 405/524-2365
www.okbar.org

OREGON
Admissions Director
5200 SW Meadows Road
P.O. Box 1689
Lake Oswego, OR 97035-0889
TEL: 503/620-0222 ext. 410
www.osbar.org

PENNSYLVANIA
Pennsylvania Board of Law Examiners
5035 Ritter Road, Suite 1100
Mechanicsburg, PA 17055
TEL: 717/795-7270
www.pable.org

PUERTO RICO
Commonwealth of Puerto Rico
Supreme Court
P.O. Box 2392
San Juan, PR 00902-2392
TEL: 787/725-5030

RHODE ISLAND
Rhode Island Board of Bar Examiners
Supreme Court
250 Benefit Street
Providence, RI 02903
TEL: 401/222-3272

SOUTH CAROLINA
South Carolina State Board of Law Examiners
P.O. Box 11330
Columbia, SC 29211
TEL: 803/734-1080

SOUTH DAKOTA
South Dakota Board of Bar Examiners
500 East Capitol
Pierre, SD 57501
TEL: 605/773-4898

TENNESSEE
Tennessee Board of Law Examiners
706 Church Street, Suite 100
Nashville, TN 37243-0740
TEL: 615/741-3234

TEXAS
Texas Board of Law Examiners
P.O. Box 13486
Austin, TX 78711-3486
TEL: 512/463-1621
www.ble.state.tx.us

UTAH
Utah State Bar
645 South 200 East
Salt Lake City, UT 84111-3834
TEL: 801/531-9077
www.utahbar.org

VERMONT
Board of Bar Examiners
109 State Street
Montpelier, VT 05609-0702
TEL: 802/828-3281
www.state.ut.us/courts

VIRGIN ISLANDS
Committee of Bar Examiners
Territorial Court of the Virgin Islands
P.O. Box 70
Charlotte Amalie,
St. Thomas, VI 00804
TEL: 809/774-5480

VIRGINIA
Virginia Board of Bar Examiners
Shockoe Center, Suite 225
11 South 12th Street
Richmond, VA 23219
TEL: 804/786-7490
www.vsb.org/barexam.html

WASHINGTON
Washington State Bar Association
2101 Fourth Avenue, 4th Fl.
Seattle, WA 98121-2330
TEL: 206/727-8210
www.wsba/prg

WEST VIRGINIA
West Virginia Board of Law Examiners
Building 1, E-400
1900 Kanawha Blvd., E.
Charleston, WV 25305-0837
TEL: 304/558-7815
www.state.wv.us/wvsca

WISCONSIN
Board of Bar Examiners
119 Martin Luther King, Jr. Boulevard, Room 405
Madison, WI 53703-3355
TEL: 608/266-9760
www.wisbar.org/sct/bbe/scr40.html

WYOMING
State Board of Law Examiners of Wyoming
P.O. Box 109
Cheyenne, WY 82003-0109
TEL: 307/632-9061
courts.state.wy.us/statebar/html/law_examiners.html

Chapter Eight

Values of the Profession

(What follows is Part II, without comments, of the Statement of Fundamental Lawyering Skills and Professional Values, written by the ABA's Section of Legal Education and Admissions to the Bar's Task Force on Law Schools and the Profession: Narrowing the Gap, chaired by Robert MacCrate. The purpose of the group was to study and improve the process by which new members of the profession are prepared for the practice of law. The Task Force was a diverse group, reflecting the various segments of the profession. It included members of the federal and state judiciary, deans and faculty members of law schools, and members of the practicing bar.)

1. Provision of Competent Representation

As a member of a profession dedicated to the service of clients, a lawyer should be committed to the values of:

1.1 *Attaining a Level of Competence in One's Own Field of Practice, including:*

(a) With regard to lawyering skills, developing a degree of proficiency that is sufficient to enable the lawyer to represent the client competently or to acquire whatever additional degree of proficiency is needed within the time available for doing so and without inappropriately burdening the client's resources;

(b) With regard to substantive knowledge (including both knowledge of the law and familiarity with the fields and disciplines other than law), acquiring sufficient knowledge to enable the lawyer to represent clients competently or to acquire whatever additional knowledge is needed within the time available for doing so and without inappropriately burdening the client's resources;

(c) Developing a realistic sense of the limits of the lawyer's own skills and knowledge;

(d) Developing practices that will enable the lawyer to represent clients consistently with the ethical rules of the profession, including the rules that require a lawyer:

(i) Work diligently and zealously on a client's behalf;

(ii) Avoid conflicts of interest that undermine or appear to undermine the lawyer's loyalty to a client;

(iii) Preserve a client's confidences and secrets;

(iv) Refrain from handling matters that are beyond the lawyer's range of competence (*see* Value §§ 1.3(a)(ii), 1.3(b)(ii) *infra*);

1.2 *Maintaining a Level of Competence in One's Own Field of Practice, including:*

(a) With regard to lawyering skills, engaging in whatever forms of study and learning are necessary to attain the degree of expertise that may be expected of any competent practitioner at the lawyer's level of experience;

(b) With regard to substantive knowledge, attending to new developments in the law or other relevant fields or disciplines, and engaging in whatever forms of study and learning are necessary to attain the degree of expertise that may be expected of any competent practitioner at the lawyer's level of experience;

(c) As the lawyer improves his or her skills and expands his or her knowledge of the field, maintaining a realistic sense of the new limits of his or her skills and knowledge;

(d) Maintaining the conditions of physical and mental alertness necessary for competence, including:

(i) Remaining constantly alert to the existence of problems that may impede or impair the lawyer's ability to provide competent representation (such as alcohol abuse, drug abuse, psychological or emotional problems, senility, or other types of health problems);

(ii) To the extent that the lawyer's ability to provide competent representation is impeded or impaired, taking whatever steps are necessary to ensure competent representation of his or her clients, including, when appropriate:

(A) Seeking treatment to remedy the problems that have resulted in the impairment of the lawyer's abilities;

(B) Until the lawyer has regained competence, enlisting whatever aid is necessary (including aid from other lawyers) to allow the lawyer to competently represent his or her clients;

(C) If the lawyer is unable to competently represent a client even with assistance, withdrawing from the representation and referring the client to another lawyer;

1.3 *Representing Clients in a Competent Manner, including,*

(a) With regard to lawyering skills:

(i) Applying his or her skills in a competent manner;

(ii) If the representation of a particular client requires types of skills or a degree of proficiency that the lawyer does not presently possess:

(A) Assessing whether the client would be best served by the lawyer's acquisition of the requisite skills (assuming it is possible to do so within the time available and without inappropriately burdening the client's resources), or by the lawyer's enlisting the aid of other lawyers or other individuals, or by referring the client to another lawyer;

(B) Advising the client of the limits of the lawyer's skills and the steps the lawyer intends to take to overcome or compensate for his or her limitations;

(b) With regard to substantive knowledge of the law or of other fields or disciplines:

(i) Applying his or her knowledge in a competent manner;

(ii) If the representation of a particular client requires knowledge that the lawyer does not presently possess:

(A) Assessing whether the client would best be served by the lawyer's acquisition of the requisite knowledge (assuming it is possible to do so with the time available and without inappropriately burdening the client's resources), or by the lawyer's enlisting the aid of other lawyers or experts from other fields, or by referring the client to another lawyer;

(B) Advising the client of the limits of the lawyer's knowledge and the steps the lawyer intends to take to overcome or compensate for his or her limitations;

(c) Devoting the time, effort, and resources necessary to competently represent the client;

(d) Representing the client in a manner that is consistent with the ethical rules of the profession.

2. Striving to Promote Justice, Fairness, and Morality

2.1 *Promoting Justice, Fairness, and Morality in One's Own Daily Practice, including:*

(a) To the extent required or permitted by the ethical rules of the profession, acting in conformance with considerations of justice, fairness, or morality when making decisions or acting on behalf of a client;

(b) To the extent required or permitted by the ethical rules of the profession, counseling clients to take considerations of justice, fairness, and morality in account when the client makes decisions or engages in conduct that may have an adverse effect on other individuals or on society;

(c) Treating other people (including clients, other attorneys, and support personnel) with dignity and respect;

2.2 *Contributing to the Profession's Fulfillment of its Responsibility to Ensure that Adequate Legal Services Are Provided to Those Who Cannot Afford to Pay for Them*;

2.3 *Contributing to the Profession's Fulfillment of its Responsibility to Enhance the Capacity of Law and Legal Institutions to Do Justice.*

3. Striving to Improve the Profession

As a member of a "self-governing" profession (AMERICAN BAR ASSOCIATION, MODEL RULES OF PROFESSIONAL CONDUCT, Preamble (1983)), a lawyer should be committed to the values of:

3.1 *Participating in Activities Designed to Improve the Profession*;

3.2 *Assist in the Training and Preparation of New Lawyers and the Continuing Education of the Bar*;

3.3 *Striving to Rid the Profession of Bias Based on Race, Religion, Ethnic Origin, Gender, Sexual Orientation, Age, or Disability, and to Rectify the Effects of These Biases.*

4. Professional Self-Development

As a member of a "learned profession" (AMERICAN BAR ASSOCIATION, MODEL RULES OF PROFESSIONAL CONDUCT, Preamble (1983)), a lawyer should be committed to the values of:

4.1 *Seeking Out and Taking Advantage of Opportunities to Increase One's Own Knowledge and Improve One's Own Skills, including:*

(a) Making use of the process of reflecting upon and learning from experience, which entails:

(i) Critically assessing one's performance so as to evaluate:

(A) The quality of the preparation for the performance, including:

(I) An assessment of the appropriateness of the goals set for the performance and an analysis of whether it would have been possible and desirable to define the goals differently;

(II) An assessment of the appropriateness of the means chosen to pursue the goals and an analysis of whether it would have been possible and desirable to employ different means;

(III) The extent to which the planning process correctly anticipated the contingencies that arose and effectively prepared for these contingencies;

(IV) The accuracy of one's assessments of the likely perspectives, concerns, and reactions of any individuals with whom one interacted (such as, for example, clients, other lawyers, judges, mediators, legislators, and government officials);

(B) The quality of the performance itself, including:

(I) The effectiveness of any applications of the lawyering skills;

(II) The quality of the execution of the plans for the performance;

(III) The appropriateness and effectiveness of one's reactions to any unexpected events;

(C) The extent to which ethical issues were properly identified and resolved;

(ii) Identifying practices that will make it possible to replicate effective aspects of the performance in the future and/or guard against repetition of ineffective ones, including:

(A) Methods of thinking or analysis that will make it possible to plan more effectively for performances;

(B) Methods of improving future performances, including one's applications of lawyering skills;

(C) Methods of improving one's own abilities to perceive or resolve ethical issues;

(b) Taking advantage of courses of study for increasing one's knowledge of one's own field of practice, other fields of legal practice, and other relevant disciplines;

(c) Employing a consistent practice of reading about new developments in the law or other relevant fields or disciplines;

(d) Periodically meeting with other lawyers in one's own field of practice or other fields for the purpose of discussing substantive law, techniques, or topical issues;

4.2 *Selecting and Maintaining Employment That Will Allow the Lawyer to Develop As A Professional and To Pursue His or Her Professional and Personal Goals.*

Chapter Nine

Geographic Location

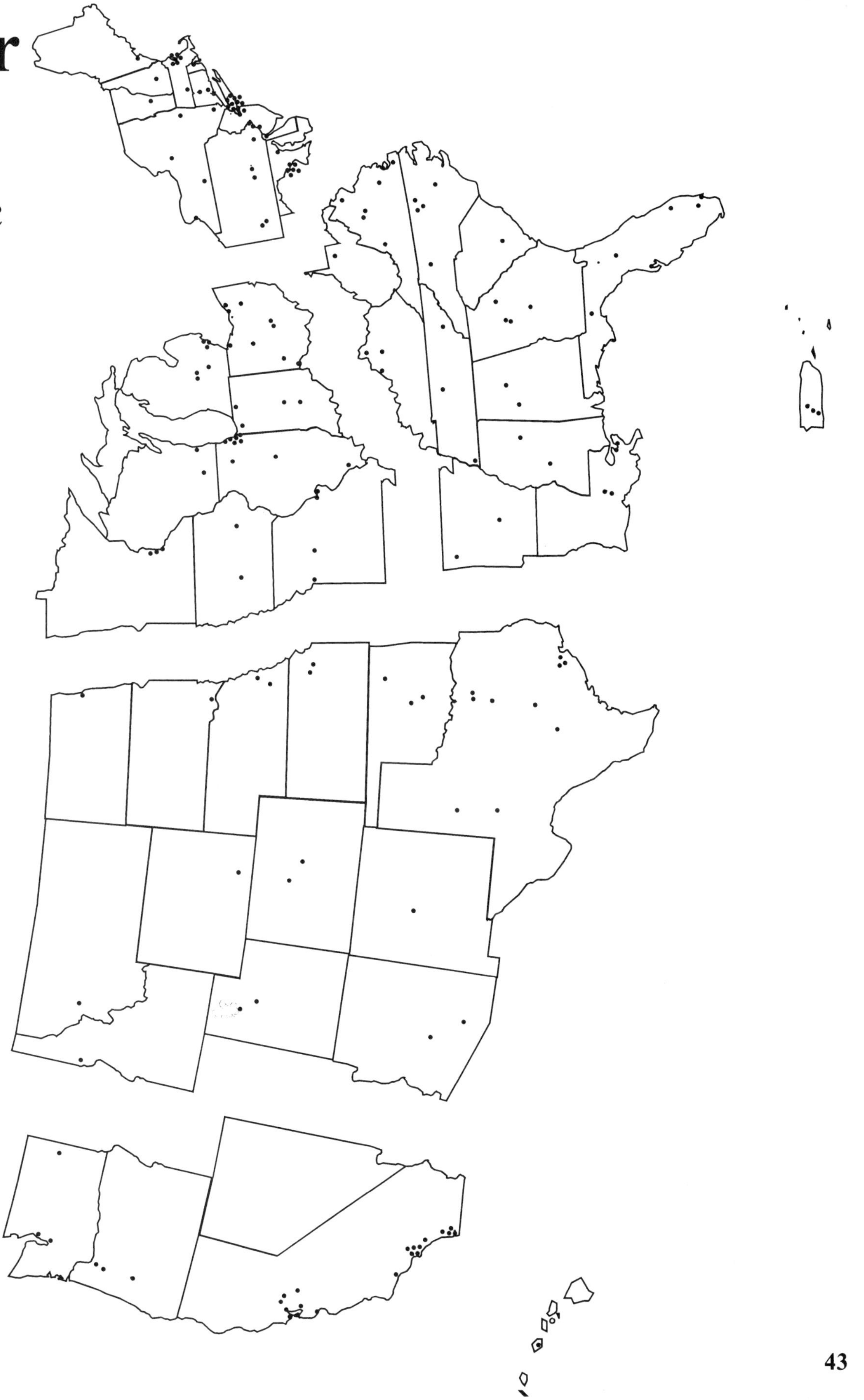

Northeast

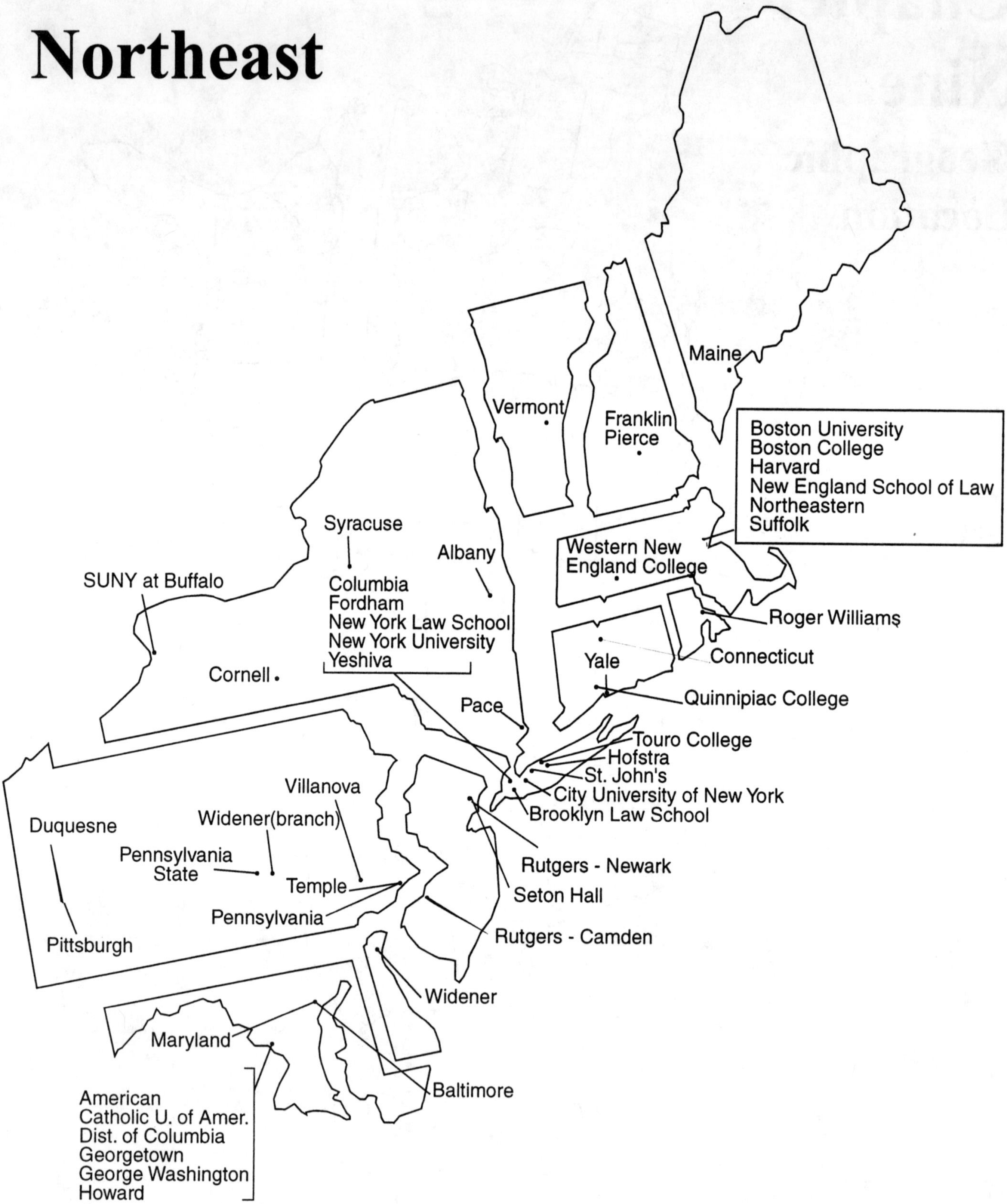
Maine
Vermont
Franklin Pierce
Boston University
Boston College
Harvard
New England School of Law
Northeastern
Suffolk
Western New England College
Roger Williams
Connecticut
Yale
Quinnipiac College
Syracuse
Albany
SUNY at Buffalo
Columbia
Fordham
New York Law School
New York University
Yeshiva
Cornell
Pace
Touro College
Hofstra
St. John's
City University of New York
Brooklyn Law School
Villanova
Duquesne
Widener(branch)
Pennsylvania State
Temple
Pennsylvania
Pittsburgh
Rutgers - Newark
Seton Hall
Rutgers - Camden
Widener
Maryland
Baltimore
American
Catholic U. of Amer.
Dist. of Columbia
Georgetown
George Washington
Howard

Midwest

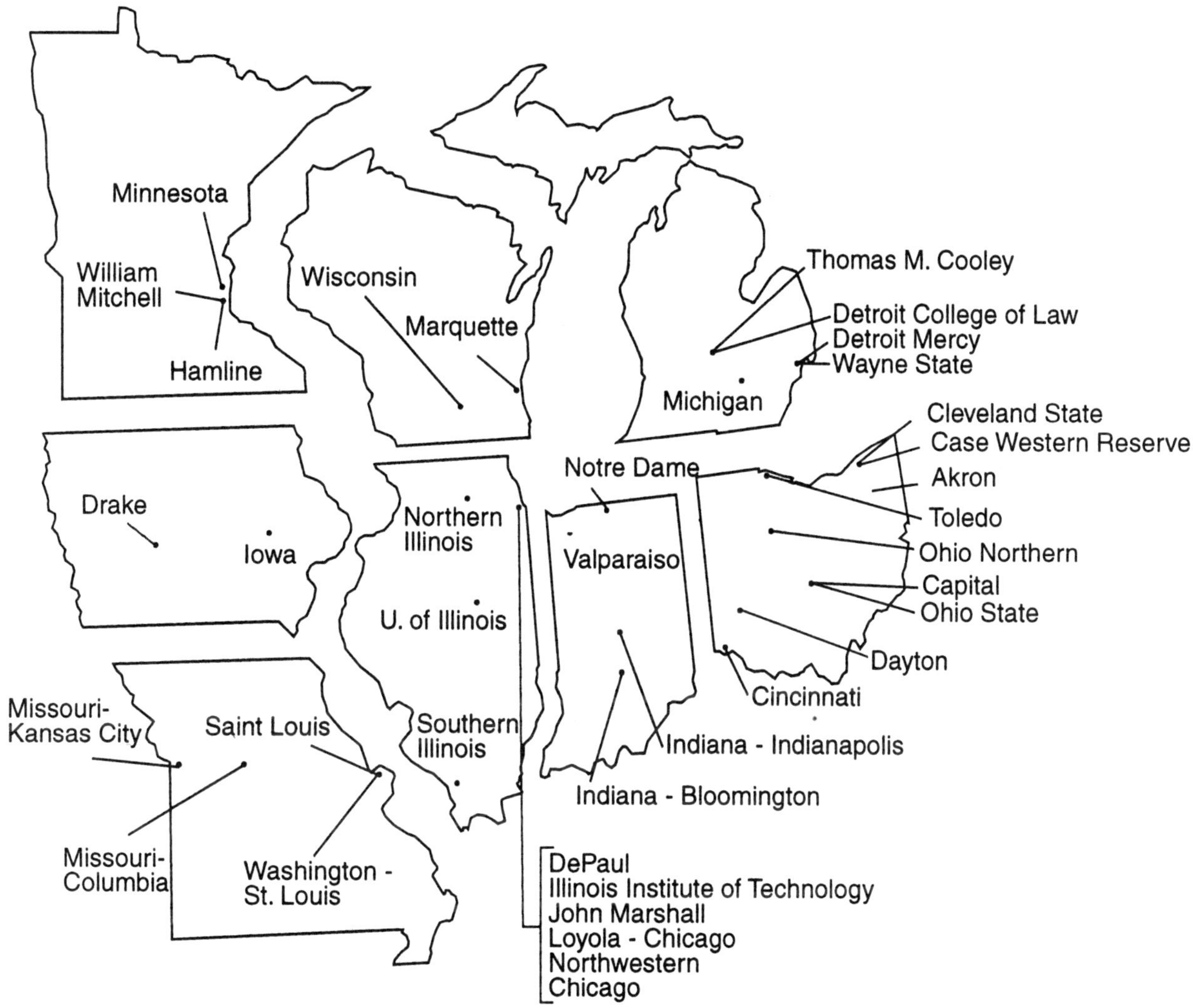
Minnesota
William Mitchell
Hamline
Wisconsin
Marquette
Thomas M. Cooley
Detroit College of Law
Detroit Mercy
Wayne State
Michigan
Cleveland State
Case Western Reserve
Akron
Toledo
Ohio Northern
Capital
Ohio State
Dayton
Cincinnati
Notre Dame
Valparaiso
Indiana - Indianapolis
Indiana - Bloomington
Drake
Iowa
Northern Illinois
U. of Illinois
Southern Illinois
Missouri-Kansas City
Saint Louis
Missouri-Columbia
Washington - St. Louis
DePaul
Illinois Institute of Technology
John Marshall
Loyola - Chicago
Northwestern
Chicago

Southeast

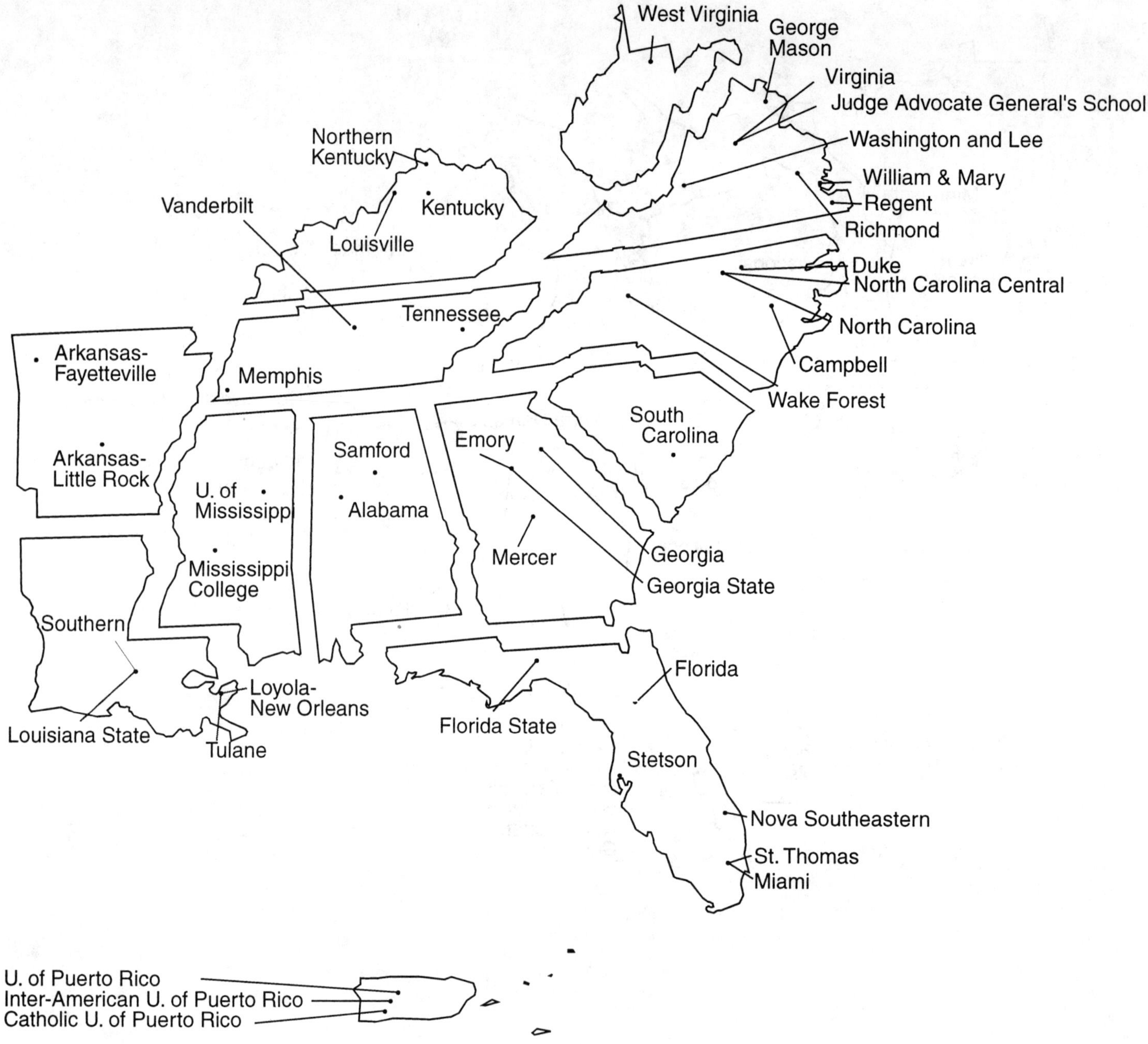
West Virginia
George Mason
Virginia
Judge Advocate General's School
Washington and Lee
William & Mary
Regent
Richmond
Northern Kentucky
Kentucky
Louisville
Vanderbilt
Duke
North Carolina Central
North Carolina
Campbell
Wake Forest
Tennessee
Memphis
Arkansas-Fayetteville
Arkansas-Little Rock
South Carolina
Samford
Emory
U. of Mississippi
Alabama
Mercer
Georgia
Georgia State
Mississippi College
Southern
Florida
Loyola-New Orleans
Louisiana State
Tulane
Florida State
Stetson
Nova Southeastern
St. Thomas
Miami
U. of Puerto Rico
Inter-American U. of Puerto Rico
Catholic U. of Puerto Rico

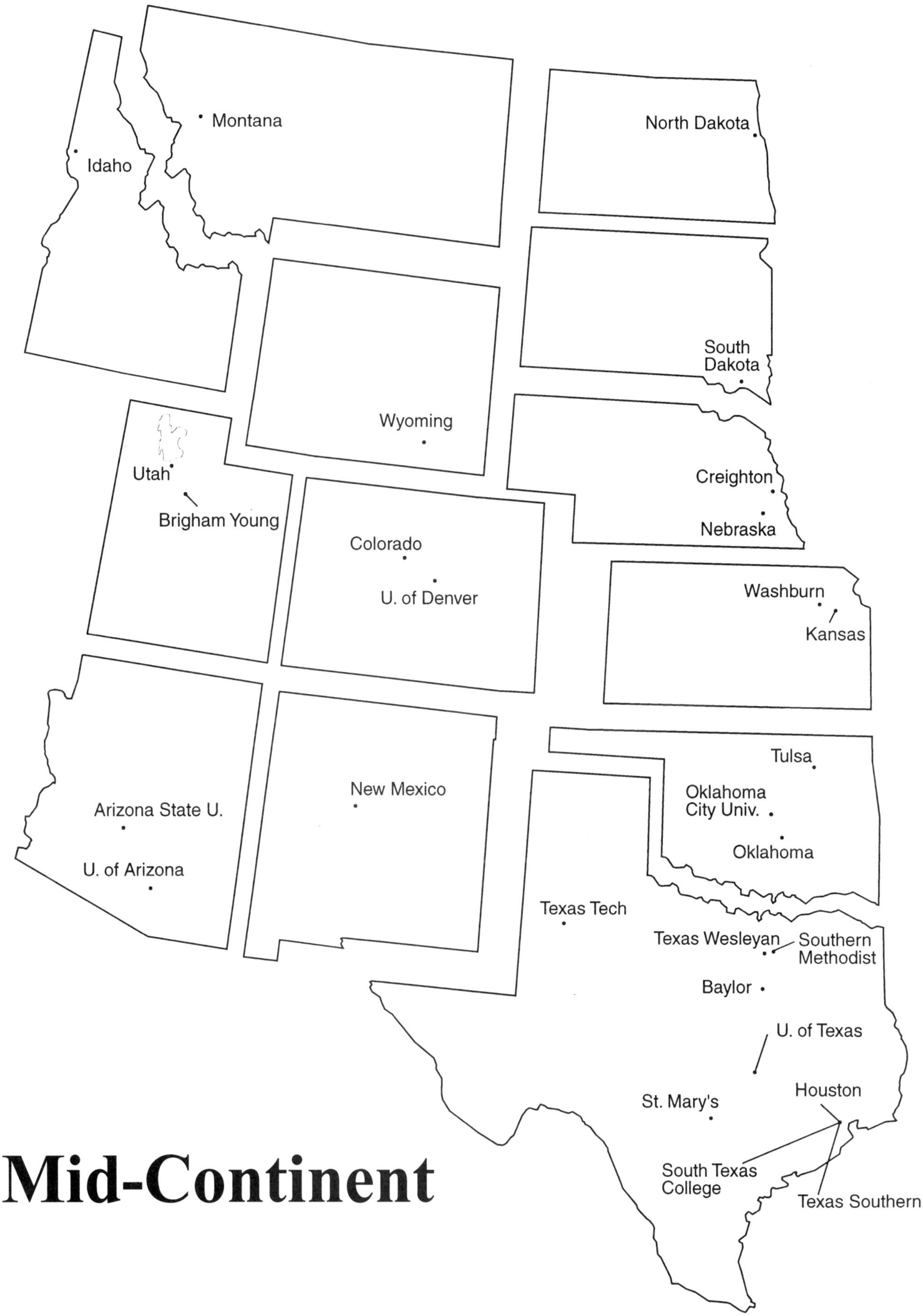

Mid-Continent

West Coast

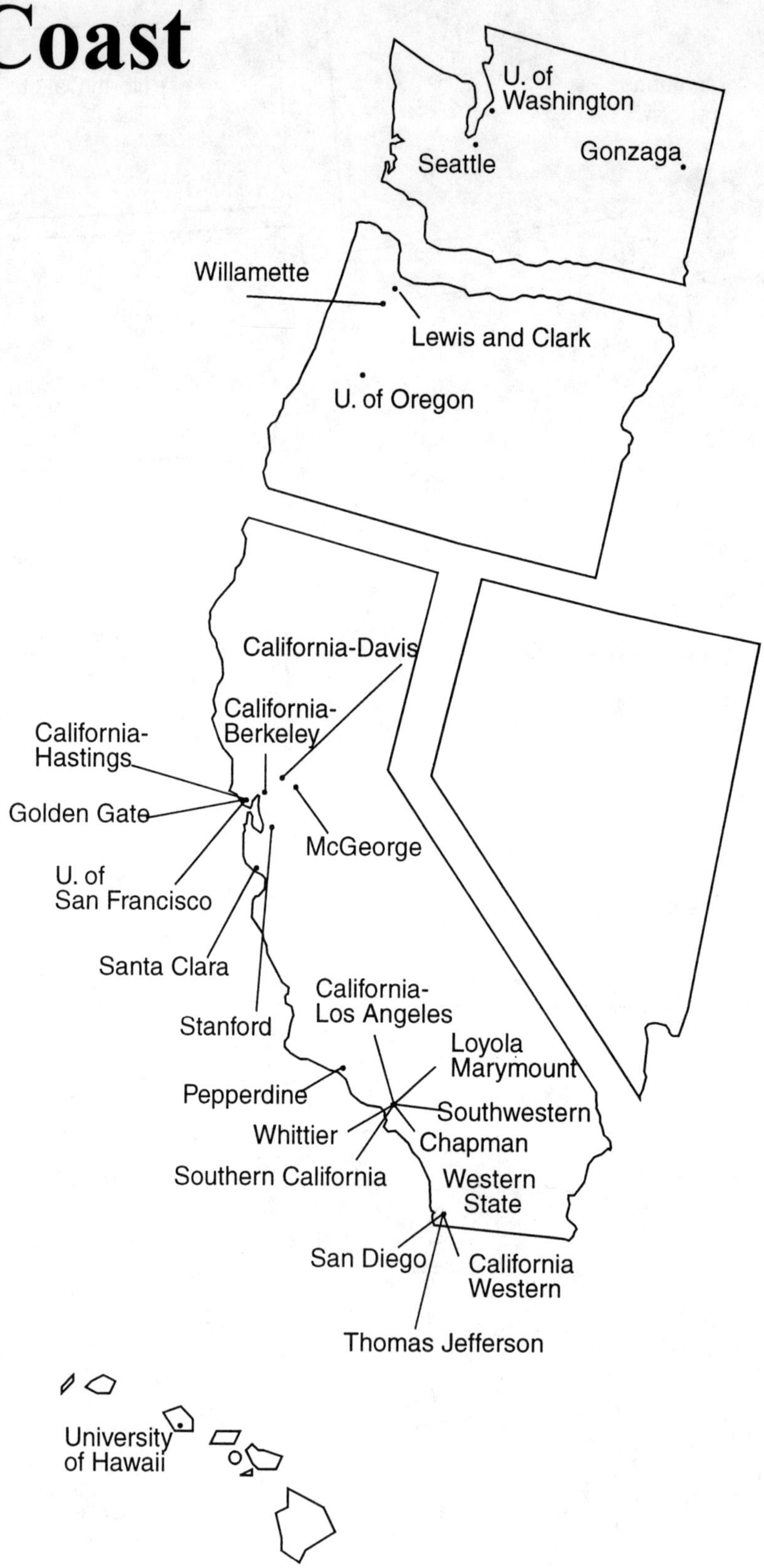
U. of Washington
Seattle
Gonzaga
Willamette
Lewis and Clark
U. of Oregon
California-Davis
California-Berkeley
California-Hastings
Golden Gate
U. of San Francisco
McGeorge
Santa Clara
Stanford
California-Los Angeles
Loyola Marymount
Pepperdine
Southwestern
Whittier
Chapman
Southern California
Western State
San Diego
California Western
Thomas Jefferson
University of Hawaii

Chapter Ten

About the Data

This book is designed to provide consumers with basic information in a simple format that will facilitate the consideration of approved law schools. Please note that applicants should not use this book as the sole source of information regarding application and admission. Rather, this book should supplement other avenues of evaluating respective schools, including making direct contact with admissions officers, professors, students, alumni or prelaw advisors.

The information made available through this publication was collected from questionnaires completed during the Fall 1998 academic semester and submitted by American Bar Association ("ABA") approved law schools to the ABA's Consultant on Legal Education as part of the accreditation process. The completed questionnaires provided to the Consultant's Office are certified by the dean of each law school. Each certification is submitted to the Consultant's Office as an assurance that the information provided accurately reflects prevailing conditions at the law school for which the certification is given. The Consultant's Office, however, does not directly audit the information submitted by the respective institutions on an annual basis.

The information contained in this book is only a small portion of what is collected in the questionnaire for accreditation purposes. Standard 509 for approved law schools, which was developed to meet United States Department of Education requirements, requires that basic information be available to consumers. As a result of these requirements, this book contains a two-page spread on each law school approved by the ABA. Each page is divided into different segments as discussed below. In addition, many of the same data are displayed on three other charts (apart from the two-page spreads) to facilitate side-by-side comparisons.

SCHOOL NAME (Provisional Approval)

The law schools are arranged in alphabetical order by each institution's primary name. Please note that some schools are known by more than one name. A law school that has completed at least one full year of successful operation may apply for provisional approval. A law school is granted provisional approval when it establishes that it substantially complies with each of the Standards and gives assurances that it will be in full compliance with all of the Standards within three years after receiving provisional approval. It is the ABA's view that students at provisionally approved law schools and persons who graduate while a school is provisionally approved are entitled to the same recognition as students and graduates of fully approved law schools. Schools listed in this publication with "Provisional" next to their name were provisionally approved as of October 1, 1998.

THE BASICS

The "Basics" section contains a variety of general information, sorted into the categories listed below.

Type of School: All ABA approved law schools are either public or private. "Public" means that the school receives money from the state in which the school is located. "Private" indicates the school is not operated by the state.

Application Deadline: Not all schools have specific deadlines for admission applications. If the item was left blank in the questionnaire completed by the school, the term "Rolling" appears, which generally means that the school considers applications on a continual basis until the class is filled.

Financial Aid Deadline: Indicates the deadline for the school's financial aid form. (The school deadline may not be the same as federal and state deadlines.) If the item was left blank in the questionnaire completed by the school, the term "Rolling" appears, which generally means schools consider financial aid applications on a continuing basis.

Student/Faculty Ratio: Indicates the number of students relative to the number of instructors for the fall term. The ratio is calculated by comparing faculty full-time equivalency (FTE) to FTE of JD enrollment. A general definition of Faculty FTE is as follows: Total "Full-time" faculty, plus "Additional Instructional Resources." Additional instructional resources include administrators who teach, as well as part-time faculty. Teaching administrators and part-time faculty are included in the faculty FTE at differing weighted factors ranging from .2 to .7. FTE of JD enrollment is calculated as follows: Full-time JD enrollment plus two-thirds of part-time JD enrollment less enrollment in semester-abroad programs. For a detailed definition of the ABA's student/faculty ratio, please consult the ABA Standards for Approval of Law Schools at **http://www.abanet.org/legaled.**

First Year Can Start Other Than Fall: Indicates whether the school has an entering class other than in the fall term.

Student Housing: Indicates whether there is housing restricted to law students and whether there is graduate housing for which law students are eligible.

Term: Indicates whether the school operates on a semester, quarter or trimester system.

FACULTY & ADMINISTRATORS

This section of the two-page spread contains detailed information on the number, gender, and race of the teachers at the school for both semesters. For fall, the information is reported as of October 1, 1998; for spring, the information is an estimate. It should be noted that some schools may have lower part-time numbers in the fall semester because at their school most of the part-time instruction occurs in the spring semester. The five categories of faculty are mutually exclusive. Teachers on "leave" or sabbatical are not included in the full-time faculty count for the term they are on leave. The "Full-time" row indicates tenured or tenure-track faculty. "Other full-time" indicates nontenured Professional Skills Instructors and nontenured Legal Writing Instructors. "Deans, librarians, & others who teach" are law school administrators who teach at least halftime. Administrators who neither teach nor hold faculty rank are not included in these numbers. Administrators who teach are typically at the school and available to students during the entire year. For this reason they are counted in fall and spring regardless of their teaching load. "Part-time during the fall semester" includes: Adjuncts, Permanent Part-time, Faculty from Another Unit, Part-time Professional Skills, and Emeritus Part-time. The "Total" row combines figures from the "Full-time" row through the "Part-time" row. "Deans, librarians, & others who teach < half" are law school administrators who teach less than halftime in the fall or spring.

J.D. ENROLLMENT & ETHNICITY

This section represents the J.D. enrollment by ethnic category, gender, year in school, and full-time/part-time status. Students are classified for purposes of enrollment statistics on the basis of whether they are carrying a full load in the division in which they are enrolled. Minority group enrollment is the total enrollment of students who classify themselves as African American; American Indian or Alaskan Native; Asian or Pacific Islander; Mexican American; Puerto Rican; and other Hispanic-American. Although Puerto Rican law students enrolled in the three approved law schools in Puerto Rico are not classified as minority students in the "Survey of Minority Group Students Enrolled in J.D. Programs in Approved Law Schools," they are counted as minorities in all other areas. Nonresident alien students ("Foreign Nationals") are not included as minority students.

J.D. Degrees Awarded: This indicates the total number of JD degrees awarded during the 1997-98 academic year.

CURRICULUM

All information in this category is based on the 12-month period beginning at the close of the prior academic year (e.g. June 1997 through May 1998). In courses where there was enrollment by both full-time and part-time students, schools were asked to classify each of those courses as "full-time" or "part-time" based on time of day and relative enrollment of full-time and part-time students. Some schools which have a part-time program experienced difficulty providing curriculum information which distinguished between full-time and part-time. In those cases, the part-time column contains zeros. A "small section" means a section of a substantive law course, which may include a legal writing component; "small section" does not mean a legal writing section standing alone. A simulation course is one in which a substantial portion of the instruction is accomplished through the use of role playing or drafting exercises, e.g., trial advocacy, corporate planning and drafting, negotiations, and estate planning and drafting. The "number of course titles beyond the first year curriculum," refers only to classroom courses offered the previous year, not to clinical or field placement possibilities. If a title is offered in both the full-time program and part-time program, the school could count it once in each column. Seminars are defined as courses requiring a written work product and having an enrollment limited to no more than 25. "Faculty-supervised clinics" are those courses or placements with other agencies in which full-time faculty have primary professional responsibility for all cases on which students are working. "Field placements" is a term in which someone other than full-time faculty has primary responsibility to the client; they are frequently called "externships" or "internships." Schools were also asked not to double count a single course by classifying it both as full-time and part-time. "Number involved in law journals/ moot court or trial competitions" reflected those students beyond the first year who participated in those activities during the previous year regardless of whether the student received credit.

GPA & LSAT SCORES

This section of the two-page spread contains statistics on the 1998 entering class. All persons in the particular category, regardless of whether they were admitted through any special admissions program rather than through the normal admissions process, were included. The admissions year was calculated from October 1, 1997 through September 30, 1998. Schools which admit in the spring and/or summer were to include those students in the totals. Figures on matriculants include all students who attended at least one class during the first week of the term in which they were admitted. For a small number of schools, applications and admitted applicants are not identified by the school as full-time or part-time. Therefore, "N/A" appears under the full-time and part-time columns, and the total application and admission offers were entered under the total column.

Percentiles of GPA and LSAT: The GPA and LSAT scores represent the 75th and 25th percentile of the entering class. For example, if the entering class has 100 students, the 75th and 25th percentile could be determined by ranking the students with the best scores first and the worst scores last. The 25th score from the top would indicate the 75th percentile, whereas the 25th score from the bottom would indicate the 25th percentile. This computation is done separately for both the LSAT and the GPA. The 75th and 25th percentiles are a better indication of the quality of a class than a simple median.

GRANTS & SCHOLARSHIPS

This indicates the number and percentage of students receiving internal grants or scholarships from law school or university sources. External grants such as state grants are not included. The percentage for full-time and part-time are based on the total number of full-time and part-time J.D. students, respectively. The total column percentage is based on total J.D. enrollment. Zeros are reported where a school did not provide data.

INFORMATIONAL & LIBRARY RESOURCES

This section of the two-page spread contains basic information about the law library. In addition, it contains brief information about the physical size of the school and the number of computers available.

Number of Volumes & Volume Equivalents: "Volumes" refers to the total number of law and law-related books held by the law school at the end of the 1997-98 fiscal year. "Volume equivalents" is also the number held at the end of the 1997-98 fiscal year. Volume equivalents are computed as follows: Microfiche, Six fiche = 1 volume. Microfilm, 1 roll = 5 volumes.
Title: Each item for which a separate shelf bibliographic unit record has been made.
Active Serial Subscription: Subscriptions where pieces/parts/ updates have been received on a regular or irregular basis during the last two years.
Study Seating Capacity Inside the Library: This indicates the number of study seats available for library users.
Square Feet of Law Library: This is the total square footage of the library.
Square Feet of Law School (Excluding Library): This is the result of subtracting the square footage of the library from the total square footage of the law school, including the library.
Number of Professional Staff: This is the number of professional librarians, including librarians who teach or hold faculty rank.
Hours Per Week With Professional Staff: This indicates the number of hours per week that professional staff are on duty in the library.
Hours Per Week Without Professional Staff: This indicates the number of hours per week the library is open (regular schedule) minus the number of hours per week professional staff are on duty. Please note that many schools also allow students to have access to the library twenty-four hours a day.
Number of Student Computer Workstations: This indicates the number of workstations (networked or stand alone) inside the library and elsewhere in the law school that are available to students. Some ABA approved law schools require their students to possess their own personal computers -- which would not be counted for these purposes.
Number of Additional Networked Connections: This number indicates the number of additional network ports (excluding those listed above) available to students inside the library and elsewhere in the law school. These are not computer workstations; this number represents the number of network ports.

Require Laptop Computer: This section simply indicates whether the school requires students entering the law school in the fall 1998 to have a laptop computer.

J.D. ATTRITION (Prior Year)

Attrition percentages were based on Fall 1997 enrollment. Academic attrition, for this purpose refers to those students not continuing their legal studies between October 1, 1997 and October 1, 1998. "Other attrition" includes: Transfers, Health, Financial, and students who leave for other reasons.

TUITION & FEES

Full-Time tuition: This represents the full-time tuition (plus annual fees) for the academic year for a typical first-year student.

Part-Time Tuition: This represents the part-time tuition (plus annual fees) for the academic year for a typical first-year student. Please note that some schools elected to report part-time tuition on a "per credit hour" basis.

LIVING EXPENSES

This represents the 1998-99 academic year total living expenses (room, board, etc.) and book expenses for full-time, single, resident students for "Living on campus," "Living off campus," and "Living at home." Tuition and fee charges are not included. The figures are used in analyzing law student budgets for loan purposes. Many schools use the same budget amount for all three categories.

PLACEMENT

This section represents statistics on the employment status of the 1997 graduating class six months after gradation. The employment percentages are based on the graduates whose employment status was "known." Hence, for the schools reporting a large percentage of graduates for whom the employment status is unknown, the percentage reported may not be a very accurate reflection of the actual percentage of the class as a whole. "Type of Employment" and "Geographic Location" percentages are based on the number of students "Employed."

BAR PASSAGE RATES

This section refers to numbers and percentages of 1997 graduates who took the Summer 1997 and the February 1998 examinations. The states' overall pass rates for first time takers were obtained by an independent survey of each state bar authority with the assistance of the National Conference of Bar Examiners. Bar examination passage rates vary considerably from state to state, and for first time and repeat test takers. For this book, schools reported data for the jurisdiction(s) in which they had the largest number of first-time takers; overall, that accounted for approximately 72% of all graduates in 1997. Reporting the second highest jurisdiction was optional. Wisconsin allows graduates of the University of Wisconsin Law School and Marquette University Law School to exercise the "diploma privilege" and be admitted to the bar without taking the examination.

Chapter Eleven

Comparison Charts

This book contains information concerning law schools that were operating as of October 1, 1998 and were approved by the ABA to confer the first degree in law. The approval status of an individual law school can change. Therefore, if you would like to confirm whether an individual law school is approved by the ABA at a specific time after October 1, you should contact the ABA directly. You can also access this information on the Section of Legal Education and Admissions to the Bar's website: http://www.abanet.org/legaled. For updates or corrections to this book, please visit the Section's website: http://www.abanet.org/legaled.

	CAREER PLACEMENT														BAR PASSAGE *		
	Employment Status					Type of Employment						Location					
	% Employment Status Known	% Employed	% Pursuing Graduate Degree	% Unemployed - Seeking	% Unemployed - Not Seeking	% in Law Firms	% in Business & Industry	% in Government	% in Public Interest	% in Judicial Clerkships	% in Academia	% Employed in State	# of States where Employed	% Employed in Foreign Nations	State where most take exam	Pass Rate for first-time test takers	State's Overall Pass Rate for first-time test takers
*** Alabama ***																	
Alabama, U. of	98.3	94.3	3.4	1.7	0.6	68.9	7.9	3.7	1.2	7.9	0.6	87.8	6	0.0	AL	91.9	76
Samford U.	95.3	90.6	4.5	1.5	3.5	64.5	8.7	14.8	1.1	9.8	0.0	51.4	16	0.0	AL	88.1	76
*** Arizona ***																	
Arizona State U.	95.4	87.0	2.1	5.5	5.5	45.7	12.6	22.0	0.8	15.7	0.8	82.7	11	0.0	AZ	80.0	80
Arizona, U. of	98.0	91.1	2.7	4.8	1.4	43.6	12.8	18.0	7.5	15.0	0.8	58.6	17	0.8	AZ	84.6	80
*** Arkansas ***																	
Arkansas, U. of Fayetteville	97.8	89.6	5.2	3.0	2.2	55.0	16.7	15.0	3.3	8.3	0.8	60.8	13	0.0	AR	77.5	75
Arkansas, U. of Little Rock	99.1	92.2	5.2	0.0	2.6	47.7	14.0	21.5	3.7	8.4	3.7	79.4	8	0.0	AR	76.6	75
*** California ***																	
California Western School of Law	90.9	85.5	3.2	7.3	4.1	55.3	12.8	26.1	1.1	3.2	1.6	77.7	14	0.5	CA	72.0	71
California-Hastings	95.5	94.7	1.1	2.9	1.3	57.8	15.0	11.1	4.2	8.9	2.5	78.1	21	1.4	CA	90.4	71
California-Los Angeles	99.7	91.0	1.9	3.1	4.0	66.8	12.9	7.8	2.4	8.8	1.4	82.7	17	0.7	CA	81.6	71
California-Berkeley	95.4	96.3	1.1	0.7	1.9	70.4	3.8	8.5	5.8	10.8	0.8	76.2	20	0.8	CA	89.2	71
California-Davis	98.8	82.7	3.7	7.4	6.2	66.4	9.0	11.2	4.5	9.0	0.0	88.1	5	0.0	CA	92.3	71
Chapman U.	0.0	0.0	0.0	0.0	0.0	0.0	0.0	0.0	0.0	0.0	0.0	0.0	1	0.0		0.0	0
Golden Gate U.	92.0	80.7	2.5	8.7	8.1	55.4	17.7	13.1	6.2	1.5	3.1	90.0	7	1.5	CA	69.5	71
Loyola Marymount U.	100.0	84.8	0.7	10.8	3.7	61.2	23.2	6.7	2.9	2.6	3.5	88.4	9	0.0	CA	81.7	71
McGeorge	94.6	81.0	3.9	14.6	0.6	54.8	14.3	22.8	2.2	4.0	1.8	87.1	15	1.1	CA	73.5	71
Pepperdine U.	83.5	75.0	7.1	15.6	2.4	81.8	11.3	4.4	1.3	0.6	0.0	86.2	9	0.0	CA	85.2	71
San Diego, U. of	88.9	86.7	7.0	5.2	1.1	64.7	11.9	16.6	2.1	2.6	0.0	86.0	13	0.0	CA	82.5	71
San Francisco, U. of	90.0	82.8	2.0	12.1	3.0	61.6	12.2	12.8	2.4	3.7	1.2	91.5	6	1.2	CA	89.3	71
Santa Clara U.	90.8	92.4	1.7	2.5	3.4	58.0	23.3	6.8	2.7	3.7	5.5	90.4	12	0.5	CA	81.1	71
Southern California, U. of	95.7	94.1	1.0	1.5	3.5	68.9	13.7	5.3	2.6	9.5	0.0	79.5	18	1.6	CA	88.1	71

* Bar Passage data are for the Summer 97 and Winter 98 exams.

	CAREER PLACEMENT														BAR PASSAGE *		
	Employment Status					Type of Employment						Location					
	% Employment Status Known	% Employed	% Pursuing Graduate Degree	% Unemployed - Seeking	% Unemployed - Not Seeking	% in Law Firms	% in Business & Industry	% in Government	% in Public Interest	% in Judicial Clerkships	% in Academia	% Employed in State	# of States where Employed	% Employed in Foreign Nations	State where most take exam	Pass Rate for first-time test takers	State's Overall Pass Rate for first-time test takers
*** California ***																	
Southwestern U.	91.3	81.8	0.3	16.0	1.8	55.6	25.9	10.2	1.5	2.3	1.1	93.2	11	0.4	CA	64.7	71
Stanford U.	98.9	96.2	1.6	1.6	0.5	56.0	8.0	2.9	4.0	28.6	0.6	57.1	25	1.1	CA	91.2	71
Thomas Jefferson School of Law	64.4	74.1	1.8	9.8	14.3	51.8	26.5	13.3	2.4	1.2	2.4	79.5	8	1.2	CA	42.7	71
Western State U.	84.5	89.4	1.2	4.1	5.3	57.7	21.8	10.9	3.6	0.5	2.3	99.5	2	0.0	CA	48.2	71
Whittier College	92.0	74.6	2.9	12.1	10.4	63.6	15.5	13.2	2.3	2.3	3.1	80.6	11	0.0	CA	68.8	71
*** Colorado ***																	
Colorado, U. of	92.6	87.3	0.0	10.0	2.7	58.0	11.5	13.0	6.1	9.9	0.8	75.6	16	0.8	CO	92.6	81
Denver, U. of	93.0	93.2	4.1	1.4	1.4	53.1	20.5	16.1	2.6	6.2	1.5	78.8	22	0.0	CO	78.5	81
*** Connecticut ***																	
Connecticut, U. of	99.0	92.8	1.0	5.7	0.5	49.4	27.2	11.1	3.3	8.3	0.6	77.8	12	1.1	CT	88.9	84
Quinnipiac College	93.4	88.4	3.1	4.9	3.6	44.2	21.6	23.1	0.0	8.0	0.5	60.3	15	1.0	CT	81.2	84
Yale U.	99.0	98.0	2.0	0.0	0.0	40.4	5.1	2.0	4.0	48.0	0.5	6.1	36	3.5	NY	98.2	76
*** Delaware ***																	
Widener U.	93.6	80.9	2.3	14.5	2.3	34.9	20.1	9.9	1.1	16.2	0.0	22.9	11	0.0	PA	74.5	79
*** District of Columbia ***																	
American U.	86.9	89.2	3.6	5.9	1.3	38.8	15.8	20.9	5.1	13.9	0.7	69.2	28	0.4	MD	69.0	72
Catholic U. of America	99.7	92.5	0.7	5.2	1.6	46.6	19.1	18.4	2.8	10.6	1.8	47.7	27	1.8	MD	67.3	72
District of Columbia, U.	86.4	66.7	5.3	24.6	3.5	34.2	28.9	15.8	18.4	2.6	0.0	63.2	8	0.0	MD	21.9	72
George Washington U.	98.1	96.5	0.2	3.0	0.2	57.0	7.0	13.0	4.0	13.9	0.9	45.1	28	0.9	MD	81.3	72
Georgetown U.	98.0	94.3	1.7	1.9	2.1	66.3	4.7	14.0	3.3	7.8	0.9	45.9	46	1.8	NY	92.1	76
Howard U.	87.2	89.2	3.9	5.9	1.0	34.1	12.1	33.0	4.4	14.3	1.1	49.5	17	2.2	MD	32.7	72

* Bar Passage data are for the Summer 97 and Winter 98 exams.

	CAREER PLACEMENT														BAR PASSAGE *		
	Employment Status					Type of Employment						Location					
	% Employment Status Known	% Employed	% Pursuing Graduate Degree	% Unemployed - Seeking	% Unemployed - Not Seeking	% in Law Firms	% in Business & Industry	% in Government	% in Public Interest	% in Judicial Clerkships	% in Academia	% Employed in State	# of States where Employed	% Employed in Foreign Nations	State where most take exam	Pass Rate for first-time test takers	State's Overall Pass Rate for first-time test takers
*** Florida ***																	
Florida State U.	88.3	89.0	1.2	8.7	1.2	55.8	4.5	18.8	10.4	7.1	1.3	81.2	6	0.0	FL	87.4	83
Florida, U. of	96.6	83.2	4.5	11.7	0.5	67.0	9.9	16.0	1.3	3.8	0.3	82.4	15	0.0	FL	87.5	83
Miami, U. of	95.0	83.9	4.5	11.1	0.5	62.8	8.7	12.9	3.0	4.2	1.5	65.5	16	0.3	FL	79.9	83
Nova Southeastern U.	74.4	72.9	4.7	16.1	6.4	55.2	6.4	30.8	2.3	1.2	1.2	84.3	12	0.6	FL	84.4	83
St. Thomas U.	85.6	84.9	5.9	4.2	5.0	53.5	11.9	32.7	1.0	0.0	1.0	87.1	15	0.0	FL	76.6	83
Stetson U.	92.8	84.9	6.0	9.2	0.0	53.0	10.3	29.2	0.5	7.0	0.0	87.0	18	0.5	FL	86.4	83
*** Georgia ***																	
Emory U.	98.8	91.6	0.8	6.8	0.8	59.0	16.2	11.8	2.2	9.2	1.7	48.0	27	3.1	GA	94.4	83
Georgia State U.	94.9	93.1	0.5	3.2	3.2	60.0	21.1	9.7	2.3	4.6	2.3	90.9	13	0.6	GA	84.5	83
Georgia, U. of	91.5	94.0	2.7	2.2	1.1	64.5	5.2	9.3	5.2	14.0	1.2	78.5	15	0.0	GA	91.1	83
Mercer U.	100.0	91.4	2.1	6.4	0.0	65.6	7.0	15.6	2.3	9.4	0.0	68.7	9	0.0	GA	90.9	83
*** Hawaii ***																	
Hawaii, U. of	96.0	90.3	2.8	1.4	5.6	36.9	15.4	12.3	6.2	26.2	1.5	80.0	8	6.2	HI	84.8	81
*** Idaho ***																	
Idaho, U. of	98.9	85.1	6.4	2.1	6.4	42.5	10.0	15.0	1.2	30.0	1.2	70.0	11	0.0	ID	70.6	75
*** Illinois ***																	
Chicago, U. of	98.9	96.1	3.9	0.0	0.0	69.9	6.4	1.2	1.2	21.4	0.0	38.7	25	0.0	IL	97.0	85
Depaul U.	96.8	89.8	0.9	3.6	5.7	47.0	17.1	12.4	3.4	2.7	1.0	72.1	19	0.0	IL	89.4	85
Illinois Institute of Technology	97.0	80.2	1.2	7.3	11.3	46.8	31.9	12.5	2.3	4.9	1.5	83.7	24	0.4	IL	0.0	85
Illinois, U. of	97.4	94.2	3.2	1.6	1.1	62.4	11.8	14.0	1.7	8.4	1.7	78.1	17	0.6	IL	94.1	85
John Marshall Law School	71.3	89.1	2.5	5.9	2.5	60.1	13.6	20.2	0.5	4.2	1.4	80.8	19	0.0	IL	78.3	85
Loyola U.-Chicago	98.8	91.7	3.1	2.0	3.1	57.9	19.3	12.9	4.7	3.9	1.3	82.4	21	0.4	IL	80.1	85
Northern Illinois U.	94.5	93.0	2.3	4.7	0.0	47.5	13.7	27.5	2.5	8.7	0.0	80.0	10	1.2	IL	82.3	85
Northwestern U.	99.0	94.1	2.0	1.5	2.4	76.2	7.3	4.7	2.6	8.8	0.5	54.9	25	1.0	IL	93.4	85

* Bar Passage data are for the Summer 97 and Winter 98 exams.

	CAREER PLACEMENT														BAR PASSAGE *		
	Employment Status					Type of Employment						Location					
	% Employment Status Known	% Employed	% Pursuing Graduate Degree	% Unemployed - Seeking	% Unemployed - Not Seeking	% in Law Firms	% in Business & Industry	% in Government	% in Public Interest	% in Judicial Clerkships	% in Academia	% Employed in State	# of States where Employed	% Employed in Foreign Nations	State where most take exam	Pass Rate for first-time test takers	State's Overall Pass Rate for first-time test takers
*** Illinois ***																	
Southern Illinois U.-Carbondale	73.5	94.2	1.2	3.5	1.2	55.6	13.6	21.0	2.5	3.7	3.7	79.0	8	0.0	IL	75.5	85
*** Indiana ***																	
Indiana U.-Bloomington	95.0	91.9	3.3	2.4	2.4	53.1	14.1	16.1	2.1	10.9	1.6	57.3	27	2.6	IN	96.5	93
Indiana U.-Indianapolis	98.2	93.4	0.0	5.2	1.4	53.3	17.6	18.1	1.5	6.5	3.0	89.9	14	1.0	IN	93.5	93
Notre Dame, U. of	98.9	94.0	3.8	1.6	0.5	63.6	7.5	15.0	2.3	11.6	0.0	6.9	29	1.2	IL	92.1	85
Valparaiso U.	99.3	97.9	0.0	1.4	0.7	51.4	13.6	19.3	5.7	9.3	0.7	42.1	17	0.7	IN	92.5	93
*** Iowa ***																	
Drake U.	96.8	93.3	3.3	3.3	0.0	48.6	12.9	24.3	5.0	8.6	0.7	49.3	21	0.0	IA	86.5	85
Iowa, U. of	99.6	86.8	3.0	4.3	6.0	57.6	14.8	12.8	3.4	8.4	3.0	29.6	31	0.5	IA	88.4	85
*** Kansas ***																	
Kansas, U. of	95.9	93.7	2.8	2.8	0.7	42.1	23.3	18.8	2.3	9.0	1.5	55.6	14	0.0	KS	89.6	87
Washburn U.	95.4	88.7	1.6	6.5	3.2	38.2	11.8	35.5	7.3	6.4	0.9	61.8	14	0.9	KS	85.4	87
*** Kentucky ***																	
Kentucky, U. of	100.0	96.5	2.1	0.7	0.7	50.4	11.7	16.1	2.2	18.2	0.7	73.7	15	0.7	KY	65.0	70
Louisville, U. of	100.0	96.4	1.4	0.7	1.4	65.9	15.6	13.3	0.0	3.7	1.5	83.7	13	0.0	KY	70.8	70
Northern Kentucky U.	57.1	93.7	1.6	4.7	0.0	48.3	20.0	21.7	0.0	5.0	1.7	43.3	8	0.0	OH	82.1	78
*** Louisiana ***																	
Louisiana State U.	91.6	89.1	2.9	7.5	0.6	59.4	1.3	12.9	1.3	22.6	0.0	91.6	6	0.6	LA	83.0	61
Loyola U.-New Orleans	90.1	85.2	5.5	0.5	8.7	55.1	7.7	17.3	1.3	14.1	1.3	78.2	18	0.0	LA	53.1	61
Southern U.	79.8	81.3	6.7	12.0	0.0	54.1	0.0	26.2	0.0	16.4	3.3	82.0	4	1.6	LA	35.8	61
Tulane U.	99.1	90.7	1.9	5.3	2.2	62.7	12.3	7.9	2.1	11.6	0.3	31.8	1	2.1	LA	71.0	61

* Bar Passage data are for the Summer 97 and Winter 98 exams.

	CAREER PLACEMENT														BAR PASSAGE *		
	Employment Status					Type of Employment						Location					
	% Employment Status Known	% Employed	% Pursuing Graduate Degree	% Unemployed - Seeking	% Unemployed - Not Seeking	% in Law Firms	% in Business & Industry	% in Government	% in Public Interest	% in Judicial Clerkships	% in Academia	% Employed in State	# of States where Employed	% Employed in Foreign Nations	State where most take exam	Pass Rate for first-time test takers	State's Overall Pass Rate for first-time test takers
*** Maine ***																	
Maine, U. of	81.3	87.8	4.1	5.4	2.7	38.5	18.5	20.0	1.5	18.5	1.5	64.6	26	0.0	ME	70.2	69
*** Maryland ***																	
Baltimore, U. of	86.0	90.0	0.7	8.5	0.7	34.2	22.2	23.0	0.4	18.9	1.2	77.0	12	0.0	MD	70.0	72
Maryland, U. of	98.7	90.3	2.5	5.9	1.3	37.6	19.2	21.6	1.9	17.4	1.9	67.1	15	0.5	MD	77.3	72
*** Massachusetts ***																	
Boston College	97.1	93.6	0.4	5.3	0.8	59.3	8.9	8.1	3.6	18.5	1.6	55.6	28	0.4	MA	91.4	82
Boston U.	98.9	87.4	3.1	7.5	2.0	68.7	9.3	12.5	2.6	6.7	0.3	38.0	29	1.9	MA	87.6	82
Harvard U.	98.2	97.4	0.2	2.4	0.0	64.2	5.8	2.4	2.3	24.9	0.4	11.1	39	1.3	NY	95.8	76
New England School of Law	90.9	89.2	2.6	6.7	1.5	40.8	28.7	16.2	0.8	8.3	1.2	79.2	20	0.0	MA	80.4	82
Northeastern U.	93.3	89.0	0.6	8.8	1.7	40.4	9.3	13.0	16.8	18.6	1.2	54.0	20	0.6	MA	85.4	82
Suffolk U.	82.4	90.4	0.8	8.1	0.8	42.1	29.5	16.0	1.1	8.4	2.5	82.6	20	0.3	MA	82.4	82
Western New England	96.3	88.1	1.0	8.6	2.4	38.9	25.9	22.2	1.6	9.2	2.2	40.0	22	0.5	MA	69.3	82
*** Michigan ***																	
Detroit College of Law At Michigan State U.	79.6	90.2	4.5	3.8	1.5	52.5	24.2	10.0	3.3	6.7	0.8	93.3	6	0.0	MI	79.8	86
Detroit Mercy, U. of	67.8	91.0	0.6	3.8	4.5	54.9	21.1	12.0	1.4	9.2	1.4	85.9	9	7.0	MI	83.8	86
Michigan, U. of	96.9	93.7	1.6	3.9	0.8	66.9	4.2	3.9	3.9	19.9	0.3	18.8	34	0.3	MI	92.1	86
Thomas Cooley Law School	76.9	83.5	4.0	12.5	0.0	58.9	12.5	15.3	4.8	7.3	1.2	43.1	32	0.0	MI	84.7	86
Wayne State U.	90.7	93.0	0.5	6.5	0.0	53.5	18.6	15.1	2.9	7.0	2.3	94.2	5	0.0	MI	95.2	86
*** Minnesota ***																	
Hamline U.	96.1	93.0	1.2	4.1	1.8	36.5	23.9	13.2	5.0	20.8	0.6	66.0	0	0.6	MN	85.8	90
Minnesota, U. of	99.2	94.2	0.8	2.3	2.7	46.9	16.5	4.1	6.6	23.0	2.9	60.5	25	2.1	MN	98.8	90
William Mitchell College of Law	90.8	93.5	0.4	5.8	0.4	40.2	28.2	13.9	2.7	14.3	0.8	92.3	14	0.0	MN	86.1	90

* Bar Passage data are for the Summer 97 and Winter 98 exams.

	CAREER PLACEMENT														BAR PASSAGE *		
	Employment Status					Type of Employment						Location					
	% Employment Status Known	% Employed	% Pursuing Graduate Degree	% Unemployed - Seeking	% Unemployed - Not Seeking	% in Law Firms	% in Business & Industry	% in Government	% in Public Interest	% in Judicial Clerkships	% in Academia	% Employed in State	# of States where Employed	% Employed in Foreign Nations	State where most take exam	Pass Rate for first-time test takers	State's Overall Pass Rate for first-time test takers
***** Mississippi *****																	
Mississippi College	98.4	92.5	3.3	0.8	3.3	63.1	4.5	11.7	1.8	18.0	0.9	59.5	13	0.0	MS	91.2	90
Mississippi, U. of	100.0	91.4	5.8	1.4	1.4	71.7	7.1	6.3	0.8	14.2	0.0	74.8	15	0.8	MS	94.8	90
***** Missouri *****																	
Missouri, U. of Kansas City	97.3	91.8	2.1	4.1	2.1	57.5	12.7	18.7	2.2	8.2	0.7	83.6	11	0.0	MO	82.0	85
Missouri, U. of Columbia	97.7	89.8	1.6	8.7	0.0	37.7	16.7	23.7	0.0	20.2	1.8	96.5	4	0.9	MO	91.3	85
St. Louis U.	94.1	92.3	1.4	4.3	1.9	55.7	16.1	14.6	1.0	8.9	2.1	74.5	19	0.5	MO	80.3	85
Washington U.	96.1	96.5	0.5	1.0	2.0	59.7	9.4	15.2	4.7	7.9	0.5	44.5	23	0.5	MO	88.9	85
***** Montana *****																	
Montana, U. of	98.7	90.5	4.1	5.4	0.0	44.8	6.0	14.9	3.0	29.9	0.0	71.6	12	0.0	MT	96.5	91
***** Nebraska *****																	
Creighton U.	97.5	86.5	5.8	1.9	5.8	50.7	24.6	11.2	3.7	7.5	0.7	50.7	23	0.0	NE	89.0	87
Nebraska, U. of	99.2	86.0	5.4	5.4	3.1	46.8	22.5	25.2	9.0	9.0	0.0	62.2	1	0.0	NE	89.6	87
***** New Hampshire *****																	
Franklin Pierce Law Center	90.3	86.6	0.9	10.7	1.8	69.1	9.3	9.3	2.1	1.0	3.1	21.6	26	2.1	NH	74.3	75
***** New Jersey *****																	
Rutgers U.- Newark	95.1	93.6	1.7	3.0	1.7	35.5	18.6	10.0	3.6	30.9	1.4	72.7	12	0.5	NJ	75.8	77
Rutgers U.- Camden	94.8	91.8	3.1	3.9	1.2	36.9	13.6	8.9	1.7	38.6	0.4	61.4	18	1.7	NJ	83.2	77
Seton Hall U.	96.1	94.4	0.6	4.4	0.6	35.6	23.2	7.1	0.6	32.8	0.0	74.3	15	0.3	NJ	78.9	77
***** New Mexico *****																	
New Mexico, U. of	100.0	90.3	1.9	6.8	1.0	45.2	16.1	26.9	3.2	8.6	0.0	75.3	18	0.0	NM	92.3	93
***** New York *****																	
Albany Law School	98.8	95.5	1.2	0.4	2.8	49.2	16.9	21.6	3.4	6.4	2.5	81.8	17	0.0	NY	80.7	76
Brooklyn Law School	97.7	92.3	1.4	4.4	1.9	58.4	15.2	17.5	3.6	3.8	1.5	92.4	11	0.5	NY	80.0	76
City U. of New York	83.6	77.9	0.8	15.6	5.7	28.4	18.9	20.0	17.9	6.3	1.1	70.5	7	0.0	NY	46.2	76
Columbia U.	98.3	98.8	0.9	0.3	0.0	69.0	3.3	3.9	2.4	21.1	1.2	68.7	23	1.8	NY	93.8	76

* Bar Passage data are for the Summer 97 and Winter 98 exams.

	CAREER PLACEMENT														BAR PASSAGE *		
	Employment Status					Type of Employment						Location					
	% Employment Status Known	% Employed	% Pursuing Graduate Degree	% Unemployed - Seeking	% Unemployed - Not Seeking	% in Law Firms	% in Business & Industry	% in Government	% in Public Interest	% in Judicial Clerkships	% in Academia	% Employed in State	# of States where Employed	% Employed in Foreign Nations	State where most take exam	Pass Rate for first-time test takers	State's Overall Pass Rate for first-time test takers
*** New York ***																	
Cornell U.	97.4	97.9	1.1	1.1	0.0	66.7	7.1	3.3	2.7	17.5	0.0	33.9	24	1.6	NY	94.5	76
Fordham U.	94.3	95.8	1.1	2.9	0.3	66.4	15.2	9.6	2.2	6.1	0.6	84.3	16	0.0	NY	83.8	76
Hofstra U.	90.2	90.7	1.2	4.4	3.6	74.7	11.1	6.7	5.3	2.2	0.0	89.8	11	0.0	NY	64.9	76
New York Law School	87.0	91.7	1.1	4.3	2.9	52.8	22.2	14.6	2.9	4.7	0.9	70.6	15	0.3	NY	66.5	76
New York U.	100.0	98.4	1.4	0.2	0.0	76.9	3.5	2.8	3.3	13.4	0.0	64.2	28	0.0	NY	95.9	76
Pace U.	89.5	84.3	0.5	11.2	4.1	56.6	17.5	12.7	4.2	4.8	0.0	69.9	13	0.6	NY	75.0	76
St. John's U.	84.3	85.0	0.6	6.9	7.5	59.5	13.0	15.5	1.4	6.7	1.4	89.8	14	0.7	NY	85.5	76
State U. of New York at Buffalo	98.4	87.9	4.4	2.4	5.2	46.3	18.8	17.9	6.4	7.3	3.2	84.9	18	0.5	NY	70.9	76
Syracuse U.	98.3	93.2	1.7	3.8	1.3	64.1	16.4	8.6	2.3	6.4	2.3	49.5	27	1.4	NY	77.6	76
Touro College	86.0	80.4	1.0	17.7	1.0	56.0	17.3	17.9	4.8	1.2	1.8	89.9	7	1.8	NY	59.4	76
Yeshiva U.	82.4	92.2	2.5	1.8	3.6	64.1	13.1	13.9	1.5	6.6	0.8	77.6	18	0.4	NY	75.6	76
*** North Carolina ***																	
Campbell U.	93.0	98.9	1.1	0.0	0.0	82.6	5.4	4.3	2.2	5.4	0.0	83.7	12	0.0	NC	94.2	82
Duke U.	100.0	97.9	0.5	0.5	1.0	73.3	3.1	4.2	1.0	18.3	0.0	6.8	32	1.0	NY	95.4	76
North Carolina Central	84.9	91.8	5.5	0.0	2.7	46.3	19.4	23.9	9.0	0.0	1.5	80.6	8	0.0	NC	81.7	82
North Carolina, U. of	98.6	96.3	1.8	0.5	1.4	56.9	12.3	12.8	2.8	13.7	1.4	64.5	23	0.5	NC	92.5	82
Wake Forest U.	96.1	95.3	0.0	2.7	2.0	66.2	10.6	10.6	1.4	11.3	0.0	63.4	21	0.0	NC	91.9	82
*** North Dakota ***																	
North Dakota, U. of	94.3	93.9	3.0	3.0	0.0	37.1	12.9	17.7	3.2	27.4	1.6	41.9	17	1.6	ND	83.3	85
*** Ohio ***																	
Akron, U. of	99.4	86.1	1.8	3.0	9.1	46.5	21.8	23.9	2.8	3.5	1.4	66.2	18	2.8	OH	77.9	78
Capital U.	99.5	88.9	0.5	7.4	3.2	44.3	28.1	20.8	0.0	5.2	1.0	89.1	19	0.0	OH	76.0	78
Case Western Reserve U.	98.0	86.5	2.5	10.0	1.0	64.2	13.9	9.2	4.0	8.7	0.0	63.0	21	1.2	OH	79.2	78

* Bar Passage data are for the Summer 97 and Winter 98 exams.

	CAREER PLACEMENT															BAR PASSAGE *		
	Employment Status					Type of Employment						Location						
	% Employment Status Known	% Employed	% Pursuing Graduate Degree	% Unemployed - Seeking	% Unemployed - Not Seeking	% in Law Firms	% in Business & Industry	% in Government	% in Public Interest	% in Judicial Clerkships	% in Academia	% Employed in State	# of States where Employed	% Employed in Foreign Nations	State where most take exam	Pass Rate for first-time test takers	State's Overall Pass Rate for first-time test takers
***** Ohio *****																		
Cincinnati, U. of	98.5	93.0	0.0	5.5	1.6	54.6	21.0	10.9	2.5	10.1	0.8	68.1	20	0.0	OH	94.2	78
Cleveland State U.	97.5	84.7	1.3	3.0	11.1	49.2	21.1	14.6	3.0	4.5	2.5	67.8	13	0.0	OH	65.0	78
Dayton, U. of	96.8	88.8	0.7	7.9	2.6	53.3	18.5	22.2	1.5	3.7	0.7	49.6	24	0.0	OH	76.1	78
Ohio Northern U.	80.4	86.7	2.2	7.8	3.3	60.3	7.7	20.5	1.3	7.7	3.8	25.6	19	0.0	OH	59.1	78
Ohio State U.	92.4	91.8	3.1	3.6	1.5	57.3	11.8	15.7	5.6	9.6	0.0	75.8	19	0.6	OH	84.8	78
Toledo, U. of	82.2	92.8	1.8	3.6	1.8	49.4	22.1	19.5	1.3	5.8	1.9	59.1	12	0.6	OH	69.1	78
***** Oklahoma *****																		
Oklahoma City U.	95.2	78.7	1.9	13.7	5.6	58.7	22.2	16.7	0.0	0.8	1.6	56.3	20	0.0	OK	81.4	82
Oklahoma, U. of	86.6	93.1	2.3	4.0	0.6	54.3	19.1	17.3	3.1	1.9	1.9	74.7	1	0.0	OK	86.7	82
Tulsa, U. of	99.0	83.4	3.1	12.4	1.0	60.2	20.5	14.9	0.6	3.1	0.6	57.1	26	1.2	OK	82.8	82
***** Oregon *****																		
Lewis & Clark College	94.5	90.8	0.0	6.3	2.9	51.6	12.2	18.6	6.9	9.6	1.1	63.3	23	0.5	OR	78.8	72
Oregon, U. of	94.3	81.2	8.1	8.1	2.7	45.5	14.0	12.4	6.6	19.8	0.8	52.1	16	1.7	OR	70.8	72
Willamette U.	97.7	82.4	1.8	14.1	1.8	57.9	17.1	15.7	2.1	2.1	2.1	57.1	16	1.4	OR	64.7	72
***** Pennsylvania *****																		
Dickinson School of Law	95.6	91.4	2.3	4.6	1.7	42.8	2.5	8.8	2.5	32.7	0.0	70.4	19	0.6	PA	88.8	79
Duquesne U.	99.4	91.1	0.6	8.3	0.0	57.5	20.3	5.9	0.7	12.4	1.3	62.1	15	0.7	PA	82.4	79
Pennsylvania, U. of	97.6	97.9	0.7	1.1	0.4	70.4	5.8	3.6	4.7	14.1	1.4	22.0	22	1.1	NY	92.3	76
Pittsburgh, U. of	92.5	82.4	3.3	2.9	11.4	52.6	9.8	6.9	1.7	13.3	0.6	57.2	22	0.6	PA	74.2	79
Temple U.	97.1	91.3	1.4	5.5	1.9	46.1	21.6	11.1	9.3	11.7	0.3	60.2	20	1.2	PA	68.2	79
Villanova U.	93.2	87.4	2.4	10.1	0.0	51.9	17.7	8.3	0.0	22.1	0.0	67.4	12	0.0	PA	79.3	79
Widener U.	92.0	80.7	0.6	14.3	4.3	28.5	15.4	27.7	3.1	17.7	0.8	62.3	14	0.0	PA	81.2	79

* Bar Passage data are for the Summer 97 and Winter 98 exams.

	CAREER PLACEMENT														BAR PASSAGE *		
	Employment Status					Type of Employment						Location					
	% Employment Status Known	% Employed	% Pursuing Graduate Degree	% Unemployed - Seeking	% Unemployed - Not Seeking	% in Law Firms	% in Business & Industry	% in Government	% in Public Interest	% in Judicial Clerkships	% in Academia	% Employed in State	# of States where Employed	% Employed in Foreign Nations	State where most take exam	Pass Rate for first-time test takers	State's Overall Pass Rate for first-time test takers
*** Puerto Rico ***																	
Inter American U. of Puerto Rico	94.5	91.0	2.6	3.2	3.2	39.0	27.0	14.2	2.1	15.6	2.1	97.2	3	0.0	PR	54.7	61
Pontifical Catholic U. of Puerto Rico	75.8	91.0	7.0	2.0	0.0	50.5	6.6	35.2	0.0	5.5	0.0	98.9	1	0.0	PR	65.3	61
Puerto Rico, U. of	90.4	90.3	2.9	4.9	1.9	55.9	1.1	28.0	1.1	11.8	0.0	91.4	1	1.1	PR	76.1	61
*** Rhode Island ***																	
Roger Williams U.	66.7	90.4	1.1	7.4	1.1	45.9	22.4	18.8	1.2	7.1	4.7	60.0	13	1.2	RI	64.1	64
*** South Carolina ***																	
South Carolina, U. of	97.4	92.1	1.7	5.7	0.4	51.2	10.9	18.0	1.4	18.5	0.0	81.0	14	0.5	SC	86.5	84
*** South Dakota ***																	
South Dakota, U. of	100.0	85.3	5.3	9.3	0.0	45.3	10.9	14.1	0.0	26.6	3.1	56.2	15	1.6	SD	91.5	89
*** Tennessee ***																	
Memphis, U. of	95.6	94.7	3.8	0.0	1.5	61.3	8.9	12.9	2.4	8.1	1.6	75.0	14	0.0	TN	83.9	80
Tennessee, U. of	98.5	93.0	4.7	1.6	0.8	67.5	5.8	11.7	0.8	11.7	2.5	79.2	10	0.0	TN	86.9	80
Vanderbilt U.	100.0	95.1	3.3	1.1	0.5	66.9	5.7	9.1	4.6	13.7	0.0	26.3	30	1.1	TN	92.3	80
*** Texas ***																	
Baylor U.	97.6	96.9	1.9	1.2	0.0	64.3	7.0	14.6	0.6	12.7	0.6	85.4	15	0.6	TX	90.0	81
Houston, U. of	95.0	90.6	1.2	7.0	1.2	62.1	19.4	11.7	1.6	3.2	1.9	89.6	18	0.3	TX	90.6	81
South Texas College of Law	73.2	77.3	1.7	19.3	1.7	71.2	13.6	9.2	0.5	2.7	1.6	90.8	8	1.1	TX	83.3	81
Southern Methodist U.	99.5	91.8	3.6	2.7	1.8	64.9	10.9	12.9	1.5	5.4	0.0	76.2	17	0.5	TX	85.0	81
St. Mary's U.	89.5	90.1	3.3	6.1	0.5	65.6	8.9	14.6	2.1	6.8	1.0	87.0	17	0.0	TX	77.6	81
Texas Southern U.	84.5	39.8	4.3	43.0	12.9	40.5	18.9	21.6	0.0	8.1	0.0	81.1	6	0.0	TX	88.0	81
Texas Tech U.	84.5	87.1	0.0	12.9	0.0	83.1	1.4	9.2	0.0	6.3	0.0	97.9	3	0.0	TX	90.9	81
Texas Wesleyan U.	91.6	80.1	1.4	7.1	11.3	41.6	35.4	8.8	3.5	6.2	4.4	94.7	4	1.8	TX	53.9	81
Texas, U. of at Austin	99.6	90.6	2.6	3.5	3.3	65.0	13.1	6.5	1.6	10.2	0.2	72.6	28	0.4	TX	89.3	81

* Bar Passage data are for the Summer 97 and Winter 98 exams.

	CAREER PLACEMENT														BAR PASSAGE *		
	Employment Status					Type of Employment						Location					
	% Employment Status Known	% Employed	% Pursuing Graduate Degree	% Unemployed - Seeking	% Unemployed - Not Seeking	% in Law Firms	% in Business & Industry	% in Government	% in Public Interest	% in Judicial Clerkships	% in Academia	% Employed in State	# of States where Employed	% Employed in Foreign Nations	State where most take exam	Pass Rate for first-time test takers	State's Overall Pass Rate for first-time test takers
*** Utah ***																	
Brigham Young U.	100.0	93.5	3.2	0.6	2.6	52.8	16.7	10.4	2.1	16.0	2.1	42.4	31	4.2	UT	95.7	93
Utah, U. of	96.9	95.2	2.4	0.0	2.4	48.3	16.1	9.3	5.1	16.9	2.5	69.5	13	0.0	UT	90.6	93
*** Vermont ***																	
Vermont Law School	98.7	85.0	3.4	8.8	2.7	37.6	24.0	16.0	11.2	8.8	1.6	17.6	35	0.0	NY	85.2	76
*** Virginia ***																	
George Mason U.	88.2	83.4	1.9	14.0	0.6	42.7	17.6	25.2	0.0	13.0	1.5	38.9	15	0.8	VA	79.5	75
Regent U.	95.1	82.5	4.1	11.3	2.1	46.2	16.2	12.5	11.2	6.2	1.2	31.2	25	1.2	VA	58.8	75
Richmond, U. of	96.3	91.0	5.1	0.0	3.8	45.1	22.5	14.8	1.4	15.5	0.7	74.6	13	0.7	VA	73.1	75
Virginia, U. of	96.2	98.4	0.8	0.8	0.0	69.2	6.2	3.8	0.8	20.0	0.0	16.2	34	0.3	VA	88.3	75
Washington & Lee U.	97.5	93.9	1.7	3.5	0.9	52.8	9.3	8.3	0.9	25.9	2.8	27.8	23	0.0	VA	91.7	75
William and Mary School of Law	98.8	89.1	6.7	1.8	2.4	52.4	9.5	18.4	2.7	17.0	0.0	32.0	26	2.7	VA	81.8	75
*** Washington ***																	
Gonzaga U.	93.4	87.7	5.8	1.9	4.5	55.9	5.9	20.6	3.7	11.8	0.7	51.5	21	0.7	WA	81.3	76
Seattle U.	89.1	86.2	1.6	9.8	2.4	55.3	17.4	15.5	2.7	3.7	1.4	88.6	14	1.4	WA	79.9	76
Washington, U. of	95.5	85.4	6.4	7.6	0.6	50.7	15.8	14.4	7.5	10.3	1.4	71.9	17	2.7	WA	86.0	76
*** West Virginia ***																	
West Virginia U.	94.2	93.9	3.1	3.1	0.0	67.5	4.1	17.1	3.3	8.1	0.0	80.5	12	0.8	WV	78.6	84
*** Wisconsin ***																	
Marquette U.	94.8	93.1	2.1	2.1	2.8	63.0	14.8	10.4	1.5	3.0	7.4	72.6	12	1.5	WI	100.0	86
Wisconsin, U. of	93.2	93.9	2.4	3.7	0.0	57.6	13.0	18.6	2.2	8.2	0.4	69.7	20	0.4	WI	100.0	86
*** Wyoming ***																	
Wyoming, U. of	94.1	84.4	0.0	14.1	1.6	48.1	3.7	25.9	3.7	16.7	1.9	68.5	10	1.9	WY	85.4	74

* Bar Passage data are for the Summer 97 and Winter 98 exams.

	EXPENSES				FACULTY						STUDENT BODY				
SECTION OF LEGAL EDUCATION AND ADMISSIONS TO THE BAR · ESTABLISHED 1893 · ABA	Full-Time Tuition Res Non-Res	Part-Time Tuition Res Non-Res	Expenses: on-campus	Expenses: off-campus	Student-Faculty Ratio	# Full-Time Faculty	# Part-Time Faculty	% Men	% Women	% Minorities	# of Full-Time Students	# of Part-Time Students	% Men	% Women	% Minorities
***** Alabama *****															
Alabama, U. of	**$4,490 $9,484**	**$0 $0**	**$10,902**	**$10,312**	**18.3/1**	**25**	**31**	**80**	**20**	**8**	**549**	**0**	**61.9**	**38.1**	**9.5**
Samford U.	**$18,350 $18,350**	**$0 $0**	**N/A**	**$11,949**	**21.0/1**	**24**	**19**	**79**	**21**	**8**	**605**	**0**	**63.1**	**36.9**	**7.9**
***** Arizona *****															
Arizona State U.	**$4,536 $11,488**	**$0 $0**	**$8,025**	**$10,625**	**17.2/1**	**23**	**21**	**83**	**17**	**13**	**475**	**0**	**52.6**	**47.4**	**21.9**
Arizona, U. of	**$4,538 $11,490**	**$0 $0**	**$8,178**	**$11,998**	**14.2/1**	**27**	**32**	**59**	**41**	**15**	**460**	**0**	**50.2**	**49.8**	**24.8**
***** Arkansas *****															
Arkansas, U. of Fayetteville	**$4,168 $9,136**	**$0 $0**	**$10,700**	**$10,700**	**13.8/1**	**22**	**10**	**68**	**32**	**14**	**364**	**0**	**60.4**	**39.6**	**7.4**
Arkansas, U. of Little Rock	**$4,418 $9,738**	**$3,196 $6,996**	**N/A**	**$9,077**	**17.0/1**	**18**	**11**	**67**	**33**	**11**	**276**	**139**	**52.5**	**47.5**	**11.8**
***** California *****															
California Western School of Law	**$20,570 $20,570**	**$14,770 $14,770**	**N/A**	**$13,582**	**17.4/1**	**33**	**32**	**58**	**42**	**18**	**666**	**33**	**46.6**	**53.4**	**27.9**
California-Hastings	**$11,167 $19,937**	**$0 $0**	**$15,635**	**$15,635**	**20.2/1**	**47**	**77**	**70**	**30**	**21**	**1,146**	**0**	**51.4**	**48.6**	**31.8**
California-Los Angeles	**$10,972 $20,356**	**$0 $0**	**N/A**	**$13,832**	**15.1/1**	**55**	**14**	**76**	**24**	**15**	**976**	**0**	**51.4**	**48.6**	**33.8**
California-Berkeley	**$10,814 $20,198**	**$0 $0**	**$12,958**	**$12,958**	**17.2/1**	**41**	**43**	**80**	**20**	**12**	**846**	**0**	**48.2**	**51.8**	**30.3**
California-Davis	**$10,859 $19,843**	**$0 $0**	**$10,544**	**$10,808**	**16.0/1**	**27**	**15**	**63**	**37**	**15**	**503**	**0**	**49.7**	**50.3**	**22.5**
Chapman U.	**$17,550 $17,550**	**$12,550 $12,550**	**N/A**	**$11,012**	**7.9/1**	**16**	**10**	**69**	**31**	**19**	**74**	**113**	**52.4**	**47.6**	**26.2**
Golden Gate U.	**$20,221 $20,221**	**$14,020 $14,020**	**N/A**	**$11,190**	**16.9/1**	**26**	**41**	**62**	**38**	**15**	**415**	**170**	**42.4**	**57.6**	**26.2**
Loyola Marymount U.	**$21,748 $21,748**	**$14,608 $14,608**	**N/A**	**$13,445**	**22.4/1**	**45**	**48**	**64**	**36**	**24**	**968**	**364**	**52.9**	**47.1**	**39.5**
McGeorge	**$20,762 $20,762**	**$13,324 $13,324**	**$13,910**	**$13,910**	**22.2/1**	**36**	**30**	**78**	**22**	**11**	**745**	**350**	**51.9**	**48.1**	**24.6**
Pepperdine U.	**$22,880 $22,880**	**$0 $0**	**$15,234**	**$15,234**	**17.6/1**	**29**	**28**	**79**	**21**	**7**	**652**	**0**	**54.8**	**45.2**	**16.3**
San Diego, U. of	**$20,980 $20,980**	**$14,890 $14,890**	**$12,538**	**$12,538**	**17.2/1**	**43**	**29**	**79**	**21**	**12**	**711**	**269**	**58.3**	**41.7**	**23.7**
San Francisco, U. of	**$21,008 $21,008**	**$15,040 $15,040**	**$11,260**	**$12,850**	**20.9/1**	**24**	**38**	**67**	**33**	**21**	**518**	**127**	**44.3**	**55.7**	**24.0**
Santa Clara U.	**$20,782 $20,782**	**$14,360 $14,360**	**$15,734**	**$15,734**	**19.5/1**	**35**	**25**	**66**	**34**	**23**	**629**	**288**	**51.0**	**49.0**	**30.4**
Southern California, U. of	**$25,052 $25,052**	**$0 $0**	**$11,344**	**$12,024**	**15.7/1**	**33**	**21**	**64**	**36**	**9**	**621**	**0**	**54.4**	**45.6**	**39.9**
Southwestern U.	**$21,040 $21,040**	**$13,362 $13,362**	**N/A**	**$11,430**	**18.1/1**	**37**	**16**	**73**	**27**	**11**	**616**	**286**	**48.7**	**51.3**	**37.1**
Stanford U.	**$25,190 $25,190**	**$0 $0**	**$11,472**	**$16,707**	**13.4/1**	**34**	**28**	**74**	**26**	**18**	**541**	**0**	**56.6**	**43.4**	**31.2**

	EXPENSES				FACULTY						STUDENT BODY				
	Res Non-Res Full-Time Tuition	Res Non-Res Part-Time Tuition	Expenses: on-campus	Expenses: off-campus	Student-Faculty Ratio	# Full-Time Faculty	# Part-Time Faculty	% Men	% Women	% Minorities	# of Full-Time Students	# of Part-Time Students	% Men	% Women	% Minorities
***** California *****															
Thomas Jefferson School of Law	**$18,880 $18,880**	**$11,680 $11,680**	**N/A**	**$13,525**	**18.4/1**	**22**	**23**	**55**	**45**	**9**	**333**	**230**	**62.2**	**37.8**	**21.3**
Western State U.	**$18,900 $18,900**	**$12,600 $12,600**	**N/A**	**$15,266**	**23.3/1**	**20**	**30**	**55**	**45**	**30**	**231**	**499**	**57.7**	**42.3**	**33.4**
Whittier College	**$21,064 $21,064**	**$12,652 $12,652**	**N/A**	**$15,219**	**17.4/1**	**27**	**25**	**59**	**41**	**11**	**392**	**259**	**51.8**	**48.2**	**36.6**
***** Colorado *****															
Colorado, U. of	**$5,412 $17,086**	**$0 $0**	**$9,110**	**$12,134**	**13.6/1**	**30**	**16**	**83**	**17**	**17**	**487**	**2**	**52.6**	**47.4**	**15.7**
Denver, U. of	**$18,780 $18,780**	**$14,085 $14,085**	**$11,893**	**$11,893**	**25.3/1**	**31**	**72**	**74**	**26**	**10**	**751**	**290**	**47.3**	**52.7**	**8.9**
***** Connecticut *****															
Connecticut, U. of	**$10,984 $22,774**	**$7,690 $15,910**	**N/A**	**$12,468**	**12.2/1**	**35**	**35**	**77**	**23**	**6**	**413**	**162**	**53.6**	**46.4**	**15.3**
Quinnipiac College	**$20,441 $20,441**	**$17,105 $17,105**	**N/A**	**$13,393**	**17.2/1**	**32**	**24**	**66**	**34**	**9**	**476**	**279**	**57.4**	**42.6**	**13.9**
Yale U.	**$25,550 $25,550**	**$0 $0**	**$11,320**	**$11,320**	**12.3/1**	**41**	**24**	**80**	**20**	**12**	**593**	**0**	**57.5**	**42.5**	**31.2**
***** Delaware *****															
Widener U.	**$18,550 $18,550**	**$13,930 $13,930**	**$11,970**	**$11,970**	**27.6/1**	**28**	**41**	**61**	**39**	**0**	**645**	**429**	**53.8**	**46.2**	**6.8**
***** District of Columbia *****															
American U.	**$22,972 $22,972**	**$16,982 $16,982**	**$12,734**	**$12,734**	**20.6/1**	**44**	**90**	**64**	**36**	**16**	**883**	**311**	**39.5**	**60.5**	**27.1**
Catholic U. of America	**$23,898 $23,898**	**$17,279 $17,279**	**$13,390**	**$13,390**	**20.6/1**	**33**	**49**	**70**	**30**	**15**	**643**	**259**	**51.0**	**49.0**	**19.8**
District of Columbia, U.	**$7,135 $14,135**	**$0 $0**	**N/A**	**$18,065**	**16.5/1**	**8**	**6**	**63**	**38**	**25**	**158**	**0**	**45.6**	**54.4**	**75.3**
George Washington U.	**$23,955 $23,955**	**$16,850 $16,850**	**N/A**	**$13,587**	**16.9/1**	**65**	**100**	**72**	**28**	**14**	**1,165**	**238**	**56.7**	**43.3**	**29.7**
Georgetown U.	**$24,530 $24,530**	**$855 $855**	**$14,720**	**$14,720**	**18.1/1**	**86**	**85**	**65**	**35**	**12**	**1,553**	**477**	**51.8**	**48.2**	**26.2**
Howard U.	**$12,785 $12,785**	**$1,187 $1,187**	**$11,079**	**$13,387**	**15.6/1**	**21**	**19**	**71**	**29**	**81**	**392**	**0**	**43.1**	**56.9**	**93.9**
***** Florida *****															
Florida State U.	**$4,650 $15,386**	**$0 $0**	**$14,100**	**$14,100**	**18.8/1**	**29**	**8**	**62**	**38**	**17**	**654**	**0**	**55.2**	**44.8**	**24.3**
Florida, U. of	**$4,311 $14,330**	**$0 $0**	**$9,195**	**$10,105**	**24.5/1**	**38**	**19**	**71**	**29**	**18**	**1,123**	**0**	**56.1**	**43.9**	**23.8**
Miami, U. of	**$21,956 $21,956**	**$16,218 $16,218**	**$14,487**	**$14,487**	**21.0/1**	**46**	**117**	**78**	**22**	**15**	**1,027**	**197**	**56.0**	**44.0**	**30.9**
Nova Southeastern U.	**$19,770 $19,770**	**$14,832 $14,832**	**$12,668**	**$13,435**	**16.2/1**	**46**	**45**	**63**	**37**	**17**	**784**	**169**	**53.8**	**46.2**	**27.9**
St. Thomas U.	**$19,974 $19,974**	**$0 $0**	**$12,065**	**$13,265**	**25.4/1**	**16**	**19**	**69**	**31**	**31**	**487**	**0**	**60.4**	**39.6**	**41.3**
Stetson U.	**$19,890 $19,890**	**$0 $0**	**$10,790**	**$12,570**	**17.2/1**	**32**	**23**	**69**	**31**	**13**	**661**	**1**	**45.3**	**54.7**	**17.8**

Section of Legal Education and Admissions to the Bar (Established 1893)	EXPENSES				FACULTY						STUDENT BODY				
	Res Non-Res Full-Time Tuition	Res Non-Res Part-Time Tuition	Expenses: on-campus	Expenses: off-campus	Student-Faculty Ratio	# Full-Time Faculty	# Part-Time Faculty	% Men	% Women	% Minorities	# of Full-Time Students	# of Part-Time Students	% Men	% Women	% Minorities
*** Georgia ***															
Emory U.	**$23,376 $23,376**	**$0 $0**	**$11,400**	**$11,400**	**19.8/1**	**27**	**55**	**93**	**7**	**7**	**642**	**0**	**50.5**	**49.5**	**19.9**
Georgia State U.	**$3,682 $13,078**	**$3,102 $10,758**	**$12,126**	**$13,280**	**16.1/1**	**30**	**6**	**73**	**27**	**13**	**414**	**248**	**48.5**	**51.5**	**24.8**
Georgia, U. of	**$4,200 $14,940**	**$0 $0**	**$7,446**	**$9,576**	**17.6/1**	**30**	**8**	**80**	**20**	**10**	**633**	**0**	**54.0**	**46.0**	**11.8**
Mercer U.	**$18,590 $18,590**	**$0 $0**	**N/A**	**$11,000**	**16.2/1**	**21**	**8**	**76**	**24**	**10**	**407**	**0**	**59.0**	**41.0**	**11.5**
*** Hawaii ***															
Hawaii, U. of	**$8,124 $14,220**	**$0 $0**	**$7,550**	**$9,729**	**11.2/1**	**17**	**15**	**53**	**47**	**24**	**228**	**0**	**49.1**	**50.9**	**67.1**
*** Idaho ***															
Idaho, U. of	**$4,076 $10,076**	**$0 $0**	**$10,244**	**$10,244**	**15.6/1**	**16**	**7**	**69**	**31**	**0**	**300**	**0**	**70.3**	**29.7**	**5.7**
*** Illinois ***															
Chicago, U. of	**$25,527 $25,527**	**$0 $0**	**$14,505**	**$14,505**	**15.1/1**	**31**	**13**	**77**	**23**	**6**	**560**	**0**	**57.9**	**42.1**	**19.5**
Depaul U.	**$19,870 $19,870**	**$13,470 $13,470**	**N/A**	**$13,032**	**23.4/1**	**35**	**45**	**60**	**40**	**9**	**766**	**327**	**49.3**	**50.7**	**15.1**
Illinois Institute of Technology	**$20,760 $20,760**	**$14,995 $14,995**	**N/A**	**$17,995**	**22.6/1**	**39**	**85**	**77**	**23**	**10**	**674**	**329**	**54.6**	**45.4**	**20.1**
Illinois, U. of	**$8,456 $18,830**	**$0 $0**	**$9,874**	**$9,874**	**15.9/1**	**31**	**17**	**71**	**29**	**16**	**592**	**0**	**59.6**	**40.4**	**29.6**
John Marshall Law School	**$18,280 $18,280**	**$6,580 $6,580**	**N/A**	**$13,149**	**15.5/1**	**54**	**106**	**72**	**28**	**7**	**725**	**425**	**55.0**	**45.0**	**20.7**
Loyola U.-Chicago	**$22,110 $22,110**	**$16,500 $16,500**	**N/A**	**$14,410**	**18.2/1**	**30**	**78**	**80**	**20**	**10**	**517**	**207**	**43.4**	**56.6**	**19.5**
Northern Illinois U.	**$6,481 $11,931**	**$0 $0**	**$8,059**	**$8,959**	**14.7/1**	**16**	**7**	**69**	**31**	**25**	**267**	**23**	**61.4**	**38.6**	**21.7**
Northwestern U.	**$23,974 $23,974**	**$0 $0**	**$16,024**	**$16,024**	**17.4/1**	**31**	**98**	**77**	**23**	**6**	**646**	**0**	**53.3**	**46.7**	**25.2**
Southern Illinois U.-Carbondale	**$5,652 $14,892**	**$0 $0**	**$8,226**	**$8,226**	**14.4/1**	**22**	**5**	**64**	**36**	**5**	**376**	**5**	**64.3**	**35.7**	**12.9**
*** Indiana ***															
Indiana U.-Bloomington	**$6,627 $16,461**	**$0 $0**	**$14,424**	**N/A**	**14.3/1**	**36**	**6**	**78**	**22**	**6**	**614**	**8**	**58.8**	**41.2**	**16.2**
Indiana U.-Indianapolis	**$6,050 $14,439**	**$4,373 $10,365**	**$8,162**	**$11,630**	**20.7/1**	**31**	**19**	**71**	**29**	**6**	**562**	**316**	**54.8**	**45.2**	**10.4**
Notre Dame, U. of	**$21,527 $21,527**	**$0 $0**	**$7,450**	**$7,450**	**16.3/1**	**26**	**18**	**85**	**15**	**8**	**538**	**0**	**61.2**	**38.8**	**17.1**
Valparaiso U.	**$17,580 $17,580**	**$13,450 $13,450**	**$4,880**	**$7,350**	**18.6/1**	**18**	**15**	**67**	**33**	**11**	**367**	**53**	**53.6**	**46.4**	**14.0**

	EXPENSES				FACULTY						STUDENT BODY				
	Res Non-Res Full-Time Tuition	Res Non-Res Part-Time Tuition	Expenses: on-campus	Expenses: off-campus	Student-Faculty Ratio	# Full-Time Faculty	# Part-Time Faculty	% Men	% Women	% Minorities	# of Full-Time Students	# of Part-Time Students	% Men	% Women	% Minorities
***** Iowa *****															
Drake U.	**$16,950 $16,950**	**$565 $565**	**N/A**	**$10,679**	**17.1/1**	**19**	**13**	**79**	**21**	**5**	**379**	**16**	**55.9**	**44.1**	**10.6**
Iowa, U. of	**$6,510 $16,426**	**$0 $0**	**$8,172**	**$9,430**	**13.5/1**	**44**	**12**	**73**	**27**	**11**	**654**	**0**	**60.6**	**39.4**	**19.4**
***** Kansas *****															
Kansas, U. of	**$5,558 $12,391**	**$0 $0**	**$10,280**	**$10,280**	**15.2/1**	**30**	**14**	**73**	**27**	**13**	**529**	**0**	**59.0**	**41.0**	**10.0**
Washburn U.	**$6,732 $10,064**	**$0 $0**	**$11,704**	**$11,704**	**16.5/1**	**22**	**16**	**68**	**32**	**27**	**435**	**0**	**56.8**	**43.2**	**11.0**
***** Kentucky *****															
Kentucky, U. of	**$5,426 $14,036**	**$0 $0**	**$10,074**	**$10,074**	**19.4/1**	**18**	**15**	**67**	**33**	**11**	**418**	**0**	**56.9**	**43.1**	**4.5**
Louisville, U. of	**$5,330 $13,940**	**$4,460 $11,630**	**$6,990**	**$9,886**	**13.9/1**	**23**	**13**	**70**	**30**	**17**	**313**	**105**	**59.6**	**40.4**	**9.6**
Northern Kentucky U.	**$5,670 $14,280**	**$4,740 $11,900**	**$10,500**	**$10,500**	**13.0/1**	**21**	**36**	**71**	**29**	**5**	**201**	**190**	**59.3**	**40.7**	**5.4**
***** Louisiana *****															
Louisiana State U.	**$4,086 $9,561**	**$2,681 $6,049**	**$10,300**	**$10,300**	**20.7/1**	**26**	**15**	**88**	**12**	**8**	**645**	**0**	**54.0**	**46.0**	**9.8**
Loyola U.- New Orleans	**$17,530 $17,530**	**$12,642 $12,642**	**$11,200**	**$11,200**	**17.2/1**	**29**	**18**	**66**	**34**	**28**	**493**	**166**	**53.6**	**46.4**	**23.7**
Southern U.	**$3,128 $7,728**	**$0 $0**	**$8,572**	**$10,016**	**11.7/1**	**24**	**7**	**58**	**42**	**58**	**311**	**0**	**50.5**	**49.5**	**66.2**
Tulane U.	**$23,588 $23,588**	**$0 $0**	**$11,540**	**$11,540**	**20.6/1**	**38**	**61**	**79**	**21**	**8**	**941**	**2**	**53.2**	**46.8**	**18.5**
***** Maine *****															
Maine, U. of	**$9,858 $17,508**	**$6,634 $11,734**	**$8,012**	**$8,012**	**20.0/1**	**12**	**8**	**75**	**25**	**0**	**286**	**2**	**58.0**	**42.0**	**5.2**
***** Maryland *****															
Baltimore, U. of	**$9,006 $15,624**	**$7,440 $12,240**	**N/A**	**$11,330**	**19.4/1**	**37**	**70**	**62**	**38**	**8**	**648**	**324**	**50.9**	**49.1**	**20.5**
Maryland, U. of	**$9,954 $17,847**	**$7,393 $13,311**	**$9,741**	**$12,630**	**15.0/1**	**42**	**38**	**60**	**40**	**17**	**581**	**266**	**46.9**	**53.1**	**27.6**
***** Massachusetts *****															
Boston College	**$23,480 $23,480**	**$0 $0**	**N/A**	**$12,460**	**14.6/1**	**47**	**27**	**64**	**36**	**19**	**823**	**0**	**48.1**	**51.9**	**19.2**
Boston U.	**$23,138 $23,138**	**$0 $0**	**$13,492**	**$13,492**	**17.0/1**	**46**	**54**	**67**	**33**	**15**	**939**	**0**	**53.4**	**46.6**	**20.1**
Harvard U.	**$24,586 $24,586**	**$0 $0**	**$13,144**	**$13,144**	**19.7/1**	**70**	**20**	**81**	**19**	**10**	**1,658**	**0**	**58.3**	**41.7**	**24.0**
New England School of Law	**$15,100 $15,100**	**$11,360 $11,360**	**N/A**	**$13,450**	**20.5/1**	**33**	**49**	**73**	**27**	**6**	**573**	**364**	**49.7**	**50.3**	**17.4**
Northeastern U.	**$22,500 $22,500**	**$0 $0**	**$13,440**	**$13,440**	**21.3/1**	**24**	**16**	**50**	**50**	**25**	**614**	**0**	**34.2**	**65.8**	**26.1**
Suffolk U.	**$20,330 $20,330**	**$15,248 $15,248**	**N/A**	**$15,018**	**23.4/1**	**53**	**61**	**83**	**17**	**8**	**991**	**754**	**51.1**	**48.9**	**9.9**

	EXPENSES				FACULTY						STUDENT BODY				
	Res Non-Res Full-Time Tuition	Res Non-Res Part-Time Tuition	Expenses: on-campus	Expenses: off-campus	Student-Faculty Ratio	# Full-Time Faculty	# Part-Time Faculty	% Men	% Women	% Minorities	# of Full-Time Students	# of Part-Time Students	% Men	% Women	% Minorities
*** Massachusetts ***															
Western New England	$18,394 $18,394	$13,570 $13,570	N/A	$11,143	16.9/1	25	24	76	24	4	357	229	49.8	50.2	11.4
*** Michigan ***															
Detroit College of Law At Michigan State U.	$15,140 $15,140	$11,369 $11,369	$9,796	$9,796	25.6/1	22	27	64	36	9	560	177	61.9	38.1	13.7
Detroit Mercy, U. of	$16,850 $16,850	$12,046 $12,046	N/A	$11,888	18.0/1	16	24	75	25	0	243	186	49.9	50.1	12.6
Michigan, U. of	$17,910 $23,880	$0 $0	$12,425	$12,425	14.9/1	58	11	72	28	3	1,030	0	60.6	39.4	22.5
Thomas Cooley Law School	$16,015 $16,015	$12,820 $12,820	N/A	$11,103	21.8/1	48	90	73	27	8	406	1,287	56.3	43.7	26.1
Wayne State U.	$7,194 $14,782	$5,178 $10,598	$15,020	$15,020	21.2/1	26	27	77	23	12	516	220	54.3	45.7	15.8
*** Minnesota ***															
Hamline U.	$16,475 $16,475	$11,867 $11,867	$7,765	$10,255	18.1/1	22	31	68	32	9	461	25	50.0	50.0	10.9
Minnesota, U. of	$9,630 $15,930	$0 $0	$9,398	$9,398	18.6/1	33	62	70	30	9	744	0	53.5	46.5	17.3
William Mitchell College of Law	$17,260 $17,260	$12,540 $0	N/A	$11,414	23.5/1	29	81	66	34	7	471	527	52.2	47.8	9.8
*** Mississippi ***															
Mississippi College	$13,248 $13,248	$0 $0	$10,336	$13,990	19.7/1	17	12	65	35	12	401	0	62.3	37.7	10.0
Mississippi, U. of	$3,760 $7,682	$0 $0	$11,028	$11,028	22.7/1	18	5	78	22	22	481	4	62.7	37.3	13.0
*** Missouri ***															
Missouri, U. of Kansas City	$8,824 $17,098	$6,352 $12,262	$10,840	$12,850	18.8/1	21	14	76	24	5	454	31	49.9	50.1	11.5
Missouri, U. of Columbia	$8,842 $17,116	$0 $0	$9,828	$12,158	18.5/1	25	7	76	24	8	555	0	59.5	40.5	9.7
St. Louis U.	$19,170 $19,170	$14,360 $14,360	$10,140	$10,980	22.9/1	26	19	81	19	15	546	253	53.3	46.7	14.8
Washington U.	$23,120 $23,120	$0 $0	N/A	$13,204	16.6/1	31	34	61	39	10	612	10	54.2	45.8	20.9
*** Montana ***															
Montana, U. of	$6,501 $11,872	$0 $0	$7,350	$7,350	19.2/1	11	14	55	45	9	253	0	58.1	41.9	8.7
*** Nebraska ***															
Creighton U.	$16,220 $16,220	$8,456 $8,456	$11,270	$11,270	15.9/1	22	25	73	27	5	409	15	59.2	40.8	9.2
Nebraska, U. of	$4,190 $8,908	$0 $0	$7,965	$9,435	14.5/1	24	11	83	17	8	392	1	58.8	41.2	7.4

	EXPENSES				FACULTY						STUDENT BODY				
	Res Non-Res Full-Time Tuition	Res Non-Res Part-Time Tuition	Expenses: on-campus	Expenses: off-campus	Student-Faculty Ratio	# Full-Time Faculty	# Part-Time Faculty	% Men	% Women	% Minorities	# of Full-Time Students	# of Part-Time Students	% Men	% Women	% Minorities
***** New Hampshire *****															
Franklin Pierce Law Center	$16,475 $16,475	$0 $0	N/A	$12,540	24.4/1	13	25	77	23	0	373	11	60.9	39.1	14.1
***** New Jersey *****															
Rutgers U.- Newark	$10,740 $15,264	$6,866 $9,915	$10,589	$11,789	15.7/1	33	27	67	33	18	493	195	54.8	45.2	32.0
Rutgers U.- Camden	$10,781 $15,305	$8,490 $12,301	$9,538	$11,789	20.0/1	29	25	76	24	7	591	158	51.3	48.7	17.4
Seton Hall U.	$19,734 $19,734	$0 $14,050	N/A	$15,370	24.5/1	37	97	59	41	19	877	317	58.0	42.0	15.8
***** New Mexico *****															
New Mexico, U. of	$3,984 $13,338	$0 $0	$9,209	$10,682	10.7/1	26	19	54	46	27	334	1	46.9	53.1	37.6
***** New York *****															
Albany Law School	$19,425 $19,425	$14,600 $14,600	$8,995	$10,325	21.0/1	27	17	63	37	19	655	37	46.5	53.5	16.5
Brooklyn Law School	$22,100 $22,100	$16,600 $16,600	$16,706	$16,706	20.3/1	52	64	56	44	8	946	484	52.2	47.8	18.4
City U. of New York	$6,602 $9,832	$0 $0	N/A	$10,349	11.4/1	27	12	44	56	44	366	6	37.1	62.9	44.6
Columbia U.	$27,156 $27,156	$0 $0	$14,225	$14,225	15.6/1	59	41	75	25	8	1,132	0	54.9	45.1	33.7
Cornell U.	$24,148 $24,148	$0 $0	$12,100	$12,100	11.8/1	41	8	73	27	7	543	0	55.8	44.2	27.6
Fordham U.	$23,790 $23,790	$17,840 $17,840	$17,330	$17,330	22.1/1	51	98	75	25	10	1,108	368	55.6	44.4	24.4
Hofstra U.	$22,210 $22,210	$0 $0	$13,280	$16,788	20.8/1	32	13	84	16	13	798	0	54.9	45.1	17.5
New York Law School	$22,114 $22,114	$16,588 $16,588	$10,745	$10,745	23.0/1	45	70	71	29	13	921	484	53.2	46.8	24.1
New York U.	$27,055 $27,055	$0 $0	$17,040	$17,040	14.1/1	80	59	73	28	11	1,355	0	53.7	46.3	22.0
Pace U.	$21,830 $21,830	$16,385 $16,385	$11,310	$13,450	15.4/1	35	38	66	34	6	446	305	45.9	54.1	17.4
St. John's U.	$22,000 $22,000	$16,500 $16,500	$8,550	$14,990	18.9/1	41	27	73	27	5	740	276	58.3	41.7	21.5
State U. of New York at Buffalo	$8,292 $13,442	$0 $0	$10,771	$10,771	16.1/1	34	43	68	32	12	657	0	52.4	47.6	18.1
Syracuse U.	$22,364 $22,364	$19,309 $19,309	$12,520	$12,520	17.8/1	35	22	60	40	17	736	15	53.8	46.2	20.6
Touro College	$20,370 $20,370	$15,900 $15,900	$16,003	$16,003	16.3/1	31	12	68	32	6	348	359	53.3	46.7	24.2
Yeshiva U.	$22,030 $22,030	$0 $0	N/A	$19,093	17.2/1	43	53	70	30	5	888	0	52.0	48.0	20.5

School	EXPENSES: Full-Time Tuition (Res / Non-Res)	EXPENSES: Part-Time Tuition (Res / Non-Res)	EXPENSES: Expenses: on-campus	EXPENSES: Expenses: off-campus	FACULTY: Student-Faculty Ratio	FACULTY: # Full-Time Faculty	FACULTY: # Part-Time Faculty	FACULTY: % Men	FACULTY: % Women	FACULTY: % Minorities	STUDENT BODY: # of Full-Time Students	STUDENT BODY: # of Part-Time Students	STUDENT BODY: % Men	STUDENT BODY: % Women	STUDENT BODY: % Minorities
***** North Carolina *****															
Campbell U.	$16,733 $16,733	$0 $0	$8,081	$9,821	17.8/1	15	9	93	7	0	320	0	55.6	44.4	3.8
Duke U.	$24,939 $24,939	$0 $0	$12,030	$12,030	15.1/1	33	20	64	36	9	608	0	55.9	44.1	19.4
North Carolina Central	$2,163 $11,089	$2,163 $11,089	$6,365	$9,950	25.7/1	11	12	55	45	55	265	112	44.3	55.7	50.1
North Carolina, U. of	$3,169 $15,269	$0 $0	$11,434	$11,434	16.8/1	35	15	60	40	9	690	0	49.4	50.6	19.7
Wake Forest U.	$20,450 $20,450	$0 $0	N/A	$11,500	15.5/1	25	19	72	28	8	460	9	60.8	39.2	7.9
***** North Dakota *****															
North Dakota, U. of	$4,243 $8,889	$0 $0	$7,400	$7,400	15.5/1	11	3	55	45	0	204	0	60.3	39.7	6.4
***** Ohio *****															
Akron, U. of	$6,733 $11,500	$4,872 $8,277	$10,568	$10,568	21.8/1	19	27	58	42	16	349	226	53.6	46.4	8.7
Capital U.	$15,370 $15,370	$10,070 $10,070	N/A	$9,748	23.0/1	24	30	79	21	13	425	360	55.2	44.8	10.7
Case Western Reserve U.	$20,540 $20,540	$0 $0	$10,730	$10,730	17.5/1	31	45	81	19	3	640	17	54.8	45.2	11.0
Cincinnati, U. of	$7,704 $14,808	$0 $0	$10,454	$10,454	13.9/1	22	25	64	36	14	365	3	48.9	51.1	14.4
Cleveland State U.	$7,460 $14,920	$5,731 $11,462	$11,180	$11,180	17.7/1	35	29	69	31	14	551	294	52.3	47.7	13.3
Dayton, U. of	$18,880 $18,880	$0 $0	$8,800	$8,800	20.8/1	20	15	65	35	5	500	0	55.6	44.4	19.0
Ohio Northern U.	$19,040 $19,040	$0 $0	$7,760	$8,700	13.5/1	20	7	70	30	0	305	0	63.6	36.4	15.4
Ohio State U.	$7,720 $17,516	$0 $0	$10,152	$10,152	14.1/1	38	26	66	34	11	637	3	51.6	48.4	18.3
Toledo, U. of	$7,350 $14,173	$6,125 $11,811	N/A	$6,039	16.6/1	26	11	65	35	12	455	95	54.5	45.5	8.4
***** Oklahoma *****															
Oklahoma City U.	$15,304 $15,304	$10,260 $10,260	$6,803	$9,156	18.2/1	21	13	81	19	5	364	142	57.9	42.1	17.6
Oklahoma, U. of	$4,744 $13,528	$3,312 $9,172	$9,673	$11,265	18.3/1	26	15	77	23	12	572	0	57.9	42.1	16.6
Tulsa, U. of	$16,064 $16,064	$10,864 $10,864	$8,400	$8,710	16.7/1	27	28	59	41	22	459	124	56.4	43.6	18.5
***** Oregon *****															
Lewis & Clark College	$18,265 $18,265	$13,697 $13,697	N/A	$11,350	14.1/1	35	25	63	37	6	490	157	53.2	46.8	11.1
Oregon, U. of	$10,236 $13,984	$0 $0	$9,308	$9,308	17.4/1	24	8	58	42	21	499	0	49.9	50.1	12.0
Willamette U.	$17,780 $17,780	$0 $0	$11,000	$11,000	18.7/1	18	11	72	28	6	401	6	55.8	44.2	12.0

	EXPENSES				FACULTY						STUDENT BODY				
	Res Non-Res Full-Time Tuition	Res Non-Res Part-Time Tuition	Expenses: on-campus	Expenses: off-campus	Student-Faculty Ratio	# Full-Time Faculty	# Part-Time Faculty	% Men	% Women	% Minorities	# of Full-Time Students	# of Part-Time Students	% Men	% Women	% Minorities
***** Pennsylvania *****															
Dickinson School of Law	$15,190 $15,190	$0 $0	$10,775	$12,875	28.2/1	15	44	73	27	7	508	0	57.3	42.7	6.7
Duquesne U.	$15,602 $15,602	$12,038 $12,038	$8,534	$8,534	25.2/1	19	20	74	26	11	356	331	55.3	44.7	4.8
Pennsylvania, U. of	$25,780 $25,780	$0 $0	$12,320	$12,320	18.8/1	34	32	79	21	3	766	0	56.9	43.1	24.5
Pittsburgh, U. of	$12,392 $19,098	$0 $0	N/A	$10,500	21.5/1	28	24	54	46	14	722	0	58.3	41.7	10.2
Temple U.	$9,236 $15,942	$7,450 $12,816	$13,382	$13,382	18.6/1	43	71	74	26	21	758	346	51.0	49.0	23.5
Villanova U.	$19,490 $19,490	$0 $0	$12,050	$14,045	21.3/1	27	24	74	26	11	689	0	54.4	45.6	15.1
Widener U.	$18,550 $18,550	$13,930 $13,930	N/A	$11,970	16.6/1	17	7	65	35	6	238	154	58.2	41.8	5.9
***** Puerto Rico *****															
Inter American U. of Puerto Rico	$11,308 $11,308	$8,508 $8,508	N/A	$8,950	23.0/1	22	27	50	50	100	379	349	46.8	53.2	100.0
Pontifical Catholic U. of Puerto Rico	$9,275 $0	$6,613 $0	$4,867	$6,327	21.7/1	17	13	59	41	100	318	185	47.1	52.9	100.0
Puerto Rico, U. of	$2,320 $3,570	$1,570 $3,500	$7,544	$6,044	20.7/1	20	31	80	20	95	352	221	43.8	56.2	99.3
***** Rhode Island *****															
Roger Williams U.	$19,100 $19,100	$11,480 $11,480	$14,655	$14,655	12.8/1	21	19	62	38	5	207	176	56.1	43.9	6.5
***** South Carolina *****															
South Carolina, U. of	$7,328 $14,986	$0 $0	$11,009	$11,009	22.8/1	31	0	87	13	0	746	0	58.4	41.6	10.1
***** South Dakota *****															
South Dakota, U. of	$4,960 $10,434	$0 $0	$8,100	$11,270	14.4/1	12	2	83	17	8	208	0	58.7	41.3	5.3
***** Tennessee *****															
Memphis, U. of	$4,580 $11,376	$3,998 $9,898	$11,272	$11,272	19.5/1	20	25	70	30	5	446	32	55.0	45.0	13.0
Tennessee, U. of	$4,502 $11,424	$0 $0	$10,927	$10,927	15.1/1	27	23	67	33	7	489	0	55.4	44.6	11.5
Vanderbilt U.	$23,010 $23,010	$0 $0	$13,870	$13,870	15.9/1	29	19	79	21	10	548	0	57.7	42.3	18.8
***** Texas *****															
Baylor U.	$12,896 $12,896	$0 $0	$8,458	$12,916	22.0/1	16	9	75	25	6	423	0	60.8	39.2	9.7
Houston, U. of	$5,880 $10,360	$4,600 $7,800	$7,920	$9,970	20.8/1	37	33	81	19	11	773	229	55.4	44.6	22.1
South Texas College of Law	$15,450 $15,450	$10,500 $10,500	N/A	$12,372	20.3/1	44	32	68	32	14	804	402	56.4	43.6	20.9
Southern Methodist U.	$20,514 $20,514	$14,920 $14,920	$9,459	$7,380	17.2/1	36	61	75	25	14	733	18	54.6	45.4	15.4

	EXPENSES				FACULTY						STUDENT BODY				
	Res Non-Res Full-Time Tuition	Res Non-Res Part-Time Tuition	Expenses: on-campus	Expenses: off-campus	Student-Faculty Ratio	# Full-Time Faculty	# Part-Time Faculty	% Men	% Women	% Minorities	# of Full-Time Students	# of Part-Time Students	% Men	% Women	% Minorities
*** Texas ***															
St. Mary's U.	$15,560 $15,560	$0 $0	$9,608	$12,296	22.2/1	29	29	72	28	17	773	0	52.3	47.7	42.3
Texas Southern U.	$5,404 $9,274	$0 $0	N/A	$9,872	20.3/1	26	7	81	19	81	626	0	52.7	47.3	84.7
Texas Tech U.	$6,621 $11,691	$0 $0	$9,488	$9,488	27.0/1	19	12	74	26	11	616	0	57.3	42.7	13.3
Texas Wesleyan U.	$13,000 $13,000	$9,400 $9,400	$7,141	$9,106	21.3/1	19	32	79	21	16	308	269	60.0	40.0	17.2
Texas, U. of at Austin	$7,234 $15,064	$0 $0	$9,264	$10,492	18.3/1	61	54	77	23	8	1,374	0	54.9	45.1	19.7
*** Utah ***															
Brigham Young U.	$5,140 $7,700	$285 $425	$11,450	$11,370	15.6/1	24	18	83	17	13	449	0	66.4	33.6	12.2
Utah, U. of	$4,857 $10,822	$0 $0	$10,041	$10,041	14.5/1	20	7	80	20	25	349	0	63.9	36.1	13.2
*** Vermont ***															
Vermont Law School	$19,490 $19,490	$0 $0	N/A	$12,626	15.5/1	26	12	50	50	4	485	0	52.2	47.8	8.2
*** Virginia ***															
George Mason U.	$7,644 $18,214	$2,730 $6,505	N/A	$15,141	23.4/1	22	41	91	9	9	379	362	60.6	39.4	11.3
Regent U.	$15,864 $15,864	$12,894 $12,894	$10,929	$10,929	19.0/1	17	17	76	24	24	365	33	56.8	43.2	13.3
Richmond, U. of	$19,195 $19,195	$0 $0	$8,855	$11,375	15.8/1	25	38	68	32	8	474	1	52.4	47.6	17.5
Virginia, U. of	$14,606 $20,706	$0 $0	$11,060	$11,060	15.3/1	63	44	79	21	6	1,105	0	63.0	37.0	13.0
Washington & Lee U.	$17,711 $17,711	$0 $0	$10,460	$10,460	11.5/1	29	4	86	14	17	366	0	59.8	40.2	8.5
William and Mary School of Law	$8,494 $17,940	$0 $0	$12,830	$12,830	18.3/1	24	27	79	21	13	528	0	55.5	44.5	19.1
*** Washington ***															
Gonzaga U.	$18,400 $18,400	$11,080 $11,080	$12,200	$12,200	19.9/1	20	13	80	20	5	461	26	56.9	43.1	15.4
Seattle U.	$17,926 $17,926	$14,932 $14,932	N/A	$11,559	22.3/1	29	26	66	34	14	652	188	44.9	55.1	21.9
Washington, U. of	$5,763 $14,169	$0 $0	$11,400	$11,400	11.4/1	39	14	54	46	8	488	1	46.8	53.2	26.4
*** West Virginia ***															
West Virginia U.	$5,296 $12,568	$0 $0	$8,440	$10,439	16.4/1	22	18	68	32	9	423	16	52.8	47.2	6.2

	EXPENSES				FACULTY						STUDENT BODY				
	Full-Time Tuition (Res / Non-Res)	Part-Time Tuition (Res / Non-Res)	Expenses: on-campus	Expenses: off-campus	Student-Faculty Ratio	# Full-Time Faculty	# Part-Time Faculty	% Men	% Women	% Minorities	# of Full-Time Students	# of Part-Time Students	% Men	% Women	% Minorities
***** Wisconsin *****															
Marquette U.	**$18,370 $18,370**	**$15,200 $15,200**	**$12,185**	**$12,185**	**18.3/1**	**23**	**25**	**65**	**35**	**9**	**438**	**101**	**56.6**	**43.4**	**7.4**
Wisconsin, U. of	**$6,206 $16,382**	**$5,170 $13,590**	**$9,950**	**$9,950**	**18.1/1**	**36**	**46**	**67**	**33**	**11**	**757**	**48**	**52.9**	**47.1**	**23.0**
***** Wyoming *****															
Wyoming, U. of	**$4,234 $9,322**	**$0 $0**	**$7,112**	**$7,112**	**14.9/1**	**13**	**3**	**54**	**46**	**0**	**224**	**0**	**59.8**	**40.2**	**4.5**

			FULL-TIME						PART-TIME						TOTAL	
ADMISSIONS	Application Deadline	Application Fee	75% GPA	25% GPA	75% LSAT	25% LSAT	% Accepted	# of Matriculants	75% GPA	25% GPA	75% LSAT	25% LSAT	% Accepted	# of Matriculants	Total % Accepted	Total Matriculants
***** Alabama *****																
Alabama, U. of	03/01	$25	3.50	2.98	159	154	46	179	0.00	0.00	0	0	N/A	0	46	179
Samford U.	05/01	$40	3.31	2.72	153	148	65	217	0.00	0.00	0	0	N/A	0	65	217
***** Arizona *****																
Arizona State U.	03/01	$45	3.59	2.96	161	154	23	162	0.00	0.00	0	0	N/A	0	23	162
Arizona, U. of	03/01	$45	3.66	3.11	164	157	27	152	0.00	0.00	0	0	N/A	0	27	152
***** Arkansas *****																
Arkansas, U. of Fayetteville	04/01	$0	3.63	2.97	157	148	53	125	0.00	0.00	0	0	N/A	0	53	125
Arkansas, U. of Little Rock	05/01	$40	3.70	3.11	156	148	69	100	3.42	2.79	154	148	39	46	57	146
***** California *****																
California Western School of Law	04/01	$45	3.42	2.81	153	146	70	300	3.31	2.65	151	147	100	17	70	317
California-Hastings	02/16	$40	3.59	3.05	164	159	30	354	0.00	0.00	0	0	N/A	0	30	354
California-Los Angeles	02/01	$40	3.78	3.45	166	161	20	270	0.00	0.00	0	0	N/A	0	20	270
California-Berkeley	02/01	$40	3.87	3.66	169	161	19	269	0.00	0.00	0	0	N/A	0	19	269
California-Davis	02/01	$40	3.62	3.24	164	158	36	183	0.00	0.00	0	0	N/A	0	36	183
Chapman U.	06/01	$40	3.36	2.70	153	146	35	33	3.42	2.61	157	147	39	26	37	59
Golden Gate U.	04/15	$40	3.35	2.78	154	146	54	168	3.29	2.66	155	147	42	37	53	205
Loyola Marymount U.	02/01	$50	3.48	3.03	160	154	40	358	3.46	3.00	158	151	43	113	40	471
McGeorge	05/15	$40	3.33	2.75	155	148	68	274	3.36	2.62	155	149	69	103	69	377
Pepperdine U.	03/01	$50	3.51	3.01	160	153	45	232	0.00	0.00	0	0	N/A	0	45	232
San Diego, U. of	02/01	$40	3.35	2.86	160	156	45	251	3.45	2.86	156	153	80	99	48	350
San Francisco, U. of	04/01	$40	3.45	3.03	159	154	42	186	3.39	2.76	159	151	65	62	44	248
Santa Clara U.	03/01	$40	3.49	2.96	158	153	51	224	3.32	2.85	160	153	49	69	51	293
Southern California, U. of	02/01	$60	3.65	3.30	165	159	24	208	0.00	0.00	0	0	N/A	0	24	208
Southwestern U.	06/30	$50	3.20	2.69	153	149	50	255	3.22	2.61	153	148	36	82	48	337
Stanford U.	02/01	$65	3.91	3.55	170	164	11	180	0.00	0.00	0	0	N/A	0	11	180

	ADMISSIONS		FULL-TIME						PART-TIME						TOTAL	
	Application Deadline	Application Fee	75% GPA	25% GPA	75% LSAT	25% LSAT	% Accepted	# of Matriculants	75% GPA	25% GPA	75% LSAT	25% LSAT	% Accepted	# of Matriculants	Total % Accepted	Total Matriculants
***** California *****																
Thomas Jefferson School of Law	**Rolling**	**$35**	**3.12**	**2.45**	**155**	**145**	**72**	**174**	**3.19**	**2.50**	**153**	**145**	**66**	**61**	**71**	**235**
Western State U.	**05/31**	**$35**	**3.17**	**2.45**	**151**	**143**	**57**	**79**	**3.13**	**2.49**	**151**	**142**	**53**	**94**	**55**	**173**
Whittier College	**03/15**	**$50**	**3.24**	**2.68**	**153**	**146**	**61**	**152**	**3.25**	**2.62**	**152**	**146**	**54**	**80**	**59**	**232**
***** Colorado *****																
Colorado, U. of	**02/15**	**$45**	**3.68**	**3.28**	**164**	**158**	**34**	**167**	**0.00**	**0.00**	**0**	**0**	**N/A**	**0**	**34**	**167**
Denver, U. of	**03/01**	**$45**	**3.42**	**2.85**	**157**	**151**	**64**	**237**	**3.50**	**2.77**	**154**	**149**	**73**	**96**	**65**	**333**
***** Connecticut *****																
Connecticut, U. of	**04/01**	**$30**	**3.54**	**3.08**	**161**	**157**	**39**	**129**	**3.40**	**2.85**	**157**	**154**	**44**	**61**	**41**	**190**
Quinnipiac College	**Rolling**	**$40**	**3.19**	**2.52**	**152**	**145**	**53**	**159**	**3.08**	**2.49**	**150**	**144**	**41**	**127**	**50**	**286**
Yale U.	**02/15**	**$65**	**3.97**	**3.75**	**175**	**168**	**7**	**185**	**0.00**	**0.00**	**0**	**0**	**N/A**	**0**	**7**	**185**
***** Delaware *****																
Widener U.	**05/15**	**$60**	**3.22**	**2.64**	**149**	**145**	**72**	**206**	**3.23**	**2.47**	**152**	**145**	**66**	**124**	**71**	**330**
***** District of Columbia *****																
American U.	**03/01**	**$55**	**3.51**	**3.09**	**158**	**153**	**40**	**296**	**3.31**	**2.85**	**155**	**148**	**65**	**97**	**43**	**393**
Catholic U. of America	**03/01**	**$55**	**3.40**	**2.80**	**157**	**151**	**51**	**219**	**3.10**	**2.50**	**156**	**151**	**48**	**71**	**50**	**290**
District of Columbia, U.	**04/01**	**$35**	**2.75**	**2.30**	**147**	**141**	**43**	**61**	**0.00**	**0.00**	**0**	**0**	**N/A**	**0**	**43**	**61**
George Washington U.	**03/01**	**$55**	**3.57**	**3.21**	**164**	**160**	**33**	**404**	**3.43**	**2.82**	**161**	**153**	**N/A**	**68**	**33**	**472**
Georgetown U.	**03/01**	**$65**	**3.76**	**3.27**	**168**	**163**	**29**	**456**	**3.71**	**3.20**	**166**	**159**	**33**	**129**	**29**	**585**
Howard U.	**04/30**	**$60**	**3.23**	**2.67**	**155**	**148**	**34**	**124**	**0.00**	**0.00**	**0**	**0**	**N/A**	**0**	**34**	**124**
***** Florida *****																
Florida State U.	**02/15**	**$20**	**3.57**	**3.07**	**159**	**153**	**33**	**225**	**0.00**	**0.00**	**0**	**0**	**N/A**	**0**	**33**	**225**
Florida, U. of	**02/01**	**$20**	**3.70**	**3.27**	**160**	**152**	**33**	**400**	**0.00**	**0.00**	**0**	**0**	**N/A**	**0**	**33**	**400**
Miami, U. of	**07/31**	**$45**	**3.41**	**2.92**	**157**	**151**	**53**	**273**	**3.31**	**2.77**	**155**	**148**	**49**	**53**	**53**	**326**
Nova Southeastern U.	**03/01**	**$50**	**3.19**	**2.59**	**151**	**144**	**54**	**263**	**3.12**	**2.53**	**150**	**144**	**54**	**73**	**54**	**336**
St. Thomas U.	**04/30**	**$40**	**3.23**	**2.55**	**151**	**146**	**71**	**190**	**0.00**	**0.00**	**0**	**0**	**N/A**	**0**	**71**	**190**
Stetson U.	**02/15**	**$50**	**3.40**	**2.91**	**154**	**146**	**47**	**291**	**0.00**	**0.00**	**0**	**0**	**N/A**	**0**	**47**	**291**

ADMISSIONS

			FULL-TIME						PART-TIME						TOTAL	
	Application Deadline	Application Fee	75% GPA	25% GPA	75% LSAT	25% LSAT	% Accepted	# of Matriculants	75% GPA	25% GPA	75% LSAT	25% LSAT	% Accepted	# of Matriculants	Total % Accepted	Total Matriculants
***** Georgia *****																
Emory U.	03/01	$50	3.59	3.25	163	159	40	235	0.00	0.00	0	0	N/A	0	40	235
Georgia State U.	03/15	$30	3.49	2.88	160	153	30	133	3.49	2.85	160	153	27	65	29	198
Georgia, U. of	03/01	$30	3.76	3.20	163	155	30	190	0.00	0.00	0	0	N/A	0	30	190
Mercer U.	03/15	$45	3.48	2.87	156	150	50	133	0.00	0.00	0	0	N/A	0	50	133
***** Hawaii *****																
Hawaii, U. of	03/01	$30	3.40	2.91	162	154	36	80	0.00	0.00	0	0	N/A	0	36	80
***** Idaho *****																
Idaho, U. of	02/01	$30	3.57	3.22	156	149	62	104	0.00	0.00	0	0	N/A	0	62	104
***** Illinois *****																
Chicago, U. of	Rolling	$60	3.81	3.55	171	167	30	182	0.00	0.00	0	0	N/A	0	30	182
Depaul U.	04/01	$40	3.37	2.87	155	149	77	293	3.13	2.69	153	146	65	99	74	392
Illinois Institute of Technology	04/01	$45	3.34	2.89	157	150	71	294	3.32	2.64	156	148	60	108	69	402
Illinois, U. of	03/15	$40	3.64	3.19	163	156	38	194	0.00	0.00	0	0	N/A	0	38	194
John Marshall Law School	03/01	$50	3.20	2.64	154	145	64	241	3.27	2.55	153	144	46	115	60	356
Loyola U.-Chicago	04/01	$45	3.56	3.06	160	155	41	169	3.34	2.78	156	150	68	66	44	235
Northern Illinois U.	05/15	$40	3.30	2.78	156	150	43	99	3.82	2.87	154	149	44	7	43	106
Northwestern U.	02/15	$80	3.67	3.28	167	162	21	204	0.00	0.00	0	0	N/A	0	21	204
Southern Illinois U.-Carbondale	03/01	$25	3.38	2.67	155	150	58	145	0.00	0.00	0	0	N/A	0	58	145
***** Indiana *****																
Indiana U.-Bloomington	03/01	$35	3.60	3.00	163	155	43	210	0.00	0.00	0	0	100	2	43	212
Indiana U.-Indianapolis	03/01	$35	3.51	2.99	156	150	60	199	3.49	2.85	157	149	42	89	55	288
Notre Dame, U. of	03/01	$50	3.67	3.20	165	160	29	185	0.00	0.00	0	0	N/A	0	29	185
Valparaiso U.	04/15	$30	3.55	2.92	157	148	72	143	3.11	2.45	151	143	64	23	71	166

	ADMISSIONS															
			FULL-TIME						PART-TIME						TOTAL	
	Application Deadline	Application Fee	75% GPA	25% GPA	75% LSAT	25% LSAT	% Accepted	# of Matriculants	75% GPA	25% GPA	75% LSAT	25% LSAT	% Accepted	# of Matriculants	Total % Accepted	Total Matriculants
*** Iowa ***																
Drake U.	03/01	$35	3.50	2.86	155	150	63	131	3.54	3.19	156	153	41	5	62	136
Iowa, U. of	03/01	$30	3.71	3.12	162	155	41	229	0.00	0.00	0	0	N/A	0	41	229
*** Kansas ***																
Kansas, U. of	03/15	$40	3.68	3.16	159	152	55	171	0.00	0.00	0	0	N/A	0	55	171
Washburn U.	03/15	$30	3.49	2.85	153	146	68	158	0.00	0.00	0	0	N/A	0	68	158
*** Kentucky ***																
Kentucky, U. of	03/01	$25	3.66	3.16	160	155	44	145	0.00	0.00	0	0	N/A	0	44	145
Louisville, U. of	03/01	$30	3.57	2.85	159	154	34	86	3.53	2.74	157	149	40	35	35	121
Northern Kentucky U.	05/15	$30	3.57	3.09	154	150	43	66	3.63	2.79	156	151	62	51	46	117
*** Louisiana ***																
Louisiana State U.	02/01	$25	3.53	3.10	156	147	65	310	0.00	0.00	0	0	N/A	0	65	310
Loyola U.- New Orleans	08/21	$20	3.25	2.67	153	148	55	185	3.28	2.62	157	148	55	54	55	239
Southern U.	03/31	$0	3.11	2.40	146	141	27	118	0.00	0.00	0	0	N/A	0	27	118
Tulane U.	05/01	$45	3.53	3.01	161	155	53	347	0.00	0.00	0	0	100	0	53	347
*** Maine ***																
Maine, U. of	02/15	$25	3.51	2.98	158	150	56	104	0.00	0.00	0	0	N/A	0	56	104
*** Maryland ***																
Baltimore, U. of	05/01	$35	3.31	2.64	152	147	58	196	3.18	2.56	153	146	49	81	56	277
Maryland, U. of	03/01	$50	3.51	3.06	158	152	42	196	3.39	2.89	159	152	31	61	41	257
*** Massachusetts ***																
Boston College	03/01	$65	3.64	3.21	164	159	28	260	0.00	0.00	0	0	N/A	0	28	260
Boston U.	03/01	$50	3.58	3.09	163	158	38	314	0.00	0.00	0	0	N/A	0	38	314
Harvard U.	02/01	$65	3.92	3.73	173	166	15	551	0.00	0.00	0	0	N/A	0	15	551
New England School of Law	06/01	$50	3.25	2.69	151	142	77	241	3.26	2.66	153	143	73	109	77	350
Northeastern U.	03/01	$55	3.37	2.77	158	151	44	230	0.00	0.00	0	0	N/A	0	44	230
Suffolk U.	03/01	$50	3.35	2.81	153	146	76	370	3.35	2.65	156	146	71	203	74	573

	ADMISSIONS															
			FULL-TIME						PART-TIME						TOTAL	
	Application Deadline	Application Fee	75% GPA	25% GPA	75% LSAT	25% LSAT	% Accepted	# of Matriculants	75% GPA	25% GPA	75% LSAT	25% LSAT	% Accepted	# of Matriculants	Total % Accepted	Total Matriculants
*** Massachusetts ***																
Western New England	Rolling	$45	3.36	2.78	151	142	69	124	3.31	2.61	151	140	69	60	69	184
*** Michigan ***																
Detroit College of Law At Michigan State U.	04/15	$50	3.40	2.85	154	147	64	154	3.42	2.80	154	145	60	52	63	206
Detroit Mercy, U. of	04/15	$50	3.42	2.77	152	144	66	110	3.17	2.57	152	145	54	41	63	151
Michigan, U. of	02/15	$70	3.73	3.36	168	163	36	341	0.00	0.00	0	0	N/A	0	36	341
Thomas Cooley Law School	Rolling	$50	3.20	2.66	145	139	85	386	3.20	2.63	147	139	81	493	83	879
Wayne State U.	03/15	$20	3.46	3.06	157	151	58	197	3.36	2.86	158	150	35	64	52	261
*** Minnesota ***																
Hamline U.	03/15	$50	3.49	2.92	157	149	61	186	3.55	2.64	154	145	44	7	61	193
Minnesota, U. of	03/01	$40	3.81	3.34	164	159	43	240	0.00	0.00	0	0	N/A	0	43	240
William Mitchell College of Law	07/01	$45	3.44	2.90	155	147	70	171	3.45	2.71	156	148	N/A	119	70	290
*** Mississippi ***																
Mississippi College	05/01	$25	3.39	2.81	152	145	60	141	0.00	0.00	0	0	N/A	0	60	141
Mississippi, U. of	03/01	$25	3.63	3.01	157	150	37	158	0.00	0.00	0	0	N/A	0	37	158
*** Missouri ***																
Missouri, U. of Kansas City	Rolling	$25	3.46	2.91	157	148	63	163	3.48	2.65	155	151	45	10	62	173
Missouri, U. of Columbia	03/01	$40	3.67	3.07	159	153	51	169	0.00	0.00	0	0	N/A	0	51	169
St. Louis U.	03/01	$40	3.60	3.00	157	150	62	180	3.41	2.77	156	148	57	68	62	248
Washington U.	03/01	$50	3.58	3.12	163	155	54	213	0.00	0.00	0	0	N/A	0	54	213
*** Montana ***																
Montana, U. of	03/01	$60	3.50	2.93	159	152	56	92	0.00	0.00	0	0	N/A	0	56	92
*** Nebraska ***																
Creighton U.	05/01	$40	3.42	2.74	153	148	66	137	3.92	3.01	158	153	39	4	65	141
Nebraska, U. of	03/01	$25	3.73	3.18	157	149	66	150	0.00	0.00	0	0	N/A	0	66	150

	ADMISSIONS															
			FULL-TIME						PART-TIME						TOTAL	
	Application Deadline	Application Fee	75% GPA	25% GPA	75% LSAT	25% LSAT	% Accepted	# of Matriculants	75% GPA	25% GPA	75% LSAT	25% LSAT	% Accepted	# of Matriculants	Total % Accepted	Total Matriculants
***** New Hampshire *****																
Franklin Pierce Law Center	**05/01**	**$45**	**3.31**	**2.60**	**155**	**146**	**65**	**114**	**0.00**	**0.00**	**0**	**0**	**100**	**1**	**65**	**115**
***** New Jersey *****																
Rutgers U.-Newark	**03/15**	**$40**	**3.42**	**2.88**	**159**	**151**	**38**	**178**	**3.32**	**3.15**	**159**	**152**	**17**	**35**	**33**	**213**
Rutgers U.-Camden	**03/01**	**$50**	**3.39**	**2.87**	**155**	**151**	**50**	**226**	**3.27**	**2.70**	**157**	**150**	**N/A**	**46**	**50**	**272**
Seton Hall U.	**04/01**	**$50**	**3.41**	**2.83**	**157**	**151**	**49**	**299**	**3.28**	**2.55**	**157**	**150**	**32**	**82**	**46**	**381**
***** New Mexico *****																
New Mexico, U. of	**02/16**	**$40**	**3.44**	**2.86**	**158**	**150**	**34**	**114**	**0.00**	**0.00**	**0**	**0**	**N/A**	**0**	**34**	**114**
***** New York *****																
Albany Law School	**Rolling**	**$50**	**3.41**	**2.90**	**153**	**145**	**68**	**247**	**0.00**	**0.00**	**0**	**0**	**N/A**	**0**	**68**	**247**
Brooklyn Law School	**Rolling**	**$60**	**3.49**	**2.95**	**158**	**152**	**50**	**291**	**3.36**	**2.72**	**154**	**150**	**47**	**157**	**49**	**448**
City U. of New York	**03/15**	**$40**	**3.41**	**2.71**	**153**	**143**	**39**	**103**	**0.00**	**0.00**	**0**	**0**	**N/A**	**0**	**39**	**103**
Columbia U.	**02/15**	**$65**	**3.74**	**3.38**	**171**	**164**	**19**	**345**	**0.00**	**0.00**	**0**	**0**	**N/A**	**0**	**19**	**345**
Cornell U.	**02/01**	**$65**	**3.72**	**3.37**	**166**	**163**	**29**	**189**	**0.00**	**0.00**	**0**	**0**	**N/A**	**0**	**29**	**189**
Fordham U.	**03/01**	**$60**	**3.63**	**3.09**	**165**	**160**	**31**	**351**	**3.51**	**2.88**	**161**	**156**	**31**	**135**	**31**	**486**
Hofstra U.	**04/15**	**$60**	**3.50**	**2.95**	**158**	**150**	**48**	**290**	**0.00**	**0.00**	**0**	**0**	**N/A**	**0**	**48**	**290**
New York Law School	**04/01**	**$50**	**3.27**	**2.77**	**154**	**148**	**52**	**360**	**3.24**	**2.78**	**154**	**147**	**41**	**143**	**50**	**503**
New York U.	**02/01**	**$65**	**3.81**	**3.56**	**171**	**166**	**24**	**448**	**0.00**	**0.00**	**0**	**0**	**N/A**	**0**	**24**	**448**
Pace U.	**02/15**	**$55**	**3.41**	**2.84**	**154**	**147**	**51**	**156**	**3.60**	**2.72**	**154**	**146**	**41**	**101**	**48**	**257**
St. John's U.	**03/01**	**$50**	**3.46**	**2.85**	**158**	**151**	**53**	**246**	**3.36**	**2.85**	**156**	**149**	**34**	**65**	**49**	**311**
State U. of New York at Buffalo	**02/15**	**$50**	**3.49**	**2.93**	**157**	**150**	**56**	**221**	**0.00**	**0.00**	**0**	**0**	**N/A**	**0**	**56**	**221**
Syracuse U.	**04/01**	**$50**	**3.40**	**2.95**	**154**	**147**	**60**	**284**	**3.38**	**3.23**	**155**	**152**	**42**	**4**	**60**	**288**
Touro College	**05/01**	**$50**	**3.20**	**2.73**	**151**	**144**	**53**	**141**	**3.31**	**2.69**	**153**	**144**	**40**	**102**	**49**	**243**
Yeshiva U.	**04/01**	**$60**	**3.57**	**3.03**	**159**	**154**	**44**	**330**	**0.00**	**0.00**	**0**	**0**	**N/A**	**0**	**44**	**330**

	ADMISSIONS															
			FULL-TIME						PART-TIME						TOTAL	
	Application Deadline	Application Fee	75% GPA	25% GPA	75% LSAT	25% LSAT	% Accepted	# of Matriculants	75% GPA	25% GPA	75% LSAT	25% LSAT	% Accepted	# of Matriculants	Total % Accepted	Total Matriculants
*** North Carolina ***																
Campbell U.	Rolling	$40	3.49	2.96	156	152	31	111	0.00	0.00	0	0	N/A	0	31	111
Duke U.	02/01	$65	3.72	3.33	170	161	28	212	0.00	0.00	0	0	N/A	0	28	212
North Carolina Central	04/15	$30	3.20	2.70	152	143	24	96	3.30	2.80	161	152	16	23	22	119
North Carolina, U. of	02/01	$60	3.81	3.32	164	153	28	231	0.00	0.00	0	0	N/A	0	28	231
Wake Forest U.	03/15	$60	3.57	3.04	162	156	45	160	0.00	0.00	0	0	N/A	0	45	160
*** North Dakota ***																
North Dakota, U. of	04/01	$35	3.43	2.95	154	148	63	71	0.00	0.00	0	0	N/A	0	63	71
*** Ohio ***																
Akron, U. of	03/01	$35	3.59	3.00	154	148	49	123	3.45	2.83	157	150	46	76	49	199
Capital U.	05/01	$35	3.33	2.80	152	146	69	148	3.33	2.82	154	145	72	105	70	253
Case Western Reserve U.	04/01	$40	3.50	2.99	161	153	61	198	0.00	0.00	0	0	21	3	59	201
Cincinnati, U. of	04/01	$35	3.66	3.01	162	154	42	121	0.00	0.00	0	0	N/A	0	42	121
Cleveland State U.	04/01	$35	3.44	2.83	153	145	56	169	3.32	2.74	154	146	50	107	55	276
Dayton, U. of	05/01	$40	3.47	2.98	153	146	61	187	0.00	0.00	0	0	N/A	0	61	187
Ohio Northern U.	Rolling	$40	3.12	2.59	150	143	68	131	0.00	0.00	0	0	N/A	0	68	131
Ohio State U.	03/15	$30	3.75	3.29	160	152	38	214	0.00	0.00	0	0	N/A	0	38	214
Toledo, U. of	03/15	$30	3.34	2.69	156	146	67	130	3.36	2.81	154	146	63	36	67	166
*** Oklahoma ***																
Oklahoma City U.	07/01	$35	3.18	2.58	148	142	80	153	3.36	2.57	152	144	62	34	76	187
Oklahoma, U. of	04/15	$50	3.42	2.74	154	146	59	204	0.00	0.00	0	0	N/A	0	59	204
Tulsa, U. of	08/15	$0	3.20	2.61	153	144	67	171	3.33	2.62	154	145	63	30	66	201
*** Oregon ***																
Lewis & Clark College	03/15	$50	3.53	3.04	162	155	67	193	3.59	2.94	161	153	57	44	66	237
Oregon, U. of	03/01	$50	3.60	3.13	159	152	52	170	0.00	0.00	0	0	N/A	0	52	170
Willamette U.	04/01	$50	3.33	2.78	157	150	74	152	0.00	0.00	0	0	100	1	74	153

	ADMISSIONS															
			FULL-TIME						PART-TIME						TOTAL	
SECTION OF LEGAL EDUCATION AND ADMISSIONS TO THE BAR · ESTABLISHED 1893 · ABA	Application Deadline	Application Fee	75% GPA	25% GPA	75% LSAT	25% LSAT	% Accepted	# of Matriculants	75% GPA	25% GPA	75% LSAT	25% LSAT	% Accepted	# of Matriculants	Total % Accepted	Total Matriculants
***** Pennsylvania *****																
Dickinson School of Law	03/01	$50	3.50	2.86	155	150	56	185	0.00	0.00	0	0	N/A	0	56	185
Duquesne U.	04/01	$50	3.50	2.88	154	147	65	120	3.39	2.74	154	144	65	98	65	218
Pennsylvania, U. of	03/01	$65	3.73	3.41	168	164	31	271	0.00	0.00	0	0	N/A	0	31	271
Pittsburgh, U. of	03/01	$40	3.50	2.80	154	150	67	250	0.00	0.00	0	0	N/A	0	67	250
Temple U.	03/01	$50	3.52	3.02	157	150	39	248	3.35	2.80	155	150	40	97	39	345
Villanova U.	03/01	$75	3.51	3.03	158	153	63	232	0.00	0.00	0	0	N/A	0	63	232
Widener U.	05/15	$60	3.37	2.62	151	144	56	86	3.31	2.53	155	145	64	62	58	148
***** Puerto Rico *****																
Inter American U. of Puerto Rico	03/31	$63	3.25	2.82	140	135	38	129	3.40	2.82	144	137	24	97	31	226
Pontifical Catholic U. of Puerto Rico	04/15	$60	3.60	2.97	140	132	40	116	3.56	2.94	139	131	35	62	38	178
Puerto Rico, U. of	02/16	$15	3.79	3.26	151	143	29	103	3.79	3.14	149	142	19	50	25	153
***** Rhode Island *****																
Roger Williams U.	05/15	$60	3.42	2.64	151	142	53	75	3.43	2.83	155	141	56	39	54	114
***** South Carolina *****																
South Carolina, U. of	02/15	$25	3.54	2.86	160	152	35	228	0.00	0.00	0	0	N/A	0	35	228
***** South Dakota *****																
South Dakota, U. of	03/01	$15	3.54	3.01	156	146	58	62	0.00	0.00	0	0	N/A	0	58	62
***** Tennessee *****																
Memphis, U. of	02/15	$15	3.63	2.84	157	150	39	152	3.46	2.81	151	141	100	13	40	165
Tennessee, U. of	02/01	$15	3.70	3.20	160	153	36	159	0.00	0.00	0	0	N/A	0	36	159
Vanderbilt U.	03/01	$50	3.81	3.41	164	157	32	190	0.00	0.00	0	0	N/A	0	32	190
***** Texas *****																
Baylor U.	03/01	$40	0.00	0.00	0	0	N/A	0	0.00	0.00	0	0	N/A	0	N/A	0
Houston, U. of	02/15	$50	3.50	3.06	160	155	43	277	3.53	3.00	161	154	35	55	42	332
South Texas College of Law	10/01	$40	3.14	2.67	153	146	61	320	3.29	2.67	152	146	66	145	62	465
Southern Methodist U.	02/01	$50	3.49	2.94	160	154	43	233	0.00	0.00	0	0	13	0	43	233

	ADMISSIONS															
			FULL-TIME						PART-TIME						TOTAL	
	Application Deadline	Application Fee	75% GPA	25% GPA	75% LSAT	25% LSAT	% Accepted	# of Matriculants	75% GPA	25% GPA	75% LSAT	25% LSAT	% Accepted	# of Matriculants	Total % Accepted	Total Matriculants
*** Texas ***																
St. Mary's U.	03/01	$45	3.12	2.61	152	146	61	269	0.00	0.00	0	0	N/A	0	61	269
Texas Southern U.	04/01	$40	3.00	2.37	144	139	55	290	0.00	0.00	0	0	N/A	0	55	290
Texas Tech U.	02/01	$50	3.59	3.12	158	151	49	217	0.00	0.00	0	0	N/A	0	49	217
Texas Wesleyan U.	03/15	$50	3.19	2.66	153	145	54	124	3.26	2.75	154	146	58	71	55	195
Texas, U. of at Austin	02/01	$65	3.77	3.40	164	158	37	468	0.00	0.00	0	0	N/A	0	37	468
*** Utah ***																
Brigham Young U.	02/01	$30	3.77	3.42	164	157	37	145	0.00	0.00	0	0	N/A	0	37	145
Utah, U. of	02/01	$40	3.76	3.19	162	155	41	123	0.00	0.00	0	0	N/A	0	41	123
*** Vermont ***																
Vermont Law School	02/01	$50	3.30	2.70	156	148	73	192	0.00	0.00	0	0	N/A	0	73	192
*** Virginia ***																
George Mason U.	03/01	$35	3.40	2.83	161	156	34	115	3.38	2.74	160	153	36	94	34	209
Regent U.	05/01	$40	3.50	2.64	153	145	59	107	3.04	2.36	152	145	74	36	62	143
Richmond, U. of	01/15	$35	3.41	2.73	158	153	43	168	0.00	0.00	0	0	N/A	0	43	168
Virginia, U. of	01/15	$65	3.78	3.51	168	163	28	358	0.00	0.00	0	0	N/A	0	28	358
Washington & Lee U.	02/01	$40	3.75	3.05	166	161	37	122	0.00	0.00	0	0	N/A	0	37	122
William and Mary School of Law	03/01	$40	3.53	3.03	164	159	34	175	0.00	0.00	0	0	N/A	0	34	175
*** Washington ***																
Gonzaga U.	03/15	$40	3.30	2.74	154	145	82	188	0.00	0.00	0	0	N/A	0	82	188
Seattle U.	04/01	$50	3.50	3.04	157	150	77	234	3.37	2.68	156	146	71	69	76	303
Washington, U. of	01/15	$50	3.72	3.38	166	158	29	173	0.00	0.00	0	0	N/A	0	29	173
*** West Virginia ***																
West Virginia U.	03/01	$45	3.62	2.96	156	150	49	142	0.00	0.00	0	0	100	7	49	149

	ADMISSIONS																
			FULL-TIME						PART-TIME						TOTAL	
	Application Deadline	Application Fee	75% GPA	25% GPA	75% LSAT	25% LSAT	% Accepted	# of Matriculants	75% GPA	25% GPA	75% LSAT	25% LSAT	% Accepted	# of Matriculants	Total % Accepted	Total Matriculants
*** Wisconsin ***																
Marquette U.	04/01	$35	3.35	2.82	157	152	67	150	3.47	2.79	159	151	56	57	65	207
Wisconsin, U. of	02/01	$45	3.66	3.25	160	154	48	273	3.56	2.64	162	154	N/A	8	48	281
*** Wyoming ***																
Wyoming, U. of	03/15	$35	3.56	3.03	157	148	70	86	0.00	0.00	0	0	N/A	0	70	86

Chapter Twelve

School Profiles

All ABA Approved Law Schools

pages 84-447

This book contains information concerning law schools that were operating as of October 1, 1998 and were approved by the ABA to confer the first degree in law. The approval status of an individual law school can change. Therefore, if you would like to confirm whether an individual law school is approved by the ABA at a specific time after October 1, you should contact the ABA directly. You can also access this information on the Section of Legal Education and Admissions to the Bar's website: http://www.abanet.org/legaled. For updates or corrections to this book, please visit the Section's website: http://www.abanet.org/legaled.

AKRON, UNIVERSITY OF

C. Blake McDowell Law Center
Akron, OH 44325-2901
800-4akron-u
http://www.uakron.edu/law/index.html

ABA Approved Since 1961

The Basics

Type of School: Public Term: Semester
Application deadline: 03/01 (Preferred)
Application fee: $35
Financial Aid deadline: 05/01 (Preferred)
Can first year start other than Fall? No
Student faculty ratio: 21.8 to 1
Does the University offer:
- housing restricted to law students? No
- graduate student housing for which law students are eligible? Yes

Faculty & Administrators

	Total		Men		Women		Minorities	
	Fall	Spr	Fall	Spr	Fall	Spr	Fall	Spr
Full-time	19	19	11	11	8	8	3	3
Other Full-Time	0	0	0	0	0	0	0	0
Deans, librarians, & others who teach > 1/2	5	5	2	2	3	3	1	1
Part-time	27	30	13	19	14	11	1	3
Total	51	54	26	32	25	22	5	7
Deans, librarians, & others who teach < 1/2	3	3	2	2	1	1	0	0

Curriculum

	Full time	Part time
Typical first-year section size	48	70
Is there typically a "small section" of the first year class, other than Legal Writing, taught by full-time faculty?	No	No
If yes, typical size offered last year	N/A	N/A
# of classroom course titles beyond 1st year curriculum	38	58
# of upper division courses, excluding seminars, with an enrollment:		
Under 25	25	31
25 - 49	6	23
50 - 74	3	4
75 - 99	5	1
100 +	0	0
# of seminars	8	8
# of seminar positions available	348	
# of seminar positions filled	106	145
# of positions available in simulation courses	253	
# of simulation positions filled	172	79
# of positions available in faculty supervised clinical courses	150	
# of fac. sup. clin. positions filled	102	17
# involved in field placements	102	17
# involved in law journals	42	10
# in moot court or trial competitions	37	6
# of credit hrs required to graduate	88	

J.D. Enrollment & Ethnicity

	Men		Women		Fl-Time		Pt-Time		1st Yr		2nd Yr		3rd Yr		4th Yr		Total		JD Degrees Awarded
	#	%	#	%	#	%	#	%	#	%	#	%	#	%	#	%	#	%	
African-American	17	5.5	14	5.2	22	6.3	9	4.0	16	8.3	9	5.5	6	3.5	0	0.0	31	5.4	4
American Indian	2	0.6	1	0.4	1	0.3	2	0.9	1	0.5	1	0.6	0	0.0	1	2.2	3	0.5	2
Asian American	3	1.0	5	1.9	5	1.4	3	1.3	3	1.6	2	1.2	2	1.2	1	2.2	8	1.4	5
Mexican American	0	0.0	0	0.0	0	0.0	0	0.0	0	0.0	0	0.0	0	0.0	0	0.0	0	0.0	0
Puerto Rican	0	0.0	0	0.0	0	0.0	0	0.0	0	0.0	0	0.0	0	0.0	0	0.0	0	0.0	0
Hispanic American	0	0.0	8	3.0	4	1.1	4	1.8	2	1.0	4	2.4	2	1.2	0	0.0	8	1.4	2
Total Minorities	22	7.1	28	10.5	32	9.2	18	8.0	22	11.5	16	9.8	10	5.8	2	4.3	50	8.7	13
Foreign Nationals	0	0.0	3	1.1	2	0.6	1	0.4	1	0.5	1	0.6	1	0.6	0	0.0	3	0.5	1
Caucasian	286	92.9	236	88.4	315	90.3	207	91.6	166	86.5	149	90.9	163	94.2	44	95.7	522	90.8	174
Total	308	53.6	267	46.4	349	60.7	226	39.3	192	33.4	164	28.5	173	30.1	46	8.0	575		188

GPA & LSAT Scores

	Full Time	Part Time	Total
# of apps	799	233	1,032
# admits	395	108	503
# of matrics	123	76	199
75% GPA	3.59	3.45	
25% GPA	3.00	2.83	
75% LSAT	154	157	
25% LSAT	148	150	

Tuition & Fees

	Resident	Non-resident
Full-Time	$6,733	$11,500
Part-Time	$4,872	$8,277

Living Expenses

Estimated living expenses for Singles		
Living on campus	Living off campus	Living at home
$10,568	$10,568	$10,568

Employment

	Total	%
Employment status known	165	99.4
Employment status unknown	1	0.6
Employed	142	86.1
Pursuing graduate degrees	3	1.8
Unemployed seeking employment	5	3.0
Unemployed not seeking employment	15	9.1
Type of Employment		
# employed in law firms	66	46.5
# employed in business & industry	31	21.8
# employed in government	34	23.9
# employed in public interest	4	2.8
# employed as judicial clerks	5	3.5
# employed in academia	2	1.4
Geographic Location		
# employed in state	94	66.2
# employed in foreign countries	4	2.8
# of states where employed	18	

Grants/Scholarships

	Full-time		Part-time		Total	
	#	%	#	%	#	%
Total # of Students	349		226		575	
Total # receiving grants	115	33.0	40	17.7	155	27.0
Less than 1/2 tuition	41	11.7	18	8.0	59	10.3
Half to full tuition	24	6.9	13	5.8	37	6.4
Full tuition	48	13.8	9	4.0	57	9.9
More than full tuition	2	0.6	0	0.0	2	0.3
Median Grant Amount	$4,000		$3,000			

Informational & Library Resources

# of volumes & volume equivalents	256,603	# of professional staff	5
# of titles	54,535	Hours per week with professional staff	79
# of active serial subscriptions	3,566	Hours per week without professional staff	16
Study seating capacity inside the library	295	# of student computer work stations for entire law school	57
Square feet of law library	34,634	# of additional networked connections	0
Square feet of law school (excl. Library)	54,709	Require Laptop Computer?	N

J.D. Attrition (from Prior Year)

	Academic	Other	TOTALS	
	#	#	#	%
1st Year	14	34	48	24%
2nd Year	9	0	9	5.1%
3rd Year	0	0	0	0.0%
4th Year	0	0	0	0.0%

Bar Passage Rates

Jurisdiction	Ohio		
Exam	Sum 97	Win 98	Total
# from school taking bar for the first time	90	23	113
School's pass rate for all first-time takers	76%	87%	78%
State's pass rate for all first-time takers	79%	75%	78%

ALABAMA, UNIVERSITY OF

P.O. Box 870382
Tuscaloosa, AL 35487
(205)348-5117
http://www.law.ua.edu

ABA Approved Since 1926

The Basics

Type of School: Public Term: Semester
Application deadline: 03/01
Application fee: $25
Financial Aid deadline: 03/01
Can first year start other than Fall? No
Student faculty ratio: 18.3 to 1
Does the University offer:
- housing restricted to law students? No
- graduate student housing for which law students are eligible? Yes

Faculty & Administrators

	Total		Men		Women		Minorities	
	Fall	Spr	Fall	Spr	Fall	Spr	Fall	Spr
Full-time	25	25	20	20	5	5	2	2
Other Full-Time	4	4	2	2	2	2	1	1
Deans, librarians, & others who teach > 1/2	1	1	1	1	0	0	0	0
Part-time	31	34	25	28	6	6	1	1
Total	61	64	48	51	13	13	4	4
Deans, librarians, & others who teach < 1/2	7	7	6	6	1	1	0	0

Curriculum

	Full time	Part time
Typical first-year section size	100	0
Is there typically a "small section" of the first year class, other than Legal Writing, taught by full-time faculty?	Yes	No
If yes, typical size offered last year	22	N/A
# of classroom course titles beyond 1st year curriculum	99	0
# of upper division courses, excluding seminars, with an enrollment:		
Under 25	65	0
25 - 49	25	0
50 - 74	17	0
75 - 99	5	0
100 +	2	0
# of seminars	17	0
# of seminar positions available	204	
# of seminar positions filled	159	0
# of positions available in simulation courses	300	
# of simulation positions filled	272	0
# of positions available in faculty supervised clinical courses	51	
# of fac. sup. clin. positions filled	51	0
# involved in field placements	46	0
# involved in law journals	90	0
# in moot court or trial competitions	90	0
# of credit hrs required to graduate	90	

J.D. Enrollment & Ethnicity

	Men		Women		Fl-Time		Pt-Time		1st Yr		2nd Yr		3rd Yr		4th Yr		Total		JD Degrees Awarded
	#	%	#	%	#	%	#	%	#	%	#	%	#	%	#	%	#	%	
African-American	12	3.5	25	12.0	37	6.7	0	0.0	20	11.2	10	5.3	7	3.8	0	0.0	37	6.7	16
American Indian	4	1.2	2	1.0	6	1.1	0	0.0	2	1.1	3	1.6	1	0.5	0	0.0	6	1.1	1
Asian American	1	0.3	3	1.4	4	0.7	0	0.0	1	0.6	2	1.1	1	0.5	0	0.0	4	0.7	1
Mexican American	0	0.0	0	0.0	0	0.0	0	0.0	0	0.0	0	0.0	0	0.0	0	0.0	0	0.0	0
Puerto Rican	0	0.0	0	0.0	0	0.0	0	0.0	0	0.0	0	0.0	0	0.0	0	0.0	0	0.0	0
Hispanic American	4	1.2	1	0.5	5	0.9	0	0.0	3	1.7	1	0.5	1	0.5	0	0.0	5	0.9	0
Total Minorities	21	6.2	31	14.8	52	9.5	0	0.0	26	14.6	16	8.6	10	5.4	0	0.0	52	9.5	18
Foreign Nationals	0	0.0	0	0.0	0	0.0	0	0.0	0	0.0	0	0.0	0	0.0	0	0.0	0	0.0	0
Caucasian	319	93.8	178	85.2	497	90.5	0	0.0	152	85.4	171	91.4	174	94.6	0	0.0	497	90.5	158
Total	340	61.9	209	38.1	549	100.0	0	0.0	178	32.4	187	34.1	184	33.5	0	0.0	549		176

GPA & LSAT Scores

	Full Time	Part Time	Total
# of apps	733	0	733
# admits	340	0	340
# of matrics	179	0	179
75% GPA	3.50	0.00	
25% GPA	2.98	0.00	
75% LSAT	159	0	
25% LSAT	154	0	

Tuition & Fees

	Resident	Non-resident
Full-Time	$4,490	$9,484
Part-Time	$0	$0

Living Expenses

Estimated living expenses for Singles		
Living on campus	Living off campus	Living at home
$10,902	$10,312	$8,746

Grants/Scholarships

	Full-time		Part-time		Total	
	#	%	#	%	#	%
Total # of Students	549		0		549	
Total # receiving grants	145	26.4	0	0.0	145	26.4
Less than 1/2 tuition	32	5.8	0	0.0	32	5.8
Half to full tuition	44	8.0	0	0.0	44	8.0
Full tuition	44	8.0	0	0.0	44	8.0
More than full tuition	25	4.6	0	0.0	25	4.6
Median Grant Amount	$2,000		$0			

Informational & Library Resources

# of volumes & volume equivalents	364,209	# of professional staff	7
# of titles	79,479	Hours per week with professional staff	57
# of active serial subscriptions	3,168	Hours per week without professional staff	45
Study seating capacity inside the library	562	# of student computer work stations for entire law school	57
Square feet of law library	65,950	# of additional networked connections	10
Square feet of law school (excl. Library)	75,892	Require Laptop Computer?	N

Employment

	Total	%
Employment status known	174	98.3
Employment status unknown	3	1.7
Employed	164	94.3
Pursuing graduate degrees	6	3.4
Unemployed seeking employment	3	1.7
Unemployed not seeking employment	1	0.6
Type of Employment		
# employed in law firms	113	68.9
# employed in business & industry	13	7.9
# employed in government	6	3.7
# employed in public interest	2	1.2
# employed as judicial clerks	13	7.9
# employed in academia	1	0.6
Geographic Location		
# employed in state	144	87.8
# employed in foreign countries	0	0.0
# of states where employed	6	

J.D. Attrition (from Prior Year)

	Academic	Other	TOTALS	
	#	#	#	%
1st Year	5	14	19	9.2%
2nd Year	0	5	5	2.7%
3rd Year	0	1	1	0.6%
4th Year	0	0	0	0.0%

Bar Passage Rates

Jurisdiction	Alabama		
Exam	Sum 97	Win 98	Total
# from school taking bar for the first time	154	31	185
School's pass rate for all first-time takers	95%	77%	92%
State's pass rate for all first-time takers	80%	68%	76%

ALBANY LAW SCHOOL

80 New Scotland Avenue
Albany, NY 12208
(518)445-2311
http://www.als.edu

ABA Approved Since 1930

The Basics

Type of School: Private Term: Semester

Application deadline: Rolling

Application fee: $50

Financial Aid deadline: Rolling

Can first year start other than Fall? No

Student faculty ratio: 21.0 to 1

Does the University offer:

- housing restricted to law students? Yes
- graduate student housing for which law students are eligible? No

Faculty & Administrators

	Total		Men		Women		Minorities	
	Fall	Spr	Fall	Spr	Fall	Spr	Fall	Spr
Full-time	27	28	17	19	10	9	5	5
Other Full-Time	4	4	1	1	3	3	0	0
Deans, librarians, & others who teach > 1/2	6	6	2	2	4	4	0	0
Part-time	17	20	13	16	4	4	2	3
Total	54	58	33	38	21	20	7	8
Deans, librarians, & others who teach < 1/2	3	3	2	2	1	1	0	0

Curriculum

	Full time	Part time
Typical first-year section size	80	0
Is there typically a "small section" of the first year class, other than Legal Writing, taught by full-time faculty?	Yes	No
If yes, typical size offered last year	48	N/A
# of classroom course titles beyond 1st year curriculum	105	0
# of upper division courses, excluding seminars, with an enrollment:		
Under 25	41	0
25 - 49	23	0
50 - 74	16	0
75 - 99	5	0
100 +	7	0
# of seminars	24	0
# of seminar positions available	436	
# of seminar positions filled	279	0
# of positions available in simulation courses	302	
# of simulation positions filled	231	0
# of positions available in faculty supervised clinical courses	95	
# of fac. sup. clin. positions filled	64	0
# involved in field placements	212	0
# involved in law journals	53	0
# in moot court or trial competitions	76	0
# of credit hrs required to graduate	87	

J.D. Enrollment & Ethnicity

	Men		Women		Fl-Time		Pt-Time		1st Yr		2nd Yr		3rd Yr		4th Yr		Total		JD Degrees Awarded
	#	%	#	%	#	%	#	%	#	%	#	%	#	%	#	%	#	%	
African-American	19	5.9	37	10.0	55	8.4	1	2.7	29	11.8	13	6.0	14	6.2	0	0.0	56	8.1	16
American Indian	3	0.9	0	0.0	3	0.5	0	0.0	0	0.0	2	0.9	1	0.4	0	0.0	3	0.4	0
Asian American	6	1.9	21	5.7	27	4.1	0	0.0	10	4.1	12	5.6	5	2.2	0	0.0	27	3.9	18
Mexican American	0	0.0	2	0.5	2	0.3	0	0.0	0	0.0	0	0.0	2	0.9	0	0.0	2	0.3	2
Puerto Rican	5	1.6	7	1.9	12	1.8	0	0.0	1	0.4	4	1.9	7	3.1	0	0.0	12	1.7	1
Hispanic American	7	2.2	7	1.9	12	1.8	2	5.4	9	3.7	1	0.5	4	1.8	0	0.0	14	2.0	6
Total Minorities	40	12.4	74	20.0	111	16.9	3	8.1	49	19.9	32	14.9	33	14.5	0	0.0	114	16.5	43
Foreign Nationals	6	1.9	3	0.8	9	1.4	0	0.0	3	1.2	2	0.9	4	1.8	0	0.0	9	1.3	3
Caucasian	276	85.7	293	79.2	535	81.7	34	91.9	194	78.9	181	84.2	190	83.7	4	100.0	569	82.2	203
Total	322	46.5	370	53.5	655	94.7	37	5.3	246	35.5	215	31.1	227	32.8	4	0.6	692		249

GPA & LSAT Scores

	Full Time	Part Time	Total
# of apps	1,174	0	1,174
# admits	804	0	804
# of matrics	247	0	247
75% GPA	3.41	0.00	
25% GPA	2.90	0.00	
75% LSAT	153	0	
25% LSAT	145	0	

Tuition & Fees

	Resident	Non-resident
Full-Time	$19,425	$19,425
Part-Time	$14,600	$14,600

Living Expenses

Estimated living expenses for Singles		
Living on campus	Living off campus	Living at home
$8,995	$10,325	$6,395

Employment

	Total	%
Employment status known	247	98.8
Employment status unknown	3	1.2
Employed	236	95.5
Pursuing graduate degrees	3	1.2
Unemployed seeking employment	1	0.4
Unemployed not seeking employment	7	2.8
Type of Employment		
# employed in law firms	116	49.2
# employed in business & industry	40	16.9
# employed in government	51	21.6
# employed in public interest	8	3.4
# employed as judicial clerks	15	6.4
# employed in academia	6	2.5
Geographic Location		
# employed in state	193	81.8
# employed in foreign countries	0	0.0
# of states where employed	17	

Grants/Scholarships

	Full-time		Part-time		Total	
	#	%	#	%	#	%
Total # of Students	655		37		692	
Total # receiving grants	319	48.7	8	21.6	327	47.3
Less than 1/2 tuition	259	39.5	8	21.6	267	38.6
Half to full tuition	52	7.9	0	0.0	52	7.5
Full tuition	8	1.2	0	0.0	8	1.2
More than full tuition	0	0.0	0	0.0	0	0.0
Median Grant Amount	$3,800		$2,400			

Informational & Library Resources

# of volumes & volume equivalents	536,218	# of professional staff	7
# of titles	80,179	Hours per week with professional staff	71
# of active serial subscriptions	3,700	Hours per week without professional staff	33
Study seating capacity inside the library	482	# of student computer work stations for entire law school	117
Square feet of law library	53,056	# of additional networked connections	0
Square feet of law school (excl. Library)	46,288	Require Laptop Computer?	N

J.D. Attrition (from Prior Year)

	Academic	Other	TOTALS	
	#	#	#	%
1st Year	11	13	24	9.6%
2nd Year	2	16	18	7.6%
3rd Year	1	0	1	0.4%
4th Year	0	0	0	0.0%

Bar Passage Rates

Jurisdiction	New York		
Exam	Sum 97	Win 98	Total
# from school taking bar for the first time	222	16	238
School's pass rate for all first-time takers	81%	81%	81%
State's pass rate for all first-time takers	78%	65%	76%

AMERICAN UNIVERSITY

Washington College of Law
4801 Massachusetts Ave, NW
Washington, DC 20016
(202)274-4000
http://www.wcl.american.edu

ABA Approved Since 1940

The Basics

Type of School: Private Term: Semester
Application deadline: 03/01
Application fee: $55
Financial Aid deadline: 03/01
Can first year start other than Fall? No
Student faculty ratio: 20.6 to 1
Does the University offer:
- housing restricted to law students? No
- graduate student housing for which law students are eligible? Yes

Faculty & Administrators

	Total		Men		Women		Minorities	
	Fall	Spr	Fall	Spr	Fall	Spr	Fall	Spr
Full-time	44	45	28	29	16	16	7	8
Other Full-Time	4	4	0	0	4	4	1	1
Deans, librarians, & others who teach > 1/2	4	4	4	4	0	0	0	0
Part-time	90	105	61	68	29	37	6	9
Total	142	158	93	101	49	57	14	18
Deans, librarians, & others who teach < 1/2	1	1	1	1	0	0	1	1

Curriculum

	Full time	Part time
Typical first-year section size	98	98
Is there typically a "small section" of the first year class, other than Legal Writing, taught by full-time faculty?	No	No
If yes, typical size offered last year	N/A	N/A
# of classroom course titles beyond 1st year curriculum	160	80
# of upper division courses, excluding seminars, with an enrollment:		
Under 25	43	43
25 - 49	29	16
50 - 74	18	7
75 - 99	9	5
100 +	0	1
# of seminars	81	31
# of seminar positions available	2,044	
# of seminar positions filled	1,106	374
# of positions available in simulation courses	367	
# of simulation positions filled	251	58
# of positions available in faculty supervised clinical courses	253	
# of fac. sup. clin. positions filled	242	11
# involved in field placements	176	19
# involved in law journals	274	47
# in moot court or trial competitions	90	16
# of credit hrs required to graduate	86	

J.D. Enrollment & Ethnicity

	Men		Women		Fl-Time		Pt-Time		1st Yr		2nd Yr		3rd Yr		4th Yr		Total		JD Degrees Awarded
	#	%	#	%	#	%	#	%	#	%	#	%	#	%	#	%	#	%	
African-American	33	7.0	77	10.7	64	7.2	46	14.8	41	9.8	37	10.9	26	7.4	6	6.9	110	9.2	20
American Indian	3	0.6	8	1.1	3	0.3	8	2.6	3	0.7	2	0.6	5	1.4	1	1.1	11	0.9	2
Asian American	47	10.0	70	9.7	99	11.2	18	5.8	47	11.2	30	8.8	35	10.0	5	5.7	117	9.8	41
Mexican American	11	2.3	16	2.2	23	2.6	4	1.3	12	2.9	9	2.7	3	0.9	3	3.4	27	2.3	3
Puerto Rican	2	0.4	4	0.6	2	0.2	4	1.3	2	0.5	2	0.6	1	0.3	1	1.1	6	0.5	1
Hispanic American	21	4.4	31	4.3	36	4.1	16	5.1	26	6.2	13	3.8	12	3.4	1	1.1	52	4.4	9
Total Minorities	117	24.8	206	28.5	227	25.7	96	30.9	131	31.3	93	27.4	82	23.4	17	19.5	323	27.1	76
Foreign Nationals	0	0.0	0	0.0	0	0.0	0	0.0	0	0.0	0	0.0	0	0.0	0	0.0	0	0.0	0
Caucasian	355	75.2	516	71.5	656	74.3	215	69.1	287	68.7	246	72.6	268	76.6	70	80.5	871	72.9	265
Total	472	39.5	722	60.5	883	74.0	311	26.0	418	35.0	339	28.4	350	29.3	87	7.3	1194		341

GPA & LSAT Scores

	Full Time	Part Time	Total
# of apps	3,949	551	4,500
# admits	1,577	358	1,935
# of matrics	296	97	393
75% GPA	3.51	3.31	
25% GPA	3.09	2.85	
75% LSAT	158	155	
25% LSAT	153	148	

Tuition & Fees

	Resident	Non-resident
Full-Time	$22,972	$22,972
Part-Time	$16,982	$16,982

Living Expenses

Estimated living expenses for Singles		
Living on campus	Living off campus	Living at home
$12,734	$12,734	$12,734

Employment

	Total	%
Employment status known	306	86.9
Employment status unknown	46	13.1
Employed	273	89.2
Pursuing graduate degrees	11	3.6
Unemployed seeking employment	18	5.9
Unemployed not seeking employment	4	1.3
Type of Employment		
# employed in law firms	106	38.8
# employed in business & industry	43	15.8
# employed in government	57	20.9
# employed in public interest	14	5.1
# employed as judicial clerks	38	13.9
# employed in academia	2	0.7
Geographic Location		
# employed in state	189	69.2
# employed in foreign countries	1	0.4
# of states where employed	28	

Grants/Scholarships

	Full-time		Part-time		Total	
	#	%	#	%	#	%
Total # of Students	883		311		1194	
Total # receiving grants	242	27.4	0	0.0	242	20.3
Less than 1/2 tuition	199	22.5	0	0.0	199	16.7
Half to full tuition	43	4.9	0	0.0	43	3.6
Full tuition	0	0.0	0	0.0	0	0.0
More than full tuition	0	0.0	0	0.0	0	0.0
Median Grant Amount	$8,456		$0			

Informational & Library Resources

# of volumes & volume equivalents	425,049	# of professional staff	9
# of titles	167,193	Hours per week with professional staff	82
# of active serial subscriptions	5,990	Hours per week without professional staff	37
Study seating capacity inside the library	649	# of student computer work stations for entire law school	0
Square feet of law library	55,000	# of additional networked connections	0
Square feet of law school (excl. Library)	84,420	Require Laptop Computer?	N

J.D. Attrition (from Prior Year)

	Academic	Other	TOTALS	
	#	#	#	%
1st Year	2	26	28	7.2%
2nd Year	1	4	5	1.4%
3rd Year	0	1	1	0.3%
4th Year	0	0	0	0.0%

Bar Passage Rates

Jurisdiction	Maryland		
Exam	Sum 97	Win 98	Total
# from school taking bar for the first time	108	37	145
School's pass rate for all first-time takers	63%	86%	69%
State's pass rate for all first-time takers	69%	83%	72%

ARIZONA STATE UNIVERSITY

P.O. Box 877906
Tempe, AZ 85287-7906
(602)965-6181
http://www.asu.edu/law

ABA Approved Since 1969

The Basics

Type of School: Public Term: Semester
Application deadline: 03/01
Application fee: $45
Financial Aid deadline: 03/01
Can first year start other than Fall? No
Student faculty ratio: 17.2 to 1
Does the University offer:
- housing restricted to law students? No
- graduate student housing for which law students are eligible? Yes

Faculty & Administrators

	Total		Men		Women		Minorities	
	Fall	Spr	Fall	Spr	Fall	Spr	Fall	Spr
Full-time	23	26	19	22	4	4	3	3
Other Full-Time	1	1	1	1	0	0	0	0
Deans, librarians, & others who teach > 1/2	3	3	1	1	2	2	0	0
Part-time	21	12	14	11	7	1	1	1
Total	48	42	35	35	13	7	4	4
Deans, librarians, & others who teach < 1/2	2	2	1	1	1	1	0	0

Curriculum

	Full time	Part time
Typical first-year section size	128	0
Is there typically a "small section" of the first year class, other than Legal Writing, taught by full-time faculty?	Yes	No
If yes, typical size offered last year	32	N/A
# of classroom course titles beyond 1st year curriculum	77	0
# of upper division courses, excluding seminars, with an enrollment:		
Under 25	41	0
25 - 49	23	0
50 - 74	11	0
75 - 99	3	0
100 +	0	0
# of seminars	22	0
# of seminar positions available	349	
# of seminar positions filled	308	0
# of positions available in simulation courses	112	
# of simulation positions filled	99	0
# of positions available in faculty supervised clinical courses	74	
# of fac. sup. clin. positions filled	71	0
# involved in field placements	83	0
# involved in law journals	138	0
# in moot court or trial competitions	80	0
# of credit hrs required to graduate	87	

J.D. Enrollment & Ethnicity

	Men		Women		Fl-Time		Pt-Time		1st Yr		2nd Yr		3rd Yr		4th Yr		Total		JD Degrees Awarded
	#	%	#	%	#	%	#	%	#	%	#	%	#	%	#	%	#	%	
African-American	9	3.6	6	2.7	15	3.2	0	0.0	4	2.5	5	3.3	6	3.7	0	0.0	15	3.2	5
American Indian	12	4.8	19	8.4	31	6.5	0	0.0	13	8.0	12	8.0	6	3.7	0	0.0	31	6.5	7
Asian American	7	2.8	4	1.8	11	2.3	0	0.0	3	1.8	3	2.0	5	3.1	0	0.0	11	2.3	6
Mexican American	19	7.6	21	9.3	40	8.4	0	0.0	13	8.0	13	8.7	14	8.6	0	0.0	40	8.4	13
Puerto Rican	0	0.0	1	0.4	1	0.2	0	0.0	1	0.6	0	0.0	0	0.0	0	0.0	1	0.2	0
Hispanic American	4	1.6	2	0.9	6	1.3	0	0.0	3	1.8	1	0.7	2	1.2	0	0.0	6	1.3	4
Total Minorities	51	20.4	53	23.6	104	21.9	0	0.0	37	22.7	34	22.7	33	20.4	0	0.0	104	21.9	35
Foreign Nationals	6	2.4	6	2.7	12	2.5	0	0.0	2	1.2	6	4.0	4	2.5	0	0.0	12	2.5	0
Caucasian	193	77.2	166	73.8	359	75.6	0	0.0	124	76.1	110	73.3	125	77.2	0	0.0	359	75.6	95
Total	250	52.6	225	47.4	475	100.0	0	0.0	163	34.3	150	31.6	162	34.1	0	0.0	475		130

GPA & LSAT Scores

	Full Time	Part Time	Total
# of apps	1,649	0	1,649
# admits	380	0	380
# of matrics	162	0	162
75% GPA	3.59	0.00	
25% GPA	2.96	0.00	
75% LSAT	161	0	
25% LSAT	154	0	

Tuition & Fees

	Resident	Non-resident
Full-Time	$4,536	$11,488
Part-Time	$0	$0

Living Expenses

Estimated living expenses for Singles		
Living on campus	Living off campus	Living at home
$8,025	$10,625	$6,000

Grants/Scholarships

	Full-time		Part-time		Total	
	#	%	#	%	#	%
Total # of Students	475		0		475	
Total # receiving grants	160	33.7	0	0.0	160	33.7
Less than 1/2 tuition	48	10.1	0	0.0	48	10.1
Half to full tuition	53	11.2	0	0.0	53	11.2
Full tuition	45	9.5	0	0.0	45	9.5
More than full tuition	14	2.9	0	0.0	14	2.9
Median Grant Amount	$4,463		$0			

Informational & Library Resources

# of volumes & volume equivalents	368,919	# of professional staff	7
# of titles	113,514	Hours per week with professional staff	73
# of active serial subscriptions	6,516	Hours per week without professional staff	37
Study seating capacity inside the library	558	# of student computer work stations for entire law school	49
Square feet of law library	60,000	# of additional networked connections	14
Square feet of law school (excl. Library)	59,645	Require Laptop Computer?	N

Employment

	Total	%
Employment status known	146	95.4
Employment status unknown	7	4.6
Employed	127	87.0
Pursuing graduate degrees	3	2.1
Unemployed seeking employment	8	5.5
Unemployed not seeking employment	8	5.5
Type of Employment		
# employed in law firms	58	45.7
# employed in business & industry	16	12.6
# employed in government	28	22.0
# employed in public interest	1	0.8
# employed as judicial clerks	20	15.7
# employed in academia	1	0.8
Geographic Location		
# employed in state	105	82.7
# employed in foreign countries	0	0.0
# of states where employed	11	

J.D. Attrition (from Prior Year)

	Academic	Other	TOTALS	
	#	#	#	%
1st Year	6	4	10	6.3%
2nd Year	0	1	1	0.7%
3rd Year	0	0	0	0.0%
4th Year	0	0	0	0.0%

Bar Passage Rates

Jurisdiction	Arizona		
Exam	Sum 97	Win 98	Total
# from school taking bar for the first time	104	21	125
School's pass rate for all first-time takers	84%	62%	80%
State's pass rate for all first-time takers	84%	72%	80%

ARIZONA, UNIVERSITY OF

James E. Rogers Law Center
P.O. Box 210176
Tucson, AZ 85721-0176
(520)621-1373
http://www.law.arizona.edu

ABA Approved Since 1930

The Basics

Type of School: Public Term: Semester

Application deadline: 03/01

Application fee: $45

Financial Aid deadline: 03/01

Can first year start other than Fall? No

Student faculty ratio: 14.2 to 1

Does the University offer:

- housing restricted to law students? No
- graduate student housing for which law students are eligible? No

Faculty & Administrators

	Total		Men		Women		Minorities	
	Fall	Spr	Fall	Spr	Fall	Spr	Fall	Spr
Full-time	27	29	16	18	11	11	4	4
Other Full-Time	1	1	1	1	0	0	0	0
Deans, librarians, & others who teach > 1/2	4	4	2	2	2	2	1	1
Part-time	32	26	22	15	10	11	3	1
Total	64	60	41	36	23	24	8	6
Deans, librarians, & others who teach < 1/2	0	0	0	0	0	0	0	0

Curriculum

	Full time	Part time
Typical first-year section size	85	0
Is there typically a "small section" of the first year class, other than Legal Writing, taught by full-time faculty?	Yes	No
If yes, typical size offered last year	25	N/A
# of classroom course titles beyond 1st year curriculum	93	0
# of upper division courses, excluding seminars, with an enrollment:		
Under 25	69	0
25 - 49	23	0
50 - 74	8	0
75 - 99	2	0
100 +	1	0
# of seminars	26	0
# of seminar positions available	397	
# of seminar positions filled	291	0
# of positions available in simulation courses	335	
# of simulation positions filled	241	0
# of positions available in faculty supervised clinical courses	57	
# of fac. sup. clin. positions filled	29	0
# involved in field placements	84	0
# involved in law journals	79	0
# in moot court or trial competitions	72	0
# of credit hrs required to graduate	85	

J.D. Enrollment & Ethnicity

	Men		Women		Fl-Time		Pt-Time		1st Yr		2nd Yr		3rd Yr		4th Yr		Total		JD Degrees Awarded
	#	%	#	%	#	%	#	%	#	%	#	%	#	%	#	%	#	%	
African-American	8	3.5	6	2.6	14	3.0	0	0.0	4	2.6	5	3.4	5	3.1	0	0.0	14	3.0	4
American Indian	7	3.0	13	5.7	20	4.3	0	0.0	9	5.9	7	4.7	4	2.5	0	0.0	20	4.3	1
Asian American	14	6.1	13	5.7	27	5.9	0	0.0	9	5.9	10	6.8	8	5.0	0	0.0	27	5.9	8
Mexican American	12	5.2	11	4.8	23	5.0	0	0.0	5	3.3	10	6.8	8	5.0	0	0.0	23	5.0	6
Puerto Rican	3	1.3	1	0.4	4	0.9	0	0.0	1	0.7	2	1.4	1	0.6	0	0.0	4	0.9	0
Hispanic American	17	7.4	9	3.9	26	5.7	0	0.0	9	5.9	7	4.7	10	6.3	0	0.0	26	5.7	11
Total Minorities	61	26.4	53	23.1	114	24.8	0	0.0	37	24.3	41	27.7	36	22.5	0	0.0	114	24.8	30
Foreign Nationals	0	0.0	3	1.3	3	0.7	0	0.0	0	0.0	1	0.7	2	1.3	0	0.0	3	0.7	0
Caucasian	170	73.6	173	75.5	343	74.6	0	0.0	115	75.7	106	71.6	122	76.3	0	0.0	343	74.6	114
Total	231	50.2	229	49.8	460	100.0	0	0.0	152	33.0	148	32.2	160	34.8	0	0.0	460		144

GPA & LSAT Scores

	Full Time	Part Time	Total
# of apps	1,499	0	1,499
# admits	408	0	408
# of matrics	152	0	152
75% GPA	3.66	0.00	
25% GPA	3.11	0.00	
75% LSAT	164	0	
25% LSAT	157	0	

Tuition & Fees

	Resident	Non-resident
Full-Time	$4,538	$11,490
Part-Time	$0	$0

Living Expenses

Estimated living expenses for Singles		
Living on campus	Living off campus	Living at home
$8,178	$11,998	$6,090

Grants/Scholarships

	Full-time		Part-time		Total	
	#	%	#	%	#	%
Total # of Students	460		0		460	
Total # receiving grants	308	67.0	0	0.0	308	67.0
Less than 1/2 tuition	95	20.7	0	0.0	95	20.7
Half to full tuition	154	33.5	0	0.0	154	33.5
Full tuition	25	5.4	0	0.0	25	5.4
More than full tuition	34	7.4	0	0.0	34	7.4
Median Grant Amount	$3,000		$0			

Informational & Library Resources

# of volumes & volume equivalents	373,075	# of professional staff	8
# of titles	64,723	Hours per week with professional staff	58
# of active serial subscriptions	4,261	Hours per week without professional staff	42
Study seating capacity inside the library	368	# of student computer work stations for entire law school	59
Square feet of law library	39,604	# of additional networked connections	66
Square feet of law school (excl. Library)	43,221	Require Laptop Computer?	N

Employment

	Total	%
Employment status known	146	98.0
Employment status unknown	3	2.0
Employed	133	91.1
Pursuing graduate degrees	4	2.7
Unemployed seeking employment	7	4.8
Unemployed not seeking employment	2	1.4
Type of Employment		
# employed in law firms	58	43.6
# employed in business & industry	17	12.8
# employed in government	24	18.0
# employed in public interest	10	7.5
# employed as judicial clerks	20	15.0
# employed in academia	1	0.8
Geographic Location		
# employed in state	78	58.6
# employed in foreign countries	1	0.8
# of states where employed	17	

J.D. Attrition (from Prior Year)

	Academic	Other	TOTALS	
	#	#	#	%
1st Year	0	0	0	0.0%
2nd Year	0	6	6	4.1%
3rd Year	0	5	5	3.1%
4th Year	0	0	0	0.0%

Bar Passage Rates

Jurisdiction	Arizona		
Exam	Sum 97	Win 98	Total
# from school taking bar for the first time	99	18	117
School's pass rate for all first-time takers	89%	61%	85%
State's pass rate for all first-time takers	84%	72%	80%

ARKANSAS, FAYETTEVILLE, UNIVERSITY OF

Waterman Hall
Leflar Law Center
Fayetteville, AR 72701-1201
(501)575-5601
http://law.uark.edu

ABA Approved Since 1926

The Basics

Type of School: Public   Term: Semester
Application deadline: 04/01
Application fee: $0
Financial Aid deadline: 04/01
Can first year start other than Fall? No
Student faculty ratio: 13.8 to 1
Does the University offer:
- housing restricted to law students? No
- graduate student housing for which law students are eligible? No

Faculty & Administrators

	Total		Men		Women		Minorities	
	Fall	Spr	Fall	Spr	Fall	Spr	Fall	Spr
Full-time	22	21	15	14	7	7	3	3
Other Full-Time	5	5	2	2	3	3	0	0
Deans, librarians, & others who teach > 1/2	4	4	2	2	2	2	0	0
Part-time	10	6	9	5	1	1	1	1
Total	41	36	28	23	13	13	4	4
Deans, librarians, & others who teach < 1/2	2	2	2	2	0	0	0	0

Curriculum

	Full time	Part time
Typical first-year section size	63	0
Is there typically a "small section" of the first year class, other than Legal Writing, taught by full-time faculty?	Yes	No
If yes, typical size offered last year	25	N/A
# of classroom course titles beyond 1st year curriculum	104	0
# of upper division courses, excluding seminars, with an enrollment:		
Under 25	73	0
25 - 49	20	0
50 - 74	7	0
75 - 99	4	0
100 +	1	0
# of seminars	7	0
# of seminar positions available	125	
# of seminar positions filled	113	0
# of positions available in simulation courses	206	
# of simulation positions filled	196	0
# of positions available in faculty supervised clinical courses	138	
# of fac. sup. clin. positions filled	91	0
# involved in field placements	15	0
# involved in law journals	43	0
# in moot court or trial competitions	98	0
# of credit hrs required to graduate	90	

J.D. Enrollment & Ethnicity

	Men		Women		Fl-Time		Pt-Time		1st Yr		2nd Yr		3rd Yr		4th Yr		Total		JD Degrees Awarded
	#	%	#	%	#	%	#	%	#	%	#	%	#	%	#	%	#	%	
African-American	5	2.3	10	6.9	15	4.1	0	0.0	3	2.5	5	4.4	7	5.4	0	0.0	15	4.1	6
American Indian	5	2.3	1	0.7	6	1.6	0	0.0	3	2.5	0	0.0	3	2.3	0	0.0	6	1.6	3
Asian American	2	0.9	2	1.4	4	1.1	0	0.0	0	0.0	4	3.5	0	0.0	0	0.0	4	1.1	2
Mexican American	0	0.0	0	0.0	0	0.0	0	0.0	0	0.0	0	0.0	0	0.0	0	0.0	0	0.0	0
Puerto Rican	0	0.0	0	0.0	0	0.0	0	0.0	0	0.0	0	0.0	0	0.0	0	0.0	0	0.0	0
Hispanic American	1	0.5	1	0.7	2	0.5	0	0.0	1	0.8	1	0.9	0	0.0	0	0.0	2	0.5	1
Total Minorities	13	5.9	14	9.7	27	7.4	0	0.0	7	5.8	10	8.8	10	7.7	0	0.0	27	7.4	12
Foreign Nationals	2	0.9	0	0.0	2	0.5	0	0.0	0	0.0	1	0.9	1	0.8	0	0.0	2	0.5	0
Caucasian	205	93.2	130	90.3	335	92.0	0	0.0	113	94.2	103	90.4	119	91.5	0	0.0	335	92.0	95
Total	220	60.4	144	39.6	364	100.0	0	0.0	120	33.0	114	31.3	130	35.7	0	0.0	364		107

GPA & LSAT Scores

	Full Time	Part Time	Total
# of apps	602	0	602
# admits	320	0	320
# of matrics	125	0	125
75% GPA	3.63	0.00	
25% GPA	2.97	0.00	
75% LSAT	157	0	
25% LSAT	148	0	

Tuition & Fees

	Resident	Non-resident
Full-Time	$4,168	$9,136
Part-Time	$0	$0

Living Expenses

Estimated living expenses for Singles

Living on campus	Living off campus	Living at home
$10,700	$10,700	$10,700

Employment

	Total	%
Employment status known	134	97.8
Employment status unknown	3	2.2
Employed	120	89.6
Pursuing graduate degrees	7	5.2
Unemployed seeking employment	4	3.0
Unemployed not seeking employment	3	2.2
Type of Employment		
# employed in law firms	66	55.0
# employed in business & industry	20	16.7
# employed in government	18	15.0
# employed in public interest	4	3.3
# employed as judicial clerks	10	8.3
# employed in academia	1	0.8
Geographic Location		
# employed in state	73	60.8
# employed in foreign countries	0	0.0
# of states where employed	13	

Grants/Scholarships

	Full-time		Part-time		Total	
	#	%	#	%	#	%
Total # of Students	364		0		364	
Total # receiving grants	96	26.4	0	0.0	96	26.4
Less than 1/2 tuition	34	9.3	0	0.0	34	9.3
Half to full tuition	29	8.0	0	0.0	29	8.0
Full tuition	0	0.0	0	0.0	0	0.0
More than full tuition	33	9.1	0	0.0	33	9.1
Median Grant Amount	$3,267		$0			

Informational & Library Resources

# of volumes & volume equivalents	251,401	# of professional staff	6
# of titles	88,349	Hours per week with professional staff	60
# of active serial subscriptions	2,319	Hours per week without professional staff	47
Study seating capacity inside the library	353	# of student computer work stations for entire law school	34
Square feet of law library	25,500	# of additional networked connections	0
Square feet of law school (excl. Library)	54,500	Require Laptop Computer?	N

J.D. Attrition (from Prior Year)

	Academic	Other	TOTALS	
	#	#	#	%
1st Year	6	14	20	15%
2nd Year	1	0	1	0.8%
3rd Year	1	0	1	0.9%
4th Year	0	0	0	0.0%

Bar Passage Rates

Jurisdiction	Arkansas		
Exam	Sum 97	Win 98	Total
# from school taking bar for the first time	82	20	102
School's pass rate for all first-time takers	74%	90%	77%
State's pass rate for all first-time takers	74%	77%	75%

ARKANSAS, LITTLE ROCK, UNIVERSITY OF

1201 McAlmont Street
Little Rock, AR 72202-5142
(501)324-9434
http://www.ualr.edu/~lawschool

ABA Approved Since 1969

The Basics

Type of School: Public

Term: Semester

Application deadline: 05/01

Application fee: $40

Financial Aid deadline: 03/01

Can first year start other than Fall? No

Student faculty ratio: 17.0 to 1

Does the University offer:
- housing restricted to law students? No
- graduate student housing for which law students are eligible? No

Faculty & Administrators

	Total		Men		Women		Minorities	
	Fall	Spr	Fall	Spr	Fall	Spr	Fall	Spr
Full-time	18	20	12	14	6	6	2	2
Other Full-Time	5	5	1	1	4	4	1	1
Deans, librarians, & others who teach > 1/2	4	4	3	3	1	1	0	0
Part-time	11	13	7	10	4	3	1	1
Total	38	42	23	28	15	14	4	4
Deans, librarians, & others who teach < 1/2	0	0	0	0	0	0	0	0

Curriculum

	Full time	Part time
Typical first-year section size	85	38
Is there typically a "small section" of the first year class, other than Legal Writing, taught by full-time faculty?	No	No
If yes, typical size offered last year	N/A	N/A
# of classroom course titles beyond 1st year curriculum	36	31
# of upper division courses, excluding seminars, with an enrollment:		
Under 25	32	26
25 - 49	9	12
50 - 74	3	0
75 - 99	5	0
100 +	0	0
# of seminars	6	5
# of seminar positions available	122	
# of seminar positions filled	76	36
# of positions available in simulation courses	232	
# of simulation positions filled	139	59
# of positions available in faculty supervised clinical courses	47	
# of fac. sup. clin. positions filled	34	0
# involved in field placements	0	0
# involved in law journals	43	13
# in moot court or trial competitions	27	3
# of credit hrs required to graduate	87	

J.D. Enrollment & Ethnicity

	Men		Women		Fl-Time		Pt-Time		1st Yr		2nd Yr		3rd Yr		4th Yr		Total		JD Degrees Awarded
	#	%	#	%	#	%	#	%	#	%	#	%	#	%	#	%	#	%	
African-American	13	6.0	23	11.7	22	8.0	14	10.1	12	8.2	15	9.6	8	8.2	1	7.1	36	8.7	7
American Indian	2	0.9	0	0.0	0	0.0	2	1.4	1	0.7	0	0.0	0	0.0	1	7.1	2	0.5	2
Asian American	1	0.5	3	1.5	4	1.4	0	0.0	2	1.4	1	0.6	1	1.0	0	0.0	4	1.0	0
Mexican American	0	0.0	0	0.0	0	0.0	0	0.0	0	0.0	0	0.0	0	0.0	0	0.0	0	0.0	0
Puerto Rican	0	0.0	0	0.0	0	0.0	0	0.0	0	0.0	0	0.0	0	0.0	0	0.0	0	0.0	0
Hispanic American	3	1.4	4	2.0	5	1.8	2	1.4	1	0.7	3	1.9	3	3.1	0	0.0	7	1.7	3
Total Minorities	19	8.7	30	15.2	31	11.2	18	12.9	16	11.0	19	12.1	12	12.2	2	14.3	49	11.8	12
Foreign Nationals	0	0.0	0	0.0	0	0.0	0	0.0	0	0.0	0	0.0	0	0.0	0	0.0	0	0.0	0
Caucasian	199	91.3	167	84.8	245	88.8	121	87.1	130	89.0	138	87.9	86	87.8	12	85.7	366	88.2	99
Total	218	52.5	197	47.5	276	66.5	139	33.5	146	35.2	157	37.8	98	23.6	14	3.4	415		111

GPA & LSAT Scores

	Full Time	Part Time	Total
# of apps	236	154	390
# admits	164	60	224
# of matrics	100	46	146
75% GPA	3.70	3.42	
25% GPA	3.11	2.79	
75% LSAT	156	154	
25% LSAT	148	148	

Tuition & Fees

	Resident	Non-resident
Full-Time	$4,418	$9,738
Part-Time	$3,196	$6,996

Living Expenses

Estimated living expenses for Singles		
Living on campus	Living off campus	Living at home
N/A	$9,077	$6,753

Grants/Scholarships

	Full-time		Part-time		Total	
	#	%	#	%	#	%
Total # of Students	276		139		415	
Total # receiving grants	55	19.9	4	2.9	59	14.2
Less than 1/2 tuition	26	9.4	3	2.2	29	7.0
Half to full tuition	12	4.3	0	0.0	12	2.9
Full tuition	0	0.0	0	0.0	0	0.0
More than full tuition	17	6.2	1	0.7	18	4.3
Median Grant Amount	$2,303		$875			

Informational & Library Resources

# of volumes & volume equivalents	261,964	# of professional staff	7
# of titles	30,076	Hours per week with professional staff	73
# of active serial subscriptions	2,987	Hours per week without professional staff	26
Study seating capacity inside the library	385	# of student computer work stations for entire law school	67
Square feet of law library	52,973	# of additional networked connections	80
Square feet of law school (excl. Library)	50,166	Require Laptop Computer?	N

Employment

	Total	%
Employment status known	116	99.1
Employment status unknown	1	0.9
Employed	107	92.2
Pursuing graduate degrees	6	5.2
Unemployed seeking employment	0	0.0
Unemployed not seeking employment	3	2.6
Type of Employment		
# employed in law firms	51	47.7
# employed in business & industry	15	14.0
# employed in government	23	21.5
# employed in public interest	4	3.7
# employed as judicial clerks	9	8.4
# employed in academia	4	3.7
Geographic Location		
# employed in state	85	79.4
# employed in foreign countries	0	0.0
# of states where employed	8	

J.D. Attrition (from Prior Year)

	Academic	Other	TOTALS	
	#	#	#	%
1st Year	3	23	26	19%
2nd Year	2	8	10	7.6%
3rd Year	0	1	1	0.9%
4th Year	0	0	0	0.0%

Bar Passage Rates

Jurisdiction	Arkansas		
Exam	Sum 97	Win 98	Total
# from school taking bar for the first time	79	32	111
School's pass rate for all first-time takers	77%	75%	77%
State's pass rate for all first-time takers	74%	77%	75%

BALTIMORE, UNIVERSITY OF

1420 North Charles Street
Baltimore, MD 21201
(410)837-4458
http://www.ubalt.edu/www/law

ABA Approved Since 1972

The Basics

Type of School: Public   Term: Semester

Application deadline: 05/01

Application fee: $35

Financial Aid deadline: 04/01

Can first year start other than Fall? No

Student faculty ratio: 19.4 to 1

Does the University offer:
- housing restricted to law students? No
- graduate student housing for which law students are eligible? No

Faculty & Administrators

	Total		Men		Women		Minorities	
	Fall	Spr	Fall	Spr	Fall	Spr	Fall	Spr
Full-time	37	35	23	21	14	14	3	4
Other Full-Time	3	3	1	1	2	2	1	1
Deans, librarians, & others who teach > 1/2	4	4	4	4	0	0	0	0
Part-time	70	80	50	59	20	21	6	7
Total	114	122	78	85	36	37	10	12
Deans, librarians, & others who teach < 1/2	1	1	1	1	0	0	0	0

Curriculum

	Full time	Part time
Typical first-year section size	75	75
Is there typically a "small section" of the first year class, other than Legal Writing, taught by full-time faculty?	No	No
If yes, typical size offered last year	N/A	N/A
# of classroom course titles beyond 1st year curriculum	69	68
# of upper division courses, excluding seminars, with an enrollment:		
Under 25	45	48
25 - 49	20	17
50 - 74	14	9
75 - 99	13	9
100 +	0	0
# of seminars	21	17
# of seminar positions available	760	
# of seminar positions filled	393	173
# of positions available in simulation courses	677	
# of simulation positions filled	396	279
# of positions available in faculty supervised clinical courses	112	
# of fac. sup. clin. positions filled	89	15
# involved in field placements	75	15
# involved in law journals	241	66
# in moot court or trial competitions	29	7
# of credit hrs required to graduate	90	

J.D. Enrollment & Ethnicity

	Men		Women		Fl-Time		Pt-Time		1st Yr		2nd Yr		3rd Yr		4th Yr		Total		JD Degrees Awarded
	#	%	#	%	#	%	#	%	#	%	#	%	#	%	#	%	#	%	
African-American	48	9.7	74	15.5	72	11.1	50	15.4	46	16.6	31	10.2	36	11.9	9	10.0	122	12.6	49
American Indian	3	0.6	4	0.8	7	1.1	0	0.0	2	0.7	1	0.3	4	1.3	0	0.0	7	0.7	1
Asian American	16	3.2	15	3.1	22	3.4	9	2.8	6	2.2	7	2.3	15	5.0	3	3.3	31	3.2	10
Mexican American	0	0.0	0	0.0	0	0.0	0	0.0	0	0.0	0	0.0	0	0.0	0	0.0	0	0.0	0
Puerto Rican	0	0.0	0	0.0	0	0.0	0	0.0	0	0.0	0	0.0	0	0.0	0	0.0	0	0.0	0
Hispanic American	12	2.4	27	5.7	28	4.3	11	3.4	9	3.2	14	4.6	15	5.0	1	1.1	39	4.0	3
Total Minorities	79	16.0	120	25.2	129	19.9	70	21.6	63	22.7	53	17.5	70	23.2	13	14.4	199	20.5	63
Foreign Nationals	7	1.4	4	0.8	10	1.5	1	0.3	1	0.4	5	1.7	5	1.7	0	0.0	11	1.1	2
Caucasian	409	82.6	353	74.0	509	78.5	253	78.1	213	76.9	245	80.9	227	75.2	77	85.6	762	78.4	251
Total	495	50.9	477	49.1	648	66.7	324	33.3	277	28.5	303	31.2	302	31.1	90	9.3	972		316

GPA & LSAT Scores

	Full Time	Part Time	Total
# of apps	1,234	331	1,565
# admits	714	163	877
# of matrics	196	81	277
75% GPA	3.31	3.18	
25% GPA	2.64	2.56	
75% LSAT	152	153	
25% LSAT	147	146	

Tuition & Fees

	Resident	Non-resident
Full-Time	$9,006	$15,624
Part-Time	$7,440	$12,240

Living Expenses

Estimated living expenses for Singles		
Living on campus	Living off campus	Living at home
N/A	$11,330	$8,092

Grants/Scholarships

	Full-time		Part-time		Total	
	#	%	#	%	#	%
Total # of Students	648		324		972	
Total # receiving grants	43	6.6	22	6.8	65	6.7
Less than 1/2 tuition	24	3.7	13	4.0	37	3.8
Half to full tuition	19	2.9	9	2.8	28	2.9
Full tuition	0	0.0	0	0.0	0	0.0
More than full tuition	0	0.0	0	0.0	0	0.0
Median Grant Amount	$4,500		$4,000			

Informational & Library Resources

# of volumes & volume equivalents	295,200	# of professional staff	7
# of titles	28,070	Hours per week with professional staff	86
# of active serial subscriptions	3,372	Hours per week without professional staff	24
Study seating capacity inside the library	339	# of student computer work stations for entire law school	71
Square feet of law library	30,000	# of additional networked connections	0
Square feet of law school (excl. Library)	88,095	Require Laptop Computer?	N

Employment

	Total	%
Employment status known	270	86.0
Employment status unknown	44	14.0
Employed	243	90.0
Pursuing graduate degrees	2	0.7
Unemployed seeking employment	23	8.5
Unemployed not seeking employment	2	0.7
Type of Employment		
# employed in law firms	83	34.2
# employed in business & industry	54	22.2
# employed in government	56	23.0
# employed in public interest	1	0.4
# employed as judicial clerks	46	18.9
# employed in academia	3	1.2
Geographic Location		
# employed in state	187	77.0
# employed in foreign countries	0	0.0
# of states where employed	12	

J.D. Attrition (from Prior Year)

	Academic	Other	TOTALS	
	#	#	#	%
1st Year	1	22	23	7.7%
2nd Year	0	1	1	0.3%
3rd Year	0	0	0	0.0%
4th Year	0	0	0	0.0%

Bar Passage Rates

Jurisdiction	Maryland		
Exam	Sum 97	Win 98	Total
# from school taking bar for the first time	239	51	290
School's pass rate for all first-time takers	68%	80%	70%
State's pass rate for all first-time takers	69%	83%	72%

BAYLOR UNIVERSITY

P.O. Box 97288
1400 S. 5th Street
Waco, TX 76798-7288
254.710.1911
http://law.baylor.edu

ABA Approved Since 1931

The Basics

Type of School: Private — Term: Quarter

Application deadline: 03/01

Application fee: $40

Financial Aid deadline: Rolling

Can first year start other than Fall? Yes

Student faculty ratio: 22.0 to 1

Does the University offer:
- housing restricted to law students? No
- graduate student housing for which law students are eligible? No

Faculty & Administrators

	Total		Men		Women		Minorities	
	Fall	Spr	Fall	Spr	Fall	Spr	Fall	Spr
Full-time	16	16	12	12	4	4	1	1
Other Full-Time	0	0	0	0	0	0	0	0
Deans, librarians, & others who teach > 1/2	2	2	1	1	1	1	0	0
Part-time	9	18	8	17	1	1	0	1
Total	27	36	21	30	6	6	1	2
Deans, librarians, & others who teach < 1/2	2	2	2	2	0	0	0	0

Curriculum

	Full time	Part time
Typical first-year section size	61	0
Is there typically a "small section" of the first year class, other than Legal Writing, taught by full-time faculty?	Yes	No
If yes, typical size offered last year	45	N/A
# of classroom course titles beyond 1st year curriculum	74	0
# of upper division courses, excluding seminars, with an enrollment:		
Under 25	53	0
25 - 49	28	0
50 - 74	13	0
75 - 99	6	0
100 +	3	0
# of seminars	2	0
# of seminar positions available	60	
# of seminar positions filled	60	0
# of positions available in simulation courses	1,215	
# of simulation positions filled	1,215	0
# of positions available in faculty supervised clinical courses	3	
# of fac. sup. clin. positions filled	0	0
# involved in field placements	67	0
# involved in law journals	65	0
# in moot court or trial competitions	30	0
# of credit hrs required to graduate	126	

J.D. Enrollment & Ethnicity

	Men		Women		Fl-Time		Pt-Time		1st Yr		2nd Yr		3rd Yr		4th Yr		Total		JD Degrees Awarded
	#	%	#	%	#	%	#	%	#	%	#	%	#	%	#	%	#	%	
African-American	0	0.0	3	1.8	3	0.7	0	0.0	2	1.3	1	0.8	0	0.0	0	0.0	3	0.7	1
American Indian	3	1.2	0	0.0	3	0.7	0	0.0	1	0.6	0	0.0	2	1.5	0	0.0	3	0.7	0
Asian American	5	1.9	3	1.8	8	1.9	0	0.0	5	3.1	1	0.8	2	1.5	0	0.0	8	1.9	1
Mexican American	17	6.6	4	2.4	21	5.0	0	0.0	6	3.8	6	4.6	9	6.8	0	0.0	21	5.0	9
Puerto Rican	0	0.0	0	0.0	0	0.0	0	0.0	0	0.0	0	0.0	0	0.0	0	0.0	0	0.0	0
Hispanic American	5	1.9	1	0.6	6	1.4	0	0.0	0	0.0	5	3.8	1	0.8	0	0.0	6	1.4	1
Total Minorities	30	11.7	11	6.6	41	9.7	0	0.0	14	8.8	13	9.9	14	10.5	0	0.0	41	9.7	12
Foreign Nationals	0	0.0	0	0.0	0	0.0	0	0.0	0	0.0	0	0.0	0	0.0	0	0.0	0	0.0	0
Caucasian	227	88.3	155	93.4	382	90.3	0	0.0	145	91.2	118	90.1	119	89.5	0	0.0	382	90.3	111
Total	257	60.8	166	39.2	423	100.0	0	0.0	159	37.6	131	31.0	133	31.4	0	0.0	423		123

GPA & LSAT Scores

	Full Time	Part Time	Total
# of apps	This school did not provide data on a basis comparable to other law schools. Please contact the school for specific information.		
# admits			
# of matrics			
75% GPA			
25% GPA			
75% LSAT			
25% LSAT			

Tuition & Fees

	Resident	Non-resident
Full-Time	$12,896	$12,896
Part-Time	$0	$0

Living Expenses

Estimated living expenses for Singles

Living on campus	Living off campus	Living at home
$8,458	$12,916	$8,395

Employment

	Total	%
Employment status known	162	97.6
Employment status unknown	4	2.4
Employed	157	96.9
Pursuing graduate degrees	3	1.9
Unemployed seeking employment	2	1.2
Unemployed not seeking employment	0	0.0
Type of Employment		
# employed in law firms	101	64.3
# employed in business & industry	11	7.0
# employed in government	23	14.6
# employed in public interest	1	0.6
# employed as judicial clerks	20	12.7
# employed in academia	1	0.6
Geographic Location		
# employed in state	134	85.4
# employed in foreign countries	1	0.6
# of states where employed	15	

Grants/Scholarships

	Full-time		Part-time		Total	
	#	%	#	%	#	%
Total # of Students						
Total # receiving grants	287	67.8	0	0.0	287	67.8
Less than 1/2 tuition	201	47.5	0	0.0	201	47.5
Half to full tuition	55	13.0	0	0.0	55	13.0
Full tuition	0	0.0	0	0.0	0	0.0
More than full tuition	31	7.3	0	0.0	31	7.3
Median Grant Amount	$2,100		$0			

Informational & Library Resources

# of volumes & volume equivalents	181,882	# of professional staff	6
# of titles	20,419	Hours per week with professional staff	55
# of active serial subscriptions	2,142	Hours per week without professional staff	55
Study seating capacity inside the library	303	# of student computer work stations for entire law school	32
Square feet of law library	17,861	# of additional networked connections	8
Square feet of law school (excl. Library)	37,413	Require Laptop Computer?	N

J.D. Attrition (from Prior Year)

	Academic	Other	TOTALS	
	#	#	#	%
1st Year	1	14	15	7.2%
2nd Year	1	1	2	1.8%
3rd Year	0	0	0	0.0%
4th Year	0	0	0	0.0%

Bar Passage Rates

Jurisdiction	Texas		
Exam	Sum 97	Win 98	Total
# from school taking bar for the first time	103	27	130
School's pass rate for all first-time takers	91%	85%	90%
State's pass rate for all first-time takers	83%	73%	81%

BOSTON COLLEGE

885 Centre Street
Newton Centre, MA 02159
(617)552-4340
http://www.bc.edu/lawschool

ABA Approved Since 1932

The Basics

Type of School: Private Term: Semester
Application deadline: 03/01
Application fee: $65
Financial Aid deadline: 03/15
Can first year start other than Fall? No
Student faculty ratio: 14.6 to 1
Does the University offer:
- housing restricted to law students? No
- graduate student housing for which law students are eligible? No

Faculty & Administrators

	Total		Men		Women		Minorities	
	Fall	Spr	Fall	Spr	Fall	Spr	Fall	Spr
Full-time	47	47	30	28	17	19	9	9
Other Full-Time	3	3	0	0	3	3	0	0
Deans, librarians, & others who teach > 1/2	0	0	0	0	0	0	0	0
Part-time	27	37	22	24	5	13	1	0
Total	77	87	52	52	25	35	10	9
Deans, librarians, & others who teach < 1/2	10	10	4	4	6	6	0	0

Curriculum

	Full time	Part time
Typical first-year section size	100	0
Is there typically a "small section" of the first year class, other than Legal Writing, taught by full-time faculty?	Yes	No
If yes, typical size offered last year	35	N/A
# of classroom course titles beyond 1st year curriculum	129	0
# of upper division courses, excluding seminars, with an enrollment:		
Under 25	90	0
25 - 49	31	0
50 - 74	14	0
75 - 99	5	0
100 +	4	0
# of seminars	46	0
# of seminar positions available	909	
# of seminar positions filled	594	0
# of positions available in simulation courses	438	
# of simulation positions filled	328	0
# of positions available in faculty supervised clinical courses	194	
# of fac. sup. clin. positions filled	175	0
# involved in field placements	5	0
# involved in law journals	90	0
# in moot court or trial competitions	147	0
# of credit hrs required to graduate	85	

J.D. Enrollment & Ethnicity

	Men		Women		Fl-Time		Pt-Time		1st Yr		2nd Yr		3rd Yr		4th Yr		Total		JD Degrees Awarded
	#	%	#	%	#	%	#	%	#	%	#	%	#	%	#	%	#	%	
African-American	33	8.3	30	7.0	63	7.7	0	0.0	21	8.2	21	7.1	21	7.7	0	0.0	63	7.7	20
American Indian	2	0.5	1	0.2	3	0.4	0	0.0	2	0.8	1	0.3	0	0.0	0	0.0	3	0.4	0
Asian American	22	5.6	35	8.2	57	6.9	0	0.0	23	9.0	20	6.8	14	5.1	0	0.0	57	6.9	16
Mexican American	2	0.5	8	1.9	10	1.2	0	0.0	3	1.2	6	2.0	1	0.4	0	0.0	10	1.2	8
Puerto Rican	1	0.3	6	1.4	7	0.9	0	0.0	1	0.4	2	0.7	4	1.5	0	0.0	7	0.9	0
Hispanic American	6	1.5	12	2.8	18	2.2	0	0.0	5	2.0	6	2.0	7	2.6	0	0.0	18	2.2	6
Total Minorities	66	16.7	92	21.5	158	19.2	0	0.0	55	21.5	56	19.0	47	17.3	0	0.0	158	19.2	50
Foreign Nationals	4	1.0	5	1.2	9	1.1	0	0.0	3	1.2	3	1.0	3	1.1	0	0.0	9	1.1	0
Caucasian	326	82.3	330	77.3	656	79.7	0	0.0	198	77.3	236	80.0	222	81.6	0	0.0	656	79.7	221
Total	396	48.1	427	51.9	823	100.0	0	0.0	256	31.1	295	35.8	272	33.0	0	0.0	823		271

GPA & LSAT Scores

	Full Time	Part Time	Total
# of apps	4,480	0	4,480
# admits	1,275	0	1,275
# of matrics	260	0	260
75% GPA	3.64	0.00	
25% GPA	3.21	0.00	
75% LSAT	164	0	
25% LSAT	159	0	

Tuition & Fees

	Resident	Non-resident
Full-Time	$23,480	$23,480
Part-Time	$0	$0

Living Expenses

Estimated living expenses for Singles		
Living on campus	Living off campus	Living at home
N/A	$12,460	$12,460

Grants/Scholarships

	Full-time		Part-time		Total	
	#	%	#	%	#	%
Total # of Students	823		0		823	
Total # receiving grants	377	45.8	0	0.0	377	45.8
Less than 1/2 tuition	260	31.6	0	0.0	260	31.6
Half to full tuition	116	14.1	0	0.0	116	14.1
Full tuition	1	0.1	0	0.0	1	0.1
More than full tuition	0	0.0	0	0.0	0	0.0
Median Grant Amount	$8,631		$0			

Informational & Library Resources

# of volumes & volume equivalents	382,628	# of professional staff	10
# of titles	55,267	Hours per week with professional staff	73
# of active serial subscriptions	6,337	Hours per week without professional staff	33
Study seating capacity inside the library	649	# of student computer work stations for entire law school	114
Square feet of law library	49,488	# of additional networked connections	475
Square feet of law school (excl. Library)	72,464	Require Laptop Computer?	N

Employment

	Total	%
Employment status known	265	97.1
Employment status unknown	8	2.9
Employed	248	93.6
Pursuing graduate degrees	1	0.4
Unemployed seeking employment	14	5.3
Unemployed not seeking employment	2	0.8
Type of Employment		
# employed in law firms	147	59.3
# employed in business & industry	22	8.9
# employed in government	20	8.1
# employed in public interest	9	3.6
# employed as judicial clerks	46	18.5
# employed in academia	4	1.6
Geographic Location		
# employed in state	138	55.6
# employed in foreign countries	1	0.4
# of states where employed	28	

J.D. Attrition (from Prior Year)

	Academic	Other	TOTALS	
	#	#	#	%
1st Year	0	3	3	1.0%
2nd Year	0	4	4	1.5%
3rd Year	0	0	0	0.0%
4th Year	0	0	0	0.0%

Bar Passage Rates

Jurisdiction	Massachusetts		
Exam	Sum 97	Win 98	Total
# from school taking bar for the first time	190	8	198
School's pass rate for all first-time takers	92%	88%	91%
State's pass rate for all first-time takers	84%	72%	82%

BOSTON UNIVERSITY

765 Commonwealth Ave
Boston, MA 02215
(617)353-3112
http://www.bu.edu/LAW

ABA Approved Since 1925

The Basics

Type of School: Private   Term: Semester

Application deadline: 03/01

Application fee: $50

Financial Aid deadline: 04/01

Can first year start other than Fall? No

Student faculty ratio: 17.0 to 1

Does the University offer:

- housing restricted to law students? No
- graduate student housing for which law students are eligible? No

Faculty & Administrators

	Total		Men		Women		Minorities	
	Fall	Spr	Fall	Spr	Fall	Spr	Fall	Spr
Full-time	46	48	31	31	15	17	7	7
Other Full-Time	0	0	0	0	0	0	0	0
Deans, librarians, & others who teach > 1/2	7	7	6	6	1	1	0	0
Part-time	54	53	37	35	16	17	5	5
Total	107	108	74	72	32	35	12	12
Deans, librarians, & others who teach < 1/2	2	2	2	2	0	0	0	0

Curriculum

	Full time	Part time
Typical first-year section size	80	0
Is there typically a "small section" of the first year class, other than Legal Writing, taught by full-time faculty?	No	No
If yes, typical size offered last year	N/A	N/A
# of classroom course titles beyond 1st year curriculum	105	0
# of upper division courses, excluding seminars, with an enrollment:		
Under 25	42	0
25 - 49	19	0
50 - 74	12	0
75 - 99	10	0
100 +	13	0
# of seminars	40	0
# of seminar positions available	716	
# of seminar positions filled	539	0
# of positions available in simulation courses	232	
# of simulation positions filled	183	0
# of positions available in faculty supervised clinical courses	160	
# of fac. sup. clin. positions filled	132	0
# involved in field placements	43	0
# involved in law journals	342	0
# in moot court or trial competitions	218	0
# of credit hrs required to graduate	84	

J.D. Enrollment & Ethnicity

	Men		Women		Fl-Time		Pt-Time		1st Yr		2nd Yr		3rd Yr		4th Yr		Total		JD Degrees Awarded
	#	%	#	%	#	%	#	%	#	%	#	%	#	%	#	%	#	%	
African-American	10	2.0	20	4.6	30	3.2	0	0.0	13	4.2	7	2.3	10	3.0	0	0.0	30	3.2	9
American Indian	1	0.2	2	0.5	3	0.3	0	0.0	0	0.0	1	0.3	2	0.6	0	0.0	3	0.3	6
Asian American	42	8.4	56	12.8	98	10.4	0	0.0	35	11.2	35	11.7	28	8.5	0	0.0	98	10.4	31
Mexican American	3	0.6	1	0.2	4	0.4	0	0.0	0	0.0	3	1.0	1	0.3	0	0.0	4	0.4	0
Puerto Rican	2	0.4	0	0.0	2	0.2	0	0.0	1	0.3	1	0.3	0	0.0	0	0.0	2	0.2	1
Hispanic American	25	5.0	27	6.2	52	5.5	0	0.0	34	10.9	12	4.0	6	1.8	0	0.0	52	5.5	17
Total Minorities	83	16.6	106	24.2	189	20.1	0	0.0	83	26.5	59	19.8	47	14.3	0	0.0	189	20.1	64
Foreign Nationals	5	1.0	5	1.1	10	1.1	0	0.0	6	1.9	2	0.7	2	0.6	0	0.0	10	1.1	4
Caucasian	413	82.4	327	74.7	740	78.8	0	0.0	224	71.6	237	79.5	279	85.1	0	0.0	740	78.8	289
Total	501	53.4	438	46.6	939	100.0	0	0.0	313	33.3	298	31.7	328	34.9	0	0.0	939		357

GPA & LSAT Scores

	Full Time	Part Time	Total
# of apps	4,233	0	4,233
# admits	1,602	0	1,602
# of matrics	314	0	314
75% GPA	3.58	0.00	
25% GPA	3.09	0.00	
75% LSAT	163	0	
25% LSAT	158	0	

Tuition & Fees

	Resident	Non-resident
Full-Time	$23,138	$23,138
Part-Time	$0	$0

Living Expenses

Estimated living expenses for Singles		
Living on campus	Living off campus	Living at home
$13,492	$13,492	$9,330

Employment

	Total	%
Employment status known	358	98.9
Employment status unknown	4	1.1
Employed	313	87.4
Pursuing graduate degrees	11	3.1
Unemployed seeking employment	27	7.5
Unemployed not seeking employment	7	2.0
Type of Employment		
# employed in law firms	215	68.7
# employed in business & industry	29	9.3
# employed in government	39	12.5
# employed in public interest	8	2.6
# employed as judicial clerks	21	6.7
# employed in academia	1	0.3
Geographic Location		
# employed in state	119	38.0
# employed in foreign countries	6	1.9
# of states where employed	29	

Grants/Scholarships

	Full-time		Part-time		Total	
	#	%	#	%	#	%
Total # of Students	939		0		939	
Total # receiving grants	443	47.2	0	0.0	443	47.2
Less than 1/2 tuition	239	25.5	0	0.0	239	25.5
Half to full tuition	186	19.8	0	0.0	186	19.8
Full tuition	0	0.0	0	0.0	0	0.0
More than full tuition	18	1.9	0	0.0	18	1.9
Median Grant Amount	$10,000		$0			

Informational & Library Resources

# of volumes & volume equivalents	543,257	# of professional staff	10
# of titles	76,423	Hours per week with professional staff	77
# of active serial subscriptions	6,484	Hours per week without professional staff	25
Study seating capacity inside the library	783	# of student computer work stations for entire law school	93
Square feet of law library	37,000	# of additional networked connections	4
Square feet of law school (excl. Library)	64,452	Require Laptop Computer?	N

J.D. Attrition (from Prior Year)

	Academic	Other	TOTALS	
	#	#	#	%
1st Year	2	24	26	8.0%
2nd Year	0	1	1	0.3%
3rd Year	2	0	2	0.6%
4th Year	0	0	0	0.0%

Bar Passage Rates

Jurisdiction	Massachusetts			New York		
Exam	Sum 97	Win 98	Total	Sum 97	Win 98	Total
# from school taking bar for the first time	161	33	194	116	22	138
School's pass rate for all first-time takers	91%	73%	88%	85%	77%	84%
State's pass rate for all first-time takers	84%	72%	82%	78%	65%	76%

BRIGHAM YOUNG UNIVERSITY

J. Reuben Clark Law School
Provo, UT 84602
(801)378-4274
http://www.law.byu.edu

ABA Approved Since 1974

The Basics

Type of School: Private Term: Semester

Application deadline: 02/01

Application fee: $30

Financial Aid deadline: 05/01

Can first year start other than Fall? No

Student faculty ratio: 15.6 to 1

Does the University offer:
- housing restricted to law students? No
- graduate student housing for which law students are eligible? No

Faculty & Administrators

	Total		Men		Women		Minorities	
	Fall	Spr	Fall	Spr	Fall	Spr	Fall	Spr
Full-time	24	23	20	19	4	4	3	3
Other Full-Time	0	0	0	0	0	0	0	0
Deans, librarians, & others who teach > 1/2	4	4	3	3	1	1	0	0
Part-time	18	19	12	13	6	6	0	0
Total	46	46	35	35	11	11	3	3
Deans, librarians, & others who teach < 1/2	0	0	0	0	0	0	0	0

Curriculum

	Full time	Part time
Typical first-year section size	115	0
Is there typically a "small section" of the first year class, other than Legal Writing, taught by full-time faculty?	Yes	No
If yes, typical size offered last year	35	N/A
# of classroom course titles beyond 1st year curriculum	46	0
# of upper division courses, excluding seminars, with an enrollment:		
Under 25	16	0
25 - 49	13	0
50 - 74	10	0
75 - 99	3	0
100 +	4	0
# of seminars	75	0
# of seminar positions available	1,996	
# of seminar positions filled	1,491	0
# of positions available in simulation courses	372	
# of simulation positions filled	304	0
# of positions available in faculty supervised clinical courses	150	
# of fac. sup. clin. positions filled	44	0
# involved in field placements	128	0
# involved in law journals	121	0
# in moot court or trial competitions	97	0
# of credit hrs required to graduate	90	

J.D. Enrollment & Ethnicity

	Men		Women		Fl-Time		Pt-Time		1st Yr		2nd Yr		3rd Yr		4th Yr		Total		JD Degrees Awarded
	#	%	#	%	#	%	#	%	#	%	#	%	#	%	#	%	#	%	
African-American	3	1.0	1	0.7	4	0.9	0	0.0	2	1.4	1	0.7	1	0.6	0	0.0	4	0.9	1
American Indian	6	2.0	3	2.0	9	2.0	0	0.0	1	0.7	3	2.0	5	3.2	0	0.0	9	2.0	2
Asian American	13	4.4	7	4.6	20	4.5	0	0.0	7	4.8	7	4.7	6	3.9	0	0.0	20	4.5	3
Mexican American	12	4.0	1	0.7	13	2.9	0	0.0	5	3.4	5	3.4	3	1.9	0	0.0	13	2.9	7
Puerto Rican	0	0.0	1	0.7	1	0.2	0	0.0	0	0.0	1	0.7	0	0.0	0	0.0	1	0.2	0
Hispanic American	4	1.3	4	2.6	8	1.8	0	0.0	1	0.7	2	1.3	5	3.2	0	0.0	8	1.8	0
Total Minorities	38	12.8	17	11.3	55	12.2	0	0.0	16	11.0	19	12.8	20	12.9	0	0.0	55	12.2	13
Foreign Nationals	4	1.3	4	2.6	8	1.8	0	0.0	2	1.4	4	2.7	2	1.3	0	0.0	8	1.8	2
Caucasian	256	85.9	130	86.1	386	86.0	0	0.0	127	87.6	126	84.6	133	85.8	0	0.0	386	86.0	129
Total	298	66.4	151	33.6	449	100.0	0	0.0	145	32.3	149	33.2	155	34.5	0	0.0	449		144

GPA & LSAT Scores

	Full Time	Part Time	Total
# of apps	591	0	591
# admits	221	0	221
# of matrics	145	0	145
75% GPA	3.77	0.00	
25% GPA	3.42	0.00	
75% LSAT	164	0	
25% LSAT	157	0	

Tuition & Fees

	LDS	Non-LDS
Full-Time	$5,140	$7,700
Part-Time	$285	$425

Living Expenses

Estimated living expenses for Singles		
Living on campus	Living off campus	Living at home
$11,450	$11,370	$8,075

Employment

	Total	%
Employment status known	154	100.0
Employment status unknown	0	0.0
Employed	144	93.5
Pursuing graduate degrees	5	3.2
Unemployed seeking employment	1	0.6
Unemployed not seeking employment	4	2.6
Type of Employment		
# employed in law firms	76	52.8
# employed in business & industry	24	16.7
# employed in government	15	10.4
# employed in public interest	3	2.1
# employed as judicial clerks	23	16.0
# employed in academia	3	2.1
Geographic Location		
# employed in state	61	42.4
# employed in foreign countries	6	4.2
# of states where employed	31	

Grants/Scholarships

	Full-time		Part-time		Total	
	#	%	#	%	#	%
Total # of Students	449		0		449	
Total # receiving grants	200	44.5	0	0.0	200	44.5
Less than 1/2 tuition	143	31.8	0	0.0	143	31.8
Half to full tuition	53	11.8	0	0.0	53	11.8
Full tuition	4	0.9	0	0.0	4	0.9
More than full tuition	0	0.0	0	0.0	0	0.0
Median Grant Amount	$2,300		$0			

Informational & Library Resources

# of volumes & volume equivalents	421,913	# of professional staff	11
# of titles	150,988	Hours per week with professional staff	45
# of active serial subscriptions	5,691	Hours per week without professional staff	60
Study seating capacity inside the library	883	# of student computer work stations for entire law school	97
Square feet of law library	90,605	# of additional networked connections	535
Square feet of law school (excl. Library)	28,073	Require Laptop Computer?	Y

J.D. Attrition (from Prior Year)

	Academic	Other	TOTALS	
	#	#	#	%
1st Year	0	0	0	0.0%
2nd Year	0	0	0	0.0%
3rd Year	0	0	0	0.0%
4th Year	0	0	0	0.0%

Bar Passage Rates

Jurisdiction	Utah			California		
Exam	Sum 97	Win 98	Total	Sum 97	Win 98	Total
# from school taking bar for the first time	74	19	93	12	0	12
School's pass rate for all first-time takers	97%	89%	96%	75%		75%
State's pass rate for all first-time takers	93%	92%	93%	75%	57%	71%

BROOKLYN LAW SCHOOL

250 Joralemon Street
Brooklyn, NY 11201
(718)625-2200
http://www.brooklaw.edu

ABA Approved Since 1937

The Basics

Type of School: Private Term: Semester
Application deadline: Rolling
Application fee: $60
Financial Aid deadline: 04/15
Can first year start other than Fall? No
Student faculty ratio: 20.3 to 1
Does the University offer:
- housing restricted to law students? Yes
- graduate student housing for which law students are eligible? No

Curriculum

	Full time	Part time
Typical first-year section size	97	116
Is there typically a "small section" of the first year class, other than Legal Writing, taught by full-time faculty?	Yes	No
If yes, typical size offered last year	38	N/A
# of classroom course titles beyond 1st year curriculum	80	60
# of upper division courses, excluding seminars, with an enrollment:		
Under 25	68	42
25 - 49	31	26
50 - 74	21	9
75 - 99	11	6
100 +	9	4
# of seminars	15	13
# of seminar positions available	495	
# of seminar positions filled	231	116
# of positions available in simulation courses	737	
# of simulation positions filled	461	170
# of positions available in faculty supervised clinical courses	278	
# of fac. sup. clin. positions filled	254	24
# involved in field placements	589	54
# involved in law journals	155	27
# in moot court or trial competitions	49	16
# of credit hrs required to graduate	86	

Faculty & Administrators

	Total		Men		Women		Minorities	
	Fall	Spr	Fall	Spr	Fall	Spr	Fall	Spr
Full-time	52	50	29	29	23	21	4	5
Other Full-Time	1	1	1	1	0	0	0	0
Deans, librarians, & others who teach > 1/2	3	3	2	2	1	1	0	0
Part-time	64	58	46	44	18	14	5	2
Total	120	112	78	76	42	36	9	7
Deans, librarians, & others who teach < 1/2	6	6	1	1	5	5	0	0

J.D. Enrollment & Ethnicity

	Men		Women		Fl-Time		Pt-Time		1st Yr		2nd Yr		3rd Yr		4th Yr		Total		JD Degrees Awarded
	#	%	#	%	#	%	#	%	#	%	#	%	#	%	#	%	#	%	
African-American	28	3.7	51	7.5	35	3.7	44	9.1	24	5.4	24	5.3	20	4.6	11	10.8	79	5.5	14
American Indian	3	0.4	1	0.1	3	0.3	1	0.2	2	0.5	0	0.0	2	0.5	0	0.0	4	0.3	0
Asian American	50	6.7	59	8.6	79	8.4	30	6.2	35	7.9	33	7.3	37	8.5	4	3.9	109	7.6	27
Mexican American	2	0.3	2	0.3	0	0.0	4	0.8	1	0.2	1	0.2	1	0.2	1	1.0	4	0.3	2
Puerto Rican	8	1.1	11	1.6	14	1.5	5	1.0	6	1.4	10	2.2	2	0.5	1	1.0	19	1.3	10
Hispanic American	17	2.3	31	4.5	26	2.7	22	4.5	15	3.4	11	2.4	19	4.4	3	2.9	48	3.4	10
Total Minorities	108	14.5	155	22.7	157	16.6	106	21.9	83	18.7	79	17.5	81	18.7	20	19.6	263	18.4	63
Foreign Nationals	9	1.2	2	0.3	8	0.8	3	0.6	4	0.9	4	0.9	3	0.7	0	0.0	11	0.8	1
Caucasian	630	84.3	526	77.0	781	82.6	375	77.5	356	80.4	368	81.6	350	80.6	82	80.4	1156	80.8	366
Total	747	52.2	683	47.8	946	66.2	484	33.8	443	31.0	451	31.5	434	30.3	102	7.1	1430		430

GPA & LSAT Scores

	Full Time	Part Time	Total
# of apps	2,174	628	2,802
# admits	1,081	295	1,376
# of matrics	291	157	448
75% GPA	3.49	3.36	
25% GPA	2.95	2.72	
75% LSAT	158	154	
25% LSAT	152	150	

Tuition & Fees

	Resident	Non-resident
Full-Time	$22,100	$22,100
Part-Time	$16,600	$16,600

Living Expenses

Estimated living expenses for Singles		
Living on campus	Living off campus	Living at home
$16,706	$16,706	$10,496

Grants/Scholarships

	Full-time		Part-time		Total	
	#	%	#	%	#	%
Total # of Students	946		484		1430	
Total # receiving grants	480	50.7	135	27.9	615	43.0
Less than 1/2 tuition	446	47.1	119	24.6	565	39.5
Half to full tuition	30	3.2	16	3.3	46	3.2
Full tuition	4	0.4	0	0.0	4	0.3
More than full tuition	0	0.0	0	0.0	0	0.0
Median Grant Amount	$5,314		$3,973			

Informational & Library Resources

# of volumes & volume equivalents	475,457	# of professional staff	9
# of titles	59,852	Hours per week with professional staff	76
# of active serial subscriptions	3,484	Hours per week without professional staff	30
Study seating capacity inside the library	702	# of student computer work stations for entire law school	83
Square feet of law library	78,082	# of additional networked connections	1350
Square feet of law school (excl. Library)	191,798	Require Laptop Computer?	N

Employment

	Total	%
Employment status known	427	97.7
Employment status unknown	10	2.3
Employed	394	92.3
Pursuing graduate degrees	6	1.4
Unemployed seeking employment	19	4.4
Unemployed not seeking employment	8	1.9
Type of Employment		
# employed in law firms	230	58.4
# employed in business & industry	60	15.2
# employed in government	69	17.5
# employed in public interest	14	3.6
# employed as judicial clerks	15	3.8
# employed in academia	6	1.5
Geographic Location		
# employed in state	364	92.4
# employed in foreign countries	2	0.5
# of states where employed	11	

J.D. Attrition (from Prior Year)

	Academic	Other	TOTALS	
	#	#	#	%
1st Year	1	6	7	1.4%
2nd Year	6	27	33	7.4%
3rd Year	1	3	4	0.9%
4th Year	0	0	0	0.0%

Bar Passage Rates

Jurisdiction	New York		
Exam	Sum 97	Win 98	Total
# from school taking bar for the first time	395	19	414
School's pass rate for all first-time takers	80%	84%	80%
State's pass rate for all first-time takers	78%	65%	76%

CALIFORNIA WESTERN SCHOOL OF LAW

225 Cedar Street
San Diego, CA 92101-3046
(619)239-0391
http://www.cwsl.edu

ABA Approved Since 1962

The Basics

Type of School: Private   Term: Trimester

Application deadline: 04/01

Application fee: $45

Financial Aid deadline: 03/15

Can first year start other than Fall? Yes

Student faculty ratio: 17.4 to 1

Does the University offer:
- housing restricted to law students? No
- graduate student housing for which law students are eligible? No

Faculty & Administrators

	Total		Men		Women		Minorities	
	Fall	Spr	Fall	Spr	Fall	Spr	Fall	Spr
Full-time	33	28	19	17	14	11	6	4
Other Full-Time	2	2	1	1	1	1	0	0
Deans, librarians, & others who teach > 1/2	2	2	0	0	2	2	0	0
Part-time	32	27	22	20	10	7	3	2
Total	69	59	42	38	27	21	9	6
Deans, librarians, & others who teach < 1/2	4	5	3	3	1	2	0	0

Curriculum

	Full time	Part time
Typical first-year section size	90	0
Is there typically a "small section" of the first year class, other than Legal Writing, taught by full-time faculty?	No	No
If yes, typical size offered last year	N/A	N/A
# of classroom course titles beyond 1st year curriculum	93	0
# of upper division courses, excluding seminars, with an enrollment:		
Under 25	81	0
25 - 49	23	0
50 - 74	12	0
75 - 99	5	0
100 +	4	0
# of seminars	24	0
# of seminar positions available	475	
# of seminar positions filled	282	0
# of positions available in simulation courses	1,382	
# of simulation positions filled	1,011	0
# of positions available in faculty supervised clinical courses	0	
# of fac. sup. clin. positions filled	0	0
# involved in field placements	125	0
# involved in law journals	67	0
# in moot court or trial competitions	49	0
# of credit hrs required to graduate	89	

J.D. Enrollment & Ethnicity

	Men		Women		Fl-Time		Pt-Time		1st Yr		2nd Yr		3rd Yr		4th Yr		Total		JD Degrees Awarded
	#	%	#	%	#	%	#	%	#	%	#	%	#	%	#	%	#	%	
African-American	8	2.5	22	5.9	23	3.5	7	21.2	13	4.9	11	4.6	6	3.1	0	0.0	30	4.3	6
American Indian	0	0.0	12	3.2	12	1.8	0	0.0	4	1.5	5	2.1	3	1.5	0	0.0	12	1.7	1
Asian American	35	10.7	45	12.1	75	11.3	5	15.2	32	12.1	29	12.0	19	9.8	0	0.0	80	11.4	24
Mexican American	26	8.0	21	5.6	46	6.9	1	3.0	24	9.1	16	6.6	7	3.6	0	0.0	47	6.7	14
Puerto Rican	0	0.0	4	1.1	4	0.6	0	0.0	1	0.4	1	0.4	2	1.0	0	0.0	4	0.6	0
Hispanic American	7	2.1	15	4.0	20	3.0	2	6.1	10	3.8	5	2.1	7	3.6	0	0.0	22	3.1	5
Total Minorities	76	23.3	119	31.9	180	27.0	15	45.5	84	31.8	67	27.8	44	22.7	0	0.0	195	27.9	50
Foreign Nationals	3	0.9	4	1.1	6	0.9	1	3.0	2	0.8	3	1.2	2	1.0	0	0.0	7	1.0	1
Caucasian	247	75.8	250	67.0	480	72.1	17	51.5	178	67.4	171	71.0	148	76.3	0	0.0	497	71.1	162
Total	326	46.6	373	53.4	666	95.3	33	4.7	264	37.8	241	34.5	194	27.8	0	0.0	699		213

GPA & LSAT Scores

	Full Time	Part Time	Total
# of apps	1,758	18	1,776
# admits	1,224	18	1,242
# of matrics	300	17	317
75% GPA	3.42	3.31	
25% GPA	2.81	2.65	
75% LSAT	153	151	
25% LSAT	146	147	

Tuition & Fees

	Resident	Non-resident
Full-Time	$20,570	$20,570
Part-Time	$14,770	$14,770

Living Expenses

Estimated living expenses for Singles		
Living on campus	Living off campus	Living at home
N/A	$13,582	$8,586

Grants/Scholarships

	Full-time		Part-time		Total	
	#	%	#	%	#	%
Total # of Students	666		33		699	
Total # receiving grants	218	32.7	0	0.0	218	31.2
Less than 1/2 tuition	88	13.2	0	0.0	88	12.6
Half to full tuition	79	11.9	0	0.0	79	11.3
Full tuition	51	7.7	0	0.0	51	7.3
More than full tuition	0	0.0	0	0.0	0	0.0
Median Grant Amount	$10,250		$0			

Informational & Library Resources

# of volumes & volume equivalents	265,077	# of professional staff	8
# of titles	42,994	Hours per week with professional staff	90
# of active serial subscriptions	3,532	Hours per week without professional staff	29
Study seating capacity inside the library	487	# of student computer work stations for entire law school	65
Square feet of law library	27,370	# of additional networked connections	16
Square feet of law school (excl. Library)	109,344	Require Laptop Computer?	N

Employment

	Total	%
Employment status known	220	90.9
Employment status unknown	22	9.1
Employed	188	85.5
Pursuing graduate degrees	7	3.2
Unemployed seeking employment	16	7.3
Unemployed not seeking employment	9	4.1
Type of Employment		
# employed in law firms	104	55.3
# employed in business & industry	24	12.8
# employed in government	49	26.1
# employed in public interest	2	1.1
# employed as judicial clerks	6	3.2
# employed in academia	3	1.6
Geographic Location		
# employed in state	146	77.7
# employed in foreign countries	1	0.5
# of states where employed	14	

J.D. Attrition (from Prior Year)

	Academic	Other	TOTALS	
	#	#	#	%
1st Year	54	31	85	29%
2nd Year	0	3	3	1.4%
3rd Year	0	0	0	0.0%
4th Year	0	0	0	0.0%

Bar Passage Rates

Jurisdiction	California			Nevada		
Exam	Sum 97	Win 98	Total	Sum 97	Win 98	Total
# from school taking bar for the first time	91	109	200	21	0	21
School's pass rate for all first-time takers	75%	70%	72%	95%		95%
State's pass rate for all first-time takers	75%	57%	71%	67%	0%	67%

CALIFORNIA-BERKELEY, UNIVERSITY OF

221 Boalt Hall
Berkeley, CA 94720
(510)642-1741
http://www.law.berkeley.edu

ABA Approved Since 1923

The Basics

Type of School: Public Term: Semester
Application deadline: 02/01
Application fee: $40
Financial Aid deadline: 03/01
Can first year start other than Fall? No
Student faculty ratio: 17.2 to 1
Does the University offer:
- housing restricted to law students? No
- graduate student housing for which law students are eligible? Yes

Faculty & Administrators

	Total		Men		Women		Minorities	
	Fall	Spr	Fall	Spr	Fall	Spr	Fall	Spr
Full-time	41	43	33	35	8	8	5	6
Other Full-Time	4	4	2	2	2	2	1	1
Deans, librarians, & others who teach > 1/2	8	8	5	5	3	3	0	0
Part-time	43	63	31	48	12	15	2	7
Total	96	118	71	90	25	28	8	14
Deans, librarians, & others who teach < 1/2	1	1	0	0	1	1	0	0

Curriculum

	Full time	Part time
Typical first-year section size	90	0
Is there typically a "small section" of the first year class, other than Legal Writing, taught by full-time faculty?	Yes	No
If yes, typical size offered last year	30	N/A
# of classroom course titles beyond 1st year curriculum	143	0
# of upper division courses, excluding seminars, with an enrollment:		
Under 25	63	0
25 - 49	23	0
50 - 74	17	0
75 - 99	11	0
100 +	7	0
# of seminars	41	0
# of seminar positions available	769	
# of seminar positions filled	554	0
# of positions available in simulation courses	280	
# of simulation positions filled	249	0
# of positions available in faculty supervised clinical courses	169	
# of fac. sup. clin. positions filled	92	0
# involved in field placements	96	0
# involved in law journals	240	0
# in moot court or trial competitions	114	0
# of credit hrs required to graduate	85	

J.D. Enrollment & Ethnicity

	Men		Women		Fl-Time		Pt-Time		1st Yr		2nd Yr		3rd Yr		4th Yr		Total		JD Degrees Awarded
	#	%	#	%	#	%	#	%	#	%	#	%	#	%	#	%	#	%	
African-American	11	2.7	17	3.9	28	3.3	0	0.0	8	3.0	2	0.7	18	6.2	0	0.0	28	3.3	25
American Indian	3	0.7	4	0.9	7	0.8	0	0.0	2	0.7	0	0.0	5	1.7	0	0.0	7	0.8	4
Asian American	67	16.4	85	19.4	152	18.0	0	0.0	48	17.8	50	17.5	54	18.6	0	0.0	152	18.0	38
Mexican American	26	6.4	20	4.6	46	5.4	0	0.0	15	5.6	7	2.4	24	8.2	0	0.0	46	5.4	26
Puerto Rican	0	0.0	0	0.0	0	0.0	0	0.0	0	0.0	0	0.0	0	0.0	0	0.0	0	0.0	0
Hispanic American	8	2.0	15	3.4	23	2.7	0	0.0	8	3.0	9	3.1	6	2.1	0	0.0	23	2.7	9
Total Minorities	115	28.2	141	32.2	256	30.3	0	0.0	81	30.1	68	23.8	107	36.8	0	0.0	256	30.3	102
Foreign Nationals	2	0.5	6	1.4	8	0.9	0	0.0	3	1.1	3	1.0	2	0.7	0	0.0	8	0.9	0
Caucasian	291	71.3	291	66.4	582	68.8	0	0.0	185	68.8	215	75.2	182	62.5	0	0.0	582	68.8	175
Total	408	48.2	438	51.8	846	100.0	0	0.0	269	31.8	286	33.8	291	34.4	0	0.0	846		277

CALIFORNIA-BERKELEY, UNIVERSITY OF

GPA & LSAT Scores

	Full Time	Part Time	Total
# of apps	4,587	0	4,587
# admits	857	0	857
# of matrics	269	0	269
75% GPA	3.87	0.00	
25% GPA	3.66	0.00	
75% LSAT	169	0	
25% LSAT	161	0	

Tuition & Fees

	Resident	Non-resident
Full-Time	$10,814	$20,198
Part-Time	$0	$0

Living Expenses

Estimated living expenses for Singles		
Living on campus	Living off campus	Living at home
$12,958	$12,958	$12,958

Employment

	Total	%
Employment status known	270	95.4
Employment status unknown	13	4.6
Employed	260	96.3
Pursuing graduate degrees	3	1.1
Unemployed seeking employment	2	0.7
Unemployed not seeking employment	5	1.9
Type of Employment		
# employed in law firms	183	70.4
# employed in business & industry	10	3.8
# employed in government	22	8.5
# employed in public interest	15	5.8
# employed as judicial clerks	28	10.8
# employed in academia	2	0.8
Geographic Location		
# employed in state	198	76.2
# employed in foreign countries	2	0.8
# of states where employed	20	

Grants/Scholarships

	Full-time		Part-time		Total	
	#	%	#	%	#	%
Total # of Students	846		0		846	
Total # receiving grants	539	63.7	0	0.0	539	63.7
Less than 1/2 tuition	220	26.0	0	0.0	220	26.0
Half to full tuition	280	33.1	0	0.0	280	33.1
Full tuition	12	1.4	0	0.0	12	1.4
More than full tuition	27	3.2	0	0.0	27	3.2
Median Grant Amount	$6,000		$0			

Informational & Library Resources

# of volumes & volume equivalents	780,666	# of professional staff	18
# of titles	215,504	Hours per week with professional staff	65
# of active serial subscriptions	7,587	Hours per week without professional staff	31
Study seating capacity inside the library	401	# of student computer work stations for entire law school	160
Square feet of law library	88,902	# of additional networked connections	49
Square feet of law school (excl. Library)	85,833	Require Laptop Computer?	N

J.D. Attrition (from Prior Year)

	Academic	Other	TOTALS	
	#	#	#	%
1st Year	0	3	3	1.1%
2nd Year	0	6	6	2.3%
3rd Year	0	1	1	0.3%
4th Year	0	0	0	0.0%

Bar Passage Rates

Jurisdiction	California		
Exam	Sum 97	Win 98	Total
# from school taking bar for the first time	220	11	231
School's pass rate for all first-time takers	89%	100%	89%
State's pass rate for all first-time takers	75%	57%	71%

CALIFORNIA-DAVIS, UNIVERSITY OF

400 Mrak Hall Drive
Davis, CA 95616-5201
(530)752-0243
http://www.kinghall.ucdavis.edu

ABA Approved Since 1968

The Basics

Type of School: Public   Term: Semester
Application deadline: 02/01
Application fee: $40
Financial Aid deadline: 03/02
Can first year start other than Fall? No
Student faculty ratio: 16.0 to 1
Does the University offer:
- housing restricted to law students? No
- graduate student housing for which law students are eligible? Yes

Faculty & Administrators

	Total		Men		Women		Minorities	
	Fall	Spr	Fall	Spr	Fall	Spr	Fall	Spr
Full-time	27	23	17	16	10	7	4	4
Other Full-Time	0	0	0	0	0	0	0	0
Deans, librarians, & others who teach > 1/2	1	1	1	1	0	0	1	1
Part-time	15	21	10	10	5	11	3	4
Total	43	45	28	27	15	18	8	9
Deans, librarians, & others who teach < 1/2	3	3	2	2	1	1	0	0

Curriculum

	Full time	Part time
Typical first-year section size	90	0
Is there typically a "small section" of the first year class, other than Legal Writing, taught by full-time faculty?	Yes	No
If yes, typical size offered last year	30	N/A
# of classroom course titles beyond 1st year curriculum	74	0
# of upper division courses, excluding seminars, with an enrollment:		
Under 25	28	0
25 - 49	30	0
50 - 74	12	0
75 - 99	6	0
100 +	0	0
# of seminars	21	0
# of seminar positions available	347	
# of seminar positions filled	240	0
# of positions available in simulation courses	292	
# of simulation positions filled	225	0
# of positions available in faculty supervised clinical courses	160	
# of fac. sup. clin. positions filled	62	0
# involved in field placements	60	0
# involved in law journals	101	0
# in moot court or trial competitions	101	0
# of credit hrs required to graduate	88	

J.D. Enrollment & Ethnicity

	Men		Women		Fl-Time		Pt-Time		1st Yr		2nd Yr		3rd Yr		4th Yr		Total		JD Degrees Awarded
	#	%	#	%	#	%	#	%	#	%	#	%	#	%	#	%	#	%	
African-American	5	2.0	9	3.6	14	2.8	0	0.0	3	1.6	5	2.9	6	4.1	0	0.0	14	2.8	5
American Indian	2	0.8	4	1.6	6	1.2	0	0.0	2	1.1	3	1.7	1	0.7	0	0.0	6	1.2	4
Asian American	22	8.8	36	14.2	58	11.5	0	0.0	23	12.6	20	11.6	15	10.1	0	0.0	58	11.5	32
Mexican American	12	4.8	13	5.1	25	5.0	0	0.0	10	5.5	5	2.9	10	6.8	0	0.0	25	5.0	10
Puerto Rican	1	0.4	2	0.8	3	0.6	0	0.0	2	1.1	0	0.0	1	0.7	0	0.0	3	0.6	0
Hispanic American	4	1.6	3	1.2	7	1.4	0	0.0	2	1.1	2	1.2	3	2.0	0	0.0	7	1.4	7
Total Minorities	46	18.4	67	26.5	113	22.5	0	0.0	42	23.1	35	20.2	36	24.3	0	0.0	113	22.5	58
Foreign Nationals	2	0.8	3	1.2	5	1.0	0	0.0	0	0.0	3	1.7	2	1.4	0	0.0	5	1.0	2
Caucasian	202	80.8	183	72.3	385	76.5	0	0.0	140	76.9	135	78.0	110	74.3	0	0.0	385	76.5	94
Total	250	49.7	253	50.3	503	100.0	0	0.0	182	36.2	173	34.4	148	29.4	0	0.0	503		154

GPA & LSAT Scores

	Full Time	Part Time	Total
# of apps	2,288	0	2,288
# admits	813	0	813
# of matrics	183	0	183
75% GPA	3.62	0.00	
25% GPA	3.24	0.00	
75% LSAT	164	0	
25% LSAT	158	0	

Tuition & Fees

	Resident	Non-resident
Full-Time	$10,859	$19,843
Part-Time	$0	$0

Living Expenses

Estimated living expenses for Singles		
Living on campus	Living off campus	Living at home
$10,544	$10,808	N/A

Grants/Scholarships

	Full-time		Part-time		Total	
	#	%	#	%	#	%
Total # of Students	503		0		503	
Total # receiving grants	376	74.8	0	0.0	376	74.8
Less than 1/2 tuition	48	9.5	0	0.0	48	9.5
Half to full tuition	312	62.0	0	0.0	312	62.0
Full tuition	1	0.2	0	0.0	1	0.2
More than full tuition	15	3.0	0	0.0	15	3.0
Median Grant Amount	$5,579		$0			

Informational & Library Resources

# of volumes & volume equivalents	401,343	# of professional staff	6
# of titles	83,829	Hours per week with professional staff	78
# of active serial subscriptions	5,228	Hours per week without professional staff	0
Study seating capacity inside the library	376	# of student computer work stations for entire law school	55
Square feet of law library	35,988	# of additional networked connections	9
Square feet of law school (excl. Library)	28,347	Require Laptop Computer?	N

Employment

	Total	%
Employment status known	162	98.8
Employment status unknown	2	1.2
Employed	134	82.7
Pursuing graduate degrees	6	3.7
Unemployed seeking employment	12	7.4
Unemployed not seeking employment	10	6.2
Type of Employment		
# employed in law firms	89	66.4
# employed in business & industry	12	9.0
# employed in government	15	11.2
# employed in public interest	6	4.5
# employed as judicial clerks	12	9.0
# employed in academia	0	0.0
Geographic Location		
# employed in state	118	88.1
# employed in foreign countries	0	0.0
# of states where employed	5	

J.D. Attrition (from Prior Year)

	Academic	Other	TOTALS	
	#	#	#	%
1st Year	0	2	2	1.2%
2nd Year	0	5	5	3.2%
3rd Year	0	1	1	0.7%
4th Year	0	0	0	0.0%

Bar Passage Rates

Jurisdiction	California			New York		
Exam	Sum 97	Win 98	Total	Sum 97	Win 98	Total
# from school taking bar for the first time	149	7	156	3	0	3
School's pass rate for all first-time takers	93%	71%	92%	100%		100%
State's pass rate for all first-time takers	75%	57%	71%	78%	65%	76%

CALIFORNIA-HASTINGS, UNIVERSITY OF

Hastings College of the Law
200 McAllister Street
San Francisco, CA 94102
(415)565-4600
http://www.uchastings.edu

ABA Approved Since 1939

The Basics

Type of School: Public — Term: Semester
Application deadline: 02/16
Application fee: $40
Financial Aid deadline: 02/16
Can first year start other than Fall? No
Student faculty ratio: 20.2 to 1
Does the University offer:
- housing restricted to law students? Yes
- graduate student housing for which law students are eligible? Yes

Faculty & Administrators

	Total		Men		Women		Minorities	
	Fall	Spr	Fall	Spr	Fall	Spr	Fall	Spr
Full-time	47	43	33	31	14	12	10	8
Other Full-Time	0	0	0	0	0	0	0	0
Deans, librarians, & others who teach > 1/2	4	4	3	3	1	1	1	1
Part-time	77	46	49	33	28	13	11	1
Total	128	93	85	67	43	26	22	10
Deans, librarians, & others who teach < 1/2	2	2	0	0	2	2	0	0

Curriculum

	Full time	Part time
Typical first-year section size	90	0
Is there typically a "small section" of the first year class, other than Legal Writing, taught by full-time faculty?	Yes	No
If yes, typical size offered last year	45	N/A
# of classroom course titles beyond 1st year curriculum	132	0
# of upper division courses, excluding seminars, with an enrollment:		
Under 25	115	0
25 - 49	38	0
50 - 74	29	0
75 - 99	15	0
100 +	6	0
# of seminars	54	0
# of seminar positions available	1,219	
# of seminar positions filled	715	0
# of positions available in simulation courses	898	
# of simulation positions filled	758	0
# of positions available in faculty supervised clinical courses	290	
# of fac. sup. clin. positions filled	223	0
# involved in field placements	213	0
# involved in law journals	372	0
# in moot court or trial competitions	177	0
# of credit hrs required to graduate	86	

J.D. Enrollment & Ethnicity

	Men		Women		Fl-Time		Pt-Time		1st Yr		2nd Yr		3rd Yr		4th Yr		Total		JD Degrees Awarded
	#	%	#	%	#	%	#	%	#	%	#	%	#	%	#	%	#	%	
African-American	24	4.1	30	5.4	54	4.7	0	0.0	19	5.3	15	4.4	20	4.4	0	0.0	54	4.7	9
American Indian	4	0.7	3	0.5	7	0.6	0	0.0	0	0.0	3	0.9	4	0.9	0	0.0	7	0.6	4
Asian American	95	16.1	125	22.4	220	19.2	0	0.0	69	19.4	55	16.3	96	21.2	0	0.0	220	19.2	56
Mexican American	25	4.2	24	4.3	49	4.3	0	0.0	14	3.9	12	3.6	23	5.1	0	0.0	49	4.3	5
Puerto Rican	1	0.2	2	0.4	3	0.3	0	0.0	0	0.0	0	0.0	3	0.7	0	0.0	3	0.3	1
Hispanic American	14	2.4	18	3.2	32	2.8	0	0.0	9	2.5	8	2.4	15	3.3	0	0.0	32	2.8	11
Total Minorities	163	27.7	202	36.3	365	31.8	0	0.0	111	31.2	93	27.5	161	35.6	0	0.0	365	31.8	86
Foreign Nationals	3	0.5	6	1.1	9	0.8	0	0.0	2	0.6	0	0.0	7	1.5	0	0.0	9	0.8	0
Caucasian	423	71.8	349	62.7	772	67.4	0	0.0	243	68.3	245	72.5	284	62.8	0	0.0	772	67.4	283
Total	589	51.4	557	48.6	1146	100.0	0	0.0	356	31.1	338	29.5	452	39.4	0	0.0	1146		369

GPA & LSAT Scores

	Full Time	Part Time	Total
# of apps	4,121	0	4,121
# admits	1,255	0	1,255
# of matrics	354	0	354
75% GPA	3.59	0.00	
25% GPA	3.05	0.00	
75% LSAT	164	0	
25% LSAT	159	0	

Tuition & Fees

	Resident	Non-resident
Full-Time	$11,167	$19,937
Part-Time	$0	$0

Living Expenses

Estimated living expenses for Singles		
Living on campus	Living off campus	Living at home
$15,635	$15,635	$15,635

Grants/Scholarships

	Full-time		Part-time		Total	
	#	%	#	%	#	%
Total # of Students	1146		0		1146	
Total # receiving grants	854	74.5	0	0.0	854	74.5
Less than 1/2 tuition	802	70.0	0	0.0	802	70.0
Half to full tuition	39	3.4	0	0.0	39	3.4
Full tuition	0	0.0	0	0.0	0	0.0
More than full tuition	13	1.1	0	0.0	13	1.1
Median Grant Amount	$4,438		$0			

Informational & Library Resources

# of volumes & volume equivalents	612,117	# of professional staff	11
# of titles	187,737	Hours per week with professional staff	62
# of active serial subscriptions	8,289	Hours per week without professional staff	40
Study seating capacity inside the library	1,295	# of student computer work stations for entire law school	146
Square feet of law library	82,750	# of additional networked connections	323
Square feet of law school (excl. Library)	120,070	Require Laptop Computer?	N

Employment

	Total	%
Employment status known	380	95.5
Employment status unknown	18	4.5
Employed	360	94.7
Pursuing graduate degrees	4	1.1
Unemployed seeking employment	11	2.9
Unemployed not seeking employment	5	1.3
Type of Employment		
# employed in law firms	208	57.8
# employed in business & industry	54	15.0
# employed in government	40	11.1
# employed in public interest	15	4.2
# employed as judicial clerks	32	8.9
# employed in academia	9	2.5
Geographic Location		
# employed in state	281	78.1
# employed in foreign countries	5	1.4
# of states where employed	21	

J.D. Attrition (from Prior Year)

	Academic	Other	TOTALS	
	#	#	#	%
1st Year	4	28	32	10%
2nd Year	1	1	2	0.4%
3rd Year	1	2	3	0.8%
4th Year	0	0	0	0.0%

Bar Passage Rates

Jurisdiction	California		
Exam	Sum 97	Win 98	Total
# from school taking bar for the first time	337	18	355
School's pass rate for all first-time takers	92%	61%	90%
State's pass rate for all first-time takers	75%	57%	71%

CALIFORNIA-LOS ANGELES, UNIVERSITY OF

405 Hilgard Avenue
Los Angeles, CA 90095
(310)825-4841
http://www.law.ucla.edu

ABA Approved Since 1950

The Basics

Type of School: Public   Term: Semester

Application deadline: 02/01

Application fee: $40

Financial Aid deadline: 03/01

Can first year start other than Fall? No

Student faculty ratio: 15.1 to 1

Does the University offer:
- housing restricted to law students? No
- graduate student housing for which law students are eligible? Yes

Faculty & Administrators

	Total		Men		Women		Minorities	
	Fall	Spr	Fall	Spr	Fall	Spr	Fall	Spr
Full-time	55	58	42	43	13	15	8	9
Other Full-Time	7	7	2	2	5	5	0	0
Deans, librarians, & others who teach > 1/2	3	3	1	1	2	2	0	0
Part-time	14	21	11	16	3	5	1	0
Total	79	89	56	62	23	27	9	9
Deans, librarians, & others who teach < 1/2	1	1	0	0	1	1	0	0

Curriculum

	Full time	Part time
Typical first-year section size	80	0
Is there typically a "small section" of the first year class, other than Legal Writing, taught by full-time faculty?	Yes	No
If yes, typical size offered last year	38	N/A
# of classroom course titles beyond 1st year curriculum	114	0
# of upper division courses, excluding seminars, with an enrollment:		
Under 25	57	0
25 - 49	26	0
50 - 74	14	0
75 - 99	8	0
100 +	11	0
# of seminars	21	0
# of seminar positions available	280	
# of seminar positions filled	249	0
# of positions available in simulation courses	81	
# of simulation positions filled	81	0
# of positions available in faculty supervised clinical courses	140	
# of fac. sup. clin. positions filled	135	0
# involved in field placements	51	0
# involved in law journals	340	0
# in moot court or trial competitions	213	0
# of credit hrs required to graduate	87	

J.D. Enrollment & Ethnicity

	Men		Women		Fl-Time		Pt-Time		1st Yr		2nd Yr		3rd Yr		4th Yr		Total		JD Degrees Awarded
	#	%	#	%	#	%	#	%	#	%	#	%	#	%	#	%	#	%	
African-American	14	2.8	24	5.1	38	3.9	0	0.0	8	2.9	8	2.2	22	6.6	0	0.0	38	3.9	19
American Indian	10	2.0	1	0.2	11	1.1	0	0.0	3	1.1	1	0.3	7	2.1	0	0.0	11	1.1	2
Asian American	73	14.5	111	23.4	184	18.9	0	0.0	49	17.9	81	22.1	54	16.1	0	0.0	184	18.9	63
Mexican American	46	9.2	49	10.3	95	9.7	0	0.0	14	5.1	36	9.8	45	13.4	0	0.0	95	9.7	20
Puerto Rican	0	0.0	0	0.0	0	0.0	0	0.0	0	0.0	0	0.0	0	0.0	0	0.0	0	0.0	0
Hispanic American	1	0.2	1	0.2	2	0.2	0	0.0	2	0.7	0	0.0	0	0.0	0	0.0	2	0.2	5
Total Minorities	144	28.7	186	39.2	330	33.8	0	0.0	76	27.7	126	34.3	128	38.2	0	0.0	330	33.8	109
Foreign Nationals	0	0.0	0	0.0	0	0.0	0	0.0	0	0.0	0	0.0	0	0.0	0	0.0	0	0.0	0
Caucasian	358	71.3	288	60.8	646	66.2	0	0.0	198	72.3	241	65.7	207	61.8	0	0.0	646	66.2	168
Total	502	51.4	474	48.6	976	100.0	0	0.0	274	28.1	367	37.6	335	34.3	0	0.0	976		277

GPA & LSAT Scores

	Full Time	Part Time	Total
# of apps	4,282	0	4,282
# admits	841	0	841
# of matrics	270	0	270
75% GPA	3.78	0.00	
25% GPA	3.45	0.00	
75% LSAT	166	0	
25% LSAT	161	0	

Tuition & Fees

	Resident	Non-resident
Full-Time	$10,972	$20,356
Part-Time	$0	$0

Living Expenses

Estimated living expenses for Singles		
Living on campus	Living off campus	Living at home
N/A	$13,832	$7,203

Grants/Scholarships

	Full-time		Part-time		Total	
	#	%	#	%	#	%
Total # of Students	976		0		976	
Total # receiving grants	528	54.1	0	0.0	528	54.1
Less than 1/2 tuition	181	18.5	0	0.0	181	18.5
Half to full tuition	329	33.7	0	0.0	329	33.7
Full tuition	5	0.5	0	0.0	5	0.5
More than full tuition	13	1.3	0	0.0	13	1.3
Median Grant Amount	$5,950		$0			

Informational & Library Resources

# of volumes & volume equivalents	544,054	# of professional staff	10
# of titles	184,025	Hours per week with professional staff	69
# of active serial subscriptions	7,238	Hours per week without professional staff	29
Study seating capacity inside the library	774	# of student computer work stations for entire law school	120
Square feet of law library	78,891	# of additional networked connections	600
Square feet of law school (excl. Library)	67,315	Require Laptop Computer?	N

Employment

	Total	%
Employment status known	324	99.7
Employment status unknown	1	0.3
Employed	295	91.0
Pursuing graduate degrees	6	1.9
Unemployed seeking employment	10	3.1
Unemployed not seeking employment	13	4.0
Type of Employment		
# employed in law firms	197	66.8
# employed in business & industry	38	12.9
# employed in government	23	7.8
# employed in public interest	7	2.4
# employed as judicial clerks	26	8.8
# employed in academia	4	1.4
Geographic Location		
# employed in state	244	82.7
# employed in foreign countries	2	0.7
# of states where employed	17	

J.D. Attrition (from Prior Year)

	Academic	Other	TOTALS	
	#	#	#	%
1st Year	1	22	23	6.1%
2nd Year	0	1	1	0.3%
3rd Year	0	1	1	0.3%
4th Year	0	0	0	0.0%

Bar Passage Rates

Jurisdiction	California			New York		
Exam	Sum 97	Win 98	Total	Sum 97	Win 98	Total
# from school taking bar for the first time	279	15	294	14	7	21
School's pass rate for all first-time takers	83%	60%	82%	100%	86%	95%
State's pass rate for all first-time takers	75%	57%	71%	78%	65%	76%

CAMPBELL UNIVERSITY

Norman Adrian Wiggins School of Law
P.O. Box 158
Buies Creek, NC 27506
(910)893-1750
http://webster.campbell.edu/culawsch

ABA Approved Since 1979

The Basics

Type of School: Private   Term: Semester

Application deadline: Rolling

Application fee: $40

Financial Aid deadline: Rolling

Can first year start other than Fall? No

Student faculty ratio: 17.8 to 1

Does the University offer:
- housing restricted to law students? No
- graduate student housing for which law students are eligible? Yes

Faculty & Administrators

	Total		Men		Women		Minorities	
	Fall	Spr	Fall	Spr	Fall	Spr	Fall	Spr
Full-time	15	15	14	14	1	1	0	0
Other Full-Time	1	1	1	1	0	0	0	0
Deans, librarians, & others who teach > 1/2	3	3	2	2	1	1	0	0
Part-time	9	13	7	10	2	3	0	0
Total	28	32	24	27	4	5	0	0
Deans, librarians, & others who teach < 1/2	0	0	0	0	0	0	0	0

Curriculum

	Full time	Part time
Typical first-year section size	72	0
Is there typically a "small section" of the first year class, other than Legal Writing, taught by full-time faculty?	Yes	No
If yes, typical size offered last year	37	N/A
# of classroom course titles beyond 1st year curriculum	61	0
# of upper division courses, excluding seminars, with an enrollment:		
Under 25	26	0
25 - 49	16	0
50 - 74	12	0
75 - 99	3	0
100 +	1	0
# of seminars	8	0
# of seminar positions available	336	
# of seminar positions filled	196	0
# of positions available in simulation courses	103	
# of simulation positions filled	103	0
# of positions available in faculty supervised clinical courses	0	
# of fac. sup. clin. positions filled	0	0
# involved in field placements	30	0
# involved in law journals	112	0
# in moot court or trial competitions	32	0
# of credit hrs required to graduate	90	

J.D. Enrollment & Ethnicity

	Men		Women		Fl-Time		Pt-Time		1st Yr		2nd Yr		3rd Yr		4th Yr		Total		JD Degrees Awarded
	#	%	#	%	#	%	#	%	#	%	#	%	#	%	#	%	#	%	
African-American	1	0.6	3	2.1	4	1.3	0	0.0	2	1.9	1	1.0	1	0.9	0	0.0	4	1.3	5
American Indian	2	1.1	2	1.4	4	1.3	0	0.0	0	0.0	3	3.1	1	0.9	0	0.0	4	1.3	0
Asian American	0	0.0	2	1.4	2	0.6	0	0.0	0	0.0	2	2.0	0	0.0	0	0.0	2	0.6	2
Mexican American	0	0.0	0	0.0	0	0.0	0	0.0	0	0.0	0	0.0	0	0.0	0	0.0	0	0.0	0
Puerto Rican	1	0.6	0	0.0	1	0.3	0	0.0	0	0.0	1	1.0	0	0.0	0	0.0	1	0.3	0
Hispanic American	0	0.0	1	0.7	1	0.3	0	0.0	0	0.0	0	0.0	1	0.9	0	0.0	1	0.3	0
Total Minorities	4	2.2	8	5.6	12	3.8	0	0.0	2	1.9	7	7.1	3	2.6	0	0.0	12	3.8	7
Foreign Nationals	0	0.0	0	0.0	0	0.0	0	0.0	0	0.0	0	0.0	0	0.0	0	0.0	0	0.0	0
Caucasian	174	97.8	134	94.4	308	96.3	0	0.0	106	98.1	91	92.9	111	97.4	0	0.0	308	96.3	97
Total	178	55.6	142	44.4	320	100.0	0	0.0	108	33.8	98	30.6	114	35.6	0	0.0	320		104

GPA & LSAT Scores

	Full Time	Part Time	Total
# of apps	655	0	655
# admits	204	0	204
# of matrics	111	0	111
75% GPA	3.49	0.00	
25% GPA	2.96	0.00	
75% LSAT	156	0	
25% LSAT	152	0	

Tuition & Fees

	Resident	Non-resident
Full-Time	$16,733	$16,733
Part-Time	$0	$0

Living Expenses

Estimated living expenses for Singles		
Living on campus	Living off campus	Living at home
$8,081	$9,821	N/A

Employment

	Total	%
Employment status known	93	93.0
Employment status unknown	7	7.0
Employed	92	98.9
Pursuing graduate degrees	1	1.1
Unemployed seeking employment	0	0.0
Unemployed not seeking employment	0	0.0
Type of Employment		
# employed in law firms	76	82.6
# employed in business & industry	5	5.4
# employed in government	4	4.3
# employed in public interest	2	2.2
# employed as judicial clerks	5	5.4
# employed in academia	0	0.0
Geographic Location		
# employed in state	77	83.7
# employed in foreign countries	0	0.0
# of states where employed	12	

Grants/Scholarships

	Full-time		Part-time		Total	
	#	%	#	%	#	%
Total # of Students	320		0		320	
Total # receiving grants	119	37.2	0	0.0	119	37.2
Less than 1/2 tuition	103	32.2	0	0.0	103	32.2
Half to full tuition	13	4.1	0	0.0	13	4.1
Full tuition	3	0.9	0	0.0	3	0.9
More than full tuition	0	0.0	0	0.0	0	0.0
Median Grant Amount	$2,000		$0			

Informational & Library Resources

# of volumes & volume equivalents	166,217	# of professional staff	5
# of titles	19,322	Hours per week with professional staff	45
# of active serial subscriptions	2,343	Hours per week without professional staff	61
Study seating capacity inside the library	412	# of student computer work stations for entire law school	55
Square feet of law library	28,143	# of additional networked connections	15
Square feet of law school (excl. Library)	50,140	Require Laptop Computer?	N

J.D. Attrition (from Prior Year)

	Academic	Other	TOTALS	
	#	#	#	%
1st Year	13	0	13	12%
2nd Year	2	3	5	4.3%
3rd Year	0	0	0	0.0%
4th Year	0	0	0	0.0%

Bar Passage Rates

Jurisdiction	North Carolina		
Exam	Sum 97	Win 98	Total
# from school taking bar for the first time	85	1	86
School's pass rate for all first-time takers	95%	0%	94%
State's pass rate for all first-time takers	85%	73%	82%

CAPITAL UNIVERSITY

303 East Broad Street
Columbus, OH 43215
(614)236-6500
http://www.law.capital.edu

ABA Approved Since 1950

The Basics

Type of School: Private
Term: Semester
Application deadline: 05/01
Application fee: $35
Financial Aid deadline: 04/01
Can first year start other than Fall? No
Student faculty ratio: 23.0 to 1
Does the University offer:
- housing restricted to law students? No
- graduate student housing for which law students are eligible? No

Faculty & Administrators

	Total		Men		Women		Minorities	
	Fall	Spr	Fall	Spr	Fall	Spr	Fall	Spr
Full-time	24	23	19	18	5	5	3	3
Other Full-Time	0	0	0	0	0	0	0	0
Deans, librarians, & others who teach > 1/2	3	4	1	2	2	2	1	1
Part-time	30	29	24	24	6	5	3	3
Total	57	56	44	44	13	12	7	7
Deans, librarians, & others who teach < 1/2	2	2	2	2	0	0	0	0

Curriculum

	Full time	Part time
Typical first-year section size	75	95
Is there typically a "small section" of the first year class, other than Legal Writing, taught by full-time faculty?	No	Yes
If yes, typical size offered last year	N/A	42
# of classroom course titles beyond 1st year curriculum	38	82
# of upper division courses, excluding seminars, with an enrollment:		
Under 25	24	54
25 - 49	6	16
50 - 74	11	6
75 - 99	10	9
100 +	1	2
# of seminars	8	6
# of seminar positions available	210	
# of seminar positions filled	92	54
# of positions available in simulation courses	516	
# of simulation positions filled	307	118
# of positions available in faculty supervised clinical courses	52	
# of fac. sup. clin. positions filled	36	6
# involved in field placements	79	30
# involved in law journals	24	23
# in moot court or trial competitions	9	1
# of credit hrs required to graduate	86	

J.D. Enrollment & Ethnicity

	Men		Women		Fl-Time		Pt-Time		1st Yr		2nd Yr		3rd Yr		4th Yr		Total		JD Degrees Awarded
	#	%	#	%	#	%	#	%	#	%	#	%	#	%	#	%	#	%	
African-American	27	6.2	33	9.4	33	7.8	27	7.5	20	8.2	18	7.3	18	8.0	4	5.8	60	7.6	11
American Indian	2	0.5	0	0.0	2	0.5	0	0.0	0	0.0	2	0.8	0	0.0	0	0.0	2	0.3	0
Asian American	6	1.4	4	1.1	7	1.6	3	0.8	2	0.8	4	1.6	4	1.8	0	0.0	10	1.3	2
Mexican American	0	0.0	0	0.0	0	0.0	0	0.0	0	0.0	0	0.0	0	0.0	0	0.0	0	0.0	0
Puerto Rican	0	0.0	0	0.0	0	0.0	0	0.0	0	0.0	0	0.0	0	0.0	0	0.0	0	0.0	0
Hispanic American	4	0.9	8	2.3	6	1.4	6	1.7	4	1.6	2	0.8	6	2.7	0	0.0	12	1.5	10
Total Minorities	39	9.0	45	12.8	48	11.3	36	10.0	26	10.7	26	10.5	28	12.4	4	5.8	84	10.7	23
Foreign Nationals	4	0.9	1	0.3	2	0.5	3	0.8	1	0.4	3	1.2	0	0.0	1	1.4	5	0.6	1
Caucasian	390	90.1	306	86.9	375	88.2	321	89.2	216	88.9	218	88.3	198	87.6	64	92.8	696	88.7	199
Total	433	55.2	352	44.8	425	54.1	360	45.9	243	31.0	247	31.5	226	28.8	69	8.8	785		223

GPA & LSAT Scores

	Full Time	Part Time	Total
# of apps	610	209	819
# admits	420	151	571
# of matrics	148	105	253
75% GPA	3.33	3.33	
25% GPA	2.80	2.82	
75% LSAT	152	154	
25% LSAT	146	145	

Tuition & Fees

	Resident	Non-resident
Full-Time	$15,370	$15,370
Part-Time	$10,070	$10,070

Living Expenses

Estimated living expenses for Singles		
Living on campus	Living off campus	Living at home
N/A	$9,748	$9,748

Employment

	Total	%
Employment status known	216	99.5
Employment status unknown	1	0.5
Employed	192	88.9
Pursuing graduate degrees	1	0.5
Unemployed seeking employment	16	7.4
Unemployed not seeking employment	7	3.2
Type of Employment		
# employed in law firms	85	44.3
# employed in business & industry	54	28.1
# employed in government	40	20.8
# employed in public interest	0	0.0
# employed as judicial clerks	10	5.2
# employed in academia	2	1.0
Geographic Location		
# employed in state	171	89.1
# employed in foreign countries	0	0.0
# of states where employed	19	

Grants/Scholarships

	Full-time		Part-time		Total	
	#	%	#	%	#	%
Total # of Students	425		360		785	
Total # receiving grants	189	44.5	100	27.8	289	36.8
Less than 1/2 tuition	173	40.7	80	22.2	253	32.2
Half to full tuition	13	3.1	16	4.4	29	3.7
Full tuition	3	0.7	4	1.1	7	0.9
More than full tuition	0	0.0	0	0.0	0	0.0
Median Grant Amount	$4,000		$3,000			

Informational & Library Resources

# of volumes & volume equivalents	250,601	# of professional staff	5
# of titles	46,296	Hours per week with professional staff	45
# of active serial subscriptions	2,447	Hours per week without professional staff	48
Study seating capacity inside the library	460	# of student computer work stations for entire law school	68
Square feet of law library	40,500	# of additional networked connections	360
Square feet of law school (excl. Library)	63,600	Require Laptop Computer?	N

J.D. Attrition (from Prior Year)

	Academic	Other	TOTALS	
	#	#	#	%
1st Year	7	38	45	16%
2nd Year	6	5	11	4.6%
3rd Year	2	0	2	1.0%
4th Year	0	0	0	0.0%

Bar Passage Rates

Jurisdiction	Ohio		
Exam	Sum 97	Win 98	Total
# from school taking bar for the first time	155	24	179
School's pass rate for all first-time takers	75%	79%	76%
State's pass rate for all first-time takers	79%	75%	78%

CASE WESTERN RESERVE UNIVERSITY

Franklin Thomas Backus School of Law
Gund Hall
Cleveland, OH 44106-7148
(216)368-6350
http://lawwww.cwru.edu

ABA Approved Since 1923

The Basics

Type of School: Private Term: Semester
Application deadline: 04/01
Application fee: $40
Financial Aid deadline: 05/01
Can first year start other than Fall? No
Student faculty ratio: 17.5 to 1
Does the University offer:
- housing restricted to law students? No
- graduate student housing for which law students are eligible? Yes

Faculty & Administrators

	Total		Men		Women		Minorities	
	Fall	Spr	Fall	Spr	Fall	Spr	Fall	Spr
Full-time	31	30	25	24	6	6	1	2
Other Full-Time	6	6	5	5	1	1	0	0
Deans, librarians, & others who teach > 1/2	1	1	1	1	0	0	0	0
Part-time	45	43	35	32	10	11	1	3
Total	83	80	66	62	17	18	2	5
Deans, librarians, & others who teach < 1/2	2	2	1	1	1	1	0	0

Curriculum

	Full time	Part time
Typical first-year section size	75	0
Is there typically a "small section" of the first year class, other than Legal Writing, taught by full-time faculty?	No	No
If yes, typical size offered last year	N/A	N/A
# of classroom course titles beyond 1st year curriculum	76	0
# of upper division courses, excluding seminars, with an enrollment:		
Under 25	64	0
25 - 49	22	0
50 - 74	20	0
75 - 99	8	0
100 +	1	0
# of seminars	18	0
# of seminar positions available	220	
# of seminar positions filled	197	0
# of positions available in simulation courses	344	
# of simulation positions filled	292	0
# of positions available in faculty supervised clinical courses	67	
# of fac. sup. clin. positions filled	55	0
# involved in field placements	36	0
# involved in law journals	136	0
# in moot court or trial competitions	30	0
# of credit hrs required to graduate	88	

J.D. Enrollment & Ethnicity

	Men		Women		Fl-Time		Pt-Time		1st Yr		2nd Yr		3rd Yr		4th Yr		Total		JD Degrees Awarded
	#	%	#	%	#	%	#	%	#	%	#	%	#	%	#	%	#	%	
African-American	14	3.9	23	7.7	34	5.3	3	17.6	9	4.4	14	6.1	14	6.3	0	0.0	37	5.6	22
American Indian	1	0.3	1	0.3	2	0.3	0	0.0	0	0.0	0	0.0	2	0.9	0	0.0	2	0.3	0
Asian American	16	4.4	15	5.1	31	4.8	0	0.0	10	4.9	12	5.2	9	4.1	0	0.0	31	4.7	15
Mexican American	0	0.0	0	0.0	0	0.0	0	0.0	0	0.0	0	0.0	0	0.0	0	0.0	0	0.0	0
Puerto Rican	0	0.0	0	0.0	0	0.0	0	0.0	0	0.0	0	0.0	0	0.0	0	0.0	0	0.0	0
Hispanic American	2	0.6	0	0.0	2	0.3	0	0.0	0	0.0	0	0.0	2	0.9	0	0.0	2	0.3	2
Total Minorities	33	9.2	39	13.1	69	10.8	3	17.6	19	9.3	26	11.3	27	12.2	0	0.0	72	11.0	39
Foreign Nationals	0	0.0	0	0.0	0	0.0	0	0.0	0	0.0	0	0.0	0	0.0	0	0.0	0	0.0	0
Caucasian	327	90.8	258	86.9	571	89.2	14	82.4	186	90.7	204	88.7	195	87.8	0	0.0	585	89.0	149
Total	360	54.8	297	45.2	640	97.4	17	2.6	205	31.2	230	35.0	222	33.8	0	0.0	657		188

CASE WESTERN RESERVE UNIVERSITY

GPA & LSAT Scores

	Full Time	Part Time	Total
# of apps	1,214	63	1,277
# admits	740	13	753
# of matrics	198	3	201
75% GPA	3.50	0.00	
25% GPA	2.99	0.00	
75% LSAT	161	0	
25% LSAT	153	0	

Tuition & Fees

	Resident	Non-resident
Full-Time	$20,540	$20,540
Part-Time	$0	$0

Living Expenses

Estimated living expenses for Singles		
Living on campus	Living off campus	Living at home
$10,730	$10,730	$10,730

Grants/Scholarships

	Full-time		Part-time		Total	
	#	%	#	%	#	%
Total # of Students	640		17		657	
Total # receiving grants	196	30.6	0	0.0	196	29.8
Less than 1/2 tuition	91	14.2	0	0.0	91	13.9
Half to full tuition	75	11.7	0	0.0	75	11.4
Full tuition	30	4.7	0	0.0	30	4.6
More than full tuition	0	0.0	0	0.0	0	0.0
Median Grant Amount	$10,200		$0			

Informational & Library Resources

# of volumes & volume equivalents	358,621	# of professional staff	11
# of titles	87,701	Hours per week with professional staff	63
# of active serial subscriptions	4,745	Hours per week without professional staff	45
Study seating capacity inside the library	467	# of student computer work stations for entire law school	60
Square feet of law library	31,495	# of additional networked connections	10
Square feet of law school (excl. Library)	64,909	Require Laptop Computer?	N

Employment

	Total	%
Employment status known	200	98.0
Employment status unknown	4	2.0
Employed	173	86.5
Pursuing graduate degrees	5	2.5
Unemployed seeking employment	20	10.0
Unemployed not seeking employment	2	1.0
Type of Employment		
# employed in law firms	111	64.2
# employed in business & industry	24	13.9
# employed in government	16	9.2
# employed in public interest	7	4.0
# employed as judicial clerks	15	8.7
# employed in academia	0	0.0
Geographic Location		
# employed in state	109	63.0
# employed in foreign countries	2	1.2
# of states where employed	21	

J.D. Attrition (from Prior Year)

	Academic	Other	TOTALS	
	#	#	#	%
1st Year	0	5	5	2.1%
2nd Year	0	10	10	4.5%
3rd Year	1	5	6	3.2%
4th Year	0	0	0	0.0%

Bar Passage Rates

Jurisdiction	Ohio		
Exam	Sum 97	Win 98	Total
# from school taking bar for the first time	125	5	130
School's pass rate for all first-time takers	79%	80%	79%
State's pass rate for all first-time takers	79%	75%	78%

CATHOLIC UNIVERSITY OF AMERICA

Columbus School of Law
Washington, DC 20064
(319)319-5140
http://www.law.cua.edu

ABA Approved Since 1925

The Basics

Type of School: Private   Term: Semester
Application deadline: 03/01
Application fee: $55
Financial Aid deadline: 03/15
Can first year start other than Fall? No
Student faculty ratio: 20.6 to 1
Does the University offer:
- housing restricted to law students? No
- graduate student housing for which law students are eligible? Yes

Faculty & Administrators

	Total		Men		Women		Minorities	
	Fall	Spr	Fall	Spr	Fall	Spr	Fall	Spr
Full-time	33	29	23	19	10	10	5	4
Other Full-Time	5	5	2	2	3	3	0	0
Deans, librarians, & others who teach > 1/2	1	1	0	0	1	1	1	1
Part-time	49	56	38	38	11	18	6	2
Total	88	91	63	59	25	32	12	7
Deans, librarians, & others who teach < 1/2	2	2	2	2	0	0	0	0

Curriculum

	Full time	Part time
Typical first-year section size	70	70
Is there typically a "small section" of the first year class, other than Legal Writing, taught by full-time faculty?	Yes	Yes
If yes, typical size offered last year	35	35
# of classroom course titles beyond 1st year curriculum	82	75
# of upper division courses, excluding seminars, with an enrollment:		
Under 25	57	56
25 - 49	26	15
50 - 74	18	6
75 - 99	2	1
100 +	1	0
# of seminars	7	4
# of seminar positions available	218	
# of seminar positions filled	124	51
# of positions available in simulation courses	416	
# of simulation positions filled	150	203
# of positions available in faculty supervised clinical courses	183	
# of fac. sup. clin. positions filled	86	16
# involved in field placements	190	64
# involved in law journals	139	40
# in moot court or trial competitions	32	11
# of credit hrs required to graduate	84	

J.D. Enrollment & Ethnicity

	Men		Women		Fl-Time		Pt-Time		1st Yr		2nd Yr		3rd Yr		4th Yr		Total		JD Degrees Awarded
	#	%	#	%	#	%	#	%	#	%	#	%	#	%	#	%	#	%	
African-American	38	8.3	75	17.0	70	10.9	43	16.6	36	12.4	41	15.0	24	8.6	12	20.3	113	12.5	23
American Indian	0	0.0	0	0.0	0	0.0	0	0.0	0	0.0	0	0.0	0	0.0	0	0.0	0	0.0	0
Asian American	15	3.3	15	3.4	19	3.0	11	4.2	10	3.4	10	3.7	9	3.2	1	1.7	30	3.3	14
Mexican American	6	1.3	5	1.1	9	1.4	2	0.8	4	1.4	4	1.5	3	1.1	0	0.0	11	1.2	3
Puerto Rican	3	0.7	8	1.8	9	1.4	2	0.8	6	2.1	1	0.4	4	1.4	0	0.0	11	1.2	1
Hispanic American	9	2.0	5	1.1	11	1.7	3	1.2	1	0.3	6	2.2	7	2.5	0	0.0	14	1.6	5
Total Minorities	71	15.4	108	24.4	118	18.4	61	23.6	57	19.7	62	22.7	47	16.8	13	22.0	179	19.8	46
Foreign Nationals	3	0.7	5	1.1	6	0.9	2	0.8	2	0.7	3	1.1	2	0.7	1	1.7	8	0.9	1
Caucasian	386	83.9	329	74.4	519	80.7	196	75.7	231	79.7	208	76.2	231	82.5	45	76.3	715	79.3	246
Total	460	51.0	442	49.0	643	71.3	259	28.7	290	32.2	273	30.3	280	31.0	59	6.5	902		293

GPA & LSAT Scores

	Full Time	Part Time	Total
# of apps	1,706	410	2,116
# admits	865	197	1,062
# of matrics	219	71	290
75% GPA	3.40	3.10	
25% GPA	2.80	2.50	
75% LSAT	157	156	
25% LSAT	151	151	

Tuition & Fees

	Resident	Non-resident
Full-Time	$23,898	$23,898
Part-Time	$17,279	$17,279

Living Expenses

Estimated living expenses for Singles		
Living on campus	Living off campus	Living at home
$13,390	$13,390	$13,390

Employment

	Total	%
Employment status known	306	99.7
Employment status unknown	1	0.3
Employed	283	92.5
Pursuing graduate degrees	2	0.7
Unemployed seeking employment	16	5.2
Unemployed not seeking employment	5	1.6
Type of Employment		
# employed in law firms	132	46.6
# employed in business & industry	54	19.1
# employed in government	52	18.4
# employed in public interest	8	2.8
# employed as judicial clerks	30	10.6
# employed in academia	5	1.8
Geographic Location		
# employed in state	135	47.7
# employed in foreign countries	5	1.8
# of states where employed	27	

Grants/Scholarships

	Full-time		Part-time		Total	
	#	%	#	%	#	%
Total # of Students	643		259		902	
Total # receiving grants	179	27.8	26	10.0	205	22.7
Less than 1/2 tuition	172	26.7	26	10.0	198	22.0
Half to full tuition	4	0.6	0	0.0	4	0.4
Full tuition	3	0.5	0	0.0	3	0.3
More than full tuition	0	0.0	0	0.0	0	0.0
Median Grant Amount	$3,000		$2,500			

Informational & Library Resources

# of volumes & volume equivalents	307,002	# of professional staff	8
# of titles	84,734	Hours per week with professional staff	86
# of active serial subscriptions	5,473	Hours per week without professional staff	29
Study seating capacity inside the library	502	# of student computer work stations for entire law school	73
Square feet of law library	50,000	# of additional networked connections	405
Square feet of law school (excl. Library)	68,575	Require Laptop Computer?	N

J.D. Attrition (from Prior Year)

	Academic	Other	TOTALS	
	#	#	#	%
1st Year	4	29	33	11%
2nd Year	4	3	7	2.4%
3rd Year	0	1	1	0.3%
4th Year	0	0	0	0.0%

Bar Passage Rates

Jurisdiction	Maryland		
Exam	Sum 97	Win 98	Total
# from school taking bar for the first time	134	25	159
School's pass rate for all first-time takers	66%	72%	67%
State's pass rate for all first-time takers	69%	83%	72%

CHAPMAN UNIVERSITY (Provisional)

1240 South State College Blvd.
Suite 200
Anaheim, CA 92806
(714)517-0300
http://www.chapman.edu/law

ABA Approved Since 1998

The Basics

Type of School: Private Term: Semester

Application deadline: 06/01

Application fee: $40

Financial Aid deadline: 04/01

Can first year start other than Fall? No

Student faculty ratio: 7.9 to 1

Does the University offer:
- housing restricted to law students? No
- graduate student housing for which law students are eligible? No

Faculty & Administrators

	Total		Men		Women		Minorities	
	Fall	Spr	Fall	Spr	Fall	Spr	Fall	Spr
Full-time	16	17	11	11	5	6	3	4
Other Full-Time	0	0	0	0	0	0	0	0
Deans, librarians, & others who teach > 1/2	0	0	0	0	0	0	0	0
Part-time	10	5	9	5	1	0	1	0
Total	26	22	20	16	6	6	4	4
Deans, librarians, & others who teach < 1/2	2	2	1	1	1	1	0	0

Curriculum

	Full time	Part time
Typical first-year section size	40	20
Is there typically a "small section" of the first year class, other than Legal Writing, taught by full-time faculty?	No	No
If yes, typical size offered last year	N/A	N/A
# of classroom course titles beyond 1st year curriculum	33	33
# of upper division courses, excluding seminars, with an enrollment:		
Under 25	19	18
25 - 49	8	12
50 - 74	0	1
75 - 99	0	0
100 +	0	0
# of seminars	6	2
# of seminar positions available	108	
# of seminar positions filled	35	11
# of positions available in simulation courses	148	
# of simulation positions filled	52	89
# of positions available in faculty supervised clinical courses	10	
# of fac. sup. clin. positions filled	10	0
# involved in field placements	18	13
# involved in law journals	20	10
# in moot court or trial competitions	30	10
# of credit hrs required to graduate	88	

J.D. Enrollment & Ethnicity

	Men		Women		Fl-Time		Pt-Time		1st Yr		2nd Yr		3rd Yr		4th Yr		Total		JD Degrees Awarded
	#	%	#	%	#	%	#	%	#	%	#	%	#	%	#	%	#	%	
African-American	1	1.0	2	2.2	2	2.7	1	0.9	1	1.7	0	0.0	1	2.6	1	1.5	3	1.6	1
American Indian	0	0.0	2	2.2	1	1.4	1	0.9	0	0.0	1	4.3	0	0.0	1	1.5	2	1.1	0
Asian American	12	12.2	14	15.7	14	18.9	12	10.6	5	8.5	5	21.7	10	25.6	6	9.1	26	13.9	5
Mexican American	0	0.0	0	0.0	0	0.0	0	0.0	0	0.0	0	0.0	0	0.0	0	0.0	0	0.0	0
Puerto Rican	0	0.0	0	0.0	0	0.0	0	0.0	0	0.0	0	0.0	0	0.0	0	0.0	0	0.0	0
Hispanic American	6	6.1	12	13.5	6	8.1	12	10.6	9	15.3	0	0.0	2	5.1	7	10.6	18	9.6	8
Total Minorities	19	19.4	30	33.7	23	31.1	26	23.0	15	25.4	6	26.1	13	33.3	15	22.7	49	26.2	14
Foreign Nationals	1	1.0	0	0.0	0	0.0	1	0.9	0	0.0	0	0.0	0	0.0	1	1.5	1	0.5	0
Caucasian	78	79.6	59	66.3	51	68.9	86	76.1	44	74.6	17	73.9	26	66.7	50	75.8	137	73.3	50
Total	98	52.4	89	47.6	74	39.6	113	60.4	59	31.6	23	12.3	39	20.9	66	35.3	187		64

CHAPMAN UNIVERSITY (Provisional)

GPA & LSAT Scores

	Full Time	Part Time	Total
# of apps	221	137	358
# admits	77	54	131
# of matrics	33	26	59
75% GPA	3.36	3.42	
25% GPA	2.70	2.61	
75% LSAT	153	157	
25% LSAT	146	147	

Tuition & Fees

	Resident	Non-resident
Full-Time	$17,550	$17,550
Part-Time	$12,550	$12,550

Living Expenses

Estimated living expenses for Singles		
Living on campus	Living off campus	Living at home
N/A	$11,012	$7,236

Employment

	Total	%
Employment status known	0	0.0
Employment status unknown	0	0.0
Employed	0	0.0
Pursuing graduate degrees	0	0.0
Unemployed seeking employment	0	0.0
Unemployed not seeking employment	0	0.0
Type of Employment		
# employed in law firms	0	0.0
# employed in business & industry	0	0.0
# employed in government	0	0.0
# employed in public interest	0	0.0
# employed as judicial clerks	0	0.0
# employed in academia	0	0.0
Geographic Location		
# employed in state	0	0.0
# employed in foreign countries	0	0.0
# of states where employed	1	

Grants/Scholarships

	Full-time		Part-time		Total	
	#	%	#	%	#	%
Total # of Students						
Total # receiving grants	48	64.9	46	40.7	94	50.3
Less than 1/2 tuition	16	21.6	29	25.7	45	24.1
Half to full tuition	15	20.3	7	6.2	22	11.8
Full tuition	12	16.2	8	7.1	20	10.7
More than full tuition	5	6.8	2	1.8	7	3.7
Median Grant Amount	$10,363		$5,702			

Informational & Library Resources

# of volumes & volume equivalents	219,386	# of professional staff	5
# of titles	89,309	Hours per week with professional staff	58
# of active serial subscriptions	4,571	Hours per week without professional staff	37
Study seating capacity inside the library	162	# of student computer work stations for entire law school	2
Square feet of law library	13,000	# of additional networked connections	20
Square feet of law school (excl. Library)	26,800	Require Laptop Computer?	N

J.D. Attrition (from Prior Year)

	Academic	Other	TOTALS	
	#	#	#	%
1st Year	7	0	7	19%
2nd Year	5	0	5	13%
3rd Year	8	0	8	5.8%
4th Year	0	0	0	0.0%

Bar Passage Rates

Jurisdiction	
Exam	
# from school taking bar for the first time	Chapman University School of Law did not graduate its first class until May 1998.
School's pass rate for all first-time takers	
State's pass rate for all first-time takers	

CHICAGO, UNIVERSITY OF

1111 East 60th Street
Chicago, IL 60637
(773)702-9494
http://www.law.uchicago.edu

ABA Approved Since 1923

The Basics

Type of School: Private   Term: Quarter

Application deadline: Rolling

Application fee: $60

Financial Aid deadline: 04/15

Can first year start other than Fall? No

Student faculty ratio: 15.1 to 1

Does the University offer:
- housing restricted to law students? No
- graduate student housing for which law students are eligible? Yes

Faculty & Administrators

	Total		Men		Women		Minorities	
	Fall	Spr	Fall	Spr	Fall	Spr	Fall	Spr
Full-time	31	33	24	25	7	8	2	2
Other Full-Time	6	6	4	4	2	2	0	0
Deans, librarians, & others who teach > 1/2	3	3	2	2	1	1	1	1
Part-time	13	16	10	11	3	5	2	0
Total	53	58	40	42	13	16	5	3
Deans, librarians, & others who teach < 1/2	0	0	0	0	0	0	0	0

Curriculum

	Full time	Part time
Typical first-year section size	90	0
Is there typically a "small section" of the first year class, other than Legal Writing, taught by full-time faculty?	No	No
If yes, typical size offered last year	N/A	N/A
# of classroom course titles beyond 1st year curriculum	59	0
# of upper division courses, excluding seminars, with an enrollment:		
Under 25	15	0
25 - 49	16	0
50 - 74	14	0
75 - 99	5	0
100 +	9	0
# of seminars	60	0
# of seminar positions available	616	
# of seminar positions filled	616	0
# of positions available in simulation courses	116	
# of simulation positions filled	116	0
# of positions available in faculty supervised clinical courses	64	
# of fac. sup. clin. positions filled	64	0
# involved in field placements	0	0
# involved in law journals	100	0
# in moot court or trial competitions	75	0
# of credit hrs required to graduate	105	

J.D. Enrollment & Ethnicity

	Men		Women		Fl-Time		Pt-Time		1st Yr		2nd Yr		3rd Yr		4th Yr		Total		JD Degrees Awarded
	#	%	#	%	#	%	#	%	#	%	#	%	#	%	#	%	#	%	
African-American	8	2.5	17	7.2	25	4.5	0	0.0	2	1.1	8	4.5	15	7.5	0	0.0	25	4.5	13
American Indian	0	0.0	0	0.0	0	0.0	0	0.0	0	0.0	0	0.0	0	0.0	0	0.0	0	0.0	1
Asian American	32	9.9	23	9.7	55	9.8	0	0.0	18	9.9	19	10.7	18	9.0	0	0.0	55	9.8	18
Mexican American	12	3.7	2	0.8	14	2.5	0	0.0	3	1.6	6	3.4	5	2.5	0	0.0	14	2.5	3
Puerto Rican	5	1.5	0	0.0	5	0.9	0	0.0	0	0.0	2	1.1	3	1.5	0	0.0	5	0.9	0
Hispanic American	5	1.5	5	2.1	10	1.8	0	0.0	4	2.2	3	1.7	3	1.5	0	0.0	10	1.8	4
Total Minorities	62	19.1	47	19.9	109	19.5	0	0.0	27	14.8	38	21.3	44	22.0	0	0.0	109	19.5	39
Foreign Nationals	0	0.0	1	0.4	1	0.2	0	0.0	1	0.5	0	0.0	0	0.0	0	0.0	1	0.2	0
Caucasian	262	80.9	188	79.7	450	80.4	0	0.0	154	84.6	140	78.7	156	78.0	0	0.0	450	80.4	139
Total	324	57.9	236	42.1	560	100.0	0	0.0	182	32.5	178	31.8	200	35.7	0	0.0	560		178

GPA & LSAT Scores

	Full Time	Part Time	Total
# of apps	2,127	0	2,127
# admits	642	0	642
# of matrics	182	0	182
75% GPA	3.81	0.00	
25% GPA	3.55	0.00	
75% LSAT	171	0	
25% LSAT	167	0	

Tuition & Fees

	Resident	Non-resident
Full-Time	$25,527	$25,527
Part-Time	$0	$0

Living Expenses

Estimated living expenses for Singles		
Living on campus	Living off campus	Living at home
$14,505	$14,505	$14,505

Employment

	Total	%
Employment status known	180	98.9
Employment status unknown	2	1.1
Employed	173	96.1
Pursuing graduate degrees	7	3.9
Unemployed seeking employment	0	0.0
Unemployed not seeking employment	0	0.0
Type of Employment		
# employed in law firms	121	69.9
# employed in business & industry	11	6.4
# employed in government	2	1.2
# employed in public interest	2	1.2
# employed as judicial clerks	37	21.4
# employed in academia	0	0.0
Geographic Location		
# employed in state	67	38.7
# employed in foreign countries	0	0.0
# of states where employed	25	

Grants/Scholarships

	Full-time		Part-time		Total	
	#	%	#	%	#	%
Total # of Students	560		0		560	
Total # receiving grants	235	42.0	0	0.0	235	42.0
Less than 1/2 tuition	195	34.8	0	0.0	195	34.8
Half to full tuition	40	7.1	0	0.0	40	7.1
Full tuition	0	0.0	0	0.0	0	0.0
More than full tuition	0	0.0	0	0.0	0	0.0
Median Grant Amount	$8,000		$0			

Informational & Library Resources

# of volumes & volume equivalents	628,773	# of professional staff	9
# of titles	247,785	Hours per week with professional staff	57
# of active serial subscriptions	8,164	Hours per week without professional staff	33
Study seating capacity inside the library	445	# of student computer work stations for entire law school	47
Square feet of law library	74,002	# of additional networked connections	200
Square feet of law school (excl. Library)	85,259	Require Laptop Computer?	N

J.D. Attrition (from Prior Year)

	Academic	Other	TOTALS	
	#	#	#	%
1st Year	0	8	8	4.6%
2nd Year	0	0	0	0.0%
3rd Year	0	0	0	0.0%
4th Year	0	0	0	0.0%

Bar Passage Rates

Jurisdiction	Illinois			New York		
Exam	Sum 97	Win 98	Total	Sum 97	Win 98	Total
# from school taking bar for the first time	63	3	66	45	5	50
School's pass rate for all first-time takers	98%	67%	97%	93%	100%	94%
State's pass rate for all first-time takers	87%	80%	85%	78%	65%	76%

CINCINNATI, UNIVERSITY OF

P.O. Box 210040
Cincinnati, OH 45221-0040
(513)556-6805
http://www.law.uc.edu

ABA Approved Since 1923

The Basics

Type of School: Public — Term: Semester
Application deadline: 04/01
Application fee: $35
Financial Aid deadline: 03/01
Can first year start other than Fall? No
Student faculty ratio: 13.9 to 1
Does the University offer:
- housing restricted to law students? No
- graduate student housing for which law students are eligible? Yes

Faculty & Administrators

	Total		Men		Women		Minorities	
	Fall	Spr	Fall	Spr	Fall	Spr	Fall	Spr
Full-time	22	20	14	13	8	7	3	3
Other Full-Time	3	3	1	1	2	2	1	1
Deans, librarians, & others who teach > 1/2	1	1	0	0	1	1	0	0
Part-time	25	32	24	24	1	8	1	2
Total	51	56	39	38	12	18	5	6
Deans, librarians, & others who teach < 1/2	2	2	1	1	1	1	0	0

Curriculum

	Full time	Part time
Typical first-year section size	22	0
Is there typically a "small section" of the first year class, other than Legal Writing, taught by full-time faculty?	Yes	No
If yes, typical size offered last year	20	N/A
# of classroom course titles beyond 1st year curriculum	83	0
# of upper division courses, excluding seminars, with an enrollment:		
Under 25	51	0
25 - 49	20	0
50 - 74	5	0
75 - 99	3	0
100 +	1	0
# of seminars	22	0
# of seminar positions available	296	
# of seminar positions filled	235	0
# of positions available in simulation courses	196	
# of simulation positions filled	154	0
# of positions available in faculty supervised clinical courses	157	
# of fac. sup. clin. positions filled	157	0
# involved in field placements	126	0
# involved in law journals	64	0
# in moot court or trial competitions	39	0
# of credit hrs required to graduate	90	

J.D. Enrollment & Ethnicity

	Men		Women		Fl-Time		Pt-Time		1st Yr		2nd Yr		3rd Yr		4th Yr		Total		JD Degrees Awarded
	#	%	#	%	#	%	#	%	#	%	#	%	#	%	#	%	#	%	
African-American	16	8.9	23	12.2	39	10.7	0	0.0	17	14.3	13	10.7	9	7.1	0	0.0	39	10.6	7
American Indian	0	0.0	1	0.5	1	0.3	0	0.0	1	0.8	0	0.0	0	0.0	0	0.0	1	0.3	0
Asian American	4	2.2	1	0.5	5	1.4	0	0.0	2	1.7	3	2.5	0	0.0	0	0.0	5	1.4	0
Mexican American	3	1.7	0	0.0	3	0.8	0	0.0	2	1.7	1	0.8	0	0.0	0	0.0	3	0.8	0
Puerto Rican	3	1.7	1	0.5	4	1.1	0	0.0	3	2.5	0	0.0	1	0.8	0	0.0	4	1.1	0
Hispanic American	1	0.6	0	0.0	1	0.3	0	0.0	1	0.8	0	0.0	0	0.0	0	0.0	1	0.3	2
Total Minorities	27	15.0	26	13.8	53	14.5	0	0.0	26	21.8	17	13.9	10	7.9	0	0.0	53	14.4	9
Foreign Nationals	1	0.6	1	0.5	2	0.5	0	0.0	0	0.0	2	1.6	0	0.0	0	0.0	2	0.5	3
Caucasian	152	84.4	161	85.6	310	84.9	3	100.0	93	78.2	103	84.4	116	92.1	1	100.0	313	85.1	103
Total	180	48.9	188	51.1	365	99.2	3	0.8	119	32.3	122	33.2	126	34.2	1	0.3	368		115

GPA & LSAT Scores

	Full Time	Part Time	Total
# of apps	917	0	917
# admits	381	0	381
# of matrics	121	0	121
75% GPA	3.66	0.00	
25% GPA	3.01	0.00	
75% LSAT	162	0	
25% LSAT	154	0	

Tuition & Fees

	Resident	Non-resident
Full-Time	$7,704	$14,808
Part-Time	$0	$0

Living Expenses

Estimated living expenses for Singles		
Living on campus	Living off campus	Living at home
$10,454	$10,454	$10,454

Grants/Scholarships

	Full-time		Part-time		Total	
	#	%	#	%	#	%
Total # of Students	365		3		368	
Total # receiving grants	201	55.1	0	0.0	201	54.6
Less than 1/2 tuition	96	26.3	0	0.0	96	26.1
Half to full tuition	53	14.5	0	0.0	53	14.4
Full tuition	44	12.1	0	0.0	44	12.0
More than full tuition	8	2.2	0	0.0	8	2.2
Median Grant Amount	$4,000		$0			

Informational & Library Resources

# of volumes & volume equivalents	379,242	# of professional staff	12
# of titles	176,918	Hours per week with professional staff	74
# of active serial subscriptions	2,570	Hours per week without professional staff	33
Study seating capacity inside the library	401	# of student computer work stations for entire law school	53
Square feet of law library	49,227	# of additional networked connections	17
Square feet of law school (excl. Library)	48,836	Require Laptop Computer?	N

Employment

	Total	%
Employment status known	128	98.5
Employment status unknown	2	1.5
Employed	119	93.0
Pursuing graduate degrees	0	0.0
Unemployed seeking employment	7	5.5
Unemployed not seeking employment	2	1.6
Type of Employment		
# employed in law firms	65	54.6
# employed in business & industry	25	21.0
# employed in government	13	10.9
# employed in public interest	3	2.5
# employed as judicial clerks	12	10.1
# employed in academia	1	0.8
Geographic Location		
# employed in state	81	68.1
# employed in foreign countries	0	0.0
# of states where employed	20	

J.D. Attrition (from Prior Year)

	Academic	Other	TOTALS	
	#	#	#	%
1st Year	1	1	2	1.7%
2nd Year	0	0	0	0.0%
3rd Year	1	0	1	0.8%
4th Year	0	0	0	0.0%

Bar Passage Rates

Jurisdiction	Ohio		
Exam	Sum 97	Win 98	Total
# from school taking bar for the first time	97	6	103
School's pass rate for all first-time takers	95%	83%	94%
State's pass rate for all first-time takers	79%	75%	78%

CITY UNIVERSITY OF NEW YORK

65-21 Main Street
Flushing, NY 11367
(718)340-4200
http://web.law.cuny.edu

ABA Approved Since 1985

The Basics

Type of School: Public — Term: Semester
Application deadline: 03/15
Application fee: $40
Financial Aid deadline: 05/01
Can first year start other than Fall? Yes
Student faculty ratio: 11.4 to 1
Does the University offer:
- housing restricted to law students? No
- graduate student housing for which law students are eligible? No

Faculty & Administrators

	Total		Men		Women		Minorities	
	Fall	Spr	Fall	Spr	Fall	Spr	Fall	Spr
Full-time	27	27	12	12	15	15	12	12
Other Full-Time	4	4	1	1	3	3	1	1
Deans, librarians, & others who teach > 1/2	2	2	0	0	2	2	0	0
Part-time	12	14	5	4	7	10	2	3
Total	45	47	18	17	27	30	15	16
Deans, librarians, & others who teach < 1/2	2	2	1	1	1	1	0	0

Curriculum

	Full time	Part time
Typical first-year section size	80	0
Is there typically a "small section" of the first year class, other than Legal Writing, taught by full-time faculty?	Yes	No
If yes, typical size offered last year	20	N/A
# of classroom course titles beyond 1st year curriculum	66	0
# of upper division courses, excluding seminars, with an enrollment:		
Under 25	20	0
25 - 49	17	0
50 - 74	5	0
75 - 99	6	0
100 +	1	0
# of seminars	10	0
# of seminar positions available	240	
# of seminar positions filled	165	0
# of positions available in simulation courses	160	
# of simulation positions filled	136	0
# of positions available in faculty supervised clinical courses	130	
# of fac. sup. clin. positions filled	111	0
# involved in field placements	35	0
# involved in law journals	15	0
# in moot court or trial competitions	25	0
# of credit hrs required to graduate	91	

J.D. Enrollment & Ethnicity

	Men		Women		Fl-Time		Pt-Time		1st Yr		2nd Yr		3rd Yr		4th Yr		Total		JD Degrees Awarded
	#	%	#	%	#	%	#	%	#	%	#	%	#	%	#	%	#	%	
African-American	23	16.7	44	18.8	66	18.0	1	16.7	19	17.3	22	16.4	26	20.3	0	0.0	67	18.0	17
American Indian	2	1.4	1	0.4	3	0.8	0	0.0	1	0.9	2	1.5	0	0.0	0	0.0	3	0.8	1
Asian American	21	15.2	23	9.8	44	12.0	0	0.0	10	9.1	21	15.7	13	10.2	0	0.0	44	11.8	9
Mexican American	0	0.0	0	0.0	0	0.0	0	0.0	0	0.0	0	0.0	0	0.0	0	0.0	0	0.0	0
Puerto Rican	11	8.0	5	2.1	16	4.4	0	0.0	7	6.4	3	2.2	6	4.7	0	0.0	16	4.3	8
Hispanic American	11	8.0	25	10.7	35	9.6	1	16.7	16	14.5	12	9.0	8	6.3	0	0.0	36	9.7	6
Total Minorities	68	49.3	98	41.9	164	44.8	2	33.3	53	48.2	60	44.8	53	41.4	0	0.0	166	44.6	41
Foreign Nationals	2	1.4	6	2.6	8	2.2	0	0.0	3	2.7	2	1.5	3	2.3	0	0.0	8	2.2	0
Caucasian	68	49.3	130	55.6	194	53.0	4	66.7	54	49.1	72	53.7	72	56.3	0	0.0	198	53.2	98
Total	138	37.1	234	62.9	366	98.4	6	1.6	110	29.6	134	36.0	128	34.4	0	0.0	372		139

GPA & LSAT Scores

	Full Time	Part Time	Total
# of apps	1,281	0	1,281
# admits	497	0	497
# of matrics	103	0	103
75% GPA	3.41	0.00	
25% GPA	2.71	0.00	
75% LSAT	153	0	
25% LSAT	143	0	

Tuition & Fees

	Resident	Non-resident
Full-Time	$6,602	$9,832
Part-Time	$0	$0

Living Expenses

Estimated living expenses for Singles		
Living on campus	Living off campus	Living at home
N/A	$10,349	$5,302

Grants/Scholarships

	Full-time		Part-time		Total	
	#	%	#	%	#	%
Total # of Students	366		6		372	
Total # receiving grants	237	64.8	0	0.0	237	63.7
Less than 1/2 tuition	227	62.0	0	0.0	227	61.0
Half to full tuition	7	1.9	0	0.0	7	1.9
Full tuition	3	0.8	0	0.0	3	0.8
More than full tuition	0	0.0	0	0.0	0	0.0
Median Grant Amount	$1,225		$0			

Informational & Library Resources

# of volumes & volume equivalents	248,189	# of professional staff	8
# of titles	27,811	Hours per week with professional staff	49
# of active serial subscriptions	2,779	Hours per week without professional staff	8
Study seating capacity inside the library	397	# of student computer work stations for entire law school	75
Square feet of law library	34,545	# of additional networked connections	0
Square feet of law school (excl. Library)	61,907	Require Laptop Computer?	N

Employment

	Total	%
Employment status known	122	83.6
Employment status unknown	24	16.4
Employed	95	77.9
Pursuing graduate degrees	1	0.8
Unemployed seeking employment	19	15.6
Unemployed not seeking employment	7	5.7
Type of Employment		
# employed in law firms	27	28.4
# employed in business & industry	18	18.9
# employed in government	19	20.0
# employed in public interest	17	17.9
# employed as judicial clerks	6	6.3
# employed in academia	1	1.1
Geographic Location		
# employed in state	67	70.5
# employed in foreign countries	0	0.0
# of states where employed	7	

J.D. Attrition (from Prior Year)

	Academic	Other	TOTALS	
	#	#	#	%
1st Year	17	18	35	21%
2nd Year	7	3	10	7.4%
3rd Year	4	1	5	3.3%
4th Year	0	0	0	0.0%

Bar Passage Rates

Jurisdiction	New York		
Exam	Sum 97	Win 98	Total
# from school taking bar for the first time	110	7	117
School's pass rate for all first-time takers	46%	43%	46%
State's pass rate for all first-time takers	78%	65%	76%

CLEVELAND STATE UNIVERSITY

Cleveland-Marshall College of Law
1801 Euclid Avenue
Cleveland, OH 44115-2223
(216)687-2344
http://www.law.csuohio.edu

ABA Approved Since 1957

The Basics

Type of School: Public — Term: Semester

Application deadline: 04/01

Application fee: $35

Financial Aid deadline: 04/01

Can first year start other than Fall? No

Student faculty ratio: 17.7 to 1

Does the University offer:
- housing restricted to law students? Yes
- graduate student housing for which law students are eligible? Yes

Faculty & Administrators

	Total		Men		Women		Minorities	
	Fall	Spr	Fall	Spr	Fall	Spr	Fall	Spr
Full-time	35	34	24	23	11	11	5	4
Other Full-Time	8	8	4	4	4	4	0	0
Deans, librarians, & others who teach > 1/2	6	6	3	3	3	3	1	1
Part-time	29	36	21	31	8	5	2	2
Total	78	84	52	61	26	23	8	7
Deans, librarians, & others who teach < 1/2	4	4	3	3	1	1	0	0

Curriculum

	Full time	Part time
Typical first-year section size	64	49
Is there typically a "small section" of the first year class, other than Legal Writing, taught by full-time faculty?	No	No
If yes, typical size offered last year	N/A	N/A
# of classroom course titles beyond 1st year curriculum	47	64
# of upper division courses, excluding seminars, with an enrollment:		
Under 25	22	50
25 - 49	25	26
50 - 74	10	10
75 - 99	2	2
100 +	1	0
# of seminars	8	6
# of seminar positions available	259	
# of seminar positions filled	84	102
# of positions available in simulation courses	292	
# of simulation positions filled	131	108
# of positions available in faculty supervised clinical courses	40	
# of fac. sup. clin. positions filled	22	6
# involved in field placements	44	2
# involved in law journals	108	19
# in moot court or trial competitions	32	14
# of credit hrs required to graduate	87	

J.D. Enrollment & Ethnicity

	Men		Women		Fl-Time		Pt-Time		1st Yr		2nd Yr		3rd Yr		4th Yr		Total		JD Degrees Awarded
	#	%	#	%	#	%	#	%	#	%	#	%	#	%	#	%	#	%	
African-American	28	6.3	52	12.9	49	8.9	31	10.5	32	11.8	20	8.4	23	8.7	5	7.2	80	9.5	18
American Indian	1	0.2	1	0.2	2	0.4	0	0.0	1	0.4	1	0.4	0	0.0	0	0.0	2	0.2	1
Asian American	8	1.8	9	2.2	11	2.0	6	2.0	5	1.8	8	3.3	4	1.5	0	0.0	17	2.0	6
Mexican American	0	0.0	0	0.0	0	0.0	0	0.0	0	0.0	0	0.0	0	0.0	0	0.0	0	0.0	0
Puerto Rican	0	0.0	0	0.0	0	0.0	0	0.0	0	0.0	0	0.0	0	0.0	0	0.0	0	0.0	0
Hispanic American	4	0.9	9	2.2	12	2.2	1	0.3	6	2.2	4	1.7	3	1.1	0	0.0	13	1.5	3
Total Minorities	41	9.3	71	17.6	74	13.4	38	12.9	44	16.2	33	13.8	30	11.3	5	7.2	112	13.3	28
Foreign Nationals	6	1.4	7	1.7	13	2.4	0	0.0	7	2.6	6	2.5	0	0.0	0	0.0	13	1.5	0
Caucasian	395	89.4	325	80.6	464	84.2	256	87.1	221	81.3	200	83.7	235	88.7	64	92.8	720	85.2	232
Total	442	52.3	403	47.7	551	65.2	294	34.8	272	32.2	239	28.3	265	31.4	69	8.2	845		260

GPA & LSAT Scores

	Full Time	Part Time	Total
# of apps	837	305	1,142
# admits	470	153	623
# of matrics	169	107	276
75% GPA	3.44	3.32	
25% GPA	2.83	2.74	
75% LSAT	153	154	
25% LSAT	145	146	

Tuition & Fees

	Resident	Non-resident
Full-Time	$7,460	$14,920
Part-Time	$5,731	$11,462

Living Expenses

Estimated living expenses for Singles		
Living on campus	Living off campus	Living at home
$11,180	$11,180	$11,180

Grants/Scholarships

	Full-time		Part-time		Total	
	#	%	#	%	#	%
Total # of Students	551		294		845	
Total # receiving grants	196	35.6	69	23.5	265	31.4
Less than 1/2 tuition	144	26.1	48	16.3	192	22.7
Half to full tuition	45	8.2	20	6.8	65	7.7
Full tuition	7	1.3	1	0.3	8	0.9
More than full tuition	0	0.0	0	0.0	0	0.0
Median Grant Amount	$1,000		$1,000			

Informational & Library Resources

# of volumes & volume equivalents	436,850	# of professional staff	12
# of titles	124,195	Hours per week with professional staff	88
# of active serial subscriptions	3,131	Hours per week without professional staff	7
Study seating capacity inside the library	396	# of student computer work stations for entire law school	65
Square feet of law library	84,670	# of additional networked connections	232
Square feet of law school (excl. Library)	55,343	Require Laptop Computer?	N

Employment

	Total	%
Employment status known	235	97.5
Employment status unknown	6	2.5
Employed	199	84.7
Pursuing graduate degrees	3	1.3
Unemployed seeking employment	7	3.0
Unemployed not seeking employment	26	11.1
Type of Employment		
# employed in law firms	98	49.2
# employed in business & industry	42	21.1
# employed in government	29	14.6
# employed in public interest	6	3.0
# employed as judicial clerks	9	4.5
# employed in academia	5	2.5
Geographic Location		
# employed in state	135	67.8
# employed in foreign countries	0	0.0
# of states where employed	13	

J.D. Attrition (from Prior Year)

	Academic	Other	TOTALS	
	#	#	#	%
1st Year	14	28	42	15%
2nd Year	4	8	12	4.9%
3rd Year	2	5	7	2.5%
4th Year	0	1	1	1.4%

Bar Passage Rates

Jurisdiction	Ohio		
Exam	Sum 97	Win 98	Total
# from school taking bar for the first time	145	35	180
School's pass rate for all first-time takers	66%	60%	65%
State's pass rate for all first-time takers	79%	75%	78%

COLORADO, UNIVERSITY OF

Campus Box 401
Boulder, CO 80309-0401
(303)492-7203
http://www.colorado.edu/law

ABA Approved Since 1923

The Basics

Type of School: Public   Term: Semester

Application deadline: 02/15

Application fee: $45

Financial Aid deadline: 03/01

Can first year start other than Fall? No

Student faculty ratio: 13.6 to 1

Does the University offer:
- housing restricted to law students? No
- graduate student housing for which law students are eligible? Yes

Faculty & Administrators

	Total		Men		Women		Minorities	
	Fall	Spr	Fall	Spr	Fall	Spr	Fall	Spr
Full-time	30	27	25	22	5	5	5	4
Other Full-Time	3	3	1	1	2	2	0	0
Deans, librarians, & others who teach > 1/2	3	3	2	2	1	1	1	1
Part-time	16	20	13	14	3	6	1	3
Total	52	53	41	39	11	14	7	8
Deans, librarians, & others who teach < 1/2	3	3	1	1	2	2	0	0

Curriculum

	Full time	Part time
Typical first-year section size	70	0
Is there typically a "small section" of the first year class, other than Legal Writing, taught by full-time faculty?	Yes	No
If yes, typical size offered last year	31	N/A
# of classroom course titles beyond 1st year curriculum	86	0
# of upper division courses, excluding seminars, with an enrollment:		
Under 25	51	0
25 - 49	31	0
50 - 74	12	0
75 - 99	6	0
100 +	0	0
# of seminars	16	0
# of seminar positions available	198	
# of seminar positions filled	178	0
# of positions available in simulation courses	274	
# of simulation positions filled	263	0
# of positions available in faculty supervised clinical courses	104	
# of fac. sup. clin. positions filled	69	0
# involved in field placements	58	0
# involved in law journals	100	0
# in moot court or trial competitions	44	0
# of credit hrs required to graduate	89	

J.D. Enrollment & Ethnicity

	Men		Women		Fl-Time		Pt-Time		1st Yr		2nd Yr		3rd Yr		4th Yr		Total		JD Degrees Awarded
	#	%	#	%	#	%	#	%	#	%	#	%	#	%	#	%	#	%	
African-American	7	2.7	8	3.4	15	3.1	0	0.0	4	2.5	6	3.5	5	3.2	0	0.0	15	3.1	8
American Indian	4	1.6	10	4.3	13	2.7	1	50.0	7	4.3	4	2.4	3	1.9	0	0.0	14	2.9	7
Asian American	11	4.3	9	3.9	20	4.1	0	0.0	8	4.9	6	3.5	6	3.8	0	0.0	20	4.1	5
Mexican American	4	1.6	8	3.4	12	2.5	0	0.0	5	3.1	3	1.8	4	2.6	0	0.0	12	2.5	9
Puerto Rican	0	0.0	1	0.4	1	0.2	0	0.0	0	0.0	1	0.6	0	0.0	0	0.0	1	0.2	0
Hispanic American	9	3.5	6	2.6	15	3.1	0	0.0	4	2.5	7	4.1	4	2.6	0	0.0	15	3.1	7
Total Minorities	35	13.6	42	18.1	76	15.6	1	50.0	28	17.2	27	15.9	22	14.1	0	0.0	77	15.7	36
Foreign Nationals	0	0.0	1	0.4	1	0.2	0	0.0	0	0.0	0	0.0	1	0.6	0	0.0	1	0.2	0
Caucasian	222	86.4	189	81.5	410	84.2	1	50.0	135	82.8	143	84.1	133	85.3	0	0.0	411	84.0	133
Total	257	52.6	232	47.4	487	99.6	2	0.4	163	33.3	170	34.8	156	31.9	0	0.0	489		169

GPA & LSAT Scores

	Full Time	Part Time	Total
# of apps	1,731	0	1,731
# admits	592	0	592
# of matrics	167	0	167
75% GPA	3.68	0.00	
25% GPA	3.28	0.00	
75% LSAT	164	0	
25% LSAT	158	0	

Tuition & Fees

	Resident	Non-resident
Full-Time	$5,412	$17,086
Part-Time	$0	$0

Living Expenses

Estimated living expenses for Singles		
Living on campus	Living off campus	Living at home
$9,110	$12,134	$8,039

Grants/Scholarships

	Full-time		Part-time		Total	
	#	%	#	%	#	%
Total # of Students	487		2		489	
Total # receiving grants	246	50.5	0	0.0	246	50.3
Less than 1/2 tuition	159	32.6	0	0.0	159	32.5
Half to full tuition	30	6.2	0	0.0	30	6.1
Full tuition	47	9.7	0	0.0	47	9.6
More than full tuition	10	2.1	0	0.0	10	2.0
Median Grant Amount	$2,000		$0			

Informational & Library Resources

# of volumes & volume equivalents	369,571	# of professional staff	7
# of titles	128,471	Hours per week with professional staff	64
# of active serial subscriptions	3,969	Hours per week without professional staff	45
Study seating capacity inside the library	333	# of student computer work stations for entire law school	86
Square feet of law library	36,000	# of additional networked connections	0
Square feet of law school (excl. Library)	68,185	Require Laptop Computer?	N

Employment

	Total	%
Employment status known	150	92.6
Employment status unknown	12	7.4
Employed	131	87.3
Pursuing graduate degrees	0	0.0
Unemployed seeking employment	15	10.0
Unemployed not seeking employment	4	2.7
Type of Employment		
# employed in law firms	76	58.0
# employed in business & industry	15	11.5
# employed in government	17	13.0
# employed in public interest	8	6.1
# employed as judicial clerks	13	9.9
# employed in academia	1	0.8
Geographic Location		
# employed in state	99	75.6
# employed in foreign countries	1	0.8
# of states where employed	16	

J.D. Attrition (from Prior Year)

	Academic	Other	TOTALS	
	#	#	#	%
1st Year	0	6	6	3.3%
2nd Year	1	8	9	5.8%
3rd Year	0	0	0	0.0%
4th Year	0	0	0	0.0%

Bar Passage Rates

Jurisdiction	Colorado		
Exam	Sum 97	Win 98	Total
# from school taking bar for the first time	122	13	135
School's pass rate for all first-time takers	97%	54%	93%
State's pass rate for all first-time takers	83%	77%	81%

COLUMBIA UNIVERSITY

435 West 116th Street
New York, NY 10027
(212)854-2640
http://www.columbia.edu/cu/law

ABA Approved Since 1923

The Basics

Type of School: Private   Term: Semester

Application deadline: 02/15

Application fee: $65

Financial Aid deadline: 03/01

Can first year start other than Fall? No

Student faculty ratio: 15.6 to 1

Does the University offer:
- housing restricted to law students? Yes
- graduate student housing for which law students are eligible? Yes

Faculty & Administrators

	Total		Men		Women		Minorities	
	Fall	Spr	Fall	Spr	Fall	Spr	Fall	Spr
Full-time	59	55	44	43	15	12	5	5
Other Full-Time	10	10	5	5	5	5	0	0
Deans, librarians, & others who teach > 1/2	3	3	3	3	0	0	1	1
Part-time	41	61	35	52	6	9	2	5
Total	113	129	87	103	26	26	8	11
Deans, librarians, & others who teach < 1/2	4	4	1	1	3	3	0	0

Curriculum

	Full time	Part time
Typical first-year section size	115	0
Is there typically a "small section" of the first year class, other than Legal Writing, taught by full-time faculty?	Yes	No
If yes, typical size offered last year	30	N/A
# of classroom course titles beyond 1st year curriculum	81	0
# of upper division courses, excluding seminars, with an enrollment:		
Under 25	23	0
25 - 49	22	0
50 - 74	16	0
75 - 99	6	0
100 +	22	0
# of seminars	106	0
# of seminar positions available	1,902	
# of seminar positions filled	1,446	0
# of positions available in simulation courses	626	
# of simulation positions filled	613	0
# of positions available in faculty supervised clinical courses	136	
# of fac. sup. clin. positions filled	136	0
# involved in field placements	90	0
# involved in law journals	550	0
# in moot court or trial competitions	102	0
# of credit hrs required to graduate	83	

J.D. Enrollment & Ethnicity

	Men		Women		Fl-Time		Pt-Time		1st Yr		2nd Yr		3rd Yr		4th Yr		Total		JD Degrees Awarded
	#	%	#	%	#	%	#	%	#	%	#	%	#	%	#	%	#	%	
African-American	56	9.0	79	15.5	135	11.9	0	0.0	40	11.6	48	12.0	47	12.1	0	0.0	135	11.9	39
American Indian	2	0.3	5	1.0	7	0.6	0	0.0	2	0.6	3	0.8	2	0.5	0	0.0	7	0.6	1
Asian American	74	11.9	81	15.9	155	13.7	0	0.0	49	14.2	54	13.5	52	13.4	0	0.0	155	13.7	53
Mexican American	11	1.8	22	4.3	33	2.9	0	0.0	10	2.9	12	3.0	11	2.8	0	0.0	33	2.9	13
Puerto Rican	6	1.0	15	2.9	21	1.9	0	0.0	10	2.9	3	0.8	8	2.1	0	0.0	21	1.9	10
Hispanic American	18	2.9	12	2.3	30	2.7	0	0.0	9	2.6	12	3.0	9	2.3	0	0.0	30	2.7	8
Total Minorities	167	26.9	214	41.9	381	33.7	0	0.0	120	34.8	132	33.1	129	33.2	0	0.0	381	33.7	124
Foreign Nationals	39	6.3	26	5.1	65	5.7	0	0.0	27	7.8	22	5.5	16	4.1	0	0.0	65	5.7	10
Caucasian	415	66.8	271	53.0	686	60.6	0	0.0	198	57.4	245	61.4	243	62.6	0	0.0	686	60.6	221
Total	621	54.9	511	45.1	1132	100.0	0	0.0	345	30.5	399	35.2	388	34.3	0	0.0	1132		355

GPA & LSAT Scores

	Full Time	Part Time	Total
# of apps	5,719	0	5,719
# admits	1,099	0	1,099
# of matrics	345	0	345
75% GPA	3.74	0.00	
25% GPA	3.38	0.00	
75% LSAT	171	0	
25% LSAT	164	0	

Tuition & Fees

	Resident	Non-resident
Full-Time	$27,156	$27,156
Part-Time	$0	$0

Living Expenses

Estimated living expenses for Singles		
Living on campus	Living off campus	Living at home
$14,225	$14,225	$3,855

Grants/Scholarships

	Full-time		Part-time		Total	
	#	%	#	%	#	%
Total # of Students	1132		0		1132	
Total # receiving grants	375	33.1	0	0.0	375	33.1
Less than 1/2 tuition	345	30.5	0	0.0	345	30.5
Half to full tuition	30	2.7	0	0.0	30	2.7
Full tuition	0	0.0	0	0.0	0	0.0
More than full tuition	0	0.0	0	0.0	0	0.0
Median Grant Amount	$10,015		$0			

Informational & Library Resources

# of volumes & volume equivalents	980,461	# of professional staff	19
# of titles	339,501	Hours per week with professional staff	74
# of active serial subscriptions	7,356	Hours per week without professional staff	28
Study seating capacity inside the library	417	# of student computer work stations for entire law school	130
Square feet of law library	68,408	# of additional networked connections	644
Square feet of law school (excl. Library)	112,788	Require Laptop Computer?	N

Employment

	Total	%
Employment status known	340	98.3
Employment status unknown	6	1.7
Employed	336	98.8
Pursuing graduate degrees	3	0.9
Unemployed seeking employment	1	0.3
Unemployed not seeking employment	0	0.0
Type of Employment		
# employed in law firms	232	69.0
# employed in business & industry	11	3.3
# employed in government	13	3.9
# employed in public interest	8	2.4
# employed as judicial clerks	71	21.1
# employed in academia	4	1.2
Geographic Location		
# employed in state	231	68.7
# employed in foreign countries	6	1.8
# of states where employed	23	

J.D. Attrition (from Prior Year)

	Academic	Other	TOTALS	
	#	#	#	%
1st Year	0	3	3	0.8%
2nd Year	0	7	7	1.8%
3rd Year	0	0	0	0.0%
4th Year	0	0	0	0.0%

Bar Passage Rates

Jurisdiction	New York		
Exam	Sum 97	Win 98	Total
# from school taking bar for the first time	273	16	289
School's pass rate for all first-time takers	95%	81%	94%
State's pass rate for all first-time takers	78%	65%	76%

CONNECTICUT, UNIVERSITY OF

55 Elizabeth Street
Hartford, CT 06105-2296
(860)570-5127
http://www.law.uconn.edu

ABA Approved Since 1933

The Basics

Type of School: Public Term: Semester

Application deadline: 04/01

Application fee: $30

Financial Aid deadline: 04/01

Can first year start other than Fall? No

Student faculty ratio: 12.2 to 1

Does the University offer:
- housing restricted to law students? No
- graduate student housing for which law students are eligible? No

Faculty & Administrators

	Total		Men		Women		Minorities	
	Fall	Spr	Fall	Spr	Fall	Spr	Fall	Spr
Full-time	35	34	27	28	8	6	2	2
Other Full-Time	4	4	2	2	2	2	0	0
Deans, librarians, & others who teach > 1/2	1	1	1	1	0	0	0	0
Part-time	35	27	30	21	5	6	1	0
Total	75	66	60	52	15	14	3	2
Deans, librarians, & others who teach < 1/2	2	2	1	1	1	1	0	0

Curriculum

	Full time	Part time
Typical first-year section size	68	55
Is there typically a "small section" of the first year class, other than Legal Writing, taught by full-time faculty?	Yes	Yes
If yes, typical size offered last year	28	27
# of classroom course titles beyond 1st year curriculum	73	36
# of upper division courses, excluding seminars, with an enrollment:		
Under 25	37	10
25 - 49	9	10
50 - 74	14	7
75 - 99	0	0
100 +	0	0
# of seminars	35	9
# of seminar positions available	688	
# of seminar positions filled	466	142
# of positions available in simulation courses	88	
# of simulation positions filled	47	34
# of positions available in faculty supervised clinical courses	135	
# of fac. sup. clin. positions filled	94	14
# involved in field placements	44	11
# involved in law journals	77	7
# in moot court or trial competitions	5	0
# of credit hrs required to graduate	86	

J.D. Enrollment & Ethnicity

	Men		Women		Fl-Time		Pt-Time		1st Yr		2nd Yr		3rd Yr		4th Yr		Total		JD Degrees Awarded
	#	%	#	%	#	%	#	%	#	%	#	%	#	%	#	%	#	%	
African-American	14	4.5	14	5.2	17	4.1	11	6.8	9	4.8	7	4.1	10	5.3	2	6.3	28	4.9	13
American Indian	0	0.0	2	0.7	2	0.5	0	0.0	0	0.0	1	0.6	1	0.5	0	0.0	2	0.3	1
Asian American	18	5.8	16	6.0	31	7.5	3	1.9	11	5.9	13	7.7	10	5.3	0	0.0	34	5.9	8
Mexican American	0	0.0	2	0.7	2	0.5	0	0.0	1	0.5	1	0.6	0	0.0	0	0.0	2	0.3	2
Puerto Rican	4	1.3	6	2.2	7	1.7	3	1.9	5	2.7	1	0.6	3	1.6	1	3.1	10	1.7	2
Hispanic American	7	2.3	5	1.9	8	1.9	4	2.5	2	1.1	7	4.1	3	1.6	0	0.0	12	2.1	0
Total Minorities	43	14.0	45	16.9	67	16.2	21	13.0	28	15.0	30	17.8	27	14.4	3	9.4	88	15.3	26
Foreign Nationals	0	0.0	0	0.0	0	0.0	0	0.0	0	0.0	0	0.0	0	0.0	0	0.0	0	0.0	0
Caucasian	265	86.0	222	83.1	346	83.8	141	87.0	159	85.0	139	82.2	160	85.6	29	90.6	487	84.7	164
Total	308	53.6	267	46.4	413	71.8	162	28.2	187	32.5	169	29.4	187	32.5	32	5.6	575		190

GPA & LSAT Scores

	Full Time	Part Time	Total
# of apps	936	429	1,365
# admits	367	189	556
# of matrics	129	61	190
75% GPA	3.54	3.40	
25% GPA	3.08	2.85	
75% LSAT	161	157	
25% LSAT	157	154	

Tuition & Fees

	Resident	Non-resident
Full-Time	$10,984	$22,774
Part-Time	$7,690	$15,910

Living Expenses

Estimated living expenses for Singles		
Living on campus	Living off campus	Living at home
N/A	$12,468	$6,490

Grants/Scholarships

	Full-time		Part-time		Total	
	#	%	#	%	#	%
Total # of Students	413		162		575	
Total # receiving grants	202	48.9	0	0.0	202	35.1
Less than 1/2 tuition	121	29.3	0	0.0	121	21.0
Half to full tuition	54	13.1	0	0.0	54	9.4
Full tuition	2	0.5	0	0.0	2	0.3
More than full tuition	25	6.1	0	0.0	25	4.3
Median Grant Amount	$6,200		$0			

Informational & Library Resources

# of volumes & volume equivalents	461,903	# of professional staff	17
# of titles	148,606	Hours per week with professional staff	70
# of active serial subscriptions	6,194	Hours per week without professional staff	22
Study seating capacity inside the library	747	# of student computer work stations for entire law school	55
Square feet of law library	97,724	# of additional networked connections	396
Square feet of law school (excl. Library)	60,810	Require Laptop Computer?	N

Employment

	Total	%
Employment status known	194	99.0
Employment status unknown	2	1.0
Employed	180	92.8
Pursuing graduate degrees	2	1.0
Unemployed seeking employment	11	5.7
Unemployed not seeking employment	1	0.5
Type of Employment		
# employed in law firms	89	49.4
# employed in business & industry	49	27.2
# employed in government	20	11.1
# employed in public interest	6	3.3
# employed as judicial clerks	15	8.3
# employed in academia	1	0.6
Geographic Location		
# employed in state	140	77.8
# employed in foreign countries	2	1.1
# of states where employed	12	

J.D. Attrition (from Prior Year)

	Academic	Other	TOTALS	
	#	#	#	%
1st Year	0	17	17	8.9%
2nd Year	0	1	1	0.5%
3rd Year	0	1	1	0.5%
4th Year	0	0	0	0.0%

Bar Passage Rates

Jurisdiction	Connecticut		
Exam	Sum 97	Win 98	Total
# from school taking bar for the first time	141	21	162
School's pass rate for all first-time takers	90%	81%	89%
State's pass rate for all first-time takers	85%	81%	84%

CORNELL LAW SCHOOL

Myron Taylor Hall
Ithaca, NY 14853-4901
(607)255-3527
http://www.law.cornell.edu/admit/admit.h

ABA Approved Since 1923

The Basics

Type of School: Private   Term: Semester
Application deadline: 02/01
Application fee: $65
Financial Aid deadline: 03/15
Can first year start other than Fall? No
Student faculty ratio: 11.8 to 1
Does the University offer:
- housing restricted to law students? Yes
- graduate student housing for which law students are eligible? Yes

Faculty & Administrators

	Total		Men		Women		Minorities	
	Fall	Spr	Fall	Spr	Fall	Spr	Fall	Spr
Full-time	41	35	30	25	11	10	3	2
Other Full-Time	2	0	1	0	1	0	0	0
Deans, librarians, & others who teach > 1/2	1	1	1	0	0	1	0	0
Part-time	8	19	8	18	0	1	0	1
Total	52	55	40	43	12	12	3	3
Deans, librarians, & others who teach < 1/2	7	7	5	5	2	2	0	0

Curriculum

	Full time	Part time
Typical first-year section size	96	0
Is there typically a "small section" of the first year class, other than Legal Writing, taught by full-time faculty?	Yes	No
If yes, typical size offered last year	27	N/A
# of classroom course titles beyond 1st year curriculum	120	0
# of upper division courses, excluding seminars, with an enrollment:		
Under 25	22	0
25 - 49	16	0
50 - 74	13	0
75 - 99	9	0
100 +	3	0
# of seminars	34	0
# of seminar positions available	533	
# of seminar positions filled	473	0
# of positions available in simulation courses	154	
# of simulation positions filled	129	0
# of positions available in faculty supervised clinical courses	73	
# of fac. sup. clin. positions filled	69	0
# involved in field placements	0	0
# involved in law journals	206	0
# in moot court or trial competitions	78	0
# of credit hrs required to graduate	84	

J.D. Enrollment & Ethnicity

	Men		Women		Fl-Time		Pt-Time		1st Yr		2nd Yr		3rd Yr		4th Yr		Total		JD Degrees Awarded
	#	%	#	%	#	%	#	%	#	%	#	%	#	%	#	%	#	%	
African-American	13	4.3	26	10.8	39	7.2	0	0.0	12	6.3	13	7.2	14	8.0	0	0.0	39	7.2	13
American Indian	6	2.0	6	2.5	12	2.2	0	0.0	3	1.6	5	2.8	4	2.3	0	0.0	12	2.2	5
Asian American	39	12.9	38	15.8	77	14.2	0	0.0	29	15.3	22	12.2	26	14.9	0	0.0	77	14.2	16
Mexican American	3	1.0	4	1.7	7	1.3	0	0.0	1	0.5	3	1.7	3	1.7	0	0.0	7	1.3	3
Puerto Rican	2	0.7	3	1.3	5	0.9	0	0.0	2	1.1	2	1.1	1	0.6	0	0.0	5	0.9	6
Hispanic American	8	2.6	2	0.8	10	1.8	0	0.0	2	1.1	5	2.8	3	1.7	0	0.0	10	1.8	3
Total Minorities	71	23.4	79	32.9	150	27.6	0	0.0	49	25.9	50	27.8	51	29.3	0	0.0	150	27.6	46
Foreign Nationals	10	3.3	10	4.2	20	3.7	0	0.0	7	3.7	9	5.0	4	2.3	0	0.0	20	3.7	8
Caucasian	222	73.3	151	62.9	373	68.7	0	0.0	133	70.4	121	67.2	119	68.4	0	0.0	373	68.7	128
Total	303	55.8	240	44.2	543	100.0	0	0.0	189	34.8	180	33.1	174	32.0	0	0.0	543		182

GPA & LSAT Scores

	Full Time	Part Time	Total
# of apps	3,014	0	3,014
# admits	863	0	863
# of matrics	189	0	189
75% GPA	3.72	0.00	
25% GPA	3.37	0.00	
75% LSAT	166	0	
25% LSAT	163	0	

Tuition & Fees

	Resident	Non-resident
Full-Time	$24,148	$24,148
Part-Time	$0	$0

Living Expenses

Estimated living expenses for Singles		
Living on campus	Living off campus	Living at home
$12,100	$12,100	$12,100

Employment

	Total	%
Employment status known	187	97.4
Employment status unknown	5	2.6
Employed	183	97.9
Pursuing graduate degrees	2	1.1
Unemployed seeking employment	2	1.1
Unemployed not seeking employment	0	0.0
Type of Employment		
# employed in law firms	122	66.7
# employed in business & industry	13	7.1
# employed in government	6	3.3
# employed in public interest	5	2.7
# employed as judicial clerks	32	17.5
# employed in academia	0	0.0
Geographic Location		
# employed in state	62	33.9
# employed in foreign countries	3	1.6
# of states where employed	24	

Grants/Scholarships

	Full-time		Part-time		Total	
	#	%	#	%	#	%
Total # of Students	543		0		543	
Total # receiving grants	217	40.0	0	0.0	217	40.0
Less than 1/2 tuition	174	32.0	0	0.0	174	32.0
Half to full tuition	43	7.9	0	0.0	43	7.9
Full tuition	0	0.0	0	0.0	0	0.0
More than full tuition	0	0.0	0	0.0	0	0.0
Median Grant Amount	$9,600		$0			

Informational & Library Resources

# of volumes & volume equivalents	600,442	# of professional staff	7
# of titles	175,914	Hours per week with professional staff	61
# of active serial subscriptions	6,238	Hours per week without professional staff	24
Study seating capacity inside the library	407	# of student computer work stations for entire law school	65
Square feet of law library	64,360	# of additional networked connections	8
Square feet of law school (excl. Library)	54,363	Require Laptop Computer?	N

J.D. Attrition (from Prior Year)

	Academic	Other	TOTALS	
	#	#	#	%
1st Year	0	5	5	2.8%
2nd Year	0	1	1	0.5%
3rd Year	0	1	1	0.6%
4th Year	0	0	0	0.0%

Bar Passage Rates

Jurisdiction	New York			California		
Exam	Sum 97	Win 98	Total	Sum 97	Win 98	Total
# from school taking bar for the first time	105	5	110	22	0	22
School's pass rate for all first-time takers	95%	80%	95%	77%		77%
State's pass rate for all first-time takers	78%	65%	76%	75%	57%	71%

CREIGHTON UNIVERSITY

2500 California Plaza
Omaha, NE 68178
(402)280-2872
http://www.creighton.edu/culaw

ABA Approved Since 1924

The Basics

Type of School: Private — Term: Semester
Application deadline: 05/01
Application fee: $40
Financial Aid deadline: 07/01
Can first year start other than Fall? No
Student faculty ratio: 15.9 to 1
Does the University offer:
- housing restricted to law students? No
- graduate student housing for which law students are eligible? Yes

Faculty & Administrators

	Total		Men		Women		Minorities	
	Fall	Spr	Fall	Spr	Fall	Spr	Fall	Spr
Full-time	22	23	16	16	6	7	1	1
Other Full-Time	0	0	0	0	0	0	0	0
Deans, librarians, & others who teach > 1/2	5	5	2	2	3	3	0	0
Part-time	25	29	15	19	10	10	2	2
Total	52	57	33	37	19	20	3	3
Deans, librarians, & others who teach < 1/2	1	1	1	1	0	0	0	0

Curriculum

	Full time	Part time
Typical first-year section size	76	0
Is there typically a "small section" of the first year class, other than Legal Writing, taught by full-time faculty?	Yes	No
If yes, typical size offered last year	25	N/A
# of classroom course titles beyond 1st year curriculum	65	0
# of upper division courses, excluding seminars, with an enrollment:		
Under 25	44	0
25 - 49	22	0
50 - 74	12	0
75 - 99	5	0
100 +	0	0
# of seminars	9	0
# of seminar positions available	176	
# of seminar positions filled	173	0
# of positions available in simulation courses	363	
# of simulation positions filled	344	0
# of positions available in faculty supervised clinical courses	20	
# of fac. sup. clin. positions filled	15	0
# involved in field placements	59	0
# involved in law journals	45	0
# in moot court or trial competitions	127	0
# of credit hrs required to graduate	94	

J.D. Enrollment & Ethnicity

	Men		Women		Fl-Time		Pt-Time		1st Yr		2nd Yr		3rd Yr		4th Yr		Total		JD Degrees Awarded
	#	%	#	%	#	%	#	%	#	%	#	%	#	%	#	%	#	%	
African-American	2	0.8	7	4.0	8	2.0	1	6.7	3	2.1	3	2.2	3	2.1	0	0.0	9	2.1	4
American Indian	2	0.8	1	0.6	3	0.7	0	0.0	0	0.0	2	1.4	1	0.7	0	0.0	3	0.7	0
Asian American	3	1.2	4	2.3	7	1.7	0	0.0	1	0.7	1	0.7	5	3.5	0	0.0	7	1.7	3
Mexican American	4	1.6	3	1.7	7	1.7	0	0.0	2	1.4	3	2.2	2	1.4	0	0.0	7	1.7	0
Puerto Rican	0	0.0	0	0.0	0	0.0	0	0.0	0	0.0	0	0.0	0	0.0	0	0.0	0	0.0	0
Hispanic American	5	2.0	8	4.6	13	3.2	0	0.0	4	2.8	5	3.6	4	2.8	0	0.0	13	3.1	5
Total Minorities	16	6.4	23	13.3	38	9.3	1	6.7	10	6.9	14	10.1	15	10.6	0	0.0	39	9.2	12
Foreign Nationals	0	0.0	0	0.0	0	0.0	0	0.0	0	0.0	0	0.0	0	0.0	0	0.0	0	0.0	0
Caucasian	235	93.6	150	86.7	371	90.7	14	93.3	134	93.1	125	89.9	126	89.4	0	0.0	385	90.8	126
Total	251	59.2	173	40.8	409	96.5	15	3.5	144	34.0	139	32.8	141	33.3	0	0.0	424		138

GPA & LSAT Scores

	Full Time	Part Time	Total
# of apps	724	18	742
# admits	478	7	485
# of matrics	137	4	141
75% GPA	3.42	3.92	
25% GPA	2.74	3.01	
75% LSAT	153	158	
25% LSAT	148	153	

Tuition & Fees

	Resident	Non-resident
Full-Time	$16,220	$16,220
Part-Time	$8,456	$8,456

Living Expenses

Estimated living expenses for Singles		
Living on campus	Living off campus	Living at home
$11,270	$11,270	$11,270

Employment

	Total	%
Employment status known	155	97.5
Employment status unknown	4	2.5
Employed	134	86.5
Pursuing graduate degrees	9	5.8
Unemployed seeking employment	3	1.9
Unemployed not seeking employment	9	5.8
Type of Employment		
# employed in law firms	68	50.7
# employed in business & industry	33	24.6
# employed in government	15	11.2
# employed in public interest	5	3.7
# employed as judicial clerks	10	7.5
# employed in academia	1	0.7
Geographic Location		
# employed in state	68	50.7
# employed in foreign countries	0	0.0
# of states where employed	23	

Grants/Scholarships

	Full-time		Part-time		Total	
	#	%	#	%	#	%
Total # of Students	409		15		424	
Total # receiving grants	143	35.0	1	6.7	144	34.0
Less than 1/2 tuition	77	18.8	1	6.7	78	18.4
Half to full tuition	49	12.0	0	0.0	49	11.6
Full tuition	16	3.9	0	0.0	16	3.8
More than full tuition	1	0.2	0	0.0	1	0.2
Median Grant Amount	$7,000		$394			

Informational & Library Resources

# of volumes & volume equivalents	245,920	# of professional staff	6
# of titles	36,912	Hours per week with professional staff	68
# of active serial subscriptions	4,165	Hours per week without professional staff	36
Study seating capacity inside the library	418	# of student computer work stations for entire law school	57
Square feet of law library	47,964	# of additional networked connections	66
Square feet of law school (excl. Library)	52,250	Require Laptop Computer?	N

J.D. Attrition (from Prior Year)

	Academic	Other	TOTALS	
	#	#	#	%
1st Year	7	14	21	13%
2nd Year	0	2	2	1.3%
3rd Year	0	0	0	0.0%
4th Year	0	0	0	0.0%

Bar Passage Rates

Jurisdiction	Nebraska			Iowa		
Exam	Sum 97	Win 98	Total	Sum 97	Win 98	Total
# from school taking bar for the first time	73	0	73	11	2	13
School's pass rate for all first-time takers	89%		89%	100%	100%	100%
State's pass rate for all first-time takers	88%	73%	87%	86%	83%	85%

DAYTON, UNIVERSITY OF

300 College Park Ave.
Dayton, OH 45469-2772
(937)229-3211
http://www.udayton.edu/~law

ABA Approved Since 1975

The Basics

Type of School: Private   Term: Semester
Application deadline: 05/01
Application fee: $40
Financial Aid deadline: 03/01
Can first year start other than Fall? No
Student faculty ratio: 20.8 to 1
Does the University offer:
- housing restricted to law students? Yes
- graduate student housing for which law students are eligible? Yes

Curriculum

	Full time	Part time
Typical first-year section size	90	0
Is there typically a "small section" of the first year class, other than Legal Writing, taught by full-time faculty?	No	No
If yes, typical size offered last year	N/A	N/A
# of classroom course titles beyond 1st year curriculum	67	0
# of upper division courses, excluding seminars, with an enrollment:		
Under 25	51	0
25 - 49	11	0
50 - 74	17	0
75 - 99	9	0
100 +	0	0
# of seminars	10	0
# of seminar positions available	200	
# of seminar positions filled	106	0
# of positions available in simulation courses	290	
# of simulation positions filled	216	0
# of positions available in faculty supervised clinical courses	70	
# of fac. sup. clin. positions filled	55	0
# involved in field placements	25	0
# involved in law journals	50	0
# in moot court or trial competitions	33	0
# of credit hrs required to graduate	87	

Faculty & Administrators

	Total		Men		Women		Minorities	
	Fall	Spr	Fall	Spr	Fall	Spr	Fall	Spr
Full-time	20	19	13	13	7	6	1	0
Other Full-Time	5	5	1	1	4	4	1	1
Deans, librarians, & others who teach > 1/2	2	2	2	2	0	0	0	0
Part-time	15	18	8	14	7	4	1	1
Total	42	44	24	30	18	14	3	2
Deans, librarians, & others who teach < 1/2	0	0	0	0	0	0	0	0

J.D. Enrollment & Ethnicity

	Men		Women		Fl-Time		Pt-Time		1st Yr		2nd Yr		3rd Yr		4th Yr		Total		JD Degrees Awarded
	#	%	#	%	#	%	#	%	#	%	#	%	#	%	#	%	#	%	
African-American	18	6.5	32	14.4	50	10.0	0	0.0	23	12.3	12	8.3	15	8.9	0	0.0	50	10.0	9
American Indian	1	0.4	1	0.5	2	0.4	0	0.0	0	0.0	1	0.7	1	0.6	0	0.0	2	0.4	0
Asian American	11	4.0	9	4.1	20	4.0	0	0.0	9	4.8	7	4.9	4	2.4	0	0.0	20	4.0	2
Mexican American	0	0.0	0	0.0	0	0.0	0	0.0	0	0.0	0	0.0	0	0.0	0	0.0	0	0.0	0
Puerto Rican	0	0.0	0	0.0	0	0.0	0	0.0	0	0.0	0	0.0	0	0.0	0	0.0	0	0.0	0
Hispanic American	14	5.0	9	4.1	23	4.6	0	0.0	10	5.3	6	4.2	7	4.1	0	0.0	23	4.6	5
Total Minorities	44	15.8	51	23.0	95	19.0	0	0.0	42	22.5	26	18.1	27	16.0	0	0.0	95	19.0	16
Foreign Nationals	1	0.4	1	0.5	2	0.4	0	0.0	0	0.0	1	0.7	1	0.6	0	0.0	2	0.4	0
Caucasian	233	83.8	170	76.6	403	80.6	0	0.0	145	77.5	117	81.3	141	83.4	0	0.0	403	80.6	123
Total	278	55.6	222	44.4	500	100.0	0	0.0	187	37.4	144	28.8	169	33.8	0	0.0	500		139

GPA & LSAT Scores

	Full Time	Part Time	Total
# of apps	1,178	0	1,178
# admits	718	0	718
# of matrics	187	0	187
75% GPA	3.47	0.00	
25% GPA	2.98	0.00	
75% LSAT	153	0	
25% LSAT	146	0	

Tuition & Fees

	Resident	Non-resident
Full-Time	$18,880	$18,880
Part-Time	$0	$0

Living Expenses

Estimated living expenses for Singles		
Living on campus	Living off campus	Living at home
$8,800	$8,800	$8,800

Employment

	Total	%
Employment status known	152	96.8
Employment status unknown	5	3.2
Employed	135	88.8
Pursuing graduate degrees	1	0.7
Unemployed seeking employment	12	7.9
Unemployed not seeking employment	4	2.6
Type of Employment		
# employed in law firms	72	53.3
# employed in business & industry	25	18.5
# employed in government	30	22.2
# employed in public interest	2	1.5
# employed as judicial clerks	5	3.7
# employed in academia	1	0.7
Geographic Location		
# employed in state	67	49.6
# employed in foreign countries	0	0.0
# of states where employed	24	

Grants/Scholarships

	Full-time		Part-time		Total	
	#	%	#	%	#	%
Total # of Students	500		0		500	
Total # receiving grants	272	54.4	0	0.0	272	54.4
Less than 1/2 tuition	116	23.2	0	0.0	116	23.2
Half to full tuition	146	29.2	0	0.0	146	29.2
Full tuition	10	2.0	0	0.0	10	2.0
More than full tuition	0	0.0	0	0.0	0	0.0
Median Grant Amount	$9,558		$0			

Informational & Library Resources

# of volumes & volume equivalents	262,739	# of professional staff	6
# of titles	36,940	Hours per week with professional staff	70
# of active serial subscriptions	4,405	Hours per week without professional staff	32
Study seating capacity inside the library	501	# of student computer work stations for entire law school	72
Square feet of law library	46,130	# of additional networked connections	1200
Square feet of law school (excl. Library)	78,401	Require Laptop Computer?	N

J.D. Attrition (from Prior Year)

	Academic	Other	TOTALS	
	#	#	#	%
1st Year	14	21	35	20%
2nd Year	4	0	4	2.3%
3rd Year	0	0	0	0.0%
4th Year	0	0	0	0.0%

Bar Passage Rates

Jurisdiction	Ohio		
Exam	Sum 97	Win 98	Total
# from school taking bar for the first time	64	7	71
School's pass rate for all first-time takers	75%	86%	76%
State's pass rate for all first-time takers	79%	75%	78%

DENVER, UNIVERSITY OF

7039 East 18th Street
Denver, CO 80220
(303)871-6000
gopher://gopher.cair.du.edu/1

ABA Approved Since 1928

The Basics

Type of School: Private — Term: Semester

Application deadline: 03/01

Application fee: $45

Financial Aid deadline: 02/15

Can first year start other than Fall? No

Student faculty ratio: 25.3 to 1

Does the University offer:
- housing restricted to law students? Yes
- graduate student housing for which law students are eligible? Yes

Faculty & Administrators

	Total		Men		Women		Minorities	
	Fall	Spr	Fall	Spr	Fall	Spr	Fall	Spr
Full-time	31	35	23	26	8	9	3	3
Other Full-Time	4	4	0	0	4	4	0	0
Deans, librarians, & others who teach > 1/2	2	2	2	2	0	0	2	2
Part-time	72	60	55	42	17	18	7	8
Total	109	101	80	70	29	31	12	13
Deans, librarians, & others who teach < 1/2	1	1	0	0	1	1	0	0

Curriculum

	Full time	Part time
Typical first-year section size	85	90
Is there typically a "small section" of the first year class, other than Legal Writing, taught by full-time faculty?	No	No
If yes, typical size offered last year	N/A	N/A
# of classroom course titles beyond 1st year curriculum	71	64
# of upper division courses, excluding seminars, with an enrollment:		
Under 25	45	47
25 - 49	12	18
50 - 74	16	6
75 - 99	10	2
100 +	3	2
# of seminars	9	7
# of seminar positions available	315	
# of seminar positions filled	117	102
# of positions available in simulation courses	370	
# of simulation positions filled	138	197
# of positions available in faculty supervised clinical courses	252	
# of fac. sup. clin. positions filled	78	25
# involved in field placements	312	99
# involved in law journals	150	22
# in moot court or trial competitions	50	37
# of credit hrs required to graduate	90	

J.D. Enrollment & Ethnicity

	Men		Women		Fl-Time		Pt-Time		1st Yr		2nd Yr		3rd Yr		4th Yr		Total		JD Degrees Awarded
	#	%	#	%	#	%	#	%	#	%	#	%	#	%	#	%	#	%	
African-American	6	1.2	8	1.5	7	0.9	7	2.4	7	2.1	2	0.7	5	1.5	0	0.0	14	1.3	4
American Indian	3	0.6	6	1.1	5	0.7	4	1.4	4	1.2	1	0.3	2	0.6	2	2.7	9	0.9	3
Asian American	18	3.7	15	2.7	22	2.9	11	3.8	10	3.0	9	3.0	12	3.6	2	2.7	33	3.2	17
Mexican American	0	0.0	0	0.0	0	0.0	0	0.0	0	0.0	0	0.0	0	0.0	0	0.0	0	0.0	0
Puerto Rican	0	0.0	0	0.0	0	0.0	0	0.0	0	0.0	0	0.0	0	0.0	0	0.0	0	0.0	0
Hispanic American	16	3.3	21	3.8	27	3.6	10	3.4	12	3.6	11	3.6	13	4.0	1	1.3	37	3.6	19
Total Minorities	43	8.7	50	9.1	61	8.1	32	11.0	33	9.9	23	7.5	32	9.7	5	6.7	93	8.9	43
Foreign Nationals	5	1.0	3	0.5	7	0.9	1	0.3	0	0.0	7	2.3	1	0.3	0	0.0	8	0.8	1
Caucasian	444	90.2	496	90.3	683	90.9	257	88.6	299	90.1	275	90.2	296	90.0	70	93.3	940	90.3	264
Total	492	47.3	549	52.7	751	72.1	290	27.9	332	31.9	305	29.3	329	31.6	75	7.2	1041		308

GPA & LSAT Scores

	Full Time	Part Time	Total
# of apps	1,446	237	1,683
# admits	926	173	1,099
# of matrics	237	96	333
75% GPA	3.42	3.50	
25% GPA	2.85	2.77	
75% LSAT	157	154	
25% LSAT	151	149	

Tuition & Fees

	Resident	Non-resident
Full-Time	$18,780	$18,780
Part-Time	$14,085	$14,085

Living Expenses

Estimated living expenses for Singles		
Living on campus	Living off campus	Living at home
$11,893	$11,893	$11,893

Employment

	Total	%
Employment status known	293	93.0
Employment status unknown	22	7.0
Employed	273	93.2
Pursuing graduate degrees	12	4.1
Unemployed seeking employment	4	1.4
Unemployed not seeking employment	4	1.4
Type of Employment		
# employed in law firms	145	53.1
# employed in business & industry	56	20.5
# employed in government	44	16.1
# employed in public interest	7	2.6
# employed as judicial clerks	17	6.2
# employed in academia	4	1.5
Geographic Location		
# employed in state	215	78.8
# employed in foreign countries	0	0.0
# of states where employed	22	

Grants/Scholarships

	Full-time		Part-time		Total	
	#	%	#	%	#	%
Total # of Students	751		290		1041	
Total # receiving grants	202	26.9	55	19.0	257	24.7
Less than 1/2 tuition	138	18.4	33	11.4	171	16.4
Half to full tuition	36	4.8	16	5.5	52	5.0
Full tuition	28	3.7	6	2.1	34	3.3
More than full tuition	0	0.0	0	0.0	0	0.0
Median Grant Amount	$6,000		$5,000			

Informational & Library Resources

# of volumes & volume equivalents	321,592	# of professional staff	10
# of titles	114,940	Hours per week with professional staff	82
# of active serial subscriptions	4,927	Hours per week without professional staff	25
Study seating capacity inside the library	657	# of student computer work stations for entire law school	93
Square feet of law library	55,000	# of additional networked connections	50
Square feet of law school (excl. Library)	127,852	Require Laptop Computer?	N

J.D. Attrition (from Prior Year)

	Academic	Other	TOTALS	
	#	#	#	%
1st Year	13	19	32	9.6%
2nd Year	0	3	3	0.9%
3rd Year	0	0	0	0.0%
4th Year	0	0	0	0.0%

Bar Passage Rates

Jurisdiction	Colorado		
Exam	Sum 97	Win 98	Total
# from school taking bar for the first time	224	69	293
School's pass rate for all first-time takers	79%	75%	78%
State's pass rate for all first-time takers	83%	77%	81%

DEPAUL UNIVERSITY

25 East Jackson Boulevard
Chicago, IL 60604-2287
(312)362-8701
http://www.law.depaul.edu

ABA Approved Since 1925

The Basics

Type of School: Private   Term: Semester

Application deadline: 04/01

Application fee: $40

Financial Aid deadline: 04/01

Can first year start other than Fall? No

Student faculty ratio: 23.4 to 1

Does the University offer:
- housing restricted to law students? No
- graduate student housing for which law students are eligible? No

Curriculum

	Full time	Part time
Typical first-year section size	85	77
Is there typically a "small section" of the first year class, other than Legal Writing, taught by full-time faculty?	No	No
If yes, typical size offered last year	N/A	N/A
# of classroom course titles beyond 1st year curriculum	68	77
# of upper division courses, excluding seminars, with an enrollment:		
Under 25	36	26
25 - 49	20	23
50 - 74	17	10
75 - 99	10	3
100 +	0	0
# of seminars	17	5
# of seminar positions available	396	
# of seminar positions filled	288	80
# of positions available in simulation courses	416	
# of simulation positions filled	23	374
# of positions available in faculty supervised clinical courses	70	
# of fac. sup. clin. positions filled	41	6
# involved in field placements	126	2
# involved in law journals	75	0
# in moot court or trial competitions	27	0
# of credit hrs required to graduate	86	

Faculty & Administrators

	Total		Men		Women		Minorities	
	Fall	Spr	Fall	Spr	Fall	Spr	Fall	Spr
Full-time	35	36	21	23	14	13	3	3
Other Full-Time	6	6	1	1	5	5	0	0
Deans, librarians, & others who teach > 1/2	6	6	2	2	4	4	1	1
Part-time	45	45	25	29	19	15	3	1
Total	92	93	49	55	42	37	7	5
Deans, librarians, & others who teach < 1/2	2	2	0	0	2	2	0	0

J.D. Enrollment & Ethnicity

	Men		Women		Fl-Time		Pt-Time		1st Yr		2nd Yr		3rd Yr		4th Yr		Total		JD Degrees Awarded
	#	%	#	%	#	%	#	%	#	%	#	%	#	%	#	%	#	%	
African-American	26	4.8	29	5.2	28	3.7	27	8.3	27	6.6	12	4.0	13	4.6	3	3.1	55	5.0	15
American Indian	1	0.2	1	0.2	1	0.1	1	0.3	1	0.2	1	0.3	0	0.0	0	0.0	2	0.2	2
Asian American	19	3.5	29	5.2	32	4.2	16	4.9	20	4.9	11	3.7	11	3.9	6	6.2	48	4.4	12
Mexican American	0	0.0	0	0.0	0	0.0	0	0.0	0	0.0	0	0.0	0	0.0	0	0.0	0	0.0	0
Puerto Rican	0	0.0	0	0.0	0	0.0	0	0.0	0	0.0	0	0.0	0	0.0	0	0.0	0	0.0	0
Hispanic American	23	4.3	37	6.7	40	5.2	20	6.1	27	6.6	17	5.6	12	4.2	4	4.1	60	5.5	16
Total Minorities	69	12.8	96	17.3	101	13.2	64	19.6	75	18.3	41	13.6	36	12.6	13	13.4	165	15.1	45
Foreign Nationals	8	1.5	4	0.7	9	1.2	3	0.9	8	2.0	2	0.7	1	0.4	1	1.0	12	1.1	5
Caucasian	462	85.7	454	81.9	656	85.6	260	79.5	327	79.8	258	85.7	248	87.0	83	85.6	916	83.8	275
Total	539	49.3	554	50.7	766	70.1	327	29.9	410	37.5	301	27.5	285	26.1	97	8.9	1093		325

GPA & LSAT Scores

	Full Time	Part Time	Total
# of apps	1,589	350	1,939
# admits	1,216	227	1,443
# of matrics	293	99	392
75% GPA	3.37	3.13	
25% GPA	2.87	2.69	
75% LSAT	155	153	
25% LSAT	149	146	

Tuition & Fees

	Resident	Non-resident
Full-Time	$19,870	$19,870
Part-Time	$13,470	$13,470

Living Expenses

Estimated living expenses for Singles		
Living on campus	Living off campus	Living at home
N/A	$13,032	$13,032

Employment

	Total	%
Employment status known	332	96.8
Employment status unknown	11	3.2
Employed	298	89.8
Pursuing graduate degrees	3	0.9
Unemployed seeking employment	12	3.6
Unemployed not seeking employment	19	5.7
Type of Employment		
# employed in law firms	140	47.0
# employed in business & industry	51	17.1
# employed in government	37	12.4
# employed in public interest	10	3.4
# employed as judicial clerks	8	2.7
# employed in academia	3	1.0
Geographic Location		
# employed in state	215	72.1
# employed in foreign countries	0	0.0
# of states where employed	19	

Grants/Scholarships

	Full-time		Part-time		Total	
	#	%	#	%	#	%
Total # of Students	766		327		1093	
Total # receiving grants	531	69.3	13	4.0	544	49.8
Less than 1/2 tuition	497	64.9	12	3.7	509	46.6
Half to full tuition	33	4.3	1	0.3	34	3.1
Full tuition	1	0.1	0	0.0	1	0.1
More than full tuition	0	0.0	0	0.0	0	0.0
Median Grant Amount	$0		$0			

Informational & Library Resources

# of volumes & volume equivalents	339,290	# of professional staff	8
# of titles	57,277	Hours per week with professional staff	76
# of active serial subscriptions	4,806	Hours per week without professional staff	18
Study seating capacity inside the library	465	# of student computer work stations for entire law school	68
Square feet of law library	36,690	# of additional networked connections	0
Square feet of law school (excl. Library)	40,063	Require Laptop Computer?	N

J.D. Attrition (from Prior Year)

	Academic	Other	TOTALS	
	#	#	#	%
1st Year	5	9	14	4.0%
2nd Year	1	0	1	0.3%
3rd Year	1	0	1	0.3%
4th Year	0	0	0	0.0%

Bar Passage Rates

Jurisdiction	Illinois		
Exam	Sum 97	Win 98	Total
# from school taking bar for the first time	238	26	264
School's pass rate for all first-time takers	89%	88%	89%
State's pass rate for all first-time takers	87%	80%	85%

DETROIT COLLEGE AT MICHIGAN STATE UNIV.

368 Law College Bldg.
East Lansing, MI 48824-1300
(517)432-6800
http://www.dcl.edu

ABA Approved Since 1941

The Basics

Type of School: Private Term: Semester
Application deadline: 04/15
Application fee: $50
Financial Aid deadline: 04/15
Can first year start other than Fall? No
Student faculty ratio: 25.6 to 1
Does the University offer:
- housing restricted to law students? No
- graduate student housing for which law students are eligible? Yes

Faculty & Administrators

	Total		Men		Women		Minorities	
	Fall	Spr	Fall	Spr	Fall	Spr	Fall	Spr
Full-time	22	22	14	15	8	7	2	2
Other Full-Time	5	5	3	3	2	2	0	0
Deans, librarians, & others who teach > 1/2	5	4	3	3	2	1	2	2
Part-time	27	13	21	12	6	1	3	0
Total	59	44	41	33	18	11	7	4
Deans, librarians, & others who teach < 1/2	0	0	0	0	0	0	0	0

Curriculum

	Full time	Part time
Typical first-year section size	51	41
Is there typically a "small section" of the first year class, other than Legal Writing, taught by full-time faculty?	No	No
If yes, typical size offered last year	N/A	N/A
# of classroom course titles beyond 1st year curriculum	48	63
# of upper division courses, excluding seminars, with an enrollment:		
Under 25	28	32
25 - 49	5	10
50 - 74	6	0
75 - 99	0	0
100 +	0	0
# of seminars	10	10
# of seminar positions available	400	
# of seminar positions filled	138	68
# of positions available in simulation courses	360	
# of simulation positions filled	195	120
# of positions available in faculty supervised clinical courses	0	
# of fac. sup. clin. positions filled	0	0
# involved in field placements	64	20
# involved in law journals	52	26
# in moot court or trial competitions	82	41
# of credit hrs required to graduate	85	

J.D. Enrollment & Ethnicity

	Men		Women		Fl-Time		Pt-Time		1st Yr		2nd Yr		3rd Yr		4th Yr		Total		JD Degrees Awarded
	#	%	#	%	#	%	#	%	#	%	#	%	#	%	#	%	#	%	
African-American	25	5.5	16	5.7	32	5.7	9	5.1	17	6.9	13	6.6	11	4.5	0	0.0	41	5.6	26
American Indian	5	1.1	3	1.1	7	1.3	1	0.6	2	0.8	3	1.5	3	1.2	0	0.0	8	1.1	1
Asian American	21	4.6	14	5.0	33	5.9	2	1.1	16	6.5	12	6.1	7	2.9	0	0.0	35	4.7	3
Mexican American	0	0.0	0	0.0	0	0.0	0	0.0	0	0.0	0	0.0	0	0.0	0	0.0	0	0.0	0
Puerto Rican	0	0.0	0	0.0	0	0.0	0	0.0	0	0.0	0	0.0	0	0.0	0	0.0	0	0.0	0
Hispanic American	11	2.4	6	2.1	13	2.3	4	2.3	5	2.0	5	2.5	7	2.9	0	0.0	17	2.3	3
Total Minorities	62	13.6	39	13.9	85	15.2	16	9.0	40	16.3	33	16.8	28	11.5	0	0.0	101	13.7	33
Foreign Nationals	0	0.0	0	0.0	0	0.0	0	0.0	0	0.0	0	0.0	0	0.0	0	0.0	0	0.0	8
Caucasian	394	86.4	242	86.1	475	84.8	161	91.0	206	83.7	164	83.2	215	88.5	51	100.0	636	86.3	201
Total	456	61.9	281	38.1	560	76.0	177	24.0	246	33.4	197	26.7	243	33.0	51	6.9	737		242

GPA & LSAT Scores

	Full Time	Part Time	Total
# of apps	793	151	944
# admits	505	91	596
# of matrics	154	52	206
75% GPA	3.40	3.42	
25% GPA	2.85	2.80	
75% LSAT	154	154	
25% LSAT	147	145	

Tuition & Fees

	Resident	Non-resident
Full-Time	$15,140	$15,140
Part-Time	$11,369	$11,369

Living Expenses

Estimated living expenses for Singles		
Living on campus	Living off campus	Living at home
$9,796	$9,796	$9,796

Grants/Scholarships

	Full-time		Part-time		Total	
	#	%	#	%	#	%
Total # of Students	560		177		737	
Total # receiving grants	54	9.6	3	1.7	57	7.7
Less than 1/2 tuition	1	0.2	0	0.0	1	0.1
Half to full tuition	38	6.8	3	1.7	41	5.6
Full tuition	9	1.6	0	0.0	9	1.2
More than full tuition	6	1.1	0	0.0	6	0.8
Median Grant Amount	$9,000		$11,355			

Informational & Library Resources

# of volumes & volume equivalents	236,906	# of professional staff	7
# of titles	107,602	Hours per week with professional staff	64
# of active serial subscriptions	2,973	Hours per week without professional staff	45
Study seating capacity inside the library	455	# of student computer work stations for entire law school	60
Square feet of law library	42,000	# of additional networked connections	1250
Square feet of law school (excl. Library)	54,713	Require Laptop Computer?	N

Employment

	Total	%
Employment status known	133	79.6
Employment status unknown	34	20.4
Employed	120	90.2
Pursuing graduate degrees	6	4.5
Unemployed seeking employment	5	3.8
Unemployed not seeking employment	2	1.5
Type of Employment		
# employed in law firms	63	52.5
# employed in business & industry	29	24.2
# employed in government	12	10.0
# employed in public interest	4	3.3
# employed as judicial clerks	8	6.7
# employed in academia	1	0.8
Geographic Location		
# employed in state	112	93.3
# employed in foreign countries	0	0.0
# of states where employed	6	

J.D. Attrition (from Prior Year)

	Academic	Other	TOTALS	
	#	#	#	%
1st Year	5	23	28	12%
2nd Year	7	17	24	12%
3rd Year	0	1	1	0.4%
4th Year	0	0	0	0.0%

Bar Passage Rates

Jurisdiction	Michigan		
Exam	Sum 97	Win 98	Total
# from school taking bar for the first time	103	75	178
School's pass rate for all first-time takers	89%	67%	80%
State's pass rate for all first-time takers	89%	79%	86%

DETROIT MERCY, UNIVERSITY OF

651 E. Jefferson
Detroit, MI 48226
(313)596-0200
http://www.law.udmercy.edu

ABA Approved Since 1933

The Basics

Type of School: Private Term: Semester

Application deadline: 04/15

Application fee: $50

Financial Aid deadline: 04/01

Can first year start other than Fall? No

Student faculty ratio: 18.0 to 1

Does the University offer:
- housing restricted to law students? No
- graduate student housing for which law students are eligible? No

Faculty & Administrators

	Total		Men		Women		Minorities	
	Fall	Spr	Fall	Spr	Fall	Spr	Fall	Spr
Full-time	16	14	12	10	4	4	0	0
Other Full-Time	3	3	0	0	3	3	1	1
Deans, librarians, & others who teach > 1/2	6	6	5	5	1	1	1	1
Part-time	24	16	19	12	5	4	3	0
Total	49	39	36	27	13	12	5	2
Deans, librarians, & others who teach < 1/2	0	0	0	0	0	0	0	0

Curriculum

	Full time	Part time
Typical first-year section size	50	39
Is there typically a "small section" of the first year class, other than Legal Writing, taught by full-time faculty?	No	No
If yes, typical size offered last year	N/A	N/A
# of classroom course titles beyond 1st year curriculum	67	49
# of upper division courses, excluding seminars, with an enrollment:		
Under 25	43	26
25 - 49	6	9
50 - 74	6	2
75 - 99	1	1
100 +	0	0
# of seminars	11	11
# of seminar positions available	352	
# of seminar positions filled	50	107
# of positions available in simulation courses	274	
# of simulation positions filled	146	64
# of positions available in faculty supervised clinical courses	196	
# of fac. sup. clin. positions filled	27	14
# involved in field placements	23	8
# involved in law journals	52	32
# in moot court or trial competitions	42	31
# of credit hrs required to graduate	90	

J.D. Enrollment & Ethnicity

	Men		Women		Fl-Time		Pt-Time		1st Yr		2nd Yr		3rd Yr		4th Yr		Total		JD Degrees Awarded
	#	%	#	%	#	%	#	%	#	%	#	%	#	%	#	%	#	%	
African-American	14	6.5	23	10.7	14	5.8	23	12.4	18	12.8	9	8.8	6	4.1	4	10.3	37	8.6	23
American Indian	1	0.5	1	0.5	1	0.4	1	0.5	2	1.4	0	0.0	0	0.0	0	0.0	2	0.5	0
Asian American	4	1.9	4	1.9	6	2.5	2	1.1	5	3.5	3	2.9	0	0.0	0	0.0	8	1.9	0
Mexican American	1	0.5	0	0.0	1	0.4	0	0.0	1	0.7	0	0.0	0	0.0	0	0.0	1	0.2	1
Puerto Rican	0	0.0	2	0.9	1	0.4	1	0.5	0	0.0	2	2.0	0	0.0	0	0.0	2	0.5	0
Hispanic American	2	0.9	2	0.9	3	1.2	1	0.5	1	0.7	1	1.0	2	1.4	0	0.0	4	0.9	0
Total Minorities	22	10.3	32	14.9	26	10.7	28	15.1	27	19.1	15	14.7	8	5.4	4	10.3	54	12.6	24
Foreign Nationals	13	6.1	15	7.0	4	1.6	24	12.9	1	0.7	1	1.0	7	4.8	19	48.7	28	6.5	15
Caucasian	179	83.6	168	78.1	213	87.7	134	72.0	113	80.1	86	84.3	132	89.8	16	41.0	347	80.9	136
Total	214	49.9	215	50.1	243	56.6	186	43.4	141	32.9	102	23.8	147	34.3	39	9.1	429		175

GPA & LSAT Scores

	Full Time	Part Time	Total
# of apps	495	184	679
# admits	326	99	425
# of matrics	110	41	151
75% GPA	3.42	3.17	
25% GPA	2.77	2.57	
75% LSAT	152	152	
25% LSAT	144	145	

Tuition & Fees

	Resident	Non-resident
Full-Time	$16,850	$16,850
Part-Time	$12,046	$12,046

Living Expenses

Estimated living expenses for Singles		
Living on campus	Living off campus	Living at home
N/A	$11,888	$7,756

Grants/Scholarships

	Full-time		Part-time		Total	
	#	%	#	%	#	%
Total # of Students	243		186		429	
Total # receiving grants	51	21.0	20	10.8	71	16.6
Less than 1/2 tuition	16	6.6	9	4.8	25	5.8
Half to full tuition	34	14.0	10	5.4	44	10.3
Full tuition	0	0.0	0	0.0	0	0.0
More than full tuition	1	0.4	1	0.5	2	0.5
Median Grant Amount	$8,000		$3,025			

Informational & Library Resources

# of volumes & volume equivalents	298,557	# of professional staff	6
# of titles	125,872	Hours per week with professional staff	92
# of active serial subscriptions	3,501	Hours per week without professional staff	0
Study seating capacity inside the library	406	# of student computer work stations for entire law school	30
Square feet of law library	23,839	# of additional networked connections	0
Square feet of law school (excl. Library)	47,241	Require Laptop Computer?	N

Employment

	Total	%
Employment status known	156	67.8
Employment status unknown	74	32.2
Employed	142	91.0
Pursuing graduate degrees	1	0.6
Unemployed seeking employment	6	3.8
Unemployed not seeking employment	7	4.5
Type of Employment		
# employed in law firms	78	54.9
# employed in business & industry	30	21.1
# employed in government	17	12.0
# employed in public interest	2	1.4
# employed as judicial clerks	13	9.2
# employed in academia	2	1.4
Geographic Location		
# employed in state	122	85.9
# employed in foreign countries	10	7.0
# of states where employed	9	

J.D. Attrition (from Prior Year)

	Academic	Other	TOTALS	
	#	#	#	%
1st Year	19	8	27	19%
2nd Year	3	2	5	4.0%
3rd Year	0	0	0	0.0%
4th Year	0	0	0	0.0%

Bar Passage Rates

Jurisdiction	Michigan		
Exam	Sum 97	Win 98	Total
# from school taking bar for the first time	142	31	173
School's pass rate for all first-time takers	88%	65%	84%
State's pass rate for all first-time takers	89%	79%	86%

DISTRICT OF COLUMBIA, UNIVERSITY OF (Provisional)

David A. Clarke School of Law
4200 Connecticut Ave., NW
Washington, DC 20008
(202)274-7400

ABA Approved Since 1998

The Basics

Type of School: Public — Term: Semester
Application deadline: 04/01
Application fee: $35
Financial Aid deadline: 05/30
Can first year start other than Fall? No
Student faculty ratio: 16.5 to 1
Does the University offer:
- housing restricted to law students? No
- graduate student housing for which law students are eligible? No

Curriculum

	Full time	Part time
Typical first-year section size	41	0
Is there typically a "small section" of the first year class, other than Legal Writing, taught by full-time faculty?	No	No
If yes, typical size offered last year	N/A	N/A
# of classroom course titles beyond 1st year curriculum	37	0
# of upper division courses, excluding seminars, with an enrollment:		
Under 25	18	0
25 - 49	10	0
50 - 74	5	0
75 - 99	1	0
100 +	0	0
# of seminars	5	0
# of seminar positions available	30	
# of seminar positions filled	26	0
# of positions available in simulation courses	108	
# of simulation positions filled	103	0
# of positions available in faculty supervised clinical courses	123	
# of fac. sup. clin. positions filled	121	0
# involved in field placements	6	0
# involved in law journals	12	0
# in moot court or trial competitions	0	0
# of credit hrs required to graduate	90	

Faculty & Administrators

	Total		Men		Women		Minorities	
	Fall	Spr	Fall	Spr	Fall	Spr	Fall	Spr
Full-time	8	8	5	5	3	3	2	2
Other Full-Time	1	1	0	0	1	1	0	0
Deans, librarians, & others who teach > 1/2	2	2	0	0	2	2	1	1
Part-time	6	10	5	9	1	1	1	4
Total	17	21	10	14	7	7	4	7
Deans, librarians, & others who teach < 1/2	4	4	2	2	2	2	1	1

J.D. Enrollment & Ethnicity

	Men		Women		Fl-Time		Pt-Time		1st Yr		2nd Yr		3rd Yr		4th Yr		Total		JD Degrees Awarded
	#	%	#	%	#	%	#	%	#	%	#	%	#	%	#	%	#	%	
African-American	44	61.1	59	68.6	103	65.2	0	0.0	41	68.3	26	66.7	36	61.0	0	0.0	103	65.2	33
American Indian	1	1.4	0	0.0	1	0.6	0	0.0	1	1.7	0	0.0	0	0.0	0	0.0	1	0.6	0
Asian American	5	6.9	3	3.5	8	5.1	0	0.0	4	6.7	1	2.6	3	5.1	0	0.0	8	5.1	4
Mexican American	1	1.4	0	0.0	1	0.6	0	0.0	0	0.0	0	0.0	1	1.7	0	0.0	1	0.6	0
Puerto Rican	1	1.4	1	1.2	2	1.3	0	0.0	0	0.0	1	2.6	1	1.7	0	0.0	2	1.3	1
Hispanic American	1	1.4	3	3.5	4	2.5	0	0.0	1	1.7	2	5.1	1	1.7	0	0.0	4	2.5	3
Total Minorities	53	73.6	66	76.7	119	75.3	0	0.0	47	78.3	30	76.9	42	71.2	0	0.0	119	75.3	41
Foreign Nationals	0	0.0	0	0.0	0	0.0	0	0.0	0	0.0	0	0.0	0	0.0	0	0.0	0	0.0	0
Caucasian	19	26.4	20	23.3	39	24.7	0	0.0	13	21.7	9	23.1	17	28.8	0	0.0	39	24.7	19
Total	72	45.6	86	54.4	158	100.0	0	0.0	60	38.0	39	24.7	59	37.3	0	0.0	158		60

DISTRICT OF COLUMBIA, UNIVERSITY OF (Provisional)

GPA & LSAT Scores

	Full Time	Part Time	Total
# of apps	386	0	386
# admits	166	0	166
# of matrics	61	0	61
75% GPA	2.75	0.00	
25% GPA	2.30	0.00	
75% LSAT	147	0	
25% LSAT	141	0	

Tuition & Fees

	Resident	Non-resident
Full-Time	$7,135	$14,135
Part-Time	$0	$0

Living Expenses

Estimated living expenses for Singles		
Living on campus	Living off campus	Living at home
N/A	$18,065	$12,065

Grants/Scholarships

	Full-time		Part-time		Total	
	#	%	#	%	#	%
Total # of Students						
Total # receiving grants	118	74.7	0	0.0	118	74.7
Less than 1/2 tuition	79	50.0	0	0.0	79	50.0
Half to full tuition	39	24.7	0	0.0	39	24.7
Full tuition	0	0.0	0	0.0	0	0.0
More than full tuition	0	0.0	0	0.0	0	0.0
Median Grant Amount	$4,000		$0			

Informational & Library Resources

# of volumes & volume equivalents	174,812	# of professional staff	3
# of titles	14,557	Hours per week with professional staff	61
# of active serial subscriptions	2,494	Hours per week without professional staff	43
Study seating capacity inside the library	150	# of student computer work stations for entire law school	25
Square feet of law library	16,000	# of additional networked connections	0
Square feet of law school (excl. Library)	26,800	Require Laptop Computer?	Y

Employment

	Total	%
Employment status known	57	86.4
Employment status unknown	9	13.6
Employed	38	66.7
Pursuing graduate degrees	3	5.3
Unemployed seeking employment	14	24.6
Unemployed not seeking employment	2	3.5
Type of Employment		
# employed in law firms	13	34.2
# employed in business & industry	11	28.9
# employed in government	6	15.8
# employed in public interest	7	18.4
# employed as judicial clerks	1	2.6
# employed in academia	0	0.0
Geographic Location		
# employed in state	24	63.2
# employed in foreign countries	0	0.0
# of states where employed	8	

J.D. Attrition (from Prior Year)

	Academic	Other	TOTALS	
	#	#	#	%
1st Year	9	5	14	34%
2nd Year	1	1	2	3.8%
3rd Year	0	0	0	0.0%
4th Year	0	0	0	0.0%

Bar Passage Rates

Jurisdiction	Maryland		
Exam	Sum 97	Win 98	Total
# from school taking bar for the first time	31	1	32
School's pass rate for all first-time takers	19%	100%	22%
State's pass rate for all first-time takers	69%	83%	72%

DRAKE UNIVERSITY

2507 University Avenue
Des Moines, IA 50311
(515)271-2824
http://www.drake.edu

ABA Approved Since 1923

The Basics

Type of School: Private   Term: Semester

Application deadline: 03/01

Application fee: $35

Financial Aid deadline: 03/01

Can first year start other than Fall? Yes

Student faculty ratio: 17.1 to 1

Does the University offer:
- housing restricted to law students? No
- graduate student housing for which law students are eligible? Yes

Faculty & Administrators

	Total		Men		Women		Minorities	
	Fall	Spr	Fall	Spr	Fall	Spr	Fall	Spr
Full-time	19	18	15	14	4	4	1	1
Other Full-Time	2	2	0	0	2	2	0	0
Deans, librarians, & others who teach > 1/2	2	2	2	2	0	0	0	0
Part-time	13	15	11	9	2	6	0	0
Total	36	37	28	25	8	12	1	1
Deans, librarians, & others who teach < 1/2	2	2	2	2	0	0	0	0

Curriculum

	Full time	Part time
Typical first-year section size	58	0
Is there typically a "small section" of the first year class, other than Legal Writing, taught by full-time faculty?	No	No
If yes, typical size offered last year	N/A	N/A
# of classroom course titles beyond 1st year curriculum	93	0
# of upper division courses, excluding seminars, with an enrollment:		
Under 25	61	0
25 - 49	13	0
50 - 74	12	0
75 - 99	4	0
100 +	0	0
# of seminars	21	0
# of seminar positions available	420	
# of seminar positions filled	279	0
# of positions available in simulation courses	772	
# of simulation positions filled	486	0
# of positions available in faculty supervised clinical courses	124	
# of fac. sup. clin. positions filled	70	0
# involved in field placements	100	0
# involved in law journals	148	0
# in moot court or trial competitions	83	0
# of credit hrs required to graduate	90	

J.D. Enrollment & Ethnicity

	Men		Women		Fl-Time		Pt-Time		1st Yr		2nd Yr		3rd Yr		4th Yr		Total		JD Degrees Awarded
	#	%	#	%	#	%	#	%	#	%	#	%	#	%	#	%	#	%	
African-American	11	5.0	8	4.6	19	5.0	0	0.0	6	4.3	6	5.3	7	4.9	0	0.0	19	4.8	1
American Indian	1	0.5	2	1.1	3	0.8	0	0.0	0	0.0	0	0.0	3	2.1	0	0.0	3	0.8	2
Asian American	3	1.4	2	1.1	5	1.3	0	0.0	1	0.7	3	2.7	1	0.7	0	0.0	5	1.3	4
Mexican American	3	1.4	2	1.1	5	1.3	0	0.0	2	1.4	1	0.9	2	1.4	0	0.0	5	1.3	1
Puerto Rican	0	0.0	1	0.6	1	0.3	0	0.0	0	0.0	0	0.0	1	0.7	0	0.0	1	0.3	0
Hispanic American	5	2.3	4	2.3	8	2.1	1	6.3	1	0.7	4	3.5	4	2.8	0	0.0	9	2.3	1
Total Minorities	23	10.4	19	10.9	41	10.8	1	6.3	10	7.2	14	12.4	18	12.5	0	0.0	42	10.6	9
Foreign Nationals	3	1.4	2	1.1	5	1.3	0	0.0	3	2.2	0	0.0	2	1.4	0	0.0	5	1.3	1
Caucasian	195	88.2	153	87.9	333	87.9	15	93.7	125	90.6	99	87.6	124	86.1	0	0.0	348	88.1	131
Total	221	55.9	174	44.1	379	95.9	16	4.1	138	34.9	113	28.6	144	36.5	0	0.0	395		141

GPA & LSAT Scores

	Full Time	Part Time	Total
# of apps	647	34	681
# admits	405	14	419
# of matrics	131	5	136
75% GPA	3.50	3.54	
25% GPA	2.86	3.19	
75% LSAT	155	156	
25% LSAT	150	153	

Tuition & Fees

	Resident	Non-resident
Full-Time	$16,950	$16,950
Part-Time	$565	$565

Living Expenses

Estimated living expenses for Singles		
Living on campus	Living off campus	Living at home
N/A	$10,679	$5,754

Grants/Scholarships

	Full-time		Part-time		Total	
	#	%	#	%	#	%
Total # of Students	379		16		395	
Total # receiving grants	184	48.5	0	0.0	184	46.6
Less than 1/2 tuition	133	35.1	0	0.0	133	33.7
Half to full tuition	16	4.2	0	0.0	16	4.1
Full tuition	35	9.2	0	0.0	35	8.9
More than full tuition	0	0.0	0	0.0	0	0.0
Median Grant Amount	$6,000		$0			

Informational & Library Resources

# of volumes & volume equivalents	273,233	# of professional staff	4
# of titles	34,622	Hours per week with professional staff	40
# of active serial subscriptions	3,077	Hours per week without professional staff	69
Study seating capacity inside the library	705	# of student computer work stations for entire law school	91
Square feet of law library	50,541	# of additional networked connections	130
Square feet of law school (excl. Library)	62,341	Require Laptop Computer?	N

Employment

	Total	%
Employment status known	150	96.8
Employment status unknown	5	3.2
Employed	140	93.3
Pursuing graduate degrees	5	3.3
Unemployed seeking employment	5	3.3
Unemployed not seeking employment	0	0.0
Type of Employment		
# employed in law firms	68	48.6
# employed in business & industry	18	12.9
# employed in government	34	24.3
# employed in public interest	7	5.0
# employed as judicial clerks	12	8.6
# employed in academia	1	0.7
Geographic Location		
# employed in state	69	49.3
# employed in foreign countries	0	0.0
# of states where employed	21	

J.D. Attrition (from Prior Year)

	Academic	Other	TOTALS	
	#	#	#	%
1st Year	0	12	12	9.8%
2nd Year	0	7	7	4.9%
3rd Year	2	0	2	1.4%
4th Year	0	0	0	0.0%

Bar Passage Rates

Jurisdiction	Iowa			Missouri		
Exam	Sum 97	Win 98	Total	Sum 97	Win 98	Total
# from school taking bar for the first time	61	13	74	11	1	12
School's pass rate for all first-time takers	90%	69%	86%	64%	100%	67%
State's pass rate for all first-time takers	86%	83%	85%	86%	81%	85%

DUKE UNIVERSITY

P.O. Box 90362
Science Drive and Toweview Road
Durham, NC 27708-0362
(919)613-7000
http://www.law.duke.edu

ABA Approved Since 1931

The Basics

Type of School: Private   Term: Semester
Application deadline: 02/01
Application fee: $65
Financial Aid deadline: 06/15
Can first year start other than Fall? No
Student faculty ratio: 15.1 to 1
Does the University offer:
- housing restricted to law students? No
- graduate student housing for which law students are eligible? No

Faculty & Administrators

	Total		Men		Women		Minorities	
	Fall	Spr	Fall	Spr	Fall	Spr	Fall	Spr
Full-time	33	29	21	19	12	10	3	3
Other Full-Time	0	0	0	0	0	0	0	0
Deans, librarians, & others who teach > 1/2	1	1	1	1	0	0	0	0
Part-time	20	17	13	15	7	2	2	1
Total	54	47	35	35	19	12	5	4
Deans, librarians, & others who teach < 1/2	10	10	2	2	8	8	0	0

Curriculum

	Full time	Part time
Typical first-year section size	90	0
Is there typically a "small section" of the first year class, other than Legal Writing, taught by full-time faculty?	Yes	No
If yes, typical size offered last year	27	N/A
# of classroom course titles beyond 1st year curriculum	107	0
# of upper division courses, excluding seminars, with an enrollment:		
Under 25	23	0
25 - 49	17	0
50 - 74	12	0
75 - 99	8	0
100 +	3	0
# of seminars	31	0
# of seminar positions available	497	
# of seminar positions filled	497	0
# of positions available in simulation courses	126	
# of simulation positions filled	102	0
# of positions available in faculty supervised clinical courses	20	
# of fac. sup. clin. positions filled	19	0
# involved in field placements	67	0
# involved in law journals	140	0
# in moot court or trial competitions	40	0
# of credit hrs required to graduate	84	

J.D. Enrollment & Ethnicity

	Men		Women		Fl-Time		Pt-Time		1st Yr		2nd Yr		3rd Yr		4th Yr		Total		JD Degrees Awarded
	#	%	#	%	#	%	#	%	#	%	#	%	#	%	#	%	#	%	
African-American	24	7.1	43	16.0	67	11.0	0	0.0	32	15.5	18	9.0	17	8.5	0	0.0	67	11.0	17
American Indian	0	0.0	0	0.0	0	0.0	0	0.0	0	0.0	0	0.0	0	0.0	0	0.0	0	0.0	0
Asian American	21	6.2	16	6.0	37	6.1	0	0.0	14	6.8	15	7.5	8	4.0	0	0.0	37	6.1	10
Mexican American	0	0.0	0	0.0	0	0.0	0	0.0	0	0.0	0	0.0	0	0.0	0	0.0	0	0.0	0
Puerto Rican	0	0.0	0	0.0	0	0.0	0	0.0	0	0.0	0	0.0	0	0.0	0	0.0	0	0.0	0
Hispanic American	7	2.1	7	2.6	14	2.3	0	0.0	4	1.9	5	2.5	5	2.5	0	0.0	14	2.3	6
Total Minorities	52	15.3	66	24.6	118	19.4	0	0.0	50	24.3	38	18.9	30	14.9	0	0.0	118	19.4	33
Foreign Nationals	14	4.1	6	2.2	20	3.3	0	0.0	6	2.9	2	1.0	12	6.0	0	0.0	20	3.3	2
Caucasian	274	80.6	196	73.1	470	77.3	0	0.0	150	72.8	161	80.1	159	79.1	0	0.0	470	77.3	180
Total	340	55.9	268	44.1	608	100.0	0	0.0	206	33.9	201	33.1	201	33.1	0	0.0	608		215

GPA & LSAT Scores

	Full Time	Part Time	Total
# of apps	3,443	0	3,443
# admits	959	0	959
# of matrics	212	0	212
75% GPA	3.72	0.00	
25% GPA	3.33	0.00	
75% LSAT	170	0	
25% LSAT	161	0	

Tuition & Fees

	Resident	Non-resident
Full-Time	$24,939	$24,939
Part-Time	$0	$0

Living Expenses

Estimated living expenses for Singles		
Living on campus	Living off campus	Living at home
$12,030	$12,030	$12,030

Grants/Scholarships

	Full-time		Part-time		Total	
	#	%	#	%	#	%
Total # of Students	608		0		608	
Total # receiving grants	363	59.7	0	0.0	363	59.7
Less than 1/2 tuition	343	56.4	0	0.0	343	56.4
Half to full tuition	16	2.6	0	0.0	16	2.6
Full tuition	4	0.7	0	0.0	4	0.7
More than full tuition	0	0.0	0	0.0	0	0.0
Median Grant Amount	$12,000		$0			

Informational & Library Resources

# of volumes & volume equivalents	521,895	# of professional staff	9
# of titles	190,547	Hours per week with professional staff	68
# of active serial subscriptions	6,843	Hours per week without professional staff	43
Study seating capacity inside the library	451	# of student computer work stations for entire law school	155
Square feet of law library	65,265	# of additional networked connections	192
Square feet of law school (excl. Library)	50,631	Require Laptop Computer?	N

Employment

	Total	%
Employment status known	195	100.0
Employment status unknown	0	0.0
Employed	191	97.9
Pursuing graduate degrees	1	0.5
Unemployed seeking employment	1	0.5
Unemployed not seeking employment	2	1.0
Type of Employment		
# employed in law firms	140	73.3
# employed in business & industry	6	3.1
# employed in government	8	4.2
# employed in public interest	2	1.0
# employed as judicial clerks	35	18.3
# employed in academia	0	0.0
Geographic Location		
# employed in state	13	6.8
# employed in foreign countries	2	1.0
# of states where employed	32	

J.D. Attrition (from Prior Year)

	Academic	Other	TOTALS	
	#	#	#	%
1st Year	0	3	3	1.5%
2nd Year	0	3	3	1.5%
3rd Year	0	0	0	0.0%
4th Year	0	0	0	0.0%

Bar Passage Rates

Jurisdiction	New York			North Carolina		
Exam	Sum 97	Win 98	Total	Sum 97	Win 98	Total
# from school taking bar for the first time	54	11	65	20	12	32
School's pass rate for all first-time takers	100%	73%	95%	100%	75%	91%
State's pass rate for all first-time takers	78%	65%	76%	85%	73%	82%

DUQUESNE UNIVERSITY

900 Locust Street
Pittsburgh, PA 15282
(412)396-6280
http://www.duq.edu/law

ABA Approved Since 1960

The Basics

Type of School: Private   Term: Semester

Application deadline: 04/01

Application fee: $50

Financial Aid deadline: 05/31

Can first year start other than Fall? No

Student faculty ratio: 25.2 to 1

Does the University offer:

- housing restricted to law students? No
- graduate student housing for which law students are eligible? Yes

Faculty & Administrators

	Total		Men		Women		Minorities	
	Fall	Spr	Fall	Spr	Fall	Spr	Fall	Spr
Full-time	19	19	14	14	5	5	2	2
Other Full-Time	1	1	1	1	0	0	0	0
Deans, librarians, & others who teach > 1/2	3	3	3	3	0	0	0	0
Part-time	20	27	17	23	3	4	2	2
Total	43	50	35	41	8	9	4	4
Deans, librarians, & others who teach < 1/2	1	1	1	1	0	0	0	0

Curriculum

	Full time	Part time
Typical first-year section size	79	87
Is there typically a "small section" of the first year class, other than Legal Writing, taught by full-time faculty?	No	Yes
If yes, typical size offered last year	N/A	44
# of classroom course titles beyond 1st year curriculum	53	53
# of upper division courses, excluding seminars, with an enrollment:		
Under 25	26	33
25 - 49	13	9
50 - 74	3	7
75 - 99	8	4
100 +	3	0
# of seminars	4	4
# of seminar positions available	140	
# of seminar positions filled	56	42
# of positions available in simulation courses	199	
# of simulation positions filled	72	81
# of positions available in faculty supervised clinical courses	60	
# of fac. sup. clin. positions filled	49	15
# involved in field placements	98	42
# involved in law journals	48	49
# in moot court or trial competitions	37	58
# of credit hrs required to graduate	86	

J.D. Enrollment & Ethnicity

	Men		Women		Fl-Time		Pt-Time		1st Yr		2nd Yr		3rd Yr		4th Yr		Total		JD Degrees Awarded
	#	%	#	%	#	%	#	%	#	%	#	%	#	%	#	%	#	%	
African-American	9	2.4	17	5.5	9	2.5	17	5.1	9	3.9	7	3.1	8	5.0	2	2.9	26	3.8	12
American Indian	0	0.0	0	0.0	0	0.0	0	0.0	0	0.0	0	0.0	0	0.0	0	0.0	0	0.0	0
Asian American	3	0.8	1	0.3	3	0.8	1	0.3	1	0.4	2	0.9	1	0.6	0	0.0	4	0.6	1
Mexican American	0	0.0	0	0.0	0	0.0	0	0.0	0	0.0	0	0.0	0	0.0	0	0.0	0	0.0	0
Puerto Rican	0	0.0	0	0.0	0	0.0	0	0.0	0	0.0	0	0.0	0	0.0	0	0.0	0	0.0	0
Hispanic American	3	0.8	0	0.0	2	0.6	1	0.3	0	0.0	1	0.4	2	1.3	0	0.0	3	0.4	2
Total Minorities	15	3.9	18	5.9	14	3.9	19	5.7	10	4.3	10	4.4	11	6.9	2	2.9	33	4.8	15
Foreign Nationals	1	0.3	2	0.7	2	0.6	1	0.3	0	0.0	0	0.0	2	1.3	1	1.4	3	0.4	1
Caucasian	364	95.8	287	93.5	340	95.5	311	94.0	220	95.7	218	95.6	147	91.9	66	95.7	651	94.8	151
Total	380	55.3	307	44.7	356	51.8	331	48.2	230	33.5	228	33.2	160	23.3	69	10.0	687		167

GPA & LSAT Scores

	Full Time	Part Time	Total
# of apps	566	194	760
# admits	367	127	494
# of matrics	120	98	218
75% GPA	3.50	3.39	
25% GPA	2.88	2.74	
75% LSAT	154	154	
25% LSAT	147	144	

Tuition & Fees

	Resident	Non-resident
Full-Time	$15,602	$15,602
Part-Time	$12,038	$12,038

Living Expenses

Estimated living expenses for Singles		
Living on campus	Living off campus	Living at home
$8,534	$8,534	$3,000

Grants/Scholarships

	Full-time		Part-time		Total	
	#	%	#	%	#	%
Total # of Students	356		331		687	
Total # receiving grants	73	20.5	21	6.3	94	13.7
Less than 1/2 tuition	44	12.4	11	3.3	55	8.0
Half to full tuition	2	0.6	10	3.0	12	1.7
Full tuition	27	7.6	0	0.0	27	3.9
More than full tuition	0	0.0	0	0.0	0	0.0
Median Grant Amount	$4,500		$3,500			

Informational & Library Resources

# of volumes & volume equivalents	225,668	# of professional staff	6
# of titles	61,268	Hours per week with professional staff	78
# of active serial subscriptions	4,586	Hours per week without professional staff	24
Study seating capacity inside the library	246	# of student computer work stations for entire law school	46
Square feet of law library	25,034	# of additional networked connections	0
Square feet of law school (excl. Library)	108,136	Require Laptop Computer?	N

Employment

	Total	%
Employment status known	168	99.4
Employment status unknown	1	0.6
Employed	153	91.1
Pursuing graduate degrees	1	0.6
Unemployed seeking employment	14	8.3
Unemployed not seeking employment	0	0.0
Type of Employment		
# employed in law firms	88	57.5
# employed in business & industry	31	20.3
# employed in government	9	5.9
# employed in public interest	1	0.7
# employed as judicial clerks	19	12.4
# employed in academia	2	1.3
Geographic Location		
# employed in state	95	62.1
# employed in foreign countries	1	0.7
# of states where employed	15	

J.D. Attrition (from Prior Year)

	Academic	Other	TOTALS	
	#	#	#	%
1st Year	11	21	32	12%
2nd Year	2	0	2	1.2%
3rd Year	0	3	3	1.8%
4th Year	0	0	0	0.0%

Bar Passage Rates

Jurisdiction	Pennsylvania		
Exam	Sum 97	Win 98	Total
# from school taking bar for the first time	138	10	148
School's pass rate for all first-time takers	83%	80%	82%
State's pass rate for all first-time takers	81%	73%	79%

EMORY UNIVERSITY

Gambrell Hall
1301 Clifton Road
Atlanta, GA 30322-2770
(404)727-6816
http://www.law.emory.edu

ABA Approved Since 1923

The Basics

Type of School: Private Term: Semester
Application deadline: 03/01
Application fee: $50
Financial Aid deadline: 04/01
Can first year start other than Fall? No
Student faculty ratio: 19.8 to 1
Does the University offer:
- housing restricted to law students? No
- graduate student housing for which law students are eligible? Yes

Faculty & Administrators

	Total		Men		Women		Minorities	
	Fall	Spr	Fall	Spr	Fall	Spr	Fall	Spr
Full-time	27	25	25	23	2	2	2	2
Other Full-Time	0	0	0	0	0	0	0	0
Deans, librarians, & others who teach > 1/2	5	5	2	2	3	3	0	0
Part-time	55	47	32	30	23	17	1	0
Total	87	77	59	55	28	22	3	2
Deans, librarians, & others who teach < 1/2	1	1	0	0	1	1	0	0

Curriculum

	Full time	Part time
Typical first-year section size	69	0
Is there typically a "small section" of the first year class, other than Legal Writing, taught by full-time faculty?	Yes	No
If yes, typical size offered last year	35	N/A
# of classroom course titles beyond 1st year curriculum	124	0
# of upper division courses, excluding seminars, with an enrollment:		
Under 25	56	0
25 - 49	28	0
50 - 74	18	0
75 - 99	9	0
100 +	1	0
# of seminars	12	0
# of seminar positions available	180	
# of seminar positions filled	110	0
# of positions available in simulation courses	738	
# of simulation positions filled	630	0
# of positions available in faculty supervised clinical courses	4	
# of fac. sup. clin. positions filled	4	0
# involved in field placements	216	0
# involved in law journals	148	0
# in moot court or trial competitions	109	0
# of credit hrs required to graduate	88	

J.D. Enrollment & Ethnicity

	Men		Women		Fl-Time		Pt-Time		1st Yr		2nd Yr		3rd Yr		4th Yr		Total		JD Degrees Awarded
	#	%	#	%	#	%	#	%	#	%	#	%	#	%	#	%	#	%	
African-American	12	3.7	42	13.2	54	8.4	0	0.0	9	3.8	27	13.0	18	9.0	0	0.0	54	8.4	16
American Indian	1	0.3	0	0.0	1	0.2	0	0.0	0	0.0	1	0.5	0	0.0	0	0.0	1	0.2	2
Asian American	17	5.2	20	6.3	37	5.8	0	0.0	16	6.8	9	4.3	12	6.0	0	0.0	37	5.8	14
Mexican American	0	0.0	0	0.0	0	0.0	0	0.0	0	0.0	0	0.0	0	0.0	0	0.0	0	0.0	0
Puerto Rican	0	0.0	0	0.0	0	0.0	0	0.0	0	0.0	0	0.0	0	0.0	0	0.0	0	0.0	0
Hispanic American	20	6.2	16	5.0	36	5.6	0	0.0	5	2.1	13	6.3	18	9.0	0	0.0	36	5.6	13
Total Minorities	50	15.4	78	24.5	128	19.9	0	0.0	30	12.8	50	24.0	48	24.0	0	0.0	128	19.9	45
Foreign Nationals	3	0.9	4	1.3	7	1.1	0	0.0	2	0.9	1	0.5	4	2.0	0	0.0	7	1.1	3
Caucasian	271	83.6	236	74.2	507	79.0	0	0.0	202	86.3	157	75.5	148	74.0	0	0.0	507	79.0	190
Total	324	50.5	318	49.5	642	100.0	0	0.0	234	36.4	208	32.4	200	31.2	0	0.0	642		238

GPA & LSAT Scores

	Full Time	Part Time	Total
# of apps	2,664	0	2,664
# admits	1,077	0	1,077
# of matrics	235	0	235
75% GPA	3.59	0.00	
25% GPA	3.25	0.00	
75% LSAT	163	0	
25% LSAT	159	0	

Tuition & Fees

	Resident	Non-resident
Full-Time	$23,376	$23,376
Part-Time	$0	$0

Living Expenses

Estimated living expenses for Singles		
Living on campus	Living off campus	Living at home
$11,400	$11,400	$11,400

Grants/Scholarships

	Full-time		Part-time		Total	
	#	%	#	%	#	%
Total # of Students	642		0		642	
Total # receiving grants	151	23.5	0	0.0	151	23.5
Less than 1/2 tuition	37	5.8	0	0.0	37	5.8
Half to full tuition	33	5.1	0	0.0	33	5.1
Full tuition	66	10.3	0	0.0	66	10.3
More than full tuition	15	2.3	0	0.0	15	2.3
Median Grant Amount	$20,700		$0			

Informational & Library Resources

# of volumes & volume equivalents	345,345	# of professional staff	7
# of titles	109,733	Hours per week with professional staff	60
# of active serial subscriptions	5,419	Hours per week without professional staff	54
Study seating capacity inside the library	490	# of student computer work stations for entire law school	74
Square feet of law library	70,000	# of additional networked connections	450
Square feet of law school (excl. Library)	61,000	Require Laptop Computer?	N

Employment

	Total	%
Employment status known	250	98.8
Employment status unknown	3	1.2
Employed	229	91.6
Pursuing graduate degrees	2	0.8
Unemployed seeking employment	17	6.8
Unemployed not seeking employment	2	0.8
Type of Employment		
# employed in law firms	135	59.0
# employed in business & industry	37	16.2
# employed in government	27	11.8
# employed in public interest	5	2.2
# employed as judicial clerks	21	9.2
# employed in academia	4	1.7
Geographic Location		
# employed in state	110	48.0
# employed in foreign countries	7	3.1
# of states where employed	27	

J.D. Attrition (from Prior Year)

	Academic	Other	TOTALS	
	#	#	#	%
1st Year	0	6	6	2.9%
2nd Year	0	9	9	4.3%
3rd Year	1	1	2	0.9%
4th Year	0	0	0	0.0%

Bar Passage Rates

Jurisdiction	Georgia		
Exam	Sum 97	Win 98	Total
# from school taking bar for the first time	130	13	143
School's pass rate for all first-time takers	95%	85%	94%
State's pass rate for all first-time takers	86%	74%	83%

FLORIDA STATE UNIVERSITY

425 W. Jefferson Street
Tallahassee, FL 32306-1601
(850)644-3400
http://www.law.fsu.edu

ABA Approved Since 1968

The Basics

Type of School: Public — Term: Semester

Application deadline: 02/15

Application fee: $20

Financial Aid deadline: 03/01

Can first year start other than Fall? No

Student faculty ratio: 18.8 to 1

Does the University offer:

- housing restricted to law students? No
- graduate student housing for which law students are eligible? Yes

Faculty & Administrators

	Total		Men		Women		Minorities	
	Fall	Spr	Fall	Spr	Fall	Spr	Fall	Spr
Full-time	29	31	18	21	11	10	5	5
Other Full-Time	6	6	1	1	5	5	0	0
Deans, librarians, & others who teach > 1/2	2	2	2	2	0	0	0	0
Part-time	8	12	4	9	4	3	1	1
Total	45	51	25	33	20	18	6	6
Deans, librarians, & others who teach < 1/2	1	1	1	1	0	0	0	0

Curriculum

	Full time	Part time
Typical first-year section size	70	0
Is there typically a "small section" of the first year class, other than Legal Writing, taught by full-time faculty?	No	No
If yes, typical size offered last year	N/A	N/A
# of classroom course titles beyond 1st year curriculum	130	0
# of upper division courses, excluding seminars, with an enrollment:		
Under 25	62	0
25 - 49	23	0
50 - 74	14	0
75 - 99	3	0
100 +	4	0
# of seminars	21	0
# of seminar positions available	344	
# of seminar positions filled	237	0
# of positions available in simulation courses	210	
# of simulation positions filled	171	0
# of positions available in faculty supervised clinical courses	38	
# of fac. sup. clin. positions filled	30	0
# involved in field placements	97	0
# involved in law journals	209	0
# in moot court or trial competitions	69	0
# of credit hrs required to graduate	88	

J.D. Enrollment & Ethnicity

	Men		Women		Fl-Time		Pt-Time		1st Yr		2nd Yr		3rd Yr		4th Yr		Total		JD Degrees Awarded
	#	%	#	%	#	%	#	%	#	%	#	%	#	%	#	%	#	%	
African-American	30	8.3	50	17.1	80	12.2	0	0.0	24	10.5	26	11.5	30	15.1	0	0.0	80	12.2	20
American Indian	4	1.1	3	1.0	7	1.1	0	0.0	1	0.4	4	1.8	2	1.0	0	0.0	7	1.1	3
Asian American	6	1.7	4	1.4	10	1.5	0	0.0	2	0.9	3	1.3	5	2.5	0	0.0	10	1.5	9
Mexican American	1	0.3	0	0.0	1	0.2	0	0.0	0	0.0	1	0.4	0	0.0	0	0.0	1	0.2	0
Puerto Rican	5	1.4	3	1.0	8	1.2	0	0.0	3	1.3	5	2.2	0	0.0	0	0.0	8	1.2	1
Hispanic American	30	8.3	23	7.8	53	8.1	0	0.0	17	7.4	17	7.5	19	9.5	0	0.0	53	8.1	17
Total Minorities	76	21.1	83	28.3	159	24.3	0	0.0	47	20.5	56	24.8	56	28.1	0	0.0	159	24.3	50
Foreign Nationals	1	0.3	1	0.3	2	0.3	0	0.0	1	0.4	0	0.0	1	0.5	0	0.0	2	0.3	0
Caucasian	284	78.7	209	71.3	493	75.4	0	0.0	181	79.0	170	75.2	142	71.4	0	0.0	493	75.4	169
Total	361	55.2	293	44.8	654	100.0	0	0.0	229	35.0	226	34.6	199	30.4	0	0.0	654		219

GPA & LSAT Scores

	Full Time	Part Time	Total
# of apps	1,879	0	1,879
# admits	625	0	625
# of matrics	225	0	225
75% GPA	3.57	0.00	
25% GPA	3.07	0.00	
75% LSAT	159	0	
25% LSAT	153	0	

Tuition & Fees

	Resident	Non-resident
Full-Time	$4,650	$15,386
Part-Time	$0	$0

Living Expenses

Estimated living expenses for Singles		
Living on campus	Living off campus	Living at home
$14,100	$14,100	$14,100

Grants/Scholarships

	Full-time		Part-time		Total	
	#	%	#	%	#	%
Total # of Students	654		0		654	
Total # receiving grants	77	11.8	0	0.0	77	11.8
Less than 1/2 tuition	70	10.7	0	0.0	70	10.7
Half to full tuition	2	0.3	0	0.0	2	0.3
Full tuition	0	0.0	0	0.0	0	0.0
More than full tuition	5	0.8	0	0.0	5	0.8
Median Grant Amount	$1,000		$0			

Informational & Library Resources

# of volumes & volume equivalents	401,020	# of professional staff	7
# of titles	147,231	Hours per week with professional staff	50
# of active serial subscriptions	5,441	Hours per week without professional staff	43
Study seating capacity inside the library	351	# of student computer work stations for entire law school	70
Square feet of law library	33,237	# of additional networked connections	0
Square feet of law school (excl. Library)	57,433	Require Laptop Computer?	N

Employment

	Total	%
Employment status known	173	88.3
Employment status unknown	23	11.7
Employed	154	89.0
Pursuing graduate degrees	2	1.2
Unemployed seeking employment	15	8.7
Unemployed not seeking employment	2	1.2
Type of Employment		
# employed in law firms	86	55.8
# employed in business & industry	7	4.5
# employed in government	29	18.8
# employed in public interest	16	10.4
# employed as judicial clerks	11	7.1
# employed in academia	2	1.3
Geographic Location		
# employed in state	125	81.2
# employed in foreign countries	0	0.0
# of states where employed	6	

J.D. Attrition (from Prior Year)

	Academic	Other	TOTALS	
	#	#	#	%
1st Year	0	3	3	1.4%
2nd Year	0	2	2	1.0%
3rd Year	1	0	1	0.5%
4th Year	0	0	0	0.0%

Bar Passage Rates

Jurisdiction	Florida		
Exam	Sum 97	Win 98	Total
# from school taking bar for the first time	142	33	175
School's pass rate for all first-time takers	90%	76%	87%
State's pass rate for all first-time takers	84%	82%	83%

FLORIDA, UNIVERSITY OF

P.O. Box 117620
Gainesville, FL 32611
(352)392-9238
http://www.law.ufl.edu

ABA Approved Since 1925

The Basics

Type of School: Public — Term: Semester

Application deadline: 02/01

Application fee: $20

Financial Aid deadline: 03/15

Can first year start other than Fall? Yes

Student faculty ratio: 24.5 to 1

Does the University offer:
- housing restricted to law students? No
- graduate student housing for which law students are eligible? No

Faculty & Administrators

	Total		Men		Women		Minorities	
	Fall	Spr	Fall	Spr	Fall	Spr	Fall	Spr
Full-time	38	42	27	29	11	13	7	7
Other Full-Time	15	15	3	3	12	12	0	0
Deans, librarians, & others who teach > 1/2	6	6	5	5	1	1	0	0
Part-time	19	18	16	16	3	2	2	1
Total	78	81	51	53	27	28	9	8
Deans, librarians, & others who teach < 1/2	2	2	2	2	0	0	0	0

Curriculum

	Full time	Part time
Typical first-year section size	100	0
Is there typically a "small section" of the first year class, other than Legal Writing, taught by full-time faculty?	No	No
If yes, typical size offered last year	N/A	N/A
# of classroom course titles beyond 1st year curriculum	80	0
# of upper division courses, excluding seminars, with an enrollment:		
Under 25	18	0
25 - 49	45	0
50 - 74	17	0
75 - 99	22	0
100 +	16	0
# of seminars	42	0
# of seminar positions available	610	
# of seminar positions filled	503	0
# of positions available in simulation courses	440	
# of simulation positions filled	438	0
# of positions available in faculty supervised clinical courses	224	
# of fac. sup. clin. positions filled	224	0
# involved in field placements	49	0
# involved in law journals	172	0
# in moot court or trial competitions	48	0
# of credit hrs required to graduate	88	

J.D. Enrollment & Ethnicity

	Men		Women		Fl-Time		Pt-Time		1st Yr		2nd Yr		3rd Yr		4th Yr		Total		JD Degrees Awarded
	#	%	#	%	#	%	#	%	#	%	#	%	#	%	#	%	#	%	
African-American	36	5.7	70	14.2	106	9.4	0	0.0	47	11.4	25	7.2	34	9.4	0	0.0	106	9.4	65
American Indian	1	0.2	4	0.8	5	0.4	0	0.0	3	0.7	1	0.3	1	0.3	0	0.0	5	0.4	1
Asian American	22	3.5	18	3.7	40	3.6	0	0.0	20	4.8	8	2.3	12	3.3	0	0.0	40	3.6	13
Mexican American	0	0.0	0	0.0	0	0.0	0	0.0	0	0.0	0	0.0	0	0.0	0	0.0	0	0.0	0
Puerto Rican	3	0.5	2	0.4	5	0.4	0	0.0	3	0.7	1	0.3	1	0.3	0	0.0	5	0.4	1
Hispanic American	64	10.2	47	9.5	111	9.9	0	0.0	38	9.2	36	10.3	37	10.2	0	0.0	111	9.9	21
Total Minorities	126	20.0	141	28.6	267	23.8	0	0.0	111	26.9	71	20.4	85	23.5	0	0.0	267	23.8	101
Foreign Nationals	2	0.3	4	0.8	6	0.5	0	0.0	2	0.5	2	0.6	2	0.6	0	0.0	6	0.5	0
Caucasian	502	79.7	348	70.6	850	75.7	0	0.0	300	72.6	275	79.0	275	76.0	0	0.0	850	75.7	267
Total	630	56.1	493	43.9	1123	100.0	0	0.0	413	36.8	348	31.0	362	32.2	0	0.0	1123		368

GPA & LSAT Scores

	Full Time	Part Time	Total
# of apps	2,352	0	2,352
# admits	770	0	770
# of matrics	400	0	400
75% GPA	3.70		
25% GPA	3.27		
75% LSAT	160		
25% LSAT	152		

U. of Florida admits multiple classes during the year. Different data may exist for each class. Applicants should contact the school for specific information.

Tuition & Fees

	Resident	Non-resident
Full-Time	$4,311	$14,330
Part-Time	$0	$0

Living Expenses

Estimated living expenses for Singles

Living on campus	Living off campus	Living at home
$9,195	$10,105	$5,035

Grants/Scholarships

	Full-time		Part-time		Total	
	#	%	#	%	#	%
Total # of Students						
Total # receiving grants	197	17.5	0	0.0	197	17.5
Less than 1/2 tuition	137	12.2	0	0.0	137	12.2
Half to full tuition	48	4.3	0	0.0	48	4.3
Full tuition	0	0.0	0	0.0	0	0.0
More than full tuition	12	1.1	0	0.0	12	1.1
Median Grant Amount	$2,006		$0			

Informational & Library Resources

# of volumes & volume equivalents	581,269	# of professional staff	11
# of titles	163,474	Hours per week with professional staff	58
# of active serial subscriptions	8,049	Hours per week without professional staff	44
Study seating capacity inside the library	812	# of student computer work stations for entire law school	97
Square feet of law library	47,654	# of additional networked connections	0
Square feet of law school (excl. Library)	96,875	Require Laptop Computer?	N

Employment

	Total	%
Employment status known	375	96.6
Employment status unknown	13	3.4
Employed	312	83.2
Pursuing graduate degrees	17	4.5
Unemployed seeking employment	44	11.7
Unemployed not seeking employment	2	0.5
Type of Employment		
# employed in law firms	209	67.0
# employed in business & industry	31	9.9
# employed in government	50	16.0
# employed in public interest	4	1.3
# employed as judicial clerks	12	3.8
# employed in academia	1	0.3
Geographic Location		
# employed in state	257	82.4
# employed in foreign countries	0	0.0
# of states where employed	15	

J.D. Attrition (from Prior Year)

	Academic	Other	TOTALS	
	#	#	#	%
1st Year	1	14	15	3.6%
2nd Year	1	6	7	1.9%
3rd Year	0	1	1	0.3%
4th Year	0	0	0	0.0%

Bar Passage Rates

Jurisdiction	Florida		
Exam	Sum 97	Win 98	Total
# from school taking bar for the first time	210	127	337
School's pass rate for all first-time takers	89%	86%	88%
State's pass rate for all first-time takers	84%	82%	83%

FORDHAM UNIVERSITY

140 West 62nd Street
New York, NY 10023-7485
(212)636-6875
http://www.fordham.edu/law/cle/law_main

ABA Approved Since 1936

The Basics

Type of School: Private Term: Semester
Application deadline: 03/01
Application fee: $60
Financial Aid deadline: 04/30
Can first year start other than Fall? No
Student faculty ratio: 22.1 to 1
Does the University offer:
- housing restricted to law students? Yes
- graduate student housing for which law students are eligible? No

Curriculum

	Full time	Part time
Typical first-year section size	69	77
Is there typically a "small section" of the first year class, other than Legal Writing, taught by full-time faculty?	Yes	Yes
If yes, typical size offered last year	35	40
# of classroom course titles beyond 1st year curriculum	110	96
# of upper division courses, excluding seminars, with an enrollment:		
Under 25	30	13
25 - 49	35	23
50 - 74	11	16
75 - 99	9	7
100 +	6	2
# of seminars	43	42
# of seminar positions available	1,739	
# of seminar positions filled	632	527
# of positions available in simulation courses	426	
# of simulation positions filled	68	358
# of positions available in faculty supervised clinical courses	146	
# of fac. sup. clin. positions filled	131	15
# involved in field placements	36	294
# involved in law journals	324	0
# in moot court or trial competitions	351	0
# of credit hrs required to graduate	83	

Faculty & Administrators

	Total		Men		Women		Minorities	
	Fall	Spr	Fall	Spr	Fall	Spr	Fall	Spr
Full-time	51	51	38	37	13	14	5	5
Other Full-Time	7	6	0	0	7	6	1	1
Deans, librarians, & others who teach > 1/2	1	1	1	1	0	0	0	0
Part-time	98	117	64	84	34	33	8	5
Total	157	175	103	122	54	53	14	11
Deans, librarians, & others who teach < 1/2	5	5	2	2	3	3	1	1

J.D. Enrollment & Ethnicity

	Men		Women		Fl-Time		Pt-Time		1st Yr		2nd Yr		3rd Yr		4th Yr		Total		JD Degrees Awarded
	#	%	#	%	#	%	#	%	#	%	#	%	#	%	#	%	#	%	
African-American	56	6.8	74	11.3	88	7.9	42	11.4	39	8.0	43	9.3	35	7.8	13	17.1	130	8.8	40
American Indian	0	0.0	0	0.0	0	0.0	0	0.0	0	0.0	0	0.0	0	0.0	0	0.0	0	0.0	1
Asian American	51	6.2	67	10.2	104	9.4	14	3.8	47	9.7	35	7.5	35	7.8	1	1.3	118	8.0	31
Mexican American	3	0.4	1	0.2	4	0.4	0	0.0	1	0.2	2	0.4	1	0.2	0	0.0	4	0.3	3
Puerto Rican	30	3.7	31	4.7	37	3.3	24	6.5	18	3.7	14	3.0	22	4.9	7	9.2	61	4.1	15
Hispanic American	23	2.8	24	3.7	34	3.1	13	3.5	17	3.5	16	3.4	12	2.7	2	2.6	47	3.2	10
Total Minorities	163	19.9	197	30.1	267	24.1	93	25.3	122	25.1	110	23.7	105	23.3	23	30.3	360	24.4	100
Foreign Nationals	0	0.0	0	0.0	0	0.0	0	0.0	0	0.0	0	0.0	0	0.0	0	0.0	0	0.0	0
Caucasian	658	80.1	458	69.9	841	75.9	275	74.7	364	74.9	354	76.3	345	76.7	53	69.7	1116	75.6	330
Total	821	55.6	655	44.4	1108	75.1	368	24.9	486	32.9	464	31.4	450	30.5	76	5.1	1476		430

GPA & LSAT Scores

	Full Time	Part Time	Total
# of apps	3,790	668	4,458
# admits	1,182	208	1,390
# of matrics	351	135	486
75% GPA	3.63	3.51	
25% GPA	3.09	2.88	
75% LSAT	165	161	
25% LSAT	160	156	

Tuition & Fees

	Resident	Non-resident
Full-Time	$23,790	$23,790
Part-Time	$17,840	$17,840

Living Expenses

Estimated living expenses for Singles		
Living on campus	Living off campus	Living at home
$17,330	$17,330	$5,080

Employment

	Total	%
Employment status known	379	94.3
Employment status unknown	23	5.7
Employed	363	95.8
Pursuing graduate degrees	4	1.1
Unemployed seeking employment	11	2.9
Unemployed not seeking employment	1	0.3
Type of Employment		
# employed in law firms	241	66.4
# employed in business & industry	55	15.2
# employed in government	35	9.6
# employed in public interest	8	2.2
# employed as judicial clerks	22	6.1
# employed in academia	2	0.6
Geographic Location		
# employed in state	306	84.3
# employed in foreign countries	0	0.0
# of states where employed	16	

Grants/Scholarships

	Full-time		Part-time		Total	
	#	%	#	%	#	%
Total # of Students	1108		368		1476	
Total # receiving grants	435	39.3	43	11.7	478	32.4
Less than 1/2 tuition	405	36.6	39	10.6	444	30.1
Half to full tuition	23	2.1	4	1.1	27	1.8
Full tuition	7	0.6	0	0.0	7	0.5
More than full tuition	0	0.0	0	0.0	0	0.0
Median Grant Amount	$8,400		$2,900			

Informational & Library Resources

# of volumes & volume equivalents	525,864	# of professional staff	14
# of titles	172,834	Hours per week with professional staff	86
# of active serial subscriptions	5,270	Hours per week without professional staff	36
Study seating capacity inside the library	465	# of student computer work stations for entire law school	42
Square feet of law library	45,755	# of additional networked connections	103
Square feet of law school (excl. Library)	129,398	Require Laptop Computer?	N

J.D. Attrition (from Prior Year)

	Academic	Other	TOTALS	
	#	#	#	%
1st Year	2	7	9	2.0%
2nd Year	2	14	16	3.5%
3rd Year	4	0	4	0.9%
4th Year	0	0	0	0.0%

Bar Passage Rates

Jurisdiction	New York		
Exam	Sum 97	Win 98	Total
# from school taking bar for the first time	369	27	396
School's pass rate for all first-time takers	86%	59%	84%
State's pass rate for all first-time takers	78%	65%	76%

FRANKLIN PIERCE LAW CENTER

2 White Street
Concord, NH 03301
(603)228-1541
http://www.fplc.edu

ABA Approved Since 1974

The Basics

Type of School: Private — Term: Semester
Application deadline: 05/01
Application fee: $45
Financial Aid deadline: 05/15
Can first year start other than Fall? Yes
Student faculty ratio: 24.4 to 1
Does the University offer:
- housing restricted to law students? No
- graduate student housing for which law students are eligible? Yes

Faculty & Administrators

	Total		Men		Women		Minorities	
	Fall	Spr	Fall	Spr	Fall	Spr	Fall	Spr
Full-time	13	12	10	10	3	2	0	0
Other Full-Time	2	2	1	1	1	1	0	0
Deans, librarians, & others who teach > 1/2	0	0	0	0	0	0	0	0
Part-time	25	43	21	26	4	13	1	0
Total	40	57	32	37	8	16	1	0
Deans, librarians, & others who teach < 1/2	6	7	4	4	2	3	0	0

Curriculum

	Full time	Part time
Typical first-year section size	114	0
Is there typically a "small section" of the first year class, other than Legal Writing, taught by full-time faculty?	Yes	No
If yes, typical size offered last year	41	N/A
# of classroom course titles beyond 1st year curriculum	97	0
# of upper division courses, excluding seminars, with an enrollment:		
Under 25	32	0
25 - 49	19	0
50 - 74	5	0
75 - 99	4	0
100 +	7	0
# of seminars	18	0
# of seminar positions available	325	
# of seminar positions filled	241	0
# of positions available in simulation courses	361	
# of simulation positions filled	283	0
# of positions available in faculty supervised clinical courses	185	
# of fac. sup. clin. positions filled	176	0
# involved in field placements	75	0
# involved in law journals	37	0
# in moot court or trial competitions	23	0
# of credit hrs required to graduate	84	

J.D. Enrollment & Ethnicity

	Men		Women		Fl-Time		Pt-Time		1st Yr		2nd Yr		3rd Yr		4th Yr		Total		JD Degrees Awarded
	#	%	#	%	#	%	#	%	#	%	#	%	#	%	#	%	#	%	
African-American	6	2.6	3	2.0	9	2.4	0	0.0	2	1.8	3	2.3	4	2.8	0	0.0	9	2.3	2
American Indian	1	0.4	2	1.3	3	0.8	0	0.0	0	0.0	3	2.3	0	0.0	0	0.0	3	0.8	2
Asian American	11	4.7	15	10.0	25	6.7	1	9.1	7	6.1	13	10.2	6	4.2	0	0.0	26	6.8	6
Mexican American	0	0.0	0	0.0	0	0.0	0	0.0	0	0.0	0	0.0	0	0.0	0	0.0	0	0.0	0
Puerto Rican	0	0.0	0	0.0	0	0.0	0	0.0	0	0.0	0	0.0	0	0.0	0	0.0	0	0.0	0
Hispanic American	13	5.6	3	2.0	16	4.3	0	0.0	9	7.9	4	3.1	3	2.1	0	0.0	16	4.2	5
Total Minorities	31	13.2	23	15.3	53	14.2	1	9.1	18	15.8	23	18.0	13	9.2	0	0.0	54	14.1	15
Foreign Nationals	11	4.7	4	2.7	15	4.0	0	0.0	0	0.0	6	4.7	9	6.3	0	0.0	15	3.9	1
Caucasian	192	82.1	123	82.0	305	81.8	10	90.9	96	84.2	99	77.3	120	84.5	0	0.0	315	82.0	103
Total	234	60.9	150	39.1	373	97.1	11	2.9	114	29.7	128	33.3	142	37.0	0	0.0	384		119

GPA & LSAT Scores

	Full Time	Part Time	Total
# of apps	781	1	782
# admits	510	1	511
# of matrics	114	1	115
75% GPA	3.31	0.00	
25% GPA	2.60	0.00	
75% LSAT	155	0	
25% LSAT	146	0	

Tuition & Fees

	Resident	Non-resident
Full-Time	$16,475	$16,475
Part-Time	$0	$0

Living Expenses

Estimated living expenses for Singles		
Living on campus	Living off campus	Living at home
N/A	$12,540	$12,540

Grants/Scholarships

	Full-time		Part-time		Total	
	#	%	#	%	#	%
Total # of Students	373		11		384	
Total # receiving grants	232	62.2	3	27.3	235	61.2
Less than 1/2 tuition	210	56.3	2	18.2	212	55.2
Half to full tuition	13	3.5	0	0.0	13	3.4
Full tuition	9	2.4	1	9.1	10	2.6
More than full tuition	0	0.0	0	0.0	0	0.0
Median Grant Amount	$2,403		$3,860			

Informational & Library Resources

# of volumes & volume equivalents	213,018	# of professional staff	6
# of titles	49,816	Hours per week with professional staff	45
# of active serial subscriptions	2,748	Hours per week without professional staff	59
Study seating capacity inside the library	267	# of student computer work stations for entire law school	75
Square feet of law library	20,016	# of additional networked connections	325
Square feet of law school (excl. Library)	53,984	Require Laptop Computer?	N

Employment

	Total	%
Employment status known	112	90.3
Employment status unknown	12	9.7
Employed	97	86.6
Pursuing graduate degrees	1	0.9
Unemployed seeking employment	12	10.7
Unemployed not seeking employment	2	1.8
Type of Employment		
# employed in law firms	67	69.1
# employed in business & industry	9	9.3
# employed in government	9	9.3
# employed in public interest	2	2.1
# employed as judicial clerks	1	1.0
# employed in academia	3	3.1
Geographic Location		
# employed in state	21	21.6
# employed in foreign countries	2	2.1
# of states where employed	26	

J.D. Attrition (from Prior Year)

	Academic	Other	TOTALS	
	#	#	#	%
1st Year	1	8	9	6.6%
2nd Year	2	4	6	4.2%
3rd Year	2	0	2	1.6%
4th Year	0	0	0	0.0%

Bar Passage Rates

Jurisdiction	New Hampshire		
Exam	Sum 97	Win 98	Total
# from school taking bar for the first time	27	8	35
School's pass rate for all first-time takers	70%	88%	74%
State's pass rate for all first-time takers	77%	71%	75%

GEORGE MASON UNIVERSITY

3401 North Fairfax Drive
Arlington, VA 22201-4498
(703)993-8000
http://www.gmu.edu/departments/law

ABA Approved Since 1980

The Basics

Type of School: Public — Term: Semester

Application deadline: 03/01

Application fee: $35

Financial Aid deadline: 03/01

Can first year start other than Fall? No

Student faculty ratio: 23.4 to 1

Does the University offer:
- housing restricted to law students? No
- graduate student housing for which law students are eligible? No

Faculty & Administrators

	Total		Men		Women		Minorities	
	Fall	Spr	Fall	Spr	Fall	Spr	Fall	Spr
Full-time	22	22	20	20	2	2	2	2
Other Full-Time	2	2	1	1	1	1	0	0
Deans, librarians, & others who teach > 1/2	0	0	0	0	0	0	0	0
Part-time	41	63	33	55	8	8	4	7
Total	65	87	54	76	11	11	6	9
Deans, librarians, & others who teach < 1/2	0	0	0	0	0	0	0	0

Curriculum

	Full time	Part time
Typical first-year section size	118	92
Is there typically a "small section" of the first year class, other than Legal Writing, taught by full-time faculty?	No	No
If yes, typical size offered last year	N/A	N/A
# of classroom course titles beyond 1st year curriculum	60	81
# of upper division courses, excluding seminars, with an enrollment:		
Under 25	34	33
25 - 49	11	22
50 - 74	0	11
75 - 99	3	3
100 +	3	1
# of seminars	6	5
# of seminar positions available	191	
# of seminar positions filled	80	101
# of positions available in simulation courses	156	
# of simulation positions filled	56	41
# of positions available in faculty supervised clinical courses	13	
# of fac. sup. clin. positions filled	10	3
# involved in field placements	59	11
# involved in law journals	20	8
# in moot court or trial competitions	9	1
# of credit hrs required to graduate	87	

J.D. Enrollment & Ethnicity

	Men		Women		Fl-Time		Pt-Time		1st Yr		2nd Yr		3rd Yr		4th Yr		Total		JD Degrees Awarded
	#	%	#	%	#	%	#	%	#	%	#	%	#	%	#	%	#	%	
African-American	10	2.2	9	3.1	8	2.1	11	3.0	5	2.4	4	1.8	4	1.9	6	5.6	19	2.6	9
American Indian	1	0.2	3	1.0	2	0.5	2	0.6	2	0.9	0	0.0	2	1.0	0	0.0	4	0.5	0
Asian American	19	4.2	22	7.5	19	5.0	22	6.1	15	7.1	9	4.1	10	4.9	7	6.5	41	5.5	6
Mexican American	0	0.0	0	0.0	0	0.0	0	0.0	0	0.0	0	0.0	0	0.0	0	0.0	0	0.0	0
Puerto Rican	0	0.0	0	0.0	0	0.0	0	0.0	0	0.0	0	0.0	0	0.0	0	0.0	0	0.0	0
Hispanic American	14	3.1	6	2.1	8	2.1	12	3.3	8	3.8	9	4.1	2	1.0	1	0.9	20	2.7	0
Total Minorities	44	9.8	40	13.7	37	9.8	47	13.0	30	14.2	22	10.1	18	8.7	14	13.1	84	11.3	15
Foreign Nationals	0	0.0	0	0.0	0	0.0	0	0.0	0	0.0	0	0.0	0	0.0	0	0.0	0	0.0	0
Caucasian	405	90.2	252	86.3	342	90.2	315	87.0	181	85.8	195	89.9	188	91.3	93	86.9	657	88.7	167
Total	449	60.6	292	39.4	379	51.1	362	48.9	211	28.5	217	29.3	206	27.8	107	14.4	741		182

GPA & LSAT Scores

	Full Time	Part Time	Total
# of apps	1,400	538	1,938
# admits	474	191	665
# of matrics	115	94	209
75% GPA	3.40	3.38	
25% GPA	2.83	2.74	
75% LSAT	161	160	
25% LSAT	156	153	

Tuition & Fees

	Resident	Non-resident
Full-Time	$7,644	$18,214
Part-Time	$2,730	$6,505

Living Expenses

Estimated living expenses for Singles		
Living on campus	Living off campus	Living at home
N/A	$15,141	N/A

Grants/Scholarships

	Full-time		Part-time		Total	
	#	%	#	%	#	%
Total # of Students	379		362		741	
Total # receiving grants	18	4.7	9	2.5	27	3.6
Less than 1/2 tuition	9	2.4	2	0.6	11	1.5
Half to full tuition	4	1.1	4	1.1	8	1.1
Full tuition	0	0.0	0	0.0	0	0.0
More than full tuition	5	1.3	3	0.8	8	1.1
Median Grant Amount	$5,000		$5,500			

Informational & Library Resources

# of volumes & volume equivalents	374,026	# of professional staff	6
# of titles	146,844	Hours per week with professional staff	85
# of active serial subscriptions	5,342	Hours per week without professional staff	8
Study seating capacity inside the library	342	# of student computer work stations for entire law school	0
Square feet of law library	29,663	# of additional networked connections	31
Square feet of law school (excl. Library)	38,025	Require Laptop Computer?	N

Employment

	Total	%
Employment status known	157	88.2
Employment status unknown	21	11.8
Employed	131	83.4
Pursuing graduate degrees	3	1.9
Unemployed seeking employment	22	14.0
Unemployed not seeking employment	1	0.6
Type of Employment		
# employed in law firms	56	42.7
# employed in business & industry	23	17.6
# employed in government	33	25.2
# employed in public interest	0	0.0
# employed as judicial clerks	17	13.0
# employed in academia	2	1.5
Geographic Location		
# employed in state	51	38.9
# employed in foreign countries	1	0.8
# of states where employed	15	

J.D. Attrition (from Prior Year)

	Academic	Other	TOTALS	
	#	#	#	%
1st Year	1	10	11	5.2%
2nd Year	0	0	0	0.0%
3rd Year	0	1	1	0.5%
4th Year	1	1	2	2.2%

Bar Passage Rates

Jurisdiction	Virginia		
Exam	Sum 97	Win 98	Total
# from school taking bar for the first time	113	19	132
School's pass rate for all first-time takers	76%	100%	80%
State's pass rate for all first-time takers	76%	68%	75%

GEORGE WASHINGTON UNIVERSITY

2000 H Street, N.W.
Washington, DC 20052
(202)994-7230
http://www.law.gwu.edu

ABA Approved Since 1923

The Basics

Type of School: Private   Term: Semester
Application deadline: 03/01
Application fee: $55
Financial Aid deadline: 03/01
Can first year start other than Fall? No
Student faculty ratio: 16.9 to 1
Does the University offer:
- housing restricted to law students? No
- graduate student housing for which law students are eligible? Yes

Faculty & Administrators

	Total		Men		Women		Minorities	
	Fall	Spr	Fall	Spr	Fall	Spr	Fall	Spr
Full-time	65	64	47	45	18	19	9	9
Other Full-Time	0	0	0	0	0	0	0	0
Deans, librarians, & others who teach > 1/2	2	2	1	1	1	1	1	1
Part-time	100	129	66	94	34	35	11	7
Total	167	195	114	140	53	55	21	17
Deans, librarians, & others who teach < 1/2	4	4	3	3	1	1	0	0

Curriculum

	Full time	Part time
Typical first-year section size	90	50
Is there typically a "small section" of the first year class, other than Legal Writing, taught by full-time faculty?	No	No
If yes, typical size offered last year	N/A	N/A
# of classroom course titles beyond 1st year curriculum	114	104
# of upper division courses, excluding seminars, with an enrollment:		
Under 25	97	79
25 - 49	38	20
50 - 74	21	11
75 - 99	14	2
100 +	15	1
# of seminars	15	11
# of seminar positions available	416	
# of seminar positions filled	156	131
# of positions available in simulation courses	722	
# of simulation positions filled	215	316
# of positions available in faculty supervised clinical courses	202	
# of fac. sup. clin. positions filled	168	4
# involved in field placements	213	5
# involved in law journals	433	26
# in moot court or trial competitions	211	18
# of credit hrs required to graduate	84	

J.D. Enrollment & Ethnicity

	Men		Women		Fl-Time		Pt-Time		1st Yr		2nd Yr		3rd Yr		4th Yr		Total		JD Degrees Awarded
	#	%	#	%	#	%	#	%	#	%	#	%	#	%	#	%	#	%	
African-American	70	8.8	116	19.1	133	11.4	53	22.3	64	13.1	54	12.8	56	12.8	12	21.8	186	13.3	61
American Indian	2	0.3	3	0.5	3	0.3	2	0.8	1	0.2	2	0.5	2	0.5	0	0.0	5	0.4	0
Asian American	62	7.8	72	11.9	117	10.0	17	7.1	54	11.1	30	7.1	48	11.0	2	3.6	134	9.6	41
Mexican American	0	0.0	0	0.0	0	0.0	0	0.0	0	0.0	0	0.0	0	0.0	0	0.0	0	0.0	0
Puerto Rican	0	0.0	0	0.0	0	0.0	0	0.0	0	0.0	0	0.0	0	0.0	0	0.0	0	0.0	0
Hispanic American	57	7.2	34	5.6	82	7.0	9	3.8	34	7.0	31	7.3	24	5.5	2	3.6	91	6.5	39
Total Minorities	191	24.0	225	37.1	335	28.8	81	34.0	153	31.4	117	27.7	130	29.7	16	29.1	416	29.7	141
Foreign Nationals	11	1.4	5	0.8	16	1.4	0	0.0	7	1.4	6	1.4	3	0.7	0	0.0	16	1.1	6
Caucasian	594	74.6	377	62.1	814	69.9	157	66.0	328	67.2	299	70.9	305	69.6	39	70.9	971	69.2	332
Total	796	56.7	607	43.3	1165	83.0	238	17.0	488	34.8	422	30.1	438	31.2	55	3.9	1403		479

GPA & LSAT Scores

	Full Time	Part Time	Total
# of apps	N/A	N/A	6,127
# admits	N/A	N/A	2,006
# of matrics	404	68	472
75% GPA	3.57	3.43	
25% GPA	3.21	2.82	
75% LSAT	164	161	
25% LSAT	160	153	

Tuition & Fees

	Resident	Non-resident
Full-Time	$23,955	$23,955
Part-Time	$16,850	$16,850

Living Expenses

Estimated living expenses for Singles		
Living on campus	Living off campus	Living at home
N/A	$13,587	$13,587

Employment

	Total	%
Employment status known	462	98.1
Employment status unknown	9	1.9
Employed	446	96.5
Pursuing graduate degrees	1	0.2
Unemployed seeking employment	14	3.0
Unemployed not seeking employment	1	0.2
Type of Employment		
# employed in law firms	254	57.0
# employed in business & industry	31	7.0
# employed in government	58	13.0
# employed in public interest	18	4.0
# employed as judicial clerks	62	13.9
# employed in academia	4	0.9
Geographic Location		
# employed in state	201	45.1
# employed in foreign countries	4	0.9
# of states where employed	28	

Grants/Scholarships

	Full-time		Part-time		Total	
	#	%	#	%	#	%
Total # of Students	1165		238		1403	
Total # receiving grants	466	40.0	22	9.2	488	34.8
Less than 1/2 tuition	71	6.1	21	8.8	92	6.6
Half to full tuition	394	33.8	1	0.4	395	28.2
Full tuition	1	0.1	0	0.0	1	0.1
More than full tuition	0	0.0	0	0.0	0	0.0
Median Grant Amount	$9,000		$4,000			

Informational & Library Resources

# of volumes & volume equivalents	509,753	# of professional staff	16
# of titles	104,457	Hours per week with professional staff	81
# of active serial subscriptions	5,516	Hours per week without professional staff	29
Study seating capacity inside the library	711	# of student computer work stations for entire law school	142
Square feet of law library	45,999	# of additional networked connections	0
Square feet of law school (excl. Library)	136,931	Require Laptop Computer?	N

J.D. Attrition (from Prior Year)

	Academic	Other	TOTALS	
	#	#	#	%
1st Year	0	18	18	3.9%
2nd Year	0	6	6	1.4%
3rd Year	0	1	1	0.2%
4th Year	0	0	0	0.0%

Bar Passage Rates

Jurisdiction	Maryland			New York		
Exam	Sum 97	Win 98	Total	Sum 97	Win 98	Total
# from school taking bar for the first time	141	30	171	105	10	115
School's pass rate for all first-time takers	80%	87%	81%	93%	70%	91%
State's pass rate for all first-time takers	69%	83%	72%	78%	65%	76%

GEORGETOWN UNIVERSITY

600 New Jersey Avenue N.W.
Washington, DC 20001
(202)662-9000
http://www.law.georgetown.edu/lc

ABA Approved Since 1924

The Basics

Type of School: Private Term: Semester

Application deadline: 03/01

Application fee: $65

Financial Aid deadline: 03/01

Can first year start other than Fall? No

Student faculty ratio: 18.1 to 1

Does the University offer:
- housing restricted to law students? Yes
- graduate student housing for which law students are eligible? No

Faculty & Administrators

	Total		Men		Women		Minorities	
	Fall	Spr	Fall	Spr	Fall	Spr	Fall	Spr
Full-time	86	87	56	57	30	30	10	11
Other Full-Time	5	5	2	2	3	3	0	0
Deans, librarians, & others who teach > 1/2	2	2	2	2	0	0	0	0
Part-time	85	104	74	84	11	20	5	4
Total	178	198	134	145	44	53	15	15
Deans, librarians, & others who teach < 1/2	5	6	4	5	1	1	1	1

Curriculum

	Full time	Part time
Typical first-year section size	112	112
Is there typically a "small section" of the first year class, other than Legal Writing, taught by full-time faculty?	Yes	Yes
If yes, typical size offered last year	32	32
# of classroom course titles beyond 1st year curriculum	152	116
# of upper division courses, excluding seminars, with an enrollment:		
Under 25	50	42
25 - 49	31	21
50 - 74	17	9
75 - 99	10	5
100 +	25	7
# of seminars	68	40
# of seminar positions available	2,130	
# of seminar positions filled	891	540
# of positions available in simulation courses	954	
# of simulation positions filled	348	421
# of positions available in faculty supervised clinical courses	266	
# of fac. sup. clin. positions filled	253	13
# involved in field placements	0	0
# involved in law journals	655	71
# in moot court or trial competitions	292	70
# of credit hrs required to graduate	83	

J.D. Enrollment & Ethnicity

	Men		Women		Fl-Time		Pt-Time		1st Yr		2nd Yr		3rd Yr		4th Yr		Total		JD Degrees Awarded
	#	%	#	%	#	%	#	%	#	%	#	%	#	%	#	%	#	%	
African-American	79	7.5	132	13.5	163	10.5	48	10.1	59	10.2	78	12.2	58	8.4	16	13.3	211	10.4	69
American Indian	5	0.5	6	0.6	9	0.6	2	0.4	4	0.7	3	0.5	2	0.3	2	1.7	11	0.5	7
Asian American	83	7.9	112	11.4	164	10.6	31	6.5	53	9.2	55	8.6	77	11.2	10	8.3	195	9.6	56
Mexican American	4	0.4	3	0.3	6	0.4	1	0.2	4	0.7	2	0.3	1	0.1	0	0.0	7	0.3	0
Puerto Rican	4	0.4	3	0.3	6	0.4	1	0.2	3	0.5	1	0.2	3	0.4	0	0.0	7	0.3	1
Hispanic American	49	4.7	51	5.2	94	6.1	6	1.3	25	4.3	46	7.2	26	3.8	3	2.5	100	4.9	37
Total Minorities	224	21.3	307	31.4	442	28.5	89	18.7	148	25.6	185	28.9	167	24.2	31	25.8	531	26.2	170
Foreign Nationals	26	2.5	21	2.1	36	2.3	11	2.3	24	4.1	9	1.4	13	1.9	1	0.8	47	2.3	6
Caucasian	801	76.2	651	66.5	1075	69.2	377	79.0	407	70.3	447	69.7	510	73.9	88	73.3	1452	71.5	489
Total	1051	51.8	979	48.2	1553	76.5	477	23.5	579	28.5	641	31.6	690	34.0	120	5.9	2030		665

GPA & LSAT Scores

	Full Time	Part Time	Total
# of apps	6,442	630	7,072
# admits	1,855	209	2,064
# of matrics	456	129	585
75% GPA	3.76	3.71	
25% GPA	3.27	3.20	
75% LSAT	168	166	
25% LSAT	163	159	

Tuition & Fees

	Resident	Non-resident
Full-Time	$24,530	$24,530
Part-Time	$855	$855

Living Expenses

Estimated living expenses for Singles		
Living on campus	Living off campus	Living at home
$14,720	$14,720	$11,080

Grants/Scholarships

	Full-time		Part-time		Total	
	#	%	#	%	#	%
Total # of Students	1553		477		2030	
Total # receiving grants	500	32.2	7	1.5	507	25.0
Less than 1/2 tuition	385	24.8	7	1.5	392	19.3
Half to full tuition	114	7.3	0	0.0	114	5.6
Full tuition	1	0.1	0	0.0	1	0.0
More than full tuition	0	0.0	0	0.0	0	0.0
Median Grant Amount	$8,400		$5,100			

Informational & Library Resources

# of volumes & volume equivalents	933,290	# of professional staff	19
# of titles	296,563	Hours per week with professional staff	76
# of active serial subscriptions	12,057	Hours per week without professional staff	31
Study seating capacity inside the library	1,075	# of student computer work stations for entire law school	184
Square feet of law library	118,000	# of additional networked connections	969
Square feet of law school (excl. Library)	382,653	Require Laptop Computer?	N

Employment

	Total	%
Employment status known	582	98.0
Employment status unknown	12	2.0
Employed	549	94.3
Pursuing graduate degrees	10	1.7
Unemployed seeking employment	11	1.9
Unemployed not seeking employment	12	2.1
Type of Employment		
# employed in law firms	364	66.3
# employed in business & industry	26	4.7
# employed in government	77	14.0
# employed in public interest	18	3.3
# employed as judicial clerks	43	7.8
# employed in academia	5	0.9
Geographic Location		
# employed in state	252	45.9
# employed in foreign countries	10	1.8
# of states where employed	46	

J.D. Attrition (from Prior Year)

	Academic	Other	TOTALS	
	#	#	#	%
1st Year	0	15	15	2.4%
2nd Year	0	4	4	0.6%
3rd Year	0	0	0	0.0%
4th Year	0	0	0	0.0%

Bar Passage Rates

Jurisdiction	New York			Maryland		
Exam	Sum 97	Win 98	Total	Sum 97	Win 98	Total
# from school taking bar for the first time	158	19	177	117	21	138
School's pass rate for all first-time takers	92%	95%	92%	84%	95%	86%
State's pass rate for all first-time takers	78%	65%	76%	69%	83%	72%

GEORGIA STATE UNIVERSITY

P.O. Box 4037
Atlanta, GA 30302-4037
(404)651-2096
http://gsulaw.gsu.edu

ABA Approved Since 1984

The Basics

Type of School: Public   Term: Semester

Application deadline: 03/15

Application fee: $30

Financial Aid deadline: 04/01

Can first year start other than Fall? No

Student faculty ratio: 16.1 to 1

Does the University offer:
- housing restricted to law students? No
- graduate student housing for which law students are eligible? Yes

Faculty & Administrators

	Total		Men		Women		Minorities	
	Fall	Spr	Fall	Spr	Fall	Spr	Fall	Spr
Full-time	30	31	22	22	8	9	4	4
Other Full-Time	4	4	0	0	4	4	1	1
Deans, librarians, & others who teach > 1/2	2	2	1	1	1	1	0	0
Part-time	6	16	4	11	2	5	1	4
Total	42	53	27	34	15	19	6	9
Deans, librarians, & others who teach < 1/2	4	4	1	1	3	3	1	1

Curriculum

	Full time	Part time
Typical first-year section size	70	70
Is there typically a "small section" of the first year class, other than Legal Writing, taught by full-time faculty?	No	No
If yes, typical size offered last year	N/A	N/A
# of classroom course titles beyond 1st year curriculum	44	47
# of upper division courses, excluding seminars, with an enrollment:		
Under 25	22	26
25 - 49	8	15
50 - 74	14	5
75 - 99	1	1
100 +	0	0
# of seminars	19	0
# of seminar positions available	288	
# of seminar positions filled	223	0
# of positions available in simulation courses	212	
# of simulation positions filled	210	0
# of positions available in faculty supervised clinical courses	150	
# of fac. sup. clin. positions filled	136	0
# involved in field placements	0	0
# involved in law journals	54	0
# in moot court or trial competitions	83	0
# of credit hrs required to graduate	90	

J.D. Enrollment & Ethnicity

	Men		Women		Fl-Time		Pt-Time		1st Yr		2nd Yr		3rd Yr		4th Yr		Total		JD Degrees Awarded
	#	%	#	%	#	%	#	%	#	%	#	%	#	%	#	%	#	%	
African-American	27	8.4	57	16.7	43	10.4	41	16.5	27	11.0	19	10.4	32	15.0	6	28.6	84	12.7	28
American Indian	0	0.0	3	0.9	1	0.2	2	0.8	1	0.4	0	0.0	2	0.9	0	0.0	3	0.5	2
Asian American	12	3.7	13	3.8	18	4.3	7	2.8	6	2.4	8	4.4	11	5.2	0	0.0	25	3.8	13
Mexican American	6	1.9	3	0.9	3	0.7	6	2.4	1	0.4	1	0.5	6	2.8	1	4.8	9	1.4	6
Puerto Rican	0	0.0	0	0.0	0	0.0	0	0.0	0	0.0	0	0.0	0	0.0	0	0.0	0	0.0	0
Hispanic American	33	10.3	10	2.9	31	7.5	12	4.8	21	8.5	12	6.6	9	4.2	1	4.8	43	6.5	4
Total Minorities	78	24.3	86	25.2	96	23.2	68	27.4	56	22.8	40	22.0	60	28.2	8	38.1	164	24.8	53
Foreign Nationals	0	0.0	0	0.0	0	0.0	0	0.0	0	0.0	0	0.0	0	0.0	0	0.0	0	0.0	0
Caucasian	243	75.7	255	74.8	318	76.8	180	72.6	190	77.2	142	78.0	153	71.8	13	61.9	498	75.2	105
Total	321	48.5	341	51.5	414	62.5	248	37.5	246	37.2	182	27.5	213	32.2	21	3.2	662		158

GPA & LSAT Scores

	Full Time	Part Time	Total
# of apps	1,219	306	1,525
# admits	361	82	443
# of matrics	133	65	198
75% GPA	3.49	3.49	
25% GPA	2.88	2.85	
75% LSAT	160	160	
25% LSAT	153	153	

Tuition & Fees

	Resident	Non-resident
Full-Time	$3,682	$13,078
Part-Time	$3,102	$10,758

Living Expenses

Estimated living expenses for Singles		
Living on campus	Living off campus	Living at home
$12,126	$13,280	$7,466

Employment

	Total	%
Employment status known	188	94.9
Employment status unknown	10	5.1
Employed	175	93.1
Pursuing graduate degrees	1	0.5
Unemployed seeking employment	6	3.2
Unemployed not seeking employment	6	3.2
Type of Employment		
# employed in law firms	105	60.0
# employed in business & industry	37	21.1
# employed in government	17	9.7
# employed in public interest	4	2.3
# employed as judicial clerks	8	4.6
# employed in academia	4	2.3
Geographic Location		
# employed in state	159	90.9
# employed in foreign countries	1	0.6
# of states where employed	13	

Grants/Scholarships

	Full-time		Part-time		Total	
	#	%	#	%	#	%
Total # of Students	414		248		662	
Total # receiving grants	24	5.8	32	12.9	56	8.5
Less than 1/2 tuition	2	0.5	1	0.4	3	0.5
Half to full tuition	17	4.1	9	3.6	26	3.9
Full tuition	5	1.2	22	8.9	27	4.1
More than full tuition	0	0.0	0	0.0	0	0.0
Median Grant Amount	$4,500		$1,800			

Informational & Library Resources

# of volumes & volume equivalents	269,240	# of professional staff	4
# of titles	50,870	Hours per week with professional staff	68
# of active serial subscriptions	3,548	Hours per week without professional staff	37
Study seating capacity inside the library	335	# of student computer work stations for entire law school	36
Square feet of law library	37,010	# of additional networked connections	0
Square feet of law school (excl. Library)	43,323	Require Laptop Computer?	N

J.D. Attrition (from Prior Year)

	Academic	Other	TOTALS	
	#	#	#	%
1st Year	7	9	16	8.2%
2nd Year	0	0	0	0.0%
3rd Year	0	0	0	0.0%
4th Year	0	0	0	0.0%

Bar Passage Rates

Jurisdiction	Georgia		
Exam	Sum 97	Win 98	Total
# from school taking bar for the first time	137	37	174
School's pass rate for all first-time takers	87%	76%	84%
State's pass rate for all first-time takers	86%	74%	83%

GEORGIA, UNIVERSITY OF

Herty Drive
Athens, GA 30602
(706)542-7140
http://www.lawsch.uga.edu

ABA Approved Since 1930

The Basics

Type of School: Public Term: Semester
Application deadline: 03/01
Application fee: $30
Financial Aid deadline: 01/31
Can first year start other than Fall? No
Student faculty ratio: 17.6 to 1
Does the University offer:
- housing restricted to law students? No
- graduate student housing for which law students are eligible? Yes

Faculty & Administrators

	Total		Men		Women		Minorities	
	Fall	Spr	Fall	Spr	Fall	Spr	Fall	Spr
Full-time	30	32	24	25	6	7	3	4
Other Full-Time	6	6	1	1	5	5	0	0
Deans, librarians, & others who teach > 1/2	4	4	4	4	0	0	0	0
Part-time	8	30	6	23	2	7	0	3
Total	48	72	35	53	13	19	3	7
Deans, librarians, & others who teach < 1/2	7	7	2	2	5	5	1	1

Curriculum

	Full time	Part time
Typical first-year section size	75	0
Is there typically a "small section" of the first year class, other than Legal Writing, taught by full-time faculty?	No	No
If yes, typical size offered last year	N/A	N/A
# of classroom course titles beyond 1st year curriculum	135	0
# of upper division courses, excluding seminars, with an enrollment:		
Under 25	59	0
25 - 49	24	0
50 - 74	13	0
75 - 99	8	0
100 +	6	0
# of seminars	24	0
# of seminar positions available	499	
# of seminar positions filled	360	0
# of positions available in simulation courses	332	
# of simulation positions filled	246	0
# of positions available in faculty supervised clinical courses	212	
# of fac. sup. clin. positions filled	192	0
# involved in field placements	78	0
# involved in law journals	143	0
# in moot court or trial competitions	240	0
# of credit hrs required to graduate	88	

J.D. Enrollment & Ethnicity

	Men		Women		Fl-Time		Pt-Time		1st Yr		2nd Yr		3rd Yr		4th Yr		Total		JD Degrees Awarded
	#	%	#	%	#	%	#	%	#	%	#	%	#	%	#	%	#	%	
African-American	15	4.4	35	12.0	50	7.9	0	0.0	24	12.8	11	4.9	15	6.8	0	0.0	50	7.9	22
American Indian	0	0.0	2	0.7	2	0.3	0	0.0	0	0.0	0	0.0	2	0.9	0	0.0	2	0.3	0
Asian American	8	2.3	9	3.1	17	2.7	0	0.0	4	2.1	5	2.2	8	3.6	0	0.0	17	2.7	2
Mexican American	0	0.0	0	0.0	0	0.0	0	0.0	0	0.0	0	0.0	0	0.0	0	0.0	0	0.0	0
Puerto Rican	0	0.0	0	0.0	0	0.0	0	0.0	0	0.0	0	0.0	0	0.0	0	0.0	0	0.0	0
Hispanic American	3	0.9	3	1.0	6	0.9	0	0.0	0	0.0	5	2.2	1	0.5	0	0.0	6	0.9	1
Total Minorities	26	7.6	49	16.8	75	11.8	0	0.0	28	14.9	21	9.4	26	11.7	0	0.0	75	11.8	25
Foreign Nationals	0	0.0	1	0.3	1	0.2	0	0.0	1	0.5	0	0.0	0	0.0	0	0.0	1	0.2	0
Caucasian	316	92.4	241	82.8	557	88.0	0	0.0	159	84.6	202	90.6	196	88.3	0	0.0	557	88.0	170
Total	342	54.0	291	46.0	633	100.0	0	0.0	188	29.7	223	35.2	222	35.1	0	0.0	633		195

GPA & LSAT Scores

	Full Time	Part Time	Total
# of apps	1,840	0	1,840
# admits	557	0	557
# of matrics	190	0	190
75% GPA	3.76	0.00	
25% GPA	3.20	0.00	
75% LSAT	163	0	
25% LSAT	155	0	

Tuition & Fees

	Resident	Non-resident
Full-Time	$4,200	$14,940
Part-Time	$0	$0

Living Expenses

Estimated living expenses for Singles

Living on campus	Living off campus	Living at home
$7,446	$9,576	$5,546

Grants/Scholarships

	Full-time		Part-time		Total	
	#	%	#	%	#	%
Total # of Students	633		0		633	
Total # receiving grants	139	22.0	0	0.0	139	22.0
Less than 1/2 tuition	75	11.8	0	0.0	75	11.8
Half to full tuition	38	6.0	0	0.0	38	6.0
Full tuition	8	1.3	0	0.0	8	1.3
More than full tuition	18	2.8	0	0.0	18	2.8
Median Grant Amount	$2,000		$0			

Informational & Library Resources

# of volumes & volume equivalents	462,731	# of professional staff	9
# of titles	123,134	Hours per week with professional staff	76
# of active serial subscriptions	6,887	Hours per week without professional staff	39
Study seating capacity inside the library	456	# of student computer work stations for entire law school	67
Square feet of law library	43,865	# of additional networked connections	0
Square feet of law school (excl. Library)	76,713	Require Laptop Computer?	N

Employment

	Total	%
Employment status known	183	91.5
Employment status unknown	17	8.5
Employed	172	94.0
Pursuing graduate degrees	5	2.7
Unemployed seeking employment	4	2.2
Unemployed not seeking employment	2	1.1
Type of Employment		
# employed in law firms	111	64.5
# employed in business & industry	9	5.2
# employed in government	16	9.3
# employed in public interest	9	5.2
# employed as judicial clerks	24	14.0
# employed in academia	2	1.2
Geographic Location		
# employed in state	135	78.5
# employed in foreign countries	0	0.0
# of states where employed	15	

J.D. Attrition (from Prior Year)

	Academic	Other	TOTALS	
	#	#	#	%
1st Year	1	8	9	3.9%
2nd Year	1	0	1	0.4%
3rd Year	0	0	0	0.0%
4th Year	0	0	0	0.0%

Bar Passage Rates

Jurisdiction	Georgia		
Exam	Sum 97	Win 98	Total
# from school taking bar for the first time	164	15	179
School's pass rate for all first-time takers	92%	80%	91%
State's pass rate for all first-time takers	86%	74%	83%

GOLDEN GATE UNIVERSITY

536 Mission Street
San Francisco, CA 94105-2968
(415)442-6600
http://www.ggu.edu/law/

ABA Approved Since 1956

The Basics

Type of School: Private Term: Semester
Application deadline: 04/15
Application fee: $40
Financial Aid deadline: 03/01
Can first year start other than Fall? Yes
Student faculty ratio: 16.9 to 1
Does the University offer:
- housing restricted to law students? No
- graduate student housing for which law students are eligible? Yes

Faculty & Administrators

	Total		Men		Women		Minorities	
	Fall	Spr	Fall	Spr	Fall	Spr	Fall	Spr
Full-time	26	25	16	14	10	11	4	5
Other Full-Time	2	2	1	1	1	1	0	0
Deans, librarians, & others who teach > 1/2	3	3	2	2	1	1	2	2
Part-time	41	60	27	35	14	25	6	5
Total	72	90	46	52	26	38	12	12
Deans, librarians, & others who teach < 1/2	6	6	2	2	4	4	0	0

Curriculum

	Full time	Part time
Typical first-year section size	75	40
Is there typically a "small section" of the first year class, other than Legal Writing, taught by full-time faculty?	Yes	No
If yes, typical size offered last year	30	N/A
# of classroom course titles beyond 1st year curriculum	83	45
# of upper division courses, excluding seminars, with an enrollment:		
Under 25	64	31
25 - 49	21	14
50 - 74	8	4
75 - 99	3	0
100 +	1	0
# of seminars	16	4
# of seminar positions available	400	
# of seminar positions filled	100	20
# of positions available in simulation courses	875	
# of simulation positions filled	417	114
# of positions available in faculty supervised clinical courses	270	
# of fac. sup. clin. positions filled	178	26
# involved in field placements	144	23
# involved in law journals	49	15
# in moot court or trial competitions	57	19
# of credit hrs required to graduate	88	

J.D. Enrollment & Ethnicity

	Men		Women		Fl-Time		Pt-Time		1st Yr		2nd Yr		3rd Yr		4th Yr		Total		JD Degrees Awarded
	#	%	#	%	#	%	#	%	#	%	#	%	#	%	#	%	#	%	
African-American	4	1.6	19	5.6	15	3.6	8	4.7	9	4.5	5	3.1	7	4.3	2	3.5	23	3.9	9
American Indian	0	0.0	3	0.9	2	0.5	1	0.6	1	0.5	1	0.6	0	0.0	1	1.8	3	0.5	0
Asian American	34	13.7	38	11.3	50	12.0	22	12.9	28	13.9	15	9.3	21	12.8	8	14.0	72	12.3	20
Mexican American	0	0.0	0	0.0	0	0.0	0	0.0	0	0.0	0	0.0	0	0.0	0	0.0	0	0.0	0
Puerto Rican	0	0.0	0	0.0	0	0.0	0	0.0	0	0.0	0	0.0	0	0.0	0	0.0	0	0.0	0
Hispanic American	21	8.5	34	10.1	41	9.9	14	8.2	14	6.9	15	9.3	18	11.0	8	14.0	55	9.4	12
Total Minorities	59	23.8	94	27.9	108	26.0	45	26.5	52	25.7	36	22.2	46	28.0	19	33.3	153	26.2	41
Foreign Nationals	3	1.2	6	1.8	8	1.9	1	0.6	4	2.0	4	2.5	1	0.6	0	0.0	9	1.5	1
Caucasian	186	75.0	237	70.3	299	72.0	124	72.9	146	72.3	122	75.3	117	71.3	38	66.7	423	72.3	141
Total	248	42.4	337	57.6	415	70.9	170	29.1	202	34.5	162	27.7	164	28.0	57	9.7	585		183

GPA & LSAT Scores

	Full Time	Part Time	Total
# of apps	1,451	166	1,617
# admits	785	70	855
# of matrics	168	37	205
75% GPA	3.35	3.29	
25% GPA	2.78	2.66	
75% LSAT	154	155	
25% LSAT	146	147	

Tuition & Fees

	Resident	Non-resident
Full-Time	$20,221	$20,221
Part-Time	$14,020	$14,020

Living Expenses

Estimated living expenses for Singles		
Living on campus	Living off campus	Living at home
N/A	$11,190	$3,765

Grants/Scholarships

	Full-time		Part-time		Total	
	#	%	#	%	#	%
Total # of Students	415		170		585	
Total # receiving grants	133	32.0	31	18.2	164	28.0
Less than 1/2 tuition	97	23.4	16	9.4	113	19.3
Half to full tuition	25	6.0	7	4.1	32	5.5
Full tuition	11	2.7	8	4.7	19	3.2
More than full tuition	0	0.0	0	0.0	0	0.0
Median Grant Amount	$6,000		$6,000			

Informational & Library Resources

# of volumes & volume equivalents	226,140	# of professional staff	5
# of titles	24,282	Hours per week with professional staff	55
# of active serial subscriptions	3,398	Hours per week without professional staff	36
Study seating capacity inside the library	322	# of student computer work stations for entire law school	75
Square feet of law library	27,296	# of additional networked connections	22
Square feet of law school (excl. Library)	36,798	Require Laptop Computer?	N

Employment

	Total	%
Employment status known	161	92.0
Employment status unknown	14	8.0
Employed	130	80.7
Pursuing graduate degrees	4	2.5
Unemployed seeking employment	14	8.7
Unemployed not seeking employment	13	8.1
Type of Employment		
# employed in law firms	72	55.4
# employed in business & industry	23	17.7
# employed in government	17	13.1
# employed in public interest	8	6.2
# employed as judicial clerks	2	1.5
# employed in academia	4	3.1
Geographic Location		
# employed in state	117	90.0
# employed in foreign countries	2	1.5
# of states where employed	7	

J.D. Attrition (from Prior Year)

	Academic	Other	TOTALS	
	#	#	#	%
1st Year	25	11	36	16%
2nd Year	8	4	12	6.7%
3rd Year	0	0	0	0.0%
4th Year	0	0	0	0.0%

Bar Passage Rates

Jurisdiction	California		
Exam	Sum 97	Win 98	Total
# from school taking bar for the first time	101	66	167
School's pass rate for all first-time takers	69%	70%	69%
State's pass rate for all first-time takers	75%	57%	71%

GONZAGA UNIVERSITY

P.O. Box 3528
Spokane, WA 99220-3528
(509)328-4220
http://www.law.gonzaga.edu

ABA Approved Since 1951

The Basics

Type of School: Private
Term: Semester
Application deadline: 03/15
Application fee: $40
Financial Aid deadline: 02/01
Can first year start other than Fall? No
Student faculty ratio: 19.9 to 1
Does the University offer:
- housing restricted to law students? No
- graduate student housing for which law students are eligible? Yes

Faculty & Administrators

	Total		Men		Women		Minorities	
	Fall	Spr	Fall	Spr	Fall	Spr	Fall	Spr
Full-time	20	20	16	14	4	6	1	1
Other Full-Time	6	6	4	4	2	2	0	0
Deans, librarians, & others who teach > 1/2	1	1	1	1	0	0	0	0
Part-time	13	15	9	12	4	3	0	1
Total	40	42	30	31	10	11	1	2
Deans, librarians, & others who teach < 1/2	6	6	4	4	2	2	1	1

Curriculum

	Full time	Part time
Typical first-year section size	88	0
Is there typically a "small section" of the first year class, other than Legal Writing, taught by full-time faculty?	No	No
If yes, typical size offered last year	N/A	N/A
# of classroom course titles beyond 1st year curriculum	79	0
# of upper division courses, excluding seminars, with an enrollment:		
Under 25	52	0
25 - 49	23	0
50 - 74	8	0
75 - 99	0	0
100 +	1	0
# of seminars	3	0
# of seminar positions available	62	
# of seminar positions filled	40	0
# of positions available in simulation courses	180	
# of simulation positions filled	112	0
# of positions available in faculty supervised clinical courses	96	
# of fac. sup. clin. positions filled	76	0
# involved in field placements	109	0
# involved in law journals	45	0
# in moot court or trial competitions	29	0
# of credit hrs required to graduate	90	

J.D. Enrollment & Ethnicity

	Men		Women		Fl-Time		Pt-Time		1st Yr		2nd Yr		3rd Yr		4th Yr		Total		JD Degrees Awarded
	#	%	#	%	#	%	#	%	#	%	#	%	#	%	#	%	#	%	
African-American	8	2.9	8	3.8	16	3.5	0	0.0	8	4.3	5	3.4	3	2.1	0	0.0	16	3.3	2
American Indian	6	2.2	5	2.4	8	1.7	3	11.5	4	2.1	3	2.0	1	0.7	3	27.3	11	2.3	6
Asian American	17	6.1	14	6.7	31	6.7	0	0.0	17	9.0	8	5.4	6	4.3	0	0.0	31	6.4	13
Mexican American	7	2.5	9	4.3	16	3.5	0	0.0	5	2.7	8	5.4	3	2.1	0	0.0	16	3.3	8
Puerto Rican	0	0.0	0	0.0	0	0.0	0	0.0	0	0.0	0	0.0	0	0.0	0	0.0	0	0.0	0
Hispanic American	0	0.0	1	0.5	1	0.2	0	0.0	1	0.5	0	0.0	0	0.0	0	0.0	1	0.2	0
Total Minorities	38	13.7	37	17.6	72	15.6	3	11.5	35	18.6	24	16.2	13	9.3	3	27.3	75	15.4	29
Foreign Nationals	0	0.0	0	0.0	0	0.0	0	0.0	0	0.0	0	0.0	0	0.0	0	0.0	0	0.0	0
Caucasian	239	86.3	173	82.4	389	84.4	23	88.5	153	81.4	124	83.8	127	90.7	8	72.7	412	84.6	158
Total	277	56.9	210	43.1	461	94.7	26	5.3	188	38.6	148	30.4	140	28.7	11	2.3	487		187

GPA & LSAT Scores

	Full Time	Part Time	Total
# of apps	875	0	875
# admits	720	0	720
# of matrics	188	0	188
75% GPA	3.30	0.00	
25% GPA	2.74	0.00	
75% LSAT	154	0	
25% LSAT	145	0	

Tuition & Fees

	Resident	Non-resident
Full-Time	$18,400	$18,400
Part-Time	$11,080	$11,080

Living Expenses

Estimated living expenses for Singles		
Living on campus	Living off campus	Living at home
$12,200	$12,200	$7,200

Employment

	Total	%
Employment status known	155	93.4
Employment status unknown	11	6.6
Employed	136	87.7
Pursuing graduate degrees	9	5.8
Unemployed seeking employment	3	1.9
Unemployed not seeking employment	7	4.5
Type of Employment		
# employed in law firms	76	55.9
# employed in business & industry	8	5.9
# employed in government	28	20.6
# employed in public interest	5	3.7
# employed as judicial clerks	16	11.8
# employed in academia	1	0.7
Geographic Location		
# employed in state	70	51.5
# employed in foreign countries	1	0.7
# of states where employed	21	

Grants/Scholarships

	Full-time		Part-time		Total	
	#	%	#	%	#	%
Total # of Students	461		26		487	
Total # receiving grants	176	38.2	0	0.0	176	36.1
Less than 1/2 tuition	141	30.6	0	0.0	141	29.0
Half to full tuition	4	0.9	0	0.0	4	0.8
Full tuition	31	6.7	0	0.0	31	6.4
More than full tuition	0	0.0	0	0.0	0	0.0
Median Grant Amount	$6,750		$0			

Informational & Library Resources

# of volumes & volume equivalents	236,192	# of professional staff	6
# of titles	35,988	Hours per week with professional staff	52
# of active serial subscriptions	2,940	Hours per week without professional staff	56
Study seating capacity inside the library	394	# of student computer work stations for entire law school	57
Square feet of law library	23,806	# of additional networked connections	0
Square feet of law school (excl. Library)	35,305	Require Laptop Computer?	N

J.D. Attrition (from Prior Year)

	Academic	Other	TOTALS	
	#	#	#	%
1st Year	5	10	15	8.8%
2nd Year	0	0	0	0.0%
3rd Year	0	0	0	0.0%
4th Year	0	0	0	0.0%

Bar Passage Rates

Jurisdiction	Washington		
Exam	Sum 97	Win 98	Total
# from school taking bar for the first time	91	16	107
School's pass rate for all first-time takers	82%	75%	81%
State's pass rate for all first-time takers	73%	83%	76%

HAMLINE UNIVERSITY

1536 Hewitt Avenue
St. Paul, MN 55104
(651)523-2941
http://web.hamline.edu/law

ABA Approved Since 1975

The Basics

Type of School: Private   Term: Semester
Application deadline: 03/15
Application fee: $50
Financial Aid deadline: Rolling
Can first year start other than Fall? No
Student faculty ratio: 18.1 to 1
Does the University offer:
- housing restricted to law students? Yes
- graduate student housing for which law students are eligible? No

Faculty & Administrators

	Total		Men		Women		Minorities	
	Fall	Spr	Fall	Spr	Fall	Spr	Fall	Spr
Full-time	22	20	15	13	7	7	2	2
Other Full-Time	4	4	2	2	2	2	0	0
Deans, librarians, & others who teach > 1/2	1	1	0	0	1	1	0	0
Part-time	31	39	21	28	10	11	4	1
Total	58	64	38	43	20	21	6	3
Deans, librarians, & others who teach < 1/2	5	5	3	3	2	2	1	1

Curriculum

	Full time	Part time
Typical first-year section size	66	0
Is there typically a "small section" of the first year class, other than Legal Writing, taught by full-time faculty?	No	No
If yes, typical size offered last year	N/A	N/A
# of classroom course titles beyond 1st year curriculum	127	127
# of upper division courses, excluding seminars, with an enrollment:		
Under 25	102	102
25 - 49	26	26
50 - 74	14	14
75 - 99	4	4
100 +	0	0
# of seminars	18	0
# of seminar positions available	294	
# of seminar positions filled	209	19
# of positions available in simulation courses	176	
# of simulation positions filled	131	8
# of positions available in faculty supervised clinical courses	105	
# of fac. sup. clin. positions filled	75	9
# involved in field placements	63	8
# involved in law journals	98	0
# in moot court or trial competitions	55	2
# of credit hrs required to graduate	88	

J.D. Enrollment & Ethnicity

	Men		Women		Fl-Time		Pt-Time		1st Yr		2nd Yr		3rd Yr		4th Yr		Total		JD Degrees Awarded
	#	%	#	%	#	%	#	%	#	%	#	%	#	%	#	%	#	%	
African-American	13	5.3	10	4.1	21	4.6	2	8.0	8	4.2	7	5.1	8	5.0	0	0.0	23	4.7	12
American Indian	2	0.8	4	1.6	5	1.1	1	4.0	3	1.6	2	1.5	1	0.6	0	0.0	6	1.2	3
Asian American	10	4.1	9	3.7	19	4.1	0	0.0	8	4.2	5	3.7	6	3.7	0	0.0	19	3.9	6
Mexican American	0	0.0	0	0.0	0	0.0	0	0.0	0	0.0	0	0.0	0	0.0	0	0.0	0	0.0	0
Puerto Rican	0	0.0	0	0.0	0	0.0	0	0.0	0	0.0	0	0.0	0	0.0	0	0.0	0	0.0	0
Hispanic American	1	0.4	4	1.6	5	1.1	0	0.0	2	1.1	3	2.2	0	0.0	0	0.0	5	1.0	3
Total Minorities	26	10.7	27	11.1	50	10.8	3	12.0	21	11.1	17	12.5	15	9.3	0	0.0	53	10.9	24
Foreign Nationals	4	1.6	2	0.8	5	1.1	1	4.0	4	2.1	0	0.0	2	1.2	0	0.0	6	1.2	5
Caucasian	213	87.7	214	88.1	406	88.1	21	84.0	164	86.8	119	87.5	144	89.4	0	0.0	427	87.9	177
Total	243	50.0	243	50.0	461	94.9	25	5.1	189	38.9	136	28.0	161	33.1	0	0.0	486		206

HAMLINE UNIVERSITY

GPA & LSAT Scores

	Full Time	Part Time	Total
# of apps	833	18	851
# admits	510	8	518
# of matrics	186	7	193
75% GPA	3.49	3.55	
25% GPA	2.92	2.64	
75% LSAT	157	154	
25% LSAT	149	145	

Tuition & Fees

	Resident	Non-resident
Full-Time	$16,475	$16,475
Part-Time	$11,867	$11,867

Living Expenses

Estimated living expenses for Singles		
Living on campus	Living off campus	Living at home
$7,765	$10,255	$10,255

Employment

	Total	%
Employment status known	171	96.1
Employment status unknown	7	3.9
Employed	159	93.0
Pursuing graduate degrees	2	1.2
Unemployed seeking employment	7	4.1
Unemployed not seeking employment	3	1.8
Type of Employment		
# employed in law firms	58	36.5
# employed in business & industry	38	23.9
# employed in government	21	13.2
# employed in public interest	8	5.0
# employed as judicial clerks	33	20.8
# employed in academia	1	0.6
Geographic Location		
# employed in state	105	66.0
# employed in foreign countries	1	0.6
# of states where employed	0	

Grants/Scholarships

	Full-time		Part-time		Total	
	#	%	#	%	#	%
Total # of Students	461		25		486	
Total # receiving grants	124	26.9	12	48.0	136	28.0
Less than 1/2 tuition	89	19.3	9	36.0	98	20.2
Half to full tuition	21	4.6	3	12.0	24	4.9
Full tuition	11	2.4	0	0.0	11	2.3
More than full tuition	3	0.7	0	0.0	3	0.6
Median Grant Amount	$5,500		$5,500			

Informational & Library Resources

# of volumes & volume equivalents	238,070	# of professional staff	5
# of titles	126,596	Hours per week with professional staff	68
# of active serial subscriptions	2,692	Hours per week without professional staff	39
Study seating capacity inside the library	374	# of student computer work stations for entire law school	47
Square feet of law library	39,500	# of additional networked connections	180
Square feet of law school (excl. Library)	93,916	Require Laptop Computer?	N

J.D. Attrition (from Prior Year)

	Academic	Other	TOTALS	
	#	#	#	%
1st Year	0	8	8	6.0%
2nd Year	0	10	10	5.8%
3rd Year	0	0	0	0.0%
4th Year	0	0	0	0.0%

Bar Passage Rates

Jurisdiction	Minnesota		
Exam	Sum 97	Win 98	Total
# from school taking bar for the first time	107	27	134
School's pass rate for all first-time takers	88%	78%	86%
State's pass rate for all first-time takers	93%	77%	90%

HARVARD UNIVERSITY

Harvard Law School
Cambridge, MA 02138
(617)495-1000
http://www.law.harvard.edu

ABA Approved Since 1923

The Basics

Type of School: Private Term: Semester

Application deadline: 02/01

Application fee: $65

Financial Aid deadline: 03/01

Can first year start other than Fall? No

Student faculty ratio: 19.7 to 1

Does the University offer:
- housing restricted to law students? Yes
- graduate student housing for which law students are eligible? Yes

Curriculum

	Full time	Part time
Typical first-year section size	138	0
Is there typically a "small section" of the first year class, other than Legal Writing, taught by full-time faculty?	Yes	No
If yes, typical size offered last year	46	N/A
# of classroom course titles beyond 1st year curriculum	215	0
# of upper division courses, excluding seminars, with an enrollment:		
Under 25	36	0
25 - 49	35	0
50 - 74	25	0
75 - 99	15	0
100 +	30	0
# of seminars	74	0
# of seminar positions available	1,502	
# of seminar positions filled	977	0
# of positions available in simulation courses	453	
# of simulation positions filled	453	0
# of positions available in faculty supervised clinical courses	615	
# of fac. sup. clin. positions filled	430	0
# involved in field placements	430	0
# involved in law journals	900	0
# in moot court or trial competitions	554	0
# of credit hrs required to graduate	80	

Faculty & Administrators

	Total		Men		Women		Minorities	
	Fall	Spr	Fall	Spr	Fall	Spr	Fall	Spr
Full-time	70	71	57	57	13	14	7	9
Other Full-Time	21	21	6	6	15	15	11	11
Deans, librarians, & others who teach > 1/2	0	0	0	0	0	0	0	0
Part-time	20	23	18	22	2	1	3	2
Total	111	115	81	85	30	30	21	22
Deans, librarians, & others who teach < 1/2	9	9	6	6	3	3	1	1

J.D. Enrollment & Ethnicity

	Men		Women		Fl-Time		Pt-Time		1st Yr		2nd Yr		3rd Yr		4th Yr		Total		JD Degrees Awarded
	#	%	#	%	#	%	#	%	#	%	#	%	#	%	#	%	#	%	
African-American	70	7.2	80	11.6	150	9.0	0	0.0	41	7.4	48	8.7	61	11.1	0	0.0	150	9.0	51
American Indian	3	0.3	7	1.0	10	0.6	0	0.0	3	0.5	4	0.7	3	0.5	0	0.0	10	0.6	3
Asian American	71	7.3	92	13.3	163	9.8	0	0.0	42	7.6	50	9.0	71	12.9	0	0.0	163	9.8	54
Mexican American	21	2.2	7	1.0	28	1.7	0	0.0	4	0.7	7	1.3	17	3.1	0	0.0	28	1.7	5
Puerto Rican	3	0.3	5	0.7	8	0.5	0	0.0	3	0.5	4	0.7	1	0.2	0	0.0	8	0.5	1
Hispanic American	22	2.3	17	2.5	39	2.4	0	0.0	9	1.6	16	2.9	14	2.5	0	0.0	39	2.4	16
Total Minorities	190	19.6	208	30.1	398	24.0	0	0.0	102	18.4	129	23.3	167	30.4	0	0.0	398	24.0	130
Foreign Nationals	46	4.8	15	2.2	61	3.7	0	0.0	19	3.4	21	3.8	21	3.8	0	0.0	61	3.7	1
Caucasian	731	75.6	468	67.7	1199	72.3	0	0.0	433	78.2	404	72.9	362	65.8	0	0.0	1199	72.3	401
Total	967	58.3	691	41.7	1658	100.0	0	0.0	554	33.4	554	33.4	550	33.2	0	0.0	1658		532

GPA & LSAT Scores

	Full Time	Part Time	Total
# of apps	5,813	0	5,813
# admits	847	0	847
# of matrics	551	0	551
75% GPA	3.92	0.00	
25% GPA	3.73	0.00	
75% LSAT	173	0	
25% LSAT	166	0	

Tuition & Fees

	Resident	Non-resident
Full-Time	$24,586	$24,586
Part-Time	$0	$0

Living Expenses

Estimated living expenses for Singles		
Living on campus	Living off campus	Living at home
$13,144	$13,144	N/A

Employment

	Total	%
Employment status known	545	98.2
Employment status unknown	10	1.8
Employed	531	97.4
Pursuing graduate degrees	1	0.2
Unemployed seeking employment	13	2.4
Unemployed not seeking employment	0	0.0
Type of Employment		
# employed in law firms	341	64.2
# employed in business & industry	31	5.8
# employed in government	13	2.4
# employed in public interest	12	2.3
# employed as judicial clerks	132	24.9
# employed in academia	2	0.4
Geographic Location		
# employed in state	59	11.1
# employed in foreign countries	7	1.3
# of states where employed	39	

Grants/Scholarships

	Full-time		Part-time		Total	
	#	%	#	%	#	%
Total # of Students	1658		0		1658	
Total # receiving grants	476	28.7	0	0.0	476	28.7
Less than 1/2 tuition	362	21.8	0	0.0	362	21.8
Half to full tuition	107	6.5	0	0.0	107	6.5
Full tuition	7	0.4	0	0.0	7	0.4
More than full tuition	0	0.0	0	0.0	0	0.0
Median Grant Amount	$7,940		$0			

Informational & Library Resources

# of volumes & volume equivalents	1,962,871	# of professional staff	32
# of titles	749,276	Hours per week with professional staff	69
# of active serial subscriptions	14,749	Hours per week without professional staff	30
Study seating capacity inside the library	761	# of student computer work stations for entire law school	167
Square feet of law library	198,640	# of additional networked connections	1250
Square feet of law school (excl. Library)	155,965	Require Laptop Computer?	N

J.D. Attrition (from Prior Year)

	Academic	Other	TOTALS	
	#	#	#	%
1st Year	0	1	1	0.2%
2nd Year	0	8	8	1.4%
3rd Year	0	6	6	1.1%
4th Year	0	0	0	0.0%

Bar Passage Rates

Jurisdiction	New York			Massachusetts		
Exam	Sum 97	Win 98	Total	Sum 97	Win 98	Total
# from school taking bar for the first time	176	16	192	10	8	18
School's pass rate for all first-time takers	97%	81%	96%	100%	100%	100%
State's pass rate for all first-time takers	78%	65%	76%	84%	72%	82%

HAWAII, UNIVERSITY OF

William S. Richardson School of Law
2515 Dole Street
Honolulu, HI 96822
(808)956-8636
gopher://gopher.hawaii.edu/11/student/ca

ABA Approved Since 1974

The Basics

Type of School: Public   Term: Semester

Application deadline: 03/01

Application fee: $30

Financial Aid deadline: 03/01

Can first year start other than Fall? No

Student faculty ratio: 11.2 to 1

Does the University offer:
- housing restricted to law students? No
- graduate student housing for which law students are eligible? Yes

Faculty & Administrators

	Total		Men		Women		Minorities	
	Fall	Spr	Fall	Spr	Fall	Spr	Fall	Spr
Full-time	17	17	9	10	8	7	4	4
Other Full-Time	0	0	0	0	0	0	0	0
Deans, librarians, & others who teach > 1/2	0	0	0	0	0	0	0	0
Part-time	15	23	12	18	3	5	5	15
Total	32	40	21	28	11	12	9	19
Deans, librarians, & others who teach < 1/2	3	3	1	1	2	2	2	2

Curriculum

	Full time	Part time
Typical first-year section size	75	0
Is there typically a "small section" of the first year class, other than Legal Writing, taught by full-time faculty?	No	No
If yes, typical size offered last year	N/A	N/A
# of classroom course titles beyond 1st year curriculum	51	0
# of upper division courses, excluding seminars, with an enrollment:		
Under 25	40	0
25 - 49	9	0
50 - 74	5	0
75 - 99	1	0
100 +	0	0
# of seminars	19	0
# of seminar positions available	254	
# of seminar positions filled	254	0
# of positions available in simulation courses	107	
# of simulation positions filled	92	0
# of positions available in faculty supervised clinical courses	36	
# of fac. sup. clin. positions filled	31	0
# involved in field placements	127	0
# involved in law journals	35	0
# in moot court or trial competitions	25	0
# of credit hrs required to graduate	89	

J.D. Enrollment & Ethnicity

	Men		Women		Fl-Time		Pt-Time		1st Yr		2nd Yr		3rd Yr		4th Yr		Total		JD Degrees Awarded
	#	%	#	%	#	%	#	%	#	%	#	%	#	%	#	%	#	%	
African-American	1	0.9	1	0.9	2	0.9	0	0.0	2	2.5	0	0.0	0	0.0	0	0.0	2	0.9	1
American Indian	2	1.8	2	1.7	4	1.8	0	0.0	3	3.8	0	0.0	1	1.3	0	0.0	4	1.8	0
Asian American	65	58.0	79	68.1	144	63.2	0	0.0	46	57.5	47	64.4	51	68.0	0	0.0	144	63.2	48
Mexican American	0	0.0	0	0.0	0	0.0	0	0.0	0	0.0	0	0.0	0	0.0	0	0.0	0	0.0	0
Puerto Rican	0	0.0	0	0.0	0	0.0	0	0.0	0	0.0	0	0.0	0	0.0	0	0.0	0	0.0	1
Hispanic American	0	0.0	3	2.6	3	1.3	0	0.0	3	3.8	0	0.0	0	0.0	0	0.0	3	1.3	0
Total Minorities	68	60.7	85	73.3	153	67.1	0	0.0	54	67.5	47	64.4	52	69.3	0	0.0	153	67.1	50
Foreign Nationals	0	0.0	3	2.6	3	1.3	0	0.0	1	1.3	1	1.4	1	1.3	0	0.0	3	1.3	1
Caucasian	44	39.3	28	24.1	72	31.6	0	0.0	25	31.3	25	34.2	22	29.3	0	0.0	72	31.6	21
Total	112	49.1	116	50.9	228	100.0	0	0.0	80	35.1	73	32.0	75	32.9	0	0.0	228		72

GPA & LSAT Scores

	Full Time	Part Time	Total
# of apps	468	0	468
# admits	168	0	168
# of matrics	80	0	80
75% GPA	3.40	0.00	
25% GPA	2.91	0.00	
75% LSAT	162	0	
25% LSAT	154	0	

Tuition & Fees

	Resident	Non-resident
Full-Time	$8,124	$14,220
Part-Time	$0	$0

Living Expenses

Estimated living expenses for Singles		
Living on campus	Living off campus	Living at home
$7,550	$9,729	$4,551

Grants/Scholarships

	Full-time		Part-time		Total	
	#	%	#	%	#	%
Total # of Students	228		0		228	
Total # receiving grants	108	47.4	0	0.0	108	47.4
Less than 1/2 tuition	26	11.4	0	0.0	26	11.4
Half to full tuition	47	20.6	0	0.0	47	20.6
Full tuition	14	6.1	0	0.0	14	6.1
More than full tuition	21	9.2	0	0.0	21	9.2
Median Grant Amount	$6,720		$0			

Informational & Library Resources

# of volumes & volume equivalents	257,679	# of professional staff	5
# of titles	30,450	Hours per week with professional staff	74
# of active serial subscriptions	2,896	Hours per week without professional staff	12
Study seating capacity inside the library	392	# of student computer work stations for entire law school	21
Square feet of law library	32,126	# of additional networked connections	1
Square feet of law school (excl. Library)	36,233	Require Laptop Computer?	Y

Employment

	Total	%
Employment status known	72	96.0
Employment status unknown	3	4.0
Employed	65	90.3
Pursuing graduate degrees	2	2.8
Unemployed seeking employment	1	1.4
Unemployed not seeking employment	4	5.6
Type of Employment		
# employed in law firms	24	36.9
# employed in business & industry	10	15.4
# employed in government	8	12.3
# employed in public interest	4	6.2
# employed as judicial clerks	17	26.2
# employed in academia	1	1.5
Geographic Location		
# employed in state	52	80.0
# employed in foreign countries	4	6.2
# of states where employed	8	

J.D. Attrition (from Prior Year)

	Academic	Other	TOTALS	
	#	#	#	%
1st Year	0	1	1	1.3%
2nd Year	0	0	0	0.0%
3rd Year	0	1	1	1.3%
4th Year	0	0	0	0.0%

Bar Passage Rates

Jurisdiction	Hawaii		
Exam	Sum 97	Win 98	Total
# from school taking bar for the first time	60	6	66
School's pass rate for all first-time takers	85%	83%	85%
State's pass rate for all first-time takers	81%	0%	81%

HOFSTRA UNIVERSITY

121 Hofstra University
Hempstead, NY 11549-1210
(516)463-5858
http://www.hofstra.edu

ABA Approved Since 1971

The Basics

Type of School: Private Term: Semester

Application deadline: 04/15

Application fee: $60

Financial Aid deadline: 06/01

Can first year start other than Fall? No

Student faculty ratio: 20.8 to 1

Does the University offer:

- housing restricted to law students? No
- graduate student housing for which law students are eligible? Yes

Curriculum

	Full time	Part time
Typical first-year section size	118	0
Is there typically a "small section" of the first year class, other than Legal Writing, taught by full-time faculty?	Yes	No
If yes, typical size offered last year	29	N/A
# of classroom course titles beyond 1st year curriculum	103	0
# of upper division courses, excluding seminars, with an enrollment:		
Under 25	50	0
25 - 49	37	0
50 - 74	7	0
75 - 99	9	0
100 +	11	0
# of seminars	29	0
# of seminar positions available	559	
# of seminar positions filled	424	0
# of positions available in simulation courses	667	
# of simulation positions filled	642	0
# of positions available in faculty supervised clinical courses	61	
# of fac. sup. clin. positions filled	54	0
# involved in field placements	60	0
# involved in law journals	129	0
# in moot court or trial competitions	48	0
# of credit hrs required to graduate	87	

Faculty & Administrators

	Total		Men		Women		Minorities	
	Fall	Spr	Fall	Spr	Fall	Spr	Fall	Spr
Full-time	32	28	27	24	5	4	4	2
Other Full-Time	6	6	1	1	5	5	0	0
Deans, librarians, & others who teach > 1/2	0	0	0	0	0	0	0	0
Part-time	13	28	10	25	3	3	0	0
Total	51	62	38	50	13	12	4	2
Deans, librarians, & others who teach < 1/2	4	4	1	1	3	3	0	0

J.D. Enrollment & Ethnicity

	Men		Women		Fl-Time		Pt-Time		1st Yr		2nd Yr		3rd Yr		4th Yr		Total		JD Degrees Awarded
	#	%	#	%	#	%	#	%	#	%	#	%	#	%	#	%	#	%	
African-American	17	3.9	32	8.9	49	6.1	0	0.0	12	4.2	20	7.2	17	7.2	0	0.0	49	6.1	17
American Indian	0	0.0	0	0.0	0	0.0	0	0.0	0	0.0	0	0.0	0	0.0	0	0.0	0	0.0	0
Asian American	22	5.0	27	7.5	49	6.1	0	0.0	22	7.7	18	6.5	9	3.8	0	0.0	49	6.1	11
Mexican American	0	0.0	1	0.3	1	0.1	0	0.0	0	0.0	0	0.0	1	0.4	0	0.0	1	0.1	0
Puerto Rican	0	0.0	0	0.0	0	0.0	0	0.0	0	0.0	0	0.0	0	0.0	0	0.0	0	0.0	0
Hispanic American	20	4.6	21	5.8	41	5.1	0	0.0	10	3.5	17	6.1	14	5.9	0	0.0	41	5.1	21
Total Minorities	59	13.5	81	22.5	140	17.5	0	0.0	44	15.4	55	19.9	41	17.4	0	0.0	140	17.5	49
Foreign Nationals	1	0.2	0	0.0	1	0.1	0	0.0	0	0.0	0	0.0	1	0.4	0	0.0	1	0.1	1
Caucasian	378	86.3	279	77.5	657	82.3	0	0.0	241	84.6	222	80.1	194	82.2	0	0.0	657	82.3	224
Total	438	54.9	360	45.1	798	100.0	0	0.0	285	35.7	277	34.7	236	29.6	0	0.0	798		274

GPA & LSAT Scores

	Full Time	Part Time	Total
# of apps	1,807	0	1,807
# admits	867	0	867
# of matrics	290	0	290
75% GPA	3.50	0.00	
25% GPA	2.95	0.00	
75% LSAT	158	0	
25% LSAT	150	0	

Tuition & Fees

	Resident	Non-resident
Full-Time	$22,210	$22,210
Part-Time	$0	$0

Living Expenses

Estimated living expenses for Singles		
Living on campus	Living off campus	Living at home
$13,280	$16,788	$7,518

Grants/Scholarships

	Full-time		Part-time		Total	
	#	%	#	%	#	%
Total # of Students	798		0		798	
Total # receiving grants	457	57.3	0	0.0	457	57.3
Less than 1/2 tuition	435	54.5	0	0.0	435	54.5
Half to full tuition	14	1.8	0	0.0	14	1.8
Full tuition	5	0.6	0	0.0	5	0.6
More than full tuition	3	0.4	0	0.0	3	0.4
Median Grant Amount	$3,952		$0			

Informational & Library Resources

# of volumes & volume equivalents	472,423	# of professional staff	8
# of titles	116,952	Hours per week with professional staff	94
# of active serial subscriptions	5,881	Hours per week without professional staff	4
Study seating capacity inside the library	595	# of student computer work stations for entire law school	101
Square feet of law library	50,665	# of additional networked connections	60
Square feet of law school (excl. Library)	59,629	Require Laptop Computer?	N

Employment

	Total	%
Employment status known	248	90.2
Employment status unknown	27	9.8
Employed	225	90.7
Pursuing graduate degrees	3	1.2
Unemployed seeking employment	11	4.4
Unemployed not seeking employment	9	3.6
Type of Employment		
# employed in law firms	168	74.7
# employed in business & industry	25	11.1
# employed in government	15	6.7
# employed in public interest	12	5.3
# employed as judicial clerks	5	2.2
# employed in academia	0	0.0
Geographic Location		
# employed in state	202	89.8
# employed in foreign countries	0	0.0
# of states where employed	11	

J.D. Attrition (from Prior Year)

	Academic	Other	TOTALS	
	#	#	#	%
1st Year	1	14	15	5.2%
2nd Year	3	5	8	3.3%
3rd Year	0	0	0	0.0%
4th Year	0	0	0	0.0%

Bar Passage Rates

Jurisdiction	New York		
Exam	Sum 97	Win 98	Total
# from school taking bar for the first time	244	24	268
School's pass rate for all first-time takers	68%	38%	65%
State's pass rate for all first-time takers	78%	65%	76%

HOUSTON, UNIVERSITY OF

4800 Calhoun
Entrance 19
Houston, TX 77004-6371
(713)743-2100
http://www.law.uh.edu

ABA Approved Since 1950

The Basics

Type of School: Public Term: Semester
Application deadline: 02/15
Application fee: $50
Financial Aid deadline: 04/01
Can first year start other than Fall? Yes
Student faculty ratio: 20.8 to 1
Does the University offer:
- housing restricted to law students? No
- graduate student housing for which law students are eligible? Yes

Faculty & Administrators

	Total		Men		Women		Minorities	
	Fall	Spr	Fall	Spr	Fall	Spr	Fall	Spr
Full-time	37	38	30	32	7	6	4	4
Other Full-Time	0	0	0	0	0	0	0	0
Deans, librarians, & others who teach > 1/2	8	8	5	5	3	3	1	1
Part-time	33	44	29	35	4	9	2	4
Total	78	90	64	72	14	18	7	9
Deans, librarians, & others who teach < 1/2	2	2	1	1	1	1	0	0

Curriculum

	Full time	Part time
Typical first-year section size	81	63
Is there typically a "small section" of the first year class, other than Legal Writing, taught by full-time faculty?	No	No
If yes, typical size offered last year	N/A	N/A
# of classroom course titles beyond 1st year curriculum	205	0
# of upper division courses, excluding seminars, with an enrollment:		
Under 25	138	0
25 - 49	45	0
50 - 74	13	0
75 - 99	15	0
100 +	1	0
# of seminars	27	0
# of seminar positions available	391	
# of seminar positions filled	283	0
# of positions available in simulation courses	366	
# of simulation positions filled	320	0
# of positions available in faculty supervised clinical courses	102	
# of fac. sup. clin. positions filled	76	0
# involved in field placements	77	0
# involved in law journals	147	0
# in moot court or trial competitions	448	0
# of credit hrs required to graduate	90	

J.D. Enrollment & Ethnicity

	Men		Women		Fl-Time		Pt-Time		1st Yr		2nd Yr		3rd Yr		4th Yr		Total		JD Degrees Awarded
	#	%	#	%	#	%	#	%	#	%	#	%	#	%	#	%	#	%	
African-American	14	2.5	19	4.3	20	2.6	13	5.7	8	2.4	8	2.6	10	3.4	7	10.0	33	3.3	18
American Indian	4	0.7	4	0.9	7	0.9	1	0.4	2	0.6	3	1.0	2	0.7	1	1.4	8	0.8	4
Asian American	39	7.0	37	8.3	61	7.9	15	6.6	32	9.7	18	5.8	25	8.6	1	1.4	76	7.6	19
Mexican American	35	6.3	27	6.0	51	6.6	11	4.8	18	5.5	21	6.8	16	5.5	7	10.0	62	6.2	16
Puerto Rican	0	0.0	0	0.0	0	0.0	0	0.0	0	0.0	0	0.0	0	0.0	0	0.0	0	0.0	0
Hispanic American	18	3.2	24	5.4	34	4.4	8	3.5	16	4.9	10	3.2	13	4.5	3	4.3	42	4.2	4
Total Minorities	110	19.8	111	24.8	173	22.4	48	21.0	76	23.1	60	19.3	66	22.6	19	27.1	221	22.1	61
Foreign Nationals	3	0.5	2	0.4	4	0.5	1	0.4	1	0.3	0	0.0	4	1.4	0	0.0	5	0.5	0
Caucasian	442	79.6	334	74.7	596	77.1	180	78.6	252	76.6	251	80.7	222	76.0	51	72.9	776	77.4	228
Total	555	55.4	447	44.6	773	77.1	229	22.9	329	32.8	311	31.0	292	29.1	70	7.0	1002		289

GPA & LSAT Scores

	Full Time	Part Time	Total
# of apps	1,927	247	2,174
# admits	834	86	920
# of matrics	277	55	332
75% GPA	3.50	3.53	
25% GPA	3.06	3.00	
75% LSAT	160	161	
25% LSAT	155	154	

Tuition & Fees

	Resident	Non-resident
Full-Time	$5,880	$10,360
Part-Time	$4,600	$7,800

Living Expenses

Estimated living expenses for Singles		
Living on campus	Living off campus	Living at home
$7,920	$9,970	$6,430

Grants/Scholarships

	Full-time		Part-time		Total	
	#	%	#	%	#	%
Total # of Students	773		229		1002	
Total # receiving grants	309	40.0	0	0.0	309	30.8
Less than 1/2 tuition	250	32.3	0	0.0	250	25.0
Half to full tuition	39	5.0	0	0.0	39	3.9
Full tuition	20	2.6	0	0.0	20	2.0
More than full tuition	0	0.0	0	0.0	0	0.0
Median Grant Amount	$2,799		$0			

Informational & Library Resources

# of volumes & volume equivalents	468,634	# of professional staff	10
# of titles	89,368	Hours per week with professional staff	62
# of active serial subscriptions	3,029	Hours per week without professional staff	43
Study seating capacity inside the library	936	# of student computer work stations for entire law school	70
Square feet of law library	87,528	# of additional networked connections	464
Square feet of law school (excl. Library)	75,585	Require Laptop Computer?	N

Employment

	Total	%
Employment status known	341	95.0
Employment status unknown	18	5.0
Employed	309	90.6
Pursuing graduate degrees	4	1.2
Unemployed seeking employment	24	7.0
Unemployed not seeking employment	4	1.2
Type of Employment		
# employed in law firms	192	62.1
# employed in business & industry	60	19.4
# employed in government	36	11.7
# employed in public interest	5	1.6
# employed as judicial clerks	10	3.2
# employed in academia	6	1.9
Geographic Location		
# employed in state	277	89.6
# employed in foreign countries	1	0.3
# of states where employed	18	

J.D. Attrition (from Prior Year)

	Academic	Other	TOTALS	
	#	#	#	%
1st Year	0	12	12	3.9%
2nd Year	1	10	11	3.7%
3rd Year	0	8	8	2.8%
4th Year	0	2	2	3.2%

Bar Passage Rates

Jurisdiction	Texas		
Exam	Sum 97	Win 98	Total
# from school taking bar for the first time	255	63	318
School's pass rate for all first-time takers	91%	90%	91%
State's pass rate for all first-time takers	83%	73%	81%

HOWARD UNIVERSITY

2900 Van Ness Street
Washington, DC 20008
(202)806-8021
http://www.law.howard.edu

ABA Approved Since 1931

The Basics

Type of School: Private — Term: Semester

Application deadline: 04/30

Application fee: $60

Financial Aid deadline: 03/01

Can first year start other than Fall? No

Student faculty ratio: 15.6 to 1

Does the University offer:
- housing restricted to law students? No
- graduate student housing for which law students are eligible? Yes

Faculty & Administrators

	Total		Men		Women		Minorities	
	Fall	Spr	Fall	Spr	Fall	Spr	Fall	Spr
Full-time	21	21	15	15	6	6	17	18
Other Full-Time	0	0	0	0	0	0	0	0
Deans, librarians, & others who teach > 1/2	0	0	0	0	0	0	0	0
Part-time	19	0	15	0	4	0	13	0
Total	40	21	30	15	10	6	30	18
Deans, librarians, & others who teach < 1/2	3	3	1	1	2	2	3	3

Curriculum

	Full time	Part time
Typical first-year section size	70	0
Is there typically a "small section" of the first year class, other than Legal Writing, taught by full-time faculty?	No	No
If yes, typical size offered last year	N/A	N/A
# of classroom course titles beyond 1st year curriculum	70	0
# of upper division courses, excluding seminars, with an enrollment:		
Under 25	49	0
25 - 49	23	0
50 - 74	9	0
75 - 99	3	0
100 +	0	0
# of seminars	28	0
# of seminar positions available	432	
# of seminar positions filled	335	0
# of positions available in simulation courses	239	
# of simulation positions filled	162	0
# of positions available in faculty supervised clinical courses	127	
# of fac. sup. clin. positions filled	76	0
# involved in field placements	27	0
# involved in law journals	63	0
# in moot court or trial competitions	57	0
# of credit hrs required to graduate	88	

J.D. Enrollment & Ethnicity

	Men		Women		Fl-Time		Pt-Time		1st Yr		2nd Yr		3rd Yr		4th Yr		Total		JD Degrees Awarded
	#	%	#	%	#	%	#	%	#	%	#	%	#	%	#	%	#	%	
African-American	148	87.6	194	87.0	342	87.2	0	0.0	108	85.0	120	88.9	114	87.7	0	0.0	342	87.2	132
American Indian	0	0.0	0	0.0	0	0.0	0	0.0	0	0.0	0	0.0	0	0.0	0	0.0	0	0.0	0
Asian American	5	3.0	9	4.0	14	3.6	0	0.0	5	3.9	6	4.4	3	2.3	0	0.0	14	3.6	1
Mexican American	0	0.0	0	0.0	0	0.0	0	0.0	0	0.0	0	0.0	0	0.0	0	0.0	0	0.0	0
Puerto Rican	0	0.0	0	0.0	0	0.0	0	0.0	0	0.0	0	0.0	0	0.0	0	0.0	0	0.0	0
Hispanic American	4	2.4	8	3.6	12	3.1	0	0.0	5	3.9	3	2.2	4	3.1	0	0.0	12	3.1	7
Total Minorities	157	92.9	211	94.6	368	93.9	0	0.0	118	92.9	129	95.6	121	93.1	0	0.0	368	93.9	140
Foreign Nationals	0	0.0	0	0.0	0	0.0	0	0.0	0	0.0	0	0.0	0	0.0	0	0.0	0	0.0	0
Caucasian	12	7.1	12	5.4	24	6.1	0	0.0	9	7.1	6	4.4	9	6.9	0	0.0	24	6.1	14
Total	169	43.1	223	56.9	392	100.0	0	0.0	127	32.4	135	34.4	130	33.2	0	0.0	392		154

GPA & LSAT Scores

	Full Time	Part Time	Total
# of apps	927	0	927
# admits	318	0	318
# of matrics	124	0	124
75% GPA	3.23	0.00	
25% GPA	2.67	0.00	
75% LSAT	155	0	
25% LSAT	148	0	

Tuition & Fees

	Resident	Non-resident
Full-Time	$12,785	$12,785
Part-Time	$1,187	$1,187

Living Expenses

Estimated living expenses for Singles		
Living on campus	Living off campus	Living at home
$11,079	$13,387	$13,387

Grants/Scholarships

	Full-time		Part-time		Total	
	#	%	#	%	#	%
Total # of Students	392		0		392	
Total # receiving grants	213	54.3	0	0.0	213	54.3
Less than 1/2 tuition	74	18.9	0	0.0	74	18.9
Half to full tuition	86	21.9	0	0.0	86	21.9
Full tuition	33	8.4	0	0.0	33	8.4
More than full tuition	20	5.1	0	0.0	20	5.1
Median Grant Amount	$9,000		$0			

Informational & Library Resources

# of volumes & volume equivalents	264,962	# of professional staff	8
# of titles	23,511	Hours per week with professional staff	62
# of active serial subscriptions	1,291	Hours per week without professional staff	49
Study seating capacity inside the library	173	# of student computer work stations for entire law school	0
Square feet of law library	29,110	# of additional networked connections	0
Square feet of law school (excl. Library)	137,070	Require Laptop Computer?	

Employment

	Total	%
Employment status known	102	87.2
Employment status unknown	15	12.8
Employed	91	89.2
Pursuing graduate degrees	4	3.9
Unemployed seeking employment	6	5.9
Unemployed not seeking employment	1	1.0
Type of Employment		
# employed in law firms	31	34.1
# employed in business & industry	11	12.1
# employed in government	30	33.0
# employed in public interest	4	4.4
# employed as judicial clerks	13	14.3
# employed in academia	1	1.1
Geographic Location		
# employed in state	45	49.5
# employed in foreign countries	2	2.2
# of states where employed	17	

J.D. Attrition (from Prior Year)

	Academic	Other	TOTALS	
	#	#	#	%
1st Year	0	6	6	4.3%
2nd Year	0	2	2	1.7%
3rd Year	1	1	2	1.2%
4th Year	0	0	0	0.0%

Bar Passage Rates

Jurisdiction	Maryland			New York		
Exam	Sum 97	Win 98	Total	Sum 97	Win 98	Total
# from school taking bar for the first time	44	11	55	14	3	17
School's pass rate for all first-time takers	32%	36%	33%	64%	67%	65%
State's pass rate for all first-time takers	69%	83%	72%	78%	65%	76%

IDAHO, UNIVERSITY OF

6th & Rayburn
Moscow, ID 83844-2321
(208)885-4977
http://www.uidaho.edu/law

ABA Approved Since 1925

The Basics

Type of School: Public   Term: Semester

Application deadline: 02/01

Application fee: $30

Financial Aid deadline: 02/01

Can first year start other than Fall? No

Student faculty ratio: 15.6 to 1

Does the University offer:
- housing restricted to law students? No
- graduate student housing for which law students are eligible? Yes

Faculty & Administrators

	Total		Men		Women		Minorities	
	Fall	Spr	Fall	Spr	Fall	Spr	Fall	Spr
Full-time	16	17	11	12	5	5	0	0
Other Full-Time	2	2	1	1	1	1	0	0
Deans, librarians, & others who teach > 1/2	2	2	1	1	1	1	0	0
Part-time	7	1	4	0	3	1	0	0
Total	27	22	17	14	10	8	0	0
Deans, librarians, & others who teach < 1/2	1	1	1	1	0	0	0	0

Curriculum

	Full time	Part time
Typical first-year section size	55	0
Is there typically a "small section" of the first year class, other than Legal Writing, taught by full-time faculty?	No	No
If yes, typical size offered last year	N/A	N/A
# of classroom course titles beyond 1st year curriculum	54	0
# of upper division courses, excluding seminars, with an enrollment:		
Under 25	37	0
25 - 49	15	0
50 - 74	7	0
75 - 99	4	0
100 +	0	0
# of seminars	6	0
# of seminar positions available	109	
# of seminar positions filled	109	0
# of positions available in simulation courses	121	
# of simulation positions filled	121	0
# of positions available in faculty supervised clinical courses	0	
# of fac. sup. clin. positions filled	40	0
# involved in field placements	58	0
# involved in law journals	19	0
# in moot court or trial competitions	6	0
# of credit hrs required to graduate	88	

J.D. Enrollment & Ethnicity

	Men		Women		Fl-Time		Pt-Time		1st Yr		2nd Yr		3rd Yr		4th Yr		Total		JD Degrees Awarded
	#	%	#	%	#	%	#	%	#	%	#	%	#	%	#	%	#	%	
African-American	0	0.0	0	0.0	0	0.0	0	0.0	0	0.0	0	0.0	0	0.0	0	0.0	0	0.0	0
American Indian	1	0.5	0	0.0	1	0.3	0	0.0	0	0.0	0	0.0	1	1.1	0	0.0	1	0.3	0
Asian American	0	0.0	2	2.2	2	0.7	0	0.0	0	0.0	2	1.8	0	0.0	0	0.0	2	0.7	5
Mexican American	2	0.9	4	4.5	6	2.0	0	0.0	2	1.9	1	0.9	3	3.4	0	0.0	6	2.0	0
Puerto Rican	0	0.0	0	0.0	0	0.0	0	0.0	0	0.0	0	0.0	0	0.0	0	0.0	0	0.0	0
Hispanic American	5	2.4	3	3.4	8	2.7	0	0.0	4	3.8	0	0.0	4	4.6	0	0.0	8	2.7	3
Total Minorities	8	3.8	9	10.1	17	5.7	0	0.0	6	5.8	3	2.8	8	9.2	0	0.0	17	5.7	8
Foreign Nationals	0	0.0	0	0.0	0	0.0	0	0.0	0	0.0	0	0.0	0	0.0	0	0.0	0	0.0	0
Caucasian	203	96.2	80	89.9	283	94.3	0	0.0	98	94.2	106	97.2	79	90.8	0	0.0	283	94.3	76
Total	211	70.3	89	29.7	300	100.0	0	0.0	104	34.7	109	36.3	87	29.0	0	0.0	300		84

GPA & LSAT Scores

	Full Time	Part Time	Total
# of apps	457	0	457
# admits	284	0	284
# of matrics	104	0	104
75% GPA	3.57	0.00	
25% GPA	3.22	0.00	
75% LSAT	156	0	
25% LSAT	149	0	

Tuition & Fees

	Resident	Non-resident
Full-Time	$4,076	$10,076
Part-Time	$0	$0

Living Expenses

Estimated living expenses for Singles		
Living on campus	Living off campus	Living at home
$10,244	$10,244	$5,424

Grants/Scholarships

	Full-time		Part-time		Total	
	#	%	#	%	#	%
Total # of Students	300		0		300	
Total # receiving grants	61	20.3	0	0.0	61	20.3
Less than 1/2 tuition	33	11.0	0	0.0	33	11.0
Half to full tuition	7	2.3	0	0.0	7	2.3
Full tuition	21	7.0	0	0.0	21	7.0
More than full tuition	0	0.0	0	0.0	0	0.0
Median Grant Amount	$2,098		$36			

Informational & Library Resources

# of volumes & volume equivalents	174,435	# of professional staff	3
# of titles	25,872	Hours per week with professional staff	45
# of active serial subscriptions	2,758	Hours per week without professional staff	47
Study seating capacity inside the library	369	# of student computer work stations for entire law school	39
Square feet of law library	24,822	# of additional networked connections	203
Square feet of law school (excl. Library)	24,150	Require Laptop Computer?	N

Employment

	Total	%
Employment status known	94	98.9
Employment status unknown	1	1.1
Employed	80	85.1
Pursuing graduate degrees	6	6.4
Unemployed seeking employment	2	2.1
Unemployed not seeking employment	6	6.4
Type of Employment		
# employed in law firms	34	42.5
# employed in business & industry	8	10.0
# employed in government	12	15.0
# employed in public interest	1	1.2
# employed as judicial clerks	24	30.0
# employed in academia	1	1.2
Geographic Location		
# employed in state	56	70.0
# employed in foreign countries	0	0.0
# of states where employed	11	

J.D. Attrition (from Prior Year)

	Academic	Other	TOTALS	
	#	#	#	%
1st Year	9	10	19	15%
2nd Year	0	0	0	0.0%
3rd Year	0	0	0	0.0%
4th Year	0	0	0	0.0%

Bar Passage Rates

Jurisdiction	Idaho			Washington		
Exam	Sum 97	Win 98	Total	Sum 97	Win 98	Total
# from school taking bar for the first time	50	18	68	13	7	20
School's pass rate for all first-time takers	72%	67%	71%	77%	43%	65%
State's pass rate for all first-time takers	75%	76%	75%	73%	83%	76%

ILLINOIS INSTITUTE OF TECHNOLOGY

Chicago-Kent College of Law
565 West Adams Street
Chicago, IL 60661
(312)906-5000
http://www.kentlaw.edu

ABA Approved Since 1936

The Basics

Type of School: Private — Term: Semester

Application deadline: 04/01

Application fee: $45

Financial Aid deadline: 04/15

Can first year start other than Fall? No

Student faculty ratio: 22.6 to 1

Does the University offer:
- housing restricted to law students? No
- graduate student housing for which law students are eligible? Yes

Faculty & Administrators

	Total		Men		Women		Minorities	
	Fall	Spr	Fall	Spr	Fall	Spr	Fall	Spr
Full-time	39	37	30	28	9	9	4	3
Other Full-Time	14	14	7	7	7	7	0	0
Deans, librarians, & others who teach > 1/2	10	10	6	6	4	4	0	0
Part-time	85	84	65	64	19	19	3	3
Total	148	145	108	105	39	39	7	6
Deans, librarians, & others who teach < 1/2	0	1	0	1	0	0	0	0

Curriculum

	Full time	Part time
Typical first-year section size	100	100
Is there typically a "small section" of the first year class, other than Legal Writing, taught by full-time faculty?	Yes	Yes
If yes, typical size offered last year	50	50
# of classroom course titles beyond 1st year curriculum	117	89
# of upper division courses, excluding seminars, with an enrollment:		
Under 25	119	43
25 - 49	25	18
50 - 74	12	7
75 - 99	4	4
100 +	5	0
# of seminars	21	7
# of seminar positions available	420	
# of seminar positions filled	169	79
# of positions available in simulation courses	542	
# of simulation positions filled	306	158
# of positions available in faculty supervised clinical courses	180	
# of fac. sup. clin. positions filled	163	8
# involved in field placements	102	5
# involved in law journals	50	5
# in moot court or trial competitions	43	17
# of credit hrs required to graduate	87	

J.D. Enrollment & Ethnicity

	Men		Women		Fl-Time		Pt-Time		1st Yr		2nd Yr		3rd Yr		4th Yr		Total		JD Degrees Awarded
	#	%	#	%	#	%	#	%	#	%	#	%	#	%	#	%	#	%	
African-American	24	4.4	40	8.8	39	5.8	25	7.6	29	6.9	18	4.9	16	4.7	1	1.9	64	6.4	15
American Indian	3	0.5	1	0.2	3	0.4	1	0.3	2	0.5	2	0.5	0	0.0	0	0.0	4	0.4	2
Asian American	44	8.0	40	8.8	67	9.9	17	5.2	27	6.5	26	7.1	29	8.5	2	3.7	84	8.4	32
Mexican American	5	0.9	11	2.4	12	1.8	4	1.2	8	1.9	5	1.4	2	0.6	1	1.9	16	1.6	7
Puerto Rican	4	0.7	5	1.1	7	1.0	2	0.6	4	1.0	3	0.8	1	0.3	1	1.9	9	0.9	2
Hispanic American	8	1.5	17	3.7	17	2.5	8	2.4	10	2.4	12	3.3	2	0.6	1	1.9	25	2.5	2
Total Minorities	88	16.1	114	25.1	145	21.5	57	17.3	80	19.1	66	18.1	50	14.7	6	11.1	202	20.1	60
Foreign Nationals	2	0.4	0	0.0	2	0.3	0	0.0	1	0.2	1	0.3	0	0.0	0	0.0	2	0.2	3
Caucasian	458	83.6	341	74.9	527	78.2	272	82.7	313	74.9	165	45.3	276	81.2	45	83.3	799	79.7	272
Total	548	54.6	455	45.4	674	67.2	329	32.8	418	41.7	364	36.3	340	33.9	54	5.4	1003		335

ILLINOIS INSTITUTE OF TECHNOLOGY

GPA & LSAT Scores

	Full Time	Part Time	Total
# of apps	1,490	391	1,881
# admits	1,060	234	1,294
# of matrics	294	108	402
75% GPA	3.34	3.32	
25% GPA	2.89	2.64	
75% LSAT	157	156	
25% LSAT	150	148	

Tuition & Fees

	Resident	Non-resident
Full-Time	$20,760	$20,760
Part-Time	$14,995	$14,995

Living Expenses

Estimated living expenses for Singles		
Living on campus	Living off campus	Living at home
N/A	$17,995	$10,390

Employment

	Total	%
Employment status known	328	97.0
Employment status unknown	10	3.0
Employed	263	80.2
Pursuing graduate degrees	4	1.2
Unemployed seeking employment	24	7.3
Unemployed not seeking employment	37	11.3
Type of Employment		
# employed in law firms	123	46.8
# employed in business & industry	84	31.9
# employed in government	33	12.5
# employed in public interest	6	2.3
# employed as judicial clerks	13	4.9
# employed in academia	4	1.5
Geographic Location		
# employed in state	220	83.7
# employed in foreign countries	1	0.4
# of states where employed	24	

Grants/Scholarships

	Full-time		Part-time		Total	
	#	%	#	%	#	%
Total # of Students	674		329		1003	
Total # receiving grants	330	49.0	111	33.7	441	44.0
Less than 1/2 tuition	249	36.9	86	26.1	335	33.4
Half to full tuition	43	6.4	20	6.1	63	6.3
Full tuition	28	4.2	5	1.5	33	3.3
More than full tuition	10	1.5	0	0.0	10	1.0
Median Grant Amount	$6,000		$3,000			

Informational & Library Resources

# of volumes & volume equivalents	548,811	# of professional staff	6
# of titles	135,858	Hours per week with professional staff	88
# of active serial subscriptions	8,182	Hours per week without professional staff	10
Study seating capacity inside the library	689	# of student computer work stations for entire law school	135
Square feet of law library	60,916	# of additional networked connections	1860
Square feet of law school (excl. Library)	190,590	Require Laptop Computer?	Y

J.D. Attrition (from Prior Year)

	Academic	Other	TOTALS	
	#	#	#	%
1st Year	7	25	32	8.0%
2nd Year	3	26	29	7.5%
3rd Year	0	4	4	1.2%
4th Year	0	1	1	1.4%

Bar Passage Rates

Jurisdiction	Illinois
Exam	
# from school taking bar for the first time	This school did not provide data on a basis comparable with other law schools. Please contact the school for specific information.
School's pass rate for all first-time takers	
State's pass rate for all first-time takers	

ILLINOIS, UNIVERSITY OF

504 East Pennsylvania Avenue
Champaign, IL 61820
(217)333-0931
http://www.law.uiuc.edu

ABA Approved Since 1923

The Basics

Type of School: Public   Term: Semester

Application deadline: 03/15

Application fee: $40

Financial Aid deadline: 03/15

Can first year start other than Fall? No

Student faculty ratio: 15.9 to 1

Does the University offer:
- housing restricted to law students? No
- graduate student housing for which law students are eligible? Yes

Faculty & Administrators

	Total		Men		Women		Minorities	
	Fall	Spr	Fall	Spr	Fall	Spr	Fall	Spr
Full-time	31	32	22	24	9	8	5	6
Other Full-Time	7	7	3	3	4	4	1	1
Deans, librarians, & others who teach > 1/2	1	1	1	1	0	0	1	1
Part-time	17	14	15	9	2	5	1	1
Total	56	54	41	37	15	17	8	9
Deans, librarians, & others who teach < 1/2	1	1	1	1	0	0	0	0

Curriculum

	Full time	Part time
Typical first-year section size	67	0
Is there typically a "small section" of the first year class, other than Legal Writing, taught by full-time faculty?	No	No
If yes, typical size offered last year	N/A	N/A
# of classroom course titles beyond 1st year curriculum	112	0
# of upper division courses, excluding seminars, with an enrollment:		
Under 25	55	0
25 - 49	34	0
50 - 74	12	0
75 - 99	7	0
100 +	4	0
# of seminars	21	0
# of seminar positions available	317	
# of seminar positions filled	253	0
# of positions available in simulation courses	407	
# of simulation positions filled	407	0
# of positions available in faculty supervised clinical courses	36	
# of fac. sup. clin. positions filled	36	0
# involved in field placements	64	0
# involved in law journals	117	0
# in moot court or trial competitions	159	0
# of credit hrs required to graduate	90	

J.D. Enrollment & Ethnicity

	Men		Women		Fl-Time		Pt-Time		1st Yr		2nd Yr		3rd Yr		4th Yr		Total		JD Degrees Awarded
	#	%	#	%	#	%	#	%	#	%	#	%	#	%	#	%	#	%	
African-American	32	9.1	42	17.6	74	12.5	0	0.0	26	13.8	23	11.4	25	12.4	0	0.0	74	12.5	24
American Indian	2	0.6	0	0.0	2	0.3	0	0.0	2	1.1	0	0.0	0	0.0	0	0.0	2	0.3	0
Asian American	30	8.5	19	7.9	49	8.3	0	0.0	19	10.1	15	7.4	15	7.5	0	0.0	49	8.3	24
Mexican American	0	0.0	0	0.0	0	0.0	0	0.0	0	0.0	0	0.0	0	0.0	0	0.0	0	0.0	0
Puerto Rican	0	0.0	0	0.0	0	0.0	0	0.0	0	0.0	0	0.0	0	0.0	0	0.0	0	0.0	0
Hispanic American	30	8.5	20	8.4	50	8.4	0	0.0	19	10.1	16	7.9	15	7.5	0	0.0	50	8.4	15
Total Minorities	94	26.6	81	33.9	175	29.6	0	0.0	66	34.9	54	26.7	55	27.4	0	0.0	175	29.6	63
Foreign Nationals	0	0.0	0	0.0	0	0.0	0	0.0	0	0.0	0	0.0	0	0.0	0	0.0	0	0.0	0
Caucasian	259	73.4	158	66.1	417	70.4	0	0.0	123	65.1	148	73.3	146	72.6	0	0.0	417	70.4	140
Total	353	59.6	239	40.4	592	100.0	0	0.0	189	31.9	202	34.1	201	34.0	0	0.0	592		203

GPA & LSAT Scores

	Full Time	Part Time	Total
# of apps	1,540	0	1,540
# admits	589	0	589
# of matrics	194	0	194
75% GPA	3.64	0.00	
25% GPA	3.19	0.00	
75% LSAT	163	0	
25% LSAT	156	0	

Tuition & Fees

	Resident	Non-resident
Full-Time	$8,456	$18,830
Part-Time	$0	$0

Living Expenses

Estimated living expenses for Singles

Living on campus	Living off campus	Living at home
$9,874	$9,874	$9,874

Grants/Scholarships

	Full-time		Part-time		Total	
	#	%	#	%	#	%
Total # of Students	592		0		592	
Total # receiving grants	246	41.6	0	0.0	246	41.6
Less than 1/2 tuition	127	21.5	0	0.0	127	21.5
Half to full tuition	77	13.0	0	0.0	77	13.0
Full tuition	27	4.6	0	0.0	27	4.6
More than full tuition	15	2.5	0	0.0	15	2.5
Median Grant Amount	$4,381		$0			

Informational & Library Resources

# of volumes & volume equivalents	687,964	# of professional staff	3
# of titles	245,124	Hours per week with professional staff	50
# of active serial subscriptions	8,289	Hours per week without professional staff	46
Study seating capacity inside the library	417	# of student computer work stations for entire law school	79
Square feet of law library	59,617	# of additional networked connections	375
Square feet of law school (excl. Library)	65,283	Require Laptop Computer?	N

Employment

	Total	%
Employment status known	189	97.4
Employment status unknown	5	2.6
Employed	178	94.2
Pursuing graduate degrees	6	3.2
Unemployed seeking employment	3	1.6
Unemployed not seeking employment	2	1.1
Type of Employment		
# employed in law firms	111	62.4
# employed in business & industry	21	11.8
# employed in government	25	14.0
# employed in public interest	3	1.7
# employed as judicial clerks	15	8.4
# employed in academia	3	1.7
Geographic Location		
# employed in state	139	78.1
# employed in foreign countries	1	0.6
# of states where employed	17	

J.D. Attrition (from Prior Year)

	Academic	Other	TOTALS	
	#	#	#	%
1st Year	0	7	7	3.5%
2nd Year	0	0	0	0.0%
3rd Year	0	0	0	0.0%
4th Year	0	0	0	0.0%

Bar Passage Rates

Jurisdiction	Illinois		
Exam	Sum 97	Win 98	Total
# from school taking bar for the first time	143	26	169
School's pass rate for all first-time takers	95%	88%	94%
State's pass rate for all first-time takers	87%	80%	85%

INDIANA UNIVERSITY - BLOOMINGTON

211 S. Indiana Avenue
Bloomington, IN 47405
(812)855-7995
http://www.law.indiana.edu

ABA Approved Since 1923

The Basics

Type of School: Public   Term: Semester

Application deadline: 03/01 (Preferred)

Application fee: $35

Financial Aid deadline: 04/01

Can first year start other than Fall? Yes

Student faculty ratio: 14.3 to 1

Does the University offer:

- housing restricted to law students? No
- graduate student housing for which law students are eligible? Yes

Faculty & Administrators

	Total		Men		Women		Minorities	
	Fall	Spr	Fall	Spr	Fall	Spr	Fall	Spr
Full-time	36	33	28	25	8	8	2	2
Other Full-Time	6	6	1	1	5	5	0	0
Deans, librarians, & others who teach > 1/2	2	2	1	1	1	1	0	0
Part-time	6	7	5	3	1	4	0	0
Total	50	48	35	30	15	18	2	2
Deans, librarians, & others who teach < 1/2	2	2	1	1	1	1	0	0

Curriculum

	Full time	Part time
Typical first-year section size	78	0
Is there typically a "small section" of the first year class, other than Legal Writing, taught by full-time faculty?	No	No
If yes, typical size offered last year	N/A	N/A
# of classroom course titles beyond 1st year curriculum	106	0
# of upper division courses, excluding seminars, with an enrollment:		
Under 25	70	0
25 - 49	25	0
50 - 74	15	0
75 - 99	4	0
100 +	5	0
# of seminars	13	0
# of seminar positions available	216	
# of seminar positions filled	160	0
# of positions available in simulation courses	224	
# of simulation positions filled	195	0
# of positions available in faculty supervised clinical courses	95	
# of fac. sup. clin. positions filled	83	0
# involved in field placements	146	0
# involved in law journals	178	0
# in moot court or trial competitions	191	0
# of credit hrs required to graduate	86	

J.D. Enrollment & Ethnicity

	Men		Women		Fl-Time		Pt-Time		1st Yr		2nd Yr		3rd Yr		4th Yr		Total		JD Degrees Awarded
	#	%	#	%	#	%	#	%	#	%	#	%	#	%	#	%	#	%	
African-American	23	6.3	23	9.0	46	7.5	0	0.0	13	6.1	14	7.4	19	8.7	0	0.0	46	7.4	21
American Indian	0	0.0	1	0.4	1	0.2	0	0.0	0	0.0	1	0.5	0	0.0	0	0.0	1	0.2	1
Asian American	14	3.8	21	8.2	35	5.7	0	0.0	10	4.7	11	5.8	14	6.4	0	0.0	35	5.6	7
Mexican American	14	3.8	5	2.0	19	3.1	0	0.0	6	2.8	7	3.7	6	2.8	0	0.0	19	3.1	16
Puerto Rican	0	0.0	0	0.0	0	0.0	0	0.0	0	0.0	0	0.0	0	0.0	0	0.0	0	0.0	0
Hispanic American	0	0.0	0	0.0	0	0.0	0	0.0	0	0.0	0	0.0	0	0.0	0	0.0	0	0.0	0
Total Minorities	51	13.9	50	19.5	101	16.4	0	0.0	29	13.6	33	17.4	39	17.9	0	0.0	101	16.2	45
Foreign Nationals	2	0.5	5	2.0	7	1.1	0	0.0	4	1.9	1	0.5	2	0.9	0	0.0	7	1.1	2
Caucasian	313	85.5	201	78.5	506	82.4	8	100.0	181	84.6	156	82.1	177	81.2	0	0.0	514	82.6	169
Total	366	58.8	256	41.2	614	98.7	8	1.3	214	34.4	190	30.5	218	35.0	0	0.0	622		216

GPA & LSAT Scores

	Full Time	Part Time	Total
# of apps	1,392	2	1,394
# admits	592	2	594
# of matrics	210	2	212
75% GPA	3.60	0.00	
25% GPA	3.00	0.00	
75% LSAT	163	0	
25% LSAT	155	0	

Tuition & Fees

	Resident	Non-resident
Full-Time	$6,627	$16,461
Part-Time	$0	$0

Living Expenses

Estimated living expenses for Singles

Living on campus	Living off campus	Living at home
$14,424	N/A	$8,754

Grants/Scholarships

	Full-time		Part-time		Total	
	#	%	#	%	#	%
Total # of Students	614		8		622	
Total # receiving grants	303	49.3	0	0.0	303	48.7
Less than 1/2 tuition	228	37.1	0	0.0	228	36.7
Half to full tuition	58	9.4	0	0.0	58	9.3
Full tuition	5	0.8	0	0.0	5	0.8
More than full tuition	12	2.0	0	0.0	12	1.9
Median Grant Amount	$4,742		$0			

Informational & Library Resources

# of volumes & volume equivalents	610,983	# of professional staff	9
# of titles	191,544	Hours per week with professional staff	65
# of active serial subscriptions	7,842	Hours per week without professional staff	50
Study seating capacity inside the library	723	# of student computer work stations for entire law school	80
Square feet of law library	65,526	# of additional networked connections	87
Square feet of law school (excl. Library)	42,787	Require Laptop Computer?	N

Employment

	Total	%
Employment status known	209	95.0
Employment status unknown	11	5.0
Employed	192	91.9
Pursuing graduate degrees	7	3.3
Unemployed seeking employment	5	2.4
Unemployed not seeking employment	5	2.4
Type of Employment		
# employed in law firms	102	53.1
# employed in business & industry	27	14.1
# employed in government	31	16.1
# employed in public interest	4	2.1
# employed as judicial clerks	21	10.9
# employed in academia	3	1.6
Geographic Location		
# employed in state	110	57.3
# employed in foreign countries	5	2.6
# of states where employed	27	

J.D. Attrition (from Prior Year)

	Academic	Other	TOTALS	
	#	#	#	%
1st Year	0	16	16	7.8%
2nd Year	0	5	5	2.2%
3rd Year	0	5	5	2.3%
4th Year	0	0	0	0.0%

Bar Passage Rates

Jurisdiction	Indiana		
Exam	Sum 97	Win 98	Total
# from school taking bar for the first time	100	15	115
School's pass rate for all first-time takers	97%	93%	97%
State's pass rate for all first-time takers	93%	92%	93%

INDIANA UNIVERSITY - INDIANAPOLIS

735 West New York Street
Indianapolis, IN 46202-5194
(317)274-8523
http://www.iulaw.indy.indiana.edu

ABA Approved Since 1936

The Basics

Type of School: Public Term: Semester
Application deadline: 03/01
Application fee: $35
Financial Aid deadline: 03/01
Can first year start other than Fall? Yes
Student faculty ratio: 20.7 to 1
Does the University offer:
- housing restricted to law students? No
- graduate student housing for which law students are eligible? No

Faculty & Administrators

	Total		Men		Women		Minorities	
	Fall	Spr	Fall	Spr	Fall	Spr	Fall	Spr
Full-time	31	33	22	24	9	9	2	2
Other Full-Time	3	3	0	0	3	3	0	0
Deans, librarians, & others who teach > 1/2	1	1	0	0	1	1	0	0
Part-time	19	24	14	18	5	6	2	0
Total	54	61	36	42	18	19	4	2
Deans, librarians, & others who teach < 1/2	2	2	2	2	0	0	0	0

Curriculum

	Full time	Part time
Typical first-year section size	90	80
Is there typically a "small section" of the first year class, other than Legal Writing, taught by full-time faculty?	Yes	Yes
If yes, typical size offered last year	45	40
# of classroom course titles beyond 1st year curriculum	58	44
# of upper division courses, excluding seminars, with an enrollment:		
Under 25	16	13
25 - 49	25	16
50 - 74	10	10
75 - 99	9	3
100 +	3	0
# of seminars	9	4
# of seminar positions available	266	
# of seminar positions filled	140	62
# of positions available in simulation courses	315	
# of simulation positions filled	185	90
# of positions available in faculty supervised clinical courses	94	
# of fac. sup. clin. positions filled	49	13
# involved in field placements	88	12
# involved in law journals	78	17
# in moot court or trial competitions	107	22
# of credit hrs required to graduate	90	

J.D. Enrollment & Ethnicity

	Men		Women		Fl-Time		Pt-Time		1st Yr		2nd Yr		3rd Yr		4th Yr		Total		JD Degrees Awarded
	#	%	#	%	#	%	#	%	#	%	#	%	#	%	#	%	#	%	
African-American	19	4.0	29	7.3	29	5.2	19	6.0	23	6.4	14	5.3	11	4.3	0	0.0	48	5.5	20
American Indian	2	0.4	3	0.8	2	0.4	3	0.9	2	0.6	2	0.8	1	0.4	0	0.0	5	0.6	1
Asian American	6	1.2	13	3.3	14	2.5	5	1.6	7	1.9	7	2.7	5	2.0	0	0.0	19	2.2	3
Mexican American	11	2.3	8	2.0	15	2.7	4	1.3	5	1.4	5	1.9	9	3.5	0	0.0	19	2.2	3
Puerto Rican	0	0.0	0	0.0	0	0.0	0	0.0	0	0.0	0	0.0	0	0.0	0	0.0	0	0.0	0
Hispanic American	0	0.0	0	0.0	0	0.0	0	0.0	0	0.0	0	0.0	0	0.0	0	0.0	0	0.0	0
Total Minorities	38	7.9	53	13.4	60	10.7	31	9.8	37	10.2	28	10.6	26	10.2	0	0.0	91	10.4	27
Foreign Nationals	14	2.9	3	0.8	14	2.5	3	0.9	8	2.2	6	2.3	3	1.2	0	0.0	17	1.9	4
Caucasian	429	89.2	341	85.9	488	86.8	282	89.2	316	87.5	229	87.1	225	88.6	0	0.0	770	87.7	211
Total	481	54.8	397	45.2	562	64.0	316	36.0	361	41.1	263	30.0	254	28.9	0	0.0	878		242

GPA & LSAT Scores

	Full Time	Part Time	Total
# of apps	733	276	1,009
# admits	442	117	559
# of matrics	199	89	288
75% GPA	3.51	3.49	
25% GPA	2.99	2.85	
75% LSAT	156	157	
25% LSAT	150	149	

Tuition & Fees

	Resident	Non-resident
Full-Time	$6,050	$14,439
Part-Time	$4,373	$10,365

Living Expenses

Estimated living expenses for Singles		
Living on campus	Living off campus	Living at home
$8,162	$11,630	$7,532

Grants/Scholarships

	Full-time		Part-time		Total	
	#	%	#	%	#	%
Total # of Students	562		316		878	
Total # receiving grants	78	13.9	21	6.6	99	11.3
Less than 1/2 tuition	51	9.1	11	3.5	62	7.1
Half to full tuition	16	2.8	5	1.6	21	2.4
Full tuition	6	1.1	1	0.3	7	0.8
More than full tuition	5	0.9	4	1.3	9	1.0
Median Grant Amount	$1,500		$1,000			

Informational & Library Resources

# of volumes & volume equivalents	502,907	# of professional staff	8
# of titles	175,916	Hours per week with professional staff	60
# of active serial subscriptions	7,037	Hours per week without professional staff	39
Study seating capacity inside the library	452	# of student computer work stations for entire law school	70
Square feet of law library	32,016	# of additional networked connections	0
Square feet of law school (excl. Library)	40,150	Require Laptop Computer?	N

Employment

	Total	%
Employment status known	213	98.2
Employment status unknown	4	1.8
Employed	199	93.4
Pursuing graduate degrees	0	0.0
Unemployed seeking employment	11	5.2
Unemployed not seeking employment	3	1.4
Type of Employment		
# employed in law firms	106	53.3
# employed in business & industry	35	17.6
# employed in government	36	18.1
# employed in public interest	3	1.5
# employed as judicial clerks	13	6.5
# employed in academia	6	3.0
Geographic Location		
# employed in state	179	89.9
# employed in foreign countries	2	1.0
# of states where employed	14	

J.D. Attrition (from Prior Year)

	Academic	Other	TOTALS	
	#	#	#	%
1st Year	4	13	17	4.8%
2nd Year	4	2	6	2.5%
3rd Year	0	3	3	1.1%
4th Year	0	0	0	0.0%

Bar Passage Rates

Jurisdiction	Indiana		
Exam	Sum 97	Win 98	Total
# from school taking bar for the first time	161	39	200
School's pass rate for all first-time takers	94%	90%	94%
State's pass rate for all first-time takers	93%	92%	93%

INTER AMERICAN UNIVERSITY OF PUERTO RICO

P.O. Box 70351
San Juan, PR 00936-8351
(787)751-1912
http://www.derecho.inter.edu

ABA Approved Since 1969

The Basics

Type of School: Private — Term: Semester
Application deadline: 03/31
Application fee: $63
Financial Aid deadline: 09/30
Can first year start other than Fall? No
Student faculty ratio: 23.0 to 1
Does the University offer:
- housing restricted to law students? No
- graduate student housing for which law students are eligible? No

Curriculum

	Full time	Part time
Typical first-year section size	55	50
Is there typically a "small section" of the first year class, other than Legal Writing, taught by full-time faculty?	No	No
If yes, typical size offered last year	N/A	N/A
# of classroom course titles beyond 1st year curriculum	47	43
# of upper division courses, excluding seminars, with an enrollment:		
Under 25	25	23
25 - 49	21	20
50 - 74	10	11
75 - 99	1	0
100 +	0	0
# of seminars	10	7
# of seminar positions available	255	
# of seminar positions filled	113	96
# of positions available in simulation courses	225	
# of simulation positions filled	66	110
# of positions available in faculty supervised clinical courses	145	
# of fac. sup. clin. positions filled	74	0
# involved in field placements	23	0
# involved in law journals	47	0
# in moot court or trial competitions	2	1
# of credit hrs required to graduate	92	

Faculty & Administrators

	Total		Men		Women		Minorities	
	Fall	Spr	Fall	Spr	Fall	Spr	Fall	Spr
Full-time	22	21	11	10	11	11	22	21
Other Full-Time	0	0	0	0	0	0	0	0
Deans, librarians, & others who teach > 1/2	2	2	2	2	0	0	2	2
Part-time	27	26	19	19	8	7	26	25
Total	51	49	32	31	19	18	50	48
Deans, librarians, & others who teach < 1/2	2	2	1	1	1	1	2	2

J.D. Enrollment & Ethnicity

	Men		Women		Fl-Time		Pt-Time		1st Yr		2nd Yr		3rd Yr		4th Yr		Total		JD Degrees Awarded
	#	%	#	%	#	%	#	%	#	%	#	%	#	%	#	%	#	%	
African-American	0	0.0	0	0.0	0	0.0	0	0.0	0	0.0	0	0.0	0	0.0	0	0.0	0	0.0	0
American Indian	0	0.0	0	0.0	0	0.0	0	0.0	0	0.0	0	0.0	0	0.0	0	0.0	0	0.0	0
Asian American	0	0.0	0	0.0	0	0.0	0	0.0	0	0.0	0	0.0	0	0.0	0	0.0	0	0.0	0
Mexican American	0	0.0	0	0.0	0	0.0	0	0.0	0	0.0	0	0.0	0	0.0	0	0.0	0	0.0	0
Puerto Rican	340	99.7	386	99.7	377	99.5	349	100.0	220	97.3	207	101.5	222	100.5	77	100.0	726	99.7	157
Hispanic American	1	0.3	1	0.3	2	0.5	0	0.0	0	0.0	1	0.5	1	0.5	0	0.0	2	0.3	0
Total Minorities	341	100.0	387	100.0	379	100.0	349	100.0	220	97.3	208	102.0	223	100.9	77	100.0	728	100.0	157
Foreign Nationals	0	0.0	0	0.0	0	0.0	0	0.0	0	0.0	0	0.0	0	0.0	0	0.0	0	0.0	0
Caucasian	0	0.0	0	0.0	0	0.0	0	0.0	0	0.0	0	0.0	0	0.0	0	0.0	0	0.0	0
Total	341	46.8	387	53.2	379	52.1	349	47.9	226	31.0	204	28.0	221	30.4	77	10.6	728		157

INTER AMERICAN UNIVERSITY OF PUERTO RICO

GPA & LSAT Scores

	Full Time	Part Time	Total
# of apps	524	534	1,058
# admits	201	130	331
# of matrics	129	97	226
75% GPA	3.25	3.40	
25% GPA	2.82	2.82	
75% LSAT	140	144	
25% LSAT	135	137	

Tuition & Fees

	Resident	Non-resident
Full-Time	$11,308	$11,308
Part-Time	$8,508	$8,508

Living Expenses

Estimated living expenses for Singles		
Living on campus	Living off campus	Living at home
N/A	$8,950	$5,450

Employment

	Total	%
Employment status known	155	94.5
Employment status unknown	9	5.5
Employed	141	91.0
Pursuing graduate degrees	4	2.6
Unemployed seeking employment	5	3.2
Unemployed not seeking employment	5	3.2
Type of Employment		
# employed in law firms	55	39.0
# employed in business & industry	38	27.0
# employed in government	20	14.2
# employed in public interest	3	2.1
# employed as judicial clerks	22	15.6
# employed in academia	3	2.1
Geographic Location		
# employed in state	137	97.2
# employed in foreign countries	0	0.0
# of states where employed	3	

Grants/Scholarships

	Full-time		Part-time		Total	
	#	%	#	%	#	%
Total # of Students	379		349		728	
Total # receiving grants	61	16.1	3	0.9	64	8.8
Less than 1/2 tuition	16	4.2	3	0.9	19	2.6
Half to full tuition	45	11.9	0	0.0	45	6.2
Full tuition	0	0.0	0	0.0	0	0.0
More than full tuition	0	0.0	0	0.0	0	0.0
Median Grant Amount	$2,456		$850			

Informational & Library Resources

# of volumes & volume equivalents	174,935	# of professional staff	16
# of titles	22,942	Hours per week with professional staff	87
# of active serial subscriptions	3,925	Hours per week without professional staff	15
Study seating capacity inside the library	329	# of student computer work stations for entire law school	39
Square feet of law library	35,136	# of additional networked connections	6
Square feet of law school (excl. Library)	174,864	Require Laptop Computer?	N

J.D. Attrition (from Prior Year)

	Academic	Other	TOTALS	
	#	#	#	%
1st Year	7	10	17	7.8%
2nd Year	1	10	11	5.4%
3rd Year	0	5	5	2.6%
4th Year	0	2	2	3.6%

Bar Passage Rates

Jurisdiction	Puerto Rico		
Exam	Sum 97	Win 98	Total
# from school taking bar for the first time	120	41	161
School's pass rate for all first-time takers	60%	39%	55%
State's pass rate for all first-time takers	63%	53%	61%

IOWA, UNIVERSITY OF

Melrose and Byington
Iowa City, IA 52242-1113
(319)335-9034
http://www.uiowa.edu/~/lawcoll

ABA Approved Since 1923

The Basics

Type of School: Public
Term: Semester
Application deadline: 03/01
Application fee: $30
Financial Aid deadline: 03/01
Can first year start other than Fall? Yes
Student faculty ratio: 13.5 to 1
Does the University offer:
- housing restricted to law students? No
- graduate student housing for which law students are eligible? Yes

Faculty & Administrators

	Total		Men		Women		Minorities	
	Fall	Spr	Fall	Spr	Fall	Spr	Fall	Spr
Full-time	44	44	32	33	12	11	5	5
Other Full-Time	0	0	0	0	0	0	0	0
Deans, librarians, & others who teach > 1/2	4	4	3	3	1	1	0	0
Part-time	12	20	11	14	1	6	0	0
Total	60	68	46	50	14	18	5	5
Deans, librarians, & others who teach < 1/2	1	1	0	0	1	1	0	0

Curriculum

	Full time	Part time
Typical first-year section size	75	0
Is there typically a "small section" of the first year class, other than Legal Writing, taught by full-time faculty?	Yes	No
If yes, typical size offered last year	20	N/A
# of classroom course titles beyond 1st year curriculum	132	0
# of upper division courses, excluding seminars, with an enrollment:		
Under 25	55	0
25 - 49	40	0
50 - 74	13	0
75 - 99	10	0
100 +	1	0
# of seminars	25	0
# of seminar positions available	260	
# of seminar positions filled	245	0
# of positions available in simulation courses	289	
# of simulation positions filled	280	0
# of positions available in faculty supervised clinical courses	86	
# of fac. sup. clin. positions filled	86	0
# involved in field placements	30	0
# involved in law journals	123	0
# in moot court or trial competitions	182	0
# of credit hrs required to graduate	90	

J.D. Enrollment & Ethnicity

	Men		Women		Fl-Time		Pt-Time		1st Yr		2nd Yr		3rd Yr		4th Yr		Total		JD Degrees Awarded
	#	%	#	%	#	%	#	%	#	%	#	%	#	%	#	%	#	%	
African-American	26	6.6	21	8.1	47	7.2	0	0.0	15	6.6	16	8.1	16	7.0	0	0.0	47	7.2	17
American Indian	8	2.0	7	2.7	15	2.3	0	0.0	6	2.6	5	2.5	4	1.7	0	0.0	15	2.3	5
Asian American	20	5.1	13	5.0	33	5.0	0	0.0	10	4.4	7	3.5	16	7.0	0	0.0	33	5.0	15
Mexican American	5	1.3	12	4.7	17	2.6	0	0.0	7	3.1	6	3.0	4	1.7	0	0.0	17	2.6	4
Puerto Rican	2	0.5	1	0.4	3	0.5	0	0.0	0	0.0	1	0.5	2	0.9	0	0.0	3	0.5	1
Hispanic American	4	1.0	8	3.1	12	1.8	0	0.0	1	0.4	4	2.0	7	3.1	0	0.0	12	1.8	4
Total Minorities	65	16.4	62	24.0	127	19.4	0	0.0	39	17.2	39	19.7	49	21.4	0	0.0	127	19.4	46
Foreign Nationals	8	2.0	5	1.9	13	2.0	0	0.0	8	3.5	3	1.5	2	0.9	0	0.0	13	2.0	3
Caucasian	323	81.6	191	74.0	514	78.6	0	0.0	180	79.3	156	78.8	178	77.7	0	0.0	514	78.6	166
Total	396	60.6	258	39.4	654	100.0	0	0.0	227	34.7	198	30.3	229	35.0	0	0.0	654		215

GPA & LSAT Scores

	Full Time	Part Time	Total
# of apps	1,110	0	1,110
# admits	457	0	457
# of matrics	229	0	229
75% GPA	3.71	0.00	
25% GPA	3.12	0.00	
75% LSAT	162	0	
25% LSAT	155	0	

Tuition & Fees

	Resident	Non-resident
Full-Time	$6,510	$16,426
Part-Time	$0	$0

Living Expenses

Estimated living expenses for Singles		
Living on campus	Living off campus	Living at home
$8,172	$9,430	$5,784

Employment

	Total	%
Employment status known	234	99.6
Employment status unknown	1	0.4
Employed	203	86.8
Pursuing graduate degrees	7	3.0
Unemployed seeking employment	10	4.3
Unemployed not seeking employment	14	6.0
Type of Employment		
# employed in law firms	117	57.6
# employed in business & industry	30	14.8
# employed in government	26	12.8
# employed in public interest	7	3.4
# employed as judicial clerks	17	8.4
# employed in academia	6	3.0
Geographic Location		
# employed in state	60	29.6
# employed in foreign countries	1	0.5
# of states where employed	31	

Grants/Scholarships

	Full-time		Part-time		Total	
	#	%	#	%	#	%
Total # of Students	654		0		654	
Total # receiving grants	261	39.9	0	0.0	261	39.9
Less than 1/2 tuition	76	11.6	0	0.0	76	11.6
Half to full tuition	25	3.8	0	0.0	25	3.8
Full tuition	156	23.9	0	0.0	156	23.9
More than full tuition	4	0.6	0	0.0	4	0.6
Median Grant Amount	$6,240		$0			

Informational & Library Resources

# of volumes & volume equivalents	909,842	# of professional staff	13
# of titles	347,169	Hours per week with professional staff	104
# of active serial subscriptions	8,373	Hours per week without professional staff	0
Study seating capacity inside the library	672	# of student computer work stations for entire law school	0
Square feet of law library	76,571	# of additional networked connections	79
Square feet of law school (excl. Library)	68,429	Require Laptop Computer?	N

J.D. Attrition (from Prior Year)

	Academic	Other	TOTALS	
	#	#	#	%
1st Year	0	10	10	4.4%
2nd Year	1	4	5	2.6%
3rd Year	1	1	2	0.8%
4th Year	0	0	0	0.0%

Bar Passage Rates

Jurisdiction	Iowa		
Exam	Sum 97	Win 98	Total
# from school taking bar for the first time	63	23	86
School's pass rate for all first-time takers	89%	87%	88%
State's pass rate for all first-time takers	86%	83%	85%

JOHN MARSHALL LAW SCHOOL

315 S. Plymouth Ct.
Chicago, IL 60604
(312)427-2737
http://www.jmls.edu

ABA Approved Since 1951

The Basics

Type of School: Private   Term: Semester
Application deadline: 03/01
Application fee: $50
Financial Aid deadline: Rolling
Can first year start other than Fall? Yes
Student faculty ratio: 15.5 to 1
Does the University offer:
- housing restricted to law students? No
- graduate student housing for which law students are eligible? No

Curriculum

	Full time	Part time
Typical first-year section size	65	66
Is there typically a "small section" of the first year class, other than Legal Writing, taught by full-time faculty?	No	No
If yes, typical size offered last year	N/A	N/A
# of classroom course titles beyond 1st year curriculum	41	65
# of upper division courses, excluding seminars, with an enrollment:		
Under 25	58	68
25 - 49	20	17
50 - 74	18	12
75 - 99	2	4
100 +	0	0
# of seminars	81	24
# of seminar positions available	683	
# of seminar positions filled	153	268
# of positions available in simulation courses	735	
# of simulation positions filled	355	305
# of positions available in faculty supervised clinical courses	80	
# of fac. sup. clin. positions filled	34	4
# involved in field placements	69	8
# involved in law journals	137	48
# in moot court or trial competitions	72	21
# of credit hrs required to graduate	90	

Faculty & Administrators

	Total		Men		Women		Minorities	
	Fall	Spr	Fall	Spr	Fall	Spr	Fall	Spr
Full-time	54	50	39	35	15	15	4	4
Other Full-Time	0	0	0	0	0	0	0	0
Deans, librarians, & others who teach > 1/2	2	2	1	1	1	1	0	0
Part-time	106	136	83	104	23	32	8	10
Total	162	188	123	140	39	48	12	14
Deans, librarians, & others who teach < 1/2	0	0	0	0	0	0	0	0

J.D. Enrollment & Ethnicity

	Men		Women		Fl-Time		Pt-Time		1st Yr		2nd Yr		3rd Yr		4th Yr		Total		JD Degrees Awarded
	#	%	#	%	#	%	#	%	#	%	#	%	#	%	#	%	#	%	
African-American	29	4.6	67	12.9	35	4.8	61	14.4	40	10.4	23	6.9	20	6.2	13	11.6	96	8.3	12
American Indian	3	0.5	6	1.2	6	0.8	3	0.7	3	0.8	4	1.2	0	0.0	2	1.8	9	0.8	1
Asian American	36	5.7	27	5.2	42	5.8	21	4.9	19	4.9	14	4.2	24	7.5	6	5.4	63	5.5	10
Mexican American	15	2.4	14	2.7	16	2.2	13	3.1	13	3.4	8	2.4	6	1.9	2	1.8	29	2.5	3
Puerto Rican	4	0.6	6	1.2	6	0.8	4	0.9	3	0.8	4	1.2	3	0.9	0	0.0	10	0.9	2
Hispanic American	14	2.2	17	3.3	11	1.5	20	4.7	11	2.9	7	2.1	7	2.2	6	5.4	31	2.7	5
Total Minorities	101	16.0	137	26.4	116	16.0	122	28.7	89	23.1	60	18.1	60	18.7	29	25.9	238	20.7	33
Foreign Nationals	10	1.6	10	1.9	15	2.1	5	1.2	11	2.9	9	2.7	0	0.0	0	0.0	20	1.7	1
Caucasian	521	82.4	371	71.6	594	81.9	298	70.1	285	74.0	263	79.2	261	81.3	83	74.1	892	77.6	232
Total	632	55.0	518	45.0	725	63.0	425	37.0	385	33.5	332	28.9	321	27.9	112	9.7	1150		266

GPA & LSAT Scores

	Full Time	Part Time	Total
# of apps	1,529	446	1,975
# admits	985	205	1,190
# of matrics	241	115	356
75% GPA	3.20	3.27	
25% GPA	2.64	2.55	
75% LSAT	154	153	
25% LSAT	145	144	

Tuition & Fees

	Resident	Non-resident
Full-Time	$18,280	$18,280
Part-Time	$6,580	$6,580

Living Expenses

Estimated living expenses for Singles		
Living on campus	Living off campus	Living at home
N/A	$13,149	$13,149

Grants/Scholarships

	Full-time		Part-time		Total	
	#	%	#	%	#	%
Total # of Students	725		425		1150	
Total # receiving grants	152	21.0	36	8.5	188	16.3
Less than 1/2 tuition	94	13.0	10	2.4	104	9.0
Half to full tuition	39	5.4	25	5.9	64	5.6
Full tuition	4	0.6	1	0.2	5	0.4
More than full tuition	15	2.1	0	0.0	15	1.3
Median Grant Amount	$12,400		$7,400			

Informational & Library Resources

# of volumes & volume equivalents	362,929	# of professional staff	9
# of titles	92,556	Hours per week with professional staff	67
# of active serial subscriptions	5,069	Hours per week without professional staff	33
Study seating capacity inside the library	624	# of student computer work stations for entire law school	80
Square feet of law library	50,000	# of additional networked connections	42
Square feet of law school (excl. Library)	76,729	Require Laptop Computer?	N

Employment

	Total	%
Employment status known	239	71.3
Employment status unknown	96	28.7
Employed	213	89.1
Pursuing graduate degrees	6	2.5
Unemployed seeking employment	14	5.9
Unemployed not seeking employment	6	2.5
Type of Employment		
# employed in law firms	128	60.1
# employed in business & industry	29	13.6
# employed in government	43	20.2
# employed in public interest	1	0.5
# employed as judicial clerks	9	4.2
# employed in academia	3	1.4
Geographic Location		
# employed in state	172	80.8
# employed in foreign countries	0	0.0
# of states where employed	19	

J.D. Attrition (from Prior Year)

	Academic	Other	TOTALS	
	#	#	#	%
1st Year	9	25	34	9.7%
2nd Year	7	14	21	6.3%
3rd Year	0	6	6	1.9%
4th Year	0	0	0	0.0%

Bar Passage Rates

Jurisdiction	Illinois		
Exam	Sum 97	Win 98	Total
# from school taking bar for the first time	178	89	267
School's pass rate for all first-time takers	79%	78%	78%
State's pass rate for all first-time takers	87%	80%	85%

KANSAS, UNIVERSITY OF

Green Hall
Lawrence, KS 66045
(785)864-4550
http://www.law.ukans.edu

ABA Approved Since 1923

The Basics

Type of School: Public Term: Semester
Application deadline: 03/15
Application fee: $40
Financial Aid deadline: 03/01
Can first year start other than Fall? Yes
Student faculty ratio: 15.2 to 1
Does the University offer:
- housing restricted to law students? No
- graduate student housing for which law students are eligible? Yes

Faculty & Administrators

	Total		Men		Women		Minorities	
	Fall	Spr	Fall	Spr	Fall	Spr	Fall	Spr
Full-time	30	30	22	23	8	7	4	3
Other Full-Time	0	0	0	0	0	0	0	0
Deans, librarians, & others who teach > 1/2	5	5	1	1	4	4	1	1
Part-time	14	16	10	13	4	3	0	1
Total	49	51	33	37	16	14	5	5
Deans, librarians, & others who teach < 1/2	0	0	0	0	0	0	0	0

Curriculum

	Full time	Part time
Typical first-year section size	90	0
Is there typically a "small section" of the first year class, other than Legal Writing, taught by full-time faculty?	Yes	No
If yes, typical size offered last year	20	N/A
# of classroom course titles beyond 1st year curriculum	86	0
# of upper division courses, excluding seminars, with an enrollment:		
Under 25	56	0
25 - 49	32	0
50 - 74	11	0
75 - 99	3	0
100 +	5	0
# of seminars	14	0
# of seminar positions available	258	
# of seminar positions filled	142	0
# of positions available in simulation courses	343	
# of simulation positions filled	294	0
# of positions available in faculty supervised clinical courses	208	
# of fac. sup. clin. positions filled	152	0
# involved in field placements	0	0
# involved in law journals	87	0
# in moot court or trial competitions	42	0
# of credit hrs required to graduate	90	

J.D. Enrollment & Ethnicity

	Men		Women		Fl-Time		Pt-Time		1st Yr		2nd Yr		3rd Yr		4th Yr		Total		JD Degrees Awarded
	#	%	#	%	#	%	#	%	#	%	#	%	#	%	#	%	#	%	
African-American	10	3.2	8	3.7	18	3.4	0	0.0	7	4.1	3	1.6	8	4.7	0	0.0	18	3.4	5
American Indian	4	1.3	5	2.3	9	1.7	0	0.0	2	1.2	3	1.6	4	2.4	0	0.0	9	1.7	3
Asian American	3	1.0	4	1.8	7	1.3	0	0.0	1	0.6	1	0.5	5	2.9	0	0.0	7	1.3	1
Mexican American	0	0.0	0	0.0	0	0.0	0	0.0	0	0.0	0	0.0	0	0.0	0	0.0	0	0.0	0
Puerto Rican	0	0.0	0	0.0	0	0.0	0	0.0	0	0.0	0	0.0	0	0.0	0	0.0	0	0.0	0
Hispanic American	13	4.2	6	2.8	19	3.6	0	0.0	8	4.7	4	2.1	7	4.1	0	0.0	19	3.6	8
Total Minorities	30	9.6	23	10.6	53	10.0	0	0.0	18	10.5	11	5.9	24	14.1	0	0.0	53	10.0	17
Foreign Nationals	3	1.0	1	0.5	4	0.8	0	0.0	0	0.0	2	1.1	2	1.2	0	0.0	4	0.8	0
Caucasian	279	89.4	193	88.9	472	89.2	0	0.0	153	89.5	175	93.1	144	84.7	0	0.0	472	89.2	150
Total	312	59.0	217	41.0	529	100.0	0	0.0	171	32.3	188	35.5	170	32.1	0	0.0	529		167

GPA & LSAT Scores

	Full Time	Part Time	Total
# of apps	758	0	758
# admits	417	0	417
# of matrics	171	0	171
75% GPA	3.68	0.00	
25% GPA	3.16	0.00	
75% LSAT	159	0	
25% LSAT	152	0	

Tuition & Fees

	Resident	Non-resident
Full-Time	$5,558	$12,391
Part-Time	$0	$0

Living Expenses

Estimated living expenses for Singles		
Living on campus	Living off campus	Living at home
$10,280	$10,280	$6,470

Employment

	Total	%
Employment status known	142	95.9
Employment status unknown	6	4.1
Employed	133	93.7
Pursuing graduate degrees	4	2.8
Unemployed seeking employment	4	2.8
Unemployed not seeking employment	1	0.7
Type of Employment		
# employed in law firms	56	42.1
# employed in business & industry	31	23.3
# employed in government	25	18.8
# employed in public interest	3	2.3
# employed as judicial clerks	12	9.0
# employed in academia	2	1.5
Geographic Location		
# employed in state	74	55.6
# employed in foreign countries	0	0.0
# of states where employed	14	

Grants/Scholarships

	Full-time		Part-time		Total	
	#	%	#	%	#	%
Total # of Students	529		0		529	
Total # receiving grants	178	33.6	0	0.0	178	33.6
Less than 1/2 tuition	93	17.6	0	0.0	93	17.6
Half to full tuition	68	12.9	0	0.0	68	12.9
Full tuition	17	3.2	0	0.0	17	3.2
More than full tuition	0	0.0	0	0.0	0	0.0
Median Grant Amount	$2,000		$0			

Informational & Library Resources

# of volumes & volume equivalents	338,233	# of professional staff	5
# of titles	118,217	Hours per week with professional staff	45
# of active serial subscriptions	4,448	Hours per week without professional staff	58
Study seating capacity inside the library	282	# of student computer work stations for entire law school	48
Square feet of law library	34,007	# of additional networked connections	20
Square feet of law school (excl. Library)	30,657	Require Laptop Computer?	N

J.D. Attrition (from Prior Year)

	Academic	Other	TOTALS	
	#	#	#	%
1st Year	0	1	1	0.6%
2nd Year	0	9	9	4.7%
3rd Year	1	2	3	1.8%
4th Year	0	0	0	0.0%

Bar Passage Rates

Jurisdiction	Kansas		
Exam	Sum 97	Win 98	Total
# from school taking bar for the first time	92	42	134
School's pass rate for all first-time takers	90%	88%	90%
State's pass rate for all first-time takers	87%	87%	87%

KENTUCKY, UNIVERSITY OF

209 Law Building
Lexington, KY 40506-0048
(606)257-1678
http://www.uky.edu/law

ABA Approved Since 1925

The Basics

Type of School: Public Term: Semester
Application deadline: 03/01
Application fee: $25
Financial Aid deadline: 04/01
Can first year start other than Fall? No
Student faculty ratio: 19.4 to 1
Does the University offer:
- housing restricted to law students? No
- graduate student housing for which law students are eligible? Yes

Faculty & Administrators

	Total		Men		Women		Minorities	
	Fall	Spr	Fall	Spr	Fall	Spr	Fall	Spr
Full-time	18	17	12	14	6	3	2	1
Other Full-Time	0	0	0	0	0	0	0	0
Deans, librarians, & others who teach > 1/2	4	4	2	2	2	2	0	0
Part-time	15	17	9	11	4	4	0	1
Total	37	38	23	27	12	9	2	2
Deans, librarians, & others who teach < 1/2	0	0	0	0	0	0	0	0

Curriculum

	Full time	Part time
Typical first-year section size	72	0
Is there typically a "small section" of the first year class, other than Legal Writing, taught by full-time faculty?	Yes	No
If yes, typical size offered last year	35	N/A
# of classroom course titles beyond 1st year curriculum	56	0
# of upper division courses, excluding seminars, with an enrollment:		
Under 25	45	0
25 - 49	19	0
50 - 74	18	0
75 - 99	1	0
100 +	0	0
# of seminars	13	0
# of seminar positions available	208	
# of seminar positions filled	157	0
# of positions available in simulation courses	100	
# of simulation positions filled	83	0
# of positions available in faculty supervised clinical courses	24	
# of fac. sup. clin. positions filled	16	0
# involved in field placements	32	0
# involved in law journals	55	0
# in moot court or trial competitions	43	0
# of credit hrs required to graduate	90	

J.D. Enrollment & Ethnicity

	Men		Women		Fl-Time		Pt-Time		1st Yr		2nd Yr		3rd Yr		4th Yr		Total		JD Degrees Awarded
	#	%	#	%	#	%	#	%	#	%	#	%	#	%	#	%	#	%	
African-American	4	1.7	10	5.6	14	3.3	0	0.0	6	4.2	6	4.3	2	1.5	0	0.0	14	3.3	9
American Indian	0	0.0	0	0.0	0	0.0	0	0.0	0	0.0	0	0.0	0	0.0	0	0.0	0	0.0	0
Asian American	4	1.7	0	0.0	4	1.0	0	0.0	2	1.4	1	0.7	1	0.7	0	0.0	4	1.0	2
Mexican American	0	0.0	0	0.0	0	0.0	0	0.0	0	0.0	0	0.0	0	0.0	0	0.0	0	0.0	0
Puerto Rican	0	0.0	0	0.0	0	0.0	0	0.0	0	0.0	0	0.0	0	0.0	0	0.0	0	0.0	0
Hispanic American	0	0.0	1	0.6	1	0.2	0	0.0	1	0.7	0	0.0	0	0.0	0	0.0	1	0.2	0
Total Minorities	8	3.4	11	6.1	19	4.5	0	0.0	9	6.3	7	5.0	3	2.2	0	0.0	19	4.5	11
Foreign Nationals	0	0.0	0	0.0	0	0.0	0	0.0	0	0.0	0	0.0	0	0.0	0	0.0	0	0.0	0
Caucasian	230	96.6	169	93.9	399	95.5	0	0.0	135	93.8	132	95.0	132	97.8	0	0.0	399	95.5	131
Total	238	56.9	180	43.1	418	100.0	0	0.0	144	34.4	139	33.3	135	32.3	0	0.0	418		142

KENTUCKY, UNIVERSITY OF

GPA & LSAT Scores

	Full Time	Part Time	Total
# of apps	755	0	755
# admits	330	0	330
# of matrics	145	0	145
75% GPA	3.66	0.00	
25% GPA	3.16	0.00	
75% LSAT	160	0	
25% LSAT	155	0	

Tuition & Fees

	Resident	Non-resident
Full-Time	$5,426	$14,036
Part-Time	$0	$0

Living Expenses

Estimated living expenses for Singles		
Living on campus	Living off campus	Living at home
$10,074	$10,074	$4,690

Employment

	Total	%
Employment status known	142	100.0
Employment status unknown	0	0.0
Employed	137	96.5
Pursuing graduate degrees	3	2.1
Unemployed seeking employment	1	0.7
Unemployed not seeking employment	1	0.7
Type of Employment		
# employed in law firms	69	50.4
# employed in business & industry	16	11.7
# employed in government	22	16.1
# employed in public interest	3	2.2
# employed as judicial clerks	25	18.2
# employed in academia	1	0.7
Geographic Location		
# employed in state	101	73.7
# employed in foreign countries	1	0.7
# of states where employed	15	

Grants/Scholarships

	Full-time		Part-time		Total	
	#	%	#	%	#	%
Total # of Students	418		0		418	
Total # receiving grants	119	28.5	0	0.0	119	28.5
Less than 1/2 tuition	66	15.8	0	0.0	66	15.8
Half to full tuition	7	1.7	0	0.0	7	1.7
Full tuition	33	7.9	0	0.0	33	7.9
More than full tuition	13	3.1	0	0.0	13	3.1
Median Grant Amount	$3,500		$0			

Informational & Library Resources

# of volumes & volume equivalents	404,058	# of professional staff	8
# of titles	51,604	Hours per week with professional staff	67
# of active serial subscriptions	3,418	Hours per week without professional staff	39
Study seating capacity inside the library	265	# of student computer work stations for entire law school	43
Square feet of law library	36,843	# of additional networked connections	40
Square feet of law school (excl. Library)	28,562	Require Laptop Computer?	N

J.D. Attrition (from Prior Year)

	Academic	Other	TOTALS	
	#	#	#	%
1st Year	3	4	7	5.0%
2nd Year	0	4	4	3.1%
3rd Year	0	0	0	0.0%
4th Year	0	0	0	0.0%

Bar Passage Rates

Jurisdiction	Kentucky		
Exam	Sum 97	Win 98	Total
# from school taking bar for the first time	106	14	120
School's pass rate for all first-time takers	63%	79%	65%
State's pass rate for all first-time takers	65%	86%	70%

LEWIS AND CLARK COLLEGE

Northwestern School of Law
10015 S.W. Terwilliger Blvd.
Portland, OR 97219-7799
(503)768-6600
http://lclark.edu/law/index.htm

ABA Approved Since 1970

The Basics

Type of School: Private Term: Semester
Application deadline: 03/15
Application fee: $50
Financial Aid deadline: 03/01
Can first year start other than Fall? No
Student faculty ratio: 14.1 to 1
Does the University offer:
- housing restricted to law students? No
- graduate student housing for which law students are eligible? No

Faculty & Administrators

	Total		Men		Women		Minorities	
	Fall	Spr	Fall	Spr	Fall	Spr	Fall	Spr
Full-time	35	35	22	22	13	13	2	2
Other Full-Time	0	0	0	0	0	0	0	0
Deans, librarians, & others who teach > 1/2	1	1	1	1	0	0	0	0
Part-time	25	29	16	21	9	8	1	1
Total	61	65	39	44	22	21	3	3
Deans, librarians, & others who teach < 1/2	5	5	2	2	3	3	0	0

Curriculum

	Full time	Part time
Typical first-year section size	74	64
Is there typically a "small section" of the first year class, other than Legal Writing, taught by full-time faculty?	Yes	Yes
If yes, typical size offered last year	37	30
# of classroom course titles beyond 1st year curriculum	61	49
# of upper division courses, excluding seminars, with an enrollment:		
Under 25	42	15
25 - 49	18	17
50 - 74	8	5
75 - 99	4	1
100 +	0	0
# of seminars	18	13
# of seminar positions available	591	
# of seminar positions filled	251	170
# of positions available in simulation courses	270	
# of simulation positions filled	158	62
# of positions available in faculty supervised clinical courses	80	
# of fac. sup. clin. positions filled	52	23
# involved in field placements	38	12
# involved in law journals	68	11
# in moot court or trial competitions	75	35
# of credit hrs required to graduate	86	

J.D. Enrollment & Ethnicity

	Men		Women		Fl-Time		Pt-Time		1st Yr		2nd Yr		3rd Yr		4th Yr		Total		JD Degrees Awarded
	#	%	#	%	#	%	#	%	#	%	#	%	#	%	#	%	#	%	
African-American	7	2.0	1	0.3	6	1.2	2	1.3	1	0.4	1	0.5	6	3.7	0	0.0	8	1.2	8
American Indian	5	1.5	1	0.3	3	0.6	3	1.9	5	2.1	1	0.5	0	0.0	0	0.0	6	0.9	2
Asian American	15	4.4	26	8.6	29	5.9	12	7.6	16	6.7	8	3.6	17	10.4	0	0.0	41	6.3	25
Mexican American	3	0.9	2	0.7	4	0.8	1	0.6	2	0.8	1	0.5	1	0.6	1	4.3	5	0.8	6
Puerto Rican	1	0.3	0	0.0	1	0.2	0	0.0	0	0.0	1	0.5	0	0.0	0	0.0	1	0.2	1
Hispanic American	4	1.2	7	2.3	8	1.6	3	1.9	4	1.7	2	0.9	5	3.0	0	0.0	11	1.7	6
Total Minorities	35	10.2	37	12.2	51	10.4	21	13.4	28	11.7	14	6.3	29	17.7	1	4.3	72	11.1	48
Foreign Nationals	9	2.6	10	3.3	9	1.8	10	6.4	10	4.2	7	3.2	2	1.2	0	0.0	19	2.9	10
Caucasian	300	87.2	256	84.5	430	87.8	126	80.3	200	83.7	200	90.5	134	81.7	22	95.7	556	85.9	164
Total	344	53.2	303	46.8	490	75.7	157	24.3	239	36.9	221	34.2	164	25.3	23	3.6	647		222

GPA & LSAT Scores

	Full Time	Part Time	Total
# of apps	1,320	137	1,457
# admits	878	78	956
# of matrics	193	44	237
75% GPA	3.53	3.59	
25% GPA	3.04	2.94	
75% LSAT	162	161	
25% LSAT	155	153	

Tuition & Fees

	Resident	Non-resident
Full-Time	$18,265	$18,265
Part-Time	$13,697	$13,697

Living Expenses

Estimated living expenses for Singles		
Living on campus	Living off campus	Living at home
N/A	$11,350	$11,350

Grants/Scholarships

	Full-time		Part-time		Total	
	#	%	#	%	#	%
Total # of Students	490		157		647	
Total # receiving grants	210	42.9	81	51.6	291	45.0
Less than 1/2 tuition	191	39.0	64	40.8	255	39.4
Half to full tuition	18	3.7	17	10.8	35	5.4
Full tuition	1	0.2	0	0.0	1	0.2
More than full tuition	0	0.0	0	0.0	0	0.0
Median Grant Amount	$5,230		$3,463			

Informational & Library Resources

# of volumes & volume equivalents	442,866	# of professional staff	8
# of titles	76,837	Hours per week with professional staff	69
# of active serial subscriptions	4,830	Hours per week without professional staff	44
Study seating capacity inside the library	194	# of student computer work stations for entire law school	63
Square feet of law library	27,939	# of additional networked connections	160
Square feet of law school (excl. Library)	59,361	Require Laptop Computer?	N

Employment

	Total	%
Employment status known	207	94.5
Employment status unknown	12	5.5
Employed	188	90.8
Pursuing graduate degrees	0	0.0
Unemployed seeking employment	13	6.3
Unemployed not seeking employment	6	2.9
Type of Employment		
# employed in law firms	97	51.6
# employed in business & industry	23	12.2
# employed in government	35	18.6
# employed in public interest	13	6.9
# employed as judicial clerks	18	9.6
# employed in academia	2	1.1
Geographic Location		
# employed in state	119	63.3
# employed in foreign countries	1	0.5
# of states where employed	23	

J.D. Attrition (from Prior Year)

	Academic	Other	TOTALS	
	#	#	#	%
1st Year	0	7	7	3.2%
2nd Year	0	9	9	5.4%
3rd Year	0	0	0	0.0%
4th Year	0	0	0	0.0%

Bar Passage Rates

Jurisdiction	Oregon			Washington		
Exam	Sum 97	Win 98	Total	Sum 97	Win 98	Total
# from school taking bar for the first time	120	31	151	13	31	44
School's pass rate for all first-time takers	82%	68%	79%	92%	77%	82%
State's pass rate for all first-time takers	74%	68%	72%	73%	83%	76%

LOUISIANA STATE UNIVERSITY

Paul M. Hebert Law Center
210 Law Center
Baton Rouge, LA 70803
(504)388-8491
http://www.lsu.edu/guests/lsulaw/index.h

ABA Approved Since 1926

The Basics

Type of School: Public **Term:** Semester
Application deadline: 02/01
Application fee: $25
Financial Aid deadline: 04/01
Can first year start other than Fall? No
Student faculty ratio: 20.7 to 1
Does the University offer:
- **housing restricted to law students?** No
- **graduate student housing for which law students are eligible?** No

Faculty & Administrators

	Total		Men		Women		Minorities	
	Fall	Spr	Fall	Spr	Fall	Spr	Fall	Spr
Full-time	26	26	23	23	3	3	2	2
Other Full-Time	4	4	0	0	4	4	1	1
Deans, librarians, & others who teach > 1/2	2	2	2	2	0	0	0	0
Part-time	15	14	14	13	1	1	1	1
Total	47	46	39	38	8	8	4	4
Deans, librarians, & others who teach < 1/2	2	2	1	1	1	1	0	0

Curriculum

	Full time	Part time
Typical first-year section size	78	0
Is there typically a "small section" of the first year class, other than Legal Writing, taught by full-time faculty?	Yes	No
If yes, typical size offered last year	39	N/A
# of classroom course titles beyond 1st year curriculum	61	0
# of upper division courses, excluding seminars, with an enrollment:		
Under 25	8	0
25 - 49	11	0
50 - 74	7	0
75 - 99	8	0
100 +	13	0
# of seminars	10	0
# of seminar positions available	200	
# of seminar positions filled	164	0
# of positions available in simulation courses	711	
# of simulation positions filled	697	0
# of positions available in faculty supervised clinical courses	0	
# of fac. sup. clin. positions filled	0	0
# involved in field placements	0	0
# involved in law journals	43	0
# in moot court or trial competitions	24	0
# of credit hrs required to graduate	97	

J.D. Enrollment & Ethnicity

	Men		Women		Fl-Time		Pt-Time		1st Yr		2nd Yr		3rd Yr		4th Yr		Total		JD Degrees Awarded
	#	%	#	%	#	%	#	%	#	%	#	%	#	%	#	%	#	%	
African-American	16	4.6	34	11.4	50	7.8	0	0.0	28	9.2	11	6.7	11	6.3	0	0.0	50	7.8	11
American Indian	1	0.3	2	0.7	3	0.5	0	0.0	0	0.0	2	1.2	1	0.6	0	0.0	3	0.5	1
Asian American	3	0.9	1	0.3	4	0.6	0	0.0	2	0.7	1	0.6	1	0.6	0	0.0	4	0.6	3
Mexican American	0	0.0	0	0.0	0	0.0	0	0.0	0	0.0	0	0.0	0	0.0	0	0.0	0	0.0	0
Puerto Rican	0	0.0	0	0.0	0	0.0	0	0.0	0	0.0	0	0.0	0	0.0	0	0.0	0	0.0	0
Hispanic American	6	1.7	0	0.0	6	0.9	0	0.0	3	1.0	1	0.6	2	1.1	0	0.0	6	0.9	1
Total Minorities	26	7.5	37	12.5	63	9.8	0	0.0	33	10.9	15	9.1	15	8.5	0	0.0	63	9.8	16
Foreign Nationals	5	1.4	4	1.3	9	1.4	0	0.0	6	2.0	2	1.2	1	0.6	0	0.0	9	1.4	0
Caucasian	317	91.1	256	86.2	573	88.8	0	0.0	265	87.2	148	89.7	160	90.9	0	0.0	573	88.8	178
Total	348	54.0	297	46.0	645	100.0	0	0.0	304	47.1	165	25.6	176	27.3	0	0.0	645		194

GPA & LSAT Scores

	Full Time	Part Time	Total
# of apps	965	0	965
# admits	630	0	630
# of matrics	310	0	310
75% GPA	3.53	0.00	
25% GPA	3.10	0.00	
75% LSAT	156	0	
25% LSAT	147	0	

Tuition & Fees

	Resident	Non-resident
Full-Time	$4,086	$9,561
Part-Time	$2,681	$6,049

Living Expenses

Estimated living expenses for Singles		
Living on campus	Living off campus	Living at home
$10,300	$10,300	$6,176

Employment

	Total	%
Employment status known	174	91.6
Employment status unknown	16	8.4
Employed	155	89.1
Pursuing graduate degrees	5	2.9
Unemployed seeking employment	13	7.5
Unemployed not seeking employment	1	0.6
Type of Employment		
# employed in law firms	92	59.4
# employed in business & industry	2	1.3
# employed in government	20	12.9
# employed in public interest	2	1.3
# employed as judicial clerks	35	22.6
# employed in academia	0	0.0
Geographic Location		
# employed in state	142	91.6
# employed in foreign countries	1	0.6
# of states where employed	6	

Grants/Scholarships

	Full-time		Part-time		Total	
	#	%	#	%	#	%
Total # of Students	645		0		645	
Total # receiving grants	130	20.2	0	0.0	130	20.2
Less than 1/2 tuition	46	7.1	0	0.0	46	7.1
Half to full tuition	68	10.5	0	0.0	68	10.5
Full tuition	0	0.0	0	0.0	0	0.0
More than full tuition	16	2.5	0	0.0	16	2.5
Median Grant Amount	$3,335		$0			

Informational & Library Resources

# of volumes & volume equivalents	578,034	# of professional staff	15
# of titles	146,741	Hours per week with professional staff	65
# of active serial subscriptions	2,979	Hours per week without professional staff	34
Study seating capacity inside the library	464	# of student computer work stations for entire law school	0
Square feet of law library	71,056	# of additional networked connections	0
Square feet of law school (excl. Library)	112,947	Require Laptop Computer?	N

J.D. Attrition (from Prior Year)

	Academic	Other	TOTALS	
	#	#	#	%
1st Year	58	26	84	36%
2nd Year	0	5	5	2.8%
3rd Year	1	1	2	1.0%
4th Year	0	0	0	0.0%

Bar Passage Rates

Jurisdiction	Louisiana		
Exam	Sum 97	Win 98	Total
# from school taking bar for the first time	169	13	182
School's pass rate for all first-time takers	85%	62%	83%
State's pass rate for all first-time takers	62%	54%	61%

LOUISVILLE, UNIVERSITY OF

Louis D. Brandeis School of Law
Louisville, KY 40292
(502)852-6879
http://www.louisville.edu/brandeislaw/

ABA Approved Since 1931

The Basics

Type of School: Public — Term: Semester
Application deadline: 03/01
Application fee: $30
Financial Aid deadline: 07/01
Can first year start other than Fall? No
Student faculty ratio: 13.9 to 1
Does the University offer:
- housing restricted to law students? No
- graduate student housing for which law students are eligible? Yes

Faculty & Administrators

	Total		Men		Women		Minorities	
	Fall	Spr	Fall	Spr	Fall	Spr	Fall	Spr
Full-time	23	22	16	15	7	7	4	4
Other Full-Time	1	1	1	1	0	0	0	0
Deans, librarians, & others who teach > 1/2	4	4	3	3	1	1	0	0
Part-time	13	6	9	5	4	1	1	0
Total	41	33	29	24	12	9	5	4
Deans, librarians, & others who teach < 1/2	1	1	1	1	0	0	0	0

Curriculum

	Full time	Part time
Typical first-year section size	45	35
Is there typically a "small section" of the first year class, other than Legal Writing, taught by full-time faculty?	No	No
If yes, typical size offered last year	N/A	N/A
# of classroom course titles beyond 1st year curriculum	61	30
# of upper division courses, excluding seminars, with an enrollment:		
Under 25	25	7
25 - 49	14	11
50 - 74	16	3
75 - 99	2	1
100 +	1	0
# of seminars	17	7
# of seminar positions available	432	
# of seminar positions filled	262	119
# of positions available in simulation courses	842	
# of simulation positions filled	488	249
# of positions available in faculty supervised clinical courses	0	
# of fac. sup. clin. positions filled	0	0
# involved in field placements	184	18
# involved in law journals	43	1
# in moot court or trial competitions	62	5
# of credit hrs required to graduate	90	

J.D. Enrollment & Ethnicity

	Men		Women		Fl-Time		Pt-Time		1st Yr		2nd Yr		3rd Yr		4th Yr		Total		JD Degrees Awarded
	#	%	#	%	#	%	#	%	#	%	#	%	#	%	#	%	#	%	
African-American	11	4.4	13	7.7	19	6.1	5	4.8	12	9.7	10	7.6	2	1.3	0	0.0	24	5.7	2
American Indian	0	0.0	1	0.6	1	0.3	0	0.0	0	0.0	1	0.8	0	0.0	0	0.0	1	0.2	0
Asian American	4	1.6	5	3.0	7	2.2	2	1.9	2	1.6	4	3.1	3	2.0	0	0.0	9	2.2	4
Mexican American	1	0.4	0	0.0	1	0.3	0	0.0	1	0.8	0	0.0	0	0.0	0	0.0	1	0.2	0
Puerto Rican	1	0.4	1	0.6	1	0.3	1	1.0	0	0.0	2	1.5	0	0.0	0	0.0	2	0.5	0
Hispanic American	3	1.2	0	0.0	3	1.0	0	0.0	0	0.0	3	2.3	0	0.0	0	0.0	3	0.7	0
Total Minorities	20	8.0	20	11.8	32	10.2	8	7.6	15	12.1	20	15.3	5	3.3	0	0.0	40	9.6	6
Foreign Nationals	2	0.8	1	0.6	3	1.0	0	0.0	1	0.8	0	0.0	2	1.3	0	0.0	3	0.7	1
Caucasian	227	91.2	148	87.6	278	88.8	97	92.4	108	87.1	111	84.7	143	95.3	13	100.0	375	89.7	149
Total	249	59.6	169	40.4	313	74.9	105	25.1	124	29.7	131	31.3	150	35.9	13	3.1	418		156

GPA & LSAT Scores

	Full Time	Part Time	Total
# of apps	724	115	839
# admits	248	46	294
# of matrics	86	35	121
75% GPA	3.57	3.53	
25% GPA	2.85	2.74	
75% LSAT	159	157	
25% LSAT	154	149	

Tuition & Fees

	Resident	Non-resident
Full-Time	$5,330	$13,940
Part-Time	$4,460	$11,630

Living Expenses

Estimated living expenses for Singles		
Living on campus	Living off campus	Living at home
$6,990	$9,886	$4,750

Grants/Scholarships

	Full-time		Part-time		Total	
	#	%	#	%	#	%
Total # of Students	313		105		418	
Total # receiving grants	109	34.8	20	19.0	129	30.9
Less than 1/2 tuition	62	19.8	8	7.6	70	16.7
Half to full tuition	15	4.8	3	2.9	18	4.3
Full tuition	25	8.0	7	6.7	32	7.7
More than full tuition	7	2.2	2	1.9	9	2.2
Median Grant Amount	$4,000		$5,165			

Informational & Library Resources

# of volumes & volume equivalents	302,838	# of professional staff	4
# of titles	39,078	Hours per week with professional staff	82
# of active serial subscriptions	5,135	Hours per week without professional staff	6
Study seating capacity inside the library	391	# of student computer work stations for entire law school	41
Square feet of law library	53,060	# of additional networked connections	6
Square feet of law school (excl. Library)	62,850	Require Laptop Computer?	N

Employment

	Total	%
Employment status known	140	100.0
Employment status unknown	0	0.0
Employed	135	96.4
Pursuing graduate degrees	2	1.4
Unemployed seeking employment	1	0.7
Unemployed not seeking employment	2	1.4
Type of Employment		
# employed in law firms	89	65.9
# employed in business & industry	21	15.6
# employed in government	18	13.3
# employed in public interest	0	0.0
# employed as judicial clerks	5	3.7
# employed in academia	2	1.5
Geographic Location		
# employed in state	113	83.7
# employed in foreign countries	0	0.0
# of states where employed	13	

J.D. Attrition (from Prior Year)

	Academic	Other	TOTALS	
	#	#	#	%
1st Year	7	5	12	9.8%
2nd Year	2	3	5	3.1%
3rd Year	0	1	1	0.6%
4th Year	0	0	0	0.0%

Bar Passage Rates

Jurisdiction	Kentucky		
Exam	Sum 97	Win 98	Total
# from school taking bar for the first time	124	20	144
School's pass rate for all first-time takers	68%	90%	71%
State's pass rate for all first-time takers	65%	86%	70%

LOYOLA MARYMOUNT UNIVERSITY-LOS ANGELES

919 South Albany Street
Los Angeles, CA 90015
(213)736-1000
http://www.lls.edu

ABA Approved Since 1935

The Basics

Type of School: Private   Term: Semester
Application deadline: 02/01
Application fee: $50
Financial Aid deadline: 03/02
Can first year start other than Fall? No
Student faculty ratio: 22.4 to 1
Does the University offer:
- housing restricted to law students? No
- graduate student housing for which law students are eligible? No

Faculty & Administrators

	Total		Men		Women		Minorities	
	Fall	Spr	Fall	Spr	Fall	Spr	Fall	Spr
Full-time	45	47	29	31	16	16	11	11
Other Full-Time	6	6	2	2	4	4	0	0
Deans, librarians, & others who teach > 1/2	0	0	0	0	0	0	0	0
Part-time	48	37	29	29	19	8	4	4
Total	99	90	60	62	39	28	15	15
Deans, librarians, & others who teach < 1/2	7	7	4	4	3	3	1	1

Curriculum

	Full time	Part time
Typical first-year section size	90	100
Is there typically a "small section" of the first year class, other than Legal Writing, taught by full-time faculty?	No	No
If yes, typical size offered last year	N/A	N/A
# of classroom course titles beyond 1st year curriculum	120	83
# of upper division courses, excluding seminars, with an enrollment:		
Under 25	41	40
25 - 49	33	23
50 - 74	7	4
75 - 99	7	3
100 +	9	3
# of seminars	15	13
# of seminar positions available	567	
# of seminar positions filled	240	203
# of positions available in simulation courses	903	
# of simulation positions filled	560	217
# of positions available in faculty supervised clinical courses	86	
# of fac. sup. clin. positions filled	50	36
# involved in field placements	236	20
# involved in law journals	412	39
# in moot court or trial competitions	165	16
# of credit hrs required to graduate	87	

J.D. Enrollment & Ethnicity

	Men		Women		Fl-Time		Pt-Time		1st Yr		2nd Yr		3rd Yr		4th Yr		Total		JD Degrees Awarded
	#	%	#	%	#	%	#	%	#	%	#	%	#	%	#	%	#	%	
African-American	22	3.1	38	6.1	42	4.3	18	4.9	17	3.8	17	4.4	20	4.9	6	6.8	60	4.5	19
American Indian	14	2.0	7	1.1	17	1.8	4	1.1	6	1.4	7	1.8	6	1.5	2	2.3	21	1.6	3
Asian American	134	19.0	150	23.9	226	23.3	58	15.9	105	23.7	80	20.5	86	20.9	13	14.8	284	21.3	89
Mexican American	54	7.7	49	7.8	72	7.4	31	8.5	27	6.1	39	10.0	30	7.3	7	8.0	103	7.7	35
Puerto Rican	0	0.0	0	0.0	0	0.0	0	0.0	0	0.0	0	0.0	0	0.0	0	0.0	0	0.0	0
Hispanic American	24	3.4	34	5.4	42	4.3	16	4.4	18	4.1	17	4.4	19	4.6	4	4.5	58	4.4	14
Total Minorities	248	35.2	278	44.3	399	41.2	127	34.9	173	39.1	160	41.0	161	39.2	32	36.4	526	39.5	160
Foreign Nationals	7	1.0	5	0.8	11	1.1	1	0.3	9	2.0	2	0.5	1	0.2	0	0.0	12	0.9	1
Caucasian	450	63.8	344	54.9	558	57.6	236	64.8	261	58.9	228	58.5	249	60.6	56	63.6	794	59.6	225
Total	705	52.9	627	47.1	968	72.7	364	27.3	443	33.3	390	29.3	411	30.9	88	6.6	1332		386

LOYOLA MARYMOUNT UNIVERSITY-LOS ANGELES

GPA & LSAT Scores

	Full Time	Part Time	Total
# of apps	2,548	422	2,970
# admits	1,021	180	1,201
# of matrics	358	113	471
75% GPA	3.48	3.46	
25% GPA	3.03	3.00	
75% LSAT	160	158	
25% LSAT	154	151	

Tuition & Fees

	Resident	Non-resident
Full-Time	$21,748	$21,748
Part-Time	$14,608	$14,608

Living Expenses

Estimated living expenses for Singles		
Living on campus	Living off campus	Living at home
N/A	$13,445	$7,960

Grants/Scholarships

	Full-time		Part-time		Total	
	#	%	#	%	#	%
Total # of Students	968		364		1332	
Total # receiving grants	132	13.6	39	10.7	171	12.8
Less than 1/2 tuition	14	1.4	6	1.6	20	1.5
Half to full tuition	79	8.2	27	7.4	106	8.0
Full tuition	15	1.5	2	0.5	17	1.3
More than full tuition	24	2.5	4	1.1	28	2.1
Median Grant Amount	$19,000		$11,700			

Informational & Library Resources

# of volumes & volume equivalents	457,733	# of professional staff	12
# of titles	209,819	Hours per week with professional staff	84
# of active serial subscriptions	6,836	Hours per week without professional staff	24
Study seating capacity inside the library	683	# of student computer work stations for entire law school	116
Square feet of law library	46,802	# of additional networked connections	30
Square feet of law school (excl. Library)	100,346	Require Laptop Computer?	N

Employment

	Total	%
Employment status known	407	100.0
Employment status unknown	0	0.0
Employed	345	84.8
Pursuing graduate degrees	3	0.7
Unemployed seeking employment	44	10.8
Unemployed not seeking employment	15	3.7
Type of Employment		
# employed in law firms	211	61.2
# employed in business & industry	80	23.2
# employed in government	23	6.7
# employed in public interest	10	2.9
# employed as judicial clerks	9	2.6
# employed in academia	12	3.5
Geographic Location		
# employed in state	305	88.4
# employed in foreign countries	0	0.0
# of states where employed	9	

J.D. Attrition (from Prior Year)

	Academic	Other	TOTALS	
	#	#	#	%
1st Year	13	21	34	8.2%
2nd Year	3	13	16	3.9%
3rd Year	3	5	8	2.0%
4th Year	2	1	3	3.0%

Bar Passage Rates

Jurisdiction	California		
Exam	Sum 97	Win 98	Total
# from school taking bar for the first time	359	23	382
School's pass rate for all first-time takers	84%	43%	82%
State's pass rate for all first-time takers	75%	57%	71%

LOYOLA UNIVERSITY-CHICAGO

One East Pearson Street
Chicago, IL 60611
(312)915-7120
gopher://gopher.luc.edu/11/loyola/colleg

ABA Approved Since 1925

The Basics

Type of School: Private Term: Semester
Application deadline: 04/01
Application fee: $45
Financial Aid deadline: 03/01
Can first year start other than Fall? Yes
Student faculty ratio: 18.2 to 1
Does the University offer:
- housing restricted to law students? No
- graduate student housing for which law students are eligible? Yes

Faculty & Administrators

	Total		Men		Women		Minorities	
	Fall	Spr	Fall	Spr	Fall	Spr	Fall	Spr
Full-time	30	31	24	25	6	6	3	3
Other Full-Time	1	1	0	0	1	1	0	0
Deans, librarians, & others who teach > 1/2	0	0	0	0	0	0	0	0
Part-time	78	66	43	41	35	25	7	5
Total	109	98	67	66	42	32	10	8
Deans, librarians, & others who teach < 1/2	5	5	3	3	2	2	0	0

Curriculum

	Full time	Part time
Typical first-year section size	55	65
Is there typically a "small section" of the first year class, other than Legal Writing, taught by full-time faculty?	No	No
If yes, typical size offered last year	N/A	N/A
# of classroom course titles beyond 1st year curriculum	82	19
# of upper division courses, excluding seminars, with an enrollment:		
Under 25	25	13
25 - 49	22	10
50 - 74	7	2
75 - 99	3	0
100 +	2	0
# of seminars	19	2
# of seminar positions available	495	
# of seminar positions filled	377	101
# of positions available in simulation courses	740	
# of simulation positions filled	480	170
# of positions available in faculty supervised clinical courses	101	
# of fac. sup. clin. positions filled	82	8
# involved in field placements	78	8
# involved in law journals	116	10
# in moot court or trial competitions	52	9
# of credit hrs required to graduate	86	

J.D. Enrollment & Ethnicity

	Men		Women		Fl-Time		Pt-Time		1st Yr		2nd Yr		3rd Yr		4th Yr		Total		JD Degrees Awarded
	#	%	#	%	#	%	#	%	#	%	#	%	#	%	#	%	#	%	
African-American	20	6.4	26	6.3	25	4.8	21	10.1	11	4.7	17	7.4	16	7.1	2	5.4	46	6.4	11
American Indian	1	0.3	5	1.2	6	1.2	0	0.0	2	0.9	1	0.4	3	1.3	0	0.0	6	0.8	0
Asian American	27	8.6	32	7.8	46	8.9	13	6.3	14	6.0	23	10.0	22	9.7	0	0.0	59	8.1	15
Mexican American	5	1.6	1	0.2	6	1.2	0	0.0	2	0.9	3	1.3	1	0.4	0	0.0	6	0.8	1
Puerto Rican	3	1.0	3	0.7	5	1.0	1	0.5	0	0.0	4	1.7	2	0.9	0	0.0	6	0.8	2
Hispanic American	5	1.6	13	3.2	17	3.3	1	0.5	5	2.2	7	3.1	6	2.7	0	0.0	18	2.5	2
Total Minorities	61	19.4	80	19.5	105	20.3	36	17.4	34	14.7	55	24.0	50	22.1	2	5.4	141	19.5	31
Foreign Nationals	10	3.2	4	1.0	11	2.1	3	1.4	4	1.7	7	3.1	3	1.3	0	0.0	14	1.9	0
Caucasian	243	77.4	326	79.5	401	77.6	168	81.2	194	83.6	167	72.9	173	76.5	35	94.6	569	78.6	185
Total	314	43.4	410	56.6	517	71.4	207	28.6	232	32.0	229	31.6	226	31.2	37	5.1	724		216

GPA & LSAT Scores

	Full Time	Part Time	Total
# of apps	1,987	259	2,246
# admits	813	177	990
# of matrics	169	66	235
75% GPA	3.56	3.34	
25% GPA	3.06	2.78	
75% LSAT	160	156	
25% LSAT	155	150	

Tuition & Fees

	Resident	Non-resident
Full-Time	$22,110	$22,110
Part-Time	$16,500	$16,500

Living Expenses

Estimated living expenses for Singles		
Living on campus	Living off campus	Living at home
N/A	$14,410	$14,410

Grants/Scholarships

	Full-time		Part-time		Total	
	#	%	#	%	#	%
Total # of Students	517		207		724	
Total # receiving grants	322	62.3	72	34.8	394	54.4
Less than 1/2 tuition	302	58.4	68	32.9	370	51.1
Half to full tuition	17	3.3	4	1.9	21	2.9
Full tuition	3	0.6	0	0.0	3	0.4
More than full tuition	0	0.0	0	0.0	0	0.0
Median Grant Amount	$2,675		$1,975			

Informational & Library Resources

# of volumes & volume equivalents	346,830	# of professional staff	10
# of titles	53,655	Hours per week with professional staff	90
# of active serial subscriptions	3,499	Hours per week without professional staff	9
Study seating capacity inside the library	380	# of student computer work stations for entire law school	81
Square feet of law library	43,900	# of additional networked connections	0
Square feet of law school (excl. Library)	39,202	Require Laptop Computer?	N

Employment

	Total	%
Employment status known	254	98.8
Employment status unknown	3	1.2
Employed	233	91.7
Pursuing graduate degrees	8	3.1
Unemployed seeking employment	5	2.0
Unemployed not seeking employment	8	3.1
Type of Employment		
# employed in law firms	135	57.9
# employed in business & industry	45	19.3
# employed in government	30	12.9
# employed in public interest	11	4.7
# employed as judicial clerks	9	3.9
# employed in academia	3	1.3
Geographic Location		
# employed in state	192	82.4
# employed in foreign countries	1	0.4
# of states where employed	21	

J.D. Attrition (from Prior Year)

	Academic	Other	TOTALS	
	#	#	#	%
1st Year	0	0	0	0.0%
2nd Year	2	12	14	6.1%
3rd Year	2	3	5	2.4%
4th Year	0	1	1	2.5%

Bar Passage Rates

Jurisdiction	Illinois		
Exam	Sum 97	Win 98	Total
# from school taking bar for the first time	185	31	216
School's pass rate for all first-time takers	82%	68%	80%
State's pass rate for all first-time takers	87%	80%	85%

LOYOLA UNIVERSITY-NEW ORLEANS

7214 St. Charles Avenue
New Orleans, LA 70118
(504)861-5550
www.loyno.edu/SchoolofLaw

ABA Approved Since 1931

The Basics

Type of School: Private　　Term: Semester

Application deadline: 08/21

Application fee: $20

Financial Aid deadline: Rolling

Can first year start other than Fall? No

Student faculty ratio: 17.2 to 1

Does the University offer:
- housing restricted to law students? No
- graduate student housing for which law students are eligible? No

Faculty & Administrators

	Total		Men		Women		Minorities	
	Fall	Spr	Fall	Spr	Fall	Spr	Fall	Spr
Full-time	29	29	19	19	10	10	8	8
Other Full-Time	1	1	0	0	1	1	0	0
Deans, librarians, & others who teach > 1/2	0	0	0	0	0	0	0	0
Part-time	18	27	15	22	3	4	0	0
Total	48	57	34	41	14	15	8	8
Deans, librarians, & others who teach < 1/2	4	4	4	4	0	0	0	0

Curriculum

	Full time	Part time
Typical first-year section size	87	44
Is there typically a "small section" of the first year class, other than Legal Writing, taught by full-time faculty?	Yes	No
If yes, typical size offered last year	40	N/A
# of classroom course titles beyond 1st year curriculum	60	36
# of upper division courses, excluding seminars, with an enrollment:		
Under 25	15	23
25 - 49	15	10
50 - 74	13	1
75 - 99	8	4
100 +	2	0
# of seminars	13	3
# of seminar positions available	325	
# of seminar positions filled	153	60
# of positions available in simulation courses	147	
# of simulation positions filled	70	49
# of positions available in faculty supervised clinical courses	113	
# of fac. sup. clin. positions filled	92	2
# involved in field placements	25	4
# involved in law journals	40	17
# in moot court or trial competitions	25	1
# of credit hrs required to graduate	90	

J.D. Enrollment & Ethnicity

	Men		Women		Fl-Time		Pt-Time		1st Yr		2nd Yr		3rd Yr		4th Yr		Total		JD Degrees Awarded
	#	%	#	%	#	%	#	%	#	%	#	%	#	%	#	%	#	%	
African-American	33	9.3	55	18.0	67	13.6	21	12.7	39	16.7	27	14.3	20	10.1	2	5.7	88	13.4	24
American Indian	2	0.6	4	1.3	6	1.2	0	0.0	2	0.9	4	2.1	0	0.0	0	0.0	6	0.9	2
Asian American	10	2.8	5	1.6	14	2.8	1	0.6	6	2.6	4	2.1	5	2.5	0	0.0	15	2.3	8
Mexican American	0	0.0	1	0.3	1	0.2	0	0.0	1	0.4	0	0.0	0	0.0	0	0.0	1	0.2	0
Puerto Rican	0	0.0	0	0.0	0	0.0	0	0.0	0	0.0	0	0.0	0	0.0	0	0.0	0	0.0	0
Hispanic American	21	5.9	25	8.2	37	7.5	9	5.4	12	5.2	16	8.5	16	8.1	2	5.7	46	7.0	21
Total Minorities	66	18.7	90	29.4	125	25.4	31	18.7	60	25.8	51	27.0	41	20.7	4	11.4	156	23.7	55
Foreign Nationals	2	0.6	1	0.3	3	0.6	0	0.0	0	0.0	2	1.1	1	0.5	0	0.0	3	0.5	0
Caucasian	285	80.7	215	70.3	365	74.0	135	81.3	173	74.2	136	72.0	160	80.8	31	88.6	500	75.9	172
Total	353	53.6	306	46.4	493	74.8	166	25.2	233	35.4	189	28.7	198	30.0	35	5.3	659		227

LOYOLA UNIVERSITY-NEW ORLEANS

GPA & LSAT Scores

	Full Time	Part Time	Total
# of apps	1,148	130	1,278
# admits	631	71	702
# of matrics	185	54	239
75% GPA	3.25	3.28	
25% GPA	2.67	2.62	
75% LSAT	153	157	
25% LSAT	148	148	

Tuition & Fees

	Resident	Non-resident
Full-Time	$17,530	$17,530
Part-Time	$12,642	$12,642

Living Expenses

Estimated living expenses for Singles		
Living on campus	Living off campus	Living at home
$11,200	$11,200	$4,400

Employment

	Total	%
Employment status known	183	90.1
Employment status unknown	20	9.9
Employed	156	85.2
Pursuing graduate degrees	10	5.5
Unemployed seeking employment	1	0.5
Unemployed not seeking employment	16	8.7
Type of Employment		
# employed in law firms	86	55.1
# employed in business & industry	12	7.7
# employed in government	27	17.3
# employed in public interest	2	1.3
# employed as judicial clerks	22	14.1
# employed in academia	2	1.3
Geographic Location		
# employed in state	122	78.2
# employed in foreign countries	0	0.0
# of states where employed	18	

Grants/Scholarships

	Full-time		Part-time		Total	
	#	%	#	%	#	%
Total # of Students	493		166		659	
Total # receiving grants	140	28.4	8	4.8	148	22.5
Less than 1/2 tuition	74	15.0	5	3.0	79	12.0
Half to full tuition	57	11.6	3	1.8	60	9.1
Full tuition	9	1.8	0	0.0	9	1.4
More than full tuition	0	0.0	0	0.0	0	0.0
Median Grant Amount	$7,320		$0			

Informational & Library Resources

# of volumes & volume equivalents	278,541	# of professional staff	8
# of titles	94,131	Hours per week with professional staff	77
# of active serial subscriptions	3,171	Hours per week without professional staff	27
Study seating capacity inside the library	525	# of student computer work stations for entire law school	34
Square feet of law library	52,168	# of additional networked connections	0
Square feet of law school (excl. Library)	47,539	Require Laptop Computer?	N

J.D. Attrition (from Prior Year)

	Academic	Other	TOTALS	
	#	#	#	%
1st Year	1	30	31	15%
2nd Year	2	13	15	7.7%
3rd Year	0	2	2	0.8%
4th Year	0	0	0	0.0%

Bar Passage Rates

Jurisdiction	Louisiana		
Exam	Sum 97	Win 98	Total
# from school taking bar for the first time	111	17	128
School's pass rate for all first-time takers	52%	59%	53%
State's pass rate for all first-time takers	62%	54%	61%

MAINE, UNIVERSITY OF

246 Deering Avenue
Portland, ME 04102
(207)780-4355
http://www.law.usm.maine.edu

ABA Approved Since 1962

The Basics

Type of School: Public   Term: Semester
Application deadline: 02/15
Application fee: $25
Financial Aid deadline: 02/01
Can first year start other than Fall? No
Student faculty ratio: 20.0 to 1
Does the University offer:
- housing restricted to law students? No
- graduate student housing for which law students are eligible? No

Faculty & Administrators

	Total		Men		Women		Minorities	
	Fall	Spr	Fall	Spr	Fall	Spr	Fall	Spr
Full-time	12	14	9	11	3	3	0	0
Other Full-Time	1	1	0	0	1	1	0	0
Deans, librarians, & others who teach > 1/2	2	2	0	0	2	2	0	0
Part-time	8	8	6	6	2	2	0	0
Total	23	25	15	17	8	8	0	0
Deans, librarians, & others who teach < 1/2	1	1	1	1	0	0	0	0

Curriculum

	Full time	Part time
Typical first-year section size	93	0
Is there typically a "small section" of the first year class, other than Legal Writing, taught by full-time faculty?	No	No
If yes, typical size offered last year	N/A	N/A
# of classroom course titles beyond 1st year curriculum	46	0
# of upper division courses, excluding seminars, with an enrollment:		
Under 25	27	0
25 - 49	17	0
50 - 74	4	0
75 - 99	3	0
100 +	0	0
# of seminars	6	0
# of seminar positions available	74	
# of seminar positions filled	59	0
# of positions available in simulation courses	120	
# of simulation positions filled	101	0
# of positions available in faculty supervised clinical courses	48	
# of fac. sup. clin. positions filled	47	0
# involved in field placements	2	0
# involved in law journals	48	0
# in moot court or trial competitions	16	0
# of credit hrs required to graduate	89	

J.D. Enrollment & Ethnicity

	Men		Women		Fl-Time		Pt-Time		1st Yr		2nd Yr		3rd Yr		4th Yr		Total		JD Degrees Awarded
	#	%	#	%	#	%	#	%	#	%	#	%	#	%	#	%	#	%	
African-American	3	1.8	3	2.5	6	2.1	0	0.0	2	2.0	2	2.3	2	2.0	0	0.0	6	2.1	1
American Indian	1	0.6	2	1.7	3	1.0	0	0.0	1	1.0	2	2.3	0	0.0	0	0.0	3	1.0	2
Asian American	1	0.6	1	0.8	2	0.7	0	0.0	0	0.0	2	2.3	0	0.0	0	0.0	2	0.7	1
Mexican American	0	0.0	0	0.0	0	0.0	0	0.0	0	0.0	0	0.0	0	0.0	0	0.0	0	0.0	0
Puerto Rican	0	0.0	0	0.0	0	0.0	0	0.0	0	0.0	0	0.0	0	0.0	0	0.0	0	0.0	0
Hispanic American	3	1.8	1	0.8	4	1.4	0	0.0	3	3.0	0	0.0	1	1.0	0	0.0	4	1.4	1
Total Minorities	8	4.8	7	5.8	15	5.2	0	0.0	6	5.9	6	7.0	3	3.0	0	0.0	15	5.2	5
Foreign Nationals	6	3.6	1	0.8	7	2.4	0	0.0	2	2.0	2	2.3	3	3.0	0	0.0	7	2.4	2
Caucasian	153	91.6	113	93.4	264	92.3	2	100.0	93	92.1	78	90.7	95	94.1	0	0.0	266	92.4	85
Total	167	58.0	121	42.0	286	99.3	2	0.7	101	35.1	86	29.9	101	35.1	0	0.0	288		92

GPA & LSAT Scores

	Full Time	Part Time	Total
# of apps	506	0	506
# admits	282	0	282
# of matrics	104	0	104
75% GPA	3.51	0.00	
25% GPA	2.98	0.00	
75% LSAT	158	0	
25% LSAT	150	0	

Tuition & Fees

	Resident	Non-resident
Full-Time	$9,858	$17,508
Part-Time	$6,634	$11,734

Living Expenses

Estimated living expenses for Singles		
Living on campus	Living off campus	Living at home
$8,012	$8,012	$4,875

Grants/Scholarships

	Full-time		Part-time		Total	
	#	%	#	%	#	%
Total # of Students	286		2		288	
Total # receiving grants	102	35.7	0	0.0	102	35.4
Less than 1/2 tuition	87	30.4	0	0.0	87	30.2
Half to full tuition	4	1.4	0	0.0	4	1.4
Full tuition	11	3.8	0	0.0	11	3.8
More than full tuition	0	0.0	0	0.0	0	0.0
Median Grant Amount	$1,500		$0			

Informational & Library Resources

# of volumes & volume equivalents	309,247	# of professional staff	7
# of titles	53,804	Hours per week with professional staff	61
# of active serial subscriptions	3,654	Hours per week without professional staff	36
Study seating capacity inside the library	172	# of student computer work stations for entire law school	18
Square feet of law library	32,800	# of additional networked connections	0
Square feet of law school (excl. Library)	30,115	Require Laptop Computer?	N

Employment

	Total	%
Employment status known	74	81.3
Employment status unknown	17	18.7
Employed	65	87.8
Pursuing graduate degrees	3	4.1
Unemployed seeking employment	4	5.4
Unemployed not seeking employment	2	2.7
Type of Employment		
# employed in law firms	25	38.5
# employed in business & industry	12	18.5
# employed in government	13	20.0
# employed in public interest	1	1.5
# employed as judicial clerks	12	18.5
# employed in academia	1	1.5
Geographic Location		
# employed in state	42	64.6
# employed in foreign countries	0	0.0
# of states where employed	26	

J.D. Attrition (from Prior Year)

	Academic	Other	TOTALS	
	#	#	#	%
1st Year	0	3	3	3.2%
2nd Year	1	9	10	9.9%
3rd Year	0	2	2	2.0%
4th Year	0	0	0	0.0%

Bar Passage Rates

Jurisdiction	Maine		
Exam	Sum 97	Win 98	Total
# from school taking bar for the first time	57	0	57
School's pass rate for all first-time takers	70%		70%
State's pass rate for all first-time takers	63%	83%	69%

MARQUETTE UNIVERSITY

Sensenbrenner Hall
P.O. Box 1881
Milwaukee, WI 53201-1881
(414)288-7090
http://www.mu.edu/dept/law

ABA Approved Since 1925

The Basics

Type of School: Private — Term: Semester

Application deadline: 04/01

Application fee: $35

Financial Aid deadline: 03/01

Can first year start other than Fall? No

Student faculty ratio: 18.3 to 1

Does the University offer:
- housing restricted to law students? No
- graduate student housing for which law students are eligible? Yes

Faculty & Administrators

	Total		Men		Women		Minorities	
	Fall	Spr	Fall	Spr	Fall	Spr	Fall	Spr
Full-time	23	23	15	15	8	8	2	3
Other Full-Time	0	0	0	0	0	0	0	0
Deans, librarians, & others who teach > 1/2	6	6	4	4	2	2	0	0
Part-time	25	0	16	0	9	0	2	0
Total	54	29	35	19	19	10	4	3
Deans, librarians, & others who teach < 1/2	1	1	1	1	0	0	0	0

Curriculum

	Full time	Part time
Typical first-year section size	75	50
Is there typically a "small section" of the first year class, other than Legal Writing, taught by full-time faculty?	Yes	Yes
If yes, typical size offered last year	37	32
# of classroom course titles beyond 1st year curriculum	101	0
# of upper division courses, excluding seminars, with an enrollment:		
Under 25	52	0
25 - 49	30	0
50 - 74	6	0
75 - 99	7	0
100 +	0	0
# of seminars	22	0
# of seminar positions available	330	
# of seminar positions filled	259	0
# of positions available in simulation courses	348	
# of simulation positions filled	278	0
# of positions available in faculty supervised clinical courses	107	
# of fac. sup. clin. positions filled	90	0
# involved in field placements	22	0
# involved in law journals	87	0
# in moot court or trial competitions	23	0
# of credit hrs required to graduate	90	

J.D. Enrollment & Ethnicity

	Men		Women		Fl-Time		Pt-Time		1st Yr		2nd Yr		3rd Yr		4th Yr		Total		JD Degrees Awarded
	#	%	#	%	#	%	#	%	#	%	#	%	#	%	#	%	#	%	
African-American	7	2.3	6	2.6	10	2.3	3	3.0	5	2.4	6	3.5	2	1.4	0	0.0	13	2.4	3
American Indian	0	0.0	0	0.0	0	0.0	0	0.0	0	0.0	0	0.0	0	0.0	0	0.0	0	0.0	2
Asian American	5	1.6	5	2.1	10	2.3	0	0.0	4	1.9	4	2.4	2	1.4	0	0.0	10	1.9	7
Mexican American	0	0.0	0	0.0	0	0.0	0	0.0	0	0.0	0	0.0	0	0.0	0	0.0	0	0.0	0
Puerto Rican	0	0.0	0	0.0	0	0.0	0	0.0	0	0.0	0	0.0	0	0.0	0	0.0	0	0.0	0
Hispanic American	5	1.6	12	5.1	15	3.4	2	2.0	3	1.4	7	4.1	7	4.8	0	0.0	17	3.2	9
Total Minorities	17	5.6	23	9.8	35	8.0	5	5.0	12	5.7	17	10.0	11	7.5	0	0.0	40	7.4	21
Foreign Nationals	0	0.0	0	0.0	0	0.0	0	0.0	0	0.0	0	0.0	0	0.0	0	0.0	0	0.0	0
Caucasian	288	94.4	211	90.2	403	92.0	96	95.0	199	93.9	154	90.6	136	92.5	10	100.0	499	92.6	121
Total	305	56.6	234	43.4	438	81.3	101	18.7	212	39.3	170	31.5	147	27.3	10	1.9	539		142

GPA & LSAT Scores

	Full Time	Part Time	Total
# of apps	709	128	837
# admits	476	72	548
# of matrics	150	57	207
75% GPA	3.35	3.47	
25% GPA	2.82	2.79	
75% LSAT	157	159	
25% LSAT	152	151	

Tuition & Fees

	Resident	Non-resident
Full-Time	$18,370	$18,370
Part-Time	$15,200	$15,200

Living Expenses

Estimated living expenses for Singles		
Living on campus	Living off campus	Living at home
$12,185	$12,185	$12,185

Employment

	Total	%
Employment status known	145	94.8
Employment status unknown	8	5.2
Employed	135	93.1
Pursuing graduate degrees	3	2.1
Unemployed seeking employment	3	2.1
Unemployed not seeking employment	4	2.8
Type of Employment		
# employed in law firms	85	63.0
# employed in business & industry	20	14.8
# employed in government	14	10.4
# employed in public interest	2	1.5
# employed as judicial clerks	4	3.0
# employed in academia	10	7.4
Geographic Location		
# employed in state	98	72.6
# employed in foreign countries	2	1.5
# of states where employed	12	

Grants/Scholarships

	Full-time		Part-time		Total	
	#	%	#	%	#	%
Total # of Students	438		101		539	
Total # receiving grants	107	24.4	18	17.8	125	23.2
Less than 1/2 tuition	88	20.1	18	17.8	106	19.7
Half to full tuition	13	3.0	0	0.0	13	2.4
Full tuition	6	1.4	0	0.0	6	1.1
More than full tuition	0	0.0	0	0.0	0	0.0
Median Grant Amount	$5,476		$3,139			

Informational & Library Resources

# of volumes & volume equivalents	262,568	# of professional staff	8
# of titles	127,095	Hours per week with professional staff	77
# of active serial subscriptions	2,840	Hours per week without professional staff	29
Study seating capacity inside the library	368	# of student computer work stations for entire law school	28
Square feet of law library	32,911	# of additional networked connections	0
Square feet of law school (excl. Library)	30,198	Require Laptop Computer?	N

J.D. Attrition (from Prior Year)

	Academic	Other	TOTALS	
	#	#	#	%
1st Year	0	2	2	1.1%
2nd Year	1	5	6	3.8%
3rd Year	0	0	0	0.0%
4th Year	0	0	0	0.0%

Bar Passage Rates

Jurisdiction	Wisconsin	Illinois		
Exam		Sum 97	Win 98	Total
# from school taking bar for the first time	All graduates were admitted to the Wisconsin bar via the diploma privilege.	5	0	5
School's pass rate for all first-time takers		100%		100%
State's pass rate for all first-time takers		87%	80%	85%

MARYLAND, UNIVERSITY OF

500 West Baltimore Street
Baltimore, MD 21201-1786
(410)706-3492
http://www.law.umaryland.edu

ABA Approved Since 1930

The Basics

Type of School: Public | Term: Semester

Application deadline: 03/01

Application fee: $50

Financial Aid deadline: 03/15

Can first year start other than Fall? No

Student faculty ratio: 15.0 to 1

Does the University offer:
- housing restricted to law students? No
- graduate student housing for which law students are eligible? Yes

Faculty & Administrators

	Total		Men		Women		Minorities	
	Fall	Spr	Fall	Spr	Fall	Spr	Fall	Spr
Full-time	42	43	25	25	17	18	7	8
Other Full-Time	1	1	1	1	0	0	0	0
Deans, librarians, & others who teach > 1/2	1	1	1	1	0	0	0	0
Part-time	38	34	28	26	9	8	2	3
Total	82	79	55	53	26	26	9	11
Deans, librarians, & others who teach < 1/2	3	3	1	1	2	2	0	0

Curriculum

	Full time	Part time
Typical first-year section size	72	62
Is there typically a "small section" of the first year class, other than Legal Writing, taught by full-time faculty?	Yes	Yes
If yes, typical size offered last year	26	31
# of classroom course titles beyond 1st year curriculum	96	45
# of upper division courses, excluding seminars, with an enrollment:		
Under 25	37	25
25 - 49	24	11
50 - 74	8	11
75 - 99	4	2
100 +	3	0
# of seminars	28	11
# of seminar positions available	559	
# of seminar positions filled	334	138
# of positions available in simulation courses	503	
# of simulation positions filled	222	219
# of positions available in faculty supervised clinical courses	297	
# of fac. sup. clin. positions filled	266	29
# involved in field placements	93	25
# involved in law journals	164	18
# in moot court or trial competitions	212	23
# of credit hrs required to graduate	85	

J.D. Enrollment & Ethnicity

	Men		Women		Fl-Time		Pt-Time		1st Yr		2nd Yr		3rd Yr		4th Yr		Total		JD Degrees Awarded
	#	%	#	%	#	%	#	%	#	%	#	%	#	%	#	%	#	%	
African-American	43	10.8	80	17.8	73	12.6	50	18.8	52	19.8	30	11.6	25	9.8	16	21.9	123	14.5	47
American Indian	2	0.5	0	0.0	1	0.2	1	0.4	0	0.0	2	0.8	0	0.0	0	0.0	2	0.2	1
Asian American	30	7.6	52	11.6	64	11.0	18	6.8	23	8.8	27	10.5	27	10.6	5	6.8	82	9.7	24
Mexican American	0	0.0	0	0.0	0	0.0	0	0.0	0	0.0	0	0.0	0	0.0	0	0.0	0	0.0	0
Puerto Rican	0	0.0	0	0.0	0	0.0	0	0.0	0	0.0	0	0.0	0	0.0	0	0.0	0	0.0	0
Hispanic American	12	3.0	15	3.3	19	3.3	8	3.0	7	2.7	10	3.9	7	2.8	3	4.1	27	3.2	5
Total Minorities	87	21.9	147	32.7	157	27.0	77	28.9	82	31.3	69	26.7	59	23.2	24	32.9	234	27.6	77
Foreign Nationals	3	0.8	6	1.3	8	1.4	1	0.4	2	0.8	1	0.4	5	2.0	1	1.4	9	1.1	0
Caucasian	307	77.3	297	66.0	416	71.6	188	70.7	178	67.9	188	72.9	190	74.8	48	65.8	604	71.3	187
Total	397	46.9	450	53.1	581	68.6	266	31.4	262	30.9	258	30.5	254	30.0	73	8.6	847		264

GPA & LSAT Scores

	Full Time	Part Time	Total
# of apps	2,057	382	2,439
# admits	873	120	993
# of matrics	196	61	257
75% GPA	3.51	3.39	
25% GPA	3.06	2.89	
75% LSAT	158	159	
25% LSAT	152	152	

Tuition & Fees

	Resident	Non-resident
Full-Time	$9,954	$17,847
Part-Time	$7,393	$13,311

Living Expenses

Estimated living expenses for Singles		
Living on campus	Living off campus	Living at home
$9,741	$12,630	$6,159

Grants/Scholarships

	Full-time		Part-time		Total	
	#	%	#	%	#	%
Total # of Students	581		266		847	
Total # receiving grants	343	59.0	60	22.6	403	47.6
Less than 1/2 tuition	342	58.9	60	22.6	402	47.5
Half to full tuition	0	0.0	0	0.0	0	0.0
Full tuition	1	0.2	0	0.0	1	0.1
More than full tuition	0	0.0	0	0.0	0	0.0
Median Grant Amount	$3,416		$2,703			

Informational & Library Resources

# of volumes & volume equivalents	375,296	# of professional staff	7
# of titles	89,950	Hours per week with professional staff	55
# of active serial subscriptions	4,123	Hours per week without professional staff	43
Study seating capacity inside the library	372	# of student computer work stations for entire law school	62
Square feet of law library	45,921	# of additional networked connections	0
Square feet of law school (excl. Library)	45,695	Require Laptop Computer?	N

Employment

	Total	%
Employment status known	236	98.7
Employment status unknown	3	1.3
Employed	213	90.3
Pursuing graduate degrees	6	2.5
Unemployed seeking employment	14	5.9
Unemployed not seeking employment	3	1.3
Type of Employment		
# employed in law firms	80	37.6
# employed in business & industry	41	19.2
# employed in government	46	21.6
# employed in public interest	4	1.9
# employed as judicial clerks	37	17.4
# employed in academia	4	1.9
Geographic Location		
# employed in state	143	67.1
# employed in foreign countries	1	0.5
# of states where employed	15	

J.D. Attrition (from Prior Year)

	Academic	Other	TOTALS	
	#	#	#	%
1st Year	0	22	22	8.0%
2nd Year	0	5	5	1.9%
3rd Year	0	4	4	1.5%
4th Year	0	4	4	5.6%

Bar Passage Rates

Jurisdiction	Maryland		
Exam	Sum 97	Win 98	Total
# from school taking bar for the first time	172	35	207
School's pass rate for all first-time takers	75%	89%	77%
State's pass rate for all first-time takers	69%	83%	72%

MCGEORGE SCHOOL OF LAW

University of the Pacific
5200 Fifth Avenue
Sacramento, CA 95817
(916)739-7105
http://www.mcgeorge.edu

ABA Approved Since 1969

The Basics

Type of School: Private Term: Semester
Application deadline: 05/15
Application fee: $40
Financial Aid deadline: Rolling
Can first year start other than Fall? No
Student faculty ratio: 22.2 to 1
Does the University offer:
- housing restricted to law students? Yes
- graduate student housing for which law students are eligible? Yes

Faculty & Administrators

	Total		Men		Women		Minorities	
	Fall	Spr	Fall	Spr	Fall	Spr	Fall	Spr
Full-time	36	34	28	26	8	8	4	4
Other Full-Time	6	6	2	2	4	4	0	0
Deans, librarians, & others who teach > 1/2	4	4	2	2	2	2	0	0
Part-time	30	46	23	37	6	8	2	5
Total	76	90	55	67	20	22	6	9
Deans, librarians, & others who teach < 1/2	5	5	2	2	3	3	0	0

Curriculum

	Full time	Part time
Typical first-year section size	90	100
Is there typically a "small section" of the first year class, other than Legal Writing, taught by full-time faculty?	No	No
If yes, typical size offered last year	N/A	N/A
# of classroom course titles beyond 1st year curriculum	67	50
# of upper division courses, excluding seminars, with an enrollment:		
Under 25	26	19
25 - 49	23	24
50 - 74	14	7
75 - 99	7	7
100 +	10	4
# of seminars	14	5
# of seminar positions available	563	
# of seminar positions filled	334	137
# of positions available in simulation courses	807	
# of simulation positions filled	589	210
# of positions available in faculty supervised clinical courses	167	
# of fac. sup. clin. positions filled	85	10
# involved in field placements	138	20
# involved in law journals	60	20
# in moot court or trial competitions	240	80
# of credit hrs required to graduate	88	

J.D. Enrollment & Ethnicity

	Men		Women		Fl-Time		Pt-Time		1st Yr		2nd Yr		3rd Yr		4th Yr		Total		JD Degrees Awarded
	#	%	#	%	#	%	#	%	#	%	#	%	#	%	#	%	#	%	
African-American	19	3.3	15	2.8	12	1.6	22	6.3	22	5.9	3	0.9	6	1.8	3	4.7	34	3.1	7
American Indian	14	2.5	6	1.1	12	1.6	8	2.3	7	1.9	4	1.2	6	1.8	3	4.7	20	1.8	8
Asian American	61	10.7	71	13.5	111	14.9	21	6.0	48	13.0	41	12.8	38	11.2	5	7.8	132	12.1	41
Mexican American	28	4.9	22	4.2	34	4.6	16	4.6	19	5.1	14	4.4	12	3.5	5	7.8	50	4.6	14
Puerto Rican	2	0.4	2	0.4	3	0.4	1	0.3	2	0.5	1	0.3	1	0.3	0	0.0	4	0.4	0
Hispanic American	15	2.6	14	2.7	18	2.4	11	3.1	13	3.5	5	1.6	8	2.4	3	4.7	29	2.6	12
Total Minorities	139	24.5	130	24.7	190	25.5	79	22.6	111	30.0	68	21.2	71	20.9	19	29.7	269	24.6	82
Foreign Nationals	0	0.0	0	0.0	0	0.0	0	0.0	0	0.0	0	0.0	0	0.0	0	0.0	0	0.0	0
Caucasian	429	75.5	397	75.3	555	74.5	271	77.4	259	70.0	253	78.8	269	79.1	45	70.3	826	75.4	263
Total	568	51.9	527	48.1	745	68.0	350	32.0	370	33.8	321	29.3	340	31.1	64	5.8	1095		345

GPA & LSAT Scores

	Full Time	Part Time	Total
# of apps	1,551	205	1,756
# admits	1,062	142	1,204
# of matrics	274	103	377
75% GPA	3.33	3.36	
25% GPA	2.75	2.62	
75% LSAT	155	155	
25% LSAT	148	149	

Tuition & Fees

	Resident	Non-resident
Full-Time	$20,762	$20,762
Part-Time	$13,324	$13,324

Living Expenses

Estimated living expenses for Singles		
Living on campus	Living off campus	Living at home
$13,910	$13,910	$6,317

Employment

	Total	%
Employment status known	336	94.6
Employment status unknown	19	5.4
Employed	272	81.0
Pursuing graduate degrees	13	3.9
Unemployed seeking employment	49	14.6
Unemployed not seeking employment	2	0.6
Type of Employment		
# employed in law firms	149	54.8
# employed in business & industry	39	14.3
# employed in government	62	22.8
# employed in public interest	6	2.2
# employed as judicial clerks	11	4.0
# employed in academia	5	1.8
Geographic Location		
# employed in state	237	87.1
# employed in foreign countries	3	1.1
# of states where employed	15	

Grants/Scholarships

	Full-time		Part-time		Total	
	#	%	#	%	#	%
Total # of Students	745		350		1095	
Total # receiving grants	387	51.9	123	35.1	510	46.6
Less than 1/2 tuition	319	42.8	97	27.7	416	38.0
Half to full tuition	59	7.9	22	6.3	81	7.4
Full tuition	9	1.2	4	1.1	13	1.2
More than full tuition	0	0.0	0	0.0	0	0.0
Median Grant Amount	$1,250		$1,000			

Informational & Library Resources

# of volumes & volume equivalents	436,384	# of professional staff	7
# of titles	95,950	Hours per week with professional staff	86
# of active serial subscriptions	4,926	Hours per week without professional staff	24
Study seating capacity inside the library	615	# of student computer work stations for entire law school	97
Square feet of law library	48,161	# of additional networked connections	0
Square feet of law school (excl. Library)	143,377	Require Laptop Computer?	N

J.D. Attrition (from Prior Year)

	Academic	Other	TOTALS	
	#	#	#	%
1st Year	35	23	58	15%
2nd Year	8	18	26	7.4%
3rd Year	1	10	11	3.2%
4th Year	0	2	2	2.9%

Bar Passage Rates

Jurisdiction	California		
Exam	Sum 97	Win 98	Total
# from school taking bar for the first time	279	30	309
School's pass rate for all first-time takers	76%	47%	73%
State's pass rate for all first-time takers	75%	57%	71%

MEMPHIS, UNIVERSITY OF

Cecil C. Humphreys School of Law
Campus Box 526513
Memphis, TN 39152-6513
(901)678-2421
http://www.people.memphis.edu/~law

ABA Approved Since 1965

The Basics

Type of School: Public — Term: Semester

Application deadline: 02/15

Application fee: $15

Financial Aid deadline: 04/01

Can first year start other than Fall? No

Student faculty ratio: 19.5 to 1

Does the University offer:
- housing restricted to law students? No
- graduate student housing for which law students are eligible? Yes

Faculty & Administrators

	Total		Men		Women		Minorities	
	Fall	Spr	Fall	Spr	Fall	Spr	Fall	Spr
Full-time	20	19	14	13	6	6	1	1
Other Full-Time	3	3	1	1	2	2	0	0
Deans, librarians, & others who teach > 1/2	1	1	1	1	0	0	0	0
Part-time	25	31	13	21	12	10	2	2
Total	49	54	29	36	20	18	3	3
Deans, librarians, & others who teach < 1/2	1	1	1	1	0	0	0	0

Curriculum

	Full time	Part time
Typical first-year section size	85	0
Is there typically a "small section" of the first year class, other than Legal Writing, taught by full-time faculty?	No	No
If yes, typical size offered last year	N/A	N/A
# of classroom course titles beyond 1st year curriculum	63	0
# of upper division courses, excluding seminars, with an enrollment:		
Under 25	40	0
25 - 49	22	0
50 - 74	19	0
75 - 99	6	0
100 +	0	0
# of seminars	10	0
# of seminar positions available	128	
# of seminar positions filled	117	0
# of positions available in simulation courses	227	
# of simulation positions filled	177	0
# of positions available in faculty supervised clinical courses	70	
# of fac. sup. clin. positions filled	59	0
# involved in field placements	49	0
# involved in law journals	28	0
# in moot court or trial competitions	40	0
# of credit hrs required to graduate	90	

J.D. Enrollment & Ethnicity

	Men		Women		Fl-Time		Pt-Time		1st Yr		2nd Yr		3rd Yr		4th Yr		Total		JD Degrees Awarded
	#	%	#	%	#	%	#	%	#	%	#	%	#	%	#	%	#	%	
African-American	16	6.1	35	16.3	41	9.2	10	31.3	21	12.7	14	8.2	16	11.7	0	0.0	51	10.7	10
American Indian	1	0.4	0	0.0	1	0.2	0	0.0	0	0.0	0	0.0	1	0.7	0	0.0	1	0.2	0
Asian American	4	1.5	1	0.5	5	1.1	0	0.0	3	1.8	2	1.2	0	0.0	0	0.0	5	1.0	1
Mexican American	1	0.4	0	0.0	1	0.2	0	0.0	0	0.0	1	0.6	0	0.0	0	0.0	1	0.2	0
Puerto Rican	0	0.0	0	0.0	0	0.0	0	0.0	0	0.0	0	0.0	0	0.0	0	0.0	0	0.0	0
Hispanic American	1	0.4	3	1.4	2	0.4	2	6.3	2	1.2	2	1.2	0	0.0	0	0.0	4	0.8	1
Total Minorities	23	8.7	39	18.1	50	11.2	12	37.5	26	15.8	19	11.1	17	12.4	0	0.0	62	13.0	12
Foreign Nationals	0	0.0	0	0.0	0	0.0	0	0.0	0	0.0	0	0.0	0	0.0	0	0.0	0	0.0	0
Caucasian	240	91.3	176	81.9	396	88.8	20	62.5	139	84.2	152	88.9	120	87.6	5	100.0	416	87.0	144
Total	263	55.0	215	45.0	446	93.3	32	6.7	165	34.5	171	35.8	137	28.7	5	1.0	478		156

GPA & LSAT Scores

	Full Time	Part Time	Total
# of apps	790	13	803
# admits	305	13	318
# of matrics	152	13	165
75% GPA	3.63	3.46	
25% GPA	2.84	2.81	
75% LSAT	157	151	
25% LSAT	150	141	

Tuition & Fees

	Resident	Non-resident
Full-Time	$4,580	$11,376
Part-Time	$3,998	$9,898

Living Expenses

Estimated living expenses for Singles

Living on campus	Living off campus	Living at home
$11,272	$11,272	$7,402

Grants/Scholarships

	Full-time		Part-time		Total	
	#	%	#	%	#	%
Total # of Students	446		32		478	
Total # receiving grants	99	22.2	14	43.8	113	23.6
Less than 1/2 tuition	8	1.8	0	0.0	8	1.7
Half to full tuition	7	1.6	0	0.0	7	1.5
Full tuition	68	15.2	14	43.8	82	17.2
More than full tuition	16	3.6	0	0.0	16	3.3
Median Grant Amount	$4,580		$3,654			

Informational & Library Resources

# of volumes & volume equivalents	272,454	# of professional staff	7
# of titles	42,791	Hours per week with professional staff	57
# of active serial subscriptions	2,295	Hours per week without professional staff	48
Study seating capacity inside the library	275	# of student computer work stations for entire law school	58
Square feet of law library	29,465	# of additional networked connections	0
Square feet of law school (excl. Library)	55,298	Require Laptop Computer?	N

Employment

	Total	%
Employment status known	131	95.6
Employment status unknown	6	4.4
Employed	124	94.7
Pursuing graduate degrees	5	3.8
Unemployed seeking employment	0	0.0
Unemployed not seeking employment	2	1.5
Type of Employment		
# employed in law firms	76	61.3
# employed in business & industry	11	8.9
# employed in government	16	12.9
# employed in public interest	3	2.4
# employed as judicial clerks	10	8.1
# employed in academia	2	1.6
Geographic Location		
# employed in state	93	75.0
# employed in foreign countries	0	0.0
# of states where employed	14	

J.D. Attrition (from Prior Year)

	Academic	Other	TOTALS	
	#	#	#	%
1st Year	19	13	32	16%
2nd Year	6	1	7	5.2%
3rd Year	0	2	2	1.2%
4th Year	0	0	0	0.0%

Bar Passage Rates

Jurisdiction	Tennessee		
Exam	Sum 97	Win 98	Total
# from school taking bar for the first time	101	17	118
School's pass rate for all first-time takers	85%	76%	84%
State's pass rate for all first-time takers	81%	76%	80%

MERCER UNIVERSITY

Walter F. George School of Law
1021 Georgia Avenue
Macon, GA 31207
(912)752-2601
http://www.law.mercer.edu/

ABA Approved Since 1925

The Basics

Type of School: Private   Term: Semester

Application deadline: 03/15

Application fee: $45

Financial Aid deadline: 04/01

Can first year start other than Fall? No

Student faculty ratio: 16.2 to 1

Does the University offer:
- housing restricted to law students? No
- graduate student housing for which law students are eligible? Yes

Faculty & Administrators

	Total		Men		Women		Minorities	
	Fall	Spr	Fall	Spr	Fall	Spr	Fall	Spr
Full-time	21	22	16	17	5	5	2	2
Other Full-Time	2	2	2	2	0	0	0	0
Deans, librarians, & others who teach > 1/2	1	1	0	0	1	1	0	0
Part-time	8	23	7	17	1	6	0	1
Total	32	48	25	36	7	12	2	3
Deans, librarians, & others who teach < 1/2	3	3	2	2	1	1	0	0

Curriculum

	Full time	Part time
Typical first-year section size	75	0
Is there typically a "small section" of the first year class, other than Legal Writing, taught by full-time faculty?	Yes	No
If yes, typical size offered last year	25	N/A
# of classroom course titles beyond 1st year curriculum	89	0
# of upper division courses, excluding seminars, with an enrollment:		
Under 25	59	0
25 - 49	16	0
50 - 74	13	0
75 - 99	3	0
100 +	1	0
# of seminars	13	0
# of seminar positions available	210	
# of seminar positions filled	129	0
# of positions available in simulation courses	740	
# of simulation positions filled	618	0
# of positions available in faculty supervised clinical courses	15	
# of fac. sup. clin. positions filled	4	0
# involved in field placements	38	0
# involved in law journals	41	0
# in moot court or trial competitions	42	0
# of credit hrs required to graduate	90	

J.D. Enrollment & Ethnicity

	Men		Women		Fl-Time		Pt-Time		1st Yr		2nd Yr		3rd Yr		4th Yr		Total		JD Degrees Awarded
	#	%	#	%	#	%	#	%	#	%	#	%	#	%	#	%	#	%	
African-American	6	2.5	20	12.0	26	6.4	0	0.0	11	8.5	7	4.9	8	5.9	0	0.0	26	6.4	8
American Indian	2	0.8	1	0.6	3	0.7	0	0.0	0	0.0	0	0.0	3	2.2	0	0.0	3	0.7	0
Asian American	7	2.9	4	2.4	11	2.7	0	0.0	5	3.8	0	0.0	6	4.4	0	0.0	11	2.7	3
Mexican American	0	0.0	1	0.6	1	0.2	0	0.0	0	0.0	0	0.0	1	0.7	0	0.0	1	0.2	1
Puerto Rican	1	0.4	0	0.0	1	0.2	0	0.0	0	0.0	1	0.7	0	0.0	0	0.0	1	0.2	0
Hispanic American	2	0.8	3	1.8	5	1.2	0	0.0	1	0.8	3	2.1	1	0.7	0	0.0	5	1.2	2
Total Minorities	18	7.5	29	17.4	47	11.5	0	0.0	17	13.1	11	7.7	19	14.1	0	0.0	47	11.5	14
Foreign Nationals	0	0.0	0	0.0	0	0.0	0	0.0	0	0.0	0	0.0	0	0.0	0	0.0	0	0.0	0
Caucasian	222	92.5	138	82.6	360	88.5	0	0.0	113	86.9	131	92.3	116	85.9	0	0.0	360	88.5	106
Total	240	59.0	167	41.0	407	100.0	0	0.0	130	31.9	142	34.9	135	33.2	0	0.0	407		120

GPA & LSAT Scores

	Full Time	Part Time	Total
# of apps	935	0	935
# admits	465	0	465
# of matrics	133	0	133
75% GPA	3.48	0.00	
25% GPA	2.87	0.00	
75% LSAT	156	0	
25% LSAT	150	0	

Tuition & Fees

	Resident	Non-resident
Full-Time	$18,590	$18,590
Part-Time	$0	$0

Living Expenses

Estimated living expenses for Singles		
Living on campus	Living off campus	Living at home
N/A	$11,000	N/A

Grants/Scholarships

	Full-time		Part-time		Total	
	#	%	#	%	#	%
Total # of Students	407		0		407	
Total # receiving grants	108	26.5	0	0.0	108	26.5
Less than 1/2 tuition	57	14.0	0	0.0	57	14.0
Half to full tuition	15	3.7	0	0.0	15	3.7
Full tuition	24	5.9	0	0.0	24	5.9
More than full tuition	12	2.9	0	0.0	12	2.9
Median Grant Amount	$7,000		$0			

Informational & Library Resources

# of volumes & volume equivalents	285,663	# of professional staff	7
# of titles	36,290	Hours per week with professional staff	69
# of active serial subscriptions	3,345	Hours per week without professional staff	3
Study seating capacity inside the library	283	# of student computer work stations for entire law school	65
Square feet of law library	35,000	# of additional networked connections	70
Square feet of law school (excl. Library)	48,800	Require Laptop Computer?	N

Employment

	Total	%
Employment status known	140	100.0
Employment status unknown	0	0.0
Employed	128	91.4
Pursuing graduate degrees	3	2.1
Unemployed seeking employment	9	6.4
Unemployed not seeking employment	0	0.0
Type of Employment		
# employed in law firms	84	65.6
# employed in business & industry	9	7.0
# employed in government	20	15.6
# employed in public interest	3	2.3
# employed as judicial clerks	12	9.4
# employed in academia	0	0.0
Geographic Location		
# employed in state	88	68.7
# employed in foreign countries	0	0.0
# of states where employed	9	

J.D. Attrition (from Prior Year)

	Academic	Other	TOTALS	
	#	#	#	%
1st Year	9	4	13	8.6%
2nd Year	0	9	9	6.7%
3rd Year	0	0	0	0.0%
4th Year	0	0	0	0.0%

Bar Passage Rates

Jurisdiction	Georgia		
Exam	Sum 97	Win 98	Total
# from school taking bar for the first time	107	3	110
School's pass rate for all first-time takers	92%	67%	91%
State's pass rate for all first-time takers	86%	74%	83%

MIAMI, UNIVERSITY OF

P.O. Box 248087
Coral Gables, FL 33124
(305)284-2394
http://www.law.miami.edu

ABA Approved Since 1941

The Basics

Type of School: Private   Term: Semester

Application deadline: 07/31

Application fee: $45

Financial Aid deadline: 03/01

Can first year start other than Fall? No

Student faculty ratio: 21.0 to 1

Does the University offer:

- housing restricted to law students? Yes
- graduate student housing for which law students are eligible? Yes

Faculty & Administrators

	Total		Men		Women		Minorities	
	Fall	Spr	Fall	Spr	Fall	Spr	Fall	Spr
Full-time	46	42	36	34	10	8	7	6
Other Full-Time	5	5	2	2	3	3	0	0
Deans, librarians, & others who teach > 1/2	1	1	1	1	0	0	0	0
Part-time	117	128	91	102	25	26	10	10
Total	169	176	130	139	38	37	17	16
Deans, librarians, & others who teach < 1/2	2	2	0	0	2	2	1	1

Curriculum

	Full time	Part time
Typical first-year section size	90	50
Is there typically a "small section" of the first year class, other than Legal Writing, taught by full-time faculty?	Yes	No
If yes, typical size offered last year	45	N/A
# of classroom course titles beyond 1st year curriculum	151	31
# of upper division courses, excluding seminars, with an enrollment:		
Under 25	30	5
25 - 49	50	11
50 - 74	12	4
75 - 99	7	1
100 +	10	6
# of seminars	42	4
# of seminar positions available	630	
# of seminar positions filled	510	120
# of positions available in simulation courses	625	
# of simulation positions filled	472	90
# of positions available in faculty supervised clinical courses	289	
# of fac. sup. clin. positions filled	289	0
# involved in field placements	194	0
# involved in law journals	142	15
# in moot court or trial competitions	51	0
# of credit hrs required to graduate	88	

J.D. Enrollment & Ethnicity

	Men		Women		Fl-Time		Pt-Time		1st Yr		2nd Yr		3rd Yr		4th Yr		Total		JD Degrees Awarded
	#	%	#	%	#	%	#	%	#	%	#	%	#	%	#	%	#	%	
African-American	40	5.8	57	10.6	81	7.9	16	8.1	21	6.8	32	7.5	42	9.0	2	9.5	97	7.9	33
American Indian	3	0.4	1	0.2	3	0.3	1	0.5	1	0.3	3	0.7	0	0.0	0	0.0	4	0.3	3
Asian American	16	2.3	19	3.5	25	2.4	10	5.1	7	2.3	13	3.1	13	2.8	2	9.5	35	2.9	7
Mexican American	0	0.0	0	0.0	0	0.0	0	0.0	0	0.0	0	0.0	0	0.0	0	0.0	0	0.0	0
Puerto Rican	0	0.0	0	0.0	0	0.0	0	0.0	0	0.0	0	0.0	0	0.0	0	0.0	0	0.0	0
Hispanic American	109	15.9	133	24.7	191	18.6	51	25.9	74	23.8	77	18.1	88	18.8	3	14.3	242	19.8	59
Total Minorities	168	24.5	210	39.0	300	29.2	78	39.6	103	33.1	125	29.4	143	30.6	7	33.3	378	30.9	102
Foreign Nationals	35	5.1	43	8.0	62	6.0	16	8.1	18	5.8	35	8.2	24	5.1	1	4.8	78	6.4	25
Caucasian	482	70.4	286	53.1	665	64.8	103	52.3	190	61.1	265	62.4	300	64.2	13	61.9	768	62.7	269
Total	685	56.0	539	44.0	1027	83.9	197	16.1	311	25.4	425	34.7	467	38.2	21	1.7	1224		396

GPA & LSAT Scores

	Full Time	Part Time	Total
# of apps	2,012	233	2,245
# admits	1,076	115	1,191
# of matrics	273	53	326
75% GPA	3.41	3.31	
25% GPA	2.92	2.77	
75% LSAT	157	155	
25% LSAT	151	148	

Tuition & Fees

	Resident	Non-resident
Full-Time	$21,956	$21,956
Part-Time	$16,218	$16,218

Living Expenses

Estimated living expenses for Singles		
Living on campus	Living off campus	Living at home
$14,487	$14,487	$8,142

Grants/Scholarships

	Full-time		Part-time		Total	
	#	%	#	%	#	%
Total # of Students	1027		197		1224	
Total # receiving grants	333	32.4	11	5.6	344	28.1
Less than 1/2 tuition	116	11.3	7	3.6	123	10.0
Half to full tuition	149	14.5	4	2.0	153	12.5
Full tuition	55	5.4	0	0.0	55	4.5
More than full tuition	13	1.3	0	0.0	13	1.1
Median Grant Amount	$10,587		$5,000			

Informational & Library Resources

# of volumes & volume equivalents	493,201	# of professional staff	9
# of titles	79,990	Hours per week with professional staff	84
# of active serial subscriptions	7,523	Hours per week without professional staff	35
Study seating capacity inside the library	765	# of student computer work stations for entire law school	160
Square feet of law library	77,446	# of additional networked connections	145
Square feet of law school (excl. Library)	119,486	Require Laptop Computer?	N

Employment

	Total	%
Employment status known	397	95.0
Employment status unknown	21	5.0
Employed	333	83.9
Pursuing graduate degrees	18	4.5
Unemployed seeking employment	44	11.1
Unemployed not seeking employment	2	0.5
Type of Employment		
# employed in law firms	209	62.8
# employed in business & industry	29	8.7
# employed in government	43	12.9
# employed in public interest	10	3.0
# employed as judicial clerks	14	4.2
# employed in academia	5	1.5
Geographic Location		
# employed in state	218	65.5
# employed in foreign countries	1	0.3
# of states where employed	16	

J.D. Attrition (from Prior Year)

	Academic	Other	TOTALS	
	#	#	#	%
1st Year	0	15	15	3.2%
2nd Year	13	33	46	9.6%
3rd Year	0	1	1	0.2%
4th Year	0	0	0	0.0%

Bar Passage Rates

Jurisdiction	Florida			New York		
Exam	Sum 97	Win 98	Total	Sum 97	Win 98	Total
# from school taking bar for the first time	308	56	364	31	11	42
School's pass rate for all first-time takers	81%	73%	80%	77%	100%	83%
State's pass rate for all first-time takers	84%	82%	83%	78%	65%	76%

MICHIGAN, UNIVERSITY OF

Hutchins Hall
625 South State Street
Ann Arbor, MI 48109-1215
(734)764-1358
http://www.law.umich.edu

ABA Approved Since 1923

The Basics

Type of School: Public   Term: Semester
Application deadline: 02/15
Application fee: $70
Financial Aid deadline: Rolling
Can first year start other than Fall? Yes
Student faculty ratio: 14.9 to 1
Does the University offer:
- housing restricted to law students? Yes
- graduate student housing for which law students are eligible? Yes

Faculty & Administrators

	Total		Men		Women		Minorities	
	Fall	Spr	Fall	Spr	Fall	Spr	Fall	Spr
Full-time	58	54	42	40	16	14	2	6
Other Full-Time	9	9	4	4	5	5	2	2
Deans, librarians, & others who teach > 1/2	3	3	0	0	3	3	0	0
Part-time	11	0	8	0	3	0	0	0
Total	81	66	54	44	27	22	4	8
Deans, librarians, & others who teach < 1/2	2	2	1	1	1	1	0	0

Curriculum

	Full time	Part time
Typical first-year section size	85	0
Is there typically a "small section" of the first year class, other than Legal Writing, taught by full-time faculty?	Yes	No
If yes, typical size offered last year	43	N/A
# of classroom course titles beyond 1st year curriculum	118	0
# of upper division courses, excluding seminars, with an enrollment:		
Under 25	25	0
25 - 49	21	0
50 - 74	19	0
75 - 99	17	0
100 +	15	0
# of seminars	42	0
# of seminar positions available	718	
# of seminar positions filled	518	0
# of positions available in simulation courses	172	
# of simulation positions filled	129	0
# of positions available in faculty supervised clinical courses	149	
# of fac. sup. clin. positions filled	149	0
# involved in field placements	22	0
# involved in law journals	315	0
# in moot court or trial competitions	178	0
# of credit hrs required to graduate	83	

J.D. Enrollment & Ethnicity

	Men		Women		Fl-Time		Pt-Time		1st Yr		2nd Yr		3rd Yr		4th Yr		Total		JD Degrees Awarded
	#	%	#	%	#	%	#	%	#	%	#	%	#	%	#	%	#	%	
African-American	41	6.6	35	8.6	76	7.4	0	0.0	24	7.0	27	7.5	25	7.6	0	0.0	76	7.4	28
American Indian	10	1.6	7	1.7	17	1.7	0	0.0	7	2.1	7	1.9	3	0.9	0	0.0	17	1.7	4
Asian American	47	7.5	42	10.3	89	8.6	0	0.0	31	9.1	35	9.7	23	7.0	0	0.0	89	8.6	22
Mexican American	21	3.4	8	2.0	29	2.8	0	0.0	9	2.6	8	2.2	12	3.6	0	0.0	29	2.8	7
Puerto Rican	5	0.8	3	0.7	8	0.8	0	0.0	1	0.3	4	1.1	3	0.9	0	0.0	8	0.8	2
Hispanic American	9	1.4	4	1.0	13	1.3	0	0.0	6	1.8	4	1.1	3	0.9	0	0.0	13	1.3	3
Total Minorities	133	21.3	99	24.4	232	22.5	0	0.0	78	22.9	85	23.6	69	21.0	0	0.0	232	22.5	66
Foreign Nationals	7	1.1	4	1.0	11	1.1	0	0.0	0	0.0	5	1.4	6	1.8	0	0.0	11	1.1	2
Caucasian	484	77.6	303	74.6	787	76.4	0	0.0	263	77.1	270	75.0	254	77.2	0	0.0	787	76.4	286
Total	624	60.6	406	39.4	1030	100.0	0	0.0	341	33.1	360	35.0	329	31.9	0	0.0	1030		354

GPA & LSAT Scores

	Full Time	Part Time	Total
# of apps	3,476	0	3,476
# admits	1,250	0	1,250
# of matrics	341	0	341
75% GPA	3.73	0.00	
25% GPA	3.36	0.00	
75% LSAT	168	0	
25% LSAT	163	0	

Tuition & Fees

	Resident	Non-resident
Full-Time	$17,910	$23,880
Part-Time	$0	$0

Living Expenses

Estimated living expenses for Singles		
Living on campus	Living off campus	Living at home
$12,425	$12,425	$7,400

Grants/Scholarships

	Full-time		Part-time		Total	
	#	%	#	%	#	%
Total # of Students	1030		0		1030	
Total # receiving grants	291	28.3	0	0.0	291	28.3
Less than 1/2 tuition	171	16.6	0	0.0	171	16.6
Half to full tuition	90	8.7	0	0.0	90	8.7
Full tuition	0	0.0	0	0.0	0	0.0
More than full tuition	30	2.9	0	0.0	30	2.9
Median Grant Amount	$7,265		$0			

Informational & Library Resources

# of volumes & volume equivalents	826,766	# of professional staff	11
# of titles	266,423	Hours per week with professional staff	68
# of active serial subscriptions	9,676	Hours per week without professional staff	44
Study seating capacity inside the library	843	# of student computer work stations for entire law school	92
Square feet of law library	100,493	# of additional networked connections	39
Square feet of law school (excl. Library)	85,476	Require Laptop Computer?	N

Employment

	Total	%
Employment status known	380	96.9
Employment status unknown	12	3.1
Employed	356	93.7
Pursuing graduate degrees	6	1.6
Unemployed seeking employment	15	3.9
Unemployed not seeking employment	3	0.8
Type of Employment		
# employed in law firms	238	66.9
# employed in business & industry	15	4.2
# employed in government	14	3.9
# employed in public interest	14	3.9
# employed as judicial clerks	71	19.9
# employed in academia	1	0.3
Geographic Location		
# employed in state	67	18.8
# employed in foreign countries	1	0.3
# of states where employed	34	

J.D. Attrition (from Prior Year)

	Academic	Other	TOTALS	
	#	#	#	%
1st Year	0	0	0	0.0%
2nd Year	0	7	7	2.1%
3rd Year	0	1	1	0.3%
4th Year	0	0	0	0.0%

Bar Passage Rates

Jurisdiction	Michigan			New York		
Exam	Sum 97	Win 98	Total	Sum 97	Win 98	Total
# from school taking bar for the first time	57	19	76	52	24	76
School's pass rate for all first-time takers	95%	84%	92%	100%	100%	100%
State's pass rate for all first-time takers	89%	79%	86%	78%	65%	76%

MINNESOTA, UNIVERSITY OF

229 - 19th Ave S.
Minneapolis, MN 55455
(612)625-1000
http://www.law.umn.edu/

ABA Approved Since 1923

The Basics

Type of School: Public Term: Semester
Application deadline: 03/01
Application fee: $40
Financial Aid deadline: 03/01
Can first year start other than Fall? No
Student faculty ratio: 18.6 to 1
Does the University offer:
- housing restricted to law students? No
- graduate student housing for which law students are eligible? No

Faculty & Administrators

	Total		Men		Women		Minorities	
	Fall	Spr	Fall	Spr	Fall	Spr	Fall	Spr
Full-time	33	35	23	23	10	12	3	2
Other Full-Time	3	3	2	2	1	1	0	0
Deans, librarians, & others who teach > 1/2	2	2	1	1	1	1	1	1
Part-time	62	85	39	54	23	31	3	3
Total	100	125	65	80	35	45	7	6
Deans, librarians, & others who teach < 1/2	7	7	3	3	4	4	1	1

Curriculum

	Full time	Part time
Typical first-year section size	100	0
Is there typically a "small section" of the first year class, other than Legal Writing, taught by full-time faculty?	Yes	No
If yes, typical size offered last year	50	N/A
# of classroom course titles beyond 1st year curriculum	149	0
# of upper division courses, excluding seminars, with an enrollment:		
Under 25	45	0
25 - 49	25	0
50 - 74	13	0
75 - 99	5	0
100 +	12	0
# of seminars	49	0
# of seminar positions available	784	
# of seminar positions filled	697	0
# of positions available in simulation courses	229	
# of simulation positions filled	225	0
# of positions available in faculty supervised clinical courses	352	
# of fac. sup. clin. positions filled	335	0
# involved in field placements	61	0
# involved in law journals	149	0
# in moot court or trial competitions	227	0
# of credit hrs required to graduate	88	

J.D. Enrollment & Ethnicity

	Men		Women		Fl-Time		Pt-Time		1st Yr		2nd Yr		3rd Yr		4th Yr		Total		JD Degrees Awarded
	#	%	#	%	#	%	#	%	#	%	#	%	#	%	#	%	#	%	
African-American	7	1.8	13	3.8	20	2.7	0	0.0	5	2.1	7	2.9	8	3.1	0	0.0	20	2.7	8
American Indian	3	0.8	5	1.4	8	1.1	0	0.0	2	0.8	3	1.2	3	1.1	0	0.0	8	1.1	1
Asian American	40	10.1	26	7.5	66	8.9	0	0.0	15	6.3	31	12.7	20	7.7	0	0.0	66	8.9	15
Mexican American	0	0.0	0	0.0	0	0.0	0	0.0	0	0.0	0	0.0	0	0.0	0	0.0	0	0.0	0
Puerto Rican	2	0.5	1	0.3	3	0.4	0	0.0	0	0.0	1	0.4	2	0.8	0	0.0	3	0.4	1
Hispanic American	16	4.0	16	4.6	32	4.3	0	0.0	8	3.4	12	4.9	12	4.6	0	0.0	32	4.3	6
Total Minorities	68	17.1	61	17.6	129	17.3	0	0.0	30	12.6	54	22.0	45	17.2	0	0.0	129	17.3	31
Foreign Nationals	7	1.8	9	2.6	16	2.2	0	0.0	5	2.1	9	3.7	2	0.8	0	0.0	16	2.2	4
Caucasian	323	81.2	276	79.8	599	80.5	0	0.0	203	85.3	183	74.7	213	81.6	0	0.0	599	80.5	216
Total	398	53.5	346	46.5	744	100.0	0	0.0	238	32.0	245	32.9	261	35.1	0	0.0	744		251

GPA & LSAT Scores

	Full Time	Part Time	Total
# of apps	1,467	0	1,467
# admits	626	0	626
# of matrics	240	0	240
75% GPA	3.81	0.00	
25% GPA	3.34	0.00	
75% LSAT	164	0	
25% LSAT	159	0	

Tuition & Fees

	Resident	Non-resident
Full-Time	$9,630	$15,930
Part-Time	$0	$0

Living Expenses

Estimated living expenses for Singles

Living on campus	Living off campus	Living at home
$9,398	$9,398	$9,398

Grants/Scholarships

	Full-time		Part-time		Total	
	#	%	#	%	#	%
Total # of Students	744		0		744	
Total # receiving grants	277	37.2	0	0.0	277	37.2
Less than 1/2 tuition	177	23.8	0	0.0	177	23.8
Half to full tuition	52	7.0	0	0.0	52	7.0
Full tuition	48	6.5	0	0.0	48	6.5
More than full tuition	0	0.0	0	0.0	0	0.0
Median Grant Amount	$6,300		$0			

Informational & Library Resources

# of volumes & volume equivalents	855,292	# of professional staff	12
# of titles	228,612	Hours per week with professional staff	67
# of active serial subscriptions	9,866	Hours per week without professional staff	14
Study seating capacity inside the library	934	# of student computer work stations for entire law school	75
Square feet of law library	95,000	# of additional networked connections	0
Square feet of law school (excl. Library)	265,000	Require Laptop Computer?	N

Employment

	Total	%
Employment status known	258	99.2
Employment status unknown	2	0.8
Employed	243	94.2
Pursuing graduate degrees	2	0.8
Unemployed seeking employment	6	2.3
Unemployed not seeking employment	7	2.7
Type of Employment		
# employed in law firms	114	46.9
# employed in business & industry	40	16.5
# employed in government	10	4.1
# employed in public interest	16	6.6
# employed as judicial clerks	56	23.0
# employed in academia	7	2.9
Geographic Location		
# employed in state	147	60.5
# employed in foreign countries	5	2.1
# of states where employed	25	

J.D. Attrition (from Prior Year)

	Academic	Other	TOTALS	
	#	#	#	%
1st Year	0	9	9	3.7%
2nd Year	0	1	1	0.4%
3rd Year	1	0	1	0.4%
4th Year	0	0	0	0.0%

Bar Passage Rates

Jurisdiction	Minnesota		
Exam	Sum 97	Win 98	Total
# from school taking bar for the first time	158	9	167
School's pass rate for all first-time takers	99%	100%	99%
State's pass rate for all first-time takers	93%	77%	90%

MISSISSIPPI COLLEGE

151 East Griffith Street
Jackson, MS 39201
(601)925-7105
http://www.mc.edu

ABA Approved Since 1980

The Basics

Type of School: Private Term: Semester
Application deadline: 05/01
Application fee: $25
Financial Aid deadline: 06/01
Can first year start other than Fall? No
Student faculty ratio: 19.7 to 1
Does the University offer:
- housing restricted to law students? No
- graduate student housing for which law students are eligible? No

Curriculum

	Full time	Part time
Typical first-year section size	70	0
Is there typically a "small section" of the first year class, other than Legal Writing, taught by full-time faculty?	Yes	No
If yes, typical size offered last year	24	N/A
# of classroom course titles beyond 1st year curriculum	72	0
# of upper division courses, excluding seminars, with an enrollment:		
Under 25	22	0
25 - 49	16	0
50 - 74	23	0
75 - 99	0	0
100 +	0	0
# of seminars	5	0
# of seminar positions available	75	
# of seminar positions filled	63	0
# of positions available in simulation courses	184	
# of simulation positions filled	163	0
# of positions available in faculty supervised clinical courses	0	
# of fac. sup. clin. positions filled	0	0
# involved in field placements	40	0
# involved in law journals	31	0
# in moot court or trial competitions	43	0
# of credit hrs required to graduate	88	

Faculty & Administrators

	Total		Men		Women		Minorities	
	Fall	Spr	Fall	Spr	Fall	Spr	Fall	Spr
Full-time	17	17	11	11	6	6	2	2
Other Full-Time	1	1	0	0	1	1	0	0
Deans, librarians, & others who teach > 1/2	1	1	1	1	0	0	0	0
Part-time	12	8	10	7	2	1	1	1
Total	31	27	22	19	9	8	3	3
Deans, librarians, & others who teach < 1/2	2	2	1	1	1	1	0	0

J.D. Enrollment & Ethnicity

	Men		Women		Fl-Time		Pt-Time		1st Yr		2nd Yr		3rd Yr		4th Yr		Total		JD Degrees Awarded
	#	%	#	%	#	%	#	%	#	%	#	%	#	%	#	%	#	%	
African-American	9	3.6	22	14.6	31	7.7	0	0.0	12	8.6	9	7.4	10	7.1	0	0.0	31	7.7	8
American Indian	1	0.4	2	1.3	3	0.7	0	0.0	1	0.7	0	0.0	2	1.4	0	0.0	3	0.7	0
Asian American	2	0.8	1	0.7	3	0.7	0	0.0	1	0.7	0	0.0	2	1.4	0	0.0	3	0.7	5
Mexican American	0	0.0	0	0.0	0	0.0	0	0.0	0	0.0	0	0.0	0	0.0	0	0.0	0	0.0	0
Puerto Rican	0	0.0	0	0.0	0	0.0	0	0.0	0	0.0	0	0.0	0	0.0	0	0.0	0	0.0	0
Hispanic American	2	0.8	1	0.7	3	0.7	0	0.0	2	1.4	0	0.0	1	0.7	0	0.0	3	0.7	1
Total Minorities	14	5.6	26	17.2	40	10.0	0	0.0	16	11.4	9	7.4	15	10.7	0	0.0	40	10.0	14
Foreign Nationals	1	0.4	0	0.0	1	0.2	0	0.0	0	0.0	0	0.0	1	0.7	0	0.0	1	0.2	0
Caucasian	235	94.0	125	82.8	360	89.8	0	0.0	124	88.6	112	92.6	124	88.6	0	0.0	360	89.8	100
Total	250	62.3	151	37.7	401	100.0	0	0.0	140	34.9	121	30.2	140	34.9	0	0.0	401		114

GPA & LSAT Scores

	Full Time	Part Time	Total
# of apps	693	0	693
# admits	414	0	414
# of matrics	141	0	141
75% GPA	3.39	0.00	
25% GPA	2.81	0.00	
75% LSAT	152	0	
25% LSAT	145	0	

Tuition & Fees

	Resident	Non-resident
Full-Time	$13,248	$13,248
Part-Time	$0	$0

Living Expenses

Estimated living expenses for Singles		
Living on campus	Living off campus	Living at home
$10,336	$13,990	$13,990

Employment

	Total	%
Employment status known	120	98.4
Employment status unknown	2	1.6
Employed	111	92.5
Pursuing graduate degrees	4	3.3
Unemployed seeking employment	1	0.8
Unemployed not seeking employment	4	3.3
Type of Employment		
# employed in law firms	70	63.1
# employed in business & industry	5	4.5
# employed in government	13	11.7
# employed in public interest	2	1.8
# employed as judicial clerks	20	18.0
# employed in academia	1	0.9
Geographic Location		
# employed in state	66	59.5
# employed in foreign countries	0	0.0
# of states where employed	13	

Grants/Scholarships

	Full-time		Part-time		Total	
	#	%	#	%	#	%
Total # of Students	401		0		401	
Total # receiving grants	118	29.4	0	0.0	118	29.4
Less than 1/2 tuition	34	8.5	0	0.0	34	8.5
Half to full tuition	33	8.2	0	0.0	33	8.2
Full tuition	44	11.0	0	0.0	44	11.0
More than full tuition	7	1.7	0	0.0	7	1.7
Median Grant Amount	$9,564		$0			

Informational & Library Resources

# of volumes & volume equivalents	289,761	# of professional staff	5
# of titles	150,782	Hours per week with professional staff	62
# of active serial subscriptions	3,509	Hours per week without professional staff	40
Study seating capacity inside the library	275	# of student computer work stations for entire law school	35
Square feet of law library	22,305	# of additional networked connections	0
Square feet of law school (excl. Library)	50,997	Require Laptop Computer?	N

J.D. Attrition (from Prior Year)

	Academic	Other	TOTALS	
	#	#	#	%
1st Year	3	0	3	2.1%
2nd Year	0	0	0	0.0%
3rd Year	0	0	0	0.0%
4th Year	0	0	0	0.0%

Bar Passage Rates

Jurisdiction	Mississippi		
Exam	Sum 97	Win 98	Total
# from school taking bar for the first time	59	9	68
School's pass rate for all first-time takers	95%	67%	91%
State's pass rate for all first-time takers	93%	82%	90%

MISSISSIPPI, UNIVERSITY OF

Office of the Dean
Law Center
University, MS 38677
(601)232-6900
http://www.olemiss.edu/depts/law_school

ABA Approved Since 1930

The Basics

Type of School: Public   Term: Semester

Application deadline: 03/01

Application fee: $25

Financial Aid deadline: 03/15

Can first year start other than Fall? Yes

Student faculty ratio: 22.7 to 1

Does the University offer:

- housing restricted to law students? No
- graduate student housing for which law students are eligible? Yes

Faculty & Administrators

	Total		Men		Women		Minorities	
	Fall	Spr	Fall	Spr	Fall	Spr	Fall	Spr
Full-time	18	17	14	13	4	4	4	3
Other Full-Time	1	1	1	1	0	0	0	0
Deans, librarians, & others who teach > 1/2	5	5	3	3	2	2	0	0
Part-time	5	6	3	5	2	1	1	0
Total	29	29	21	22	8	7	5	3
Deans, librarians, & others who teach < 1/2	0	0	0	0	0	0	0	0

Curriculum

	Full time	Part time
Typical first-year section size	57	0
Is there typically a "small section" of the first year class, other than Legal Writing, taught by full-time faculty?	No	No
If yes, typical size offered last year	N/A	N/A
# of classroom course titles beyond 1st year curriculum	44	0
# of upper division courses, excluding seminars, with an enrollment:		
Under 25	23	0
25 - 49	18	0
50 - 74	15	0
75 - 99	6	0
100 +	4	0
# of seminars	8	0
# of seminar positions available	162	
# of seminar positions filled	96	0
# of positions available in simulation courses	169	
# of simulation positions filled	168	0
# of positions available in faculty supervised clinical courses	0	
# of fac. sup. clin. positions filled	0	0
# involved in field placements	66	0
# involved in law journals	66	0
# in moot court or trial competitions	116	0
# of credit hrs required to graduate	90	

J.D. Enrollment & Ethnicity

	Men		Women		Fl-Time		Pt-Time		1st Yr		2nd Yr		3rd Yr		4th Yr		Total		JD Degrees Awarded
	#	%	#	%	#	%	#	%	#	%	#	%	#	%	#	%	#	%	
African-American	17	5.6	30	16.6	47	9.8	0	0.0	18	11.4	8	5.3	21	11.9	0	0.0	47	9.7	17
American Indian	7	2.3	1	0.6	8	1.7	0	0.0	3	1.9	2	1.3	3	1.7	0	0.0	8	1.6	0
Asian American	1	0.3	3	1.7	4	0.8	0	0.0	2	1.3	2	1.3	0	0.0	0	0.0	4	0.8	2
Mexican American	0	0.0	0	0.0	0	0.0	0	0.0	0	0.0	0	0.0	0	0.0	0	0.0	0	0.0	0
Puerto Rican	0	0.0	0	0.0	0	0.0	0	0.0	0	0.0	0	0.0	0	0.0	0	0.0	0	0.0	0
Hispanic American	3	1.0	1	0.6	4	0.8	0	0.0	1	0.6	2	1.3	1	0.6	0	0.0	4	0.8	1
Total Minorities	28	9.2	35	19.3	63	13.1	0	0.0	24	15.2	14	9.3	25	14.2	0	0.0	63	13.0	20
Foreign Nationals	0	0.0	0	0.0	0	0.0	0	0.0	0	0.0	0	0.0	0	0.0	0	0.0	0	0.0	0
Caucasian	276	90.8	146	80.7	418	86.9	4	100.0	134	84.8	137	90.7	151	85.8	0	0.0	422	87.0	128
Total	304	62.7	181	37.3	481	99.2	4	0.8	158	32.6	151	31.1	176	36.3	0	0.0	485		148

GPA & LSAT Scores

	Full Time	Part Time	Total
# of apps	1,203	0	1,203
# admits	446	0	446
# of matrics	158	0	158
75% GPA	3.63	0.00	
25% GPA	3.01	0.00	
75% LSAT	157	0	
25% LSAT	150	0	

Tuition & Fees

	Resident	Non-resident
Full-Time	$3,760	$7,682
Part-Time	$0	$0

Living Expenses

Estimated living expenses for Singles		
Living on campus	Living off campus	Living at home
$11,028	$11,028	$11,028

Grants/Scholarships

	Full-time		Part-time		Total	
	#	%	#	%	#	%
Total # of Students	481		4		485	
Total # receiving grants	51	10.6	0	0.0	51	10.5
Less than 1/2 tuition	0	0.0	0	0.0	0	0.0
Half to full tuition	0	0.0	0	0.0	0	0.0
Full tuition	51	10.6	0	0.0	51	10.5
More than full tuition	0	0.0	0	0.0	0	0.0
Median Grant Amount	$2,847		$0			

Informational & Library Resources

# of volumes & volume equivalents	296,063	# of professional staff	5
# of titles	63,727	Hours per week with professional staff	60
# of active serial subscriptions	2,916	Hours per week without professional staff	42
Study seating capacity inside the library	397	# of student computer work stations for entire law school	63
Square feet of law library	29,908	# of additional networked connections	35
Square feet of law school (excl. Library)	39,441	Require Laptop Computer?	N

Employment

	Total	%
Employment status known	139	100.0
Employment status unknown	0	0.0
Employed	127	91.4
Pursuing graduate degrees	8	5.8
Unemployed seeking employment	2	1.4
Unemployed not seeking employment	2	1.4
Type of Employment		
# employed in law firms	91	71.7
# employed in business & industry	9	7.1
# employed in government	8	6.3
# employed in public interest	1	0.8
# employed as judicial clerks	18	14.2
# employed in academia	0	0.0
Geographic Location		
# employed in state	95	74.8
# employed in foreign countries	1	0.8
# of states where employed	15	

J.D. Attrition (from Prior Year)

	Academic	Other	TOTALS	
	#	#	#	%
1st Year	12	7	19	11%
2nd Year	1	4	5	2.7%
3rd Year	0	0	0	0.0%
4th Year	0	0	0	0.0%

Bar Passage Rates

Jurisdiction	Mississippi		
Exam	Sum 97	Win 98	Total
# from school taking bar for the first time	88	28	116
School's pass rate for all first-time takers	98%	86%	95%
State's pass rate for all first-time takers	93%	82%	90%

MISSOURI-COLUMBIA, UNIVERSITY OF

203 Hulston Hall
University of Missouri-Columbia
Columbia, MO 65211
(573)882-6487
http://www.law.missouri.edu

ABA Approved Since 1923

The Basics

Type of School: Public **Term:** Semester

Application deadline: 03/01

Application fee: $40

Financial Aid deadline: 03/01

Can first year start other than Fall? No

Student faculty ratio: 18.5 to 1

Does the University offer:
- **housing restricted to law students?** No
- **graduate student housing for which law students are eligible?** Yes

Faculty & Administrators

	Total		Men		Women		Minorities	
	Fall	Spr	Fall	Spr	Fall	Spr	Fall	Spr
Full-time	25	24	19	19	6	5	2	2
Other Full-Time	2	2	1	1	1	1	0	0
Deans, librarians, & others who teach > 1/2	3	3	2	2	1	1	0	0
Part-time	7	9	4	6	3	3	0	0
Total	37	38	26	28	11	10	2	2
Deans, librarians, & others who teach < 1/2	5	5	4	4	1	1	0	0

Curriculum

	Full time	Part time
Typical first-year section size	65	0
Is there typically a "small section" of the first year class, other than Legal Writing, taught by full-time faculty?	No	No
If yes, typical size offered last year	N/A	N/A
# of classroom course titles beyond 1st year curriculum	86	0
# of upper division courses, excluding seminars, with an enrollment:		
Under 25	50	0
25 - 49	21	0
50 - 74	12	0
75 - 99	7	0
100 +	3	0
# of seminars	7	0
# of seminar positions available	105	
# of seminar positions filled	75	0
# of positions available in simulation courses	217	
# of simulation positions filled	185	0
# of positions available in faculty supervised clinical courses	46	
# of fac. sup. clin. positions filled	39	0
# involved in field placements	60	0
# involved in law journals	128	0
# in moot court or trial competitions	200	0
# of credit hrs required to graduate	89	

J.D. Enrollment & Ethnicity

	Men		Women		Fl-Time		Pt-Time		1st Yr		2nd Yr		3rd Yr		4th Yr		Total		JD Degrees Awarded
	#	%	#	%	#	%	#	%	#	%	#	%	#	%	#	%	#	%	
African-American	11	3.3	18	8.0	29	5.2	0	0.0	18	10.5	8	4.3	3	1.5	0	0.0	29	5.2	9
American Indian	1	0.3	3	1.3	4	0.7	0	0.0	1	0.6	1	0.5	2	1.0	0	0.0	4	0.7	2
Asian American	7	2.1	6	2.7	13	2.3	0	0.0	3	1.7	5	2.7	5	2.6	0	0.0	13	2.3	3
Mexican American	0	0.0	0	0.0	0	0.0	0	0.0	0	0.0	0	0.0	0	0.0	0	0.0	0	0.0	0
Puerto Rican	0	0.0	0	0.0	0	0.0	0	0.0	0	0.0	0	0.0	0	0.0	0	0.0	0	0.0	0
Hispanic American	5	1.5	3	1.3	8	1.4	0	0.0	2	1.2	4	2.1	2	1.0	0	0.0	8	1.4	4
Total Minorities	24	7.3	30	13.3	54	9.7	0	0.0	24	14.0	18	9.6	12	6.2	0	0.0	54	9.7	18
Foreign Nationals	0	0.0	0	0.0	0	0.0	0	0.0	0	0.0	0	0.0	0	0.0	0	0.0	0	0.0	0
Caucasian	306	92.7	195	86.7	501	90.3	0	0.0	148	86.0	170	90.4	183	93.8	0	0.0	501	90.3	116
Total	330	59.5	225	40.5	555	100.0	0	0.0	172	31.0	188	33.9	195	35.1	0	0.0	555		134

GPA & LSAT Scores

	Full Time	Part Time	Total
# of apps	798	0	798
# admits	410	0	410
# of matrics	169	0	169
75% GPA	3.67	0.00	
25% GPA	3.07	0.00	
75% LSAT	159	0	
25% LSAT	153	0	

Tuition & Fees

	Resident	Non-resident
Full-Time	$8,842	$17,116
Part-Time	$0	$0

Living Expenses

Estimated living expenses for Singles		
Living on campus	Living off campus	Living at home
$9,828	$12,158	N/A

Grants/Scholarships

	Full-time		Part-time		Total	
	#	%	#	%	#	%
Total # of Students	555		0		555	
Total # receiving grants	230	41.4	0	0.0	230	41.4
Less than 1/2 tuition	179	32.3	0	0.0	179	32.3
Half to full tuition	36	6.5	0	0.0	36	6.5
Full tuition	2	0.4	0	0.0	2	0.4
More than full tuition	13	2.3	0	0.0	13	2.3
Median Grant Amount	$2,000		$0			

Informational & Library Resources

# of volumes & volume equivalents	316,625	# of professional staff	8
# of titles	166,381	Hours per week with professional staff	66
# of active serial subscriptions	5,184	Hours per week without professional staff	23
Study seating capacity inside the library	376	# of student computer work stations for entire law school	39
Square feet of law library	61,851	# of additional networked connections	6
Square feet of law school (excl. Library)	30,699	Require Laptop Computer?	N

Employment

	Total	%
Employment status known	127	97.7
Employment status unknown	3	2.3
Employed	114	89.8
Pursuing graduate degrees	2	1.6
Unemployed seeking employment	11	8.7
Unemployed not seeking employment	0	0.0
Type of Employment		
# employed in law firms	43	37.7
# employed in business & industry	19	16.7
# employed in government	27	23.7
# employed in public interest	0	0.0
# employed as judicial clerks	23	20.2
# employed in academia	2	1.8
Geographic Location		
# employed in state	110	96.5
# employed in foreign countries	1	0.9
# of states where employed	4	

J.D. Attrition (from Prior Year)

	Academic	Other	TOTALS	
	#	#	#	%
1st Year	6	9	15	7.4%
2nd Year	0	2	2	1.0%
3rd Year	0	0	0	0.0%
4th Year	0	0	0	0.0%

Bar Passage Rates

Jurisdiction	Missouri		
Exam	Sum 97	Win 98	Total
# from school taking bar for the first time	115	11	126
School's pass rate for all first-time takers	92%	82%	91%
State's pass rate for all first-time takers	86%	81%	85%

MISSOURI-KANSAS CITY, UNIVERSITY OF

5100 Rockhill Road
Kansas City, MO 64110
(816)235-1644
http://www.law.umkc.edu

ABA Approved Since 1936

The Basics

Type of School: Public Term: Semester
Application deadline: Rolling
Application fee: $25
Financial Aid deadline: 03/01
Can first year start other than Fall? No
Student faculty ratio: 18.8 to 1
Does the University offer:
- housing restricted to law students? No
- graduate student housing for which law students are eligible? No

Faculty & Administrators

	Total		Men		Women		Minorities	
	Fall	Spr	Fall	Spr	Fall	Spr	Fall	Spr
Full-time	21	23	16	16	5	7	1	1
Other Full-Time	1	1	0	0	1	1	0	0
Deans, librarians, & others who teach > 1/2	4	4	2	2	2	2	1	1
Part-time	14	33	13	25	1	8	1	2
Total	40	61	31	43	9	18	3	4
Deans, librarians, & others who teach < 1/2	0	0	0	0	0	0	0	0

Curriculum

	Full time	Part time
Typical first-year section size	56	0
Is there typically a "small section" of the first year class, other than Legal Writing, taught by full-time faculty?	No	No
If yes, typical size offered last year	N/A	N/A
# of classroom course titles beyond 1st year curriculum	89	0
# of upper division courses, excluding seminars, with an enrollment:		
Under 25	48	0
25 - 49	27	0
50 - 74	13	0
75 - 99	7	0
100 +	0	0
# of seminars	20	0
# of seminar positions available	336	
# of seminar positions filled	256	0
# of positions available in simulation courses	518	
# of simulation positions filled	394	0
# of positions available in faculty supervised clinical courses	0	
# of fac. sup. clin. positions filled	0	0
# involved in field placements	46	0
# involved in law journals	104	0
# in moot court or trial competitions	59	0
# of credit hrs required to graduate	91	

J.D. Enrollment & Ethnicity

	Men		Women		Fl-Time		Pt-Time		1st Yr		2nd Yr		3rd Yr		4th Yr		Total		JD Degrees Awarded
	#	%	#	%	#	%	#	%	#	%	#	%	#	%	#	%	#	%	
African-American	8	3.3	15	6.2	22	4.8	1	3.2	9	5.2	6	3.8	8	5.2	0	0.0	23	4.7	5
American Indian	5	2.1	2	0.8	6	1.3	1	3.2	4	2.3	1	0.6	2	1.3	0	0.0	7	1.4	3
Asian American	7	2.9	3	1.2	9	2.0	1	3.2	4	2.3	4	2.5	2	1.3	0	0.0	10	2.1	3
Mexican American	9	3.7	7	2.9	16	3.5	0	0.0	6	3.4	5	3.2	5	3.3	0	0.0	16	3.3	1
Puerto Rican	0	0.0	0	0.0	0	0.0	0	0.0	0	0.0	0	0.0	0	0.0	0	0.0	0	0.0	0
Hispanic American	0	0.0	0	0.0	0	0.0	0	0.0	0	0.0	0	0.0	0	0.0	0	0.0	0	0.0	0
Total Minorities	29	12.0	27	11.1	53	11.7	3	9.7	23	13.2	16	10.1	17	11.1	0	0.0	56	11.5	12
Foreign Nationals	0	0.0	1	0.4	1	0.2	0	0.0	0	0.0	1	0.6	0	0.0	0	0.0	1	0.2	3
Caucasian	213	88.0	215	88.5	400	88.1	28	90.3	151	86.8	141	89.2	136	88.9	0	0.0	428	88.2	130
Total	242	49.9	243	50.1	454	93.6	31	6.4	174	35.9	158	32.6	153	31.5	0	0.0	485		145

GPA & LSAT Scores

	Full Time	Part Time	Total
# of apps	657	55	712
# admits	414	25	439
# of matrics	163	10	173
75% GPA	3.46	3.48	
25% GPA	2.91	2.65	
75% LSAT	157	155	
25% LSAT	148	151	

Tuition & Fees

	Resident	Non-resident
Full-Time	$8,824	$17,098
Part-Time	$6,352	$12,262

Living Expenses

Estimated living expenses for Singles		
Living on campus	Living off campus	Living at home
$10,840	$12,850	$7,580

Grants/Scholarships

	Full-time		Part-time		Total	
	#	%	#	%	#	%
Total # of Students	454		31		485	
Total # receiving grants	104	22.9	0	0.0	104	21.4
Less than 1/2 tuition	79	17.4	0	0.0	79	16.3
Half to full tuition	17	3.7	0	0.0	17	3.5
Full tuition	8	1.8	0	0.0	8	1.6
More than full tuition	0	0.0	0	0.0	0	0.0
Median Grant Amount	$4,310		$0			

Informational & Library Resources

# of volumes & volume equivalents	277,843	# of professional staff	5
# of titles	48,753	Hours per week with professional staff	43
# of active serial subscriptions	1,754	Hours per week without professional staff	45
Study seating capacity inside the library	521	# of student computer work stations for entire law school	50
Square feet of law library	33,456	# of additional networked connections	0
Square feet of law school (excl. Library)	84,921	Require Laptop Computer?	N

Employment

	Total	%
Employment status known	146	97.3
Employment status unknown	4	2.7
Employed	134	91.8
Pursuing graduate degrees	3	2.1
Unemployed seeking employment	6	4.1
Unemployed not seeking employment	3	2.1
Type of Employment		
# employed in law firms	77	57.5
# employed in business & industry	17	12.7
# employed in government	25	18.7
# employed in public interest	3	2.2
# employed as judicial clerks	11	8.2
# employed in academia	1	0.7
Geographic Location		
# employed in state	112	83.6
# employed in foreign countries	0	0.0
# of states where employed	11	

J.D. Attrition (from Prior Year)

	Academic	Other	TOTALS	
	#	#	#	%
1st Year	5	6	11	6.4%
2nd Year	3	7	10	6.0%
3rd Year	1	0	1	0.6%
4th Year	0	0	0	0.0%

Bar Passage Rates

Jurisdiction	Missouri			Kansas		
Exam	Sum 97	Win 98	Total	Sum 97	Win 98	Total
# from school taking bar for the first time	116	17	133	38	69	107
School's pass rate for all first-time takers	84%	65%	82%	84%	86%	85%
State's pass rate for all first-time takers	86%	81%	85%	87%	87%	87%

MONTANA, UNIVERSITY OF

School of Law
Missoula, MT 59812
(406)243-4311
http://www.umt.edu/law/homepage.htm

ABA Approved Since 1923

The Basics

Type of School: Public — Term: Semester
Application deadline: 03/01
Application fee: $60
Financial Aid deadline: 03/01
Can first year start other than Fall? No
Student faculty ratio: 19.2 to 1
Does the University offer:
- housing restricted to law students? No
- graduate student housing for which law students are eligible? No

Curriculum

	Full time	Part time
Typical first-year section size	40	0
Is there typically a "small section" of the first year class, other than Legal Writing, taught by full-time faculty?	No	No
If yes, typical size offered last year	N/A	N/A
# of classroom course titles beyond 1st year curriculum	54	0
# of upper division courses, excluding seminars, with an enrollment:		
Under 25	29	0
25 - 49	11	0
50 - 74	7	0
75 - 99	5	0
100 +	0	0
# of seminars	19	0
# of seminar positions available	475	
# of seminar positions filled	214	0
# of positions available in simulation courses	192	
# of simulation positions filled	178	0
# of positions available in faculty supervised clinical courses	22	
# of fac. sup. clin. positions filled	21	0
# involved in field placements	54	0
# involved in law journals	26	0
# in moot court or trial competitions	38	0
# of credit hrs required to graduate	90	

Faculty & Administrators

	Total		Men		Women		Minorities	
	Fall	Spr	Fall	Spr	Fall	Spr	Fall	Spr
Full-time	11	12	6	7	5	5	1	1
Other Full-Time	2	2	1	1	1	1	0	0
Deans, librarians, & others who teach > 1/2	2	2	1	1	1	1	0	0
Part-time	14	13	8	9	6	4	0	0
Total	29	29	16	18	13	11	1	1
Deans, librarians, & others who teach < 1/2	1	1	1	1	0	0	0	0

J.D. Enrollment & Ethnicity

	Men		Women		Fl-Time		Pt-Time		1st Yr		2nd Yr		3rd Yr		4th Yr		Total		JD Degrees Awarded
	#	%	#	%	#	%	#	%	#	%	#	%	#	%	#	%	#	%	
African-American	1	0.7	0	0.0	1	0.4	0	0.0	0	0.0	0	0.0	1	1.2	0	0.0	1	0.4	1
American Indian	7	4.8	5	4.7	12	4.7	0	0.0	6	6.5	1	1.3	5	6.0	0	0.0	12	4.7	1
Asian American	1	0.7	2	1.9	3	1.2	0	0.0	1	1.1	1	1.3	1	1.2	0	0.0	3	1.2	0
Mexican American	0	0.0	1	0.9	1	0.4	0	0.0	1	1.1	0	0.0	0	0.0	0	0.0	1	0.4	0
Puerto Rican	0	0.0	0	0.0	0	0.0	0	0.0	0	0.0	0	0.0	0	0.0	0	0.0	0	0.0	0
Hispanic American	2	1.4	3	2.8	5	2.0	0	0.0	2	2.2	2	2.6	1	1.2	0	0.0	5	2.0	2
Total Minorities	11	7.5	11	10.4	22	8.7	0	0.0	10	10.8	4	5.3	8	9.5	0	0.0	22	8.7	4
Foreign Nationals	2	1.4	2	1.9	4	1.6	0	0.0	0	0.0	0	0.0	4	4.8	0	0.0	4	1.6	0
Caucasian	134	91.2	93	87.7	227	89.7	0	0.0	83	89.2	72	94.7	72	85.7	0	0.0	227	89.7	65
Total	147	58.1	106	41.9	253	100.0	0	0.0	93	36.8	76	30.0	84	33.2	0	0.0	253		69

GPA & LSAT Scores

	Full Time	Part Time	Total
# of apps	409	0	409
# admits	227	0	227
# of matrics	92	0	92
75% GPA	3.50	0.00	
25% GPA	2.93	0.00	
75% LSAT	159	0	
25% LSAT	152	0	

Tuition & Fees

	Resident	Non-resident
Full-Time	$6,501	$11,872
Part-Time	$0	$0

Living Expenses

Estimated living expenses for Singles		
Living on campus	Living off campus	Living at home
$7,350	$7,350	$5,250

Grants/Scholarships

	Full-time		Part-time		Total	
	#	%	#	%	#	%
Total # of Students	253		0		253	
Total # receiving grants	106	41.9	0	0.0	106	41.9
Less than 1/2 tuition	100	39.5	0	0.0	100	39.5
Half to full tuition	6	2.4	0	0.0	6	2.4
Full tuition	0	0.0	0	0.0	0	0.0
More than full tuition	0	0.0	0	0.0	0	0.0
Median Grant Amount	$1,192		$0			

Informational & Library Resources

# of volumes & volume equivalents	104,419	# of professional staff	3
# of titles	18,979	Hours per week with professional staff	40
# of active serial subscriptions	1,795	Hours per week without professional staff	53
Study seating capacity inside the library	212	# of student computer work stations for entire law school	53
Square feet of law library	18,716	# of additional networked connections	24
Square feet of law school (excl. Library)	40,034	Require Laptop Computer?	N

Employment

	Total	%
Employment status known	74	98.7
Employment status unknown	1	1.3
Employed	67	90.5
Pursuing graduate degrees	3	4.1
Unemployed seeking employment	4	5.4
Unemployed not seeking employment	0	0.0
Type of Employment		
# employed in law firms	30	44.8
# employed in business & industry	4	6.0
# employed in government	10	14.9
# employed in public interest	2	3.0
# employed as judicial clerks	20	29.9
# employed in academia	0	0.0
Geographic Location		
# employed in state	48	71.6
# employed in foreign countries	0	0.0
# of states where employed	12	

J.D. Attrition (from Prior Year)

	Academic	Other	TOTALS	
	#	#	#	%
1st Year	0	0	0	0.0%
2nd Year	3	4	7	8.8%
3rd Year	3	0	3	4.1%
4th Year	0	0	0	0.0%

Bar Passage Rates

Jurisdiction	Montana		
Exam	Sum 97	Win 98	Total
# from school taking bar for the first time	57	0	57
School's pass rate for all first-time takers	96%		96%
State's pass rate for all first-time takers	91%	90%	91%

NEBRASKA, UNIVERSITY OF

P.O. Box 830902
Lincoln, NE 68583-0902
(402)472-2161
http://www.unl.edu/lawcoll

ABA Approved Since 1923

The Basics

Type of School: Public   Term: Semester

Application deadline: 03/01

Application fee: $25

Financial Aid deadline: 05/01

Can first year start other than Fall? No

Student faculty ratio: 14.5 to 1

Does the University offer:
- housing restricted to law students? No
- graduate student housing for which law students are eligible? Yes

Faculty & Administrators

	Total		Men		Women		Minorities	
	Fall	Spr	Fall	Spr	Fall	Spr	Fall	Spr
Full-time	24	25	20	21	4	4	2	2
Other Full-Time	0	0	0	0	0	0	0	0
Deans, librarians, & others who teach > 1/2	0	0	0	0	0	0	0	0
Part-time	11	24	6	18	5	6	1	1
Total	35	49	26	39	9	10	3	3
Deans, librarians, & others who teach < 1/2	3	3	0	0	3	3	0	0

Curriculum

	Full time	Part time
Typical first-year section size	70	0
Is there typically a "small section" of the first year class, other than Legal Writing, taught by full-time faculty?	No	No
If yes, typical size offered last year	N/A	N/A
# of classroom course titles beyond 1st year curriculum	65	0
# of upper division courses, excluding seminars, with an enrollment:		
Under 25	49	0
25 - 49	21	0
50 - 74	4	0
75 - 99	4	0
100 +	2	0
# of seminars	10	0
# of seminar positions available	122	
# of seminar positions filled	107	0
# of positions available in simulation courses	406	
# of simulation positions filled	344	0
# of positions available in faculty supervised clinical courses	88	
# of fac. sup. clin. positions filled	56	0
# involved in field placements	0	0
# involved in law journals	20	0
# in moot court or trial competitions	40	0
# of credit hrs required to graduate	96	

J.D. Enrollment & Ethnicity

	Men		Women		Fl-Time		Pt-Time		1st Yr		2nd Yr		3rd Yr		4th Yr		Total		JD Degrees Awarded
	#	%	#	%	#	%	#	%	#	%	#	%	#	%	#	%	#	%	
African-American	6	2.6	5	3.1	11	2.8	0	0.0	6	4.0	1	0.8	4	3.3	0	0.0	11	2.8	0
American Indian	1	0.4	0	0.0	1	0.3	0	0.0	0	0.0	1	0.8	0	0.0	0	0.0	1	0.3	4
Asian American	4	1.7	6	3.7	10	2.6	0	0.0	3	2.0	3	2.4	4	3.3	0	0.0	10	2.5	2
Mexican American	1	0.4	3	1.9	4	1.0	0	0.0	1	0.7	1	0.8	2	1.7	0	0.0	4	1.0	1
Puerto Rican	1	0.4	1	0.6	2	0.5	0	0.0	0	0.0	2	1.6	0	0.0	0	0.0	2	0.5	1
Hispanic American	0	0.0	1	0.6	1	0.3	0	0.0	0	0.0	0	0.0	1	0.8	0	0.0	1	0.3	0
Total Minorities	13	5.6	16	9.9	29	7.4	0	0.0	10	6.7	8	6.5	11	9.2	0	0.0	29	7.4	8
Foreign Nationals	3	1.3	1	0.6	4	1.0	0	0.0	1	0.7	1	0.8	2	1.7	0	0.0	4	1.0	3
Caucasian	215	93.1	145	89.5	359	91.6	1	100.0	138	92.6	115	92.7	107	89.2	0	0.0	360	91.6	99
Total	231	58.8	162	41.2	392	99.7	1	0.3	149	37.9	124	31.6	120	30.5	0	0.0	393		110

GPA & LSAT Scores

	Full Time	Part Time	Total
# of apps	568	0	568
# admits	373	0	373
# of matrics	150	0	150
75% GPA	3.73	0.00	
25% GPA	3.18	0.00	
75% LSAT	157	0	
25% LSAT	149	0	

Tuition & Fees

	Resident	Non-resident
Full-Time	$4,190	$8,908
Part-Time	$0	$0

Living Expenses

Estimated living expenses for Singles		
Living on campus	Living off campus	Living at home
$7,965	$9,435	$5,674

Grants/Scholarships

	Full-time		Part-time		Total	
	#	%	#	%	#	%
Total # of Students						
Total # receiving grants	199	50.8	0	0.0	199	50.6
Less than 1/2 tuition	99	25.3	0	0.0	99	25.2
Half to full tuition	42	10.7	0	0.0	42	10.7
Full tuition	12	3.1	0	0.0	12	3.1
More than full tuition	46	11.7	0	0.0	46	11.7
Median Grant Amount	$2,696		$0			

Informational & Library Resources

# of volumes & volume equivalents	349,418	# of professional staff	7
# of titles	51,127	Hours per week with professional staff	65
# of active serial subscriptions	2,997	Hours per week without professional staff	44
Study seating capacity inside the library	339	# of student computer work stations for entire law school	54
Square feet of law library	30,872	# of additional networked connections	0
Square feet of law school (excl. Library)	56,500	Require Laptop Computer?	N

Employment

	Total	%
Employment status known	129	99.2
Employment status unknown	1	0.8
Employed	111	86.0
Pursuing graduate degrees	7	5.4
Unemployed seeking employment	7	5.4
Unemployed not seeking employment	4	3.1
Type of Employment		
# employed in law firms	52	46.8
# employed in business & industry	25	22.5
# employed in government	28	25.2
# employed in public interest	10	9.0
# employed as judicial clerks	10	9.0
# employed in academia	0	0.0
Geographic Location		
# employed in state	69	62.2
# employed in foreign countries	0	0.0
# of states where employed	1	

J.D. Attrition (from Prior Year)

	Academic	Other	TOTALS	
	#	#	#	%
1st Year	9	7	16	11%
2nd Year	0	2	2	1.6%
3rd Year	0	0	0	0.0%
4th Year	0	0	0	0.0%

Bar Passage Rates

Jurisdiction	Nebraska		
Exam	Sum 97	Win 98	Total
# from school taking bar for the first time	71	6	77
School's pass rate for all first-time takers	89%	100%	90%
State's pass rate for all first-time takers	88%	73%	87%

NEW ENGLAND SCHOOL OF LAW

154 Stuart Street
Boston, MA 02116
(617)451-0010
http://www.nesl.edu

ABA Approved Since 1969

The Basics

Type of School: Private
Term: Semester
Application deadline: 06/01
Application fee: $50
Financial Aid deadline: 04/15
Can first year start other than Fall? No
Student faculty ratio: 20.5 to 1
Does the University offer:
- housing restricted to law students? No
- graduate student housing for which law students are eligible? No

Faculty & Administrators

	Total		Men		Women		Minorities	
	Fall	Spr	Fall	Spr	Fall	Spr	Fall	Spr
Full-time	33	30	24	23	9	7	2	2
Other Full-Time	0	0	0	0	0	0	0	0
Deans, librarians, & others who teach > 1/2	0	0	0	0	0	0	0	0
Part-time	49	61	31	41	18	20	1	2
Total	82	91	55	64	27	27	3	4
Deans, librarians, & others who teach < 1/2	3	3	3	3	0	0	1	1

Curriculum

	Full time	Part time
Typical first-year section size	120	110
Is there typically a "small section" of the first year class, other than Legal Writing, taught by full-time faculty?	No	No
If yes, typical size offered last year	N/A	N/A
# of classroom course titles beyond 1st year curriculum	82	72
# of upper division courses, excluding seminars, with an enrollment:		
Under 25	18	27
25 - 49	23	17
50 - 74	13	8
75 - 99	7	4
100 +	0	0
# of seminars	18	14
# of seminar positions available	672	
# of seminar positions filled	207	107
# of positions available in simulation courses	440	
# of simulation positions filled	174	99
# of positions available in faculty supervised clinical courses	66	
# of fac. sup. clin. positions filled	34	16
# involved in field placements	185	14
# involved in law journals	84	23
# in moot court or trial competitions	13	4
# of credit hrs required to graduate	84	

J.D. Enrollment & Ethnicity

	Men		Women		Fl-Time		Pt-Time		1st Yr		2nd Yr		3rd Yr		4th Yr		Total		JD Degrees Awarded
	#	%	#	%	#	%	#	%	#	%	#	%	#	%	#	%	#	%	
African-American	28	6.0	28	5.9	43	7.5	13	3.6	24	6.9	15	6.3	14	5.7	3	2.8	56	6.0	14
American Indian	4	0.9	5	1.1	1	0.2	8	2.2	2	0.6	2	0.8	3	1.2	2	1.9	9	1.0	2
Asian American	17	3.6	31	6.6	44	7.7	4	1.1	17	4.9	15	6.3	14	5.7	2	1.9	48	5.1	10
Mexican American	4	0.9	5	1.1	7	1.2	2	0.5	4	1.1	2	0.8	1	0.4	2	1.9	9	1.0	1
Puerto Rican	3	0.6	5	1.1	5	0.9	3	0.8	5	1.4	2	0.8	1	0.4	0	0.0	8	0.9	1
Hispanic American	15	3.2	18	3.8	30	5.2	3	0.8	11	3.2	13	5.4	8	3.3	1	0.9	33	3.5	11
Total Minorities	71	15.2	92	19.5	130	22.7	33	9.1	63	18.1	49	20.5	41	16.8	10	9.4	163	17.4	39
Foreign Nationals	6	1.3	6	1.3	8	1.4	4	1.1	5	1.4	3	1.3	4	1.6	0	0.0	12	1.3	4
Caucasian	389	83.5	373	79.2	435	75.9	327	89.8	280	80.5	187	78.2	199	81.6	96	90.6	762	81.3	259
Total	466	49.7	471	50.3	573	61.2	364	38.8	348	37.1	239	25.5	244	26.0	106	11.3	937		302

GPA & LSAT Scores

	Full Time	Part Time	Total
# of apps	1,562	339	1,901
# admits	1,210	247	1,457
# of matrics	241	109	350
75% GPA	3.25	3.26	
25% GPA	2.69	2.66	
75% LSAT	151	153	
25% LSAT	142	143	

Tuition & Fees

	Resident	Non-resident
Full-Time	$15,100	$15,100
Part-Time	$11,360	$11,360

Living Expenses

Estimated living expenses for Singles		
Living on campus	Living off campus	Living at home
N/A	$13,450	$9,290

Employment

	Total	%
Employment status known	269	90.9
Employment status unknown	27	9.1
Employed	240	89.2
Pursuing graduate degrees	7	2.6
Unemployed seeking employment	18	6.7
Unemployed not seeking employment	4	1.5
Type of Employment		
# employed in law firms	98	40.8
# employed in business & industry	69	28.7
# employed in government	39	16.2
# employed in public interest	2	0.8
# employed as judicial clerks	20	8.3
# employed in academia	3	1.2
Geographic Location		
# employed in state	190	79.2
# employed in foreign countries	0	0.0
# of states where employed	20	

Grants/Scholarships

	Full-time		Part-time		Total	
	#	%	#	%	#	%
Total # of Students	573		364		937	
Total # receiving grants	323	56.4	86	23.6	409	43.6
Less than 1/2 tuition	261	45.5	48	13.2	309	33.0
Half to full tuition	18	3.1	15	4.1	33	3.5
Full tuition	44	7.7	23	6.3	67	7.2
More than full tuition	0	0.0	0	0.0	0	0.0
Median Grant Amount	$3,590		$5,268			

Informational & Library Resources

# of volumes & volume equivalents	288,412	# of professional staff	9
# of titles	42,488	Hours per week with professional staff	78
# of active serial subscriptions	3,080	Hours per week without professional staff	23
Study seating capacity inside the library	398	# of student computer work stations for entire law school	79
Square feet of law library	28,087	# of additional networked connections	0
Square feet of law school (excl. Library)	45,264	Require Laptop Computer?	N

J.D. Attrition (from Prior Year)

	Academic	Other	TOTALS	
	#	#	#	%
1st Year	12	10	22	7.5%
2nd Year	0	26	26	11%
3rd Year	0	6	6	2.0%
4th Year	0	1	1	0.9%

Bar Passage Rates

Jurisdiction	Massachusetts		
Exam	Sum 97	Win 98	Total
# from school taking bar for the first time	224	26	250
School's pass rate for all first-time takers	83%	54%	80%
State's pass rate for all first-time takers	84%	72%	82%

NEW MEXICO, UNIVERSITY OF

1117 Stanford, N.E.
Albuquerque, NM 87131-1431
(505)277-2146
http://lawschool.unm.edu/law.htm

ABA Approved Since 1948

The Basics

Type of School: Public — Term: Semester

Application deadline: 02/16

Application fee: $40

Financial Aid deadline: 03/01

Can first year start other than Fall? No

Student faculty ratio: 10.7 to 1

Does the University offer:
- housing restricted to law students? No
- graduate student housing for which law students are eligible? No

Faculty & Administrators

	Total		Men		Women		Minorities	
	Fall	Spr	Fall	Spr	Fall	Spr	Fall	Spr
Full-time	26	27	14	14	12	13	7	6
Other Full-Time	2	2	0	0	2	2	1	1
Deans, librarians, & others who teach > 1/2	4	4	3	3	1	1	2	2
Part-time	19	15	7	6	12	9	4	2
Total	51	48	24	23	27	25	14	11
Deans, librarians, & others who teach < 1/2	1	1	1	1	0	0	0	0

Curriculum

	Full time	Part time
Typical first-year section size	57	0
Is there typically a "small section" of the first year class, other than Legal Writing, taught by full-time faculty?	Yes	No
If yes, typical size offered last year	28	N/A
# of classroom course titles beyond 1st year curriculum	86	0
# of upper division courses, excluding seminars, with an enrollment:		
Under 25	35	0
25 - 49	15	0
50 - 74	6	0
75 - 99	2	0
100 +	0	0
# of seminars	26	0
# of seminar positions available	367	
# of seminar positions filled	224	0
# of positions available in simulation courses	108	
# of simulation positions filled	96	0
# of positions available in faculty supervised clinical courses	83	
# of fac. sup. clin. positions filled	75	0
# involved in field placements	42	0
# involved in law journals	89	0
# in moot court or trial competitions	28	0
# of credit hrs required to graduate	86	

J.D. Enrollment & Ethnicity

	Men		Women		Fl-Time		Pt-Time		1st Yr		2nd Yr		3rd Yr		4th Yr		Total		JD Degrees Awarded
	#	%	#	%	#	%	#	%	#	%	#	%	#	%	#	%	#	%	
African-American	2	1.3	6	3.4	8	2.4	0	0.0	3	2.7	3	2.7	2	1.8	0	0.0	8	2.4	4
American Indian	6	3.8	14	7.9	20	6.0	0	0.0	6	5.3	9	8.1	5	4.5	0	0.0	20	6.0	10
Asian American	2	1.3	7	3.9	9	2.7	0	0.0	4	3.5	1	0.9	4	3.6	0	0.0	9	2.7	4
Mexican American	49	31.2	40	22.5	89	26.6	0	0.0	29	25.7	33	29.7	27	24.3	0	0.0	89	26.6	32
Puerto Rican	0	0.0	0	0.0	0	0.0	0	0.0	0	0.0	0	0.0	0	0.0	0	0.0	0	0.0	0
Hispanic American	0	0.0	0	0.0	0	0.0	0	0.0	0	0.0	0	0.0	0	0.0	0	0.0	0	0.0	0
Total Minorities	59	37.6	67	37.6	126	37.7	0	0.0	42	37.2	46	41.4	38	34.2	0	0.0	126	37.6	50
Foreign Nationals	0	0.0	0	0.0	0	0.0	0	0.0	0	0.0	0	0.0	0	0.0	0	0.0	0	0.0	0
Caucasian	98	62.4	111	62.4	208	62.3	1	100.0	71	62.8	65	58.6	73	65.8	0	0.0	209	62.4	59
Total	157	46.9	178	53.1	334	99.7	1	0.3	113	33.7	111	33.1	111	33.1	0	0.0	335		109

GPA & LSAT Scores

	Full Time	Part Time	Total
# of apps	791	0	791
# admits	267	0	267
# of matrics	114	0	114
75% GPA	3.44	0.00	
25% GPA	2.86	0.00	
75% LSAT	158	0	
25% LSAT	150	0	

Tuition & Fees

	Resident	Non-resident
Full-Time	$3,984	$13,338
Part-Time	$0	$0

Living Expenses

Estimated living expenses for Singles		
Living on campus	Living off campus	Living at home
$9,209	$10,682	$6,448

Grants/Scholarships

	Full-time		Part-time		Total	
	#	%	#	%	#	%
Total # of Students	334		1		335	
Total # receiving grants	42	12.6	0	0.0	42	12.5
Less than 1/2 tuition	6	1.8	0	0.0	6	1.8
Half to full tuition	11	3.3	0	0.0	11	3.3
Full tuition	16	4.8	0	0.0	16	4.8
More than full tuition	9	2.7	0	0.0	9	2.7
Median Grant Amount	$3,984		$0			

Informational & Library Resources

# of volumes & volume equivalents	364,270	# of professional staff	4
# of titles	82,875	Hours per week with professional staff	62
# of active serial subscriptions	3,208	Hours per week without professional staff	41
Study seating capacity inside the library	329	# of student computer work stations for entire law school	77
Square feet of law library	32,443	# of additional networked connections	98
Square feet of law school (excl. Library)	36,005	Require Laptop Computer?	N

Employment

	Total	%
Employment status known	103	100.0
Employment status unknown	0	0.0
Employed	93	90.3
Pursuing graduate degrees	2	1.9
Unemployed seeking employment	7	6.8
Unemployed not seeking employment	1	1.0
Type of Employment		
# employed in law firms	42	45.2
# employed in business & industry	15	16.1
# employed in government	25	26.9
# employed in public interest	3	3.2
# employed as judicial clerks	8	8.6
# employed in academia	0	0.0
Geographic Location		
# employed in state	70	75.3
# employed in foreign countries	0	0.0
# of states where employed	18	

J.D. Attrition (from Prior Year)

	Academic	Other	TOTALS	
	#	#	#	%
1st Year	3	5	8	7.0%
2nd Year	3	4	7	6.3%
3rd Year	0	0	0	0.0%
4th Year	0	0	0	0.0%

Bar Passage Rates

Jurisdiction	New Mexico		
Exam	Sum 97	Win 98	Total
# from school taking bar for the first time	68	10	78
School's pass rate for all first-time takers	94%	80%	92%
State's pass rate for all first-time takers	94%	92%	93%

NEW YORK LAW SCHOOL

57 Worth Street
New York, NY 10013-2960
(212)431-2100
http://www.nyls.edu

ABA Approved Since 1954

The Basics

Type of School: Private Term: Semester
Application deadline: 04/01
Application fee: $50
Financial Aid deadline: 04/15
Can first year start other than Fall? No
Student faculty ratio: 23.0 to 1
Does the University offer:
- housing restricted to law students? No
- graduate student housing for which law students are eligible? Yes

Faculty & Administrators

	Total		Men		Women		Minorities	
	Fall	Spr	Fall	Spr	Fall	Spr	Fall	Spr
Full-time	45	41	32	29	13	12	6	5
Other Full-Time	0	0	0	0	0	0	0	0
Deans, librarians, & others who teach > 1/2	0	0	0	0	0	0	0	0
Part-time	70	70	47	48	23	22	2	5
Total	115	111	79	77	36	34	8	10
Deans, librarians, & others who teach < 1/2	5	5	2	2	3	3	0	0

Curriculum

	Full time	Part time
Typical first-year section size	110	118
Is there typically a "small section" of the first year class, other than Legal Writing, taught by full-time faculty?	Yes	Yes
If yes, typical size offered last year	37	40
# of classroom course titles beyond 1st year curriculum	98	72
# of upper division courses, excluding seminars, with an enrollment:		
Under 25	25	24
25 - 49	24	15
50 - 74	9	12
75 - 99	11	8
100 +	6	5
# of seminars	49	19
# of seminar positions available	1,115	
# of seminar positions filled	518	219
# of positions available in simulation courses	264	
# of simulation positions filled	16	220
# of positions available in faculty supervised clinical courses	50	
# of fac. sup. clin. positions filled	47	0
# involved in field placements	174	42
# involved in law journals	119	40
# in moot court or trial competitions	51	7
# of credit hrs required to graduate	86	

J.D. Enrollment & Ethnicity

	Men		Women		Fl-Time		Pt-Time		1st Yr		2nd Yr		3rd Yr		4th Yr		Total		JD Degrees Awarded
	#	%	#	%	#	%	#	%	#	%	#	%	#	%	#	%	#	%	
African-American	57	7.6	70	10.6	57	6.2	70	14.5	54	10.6	34	7.9	27	7.8	12	10.1	127	9.0	30
American Indian	1	0.1	4	0.6	4	0.4	1	0.2	2	0.4	1	0.2	1	0.3	1	0.8	5	0.4	1
Asian American	44	5.9	53	8.1	70	7.6	27	5.6	48	9.4	28	6.5	16	4.7	5	4.2	97	6.9	27
Mexican American	4	0.5	2	0.3	6	0.7	0	0.0	3	0.6	0	0.0	3	0.9	0	0.0	6	0.4	0
Puerto Rican	7	0.9	10	1.5	8	0.9	9	1.9	2	0.4	6	1.4	6	1.7	3	2.5	17	1.2	0
Hispanic American	44	5.9	42	6.4	61	6.6	25	5.2	37	7.3	25	5.8	19	5.5	5	4.2	86	6.1	22
Total Minorities	157	21.0	181	27.5	206	22.4	132	27.3	146	28.7	94	21.7	72	20.9	26	21.8	338	24.1	80
Foreign Nationals	6	0.8	6	0.9	12	1.3	0	0.0	3	0.6	7	1.6	2	0.6	0	0.0	12	0.9	6
Caucasian	584	78.2	471	71.6	703	76.3	352	72.7	360	70.7	332	76.7	270	78.5	93	78.2	1055	75.1	317
Total	747	53.2	658	46.8	921	65.6	484	34.4	509	36.2	433	30.8	344	24.5	119	8.5	1405		403

GPA & LSAT Scores

	Full Time	Part Time	Total
# of apps	3,313	927	4,240
# admits	1,739	376	2,115
# of matrics	360	143	503
75% GPA	3.27	3.24	
25% GPA	2.77	2.78	
75% LSAT	154	154	
25% LSAT	148	147	

Tuition & Fees

	Resident	Non-resident
Full-Time	$22,114	$22,114
Part-Time	$16,588	$16,588

Living Expenses

Estimated living expenses for Singles		
Living on campus	Living off campus	Living at home
$10,745	$10,745	$5,300

Grants/Scholarships

	Full-time		Part-time		Total	
	#	%	#	%	#	%
Total # of Students	921		484		1405	
Total # receiving grants	361	39.2	101	20.9	462	32.9
Less than 1/2 tuition	320	34.7	73	15.1	393	28.0
Half to full tuition	39	4.2	28	5.8	67	4.8
Full tuition	2	0.2	0	0.0	2	0.1
More than full tuition	0	0.0	0	0.0	0	0.0
Median Grant Amount	$7,143		$7,492			

Informational & Library Resources

# of volumes & volume equivalents	451,199	# of professional staff	13
# of titles	135,900	Hours per week with professional staff	79
# of active serial subscriptions	5,084	Hours per week without professional staff	19
Study seating capacity inside the library	616	# of student computer work stations for entire law school	115
Square feet of law library	48,464	# of additional networked connections	70
Square feet of law school (excl. Library)	101,036	Require Laptop Computer?	N

Employment

	Total	%
Employment status known	374	87.0
Employment status unknown	56	13.0
Employed	343	91.7
Pursuing graduate degrees	4	1.1
Unemployed seeking employment	16	4.3
Unemployed not seeking employment	11	2.9
Type of Employment		
# employed in law firms	181	52.8
# employed in business & industry	76	22.2
# employed in government	50	14.6
# employed in public interest	10	2.9
# employed as judicial clerks	16	4.7
# employed in academia	3	0.9
Geographic Location		
# employed in state	242	70.6
# employed in foreign countries	1	0.3
# of states where employed	15	

J.D. Attrition (from Prior Year)

	Academic	Other	TOTALS	
	#	#	#	%
1st Year	26	35	61	13%
2nd Year	3	5	8	2.0%
3rd Year	1	3	4	1.0%
4th Year	0	2	2	1.7%

Bar Passage Rates

Jurisdiction	New York		
Exam	Sum 97	Win 98	Total
# from school taking bar for the first time	343	42	385
School's pass rate for all first-time takers	67%	60%	66%
State's pass rate for all first-time takers	78%	65%	76%

NEW YORK UNIVERSITY

40 Washington Square South
New York, NY 10012
(212)998-6100
http://www.law.nyu.edu

ABA Approved Since 1930

The Basics

Type of School: Private   Term: Semester

Application deadline: 02/01

Application fee: $65

Financial Aid deadline: 04/01

Can first year start other than Fall? No

Student faculty ratio: 14.1 to 1

Does the University offer:
- housing restricted to law students? No
- graduate student housing for which law students are eligible? Yes

Faculty & Administrators

	Total		Men		Women		Minorities	
	Fall	Spr	Fall	Spr	Fall	Spr	Fall	Spr
Full-time	80	75	58	53	22	22	9	7
Other Full-Time	19	21	4	5	15	16	4	5
Deans, librarians, & others who teach > 1/2	4	4	4	4	0	0	0	0
Part-time	59	61	49	43	10	18	5	2
Total	162	161	115	105	47	56	18	14
Deans, librarians, & others who teach < 1/2	0	0	0	0	0	0	0	0

Curriculum

	Full time	Part time
Typical first-year section size	110	0
Is there typically a "small section" of the first year class, other than Legal Writing, taught by full-time faculty?	No	No
If yes, typical size offered last year	N/A	N/A
# of classroom course titles beyond 1st year curriculum	0	0
# of upper division courses, excluding seminars, with an enrollment:		
Under 25	27	0
25 - 49	59	0
50 - 74	34	0
75 - 99	22	0
100 +	26	0
# of seminars	168	0
# of seminar positions available	2,775	
# of seminar positions filled	2,034	0
# of positions available in simulation courses	214	
# of simulation positions filled	204	0
# of positions available in faculty supervised clinical courses	110	
# of fac. sup. clin. positions filled	110	0
# involved in field placements	325	0
# involved in law journals	453	0
# in moot court or trial competitions	161	0
# of credit hrs required to graduate	82	

J.D. Enrollment & Ethnicity

	Men		Women		Fl-Time		Pt-Time		1st Yr		2nd Yr		3rd Yr		4th Yr		Total		JD Degrees Awarded
	#	%	#	%	#	%	#	%	#	%	#	%	#	%	#	%	#	%	
African-American	34	4.7	50	8.0	84	6.2	0	0.0	35	7.9	18	4.1	31	6.5	0	0.0	84	6.2	21
American Indian	0	0.0	0	0.0	0	0.0	0	0.0	0	0.0	0	0.0	0	0.0	0	0.0	0	0.0	1
Asian American	50	6.9	81	12.9	131	9.7	0	0.0	46	10.4	40	9.2	45	9.5	0	0.0	131	9.7	49
Mexican American	5	0.7	4	0.6	9	0.7	0	0.0	6	1.4	1	0.2	2	0.4	0	0.0	9	0.7	5
Puerto Rican	7	1.0	11	1.8	18	1.3	0	0.0	5	1.1	9	2.1	4	0.8	0	0.0	18	1.3	4
Hispanic American	32	4.4	24	3.8	56	4.1	0	0.0	29	6.5	12	2.8	15	3.2	0	0.0	56	4.1	13
Total Minorities	128	17.6	170	27.1	298	22.0	0	0.0	121	27.3	80	18.4	97	20.4	0	0.0	298	22.0	93
Foreign Nationals	33	4.5	22	3.5	55	4.1	0	0.0	18	4.1	17	3.9	20	4.2	0	0.0	55	4.1	17
Caucasian	567	77.9	435	69.4	1002	73.9	0	0.0	305	68.7	338	77.7	359	75.4	0	0.0	1002	73.9	347
Total	728	53.7	627	46.3	1355	100.0	0	0.0	444	32.8	435	32.1	476	35.1	0	0.0	1355		457

GPA & LSAT Scores

	Full Time	Part Time	Total
# of apps	6,374	0	6,374
# admits	1,555	0	1,555
# of matrics	448	0	448
75% GPA	3.81	0.00	
25% GPA	3.56	0.00	
75% LSAT	171	0	
25% LSAT	166	0	

Tuition & Fees

	Resident	Non-resident
Full-Time	$27,055	$27,055
Part-Time	$0	$0

Living Expenses

Estimated living expenses for Singles		
Living on campus	Living off campus	Living at home
$17,040	$17,040	$8,445

Grants/Scholarships

	Full-time		Part-time		Total	
	#	%	#	%	#	%
Total # of Students	1355		0		1355	
Total # receiving grants	437	32.3	0	0.0	437	32.3
Less than 1/2 tuition	229	16.9	0	0.0	229	16.9
Half to full tuition	152	11.2	0	0.0	152	11.2
Full tuition	56	4.1	0	0.0	56	4.1
More than full tuition	0	0.0	0	0.0	0	0.0
Median Grant Amount	$10,000		$0			

Informational & Library Resources

# of volumes & volume equivalents	975,696	# of professional staff	13
# of titles	165,460	Hours per week with professional staff	65
# of active serial subscriptions	6,385	Hours per week without professional staff	36
Study seating capacity inside the library	897	# of student computer work stations for entire law school	225
Square feet of law library	82,000	# of additional networked connections	1000
Square feet of law school (excl. Library)	197,100	Require Laptop Computer?	N

Employment

	Total	%
Employment status known	432	100.0
Employment status unknown	0	0.0
Employed	425	98.4
Pursuing graduate degrees	6	1.4
Unemployed seeking employment	1	0.2
Unemployed not seeking employment	0	0.0
Type of Employment		
# employed in law firms	327	76.9
# employed in business & industry	15	3.5
# employed in government	12	2.8
# employed in public interest	14	3.3
# employed as judicial clerks	57	13.4
# employed in academia	0	0.0
Geographic Location		
# employed in state	273	64.2
# employed in foreign countries	0	0.0
# of states where employed	28	

J.D. Attrition (from Prior Year)

	Academic	Other	TOTALS	
	#	#	#	%
1st Year	0	8	8	2.1%
2nd Year	0	5	5	1.1%
3rd Year	0	0	0	0.0%
4th Year	0	0	0	0.0%

Bar Passage Rates

Jurisdiction	New York		
Exam	Sum 97	Win 98	Total
# from school taking bar for the first time	328	15	343
School's pass rate for all first-time takers	96%	100%	96%
State's pass rate for all first-time takers	78%	65%	76%

NORTH CAROLINA CENTRAL UNIVERSITY

1512 South Alston Avenue
Durham, NC 27707
(919)560-6333
http://www.nccu.edu/law

ABA Approved Since 1950

The Basics

Type of School: Public Term: Semester
Application deadline: 04/15
Application fee: $30
Financial Aid deadline: 02/01
Can first year start other than Fall? No
Student faculty ratio: 25.7 to 1
Does the University offer:
- housing restricted to law students? No
- graduate student housing for which law students are eligible? Yes

Faculty & Administrators

	Total		Men		Women		Minorities	
	Fall	Spr	Fall	Spr	Fall	Spr	Fall	Spr
Full-time	11	12	6	6	5	6	6	6
Other Full-Time	0	0	0	0	0	0	0	0
Deans, librarians, & others who teach > 1/2	2	2	0	0	2	2	1	1
Part-time	12	8	8	6	3	1	2	1
Total	25	22	14	12	10	9	9	8
Deans, librarians, & others who teach < 1/2	5	5	0	0	5	5	4	4

Curriculum

	Full time	Part time
Typical first-year section size	50	30
Is there typically a "small section" of the first year class, other than Legal Writing, taught by full-time faculty?	No	No
If yes, typical size offered last year	N/A	N/A
# of classroom course titles beyond 1st year curriculum	38	13
# of upper division courses, excluding seminars, with an enrollment:		
Under 25	36	5
25 - 49	8	6
50 - 74	4	3
75 - 99	6	1
100 +	1	0
# of seminars	7	2
# of seminar positions available	225	
# of seminar positions filled	132	26
# of positions available in simulation courses	999	
# of simulation positions filled	217	44
# of positions available in faculty supervised clinical courses	999	
# of fac. sup. clin. positions filled	70	0
# involved in field placements	18	0
# involved in law journals	31	7
# in moot court or trial competitions	44	0
# of credit hrs required to graduate	88	

J.D. Enrollment & Ethnicity

	Men		Women		Fl-Time		Pt-Time		1st Yr		2nd Yr		3rd Yr		4th Yr		Total		JD Degrees Awarded
	#	%	#	%	#	%	#	%	#	%	#	%	#	%	#	%	#	%	
African-American	58	34.7	113	53.8	141	53.2	30	26.8	59	50.4	51	44.3	55	45.8	6	24.0	171	45.4	48
American Indian	2	1.2	1	0.5	3	1.1	0	0.0	1	0.9	1	0.9	1	0.8	0	0.0	3	0.8	0
Asian American	3	1.8	7	3.3	8	3.0	2	1.8	5	4.3	1	0.9	4	3.3	0	0.0	10	2.7	0
Mexican American	0	0.0	0	0.0	0	0.0	0	0.0	0	0.0	0	0.0	0	0.0	0	0.0	0	0.0	0
Puerto Rican	0	0.0	1	0.5	1	0.4	0	0.0	0	0.0	0	0.0	1	0.8	0	0.0	1	0.3	0
Hispanic American	1	0.6	3	1.4	3	1.1	1	0.9	0	0.0	2	1.7	2	1.7	0	0.0	4	1.1	0
Total Minorities	64	38.3	125	59.5	156	58.9	33	29.5	65	55.6	55	47.8	63	52.5	6	24.0	189	50.1	48
Foreign Nationals	1	0.6	2	1.0	3	1.1	0	0.0	1	0.9	0	0.0	2	1.7	0	0.0	3	0.8	1
Caucasian	102	61.1	83	39.5	106	40.0	79	70.5	51	43.6	60	52.2	55	45.8	19	76.0	185	49.1	46
Total	167	44.3	210	55.7	265	70.3	112	29.7	117	31.0	115	30.5	120	31.8	25	6.6	377		95

NORTH CAROLINA CENTRAL UNIVERSITY

GPA & LSAT Scores

	Full Time	Part Time	Total
# of apps	896	192	1,088
# admits	211	31	242
# of matrics	96	23	119
75% GPA	3.20	3.30	
25% GPA	2.70	2.80	
75% LSAT	152	161	
25% LSAT	143	152	

Tuition & Fees

	Resident	Non-resident
Full-Time	$2,163	$11,089
Part-Time	$2,163	$11,089

Living Expenses

Estimated living expenses for Singles		
Living on campus	Living off campus	Living at home
$6,365	$9,950	$1,250

Employment

	Total	%
Employment status known	73	84.9
Employment status unknown	13	15.1
Employed	67	91.8
Pursuing graduate degrees	4	5.5
Unemployed seeking employment	0	0.0
Unemployed not seeking employment	2	2.7
Type of Employment		
# employed in law firms	31	46.3
# employed in business & industry	13	19.4
# employed in government	16	23.9
# employed in public interest	6	9.0
# employed as judicial clerks	0	0.0
# employed in academia	1	1.5
Geographic Location		
# employed in state	54	80.6
# employed in foreign countries	0	0.0
# of states where employed	8	

Grants/Scholarships

	Full-time		Part-time		Total	
	#	%	#	%	#	%
Total # of Students	265		112		377	
Total # receiving grants	77	29.1	0	0.0	77	20.4
Less than 1/2 tuition	57	21.5	0	0.0	57	15.1
Half to full tuition	3	1.1	0	0.0	3	0.8
Full tuition	0	0.0	0	0.0	0	0.0
More than full tuition	17	6.4	0	0.0	17	4.5
Median Grant Amount	$1,790		$0			

Informational & Library Resources

# of volumes & volume equivalents	292,173	# of professional staff	7
# of titles	57,915	Hours per week with professional staff	59
# of active serial subscriptions	3,656	Hours per week without professional staff	41
Study seating capacity inside the library	287	# of student computer work stations for entire law school	46
Square feet of law library	28,674	# of additional networked connections	28
Square feet of law school (excl. Library)	47,660	Require Laptop Computer?	N

J.D. Attrition (from Prior Year)

	Academic	Other	TOTALS	
	#	#	#	%
1st Year	6	2	8	6.1%
2nd Year	0	6	6	5.1%
3rd Year	1	0	1	1.0%
4th Year	0	0	0	0.0%

Bar Passage Rates

Jurisdiction	North Carolina		
Exam	Sum 97	Win 98	Total
# from school taking bar for the first time	68	3	71
School's pass rate for all first-time takers	82%	67%	82%
State's pass rate for all first-time takers	85%	73%	82%

NORTH CAROLINA, UNIVERSITY OF

Campus Box 3380
Van Hecke-Wettach Hall
Chapel Hill, NC 27599-3380
(919)962-5106
http://www.law.unc.edu

ABA Approved Since 1923

The Basics

Type of School: Public   Term: Semester
Application deadline: 02/01
Application fee: $60
Financial Aid deadline: 03/01
Can first year start other than Fall? No
Student faculty ratio: 16.8 to 1
Does the University offer:
- housing restricted to law students? No
- graduate student housing for which law students are eligible? Yes

Faculty & Administrators

	Total		Men		Women		Minorities	
	Fall	Spr	Fall	Spr	Fall	Spr	Fall	Spr
Full-time	35	33	21	19	14	14	3	3
Other Full-Time	2	2	1	1	1	1	0	0
Deans, librarians, & others who teach > 1/2	4	3	2	1	2	2	0	0
Part-time	15	27	9	18	6	9	2	1
Total	56	65	33	39	23	26	5	4
Deans, librarians, & others who teach < 1/2	1	1	0	0	1	1	0	0

Curriculum

	Full time	Part time
Typical first-year section size	77	0
Is there typically a "small section" of the first year class, other than Legal Writing, taught by full-time faculty?	Yes	No
If yes, typical size offered last year	26	N/A
# of classroom course titles beyond 1st year curriculum	81	0
# of upper division courses, excluding seminars, with an enrollment:		
Under 25	45	0
25 - 49	33	0
50 - 74	9	0
75 - 99	10	0
100 +	3	0
# of seminars	19	0
# of seminar positions available	276	
# of seminar positions filled	265	0
# of positions available in simulation courses	533	
# of simulation positions filled	471	0
# of positions available in faculty supervised clinical courses	60	
# of fac. sup. clin. positions filled	57	0
# involved in field placements	0	0
# involved in law journals	140	0
# in moot court or trial competitions	48	0
# of credit hrs required to graduate	86	

J.D. Enrollment & Ethnicity

	Men		Women		Fl-Time		Pt-Time		1st Yr		2nd Yr		3rd Yr		4th Yr		Total		JD Degrees Awarded
	#	%	#	%	#	%	#	%	#	%	#	%	#	%	#	%	#	%	
African-American	25	7.3	66	18.9	91	13.2	0	0.0	28	12.3	25	11.0	38	16.2	0	0.0	91	13.2	25
American Indian	1	0.3	3	0.9	4	0.6	0	0.0	0	0.0	1	0.4	3	1.3	0	0.0	4	0.6	5
Asian American	7	2.1	23	6.6	30	4.3	0	0.0	7	3.1	15	6.6	8	3.4	0	0.0	30	4.3	12
Mexican American	0	0.0	0	0.0	0	0.0	0	0.0	0	0.0	0	0.0	0	0.0	0	0.0	0	0.0	0
Puerto Rican	0	0.0	0	0.0	0	0.0	0	0.0	0	0.0	0	0.0	0	0.0	0	0.0	0	0.0	0
Hispanic American	6	1.8	5	1.4	11	1.6	0	0.0	3	1.3	3	1.3	5	2.1	0	0.0	11	1.6	5
Total Minorities	39	11.4	97	27.8	136	19.7	0	0.0	38	16.7	44	19.3	54	23.0	0	0.0	136	19.7	47
Foreign Nationals	3	0.9	3	0.9	6	0.9	0	0.0	1	0.4	3	1.3	2	0.9	0	0.0	6	0.9	0
Caucasian	299	87.7	249	71.3	548	79.4	0	0.0	188	82.8	181	79.4	179	76.2	0	0.0	548	79.4	168
Total	341	49.4	349	50.6	690	100.0	0	0.0	227	32.9	228	33.0	235	34.1	0	0.0	690		215

GPA & LSAT Scores

	Full Time	Part Time	Total
# of apps	2,192	0	2,192
# admits	603	0	603
# of matrics	231	0	231
75% GPA	3.81	0.00	
25% GPA	3.32	0.00	
75% LSAT	164	0	
25% LSAT	153	0	

Tuition & Fees

	Resident	Non-resident
Full-Time	$3,169	$15,269
Part-Time	$0	$0

Living Expenses

Estimated living expenses for Singles		
Living on campus	Living off campus	Living at home
$11,434	$11,434	$5,289

Grants/Scholarships

	Full-time		Part-time		Total	
	#	%	#	%	#	%
Total # of Students	690		0		690	
Total # receiving grants	125	18.1	0	0.0	125	18.1
Less than 1/2 tuition	27	3.9	0	0.0	27	3.9
Half to full tuition	46	6.7	0	0.0	46	6.7
Full tuition	0	0.0	0	0.0	0	0.0
More than full tuition	52	7.5	0	0.0	52	7.5
Median Grant Amount	$2,800		$0			

Informational & Library Resources

# of volumes & volume equivalents	456,558	# of professional staff	9
# of titles	83,811	Hours per week with professional staff	66
# of active serial subscriptions	6,102	Hours per week without professional staff	43
Study seating capacity inside the library	407	# of student computer work stations for entire law school	62
Square feet of law library	41,081	# of additional networked connections	0
Square feet of law school (excl. Library)	35,962	Require Laptop Computer?	N

Employment

	Total	%
Employment status known	219	98.6
Employment status unknown	3	1.4
Employed	211	96.3
Pursuing graduate degrees	4	1.8
Unemployed seeking employment	1	0.5
Unemployed not seeking employment	3	1.4
Type of Employment		
# employed in law firms	120	56.9
# employed in business & industry	26	12.3
# employed in government	27	12.8
# employed in public interest	6	2.8
# employed as judicial clerks	29	13.7
# employed in academia	3	1.4
Geographic Location		
# employed in state	136	64.5
# employed in foreign countries	1	0.5
# of states where employed	23	

J.D. Attrition (from Prior Year)

	Academic	Other	TOTALS	
	#	#	#	%
1st Year	0	7	7	3.0%
2nd Year	0	0	0	0.0%
3rd Year	0	0	0	0.0%
4th Year	0	0	0	0.0%

Bar Passage Rates

Jurisdiction	North Carolina			New York		
Exam	Sum 97	Win 98	Total	Sum 97	Win 98	Total
# from school taking bar for the first time	140	20	160	20	2	22
School's pass rate for all first-time takers	91%	100%	93%	100%	100%	100%
State's pass rate for all first-time takers	85%	73%	82%	78%	65%	76%

NORTH DAKOTA, UNIVERSITY OF

Centennial Drive
P.O. Box 9003
Grand Forks, ND 58202
(701)777-2104
http://www.law.und.nodak.edu

ABA Approved Since 1923

The Basics

Type of School: Public　　Term: Semester
Application deadline: 04/01
Application fee: $35
Financial Aid deadline: 04/15
Can first year start other than Fall? No
Student faculty ratio: 15.5 to 1
Does the University offer:
- housing restricted to law students? No
- graduate student housing for which law students are eligible? No

Faculty & Administrators

	Total		Men		Women		Minorities	
	Fall	Spr	Fall	Spr	Fall	Spr	Fall	Spr
Full-time	11	9	6	5	5	4	0	0
Other Full-Time	1	1	0	0	1	1	0	0
Deans, librarians, & others who teach > 1/2	1	1	1	1	0	0	0	0
Part-time	3	3	3	3	0	0	0	0
Total	16	14	10	9	6	5	0	0
Deans, librarians, & others who teach < 1/2	5	5	3	3	2	2	0	0

Curriculum

	Full time	Part time
Typical first-year section size	70	0
Is there typically a "small section" of the first year class, other than Legal Writing, taught by full-time faculty?	No	No
If yes, typical size offered last year	N/A	N/A
# of classroom course titles beyond 1st year curriculum	51	0
# of upper division courses, excluding seminars, with an enrollment:		
Under 25	37	0
25 - 49	17	0
50 - 74	5	0
75 - 99	1	0
100 +	0	0
# of seminars	2	0
# of seminar positions available	32	
# of seminar positions filled	19	0
# of positions available in simulation courses	74	
# of simulation positions filled	73	0
# of positions available in faculty supervised clinical courses	0	
# of fac. sup. clin. positions filled	47	0
# involved in field placements	20	0
# involved in law journals	37	0
# in moot court or trial competitions	30	0
# of credit hrs required to graduate	90	

J.D. Enrollment & Ethnicity

	Men		Women		Fl-Time		Pt-Time		1st Yr		2nd Yr		3rd Yr		4th Yr		Total		JD Degrees Awarded
	#	%	#	%	#	%	#	%	#	%	#	%	#	%	#	%	#	%	
African-American	1	0.8	0	0.0	1	0.5	0	0.0	0	0.0	0	0.0	1	1.4	0	0.0	1	0.5	0
American Indian	4	3.3	3	3.7	7	3.4	0	0.0	2	2.9	1	1.6	4	5.6	0	0.0	7	3.4	1
Asian American	0	0.0	3	3.7	3	1.5	0	0.0	1	1.4	1	1.6	1	1.4	0	0.0	3	1.5	0
Mexican American	1	0.8	0	0.0	1	0.5	0	0.0	0	0.0	0	0.0	1	1.4	0	0.0	1	0.5	0
Puerto Rican	0	0.0	0	0.0	0	0.0	0	0.0	0	0.0	0	0.0	0	0.0	0	0.0	0	0.0	0
Hispanic American	0	0.0	1	1.2	1	0.5	0	0.0	1	1.4	0	0.0	0	0.0	0	0.0	1	0.5	0
Total Minorities	6	4.9	7	8.6	13	6.4	0	0.0	4	5.8	2	3.2	7	9.7	0	0.0	13	6.4	1
Foreign Nationals	4	3.3	7	8.6	11	5.4	0	0.0	5	7.2	4	6.3	2	2.8	0	0.0	11	5.4	3
Caucasian	113	91.9	67	82.7	180	88.2	0	0.0	60	87.0	57	90.5	63	87.5	0	0.0	180	88.2	54
Total	123	60.3	81	39.7	204	100.0	0	0.0	69	33.8	63	30.9	72	35.3	0	0.0	204		58

GPA & LSAT Scores

	Full Time	Part Time	Total
# of apps	231	0	231
# admits	145	0	145
# of matrics	71	0	71
75% GPA	3.43	0.00	
25% GPA	2.95	0.00	
75% LSAT	154	0	
25% LSAT	148	0	

Tuition & Fees

	Resident	Non-resident
Full-Time	$4,243	$8,889
Part-Time	$0	$0

Living Expenses

Estimated living expenses for Singles

Living on campus	Living off campus	Living at home
$7,400	$7,400	$7,400

Grants/Scholarships

	Full-time #	Full-time %	Part-time #	Part-time %	Total #	Total %
Total # of Students						
Total # receiving grants	63	30.9	0	0.0	63	30.9
Less than 1/2 tuition	31	15.2	0	0.0	31	15.2
Half to full tuition	5	2.5	0	0.0	5	2.5
Full tuition	27	13.2	0	0.0	27	13.2
More than full tuition	0	0.0	0	0.0	0	0.0
Median Grant Amount	$2,075		$0			

Informational & Library Resources

# of volumes & volume equivalents	255,991	# of professional staff	2
# of titles	71,685	Hours per week with professional staff	45
# of active serial subscriptions	2,747	Hours per week without professional staff	48
Study seating capacity inside the library	279	# of student computer work stations for entire law school	30
Square feet of law library	21,582	# of additional networked connections	170
Square feet of law school (excl. Library)	19,409	Require Laptop Computer?	N

Employment

	Total	%
Employment status known	66	94.3
Employment status unknown	4	5.7
Employed	62	93.9
Pursuing graduate degrees	2	3.0
Unemployed seeking employment	2	3.0
Unemployed not seeking employment	0	0.0
Type of Employment		
# employed in law firms	23	37.1
# employed in business & industry	8	12.9
# employed in government	11	17.7
# employed in public interest	2	3.2
# employed as judicial clerks	17	27.4
# employed in academia	1	1.6
Geographic Location		
# employed in state	26	41.9
# employed in foreign countries	1	1.6
# of states where employed	17	

J.D. Attrition (from Prior Year)

	Academic #	Other #	TOTALS #	TOTALS %
1st Year	2	2	4	6.2%
2nd Year	0	0	0	0.0%
3rd Year	0	1	1	1.8%
4th Year	0	0	0	0.0%

Bar Passage Rates

Jurisdiction	North Dakota			Minnesota		
Exam	Sum 97	Win 98	Total	Sum 97	Win 98	Total
# from school taking bar for the first time	42	0	42	36	4	40
School's pass rate for all first-time takers	83%		83%	94%	75%	93%
State's pass rate for all first-time takers	85%	0%	85%	93%	77%	90%

NORTHEASTERN UNIVERSITY

400 Huntington Avenue
Boston, MA 02115
(617)373-5149
http://www.slaw.neu.edu

ABA Approved Since 1969

The Basics

Type of School: Private   Term: Quarter
Application deadline: 03/01
Application fee: $55
Financial Aid deadline: 03/01
Can first year start other than Fall? No
Student faculty ratio: 21.3 to 1
Does the University offer:
- housing restricted to law students? No
- graduate student housing for which law students are eligible? Yes

Faculty & Administrators

	Total		Men		Women		Minorities	
	Fall	Spr	Fall	Spr	Fall	Spr	Fall	Spr
Full-time	24	22	12	13	12	9	6	6
Other Full-Time	3	3	1	1	2	2	1	1
Deans, librarians, & others who teach > 1/2	4	5	2	2	2	3	0	0
Part-time	16	9	8	6	8	3	2	1
Total	47	39	23	22	24	17	9	8
Deans, librarians, & others who teach < 1/2	0	0	0	0	0	0	0	0

Curriculum

	Full time	Part time
Typical first-year section size	53	0
Is there typically a "small section" of the first year class, other than Legal Writing, taught by full-time faculty?	No	No
If yes, typical size offered last year	N/A	N/A
# of classroom course titles beyond 1st year curriculum	75	0
# of upper division courses, excluding seminars, with an enrollment:		
Under 25	67	0
25 - 49	29	0
50 - 74	5	0
75 - 99	4	0
100 +	4	0
# of seminars	7	0
# of seminar positions available	116	
# of seminar positions filled	109	0
# of positions available in simulation courses	270	
# of simulation positions filled	238	0
# of positions available in faculty supervised clinical courses	134	
# of fac. sup. clin. positions filled	111	0
# involved in field placements	386	0
# involved in law journals	30	0
# in moot court or trial competitions	45	0
# of credit hrs required to graduate	99	

J.D. Enrollment & Ethnicity

	Men		Women		Fl-Time		Pt-Time		1st Yr		2nd Yr		3rd Yr		4th Yr		Total		JD Degrees Awarded
	#	%	#	%	#	%	#	%	#	%	#	%	#	%	#	%	#	%	
African-American	18	8.6	42	10.4	60	9.8	0	0.0	23	10.0	14	8.3	23	10.7	0	0.0	60	9.8	19
American Indian	1	0.5	2	0.5	3	0.5	0	0.0	2	0.9	0	0.0	1	0.5	0	0.0	3	0.5	0
Asian American	12	5.7	45	11.1	57	9.3	0	0.0	20	8.7	14	8.3	23	10.7	0	0.0	57	9.3	21
Mexican American	2	1.0	6	1.5	8	1.3	0	0.0	4	1.7	1	0.6	3	1.4	0	0.0	8	1.3	1
Puerto Rican	3	1.4	5	1.2	8	1.3	0	0.0	3	1.3	2	1.2	3	1.4	0	0.0	8	1.3	0
Hispanic American	6	2.9	18	4.5	24	3.9	0	0.0	10	4.3	10	5.9	4	1.9	0	0.0	24	3.9	13
Total Minorities	42	20.0	118	29.2	160	26.1	0	0.0	62	27.0	41	24.3	57	26.5	0	0.0	160	26.1	54
Foreign Nationals	4	1.9	4	1.0	8	1.3	0	0.0	6	2.6	1	0.6	1	0.5	0	0.0	8	1.3	0
Caucasian	164	78.1	282	69.8	446	72.6	0	0.0	162	70.4	127	75.1	157	73.0	0	0.0	446	72.6	141
Total	210	34.2	404	65.8	614	100.0	0	0.0	230	37.5	169	27.5	215	35.0	0	0.0	614		195

GPA & LSAT Scores

	Full Time	Part Time	Total
# of apps	1,733	0	1,733
# admits	756	0	756
# of matrics	230	0	230
75% GPA	3.37	0.00	
25% GPA	2.77	0.00	
75% LSAT	158	0	
25% LSAT	151	0	

Tuition & Fees

	Resident	Non-resident
Full-Time	$22,500	$22,500
Part-Time	$0	$0

Living Expenses

Estimated living expenses for Singles		
Living on campus	Living off campus	Living at home
$13,440	$13,440	$7,000

Employment

	Total	%
Employment status known	181	93.3
Employment status unknown	13	6.7
Employed	161	89.0
Pursuing graduate degrees	1	0.6
Unemployed seeking employment	16	8.8
Unemployed not seeking employment	3	1.7
Type of Employment		
# employed in law firms	65	40.4
# employed in business & industry	15	9.3
# employed in government	21	13.0
# employed in public interest	27	16.8
# employed as judicial clerks	30	18.6
# employed in academia	2	1.2
Geographic Location		
# employed in state	87	54.0
# employed in foreign countries	1	0.6
# of states where employed	20	

Grants/Scholarships

	Full-time		Part-time		Total	
	#	%	#	%	#	%
Total # of Students	614		0		614	
Total # receiving grants	345	56.2	0	0.0	345	56.2
Less than 1/2 tuition	296	48.2	0	0.0	296	48.2
Half to full tuition	40	6.5	0	0.0	40	6.5
Full tuition	9	1.5	0	0.0	9	1.5
More than full tuition	0	0.0	0	0.0	0	0.0
Median Grant Amount	$3,000		$0			

Informational & Library Resources

# of volumes & volume equivalents	234,314	# of professional staff	8
# of titles	33,601	Hours per week with professional staff	73
# of active serial subscriptions	3,116	Hours per week without professional staff	22
Study seating capacity inside the library	388	# of student computer work stations for entire law school	82
Square feet of law library	23,845	# of additional networked connections	0
Square feet of law school (excl. Library)	59,077	Require Laptop Computer?	N

J.D. Attrition (from Prior Year)

	Academic	Other	TOTALS	
	#	#	#	%
1st Year	0	11	11	6.3%
2nd Year	1	1	2	0.9%
3rd Year	0	0	0	0.0%
4th Year	0	0	0	0.0%

Bar Passage Rates

Jurisdiction	Massachusetts		
Exam	Sum 97	Win 98	Total
# from school taking bar for the first time	110	13	123
School's pass rate for all first-time takers	86%	77%	85%
State's pass rate for all first-time takers	84%	72%	82%

NORTHERN ILLINOIS UNIVERSITY

College of Law
DeKalb, IL 60115
(815)753-1420
http://www.niu.edu/claw

ABA Approved Since 1978

The Basics

Type of School: Public Term: Semester
Application deadline: 05/15
Application fee: $40
Financial Aid deadline: 03/01
Can first year start other than Fall? No
Student faculty ratio: 14.7 to 1
Does the University offer:
- housing restricted to law students? Yes
- graduate student housing for which law students are eligible? No

Faculty & Administrators

	Total		Men		Women		Minorities	
	Fall	Spr	Fall	Spr	Fall	Spr	Fall	Spr
Full-time	16	16	11	11	5	5	4	4
Other Full-Time	2	2	0	0	2	2	0	0
Deans, librarians, & others who teach > 1/2	1	1	1	1	0	0	0	0
Part-time	7	5	6	4	1	1	0	1
Total	26	24	18	16	8	8	4	5
Deans, librarians, & others who teach < 1/2	4	4	4	4	0	0	1	1

Curriculum

	Full time	Part time
Typical first-year section size	53	0
Is there typically a "small section" of the first year class, other than Legal Writing, taught by full-time faculty?	No	No
If yes, typical size offered last year	N/A	N/A
# of classroom course titles beyond 1st year curriculum	63	0
# of upper division courses, excluding seminars, with an enrollment:		
Under 25	60	0
25 - 49	37	0
50 - 74	8	0
75 - 99	1	0
100 +	0	0
# of seminars	9	0
# of seminar positions available	108	
# of seminar positions filled	84	0
# of positions available in simulation courses	214	
# of simulation positions filled	171	0
# of positions available in faculty supervised clinical courses	0	
# of fac. sup. clin. positions filled	0	0
# involved in field placements	33	0
# involved in law journals	33	0
# in moot court or trial competitions	64	0
# of credit hrs required to graduate	90	

J.D. Enrollment & Ethnicity

	Men		Women		Fl-Time		Pt-Time		1st Yr		2nd Yr		3rd Yr		4th Yr		Total		JD Degrees Awarded
	#	%	#	%	#	%	#	%	#	%	#	%	#	%	#	%	#	%	
African-American	12	6.7	9	8.0	21	7.9	0	0.0	9	8.5	5	6.3	7	6.7	0	0.0	21	7.2	9
American Indian	1	0.6	0	0.0	1	0.4	0	0.0	1	0.9	0	0.0	0	0.0	0	0.0	1	0.3	0
Asian American	18	10.1	7	6.3	25	9.4	0	0.0	9	8.5	8	10.0	8	7.7	0	0.0	25	8.6	5
Mexican American	8	4.5	8	7.1	16	6.0	0	0.0	9	8.5	3	3.8	4	3.8	0	0.0	16	5.5	7
Puerto Rican	0	0.0	0	0.0	0	0.0	0	0.0	0	0.0	0	0.0	0	0.0	0	0.0	0	0.0	0
Hispanic American	0	0.0	0	0.0	0	0.0	0	0.0	0	0.0	0	0.0	0	0.0	0	0.0	0	0.0	0
Total Minorities	39	21.9	24	21.4	63	23.6	0	0.0	28	26.4	16	20.0	19	18.3	0	0.0	63	21.7	21
Foreign Nationals	2	1.1	0	0.0	2	0.7	0	0.0	0	0.0	0	0.0	2	1.9	0	0.0	2	0.7	0
Caucasian	137	77.0	88	78.6	202	75.7	23	100.0	78	73.6	64	80.0	83	79.8	0	0.0	225	77.6	71
Total	178	61.4	112	38.6	267	92.1	23	7.9	106	36.6	80	27.6	104	35.9	0	0.0	290		92

NORTHERN ILLINOIS UNIVERSITY

GPA & LSAT Scores

	Full Time	Part Time	Total
# of apps	778	36	814
# admits	336	16	352
# of matrics	99	7	106
75% GPA	3.30	3.82	
25% GPA	2.78	2.87	
75% LSAT	156	154	
25% LSAT	150	149	

Tuition & Fees

	Resident	Non-resident
Full-Time	$6,481	$11,931
Part-Time	$0	$0

Living Expenses

Estimated living expenses for Singles		
Living on campus	Living off campus	Living at home
$8,059	$8,959	$8,959

Employment

	Total	%
Employment status known	86	94.5
Employment status unknown	5	5.5
Employed	80	93.0
Pursuing graduate degrees	2	2.3
Unemployed seeking employment	4	4.7
Unemployed not seeking employment	0	0.0
Type of Employment		
# employed in law firms	38	47.5
# employed in business & industry	11	13.7
# employed in government	22	27.5
# employed in public interest	2	2.5
# employed as judicial clerks	7	8.7
# employed in academia	0	0.0
Geographic Location		
# employed in state	64	80.0
# employed in foreign countries	1	1.2
# of states where employed	10	

Grants/Scholarships

	Full-time		Part-time		Total	
	#	%	#	%	#	%
Total # of Students	267		23		290	
Total # receiving grants	61	22.8	0	0.0	61	21.0
Less than 1/2 tuition	28	10.5	0	0.0	28	9.7
Half to full tuition	18	6.7	0	0.0	18	6.2
Full tuition	15	5.6	0	0.0	15	5.2
More than full tuition	0	0.0	0	0.0	0	0.0
Median Grant Amount	$3,000		$0			

Informational & Library Resources

# of volumes & volume equivalents	203,102	# of professional staff	4
# of titles	32,982	Hours per week with professional staff	50
# of active serial subscriptions	3,233	Hours per week without professional staff	47
Study seating capacity inside the library	210	# of student computer work stations for entire law school	30
Square feet of law library	24,700	# of additional networked connections	0
Square feet of law school (excl. Library)	18,600	Require Laptop Computer?	N

J.D. Attrition (from Prior Year)

	Academic	Other	TOTALS	
	#	#	#	%
1st Year	0	1	1	1.1%
2nd Year	7	4	11	11%
3rd Year	0	1	1	1.0%
4th Year	0	0	0	0.0%

Bar Passage Rates

Jurisdiction	Illinois		
Exam	Sum 97	Win 98	Total
# from school taking bar for the first time	74	5	79
School's pass rate for all first-time takers	85%	40%	82%
State's pass rate for all first-time takers	87%	80%	85%

NORTHERN KENTUCKY UNIVERSITY

Salmon P. Chase College of Law
Nunn Drive
Highland Heights, KY 41099
(606)572-5340
http://www.eku.edu/~chase

ABA Approved Since 1954

The Basics

Type of School: Public Term: Semester
Application deadline: 05/15
Application fee: $30
Financial Aid deadline: 04/01
Can first year start other than Fall? No
Student faculty ratio: 13.0 to 1
Does the University offer:
- housing restricted to law students? No
- graduate student housing for which law students are eligible? Yes

Faculty & Administrators

	Total		Men		Women		Minorities	
	Fall	Spr	Fall	Spr	Fall	Spr	Fall	Spr
Full-time	21	19	15	14	6	5	1	1
Other Full-Time	1	1	1	1	0	0	0	0
Deans, librarians, & others who teach > 1/2	2	2	1	1	1	1	0	0
Part-time	36	27	27	19	9	8	1	1
Total	60	49	44	35	16	14	2	2
Deans, librarians, & others who teach < 1/2	1	1	1	1	0	0	0	0

Curriculum

	Full time	Part time
Typical first-year section size	50	50
Is there typically a "small section" of the first year class, other than Legal Writing, taught by full-time faculty?	Yes	Yes
If yes, typical size offered last year	20	25
# of classroom course titles beyond 1st year curriculum	35	66
# of upper division courses, excluding seminars, with an enrollment:		
Under 25	27	41
25 - 49	7	20
50 - 74	5	3
75 - 99	0	0
100 +	0	0
# of seminars	4	2
# of seminar positions available	150	
# of seminar positions filled	42	16
# of positions available in simulation courses	213	
# of simulation positions filled	55	131
# of positions available in faculty supervised clinical courses	20	
# of fac. sup. clin. positions filled	6	1
# involved in field placements	17	9
# involved in law journals	20	7
# in moot court or trial competitions	26	8
# of credit hrs required to graduate	90	

J.D. Enrollment & Ethnicity

	Men		Women		Fl-Time		Pt-Time		1st Yr		2nd Yr		3rd Yr		4th Yr		Total		JD Degrees Awarded
	#	%	#	%	#	%	#	%	#	%	#	%	#	%	#	%	#	%	
African-American	11	4.7	4	2.5	2	1.0	13	6.8	3	2.5	3	2.8	5	4.1	4	9.3	15	3.8	4
American Indian	1	0.4	1	0.6	0	0.0	2	1.1	1	0.8	1	0.9	0	0.0	0	0.0	2	0.5	0
Asian American	0	0.0	0	0.0	0	0.0	0	0.0	0	0.0	0	0.0	0	0.0	0	0.0	0	0.0	1
Mexican American	0	0.0	0	0.0	0	0.0	0	0.0	0	0.0	0	0.0	0	0.0	0	0.0	0	0.0	0
Puerto Rican	0	0.0	0	0.0	0	0.0	0	0.0	0	0.0	0	0.0	0	0.0	0	0.0	0	0.0	0
Hispanic American	3	1.3	1	0.6	1	0.5	3	1.6	0	0.0	2	1.9	2	1.6	0	0.0	4	1.0	0
Total Minorities	15	6.5	6	3.8	3	1.5	18	9.5	4	3.4	6	5.6	7	5.7	4	9.3	21	5.4	5
Foreign Nationals	0	0.0	0	0.0	0	0.0	0	0.0	0	0.0	0	0.0	0	0.0	0	0.0	0	0.0	0
Caucasian	217	93.5	153	96.2	198	98.5	172	90.5	114	96.6	101	94.4	116	94.3	39	90.7	370	94.6	105
Total	232	59.3	159	40.7	201	51.4	190	48.6	118	30.2	107	27.4	123	31.5	43	11.0	391		110

GPA & LSAT Scores

	Full Time	Part Time	Total
# of apps	542	106	648
# admits	235	66	301
# of matrics	66	51	117
75% GPA	3.57	3.63	
25% GPA	3.09	2.79	
75% LSAT	154	156	
25% LSAT	150	151	

Tuition & Fees

	Resident	Non-resident
Full-Time	$5,670	$14,280
Part-Time	$4,740	$11,900

Living Expenses

Estimated living expenses for Singles

Living on campus	Living off campus	Living at home
$10,500	$10,500	$10,500

Grants/Scholarships

	Full-time		Part-time		Total	
	#	%	#	%	#	%
Total # of Students	201		190		391	
Total # receiving grants	76	37.8	77	40.5	153	39.1
Less than 1/2 tuition	41	20.4	40	21.1	81	20.7
Half to full tuition	5	2.5	24	12.6	29	7.4
Full tuition	30	14.9	13	6.8	43	11.0
More than full tuition	0	0.0	0	0.0	0	0.0
Median Grant Amount	$5,160		$4,681			

Informational & Library Resources

# of volumes & volume equivalents	248,648	# of professional staff	6
# of titles	33,107	Hours per week with professional staff	67
# of active serial subscriptions	1,961	Hours per week without professional staff	33
Study seating capacity inside the library	200	# of student computer work stations for entire law school	27
Square feet of law library	25,897	# of additional networked connections	0
Square feet of law school (excl. Library)	56,492	Require Laptop Computer?	N

Employment

	Total	%
Employment status known	64	57.1
Employment status unknown	48	42.9
Employed	60	93.7
Pursuing graduate degrees	1	1.6
Unemployed seeking employment	3	4.7
Unemployed not seeking employment	0	0.0
Type of Employment		
# employed in law firms	29	48.3
# employed in business & industry	12	20.0
# employed in government	13	21.7
# employed in public interest	0	0.0
# employed as judicial clerks	3	5.0
# employed in academia	1	1.7
Geographic Location		
# employed in state	26	43.3
# employed in foreign countries	0	0.0
# of states where employed	8	

J.D. Attrition (from Prior Year)

	Academic	Other	TOTALS	
	#	#	#	%
1st Year	6	13	19	16%
2nd Year	3	12	15	13%
3rd Year	2	2	4	3.4%
4th Year	0	0	0	0.0%

Bar Passage Rates

Jurisdiction	Ohio			Kentucky		
Exam	Sum 97	Win 98	Total	Sum 97	Win 98	Total
# from school taking bar for the first time	53	14	67	36	24	60
School's pass rate for all first-time takers	83%	79%	82%	50%	83%	63%
State's pass rate for all first-time takers	79%	75%	78%	65%	86%	70%

NORTHWESTERN UNIVERSITY

357 East Chicago Avenue
Chicago, IL 60611
(312)503-8462

ABA Approved Since 1923

The Basics

Type of School: Private   Term: Semester
Application deadline: 02/15
Application fee: $80
Financial Aid deadline: 03/15
Can first year start other than Fall? No
Student faculty ratio: 17.4 to 1
Does the University offer:
- housing restricted to law students? No
- graduate student housing for which law students are eligible? Yes

Faculty & Administrators

	Total		Men		Women		Minorities	
	Fall	Spr	Fall	Spr	Fall	Spr	Fall	Spr
Full-time	31	30	24	23	7	7	2	2
Other Full-Time	15	15	4	4	11	11	1	1
Deans, librarians, & others who teach > 1/2	1	1	1	1	0	0	0	0
Part-time	98	39	67	31	30	7	5	1
Total	145	85	96	59	48	25	8	4
Deans, librarians, & others who teach < 1/2	3	3	3	3	0	0	0	0

Curriculum

	Full time	Part time
Typical first-year section size	50	0
Is there typically a "small section" of the first year class, other than Legal Writing, taught by full-time faculty?	Yes	No
If yes, typical size offered last year	50	N/A
# of classroom course titles beyond 1st year curriculum	153	0
# of upper division courses, excluding seminars, with an enrollment:		
Under 25	82	0
25 - 49	43	0
50 - 74	26	0
75 - 99	23	0
100 +	7	0
# of seminars	54	0
# of seminar positions available	1,156	
# of seminar positions filled	760	0
# of positions available in simulation courses	626	
# of simulation positions filled	571	0
# of positions available in faculty supervised clinical courses	238	
# of fac. sup. clin. positions filled	194	0
# involved in field placements	60	0
# involved in law journals	165	0
# in moot court or trial competitions	38	0
# of credit hrs required to graduate	86	

J.D. Enrollment & Ethnicity

	Men		Women		Fl-Time		Pt-Time		1st Yr		2nd Yr		3rd Yr		4th Yr		Total		JD Degrees Awarded
	#	%	#	%	#	%	#	%	#	%	#	%	#	%	#	%	#	%	
African-American	14	4.1	30	9.9	44	6.8	0	0.0	16	7.8	15	6.8	13	5.8	0	0.0	44	6.8	12
American Indian	4	1.2	1	0.3	5	0.8	0	0.0	3	1.5	0	0.0	2	0.9	0	0.0	5	0.8	2
Asian American	34	9.9	29	9.6	63	9.8	0	0.0	24	11.8	23	10.5	16	7.2	0	0.0	63	9.8	16
Mexican American	7	2.0	3	1.0	10	1.5	0	0.0	4	2.0	0	0.0	6	2.7	0	0.0	10	1.5	6
Puerto Rican	2	0.6	3	1.0	5	0.8	0	0.0	1	0.5	4	1.8	0	0.0	0	0.0	5	0.8	0
Hispanic American	19	5.5	17	5.6	36	5.6	0	0.0	12	5.9	10	4.6	14	6.3	0	0.0	36	5.6	14
Total Minorities	80	23.3	83	27.5	163	25.2	0	0.0	60	29.4	52	23.7	51	22.9	0	0.0	163	25.2	50
Foreign Nationals	0	0.0	0	0.0	0	0.0	0	0.0	0	0.0	0	0.0	0	0.0	0	0.0	0	0.0	4
Caucasian	264	76.7	219	72.5	483	74.8	0	0.0	144	70.6	167	76.3	172	77.1	0	0.0	483	74.8	161
Total	344	53.3	302	46.7	646	100.0	0	0.0	204	31.6	219	33.9	223	34.5	0	0.0	646		215

GPA & LSAT Scores

	Full Time	Part Time	Total
# of apps	3,557	0	3,557
# admits	755	0	755
# of matrics	204	0	204
75% GPA	3.67	0.00	
25% GPA	3.28	0.00	
75% LSAT	167	0	
25% LSAT	162	0	

Tuition & Fees

	Resident	Non-resident
Full-Time	$23,974	$23,974
Part-Time	$0	$0

Living Expenses

Estimated living expenses for Singles

Living on campus	Living off campus	Living at home
$16,024	$16,024	$9,724

Grants/Scholarships

	Full-time		Part-time		Total	
	#	%	#	%	#	%
Total # of Students	646		0		646	
Total # receiving grants	273	42.3	0	0.0	273	42.3
Less than 1/2 tuition	159	24.6	0	0.0	159	24.6
Half to full tuition	106	16.4	0	0.0	106	16.4
Full tuition	5	0.8	0	0.0	5	0.8
More than full tuition	3	0.5	0	0.0	3	0.5
Median Grant Amount	$10,000		$0			

Informational & Library Resources

# of volumes & volume equivalents	646,189	# of professional staff	10
# of titles	192,161	Hours per week with professional staff	75
# of active serial subscriptions	8,282	Hours per week without professional staff	30
Study seating capacity inside the library	719	# of student computer work stations for entire law school	71
Square feet of law library	93,900	# of additional networked connections	157
Square feet of law school (excl. Library)	83,254	Require Laptop Computer?	N

Employment

	Total	%
Employment status known	205	99.0
Employment status unknown	2	1.0
Employed	193	94.1
Pursuing graduate degrees	4	2.0
Unemployed seeking employment	3	1.5
Unemployed not seeking employment	5	2.4
Type of Employment		
# employed in law firms	147	76.2
# employed in business & industry	14	7.3
# employed in government	9	4.7
# employed in public interest	5	2.6
# employed as judicial clerks	17	8.8
# employed in academia	1	0.5
Geographic Location		
# employed in state	106	54.9
# employed in foreign countries	2	1.0
# of states where employed	25	

J.D. Attrition (from Prior Year)

	Academic	Other	TOTALS	
	#	#	#	%
1st Year	0	5	5	2.5%
2nd Year	0	0	0	0.0%
3rd Year	0	0	0	0.0%
4th Year	0	0	0	0.0%

Bar Passage Rates

Jurisdiction	Illinois		
Exam	Sum 97	Win 98	Total
# from school taking bar for the first time	122	15	137
School's pass rate for all first-time takers	94%	87%	93%
State's pass rate for all first-time takers	87%	80%	85%

NOTRE DAME, UNIVERSITY OF

P.O. Box R
Notre Dame, IN 46556
(219)631-6627
http://www.nd.edu/~ndlaw

ABA Approved Since 1925

The Basics

Type of School: Private   Term: Semester
Application deadline: 03/01
Application fee: $50
Financial Aid deadline: 03/01
Can first year start other than Fall? No
Student faculty ratio: 16.3 to 1
Does the University offer:
- housing restricted to law students? No
- graduate student housing for which law students are eligible? Yes

Faculty & Administrators

	Total		Men		Women		Minorities	
	Fall	Spr	Fall	Spr	Fall	Spr	Fall	Spr
Full-time	26	23	22	20	4	3	2	2
Other Full-Time	5	5	1	1	4	4	0	0
Deans, librarians, & others who teach > 1/2	5	5	4	4	1	1	1	1
Part-time	18	21	14	16	4	5	0	0
Total	54	54	41	41	13	13	3	3
Deans, librarians, & others who teach < 1/2	11	11	6	6	5	5	1	1

Curriculum

	Full time	Part time
Typical first-year section size	92	0
Is there typically a "small section" of the first year class, other than Legal Writing, taught by full-time faculty?	No	No
If yes, typical size offered last year	N/A	N/A
# of classroom course titles beyond 1st year curriculum	83	0
# of upper division courses, excluding seminars, with an enrollment:		
Under 25	95	0
25 - 49	24	0
50 - 74	5	0
75 - 99	10	0
100 +	1	0
# of seminars	7	0
# of seminar positions available	225	
# of seminar positions filled	218	0
# of positions available in simulation courses	220	
# of simulation positions filled	176	0
# of positions available in faculty supervised clinical courses	120	
# of fac. sup. clin. positions filled	95	0
# involved in field placements	106	0
# involved in law journals	122	0
# in moot court or trial competitions	102	0
# of credit hrs required to graduate	90	

J.D. Enrollment & Ethnicity

	Men		Women		Fl-Time		Pt-Time		1st Yr		2nd Yr		3rd Yr		4th Yr		Total		JD Degrees Awarded
	#	%	#	%	#	%	#	%	#	%	#	%	#	%	#	%	#	%	
African-American	7	2.1	11	5.3	18	3.3	0	0.0	5	2.7	8	4.5	5	2.8	0	0.0	18	3.3	2
American Indian	8	2.4	2	1.0	10	1.9	0	0.0	1	0.5	5	2.8	4	2.3	0	0.0	10	1.9	1
Asian American	18	5.5	11	5.3	29	5.4	0	0.0	9	4.9	11	6.2	9	5.1	0	0.0	29	5.4	11
Mexican American	8	2.4	4	1.9	12	2.2	0	0.0	4	2.2	3	1.7	5	2.8	0	0.0	12	2.2	1
Puerto Rican	0	0.0	0	0.0	0	0.0	0	0.0	0	0.0	0	0.0	0	0.0	0	0.0	0	0.0	0
Hispanic American	15	4.6	8	3.8	23	4.3	0	0.0	5	2.7	11	6.2	7	4.0	0	0.0	23	4.3	9
Total Minorities	56	17.0	36	17.2	92	17.1	0	0.0	24	13.0	38	21.5	30	17.0	0	0.0	92	17.1	24
Foreign Nationals	0	0.0	0	0.0	0	0.0	0	0.0	0	0.0	0	0.0	0	0.0	0	0.0	0	0.0	0
Caucasian	273	83.0	173	82.8	446	82.9	0	0.0	161	87.0	139	78.5	146	83.0	0	0.0	446	82.9	137
Total	329	61.2	209	38.8	538	100.0	0	0.0	185	34.4	177	32.9	176	32.7	0	0.0	538		161

GPA & LSAT Scores

	Full Time	Part Time	Total
# of apps	1,629	0	1,629
# admits	477	0	477
# of matrics	185	0	185
75% GPA	3.67	0.00	
25% GPA	3.20	0.00	
75% LSAT	165	0	
25% LSAT	160	0	

Tuition & Fees

	Resident	Non-resident
Full-Time	$21,527	$21,527
Part-Time	$0	$0

Living Expenses

Estimated living expenses for Singles		
Living on campus	Living off campus	Living at home
$7,450	$7,450	$7,450

Grants/Scholarships

	Full-time		Part-time		Total	
	#	%	#	%	#	%
Total # of Students	538		0		538	
Total # receiving grants	208	38.7	0	0.0	208	38.7
Less than 1/2 tuition	166	30.9	0	0.0	166	30.9
Half to full tuition	15	2.8	0	0.0	15	2.8
Full tuition	24	4.5	0	0.0	24	4.5
More than full tuition	3	0.6	0	0.0	3	0.6
Median Grant Amount	$7,500		$0			

Informational & Library Resources

# of volumes & volume equivalents	484,367	# of professional staff	10
# of titles	85,415	Hours per week with professional staff	74
# of active serial subscriptions	5,371	Hours per week without professional staff	12
Study seating capacity inside the library	509	# of student computer work stations for entire law school	60
Square feet of law library	37,222	# of additional networked connections	48
Square feet of law school (excl. Library)	46,674	Require Laptop Computer?	N

Employment

	Total	%
Employment status known	184	98.9
Employment status unknown	2	1.1
Employed	173	94.0
Pursuing graduate degrees	7	3.8
Unemployed seeking employment	3	1.6
Unemployed not seeking employment	1	0.5
Type of Employment		
# employed in law firms	110	63.6
# employed in business & industry	13	7.5
# employed in government	26	15.0
# employed in public interest	4	2.3
# employed as judicial clerks	20	11.6
# employed in academia	0	0.0
Geographic Location		
# employed in state	12	6.9
# employed in foreign countries	2	1.2
# of states where employed	29	

J.D. Attrition (from Prior Year)

	Academic	Other	TOTALS	
	#	#	#	%
1st Year	0	1	1	0.6%
2nd Year	0	3	3	1.8%
3rd Year	0	2	2	1.2%
4th Year	0	0	0	0.0%

Bar Passage Rates

Jurisdiction	Illinois		
Exam	Sum 97	Win 98	Total
# from school taking bar for the first time	33	5	38
School's pass rate for all first-time takers	94%	80%	92%
State's pass rate for all first-time takers	87%	80%	85%

NOVA SOUTHEASTERN UNIVERSITY

Shepard Broad Law Center
3305 College Avenue
Fort Lauderdale, FL 33314-7721
(954)262-6100
http://www.nsulaw.nova.edu

ABA Approved Since 1975

The Basics

Type of School: Private

Term: Semester

Application deadline: 03/01

Application fee: $50

Financial Aid deadline: 03/01

Can first year start other than Fall? No

Student faculty ratio: 16.2 to 1

Does the University offer:
- housing restricted to law students? No
- graduate student housing for which law students are eligible? Yes

Faculty & Administrators

	Total		Men		Women		Minorities	
	Fall	Spr	Fall	Spr	Fall	Spr	Fall	Spr
Full-time	46	44	29	27	17	17	8	8
Other Full-Time	0	0	0	0	0	0	0	0
Deans, librarians, & others who teach > 1/2	2	2	0	0	2	2	0	0
Part-time	45	53	34	38	11	15	4	4
Total	93	99	63	65	30	34	12	12
Deans, librarians, & others who teach < 1/2	5	5	2	2	3	3	0	0

Curriculum

	Full time	Part time
Typical first-year section size	49	61
Is there typically a "small section" of the first year class, other than Legal Writing, taught by full-time faculty?	No	No
If yes, typical size offered last year	N/A	N/A
# of classroom course titles beyond 1st year curriculum	109	10
# of upper division courses, excluding seminars, with an enrollment:		
Under 25	98	2
25 - 49	27	5
50 - 74	26	3
75 - 99	10	1
100 +	0	0
# of seminars	17	0
# of seminar positions available	330	
# of seminar positions filled	250	0
# of positions available in simulation courses	1,183	
# of simulation positions filled	937	0
# of positions available in faculty supervised clinical courses	125	
# of fac. sup. clin. positions filled	16	0
# involved in field placements	191	0
# involved in law journals	115	8
# in moot court or trial competitions	108	9
# of credit hrs required to graduate	90	

J.D. Enrollment & Ethnicity

	Men		Women		Fl-Time		Pt-Time		1st Yr		2nd Yr		3rd Yr		4th Yr		Total		JD Degrees Awarded
	#	%	#	%	#	%	#	%	#	%	#	%	#	%	#	%	#	%	
African-American	22	4.3	52	11.8	61	7.8	13	7.7	31	9.6	26	9.2	17	4.9	0	0.0	74	7.8	25
American Indian	2	0.4	1	0.2	3	0.4	0	0.0	1	0.3	0	0.0	2	0.6	0	0.0	3	0.3	1
Asian American	13	2.5	8	1.8	17	2.2	4	2.4	8	2.5	2	0.7	11	3.2	0	0.0	21	2.2	0
Mexican American	0	0.0	3	0.7	3	0.4	0	0.0	2	0.6	1	0.4	0	0.0	0	0.0	3	0.3	0
Puerto Rican	10	1.9	9	2.0	15	1.9	4	2.4	10	3.1	3	1.1	6	1.7	0	0.0	19	2.0	2
Hispanic American	72	14.0	74	16.8	118	15.1	28	16.6	51	15.7	47	16.7	48	14.0	0	0.0	146	15.3	37
Total Minorities	119	23.2	147	33.4	217	27.7	49	29.0	103	31.8	79	28.0	84	24.4	0	0.0	266	27.9	65
Foreign Nationals	2	0.4	1	0.2	3	0.4	0	0.0	0	0.0	3	1.1	0	0.0	0	0.0	3	0.3	4
Caucasian	392	76.4	292	66.4	564	71.9	120	71.0	221	68.2	200	70.9	260	75.6	3	100.0	684	71.8	189
Total	513	53.8	440	46.2	784	82.3	169	17.7	324	34.0	282	29.6	344	36.1	3	0.3	953		258

GPA & LSAT Scores

	Full Time	Part Time	Total
# of apps	1,232	215	1,447
# admits	669	117	786
# of matrics	263	73	336
75% GPA	3.19	3.12	
25% GPA	2.59	2.53	
75% LSAT	151	150	
25% LSAT	144	144	

Tuition & Fees

	Resident	Non-resident
Full-Time	$19,770	$19,770
Part-Time	$14,832	$14,832

Living Expenses

Estimated living expenses for Singles		
Living on campus	Living off campus	Living at home
$12,668	$13,435	$8,500

Grants/Scholarships

	Full-time		Part-time		Total	
	#	%	#	%	#	%
Total # of Students	784		169		953	
Total # receiving grants	140	17.9	8	4.7	148	15.5
Less than 1/2 tuition	37	4.7	8	4.7	45	4.7
Half to full tuition	82	10.5	0	0.0	82	8.6
Full tuition	21	2.7	0	0.0	21	2.2
More than full tuition	0	0.0	0	0.0	0	0.0
Median Grant Amount	$10,000		$3,708			

Informational & Library Resources

# of volumes & volume equivalents	300,689	# of professional staff	12
# of titles	123,631	Hours per week with professional staff	75
# of active serial subscriptions	5,504	Hours per week without professional staff	29
Study seating capacity inside the library	565	# of student computer work stations for entire law school	59
Square feet of law library	42,372	# of additional networked connections	172
Square feet of law school (excl. Library)	77,215	Require Laptop Computer?	Y

Employment

	Total	%
Employment status known	236	74.4
Employment status unknown	81	25.6
Employed	172	72.9
Pursuing graduate degrees	11	4.7
Unemployed seeking employment	38	16.1
Unemployed not seeking employment	15	6.4
Type of Employment		
# employed in law firms	95	55.2
# employed in business & industry	11	6.4
# employed in government	53	30.8
# employed in public interest	4	2.3
# employed as judicial clerks	2	1.2
# employed in academia	2	1.2
Geographic Location		
# employed in state	145	84.3
# employed in foreign countries	1	0.6
# of states where employed	12	

J.D. Attrition (from Prior Year)

	Academic	Other	TOTALS	
	#	#	#	%
1st Year	11	20	31	10%
2nd Year	10	6	16	4.4%
3rd Year	0	0	0	0.0%
4th Year	0	0	0	0.0%

Bar Passage Rates

Jurisdiction	Florida		
Exam	Sum 97	Win 98	Total
# from school taking bar for the first time	230	40	270
School's pass rate for all first-time takers	84%	85%	84%
State's pass rate for all first-time takers	84%	82%	83%

OHIO NORTHERN UNIVERSITY

Pettit College of Law
525 S. Main Street
Ada, OH 45810-1599
(419)772-2205
http://www.law.onu.edu

ABA Approved Since 1948

The Basics

Type of School: Private Term: Semester
Application deadline: Rolling
Application fee: $40
Financial Aid deadline: 06/01
Can first year start other than Fall? No
Student faculty ratio: 13.5 to 1
Does the University offer:
- housing restricted to law students? Yes
- graduate student housing for which law students are eligible? No

Faculty & Administrators

	Total		Men		Women		Minorities	
	Fall	Spr	Fall	Spr	Fall	Spr	Fall	Spr
Full-time	20	20	14	14	6	6	0	0
Other Full-Time	0	0	0	0	0	0	0	0
Deans, librarians, & others who teach > 1/2	3	3	3	3	0	0	0	0
Part-time	7	12	4	8	3	4	0	0
Total	30	35	21	25	9	10	0	0
Deans, librarians, & others who teach < 1/2	0	0	0	0	0	0	0	0

Curriculum

	Full time	Part time
Typical first-year section size	41	0
Is there typically a "small section" of the first year class, other than Legal Writing, taught by full-time faculty?	No	No
If yes, typical size offered last year	N/A	N/A
# of classroom course titles beyond 1st year curriculum	67	0
# of upper division courses, excluding seminars, with an enrollment:		
Under 25	32	0
25 - 49	18	0
50 - 74	8	0
75 - 99	0	0
100 +	0	0
# of seminars	9	0
# of seminar positions available	135	
# of seminar positions filled	14	0
# of positions available in simulation courses	121	
# of simulation positions filled	121	0
# of positions available in faculty supervised clinical courses	12	
# of fac. sup. clin. positions filled	11	0
# involved in field placements	50	0
# involved in law journals	22	0
# in moot court or trial competitions	44	0
# of credit hrs required to graduate	87	

J.D. Enrollment & Ethnicity

	Men		Women		Fl-Time		Pt-Time		1st Yr		2nd Yr		3rd Yr		4th Yr		Total		JD Degrees Awarded
	#	%	#	%	#	%	#	%	#	%	#	%	#	%	#	%	#	%	
African-American	12	6.2	13	11.7	25	8.2	0	0.0	10	8.1	8	9.3	7	7.4	0	0.0	25	8.2	8
American Indian	0	0.0	0	0.0	0	0.0	0	0.0	0	0.0	0	0.0	0	0.0	0	0.0	0	0.0	1
Asian American	5	2.6	6	5.4	11	3.6	0	0.0	6	4.8	1	1.2	4	4.2	0	0.0	11	3.6	4
Mexican American	0	0.0	1	0.9	1	0.3	0	0.0	1	0.8	0	0.0	0	0.0	0	0.0	1	0.3	2
Puerto Rican	0	0.0	0	0.0	0	0.0	0	0.0	0	0.0	0	0.0	0	0.0	0	0.0	0	0.0	0
Hispanic American	7	3.6	3	2.7	10	3.3	0	0.0	4	3.2	4	4.7	2	2.1	0	0.0	10	3.3	4
Total Minorities	24	12.4	23	20.7	47	15.4	0	0.0	21	16.9	13	15.1	13	13.7	0	0.0	47	15.4	19
Foreign Nationals	1	0.5	2	1.8	3	1.0	0	0.0	3	2.4	0	0.0	0	0.0	0	0.0	3	1.0	0
Caucasian	169	87.1	86	77.5	255	83.6	0	0.0	100	80.6	73	84.9	82	86.3	0	0.0	255	83.6	86
Total	194	63.6	111	36.4	305	100.0	0	0.0	124	40.7	86	28.2	95	31.1	0	0.0	305		105

GPA & LSAT Scores

	Full Time	Part Time	Total
# of apps	818	0	818
# admits	557	0	557
# of matrics	131	0	131
75% GPA	3.12	0.00	
25% GPA	2.59	0.00	
75% LSAT	150	0	
25% LSAT	143	0	

Tuition & Fees

	Resident	Non-resident
Full-Time	$19,040	$19,040
Part-Time	$0	$0

Living Expenses

Estimated living expenses for Singles

Living on campus	Living off campus	Living at home
$7,760	$8,700	$4,020

Grants/Scholarships

	Full-time		Part-time		Total	
	#	%	#	%	#	%
Total # of Students	305		0		305	
Total # receiving grants	94	30.8	0	0.0	94	30.8
Less than 1/2 tuition	60	19.7	0	0.0	60	19.7
Half to full tuition	34	11.1	0	0.0	34	11.1
Full tuition	0	0.0	0	0.0	0	0.0
More than full tuition	0	0.0	0	0.0	0	0.0
Median Grant Amount	$10,000		$0			

Informational & Library Resources

# of volumes & volume equivalents	270,215	# of professional staff	4
# of titles	75,341	Hours per week with professional staff	59
# of active serial subscriptions	2,993	Hours per week without professional staff	49
Study seating capacity inside the library	310	# of student computer work stations for entire law school	41
Square feet of law library	29,670	# of additional networked connections	48
Square feet of law school (excl. Library)	24,485	Require Laptop Computer?	N

Employment

	Total	%
Employment status known	90	80.4
Employment status unknown	22	19.6
Employed	78	86.7
Pursuing graduate degrees	2	2.2
Unemployed seeking employment	7	7.8
Unemployed not seeking employment	3	3.3
Type of Employment		
# employed in law firms	47	60.3
# employed in business & industry	6	7.7
# employed in government	16	20.5
# employed in public interest	1	1.3
# employed as judicial clerks	6	7.7
# employed in academia	3	3.8
Geographic Location		
# employed in state	20	25.6
# employed in foreign countries	0	0.0
# of states where employed	19	

J.D. Attrition (from Prior Year)

	Academic	Other	TOTALS	
	#	#	#	%
1st Year	8	39	47	37%
2nd Year	0	1	1	1.0%
3rd Year	0	0	0	0.0%
4th Year	0	0	0	0.0%

Bar Passage Rates

Jurisdiction	Ohio			Pennsylvania		
Exam	Sum 97	Win 98	Total	Sum 97	Win 98	Total
# from school taking bar for the first time	40	4	44	10	0	10
School's pass rate for all first-time takers	58%	75%	59%	80%		80%
State's pass rate for all first-time takers	79%	75%	78%	81%	73%	79%

OHIO STATE UNIVERSITY

55 W. 12th Avenue
Columbus, OH 43210
(614)292-2631
http://www.osu.edu/units/law

ABA Approved Since 1923

The Basics

Type of School: Public   Term: Semester
Application deadline: 03/15
Application fee: $30
Financial Aid deadline: 03/01
Can first year start other than Fall? No
Student faculty ratio: 14.1 to 1
Does the University offer:
- housing restricted to law students? No
- graduate student housing for which law students are eligible? Yes

Faculty & Administrators

	Total		Men		Women		Minorities	
	Fall	Spr	Fall	Spr	Fall	Spr	Fall	Spr
Full-time	38	37	25	26	13	11	4	4
Other Full-Time	0	0	0	0	0	0	0	0
Deans, librarians, & others who teach > 1/2	1	1	0	0	1	1	0	0
Part-time	26	14	15	11	11	3	5	2
Total	65	52	40	37	25	15	9	6
Deans, librarians, & others who teach < 1/2	6	6	3	3	3	3	2	2

Curriculum

	Full time	Part time
Typical first-year section size	72	0
Is there typically a "small section" of the first year class, other than Legal Writing, taught by full-time faculty?	Yes	No
If yes, typical size offered last year	30	N/A
# of classroom course titles beyond 1st year curriculum	66	0
# of upper division courses, excluding seminars, with an enrollment:		
Under 25	40	0
25 - 49	15	0
50 - 74	24	0
75 - 99	6	0
100 +	1	0
# of seminars	22	0
# of seminar positions available	440	
# of seminar positions filled	351	0
# of positions available in simulation courses	146	
# of simulation positions filled	136	0
# of positions available in faculty supervised clinical courses	102	
# of fac. sup. clin. positions filled	95	0
# involved in field placements	52	0
# involved in law journals	140	0
# in moot court or trial competitions	208	0
# of credit hrs required to graduate	88	

J.D. Enrollment & Ethnicity

	Men		Women		Fl-Time		Pt-Time		1st Yr		2nd Yr		3rd Yr		4th Yr		Total		JD Degrees Awarded
	#	%	#	%	#	%	#	%	#	%	#	%	#	%	#	%	#	%	
African-American	18	5.5	32	10.3	50	7.8	0	0.0	21	9.9	13	6.4	16	7.1	0	0.0	50	7.8	22
American Indian	0	0.0	2	0.6	2	0.3	0	0.0	0	0.0	0	0.0	2	0.9	0	0.0	2	0.3	0
Asian American	24	7.3	27	8.7	51	8.0	0	0.0	23	10.8	15	7.4	13	5.8	0	0.0	51	8.0	11
Mexican American	0	0.0	0	0.0	0	0.0	0	0.0	0	0.0	0	0.0	0	0.0	0	0.0	0	0.0	0
Puerto Rican	0	0.0	0	0.0	0	0.0	0	0.0	0	0.0	0	0.0	0	0.0	0	0.0	0	0.0	0
Hispanic American	6	1.8	8	2.6	14	2.2	0	0.0	3	1.4	6	2.9	5	2.2	0	0.0	14	2.2	6
Total Minorities	48	14.5	69	22.3	117	18.4	0	0.0	47	22.2	34	16.7	36	16.1	0	0.0	117	18.3	39
Foreign Nationals	1	0.3	0	0.0	1	0.2	0	0.0	0	0.0	0	0.0	1	0.4	0	0.0	1	0.2	0
Caucasian	281	85.2	241	77.7	519	81.5	3	100.0	165	77.8	170	83.3	187	83.5	0	0.0	522	81.6	186
Total	330	51.6	310	48.4	637	99.5	3	0.5	212	33.1	204	31.9	224	35.0	0	0.0	640		225

GPA & LSAT Scores

	Full Time	Part Time	Total
# of apps	1,520	0	1,520
# admits	572	0	572
# of matrics	214	0	214
75% GPA	3.75	0.00	
25% GPA	3.29	0.00	
75% LSAT	160	0	
25% LSAT	152	0	

Tuition & Fees

	Resident	Non-resident
Full-Time	$7,720	$17,516
Part-Time	$0	$0

Living Expenses

Estimated living expenses for Singles		
Living on campus	Living off campus	Living at home
$10,152	$10,152	N/A

Employment

	Total	%
Employment status known	194	92.4
Employment status unknown	16	7.6
Employed	178	91.8
Pursuing graduate degrees	6	3.1
Unemployed seeking employment	7	3.6
Unemployed not seeking employment	3	1.5
Type of Employment		
# employed in law firms	102	57.3
# employed in business & industry	21	11.8
# employed in government	28	15.7
# employed in public interest	10	5.6
# employed as judicial clerks	17	9.6
# employed in academia	0	0.0
Geographic Location		
# employed in state	135	75.8
# employed in foreign countries	1	0.6
# of states where employed	19	

Grants/Scholarships

	Full-time		Part-time		Total	
	#	%	#	%	#	%
Total # of Students	637		3		640	
Total # receiving grants	449	70.5	0	0.0	449	70.2
Less than 1/2 tuition	429	67.3	0	0.0	429	67.0
Half to full tuition	7	1.1	0	0.0	7	1.1
Full tuition	6	0.9	0	0.0	6	0.9
More than full tuition	7	1.1	0	0.0	7	1.1
Median Grant Amount	$1,500		$0			

Informational & Library Resources

# of volumes & volume equivalents	665,317	# of professional staff	7
# of titles	158,095	Hours per week with professional staff	68
# of active serial subscriptions	8,017	Hours per week without professional staff	39
Study seating capacity inside the library	660	# of student computer work stations for entire law school	71
Square feet of law library	81,340	# of additional networked connections	0
Square feet of law school (excl. Library)	78,009	Require Laptop Computer?	N

J.D. Attrition (from Prior Year)

	Academic	Other	TOTALS	
	#	#	#	%
1st Year	1	13	14	6.6%
2nd Year	0	5	5	2.2%
3rd Year	0	0	0	0.0%
4th Year	0	0	0	0.0%

Bar Passage Rates

Jurisdiction	Ohio		
Exam	Sum 97	Win 98	Total
# from school taking bar for the first time	149	16	165
School's pass rate for all first-time takers	86%	75%	85%
State's pass rate for all first-time takers	79%	75%	78%

OKLAHOMA CITY UNIVERSITY

2501 North Blackwelder
Oklahoma City, OK 73106
(405)521-5354
http://www.okcu.edu/law

ABA Approved Since 1960

The Basics

Type of School: Private   Term: Semester
Application deadline: 07/01
Application fee: $35
Financial Aid deadline: 03/01
Can first year start other than Fall? No
Student faculty ratio: 18.2 to 1
Does the University offer:
- housing restricted to law students? No
- graduate student housing for which law students are eligible? No

Faculty & Administrators

	Total		Men		Women		Minorities	
	Fall	Spr	Fall	Spr	Fall	Spr	Fall	Spr
Full-time	21	21	17	17	4	4	1	1
Other Full-Time	4	4	1	1	3	3	0	0
Deans, librarians, & others who teach > 1/2	4	4	2	2	2	2	1	1
Part-time	13	16	9	12	4	4	1	1
Total	42	45	29	32	13	13	3	3
Deans, librarians, & others who teach < 1/2	1	1	0	0	1	1	0	0

Curriculum

	Full time	Part time
Typical first-year section size	75	45
Is there typically a "small section" of the first year class, other than Legal Writing, taught by full-time faculty?	No	No
If yes, typical size offered last year	N/A	N/A
# of classroom course titles beyond 1st year curriculum	63	45
# of upper division courses, excluding seminars, with an enrollment:		
Under 25	35	26
25 - 49	23	21
50 - 74	9	3
75 - 99	2	1
100 +	0	0
# of seminars	5	4
# of seminar positions available	153	
# of seminar positions filled	78	24
# of positions available in simulation courses	260	
# of simulation positions filled	98	124
# of positions available in faculty supervised clinical courses	0	
# of fac. sup. clin. positions filled	0	0
# involved in field placements	57	0
# involved in law journals	28	10
# in moot court or trial competitions	10	0
# of credit hrs required to graduate	90	

J.D. Enrollment & Ethnicity

	Men		Women		Fl-Time		Pt-Time		1st Yr		2nd Yr		3rd Yr		4th Yr		Total		JD Degrees Awarded
	#	%	#	%	#	%	#	%	#	%	#	%	#	%	#	%	#	%	
African-American	6	2.0	13	6.1	16	4.4	3	2.1	11	6.1	4	2.8	4	2.7	0	0.0	19	3.8	5
American Indian	18	6.1	14	6.6	21	5.8	11	7.7	11	6.1	8	5.7	12	8.1	1	2.8	32	6.3	10
Asian American	9	3.1	8	3.8	14	3.8	3	2.1	8	4.4	3	2.1	6	4.1	0	0.0	17	3.4	4
Mexican American	0	0.0	0	0.0	0	0.0	0	0.0	0	0.0	0	0.0	0	0.0	0	0.0	0	0.0	0
Puerto Rican	0	0.0	0	0.0	0	0.0	0	0.0	0	0.0	0	0.0	0	0.0	0	0.0	0	0.0	0
Hispanic American	14	4.8	7	3.3	19	5.2	2	1.4	8	4.4	8	5.7	4	2.7	1	2.8	21	4.2	4
Total Minorities	47	16.0	42	19.7	70	19.2	19	13.4	38	21.0	23	16.3	26	17.6	2	5.6	89	17.6	23
Foreign Nationals	1	0.3	0	0.0	1	0.3	0	0.0	0	0.0	0	0.0	1	0.7	0	0.0	1	0.2	0
Caucasian	245	83.6	171	80.3	293	80.5	123	86.6	143	79.0	118	83.7	121	81.8	34	94.4	416	82.2	160
Total	293	57.9	213	42.1	364	71.9	142	28.1	181	35.8	141	27.9	148	29.2	36	7.1	506		183

OKLAHOMA CITY UNIVERSITY

GPA & LSAT Scores

	Full Time	Part Time	Total
# of apps	569	177	746
# admits	455	110	565
# of matrics	153	34	187
75% GPA	3.18	3.36	
25% GPA	2.58	2.57	
75% LSAT	148	152	
25% LSAT	142	144	

Tuition & Fees

	Resident	Non-resident
Full-Time	$15,304	$15,304
Part-Time	$10,260	$10,260

Living Expenses

Estimated living expenses for Singles		
Living on campus	Living off campus	Living at home
$6,803	$9,156	$6,212

Employment

	Total	%
Employment status known	160	95.2
Employment status unknown	8	4.8
Employed	126	78.7
Pursuing graduate degrees	3	1.9
Unemployed seeking employment	22	13.7
Unemployed not seeking employment	9	5.6
Type of Employment		
# employed in law firms	74	58.7
# employed in business & industry	28	22.2
# employed in government	21	16.7
# employed in public interest	0	0.0
# employed as judicial clerks	1	0.8
# employed in academia	2	1.6
Geographic Location		
# employed in state	71	56.3
# employed in foreign countries	0	0.0
# of states where employed	20	

Grants/Scholarships

	Full-time		Part-time		Total	
	#	%	#	%	#	%
Total # of Students	364		142		506	
Total # receiving grants	44	12.1	13	9.2	57	11.3
Less than 1/2 tuition	15	4.1	10	7.0	25	4.9
Half to full tuition	12	3.3	0	0.0	12	2.4
Full tuition	4	1.1	3	2.1	7	1.4
More than full tuition	13	3.6	0	0.0	13	2.6
Median Grant Amount	$10,000		$3,000			

Informational & Library Resources

# of volumes & volume equivalents	262,218	# of professional staff	7
# of titles	64,073	Hours per week with professional staff	82
# of active serial subscriptions	4,045	Hours per week without professional staff	20
Study seating capacity inside the library	364	# of student computer work stations for entire law school	52
Square feet of law library	36,802	# of additional networked connections	44
Square feet of law school (excl. Library)	67,650	Require Laptop Computer?	N

J.D. Attrition (from Prior Year)

	Academic	Other	TOTALS	
	#	#	#	%
1st Year	16	38	54	28%
2nd Year	4	2	6	4.3%
3rd Year	0	3	3	1.6%
4th Year	0	0	0	0.0%

Bar Passage Rates

Jurisdiction	Oklahoma		
Exam	Sum 97	Win 98	Total
# from school taking bar for the first time	69	17	86
School's pass rate for all first-time takers	80%	88%	81%
State's pass rate for all first-time takers	81%	87%	82%

OKLAHOMA, UNIVERSITY OF

300 Timberdell Road
Norman, OK 73019-5081
(405)325-4699
http://www.law.ou.edu

ABA Approved Since 1923

The Basics

Type of School: Public
Term: Semester
Application deadline: 04/15
Application fee: $50
Financial Aid deadline: 03/01
Can first year start other than Fall? No
Student faculty ratio: 18.3 to 1
Does the University offer:
- housing restricted to law students? No
- graduate student housing for which law students are eligible? No

Faculty & Administrators

	Total		Men		Women		Minorities	
	Fall	Spr	Fall	Spr	Fall	Spr	Fall	Spr
Full-time	26	28	20	21	6	7	3	3
Other Full-Time	1	1	0	0	1	1	0	0
Deans, librarians, & others who teach > 1/2	4	4	3	3	1	1	0	0
Part-time	15	17	10	12	5	5	0	0
Total	46	50	33	36	13	14	3	3
Deans, librarians, & others who teach < 1/2	1	1	1	1	0	0	0	0

Curriculum

	Full time	Part time
Typical first-year section size	52	0
Is there typically a "small section" of the first year class, other than Legal Writing, taught by full-time faculty?	No	No
If yes, typical size offered last year	N/A	N/A
# of classroom course titles beyond 1st year curriculum	128	0
# of upper division courses, excluding seminars, with an enrollment:		
Under 25	75	0
25 - 49	32	0
50 - 74	20	0
75 - 99	2	0
100 +	0	0
# of seminars	16	0
# of seminar positions available	288	
# of seminar positions filled	223	0
# of positions available in simulation courses	172	
# of simulation positions filled	149	0
# of positions available in faculty supervised clinical courses	82	
# of fac. sup. clin. positions filled	80	0
# involved in field placements	115	0
# involved in law journals	54	0
# in moot court or trial competitions	34	0
# of credit hrs required to graduate	90	

J.D. Enrollment & Ethnicity

	Men		Women		Fl-Time		Pt-Time		1st Yr		2nd Yr		3rd Yr		4th Yr		Total		JD Degrees Awarded
	#	%	#	%	#	%	#	%	#	%	#	%	#	%	#	%	#	%	
African-American	6	1.8	9	3.7	15	2.6	0	0.0	5	2.5	8	3.9	2	1.2	0	0.0	15	2.6	4
American Indian	24	7.3	15	6.2	39	6.8	0	0.0	16	7.8	13	6.4	10	6.1	0	0.0	39	6.8	8
Asian American	8	2.4	15	6.2	23	4.0	0	0.0	8	3.9	7	3.4	8	4.8	0	0.0	23	4.0	5
Mexican American	6	1.8	6	2.5	12	2.1	0	0.0	0	0.0	8	3.9	4	2.4	0	0.0	12	2.1	6
Puerto Rican	0	0.0	0	0.0	0	0.0	0	0.0	0	0.0	0	0.0	0	0.0	0	0.0	0	0.0	0
Hispanic American	1	0.3	5	2.1	6	1.0	0	0.0	6	2.9	0	0.0	0	0.0	0	0.0	6	1.0	0
Total Minorities	45	13.6	50	20.7	95	16.6	0	0.0	35	17.2	36	17.7	24	14.5	0	0.0	95	16.6	23
Foreign Nationals	1	0.3	1	0.4	2	0.3	0	0.0	1	0.5	1	0.5	0	0.0	0	0.0	2	0.3	0
Caucasian	285	86.1	190	78.8	475	83.0	0	0.0	168	82.4	166	81.8	141	85.5	0	0.0	475	83.0	140
Total	331	57.9	241	42.1	572	100.0	0	0.0	204	35.7	203	35.5	165	28.8	0	0.0	572		163

GPA & LSAT Scores

	Full Time	Part Time	Total
# of apps	526	0	526
# admits	311	0	311
# of matrics	204	0	204
75% GPA	3.42	0.00	
25% GPA	2.74	0.00	
75% LSAT	154	0	
25% LSAT	146	0	

Tuition & Fees

	Resident	Non-resident
Full-Time	$4,744	$13,528
Part-Time	$3,312	$9,172

Living Expenses

Estimated living expenses for Singles		
Living on campus	Living off campus	Living at home
$9,673	$11,265	$7,728

Employment

	Total	%
Employment status known	174	86.6
Employment status unknown	27	13.4
Employed	162	93.1
Pursuing graduate degrees	4	2.3
Unemployed seeking employment	7	4.0
Unemployed not seeking employment	1	0.6
Type of Employment		
# employed in law firms	88	54.3
# employed in business & industry	31	19.1
# employed in government	28	17.3
# employed in public interest	5	3.1
# employed as judicial clerks	3	1.9
# employed in academia	3	1.9
Geographic Location		
# employed in state	121	74.7
# employed in foreign countries	0	0.0
# of states where employed	1	

Grants/Scholarships

	Full-time		Part-time		Total	
	#	%	#	%	#	%
Total # of Students	572		0		572	
Total # receiving grants	263	46.0	0	0.0	263	46.0
Less than 1/2 tuition	214	37.4	0	0.0	214	37.4
Half to full tuition	30	5.2	0	0.0	30	5.2
Full tuition	5	0.9	0	0.0	5	0.9
More than full tuition	14	2.4	0	0.0	14	2.4
Median Grant Amount	$2,000		$0			

Informational & Library Resources

# of volumes & volume equivalents	309,631	# of professional staff	5
# of titles	134,113	Hours per week with professional staff	54
# of active serial subscriptions	4,334	Hours per week without professional staff	44
Study seating capacity inside the library	374	# of student computer work stations for entire law school	30
Square feet of law library	28,733	# of additional networked connections	0
Square feet of law school (excl. Library)	58,063	Require Laptop Computer?	N

J.D. Attrition (from Prior Year)

	Academic	Other	TOTALS	
	#	#	#	%
1st Year	5	6	11	5.3%
2nd Year	0	2	2	1.2%
3rd Year	0	0	0	0.0%
4th Year	0	0	0	0.0%

Bar Passage Rates

Jurisdiction	Oklahoma		
Exam	Sum 97	Win 98	Total
# from school taking bar for the first time	141	17	158
School's pass rate for all first-time takers	86%	94%	87%
State's pass rate for all first-time takers	81%	87%	82%

OREGON, UNIVERSITY OF

1221 University of Oregon
Eugene, OR 97403-1221
(541)346-3852
http://www.law.uoregon.edu

ABA Approved Since 1923

The Basics

Type of School: Public Term: Semester
Application deadline: 03/01
Application fee: $50
Financial Aid deadline: 03/01
Can first year start other than Fall? No
Student faculty ratio: 17.4 to 1
Does the University offer:
- housing restricted to law students? No
- graduate student housing for which law students are eligible? Yes

Faculty & Administrators

	Total		Men		Women		Minorities	
	Fall	Spr	Fall	Spr	Fall	Spr	Fall	Spr
Full-time	24	24	14	16	10	8	5	4
Other Full-Time	3	3	2	2	1	1	0	0
Deans, librarians, & others who teach > 1/2	1	1	1	1	0	0	0	0
Part-time	8	8	8	6	0	2	0	0
Total	36	36	25	25	11	11	5	4
Deans, librarians, & others who teach < 1/2	1	1	1	1	0	0	1	1

Curriculum

	Full time	Part time
Typical first-year section size	56	0
Is there typically a "small section" of the first year class, other than Legal Writing, taught by full-time faculty?	No	No
If yes, typical size offered last year	N/A	N/A
# of classroom course titles beyond 1st year curriculum	73	0
# of upper division courses, excluding seminars, with an enrollment:		
Under 25	29	0
25 - 49	10	0
50 - 74	7	0
75 - 99	13	0
100 +	1	0
# of seminars	13	0
# of seminar positions available	263	
# of seminar positions filled	204	0
# of positions available in simulation courses	175	
# of simulation positions filled	120	0
# of positions available in faculty supervised clinical courses	102	
# of fac. sup. clin. positions filled	82	0
# involved in field placements	10	0
# involved in law journals	83	0
# in moot court or trial competitions	112	0
# of credit hrs required to graduate	85	

J.D. Enrollment & Ethnicity

	Men		Women		Fl-Time		Pt-Time		1st Yr		2nd Yr		3rd Yr		4th Yr		Total		JD Degrees Awarded
	#	%	#	%	#	%	#	%	#	%	#	%	#	%	#	%	#	%	
African-American	4	1.6	10	4.0	14	2.8	0	0.0	5	3.0	4	2.2	5	3.3	0	0.0	14	2.8	5
American Indian	3	1.2	2	0.8	5	1.0	0	0.0	3	1.8	0	0.0	2	1.3	0	0.0	5	1.0	1
Asian American	10	4.0	18	7.2	28	5.6	0	0.0	13	7.7	8	4.4	7	4.7	0	0.0	28	5.6	14
Mexican American	0	0.0	2	0.8	2	0.4	0	0.0	0	0.0	0	0.0	2	1.3	0	0.0	2	0.4	0
Puerto Rican	0	0.0	0	0.0	0	0.0	0	0.0	0	0.0	0	0.0	0	0.0	0	0.0	0	0.0	2
Hispanic American	8	3.2	3	1.2	11	2.2	0	0.0	4	2.4	4	2.2	3	2.0	0	0.0	11	2.2	6
Total Minorities	25	10.0	35	14.0	60	12.0	0	0.0	25	14.9	16	8.8	19	12.7	0	0.0	60	12.0	28
Foreign Nationals	5	2.0	3	1.2	8	1.6	0	0.0	2	1.2	3	1.7	3	2.0	0	0.0	8	1.6	6
Caucasian	219	88.0	212	84.8	431	86.4	0	0.0	141	83.9	162	89.5	128	85.3	0	0.0	431	86.4	146
Total	249	49.9	250	50.1	499	100.0	0	0.0	168	33.7	181	36.3	150	30.1	0	0.0	499		180

GPA & LSAT Scores

	Full Time	Part Time	Total
# of apps	1,050	0	1,050
# admits	548	0	548
# of matrics	170	0	170
75% GPA	3.60	0.00	
25% GPA	3.13	0.00	
75% LSAT	159	0	
25% LSAT	152	0	

Tuition & Fees

	Resident	Non-resident
Full-Time	$10,236	$13,984
Part-Time	$0	$0

Living Expenses

Estimated living expenses for Singles		
Living on campus	Living off campus	Living at home
$9,308	$9,308	$5,263

Grants/Scholarships

	Full-time		Part-time		Total	
	#	%	#	%	#	%
Total # of Students	499		0		499	
Total # receiving grants	215	43.1	0	0.0	215	43.1
Less than 1/2 tuition	202	40.5	0	0.0	202	40.5
Half to full tuition	13	2.6	0	0.0	13	2.6
Full tuition	0	0.0	0	0.0	0	0.0
More than full tuition	0	0.0	0	0.0	0	0.0
Median Grant Amount	$2,058		$0			

Informational & Library Resources

# of volumes & volume equivalents	355,108	# of professional staff	6
# of titles	46,234	Hours per week with professional staff	67
# of active serial subscriptions	3,343	Hours per week without professional staff	43
Study seating capacity inside the library	227	# of student computer work stations for entire law school	30
Square feet of law library	24,714	# of additional networked connections	350
Square feet of law school (excl. Library)	32,685	Require Laptop Computer?	Y

Employment

	Total	%
Employment status known	149	94.3
Employment status unknown	9	5.7
Employed	121	81.2
Pursuing graduate degrees	12	8.1
Unemployed seeking employment	12	8.1
Unemployed not seeking employment	4	2.7
Type of Employment		
# employed in law firms	55	45.5
# employed in business & industry	17	14.0
# employed in government	15	12.4
# employed in public interest	8	6.6
# employed as judicial clerks	24	19.8
# employed in academia	1	0.8
Geographic Location		
# employed in state	63	52.1
# employed in foreign countries	2	1.7
# of states where employed	16	

J.D. Attrition (from Prior Year)

	Academic	Other	TOTALS	
	#	#	#	%
1st Year	0	4	4	2.1%
2nd Year	0	10	10	6.4%
3rd Year	1	1	2	1.2%
4th Year	0	0	0	0.0%

Bar Passage Rates

Jurisdiction	Oregon			Washington		
Exam	Sum 97	Win 98	Total	Sum 97	Win 98	Total
# from school taking bar for the first time	85	4	89	24	18	42
School's pass rate for all first-time takers	69%	100%	71%	71%	83%	76%
State's pass rate for all first-time takers	74%	68%	72%	73%	83%	76%

PACE UNIVERSITY

78 North Broadway
White Plains, NY 10603
(914)422-4210
http://www.law.pace.edu

ABA Approved Since 1978

The Basics

Type of School: Private   Term: Semester

Application deadline: 02/15

Application fee: $55

Financial Aid deadline: 03/15

Can first year start other than Fall? No

Student faculty ratio: 15.4 to 1

Does the University offer:
- housing restricted to law students? No
- graduate student housing for which law students are eligible? Yes

Faculty & Administrators

	Total		Men		Women		Minorities	
	Fall	Spr	Fall	Spr	Fall	Spr	Fall	Spr
Full-time	35	35	23	23	12	12	2	3
Other Full-Time	0	0	0	0	0	0	0	0
Deans, librarians, & others who teach > 1/2	3	3	2	2	1	1	0	0
Part-time	38	52	23	39	15	13	2	1
Total	76	90	48	64	28	26	4	4
Deans, librarians, & others who teach < 1/2	2	2	1	1	1	1	0	0

Curriculum

	Full time	Part time
Typical first-year section size	82	88
Is there typically a "small section" of the first year class, other than Legal Writing, taught by full-time faculty?	Yes	Yes
If yes, typical size offered last year	24	23
# of classroom course titles beyond 1st year curriculum	67	73
# of upper division courses, excluding seminars, with an enrollment:		
Under 25	35	48
25 - 49	17	24
50 - 74	6	16
75 - 99	3	1
100 +	1	1
# of seminars	13	8
# of seminar positions available	489	
# of seminar positions filled	123	109
# of positions available in simulation courses	380	
# of simulation positions filled	191	142
# of positions available in faculty supervised clinical courses	76	
# of fac. sup. clin. positions filled	52	22
# involved in field placements	72	40
# involved in law journals	120	41
# in moot court or trial competitions	53	29
# of credit hrs required to graduate	90	

J.D. Enrollment & Ethnicity

	Men		Women		Fl-Time		Pt-Time		1st Yr		2nd Yr		3rd Yr		4th Yr		Total		JD Degrees Awarded
	#	%	#	%	#	%	#	%	#	%	#	%	#	%	#	%	#	%	
African-American	21	6.1	29	7.1	23	5.2	27	8.9	22	8.8	16	6.8	12	6.0	0	0.0	50	6.7	13
American Indian	2	0.6	0	0.0	0	0.0	2	0.7	2	0.8	0	0.0	0	0.0	0	0.0	2	0.3	1
Asian American	13	3.8	22	5.4	27	6.1	8	2.6	13	5.2	10	4.3	10	5.0	2	2.9	35	4.7	10
Mexican American	0	0.0	1	0.2	1	0.2	0	0.0	1	0.4	0	0.0	0	0.0	0	0.0	1	0.1	0
Puerto Rican	6	1.7	13	3.2	13	2.9	6	2.0	7	2.8	9	3.8	2	1.0	1	1.5	19	2.5	7
Hispanic American	7	2.0	17	4.2	14	3.1	10	3.3	4	1.6	11	4.7	7	3.5	2	2.9	24	3.2	8
Total Minorities	49	14.2	82	20.2	78	17.5	53	17.4	49	19.7	46	19.7	31	15.5	5	7.4	131	17.4	39
Foreign Nationals	0	0.0	0	0.0	0	0.0	0	0.0	0	0.0	0	0.0	0	0.0	0	0.0	0	0.0	2
Caucasian	296	85.8	324	79.8	368	82.5	252	82.6	200	80.3	188	80.3	169	84.5	63	92.6	620	82.6	235
Total	345	45.9	406	54.1	446	59.4	305	40.6	249	33.2	234	31.2	200	26.6	68	9.1	751		276

GPA & LSAT Scores

	Full Time	Part Time	Total
# of apps	1,413	420	1,833
# admits	716	171	887
# of matrics	156	101	257
75% GPA	3.41	3.60	
25% GPA	2.84	2.72	
75% LSAT	154	154	
25% LSAT	147	146	

Tuition & Fees

	Resident	Non-resident
Full-Time	$21,830	$21,830
Part-Time	$16,385	$16,385

Living Expenses

Estimated living expenses for Singles		
Living on campus	Living off campus	Living at home
$11,310	$13,450	$5,510

Employment

	Total	%
Employment status known	197	89.5
Employment status unknown	23	10.5
Employed	166	84.3
Pursuing graduate degrees	1	0.5
Unemployed seeking employment	22	11.2
Unemployed not seeking employment	8	4.1
Type of Employment		
# employed in law firms	94	56.6
# employed in business & industry	29	17.5
# employed in government	21	12.7
# employed in public interest	7	4.2
# employed as judicial clerks	8	4.8
# employed in academia	0	0.0
Geographic Location		
# employed in state	116	69.9
# employed in foreign countries	1	0.6
# of states where employed	13	

Grants/Scholarships

	Full-time		Part-time		Total	
	#	%	#	%	#	%
Total # of Students	446		305		751	
Total # receiving grants	136	30.5	59	19.3	195	26.0
Less than 1/2 tuition	100	22.4	41	13.4	141	18.8
Half to full tuition	31	7.0	18	5.9	49	6.5
Full tuition	1	0.2	0	0.0	1	0.1
More than full tuition	4	0.9	0	0.0	4	0.5
Median Grant Amount	$5,750		$7,000			

Informational & Library Resources

# of volumes & volume equivalents	318,430	# of professional staff	9
# of titles	124,270	Hours per week with professional staff	76
# of active serial subscriptions	3,837	Hours per week without professional staff	26
Study seating capacity inside the library	358	# of student computer work stations for entire law school	80
Square feet of law library	34,585	# of additional networked connections	500
Square feet of law school (excl. Library)	143,365	Require Laptop Computer?	N

J.D. Attrition (from Prior Year)

	Academic	Other	TOTALS	
	#	#	#	%
1st Year	0	16	16	6.2%
2nd Year	5	29	34	16%
3rd Year	3	7	10	4.3%
4th Year	0	1	1	1.1%

Bar Passage Rates

Jurisdiction	New York		
Exam	Sum 97	Win 98	Total
# from school taking bar for the first time	178	26	204
School's pass rate for all first-time takers	75%	73%	75%
State's pass rate for all first-time takers	78%	65%	76%

PENNSYLVANIA STATE UNIVERSITY

The Dickinson School of Law
150 S. College Street
Carlisle, PA 17013-2899
(717)240-5000
http://www.dsl.edu

ABA Approved Since 1931

The Basics

Type of School: Public   Term: Semester
Application deadline: 03/01
Application fee: $50
Financial Aid deadline: 02/15
Can first year start other than Fall? No
Student faculty ratio: 28.2 to 1
Does the University offer:
- housing restricted to law students? Yes
- graduate student housing for which law students are eligible? No

Faculty & Administrators

	Total		Men		Women		Minorities	
	Fall	Spr	Fall	Spr	Fall	Spr	Fall	Spr
Full-time	15	16	11	12	4	4	1	1
Other Full-Time	4	4	2	2	2	2	0	0
Deans, librarians, & others who teach > 1/2	5	6	4	5	1	1	1	1
Part-time	44	24	38	19	6	5	0	0
Total	68	50	55	38	13	12	2	2
Deans, librarians, & others who teach < 1/2	0	0	0	0	0	0	0	0

Curriculum

	Full time	Part time
Typical first-year section size	60	0
Is there typically a "small section" of the first year class, other than Legal Writing, taught by full-time faculty?	Yes	No
If yes, typical size offered last year	43	N/A
# of classroom course titles beyond 1st year curriculum	101	0
# of upper division courses, excluding seminars, with an enrollment:		
Under 25	49	0
25 - 49	26	0
50 - 74	14	0
75 - 99	12	0
100 +	0	0
# of seminars	22	0
# of seminar positions available	432	
# of seminar positions filled	265	0
# of positions available in simulation courses	552	
# of simulation positions filled	483	0
# of positions available in faculty supervised clinical courses	53	
# of fac. sup. clin. positions filled	42	0
# involved in field placements	67	0
# involved in law journals	109	0
# in moot court or trial competitions	26	0
# of credit hrs required to graduate	88	

J.D. Enrollment & Ethnicity

	Men		Women		Fl-Time		Pt-Time		1st Yr		2nd Yr		3rd Yr		4th Yr		Total		JD Degrees Awarded
	#	%	#	%	#	%	#	%	#	%	#	%	#	%	#	%	#	%	
African-American	5	1.7	10	4.6	15	3.0	0	0.0	2	1.1	6	3.7	7	4.3	0	0.0	15	3.0	2
American Indian	1	0.3	1	0.5	2	0.4	0	0.0	0	0.0	0	0.0	2	1.2	0	0.0	2	0.4	2
Asian American	4	1.4	5	2.3	9	1.8	0	0.0	4	2.2	4	2.4	1	0.6	0	0.0	9	1.8	5
Mexican American	0	0.0	0	0.0	0	0.0	0	0.0	0	0.0	0	0.0	0	0.0	0	0.0	0	0.0	0
Puerto Rican	1	0.3	0	0.0	1	0.2	0	0.0	0	0.0	1	0.6	0	0.0	0	0.0	1	0.2	0
Hispanic American	4	1.4	3	1.4	7	1.4	0	0.0	2	1.1	1	0.6	4	2.4	0	0.0	7	1.4	3
Total Minorities	15	5.2	19	8.8	34	6.7	0	0.0	8	4.4	12	7.3	14	8.5	0	0.0	34	6.7	12
Foreign Nationals	0	0.0	0	0.0	0	0.0	0	0.0	0	0.0	0	0.0	0	0.0	0	0.0	0	0.0	0
Caucasian	276	94.8	198	91.2	474	93.3	0	0.0	172	95.6	152	92.7	150	91.5	0	0.0	474	93.3	149
Total	291	57.3	217	42.7	508	100.0	0	0.0	180	35.4	164	32.3	164	32.3	0	0.0	508		161

GPA & LSAT Scores

	Full Time	Part Time	Total
# of apps	1,150	0	1,150
# admits	649	0	649
# of matrics	185	0	185
75% GPA	3.50	0.00	
25% GPA	2.86	0.00	
75% LSAT	155	0	
25% LSAT	150	0	

Tuition & Fees

	Resident	Non-resident
Full-Time	$15,190	$15,190
Part-Time	$0	$0

Living Expenses

Estimated living expenses for Singles		
Living on campus	Living off campus	Living at home
$10,775	$12,875	$10,375

Grants/Scholarships

	Full-time		Part-time		Total	
	#	%	#	%	#	%
Total # of Students	508		0		508	
Total # receiving grants	180	35.4	0	0.0	180	35.4
Less than 1/2 tuition	132	26.0	0	0.0	132	26.0
Half to full tuition	33	6.5	0	0.0	33	6.5
Full tuition	14	2.8	0	0.0	14	2.8
More than full tuition	1	0.2	0	0.0	1	0.2
Median Grant Amount	$2,200		$0			

Informational & Library Resources

# of volumes & volume equivalents	409,216	# of professional staff	6
# of titles	77,749	Hours per week with professional staff	81
# of active serial subscriptions	4,159	Hours per week without professional staff	5
Study seating capacity inside the library	415	# of student computer work stations for entire law school	101
Square feet of law library	38,114	# of additional networked connections	88
Square feet of law school (excl. Library)	43,867	Require Laptop Computer?	N

Employment

	Total	%
Employment status known	174	95.6
Employment status unknown	8	4.4
Employed	159	91.4
Pursuing graduate degrees	4	2.3
Unemployed seeking employment	8	4.6
Unemployed not seeking employment	3	1.7
Type of Employment		
# employed in law firms	68	42.8
# employed in business & industry	4	2.5
# employed in government	14	8.8
# employed in public interest	4	2.5
# employed as judicial clerks	52	32.7
# employed in academia	0	0.0
Geographic Location		
# employed in state	112	70.4
# employed in foreign countries	1	0.6
# of states where employed	19	

J.D. Attrition (from Prior Year)

	Academic	Other	TOTALS	
	#	#	#	%
1st Year	3	17	20	11%
2nd Year	0	1	1	0.6%
3rd Year	0	0	0	0.0%
4th Year	0	0	0	0.0%

Bar Passage Rates

Jurisdiction	Pennsylvania		
Exam	Sum 97	Win 98	Total
# from school taking bar for the first time	140	3	143
School's pass rate for all first-time takers	89%	67%	89%
State's pass rate for all first-time takers	81%	73%	79%

PENNSYLVANIA, UNIVERSITY OF

3400 Chestnut Street
Philadelphia, PA 19104-6204
(215)898-7483
http://www.law.upenn.edu

ABA Approved Since 1923

The Basics

Type of School: Private   Term: Semester

Application deadline: 03/01

Application fee: $65

Financial Aid deadline: 03/01

Can first year start other than Fall? No

Student faculty ratio: 18.8 to 1

Does the University offer:
- housing restricted to law students? Yes
- graduate student housing for which law students are eligible? Yes

Faculty & Administrators

	Total		Men		Women		Minorities	
	Fall	Spr	Fall	Spr	Fall	Spr	Fall	Spr
Full-time	34	40	27	31	7	9	1	3
Other Full-Time	3	2	0	0	3	2	0	0
Deans, librarians, & others who teach > 1/2	2	2	2	2	0	0	0	0
Part-time	32	37	22	28	10	9	6	5
Total	71	81	51	61	20	20	7	8
Deans, librarians, & others who teach < 1/2	0	0	0	0	0	0	0	0

Curriculum

	Full time	Part time
Typical first-year section size	91	0
Is there typically a "small section" of the first year class, other than Legal Writing, taught by full-time faculty?	Yes	No
If yes, typical size offered last year	57	N/A
# of classroom course titles beyond 1st year curriculum	76	0
# of upper division courses, excluding seminars, with an enrollment:		
Under 25	38	0
25 - 49	27	0
50 - 74	16	0
75 - 99	8	0
100 +	5	0
# of seminars	33	0
# of seminar positions available	594	
# of seminar positions filled	384	0
# of positions available in simulation courses	265	
# of simulation positions filled	214	0
# of positions available in faculty supervised clinical courses	110	
# of fac. sup. clin. positions filled	74	0
# involved in field placements	22	0
# involved in law journals	223	0
# in moot court or trial competitions	115	0
# of credit hrs required to graduate	89	

J.D. Enrollment & Ethnicity

	Men		Women		Fl-Time		Pt-Time		1st Yr		2nd Yr		3rd Yr		4th Yr		Total		JD Degrees Awarded
	#	%	#	%	#	%	#	%	#	%	#	%	#	%	#	%	#	%	
African-American	32	7.3	36	10.9	68	8.9	0	0.0	21	7.7	26	10.9	21	8.2	0	0.0	68	8.9	16
American Indian	3	0.7	1	0.3	4	0.5	0	0.0	0	0.0	0	0.0	4	1.6	0	0.0	4	0.5	0
Asian American	30	6.9	32	9.7	62	8.1	0	0.0	23	8.5	16	6.7	23	8.9	0	0.0	62	8.1	20
Mexican American	1	0.2	2	0.6	3	0.4	0	0.0	1	0.4	0	0.0	2	0.8	0	0.0	3	0.4	4
Puerto Rican	7	1.6	6	1.8	13	1.7	0	0.0	4	1.5	4	1.7	5	1.9	0	0.0	13	1.7	4
Hispanic American	22	5.0	16	4.8	38	5.0	0	0.0	13	4.8	12	5.0	13	5.1	0	0.0	38	5.0	15
Total Minorities	95	21.8	93	28.2	188	24.5	0	0.0	62	22.9	58	24.4	68	26.5	0	0.0	188	24.5	59
Foreign Nationals	11	2.5	9	2.7	20	2.6	0	0.0	6	2.2	5	2.1	9	3.5	0	0.0	20	2.6	4
Caucasian	330	75.7	228	69.1	558	72.8	0	0.0	203	74.9	175	73.5	180	70.0	0	0.0	558	72.8	160
Total	436	56.9	330	43.1	766	100.0	0	0.0	271	35.4	238	31.1	257	33.6	0	0.0	766		223

GPA & LSAT Scores

	Full Time	Part Time	Total
# of apps	3,771	0	3,771
# admits	1,178	0	1,178
# of matrics	271	0	271
75% GPA	3.73	0.00	
25% GPA	3.41	0.00	
75% LSAT	168	0	
25% LSAT	164	0	

Tuition & Fees

	Resident	Non-resident
Full-Time	$25,780	$25,780
Part-Time	$0	$0

Living Expenses

Estimated living expenses for Singles		
Living on campus	Living off campus	Living at home
$12,320	$12,320	$6,570

Grants/Scholarships

	Full-time		Part-time		Total	
	#	%	#	%	#	%
Total # of Students	766		0		766	
Total # receiving grants	233	30.4	0	0.0	233	30.4
Less than 1/2 tuition	156	20.4	0	0.0	156	20.4
Half to full tuition	68	8.9	0	0.0	68	8.9
Full tuition	8	1.0	0	0.0	8	1.0
More than full tuition	1	0.1	0	0.0	1	0.1
Median Grant Amount	$9,780		$0			

Informational & Library Resources

# of volumes & volume equivalents	663,947	# of professional staff	12
# of titles	172,112	Hours per week with professional staff	76
# of active serial subscriptions	7,385	Hours per week without professional staff	35
Study seating capacity inside the library	550	# of student computer work stations for entire law school	132
Square feet of law library	72,000	# of additional networked connections	1006
Square feet of law school (excl. Library)	76,800	Require Laptop Computer?	N

Employment

	Total	%
Employment status known	283	97.6
Employment status unknown	7	2.4
Employed	277	97.9
Pursuing graduate degrees	2	0.7
Unemployed seeking employment	3	1.1
Unemployed not seeking employment	1	0.4
Type of Employment		
# employed in law firms	195	70.4
# employed in business & industry	16	5.8
# employed in government	10	3.6
# employed in public interest	13	4.7
# employed as judicial clerks	39	14.1
# employed in academia	4	1.4
Geographic Location		
# employed in state	61	22.0
# employed in foreign countries	3	1.1
# of states where employed	22	

J.D. Attrition (from Prior Year)

	Academic	Other	TOTALS	
	#	#	#	%
1st Year	0	9	9	3.9%
2nd Year	0	0	0	0.0%
3rd Year	0	0	0	0.0%
4th Year	0	0	0	0.0%

Bar Passage Rates

Jurisdiction	New York			Pennsylvania		
Exam	Sum 97	Win 98	Total	Sum 97	Win 98	Total
# from school taking bar for the first time	141	14	155	64	12	76
School's pass rate for all first-time takers	94%	71%	92%	97%	100%	97%
State's pass rate for all first-time takers	78%	65%	76%	81%	73%	79%

PEPPERDINE UNIVERSITY

24255 Pacific Coast Highway
Malibu, CA 90263
(310)456-4611
http://law.pepperdine.edu

ABA Approved Since 1972

The Basics

Type of School: Private — Term: Semester
Application deadline: 03/01
Application fee: $50
Financial Aid deadline: 04/11
Can first year start other than Fall? No
Student faculty ratio: 17.6 to 1
Does the University offer:
- housing restricted to law students? No
- graduate student housing for which law students are eligible? Yes

Faculty & Administrators

	Total		Men		Women		Minorities	
	Fall	Spr	Fall	Spr	Fall	Spr	Fall	Spr
Full-time	29	28	23	23	6	5	2	2
Other Full-Time	0	0	0	0	0	0	0	0
Deans, librarians, & others who teach > 1/2	4	4	3	3	1	1	0	0
Part-time	28	23	18	17	10	6	3	1
Total	61	55	44	43	17	12	5	3
Deans, librarians, & others who teach < 1/2	4	4	3	3	1	1	0	0

Curriculum

	Full time	Part time
Typical first-year section size	80	0
Is there typically a "small section" of the first year class, other than Legal Writing, taught by full-time faculty?	No	No
If yes, typical size offered last year	N/A	N/A
# of classroom course titles beyond 1st year curriculum	96	0
# of upper division courses, excluding seminars, with an enrollment:		
Under 25	84	0
25 - 49	26	0
50 - 74	7	0
75 - 99	10	0
100 +	5	0
# of seminars	19	0
# of seminar positions available	407	
# of seminar positions filled	269	0
# of positions available in simulation courses	1,132	
# of simulation positions filled	956	0
# of positions available in faculty supervised clinical courses	93	
# of fac. sup. clin. positions filled	93	0
# involved in field placements	218	0
# involved in law journals	75	0
# in moot court or trial competitions	203	0
# of credit hrs required to graduate	88	

J.D. Enrollment & Ethnicity

	Men		Women		Fl-Time		Pt-Time		1st Yr		2nd Yr		3rd Yr		4th Yr		Total		JD Degrees Awarded
	#	%	#	%	#	%	#	%	#	%	#	%	#	%	#	%	#	%	
African-American	18	5.0	17	5.8	35	5.4	0	0.0	14	6.1	13	5.8	8	4.1	0	0.0	35	5.4	5
American Indian	3	0.8	3	1.0	6	0.9	0	0.0	2	0.9	1	0.4	3	1.5	0	0.0	6	0.9	3
Asian American	21	5.9	20	6.8	41	6.3	0	0.0	12	5.2	8	3.6	21	10.7	0	0.0	41	6.3	20
Mexican American	12	3.4	12	4.1	24	3.7	0	0.0	8	3.5	6	2.7	10	5.1	0	0.0	24	3.7	8
Puerto Rican	0	0.0	0	0.0	0	0.0	0	0.0	0	0.0	0	0.0	0	0.0	0	0.0	0	0.0	0
Hispanic American	0	0.0	0	0.0	0	0.0	0	0.0	0	0.0	0	0.0	0	0.0	0	0.0	0	0.0	0
Total Minorities	54	15.1	52	17.6	106	16.3	0	0.0	36	15.6	28	12.5	42	21.3	0	0.0	106	16.3	36
Foreign Nationals	0	0.0	0	0.0	0	0.0	0	0.0	0	0.0	0	0.0	0	0.0	0	0.0	0	0.0	0
Caucasian	303	84.9	243	82.4	546	83.7	0	0.0	195	84.4	196	87.5	155	78.7	0	0.0	546	83.7	180
Total	357	54.8	295	45.2	652	100.0	0	0.0	231	35.4	224	34.4	197	30.2	0	0.0	652		216

GPA & LSAT Scores

	Full Time	Part Time	Total
# of apps	2,395	0	2,395
# admits	1,071	0	1,071
# of matrics	232	0	232
75% GPA	3.51	0.00	
25% GPA	3.01	0.00	
75% LSAT	160	0	
25% LSAT	153	0	

Tuition & Fees

	Resident	Non-resident
Full-Time	$22,880	$22,880
Part-Time	$0	$0

Living Expenses

Estimated living expenses for Singles		
Living on campus	Living off campus	Living at home
$15,234	$15,234	$15,234

Employment

	Total	%
Employment status known	212	83.5
Employment status unknown	42	16.5
Employed	159	75.0
Pursuing graduate degrees	15	7.1
Unemployed seeking employment	33	15.6
Unemployed not seeking employment	5	2.4
Type of Employment		
# employed in law firms	130	81.8
# employed in business & industry	18	11.3
# employed in government	7	4.4
# employed in public interest	2	1.3
# employed as judicial clerks	1	0.6
# employed in academia	0	0.0
Geographic Location		
# employed in state	137	86.2
# employed in foreign countries	0	0.0
# of states where employed	9	

Grants/Scholarships

	Full-time		Part-time		Total	
	#	%	#	%	#	%
Total # of Students	652		0		652	
Total # receiving grants	465	71.3	0	0.0	465	71.3
Less than 1/2 tuition	336	51.5	0	0.0	336	51.5
Half to full tuition	91	14.0	0	0.0	91	14.0
Full tuition	4	0.6	0	0.0	4	0.6
More than full tuition	34	5.2	0	0.0	34	5.2
Median Grant Amount	$9,110		$0			

Informational & Library Resources

# of volumes & volume equivalents	312,404	# of professional staff	6
# of titles	111,045	Hours per week with professional staff	74
# of active serial subscriptions	3,591	Hours per week without professional staff	35
Study seating capacity inside the library	500	# of student computer work stations for entire law school	52
Square feet of law library	40,915	# of additional networked connections	70
Square feet of law school (excl. Library)	81,190	Require Laptop Computer?	N

J.D. Attrition (from Prior Year)

	Academic	Other	TOTALS	
	#	#	#	%
1st Year	9	10	19	7.9%
2nd Year	0	0	0	0.0%
3rd Year	0	0	0	0.0%
4th Year	0	0	0	0.0%

Bar Passage Rates

Jurisdiction	California		
Exam	Sum 97	Win 98	Total
# from school taking bar for the first time	209	28	237
School's pass rate for all first-time takers	87%	71%	85%
State's pass rate for all first-time takers	75%	57%	71%

PITTSBURGH, UNIVERSITY OF

3900 Forbes Avenue
Pittsburgh, PA 15260
(412)648-1400
http://www.law.pitt.edu

ABA Approved Since 1923

The Basics

Type of School: Public   Term: Semester
Application deadline: 03/01
Application fee: $40
Financial Aid deadline: 03/01
Can first year start other than Fall? No
Student faculty ratio: 21.5 to 1
Does the University offer:
- housing restricted to law students? No
- graduate student housing for which law students are eligible? No

Faculty & Administrators

	Total		Men		Women		Minorities	
	Fall	Spr	Fall	Spr	Fall	Spr	Fall	Spr
Full-time	28	29	15	15	13	14	4	4
Other Full-Time	0	0	0	0	0	0	0	0
Deans, librarians, & others who teach > 1/2	6	5	5	4	1	1	0	0
Part-time	24	36	17	28	7	8	3	4
Total	58	70	37	47	21	23	7	8
Deans, librarians, & others who teach < 1/2	2	2	2	2	0	0	0	0

Curriculum

	Full time	Part time
Typical first-year section size	84	0
Is there typically a "small section" of the first year class, other than Legal Writing, taught by full-time faculty?	Yes	No
If yes, typical size offered last year	25	N/A
# of classroom course titles beyond 1st year curriculum	92	0
# of upper division courses, excluding seminars, with an enrollment:		
Under 25	74	0
25 - 49	18	0
50 - 74	12	0
75 - 99	12	0
100 +	6	0
# of seminars	19	0
# of seminar positions available	236	
# of seminar positions filled	190	0
# of positions available in simulation courses	382	
# of simulation positions filled	255	0
# of positions available in faculty supervised clinical courses	84	
# of fac. sup. clin. positions filled	71	0
# involved in field placements	232	0
# involved in law journals	85	0
# in moot court or trial competitions	115	0
# of credit hrs required to graduate	88	

J.D. Enrollment & Ethnicity

	Men		Women		Fl-Time		Pt-Time		1st Yr		2nd Yr		3rd Yr		4th Yr		Total		JD Degrees Awarded
	#	%	#	%	#	%	#	%	#	%	#	%	#	%	#	%	#	%	
African-American	11	2.6	26	8.6	37	5.1	0	0.0	22	8.9	5	2.4	10	3.8	0	0.0	37	5.1	17
American Indian	6	1.4	2	0.7	8	1.1	0	0.0	3	1.2	1	0.5	4	1.5	0	0.0	8	1.1	2
Asian American	7	1.7	7	2.3	14	1.9	0	0.0	11	4.4	2	0.9	1	0.4	0	0.0	14	1.9	1
Mexican American	0	0.0	0	0.0	0	0.0	0	0.0	0	0.0	0	0.0	0	0.0	0	0.0	0	0.0	0
Puerto Rican	1	0.2	0	0.0	1	0.1	0	0.0	0	0.0	0	0.0	1	0.4	0	0.0	1	0.1	0
Hispanic American	7	1.7	7	2.3	14	1.9	0	0.0	8	3.2	1	0.5	5	1.9	0	0.0	14	1.9	14
Total Minorities	32	7.6	42	14.0	74	10.2	0	0.0	44	17.7	9	4.2	21	8.0	0	0.0	74	10.2	34
Foreign Nationals	0	0.0	0	0.0	0	0.0	0	0.0	0	0.0	0	0.0	0	0.0	0	0.0	0	0.0	0
Caucasian	389	92.4	259	86.0	648	89.8	0	0.0	204	82.3	203	95.8	241	92.0	0	0.0	648	89.8	203
Total	421	58.3	301	41.7	722	100.0	0	0.0	248	34.3	212	29.4	262	36.3	0	0.0	722		237

GPA & LSAT Scores

	Full Time	Part Time	Total
# of apps	1,228	0	1,228
# admits	826	0	826
# of matrics	250	0	250
75% GPA	3.50	0.00	
25% GPA	2.80	0.00	
75% LSAT	154	0	
25% LSAT	150	0	

Tuition & Fees

	Resident	Non-resident
Full-Time	$12,392	$19,098
Part-Time	$0	$0

Living Expenses

Estimated living expenses for Singles

Living on campus	Living off campus	Living at home
N/A	$10,500	$9,200

Grants/Scholarships

	Full-time		Part-time		Total	
	#	%	#	%	#	%
Total # of Students	722		0		722	
Total # receiving grants	466	64.5	0	0.0	466	64.5
Less than 1/2 tuition	163	22.6	0	0.0	163	22.6
Half to full tuition	67	9.3	0	0.0	67	9.3
Full tuition	3	0.4	0	0.0	3	0.4
More than full tuition	233	32.3	0	0.0	233	32.3
Median Grant Amount	$4,695		$0			

Informational & Library Resources

# of volumes & volume equivalents	378,167	# of professional staff	7
# of titles	152,231	Hours per week with professional staff	61
# of active serial subscriptions	5,038	Hours per week without professional staff	41
Study seating capacity inside the library	454	# of student computer work stations for entire law school	60
Square feet of law library	43,050	# of additional networked connections	0
Square feet of law school (excl. Library)	41,455	Require Laptop Computer?	N

Employment

	Total	%
Employment status known	210	92.5
Employment status unknown	17	7.5
Employed	173	82.4
Pursuing graduate degrees	7	3.3
Unemployed seeking employment	6	2.9
Unemployed not seeking employment	24	11.4
Type of Employment		
# employed in law firms	91	52.6
# employed in business & industry	17	9.8
# employed in government	12	6.9
# employed in public interest	3	1.7
# employed as judicial clerks	23	13.3
# employed in academia	1	0.6
Geographic Location		
# employed in state	99	57.2
# employed in foreign countries	1	0.6
# of states where employed	22	

J.D. Attrition (from Prior Year)

	Academic	Other	TOTALS	
	#	#	#	%
1st Year	0	0	0	0.0%
2nd Year	0	0	0	0.0%
3rd Year	0	0	0	0.0%
4th Year	0	0	0	0.0%

Bar Passage Rates

Jurisdiction	Pennsylvania		
Exam	Sum 97	Win 98	Total
# from school taking bar for the first time	152	38	190
School's pass rate for all first-time takers	84%	37%	74%
State's pass rate for all first-time takers	81%	73%	79%

PONTIFICAL CATHOLIC UNIVERSITY OF P.R.

2250 Las Americas Avenue Suite 543
Ponce, PR 00717-0777
(787)841-2000

ABA Approved Since 1967

The Basics

Type of School: Private
Term: Semester
Application deadline: 04/15
Application fee: $60
Financial Aid deadline: Rolling
Can first year start other than Fall? Yes
Student faculty ratio: 21.7 to 1
Does the University offer:
- housing restricted to law students? No
- graduate student housing for which law students are eligible? No

Faculty & Administrators

	Total		Men		Women		Minorities	
	Fall	Spr	Fall	Spr	Fall	Spr	Fall	Spr
Full-time	17	17	10	10	7	7	17	17
Other Full-Time	0	0	0	0	0	0	0	0
Deans, librarians, & others who teach > 1/2	0	0	0	0	0	0	0	0
Part-time	13	0	11	0	2	0	13	0
Total	30	17	21	10	9	7	30	17
Deans, librarians, & others who teach < 1/2	3	3	1	1	2	2	3	3

Curriculum

	Full time	Part time
Typical first-year section size	60	50
Is there typically a "small section" of the first year class, other than Legal Writing, taught by full-time faculty?	Yes	Yes
If yes, typical size offered last year	20	20
# of classroom course titles beyond 1st year curriculum	24	21
# of upper division courses, excluding seminars, with an enrollment:		
Under 25	5	5
25 - 49	7	10
50 - 74	13	1
75 - 99	0	0
100 +	0	0
# of seminars	1	1
# of seminar positions available	45	
# of seminar positions filled	25	10
# of positions available in simulation courses	50	
# of simulation positions filled	0	45
# of positions available in faculty supervised clinical courses	6	
# of fac. sup. clin. positions filled	4	0
# involved in field placements	73	0
# involved in law journals	0	0
# in moot court or trial competitions	0	0
# of credit hrs required to graduate	94	

J.D. Enrollment & Ethnicity

	Men		Women		Fl-Time		Pt-Time		1st Yr		2nd Yr		3rd Yr		4th Yr		Total		JD Degrees Awarded
	#	%	#	%	#	%	#	%	#	%	#	%	#	%	#	%	#	%	
African-American	0	0.0	0	0.0	0	0.0	0	0.0	0	0.0	0	0.0	0	0.0	0	0.0	0	0.0	0
American Indian	0	0.0	0	0.0	0	0.0	0	0.0	0	0.0	0	0.0	0	0.0	0	0.0	0	0.0	0
Asian American	0	0.0	0	0.0	0	0.0	0	0.0	0	0.0	0	0.0	0	0.0	0	0.0	0	0.0	0
Mexican American	0	0.0	0	0.0	0	0.0	0	0.0	0	0.0	0	0.0	0	0.0	0	0.0	0	0.0	0
Puerto Rican	237	100.0	266	100.0	318	100.0	185	100.0	178	100.0	142	100.0	144	100.0	39	100.0	503	100.0	121
Hispanic American	0	0.0	0	0.0	0	0.0	0	0.0	0	0.0	0	0.0	0	0.0	0	0.0	0	0.0	0
Total Minorities	237	100.0	266	100.0	318	100.0	185	100.0	178	100.0	142	100.0	144	100.0	39	100.0	503	100.0	121
Foreign Nationals	0	0.0	0	0.0	0	0.0	0	0.0	0	0.0	0	0.0	0	0.0	0	0.0	0	0.0	0
Caucasian	0	0.0	0	0.0	0	0.0	0	0.0	0	0.0	0	0.0	0	0.0	0	0.0	0	0.0	0
Total	237	47.1	266	52.9	318	63.2	185	36.8	178	35.4	142	28.2	144	28.6	39	7.8	503		121

GPA & LSAT Scores

	Full Time	Part Time	Total
# of apps	417	222	639
# admits	166	77	243
# of matrics	116	62	178
75% GPA	3.60	3.56	
25% GPA	2.97	2.94	
75% LSAT	140	139	
25% LSAT	132	131	

Tuition & Fees

	Resident	Non-resident
Full-Time	$9,275	$0
Part-Time	$6,613	$0

Living Expenses

Estimated living expenses for Singles		
Living on campus	Living off campus	Living at home
$4,867	$6,327	$3,627

Grants/Scholarships

	Full-time		Part-time		Total	
	#	%	#	%	#	%
Total # of Students	318		185		503	
Total # receiving grants	72	22.6	22	11.9	94	18.7
Less than 1/2 tuition	0	0.0	0	0.0	0	0.0
Half to full tuition	56	17.6	20	10.8	76	15.1
Full tuition	16	5.0	2	1.1	18	3.6
More than full tuition	0	0.0	0	0.0	0	0.0
Median Grant Amount	$135,99		$27,740			

Informational & Library Resources

# of volumes & volume equivalents	182,603	# of professional staff	4
# of titles	23,064	Hours per week with professional staff	90
# of active serial subscriptions	2,274	Hours per week without professional staff	13
Study seating capacity inside the library	169	# of student computer work stations for entire law school	2
Square feet of law library	20,393	# of additional networked connections	33
Square feet of law school (excl. Library)	28,612	Require Laptop Computer?	N

Employment

	Total	%
Employment status known	100	75.8
Employment status unknown	32	24.2
Employed	91	91.0
Pursuing graduate degrees	7	7.0
Unemployed seeking employment	2	2.0
Unemployed not seeking employment	0	0.0
Type of Employment		
# employed in law firms	46	50.5
# employed in business & industry	6	6.6
# employed in government	32	35.2
# employed in public interest	0	0.0
# employed as judicial clerks	5	5.5
# employed in academia	0	0.0
Geographic Location		
# employed in state	90	98.9
# employed in foreign countries	0	0.0
# of states where employed	1	

J.D. Attrition (from Prior Year)

	Academic	Other	TOTALS	
	#	#	#	%
1st Year	21	11	32	19%
2nd Year	4	1	5	3.4%
3rd Year	0	0	0	0.0%
4th Year	0	0	0	0.0%

Bar Passage Rates

Jurisdiction	Puerto Rico		
Exam	Sum 97	Win 98	Total
# from school taking bar for the first time	104	115	219
School's pass rate for all first-time takers	63%	68%	65%
State's pass rate for all first-time takers	63%	53%	61%

PUERTO RICO, UNIVERSITY OF

P.O. Box 23349
San Juan, PR 00931-3349
(787)764-2680

ABA Approved Since 1945

The Basics

Type of School: Public   Term: Semester
Application deadline: 02/16
Application fee: $15
Financial Aid deadline: 05/01
Can first year start other than Fall? No
Student faculty ratio: 20.7 to 1
Does the University offer:
- housing restricted to law students? No
- graduate student housing for which law students are eligible? No

Faculty & Administrators

	Total		Men		Women		Minorities	
	Fall	Spr	Fall	Spr	Fall	Spr	Fall	Spr
Full-time	20	21	16	17	4	4	19	20
Other Full-Time	0	0	0	0	0	0	0	0
Deans, librarians, & others who teach > 1/2	3	3	1	1	2	2	3	3
Part-time	31	22	16	16	15	6	30	18
Total	54	46	33	34	21	12	52	41
Deans, librarians, & others who teach < 1/2	3	3	2	2	1	1	2	2

Curriculum

	Full time	Part time
Typical first-year section size	50	30
Is there typically a "small section" of the first year class, other than Legal Writing, taught by full-time faculty?	No	No
If yes, typical size offered last year	N/A	N/A
# of classroom course titles beyond 1st year curriculum	49	35
# of upper division courses, excluding seminars, with an enrollment:		
Under 25	26	16
25 - 49	16	5
50 - 74	12	9
75 - 99	2	3
100 +	0	0
# of seminars	16	8
# of seminar positions available	360	
# of seminar positions filled	172	91
# of positions available in simulation courses	40	
# of simulation positions filled	27	13
# of positions available in faculty supervised clinical courses	165	
# of fac. sup. clin. positions filled	85	32
# involved in field placements	21	4
# involved in law journals	29	10
# in moot court or trial competitions	5	0
# of credit hrs required to graduate	92	

J.D. Enrollment & Ethnicity

	Men		Women		Fl-Time		Pt-Time		1st Yr		2nd Yr		3rd Yr		4th Yr		Total		JD Degrees Awarded
	#	%	#	%	#	%	#	%	#	%	#	%	#	%	#	%	#	%	
African-American	0	0.0	0	0.0	0	0.0	0	0.0	0	0.0	0	0.0	0	0.0	0	0.0	0	0.0	0
American Indian	0	0.0	0	0.0	0	0.0	0	0.0	0	0.0	0	0.0	0	0.0	0	0.0	0	0.0	0
Asian American	0	0.0	0	0.0	0	0.0	0	0.0	0	0.0	0	0.0	0	0.0	0	0.0	0	0.0	0
Mexican American	0	0.0	0	0.0	0	0.0	0	0.0	0	0.0	0	0.0	0	0.0	0	0.0	0	0.0	0
Puerto Rican	250	99.6	316	98.1	345	98.0	221	100.0	151	98.7	177	97.3	179	100.0	59	100.0	566	98.8	109
Hispanic American	1	0.4	2	0.6	3	0.9	0	0.0	1	0.7	2	1.1	0	0.0	0	0.0	3	0.5	0
Total Minorities	251	100.0	318	98.8	348	98.9	221	100.0	152	99.3	179	98.4	179	100.0	59	100.0	569	99.3	109
Foreign Nationals	0	0.0	4	1.2	4	1.1	0	0.0	1	0.7	3	1.6	0	0.0	0	0.0	4	0.7	4
Caucasian	0	0.0	0	0.0	0	0.0	0	0.0	0	0.0	0	0.0	0	0.0	0	0.0	0	0.0	0
Total	251	43.8	322	56.2	352	61.4	221	38.6	153	26.7	182	31.8	179	31.2	59	10.3	573		113

GPA & LSAT Scores

	Full Time	Part Time	Total
# of apps	421	299	720
# admits	123	56	179
# of matrics	103	50	153
75% GPA	3.79	3.79	
25% GPA	3.26	3.14	
75% LSAT	151	149	
25% LSAT	143	142	

Tuition & Fees

	Resident	Non-resident
Full-Time	$2,320	$3,570
Part-Time	$1,570	$3,500

Living Expenses

Estimated living expenses for Singles		
Living on campus	Living off campus	Living at home
$7,544	$6,044	$5,144

Grants/Scholarships

	Full-time		Part-time		Total	
	#	%	#	%	#	%
Total # of Students	352		221		573	
Total # receiving grants	131	37.2	21	9.5	152	26.5
Less than 1/2 tuition	5	1.4	0	0.0	5	0.9
Half to full tuition	79	22.4	19	8.6	98	17.1
Full tuition	12	3.4	0	0.0	12	2.1
More than full tuition	35	9.9	2	0.9	37	6.5
Median Grant Amount	$2,000		$2,000			

Informational & Library Resources

# of volumes & volume equivalents	328,113	# of professional staff	9
# of titles	66,798	Hours per week with professional staff	95
# of active serial subscriptions	4,451	Hours per week without professional staff	17
Study seating capacity inside the library	407	# of student computer work stations for entire law school	28
Square feet of law library	72,674	# of additional networked connections	0
Square feet of law school (excl. Library)	41,436	Require Laptop Computer?	N

Employment

	Total	%
Employment status known	103	90.4
Employment status unknown	11	9.6
Employed	93	90.3
Pursuing graduate degrees	3	2.9
Unemployed seeking employment	5	4.9
Unemployed not seeking employment	2	1.9
Type of Employment		
# employed in law firms	52	55.9
# employed in business & industry	1	1.1
# employed in government	26	28.0
# employed in public interest	1	1.1
# employed as judicial clerks	11	11.8
# employed in academia	0	0.0
Geographic Location		
# employed in state	85	91.4
# employed in foreign countries	1	1.1
# of states where employed	1	

J.D. Attrition (from Prior Year)

	Academic	Other	TOTALS	
	#	#	#	%
1st Year	3	9	12	8.0%
2nd Year	6	13	19	10%
3rd Year	0	4	4	2.6%
4th Year	0	3	3	5.5%

Bar Passage Rates

Jurisdiction	Puerto Rico		
Exam	Sum 97	Win 98	Total
# from school taking bar for the first time	101	12	113
School's pass rate for all first-time takers	77%	67%	76%
State's pass rate for all first-time takers	63%	53%	61%

QUINNIPIAC COLLEGE

275 Mount Carmel Avenue
Hamden, CT 06518-1950
(203)287-3400
http://www.quinnipiac.edu/law

ABA Approved Since 1992

The Basics

Type of School: Private   Term: Semester
Application deadline: Rolling
Application fee: $40
Financial Aid deadline: 05/01
Can first year start other than Fall? Yes
Student faculty ratio: 17.2 to 1
Does the University offer:
- housing restricted to law students? No
- graduate student housing for which law students are eligible? No

Curriculum

	Full time	Part time
Typical first-year section size	85	65
Is there typically a "small section" of the first year class, other than Legal Writing, taught by full-time faculty?	No	No
If yes, typical size offered last year	N/A	N/A
# of classroom course titles beyond 1st year curriculum	64	47
# of upper division courses, excluding seminars, with an enrollment:		
Under 25	32	31
25 - 49	18	16
50 - 74	9	4
75 - 99	4	5
100 +	0	0
# of seminars	11	5
# of seminar positions available	316	
# of seminar positions filled	169	84
# of positions available in simulation courses	377	
# of simulation positions filled	126	211
# of positions available in faculty supervised clinical courses	80	
# of fac. sup. clin. positions filled	67	0
# involved in field placements	97	0
# involved in law journals	50	24
# in moot court or trial competitions	55	19
# of credit hrs required to graduate	86	

Faculty & Administrators

	Total		Men		Women		Minorities	
	Fall	Spr	Fall	Spr	Fall	Spr	Fall	Spr
Full-time	32	33	21	21	11	12	3	3
Other Full-Time	4	4	0	0	4	4	0	0
Deans, librarians, & others who teach > 1/2	2	2	1	1	1	1	0	0
Part-time	24	34	19	26	4	7	1	1
Total	62	73	41	48	20	24	4	4
Deans, librarians, & others who teach < 1/2	2	2	1	1	1	1	0	0

J.D. Enrollment & Ethnicity

	Men		Women		Fl-Time		Pt-Time		1st Yr		2nd Yr		3rd Yr		4th Yr		Total		JD Degrees Awarded
	#	%	#	%	#	%	#	%	#	%	#	%	#	%	#	%	#	%	
African-American	18	4.2	24	7.5	24	5.0	18	6.5	19	7.6	8	3.3	14	6.5	1	1.9	42	5.6	15
American Indian	2	0.5	3	0.9	3	0.6	2	0.7	3	1.2	2	0.8	0	0.0	0	0.0	5	0.7	1
Asian American	14	3.2	10	3.1	21	4.4	3	1.1	11	4.4	6	2.5	7	3.3	0	0.0	24	3.2	6
Mexican American	0	0.0	0	0.0	0	0.0	0	0.0	0	0.0	0	0.0	0	0.0	0	0.0	0	0.0	0
Puerto Rican	0	0.0	0	0.0	0	0.0	0	0.0	0	0.0	0	0.0	0	0.0	0	0.0	0	0.0	0
Hispanic American	19	4.4	15	4.7	20	4.2	14	5.0	17	6.8	12	5.0	4	1.9	1	1.9	34	4.5	5
Total Minorities	53	12.2	52	16.1	68	14.3	37	13.3	50	20.0	28	11.7	25	11.7	2	3.8	105	13.9	27
Foreign Nationals	2	0.5	0	0.0	2	0.4	0	0.0	0	0.0	0	0.0	2	0.9	0	0.0	2	0.3	2
Caucasian	378	87.3	270	83.9	406	85.3	242	86.7	200	80.0	211	88.3	187	87.4	50	96.2	648	85.8	206
Total	433	57.4	322	42.6	476	63.0	279	37.0	250	33.1	239	31.7	214	28.3	52	6.9	755		235

GPA & LSAT Scores

	Full Time	Part Time	Total
# of apps	1,434	547	1,981
# admits	758	226	984
# of matrics	159	127	286
75% GPA	3.19	3.08	
25% GPA	2.52	2.49	
75% LSAT	152	150	
25% LSAT	145	144	

Tuition & Fees

	Resident	Non-resident
Full-Time	$20,441	$20,441
Part-Time	$17,105	$17,105

Living Expenses

Estimated living expenses for Singles		
Living on campus	Living off campus	Living at home
N/A	$13,393	$9,013

Employment

	Total	%
Employment status known	225	93.4
Employment status unknown	16	6.6
Employed	199	88.4
Pursuing graduate degrees	7	3.1
Unemployed seeking employment	11	4.9
Unemployed not seeking employment	8	3.6
Type of Employment		
# employed in law firms	88	44.2
# employed in business & industry	43	21.6
# employed in government	46	23.1
# employed in public interest	0	0.0
# employed as judicial clerks	16	8.0
# employed in academia	1	0.5
Geographic Location		
# employed in state	120	60.3
# employed in foreign countries	2	1.0
# of states where employed	15	

Grants/Scholarships

	Full-time		Part-time		Total	
	#	%	#	%	#	%
Total # of Students	476		279		755	
Total # receiving grants	220	46.2	85	30.5	305	40.4
Less than 1/2 tuition	164	34.5	66	23.7	230	30.5
Half to full tuition	43	9.0	16	5.7	59	7.8
Full tuition	9	1.9	2	0.7	11	1.5
More than full tuition	4	0.8	1	0.4	5	0.7
Median Grant Amount	$7,468		$6,000			

Informational & Library Resources

# of volumes & volume equivalents	333,979	# of professional staff	6
# of titles	37,721	Hours per week with professional staff	64
# of active serial subscriptions	3,013	Hours per week without professional staff	32
Study seating capacity inside the library	400	# of student computer work stations for entire law school	121
Square feet of law library	46,000	# of additional networked connections	750
Square feet of law school (excl. Library)	84,000	Require Laptop Computer?	N

J.D. Attrition (from Prior Year)

	Academic	Other	TOTALS	
	#	#	#	%
1st Year	14	20	34	13%
2nd Year	1	4	5	2.0%
3rd Year	0	0	0	0.0%
4th Year	0	0	0	0.0%

Bar Passage Rates

Jurisdiction	Connecticut		
Exam	Sum 97	Win 98	Total
# from school taking bar for the first time	150	31	181
School's pass rate for all first-time takers	83%	74%	81%
State's pass rate for all first-time takers	85%	81%	84%

REGENT UNIVERSITY

1000 Regent University Drive
Virginia Beach, VA 23464
(757)226-4040
http://www.regent.edu/acad/schlaw

ABA Approved Since 1989

The Basics

Type of School: Private   Term: Semester

Application deadline: 05/01

Application fee: $40

Financial Aid deadline: 03/01

Can first year start other than Fall? No

Student faculty ratio: 19.0 to 1

Does the University offer:
- housing restricted to law students? No
- graduate student housing for which law students are eligible? Yes

Faculty & Administrators

	Total		Men		Women		Minorities	
	Fall	Spr	Fall	Spr	Fall	Spr	Fall	Spr
Full-time	17	17	13	13	4	4	4	4
Other Full-Time	1	1	1	1	0	0	0	0
Deans, librarians, & others who teach > 1/2	4	4	4	4	0	0	1	1
Part-time	17	15	12	9	5	6	0	0
Total	39	37	30	27	9	10	5	5
Deans, librarians, & others who teach < 1/2	2	2	2	2	0	0	0	0

Curriculum

	Full time	Part time
Typical first-year section size	68	0
Is there typically a "small section" of the first year class, other than Legal Writing, taught by full-time faculty?	No	No
If yes, typical size offered last year	N/A	N/A
# of classroom course titles beyond 1st year curriculum	62	0
# of upper division courses, excluding seminars, with an enrollment:		
Under 25	41	0
25 - 49	29	0
50 - 74	10	0
75 - 99	0	0
100 +	0	0
# of seminars	5	0
# of seminar positions available	130	
# of seminar positions filled	73	0
# of positions available in simulation courses	396	
# of simulation positions filled	375	0
# of positions available in faculty supervised clinical courses	117	
# of fac. sup. clin. positions filled	40	0
# involved in field placements	40	0
# involved in law journals	28	0
# in moot court or trial competitions	60	0
# of credit hrs required to graduate	90	

J.D. Enrollment & Ethnicity

	Men		Women		Fl-Time		Pt-Time		1st Yr		2nd Yr		3rd Yr		4th Yr		Total		JD Degrees Awarded
	#	%	#	%	#	%	#	%	#	%	#	%	#	%	#	%	#	%	
African-American	8	3.5	20	11.6	23	6.3	5	15.2	12	8.6	13	9.8	3	2.4	0	0.0	28	7.0	6
American Indian	1	0.4	1	0.6	1	0.3	1	3.0	1	0.7	0	0.0	1	0.8	0	0.0	2	0.5	1
Asian American	8	3.5	4	2.3	12	3.3	0	0.0	5	3.6	5	3.8	2	1.6	0	0.0	12	3.0	2
Mexican American	1	0.4	2	1.2	3	0.8	0	0.0	3	2.2	0	0.0	0	0.0	0	0.0	3	0.8	0
Puerto Rican	0	0.0	1	0.6	1	0.3	0	0.0	1	0.7	0	0.0	0	0.0	0	0.0	1	0.3	1
Hispanic American	4	1.8	3	1.7	7	1.9	0	0.0	1	0.7	1	0.8	5	3.9	0	0.0	7	1.8	0
Total Minorities	22	9.7	31	18.0	47	12.9	6	18.2	23	16.5	19	14.4	11	8.7	0	0.0	53	13.3	10
Foreign Nationals	3	1.3	5	2.9	8	2.2	0	0.0	4	2.9	4	3.0	0	0.0	0	0.0	8	2.0	0
Caucasian	201	88.9	136	79.1	310	84.9	27	81.8	112	80.6	109	82.6	116	91.3	0	0.0	337	84.7	110
Total	226	56.8	172	43.2	365	91.7	33	8.3	139	34.9	132	33.2	127	31.9	0	0.0	398		120

GPA & LSAT Scores

	Full Time	Part Time	Total
# of apps	337	66	403
# admits	199	49	248
# of matrics	107	36	143
75% GPA	3.50	3.04	
25% GPA	2.64	2.36	
75% LSAT	153	152	
25% LSAT	145	145	

Tuition & Fees

	Resident	Non-resident
Full-Time	$15,864	$15,864
Part-Time	$12,894	$12,894

Living Expenses

Estimated living expenses for Singles		
Living on campus	Living off campus	Living at home
$10,929	$10,929	$10,929

Employment

	Total	%
Employment status known	97	95.1
Employment status unknown	5	4.9
Employed	80	82.5
Pursuing graduate degrees	4	4.1
Unemployed seeking employment	11	11.3
Unemployed not seeking employment	2	2.1
Type of Employment		
# employed in law firms	37	46.2
# employed in business & industry	13	16.2
# employed in government	10	12.5
# employed in public interest	9	11.2
# employed as judicial clerks	5	6.2
# employed in academia	1	1.2
Geographic Location		
# employed in state	25	31.2
# employed in foreign countries	1	1.2
# of states where employed	25	

Grants/Scholarships

	Full-time		Part-time		Total	
	#	%	#	%	#	%
Total # of Students	365		33		398	
Total # receiving grants	302	82.7	16	48.5	318	79.9
Less than 1/2 tuition	255	69.9	14	42.4	269	67.6
Half to full tuition	36	9.9	2	6.1	38	9.5
Full tuition	11	3.0	0	0.0	11	2.8
More than full tuition	0	0.0	0	0.0	0	0.0
Median Grant Amount	$2,772		$2,500			

Informational & Library Resources

# of volumes & volume equivalents	308,355	# of professional staff	7
# of titles	40,936	Hours per week with professional staff	60
# of active serial subscriptions	4,439	Hours per week without professional staff	39
Study seating capacity inside the library	271	# of student computer work stations for entire law school	34
Square feet of law library	38,730	# of additional networked connections	30
Square feet of law school (excl. Library)	71,970	Require Laptop Computer?	N

J.D. Attrition (from Prior Year)

	Academic	Other	TOTALS	
	#	#	#	%
1st Year	4	13	17	12%
2nd Year	0	4	4	3.0%
3rd Year	0	0	0	0.0%
4th Year	0	0	0	0.0%

Bar Passage Rates

Jurisdiction	Virginia			North Carolina		
Exam	Sum 97	Win 98	Total	Sum 97	Win 98	Total
# from school taking bar for the first time	40	11	51	9	1	10
School's pass rate for all first-time takers	65%	36%	59%	56%	100%	60%
State's pass rate for all first-time takers	76%	68%	75%	85%	73%	82%

RICHMOND, UNIVERSITY OF

T.C. Williams School of Law
Richmond, VA 23173
(804)289-8740
http://law.richmond.edu

ABA Approved Since 1928

The Basics

Type of School: Private Term: Semester
Application deadline: 01/15
Application fee: $35
Financial Aid deadline: 02/25
Can first year start other than Fall? Yes
Student faculty ratio: 15.8 to 1
Does the University offer:
- housing restricted to law students? Yes
- graduate student housing for which law students are eligible? Yes

Faculty & Administrators

	Total		Men		Women		Minorities	
	Fall	Spr	Fall	Spr	Fall	Spr	Fall	Spr
Full-time	25	24	17	17	8	7	2	2
Other Full-Time	0	0	0	0	0	0	0	0
Deans, librarians, & others who teach > 1/2	2	2	2	2	0	0	0	0
Part-time	38	52	22	33	16	19	4	5
Total	65	78	41	52	24	26	6	7
Deans, librarians, & others who teach < 1/2	1	1	0	0	1	1	0	0

Curriculum

	Full time	Part time
Typical first-year section size	75	0
Is there typically a "small section" of the first year class, other than Legal Writing, taught by full-time faculty?	Yes	No
If yes, typical size offered last year	50	N/A
# of classroom course titles beyond 1st year curriculum	104	0
# of upper division courses, excluding seminars, with an enrollment:		
Under 25	95	0
25 - 49	18	0
50 - 74	12	0
75 - 99	4	0
100 +	0	0
# of seminars	14	0
# of seminar positions available	224	
# of seminar positions filled	144	0
# of positions available in simulation courses	528	
# of simulation positions filled	449	0
# of positions available in faculty supervised clinical courses	40	
# of fac. sup. clin. positions filled	27	0
# involved in field placements	67	0
# involved in law journals	115	0
# in moot court or trial competitions	390	0
# of credit hrs required to graduate	86	

J.D. Enrollment & Ethnicity

	Men		Women		Fl-Time		Pt-Time		1st Yr		2nd Yr		3rd Yr		4th Yr		Total		JD Degrees Awarded
	#	%	#	%	#	%	#	%	#	%	#	%	#	%	#	%	#	%	
African-American	13	5.2	29	12.8	42	8.9	0	0.0	19	11.2	16	10.0	7	4.8	0	0.0	42	8.8	18
American Indian	1	0.4	0	0.0	1	0.2	0	0.0	0	0.0	0	0.0	1	0.7	0	0.0	1	0.2	2
Asian American	14	5.6	18	8.0	32	6.8	0	0.0	17	10.0	5	3.1	10	6.9	0	0.0	32	6.7	13
Mexican American	0	0.0	0	0.0	0	0.0	0	0.0	0	0.0	0	0.0	0	0.0	0	0.0	0	0.0	0
Puerto Rican	0	0.0	0	0.0	0	0.0	0	0.0	0	0.0	0	0.0	0	0.0	0	0.0	0	0.0	0
Hispanic American	5	2.0	3	1.3	8	1.7	0	0.0	3	1.8	2	1.3	3	2.1	0	0.0	8	1.7	6
Total Minorities	33	13.3	50	22.1	83	17.5	0	0.0	39	22.9	23	14.4	21	14.5	0	0.0	83	17.5	39
Foreign Nationals	3	1.2	1	0.4	4	0.8	0	0.0	4	2.4	0	0.0	0	0.0	0	0.0	4	0.8	2
Caucasian	213	85.5	175	77.4	387	81.6	1	100.0	127	74.7	137	85.6	124	85.5	0	0.0	388	81.7	121
Total	249	52.4	226	47.6	474	99.8	1	0.2	170	35.8	160	33.7	145	30.5	0	0.0	475		162

GPA & LSAT Scores

	Full Time	Part Time	Total
# of apps	1,305	0	1,305
# admits	564	0	564
# of matrics	168	0	168
75% GPA	3.41	0.00	
25% GPA	2.73	0.00	
75% LSAT	158	0	
25% LSAT	153	0	

Tuition & Fees

	Resident	Non-resident
Full-Time	$19,195	$19,195
Part-Time	$0	$0

Living Expenses

Estimated living expenses for Singles		
Living on campus	Living off campus	Living at home
$8,855	$11,375	$6,215

Employment

	Total	%
Employment status known	156	96.3
Employment status unknown	6	3.7
Employed	142	91.0
Pursuing graduate degrees	8	5.1
Unemployed seeking employment	0	0.0
Unemployed not seeking employment	6	3.8
Type of Employment		
# employed in law firms	64	45.1
# employed in business & industry	32	22.5
# employed in government	21	14.8
# employed in public interest	2	1.4
# employed as judicial clerks	22	15.5
# employed in academia	1	0.7
Geographic Location		
# employed in state	106	74.6
# employed in foreign countries	1	0.7
# of states where employed	13	

Grants/Scholarships

	Full-time		Part-time		Total	
	#	%	#	%	#	%
Total # of Students	474		1		475	
Total # receiving grants	372	78.5	0	0.0	372	78.3
Less than 1/2 tuition	332	70.0	0	0.0	332	69.9
Half to full tuition	31	6.5	0	0.0	31	6.5
Full tuition	8	1.7	0	0.0	8	1.7
More than full tuition	1	0.2	0	0.0	1	0.2
Median Grant Amount	$2,490		$0			

Informational & Library Resources

# of volumes & volume equivalents	267,243	# of professional staff	6
# of titles	119,680	Hours per week with professional staff	66
# of active serial subscriptions	4,317	Hours per week without professional staff	40
Study seating capacity inside the library	619	# of student computer work stations for entire law school	18
Square feet of law library	49,000	# of additional networked connections	590
Square feet of law school (excl. Library)	41,745	Require Laptop Computer?	Y

J.D. Attrition (from Prior Year)

	Academic	Other	TOTALS	
	#	#	#	%
1st Year	1	12	13	7.8%
2nd Year	0	0	0	0.0%
3rd Year	0	0	0	0.0%
4th Year	0	0	0	0.0%

Bar Passage Rates

Jurisdiction	Virginia		
Exam	Sum 97	Win 98	Total
# from school taking bar for the first time	105	25	130
School's pass rate for all first-time takers	71%	80%	73%
State's pass rate for all first-time takers	76%	68%	75%

ROGER WILLIAMS UNIVERSITY

Ralph R. Papitto School of Law
Ten Metacom Avenue
Bristol, RI 02809
(401)254-4500
www.rwu.edu/law

ABA Approved Since 1995

The Basics

Type of School: Private   Term: Semester

Application deadline: 05/15

Application fee: $60

Financial Aid deadline: 05/15

Can first year start other than Fall? No

Student faculty ratio: 12.8 to 1

Does the University offer:
- housing restricted to law students? Yes
- graduate student housing for which law students are eligible? No

Faculty & Administrators

	Total		Men		Women		Minorities	
	Fall	Spr	Fall	Spr	Fall	Spr	Fall	Spr
Full-time	21	21	13	14	8	7	1	1
Other Full-Time	0	0	0	0	0	0	0	0
Deans, librarians, & others who teach > 1/2	2	2	2	2	0	0	0	0
Part-time	19	15	15	13	4	2	0	0
Total	42	38	30	29	12	9	1	1
Deans, librarians, & others who teach < 1/2	0	0	0	0	0	0	0	0

Curriculum

	Full time	Part time
Typical first-year section size	80	40
Is there typically a "small section" of the first year class, other than Legal Writing, taught by full-time faculty?	Yes	No
If yes, typical size offered last year	40	N/A
# of classroom course titles beyond 1st year curriculum	54	37
# of upper division courses, excluding seminars, with an enrollment:		
Under 25	30	18
25 - 49	11	7
50 - 74	5	6
75 - 99	0	0
100 +	0	0
# of seminars	6	5
# of seminar positions available	199	
# of seminar positions filled	113	63
# of positions available in simulation courses	196	
# of simulation positions filled	129	46
# of positions available in faculty supervised clinical courses	48	
# of fac. sup. clin. positions filled	44	0
# involved in field placements	30	2
# involved in law journals	16	4
# in moot court or trial competitions	12	3
# of credit hrs required to graduate	90	

J.D. Enrollment & Ethnicity

	Men		Women		Fl-Time		Pt-Time		1st Yr		2nd Yr		3rd Yr		4th Yr		Total		JD Degrees Awarded
	#	%	#	%	#	%	#	%	#	%	#	%	#	%	#	%	#	%	
African-American	4	1.9	10	6.0	8	3.9	6	3.4	5	4.6	7	5.8	2	1.9	0	0.0	14	3.7	5
American Indian	0	0.0	0	0.0	0	0.0	0	0.0	0	0.0	0	0.0	0	0.0	0	0.0	0	0.0	0
Asian American	4	1.9	1	0.6	3	1.4	2	1.1	3	2.8	2	1.7	0	0.0	0	0.0	5	1.3	1
Mexican American	0	0.0	0	0.0	0	0.0	0	0.0	0	0.0	0	0.0	0	0.0	0	0.0	0	0.0	0
Puerto Rican	0	0.0	0	0.0	0	0.0	0	0.0	0	0.0	0	0.0	0	0.0	0	0.0	0	0.0	0
Hispanic American	3	1.4	3	1.8	3	1.4	3	1.7	2	1.8	3	2.5	1	1.0	0	0.0	6	1.6	2
Total Minorities	11	5.1	14	8.3	14	6.8	11	6.3	10	9.2	12	9.9	3	2.9	0	0.0	25	6.5	8
Foreign Nationals	1	0.5	0	0.0	0	0.0	1	0.6	0	0.0	1	0.8	0	0.0	0	0.0	1	0.3	0
Caucasian	203	94.4	154	91.7	193	93.2	164	93.2	99	90.8	108	89.3	100	97.1	50	100.0	357	93.2	130
Total	215	56.1	168	43.9	207	54.0	176	46.0	109	28.5	121	31.6	103	26.9	50	13.1	383		138

GPA & LSAT Scores

	Full Time	Part Time	Total
# of apps	556	105	661
# admits	295	59	354
# of matrics	75	39	114
75% GPA	3.42	3.43	
25% GPA	2.64	2.83	
75% LSAT	151	155	
25% LSAT	142	141	

Tuition & Fees

	Resident	Non-resident
Full-Time	$19,100	$19,100
Part-Time	$11,480	$11,480

Living Expenses

Estimated living expenses for Singles		
Living on campus	Living off campus	Living at home
$14,655	$14,655	$14,655

Grants/Scholarships

	Full-time		Part-time		Total	
	#	%	#	%	#	%
Total # of Students	207		176		383	
Total # receiving grants	37	17.9	19	10.8	56	14.6
Less than 1/2 tuition	36	17.4	18	10.2	54	14.1
Half to full tuition	0	0.0	1	0.6	1	0.3
Full tuition	1	0.5	0	0.0	1	0.3
More than full tuition	0	0.0	0	0.0	0	0.0
Median Grant Amount	$3,000		$2,300			

Informational & Library Resources

# of volumes & volume equivalents	222,318	# of professional staff	6
# of titles	94,718	Hours per week with professional staff	61
# of active serial subscriptions	3,426	Hours per week without professional staff	49
Study seating capacity inside the library	383	# of student computer work stations for entire law school	77
Square feet of law library	30,083	# of additional networked connections	150
Square feet of law school (excl. Library)	91,617	Require Laptop Computer?	N

Employment

	Total	%
Employment status known	94	66.7
Employment status unknown	47	33.3
Employed	85	90.4
Pursuing graduate degrees	1	1.1
Unemployed seeking employment	7	7.4
Unemployed not seeking employment	1	1.1
Type of Employment		
# employed in law firms	39	45.9
# employed in business & industry	19	22.4
# employed in government	16	18.8
# employed in public interest	1	1.2
# employed as judicial clerks	6	7.1
# employed in academia	4	4.7
Geographic Location		
# employed in state	51	60.0
# employed in foreign countries	1	1.2
# of states where employed	13	

J.D. Attrition (from Prior Year)

	Academic	Other	TOTALS	
	#	#	#	%
1st Year	18	6	24	17%
2nd Year	2	3	5	4.2%
3rd Year	0	0	0	0.0%
4th Year	0	0	0	0.0%

Bar Passage Rates

Jurisdiction	Rhode Island			Massachusetts		
Exam	Sum 97	Win 98	Total	Sum 97	Win 98	Total
# from school taking bar for the first time	78	14	92	43	22	65
School's pass rate for all first-time takers	63%	71%	64%	67%	68%	68%
State's pass rate for all first-time takers	61%	69%	64%	84%	72%	82%

RUTGERS UNIVERSITY-CAMDEN

217 North Fifth Street
Camden, NJ 08102-1203
(609)225-6102
http://www-camlaw.rutgers.edu

ABA Approved Since 1951

The Basics

Type of School: Public   Term: Semester
Application deadline: 03/01
Application fee: $50
Financial Aid deadline: 03/01
Can first year start other than Fall? No
Student faculty ratio: 20.0 to 1
Does the University offer:
- housing restricted to law students? No
- graduate student housing for which law students are eligible? Yes

Faculty & Administrators

	Total		Men		Women		Minorities	
	Fall	Spr	Fall	Spr	Fall	Spr	Fall	Spr
Full-time	29	33	22	25	7	8	2	2
Other Full-Time	4	4	1	1	3	3	0	0
Deans, librarians, & others who teach > 1/2	4	4	1	1	3	3	0	0
Part-time	25	37	19	31	6	6	1	4
Total	62	78	43	58	19	20	3	6
Deans, librarians, & others who teach < 1/2	2	2	1	1	1	1	0	0

Curriculum

	Full time	Part time
Typical first-year section size	94	43
Is there typically a "small section" of the first year class, other than Legal Writing, taught by full-time faculty?	No	No
If yes, typical size offered last year	N/A	N/A
# of classroom course titles beyond 1st year curriculum	48	39
# of upper division courses, excluding seminars, with an enrollment:		
Under 25	18	44
25 - 49	15	10
50 - 74	15	4
75 - 99	5	0
100 +	2	0
# of seminars	15	2
# of seminar positions available	238	
# of seminar positions filled	161	31
# of positions available in simulation courses	629	
# of simulation positions filled	426	126
# of positions available in faculty supervised clinical courses	34	
# of fac. sup. clin. positions filled	18	6
# involved in field placements	67	6
# involved in law journals	58	5
# in moot court or trial competitions	163	9
# of credit hrs required to graduate	84	

J.D. Enrollment & Ethnicity

	Men		Women		Fl-Time		Pt-Time		1st Yr		2nd Yr		3rd Yr		4th Yr		Total		JD Degrees Awarded
	#	%	#	%	#	%	#	%	#	%	#	%	#	%	#	%	#	%	
African-American	24	6.3	36	9.9	44	7.4	16	10.1	13	4.8	21	8.9	23	11.5	3	7.5	60	8.0	23
American Indian	0	0.0	1	0.3	1	0.2	0	0.0	0	0.0	0	0.0	1	0.5	0	0.0	1	0.1	0
Asian American	23	6.0	22	6.0	42	7.1	3	1.9	25	9.2	9	3.8	9	4.5	2	5.0	45	6.0	16
Mexican American	1	0.3	3	0.8	4	0.7	0	0.0	2	0.7	1	0.4	1	0.5	0	0.0	4	0.5	0
Puerto Rican	3	0.8	5	1.4	7	1.2	1	0.6	3	1.1	2	0.8	2	1.0	1	2.5	8	1.1	5
Hispanic American	7	1.8	5	1.4	8	1.4	4	2.5	5	1.8	2	0.8	4	2.0	1	2.5	12	1.6	5
Total Minorities	58	15.1	72	19.7	106	17.9	24	15.2	48	17.6	35	14.8	40	20.0	7	17.5	130	17.4	49
Foreign Nationals	5	1.3	8	2.2	11	1.9	2	1.3	4	1.5	6	2.5	3	1.5	0	0.0	13	1.7	2
Caucasian	321	83.6	285	78.1	474	80.2	132	83.5	220	80.9	196	82.7	157	78.5	33	82.5	606	80.9	181
Total	384	51.3	365	48.7	591	78.9	158	21.1	272	36.3	237	31.6	200	26.7	40	5.3	749		232

GPA & LSAT Scores

	Full Time	Part Time	Total
# of apps	N/A	N/A	1,444
# admits	N/A	N/A	716
# of matrics	226	46	272
75% GPA	3.39	3.27	
25% GPA	2.87	2.70	
75% LSAT	155	157	
25% LSAT	151	150	

Tuition & Fees

	Resident	Non-resident
Full-Time	$10,781	$15,305
Part-Time	$8,490	$12,301

Living Expenses

Estimated living expenses for Singles		
Living on campus	Living off campus	Living at home
$9,538	$11,789	$5,489

Employment

	Total	%
Employment status known	257	94.8
Employment status unknown	14	5.2
Employed	236	91.8
Pursuing graduate degrees	8	3.1
Unemployed seeking employment	10	3.9
Unemployed not seeking employment	3	1.2
Type of Employment		
# employed in law firms	87	36.9
# employed in business & industry	32	13.6
# employed in government	21	8.9
# employed in public interest	4	1.7
# employed as judicial clerks	91	38.6
# employed in academia	1	0.4
Geographic Location		
# employed in state	145	61.4
# employed in foreign countries	4	1.7
# of states where employed	18	

Grants/Scholarships

	Full-time		Part-time		Total	
	#	%	#	%	#	%
Total # of Students	591		158		749	
Total # receiving grants	65	11.0	7	4.4	72	9.6
Less than 1/2 tuition	60	10.2	7	4.4	67	8.9
Half to full tuition	2	0.3	0	0.0	2	0.3
Full tuition	1	0.2	0	0.0	1	0.1
More than full tuition	2	0.3	0	0.0	2	0.3
Median Grant Amount	$2,250		$1,500			

Informational & Library Resources

# of volumes & volume equivalents	404,076	# of professional staff	7
# of titles	74,728	Hours per week with professional staff	48
# of active serial subscriptions	3,106	Hours per week without professional staff	52
Study seating capacity inside the library	402	# of student computer work stations for entire law school	50
Square feet of law library	46,856	# of additional networked connections	10
Square feet of law school (excl. Library)	48,852	Require Laptop Computer?	N

J.D. Attrition (from Prior Year)

	Academic	Other	TOTALS	
	#	#	#	%
1st Year	1	15	16	6.8%
2nd Year	0	1	1	0.5%
3rd Year	1	1	2	0.9%
4th Year	0	0	0	0.0%

Bar Passage Rates

Jurisdiction	New Jersey		
Exam	Sum 97	Win 98	Total
# from school taking bar for the first time	206	20	226
School's pass rate for all first-time takers	85%	65%	83%
State's pass rate for all first-time takers	77%	0%	77%

RUTGERS UNIVERSITY-NEWARK

15 Washington Street
Newark, NJ 07102-3192
(973)353-5561
http://info.rutgers.edu/RUSLN/rulnindx

ABA Approved Since 1941

The Basics

Type of School: Public   Term: Semester
Application deadline: 03/15
Application fee: $40
Financial Aid deadline: 03/01
Can first year start other than Fall? No
Student faculty ratio: 15.7 to 1
Does the University offer:
- housing restricted to law students? No
- graduate student housing for which law students are eligible? Yes

Curriculum

	Full time	Part time
Typical first-year section size	80	35
Is there typically a "small section" of the first year class, other than Legal Writing, taught by full-time faculty?	Yes	Yes
If yes, typical size offered last year	27	27
# of classroom course titles beyond 1st year curriculum	86	25
# of upper division courses, excluding seminars, with an enrollment:		
Under 25	52	8
25 - 49	16	6
50 - 74	11	4
75 - 99	2	1
100 +	2	3
# of seminars	21	2
# of seminar positions available	368	
# of seminar positions filled	230	23
# of positions available in simulation courses	160	
# of simulation positions filled	83	39
# of positions available in faculty supervised clinical courses	240	
# of fac. sup. clin. positions filled	162	23
# involved in field placements	103	2
# involved in law journals	140	11
# in moot court or trial competitions	93	9
# of credit hrs required to graduate	84	

Faculty & Administrators

	Total		Men		Women		Minorities	
	Fall	Spr	Fall	Spr	Fall	Spr	Fall	Spr
Full-time	33	37	22	26	11	11	6	8
Other Full-Time	1	1	1	1	0	0	0	0
Deans, librarians, & others who teach > 1/2	1	1	1	1	0	0	1	1
Part-time	27	26	18	17	8	9	4	7
Total	62	65	42	45	19	20	11	16
Deans, librarians, & others who teach < 1/2	4	4	1	1	3	3	0	0

J.D. Enrollment & Ethnicity

	Men		Women		Fl-Time		Pt-Time		1st Yr		2nd Yr		3rd Yr		4th Yr		Total		JD Degrees Awarded
	#	%	#	%	#	%	#	%	#	%	#	%	#	%	#	%	#	%	
African-American	45	11.9	52	16.7	63	12.8	34	17.4	31	14.8	27	14.0	30	13.0	9	16.1	97	14.1	25
American Indian	0	0.0	0	0.0	0	0.0	0	0.0	0	0.0	0	0.0	0	0.0	0	0.0	0	0.0	0
Asian American	31	8.2	24	7.7	48	9.7	7	3.6	14	6.7	11	5.7	28	12.2	2	3.6	55	8.0	16
Mexican American	2	0.5	0	0.0	2	0.4	0	0.0	0	0.0	1	0.5	1	0.4	0	0.0	2	0.3	0
Puerto Rican	17	4.5	9	2.9	17	3.4	9	4.6	4	1.9	10	5.2	11	4.8	1	1.8	26	3.8	17
Hispanic American	22	5.8	18	5.8	25	5.1	15	7.7	12	5.7	13	6.7	12	5.2	3	5.4	40	5.8	7
Total Minorities	117	31.0	103	33.1	155	31.4	65	33.3	61	29.2	62	32.1	82	35.7	15	26.8	220	32.0	65
Foreign Nationals	21	5.6	14	4.5	27	5.5	8	4.1	16	7.7	8	4.1	9	3.9	2	3.6	35	5.1	12
Caucasian	239	63.4	194	62.4	311	63.1	122	62.6	132	63.2	123	63.7	139	60.4	39	69.6	433	62.9	153
Total	377	54.8	311	45.2	493	71.7	195	28.3	209	30.4	193	28.1	230	33.4	56	8.1	688		230

GPA & LSAT Scores

	Full Time	Part Time	Total
# of apps	1,603	456	2,059
# admits	607	79	686
# of matrics	178	35	213
75% GPA	3.42	3.32	
25% GPA	2.88	3.15	
75% LSAT	159	159	
25% LSAT	151	152	

Tuition & Fees

	Resident	Non-resident
Full-Time	$10,740	$15,264
Part-Time	$6,866	$9,915

Living Expenses

Estimated living expenses for Singles		
Living on campus	Living off campus	Living at home
$10,589	$11,789	$5,489

Employment

	Total	%
Employment status known	235	95.1
Employment status unknown	12	4.9
Employed	220	93.6
Pursuing graduate degrees	4	1.7
Unemployed seeking employment	7	3.0
Unemployed not seeking employment	4	1.7
Type of Employment		
# employed in law firms	78	35.5
# employed in business & industry	41	18.6
# employed in government	22	10.0
# employed in public interest	8	3.6
# employed as judicial clerks	68	30.9
# employed in academia	3	1.4
Geographic Location		
# employed in state	160	72.7
# employed in foreign countries	1	0.5
# of states where employed	12	

Grants/Scholarships

	Full-time		Part-time		Total	
	#	%	#	%	#	%
Total # of Students	493		195		688	
Total # receiving grants	217	44.0	13	6.7	230	33.4
Less than 1/2 tuition	204	41.4	12	6.2	216	31.4
Half to full tuition	7	1.4	0	0.0	7	1.0
Full tuition	5	1.0	1	0.5	6	0.9
More than full tuition	1	0.2	0	0.0	1	0.1
Median Grant Amount	$1,000		$500			

Informational & Library Resources

# of volumes & volume equivalents	419,259	# of professional staff	11
# of titles	117,339	Hours per week with professional staff	56
# of active serial subscriptions	2,959	Hours per week without professional staff	51
Study seating capacity inside the library	397	# of student computer work stations for entire law school	89
Square feet of law library	44,523	# of additional networked connections	0
Square feet of law school (excl. Library)	77,367	Require Laptop Computer?	N

J.D. Attrition (from Prior Year)

	Academic	Other	TOTALS	
	#	#	#	%
1st Year	1	30	31	15%
2nd Year	0	6	6	2.7%
3rd Year	0	2	2	0.8%
4th Year	0	0	0	0.0%

Bar Passage Rates

Jurisdiction	New Jersey			New York		
Exam	Sum 97	Win 98	Total	Sum 97	Win 98	Total
# from school taking bar for the first time	192	19	211	162	10	172
School's pass rate for all first-time takers	79%	47%	76%	75%	50%	74%
State's pass rate for all first-time takers	77%	0%	77%	78%	65%	76%

SAMFORD UNIVERSITY

800 Lakeshore Drive
Birmingham, AL 35229
(205)870-2400
http://cumberland.samford.edu

ABA Approved Since 1949

The Basics

Type of School: Private   Term: Semester
Application deadline: 05/01
Application fee: $40
Financial Aid deadline: 03/01
Can first year start other than Fall? No
Student faculty ratio: 21.0 to 1
Does the University offer:
- housing restricted to law students? No
- graduate student housing for which law students are eligible? No

Curriculum

	Full time	Part time
Typical first-year section size	70	0
Is there typically a "small section" of the first year class, other than Legal Writing, taught by full-time faculty?	No	No
If yes, typical size offered last year	N/A	N/A
# of classroom course titles beyond 1st year curriculum	75	0
# of upper division courses, excluding seminars, with an enrollment:		
Under 25	17	0
25 - 49	34	0
50 - 74	26	0
75 - 99	1	0
100 +	1	0
# of seminars	28	0
# of seminar positions available	700	
# of seminar positions filled	553	0
# of positions available in simulation courses	483	
# of simulation positions filled	407	0
# of positions available in faculty supervised clinical courses	324	
# of fac. sup. clin. positions filled	242	0
# involved in field placements	109	0
# involved in law journals	106	0
# in moot court or trial competitions	41	0
# of credit hrs required to graduate	90	

Faculty & Administrators

	Total		Men		Women		Minorities	
	Fall	Spr	Fall	Spr	Fall	Spr	Fall	Spr
Full-time	24	23	19	19	5	4	2	2
Other Full-Time	0	0	0	0	0	0	0	0
Deans, librarians, & others who teach > 1/2	2	2	1	1	1	1	1	1
Part-time	19	27	10	22	9	5	3	3
Total	45	52	30	42	15	10	6	6
Deans, librarians, & others who teach < 1/2	1	1	1	1	0	0	0	0

J.D. Enrollment & Ethnicity

	Men		Women		Fl-Time		Pt-Time		1st Yr		2nd Yr		3rd Yr		4th Yr		Total		JD Degrees Awarded
	#	%	#	%	#	%	#	%	#	%	#	%	#	%	#	%	#	%	
African-American	14	3.7	22	9.9	36	6.0	0	0.0	15	6.9	6	3.0	15	7.9	0	0.0	36	6.0	20
American Indian	0	0.0	0	0.0	0	0.0	0	0.0	0	0.0	0	0.0	0	0.0	0	0.0	0	0.0	0
Asian American	0	0.0	4	1.8	4	0.7	0	0.0	2	0.9	1	0.5	1	0.5	0	0.0	4	0.7	0
Mexican American	0	0.0	0	0.0	0	0.0	0	0.0	0	0.0	0	0.0	0	0.0	0	0.0	0	0.0	0
Puerto Rican	0	0.0	0	0.0	0	0.0	0	0.0	0	0.0	0	0.0	0	0.0	0	0.0	0	0.0	0
Hispanic American	5	1.3	3	1.3	8	1.3	0	0.0	3	1.4	4	2.0	1	0.5	0	0.0	8	1.3	1
Total Minorities	19	5.0	29	13.0	48	7.9	0	0.0	20	9.3	11	5.5	17	8.9	0	0.0	48	7.9	21
Foreign Nationals	0	0.0	0	0.0	0	0.0	0	0.0	0	0.0	0	0.0	0	0.0	0	0.0	0	0.0	0
Caucasian	363	95.0	194	87.0	557	92.1	0	0.0	196	90.7	188	94.5	173	91.1	0	0.0	557	92.1	184
Total	382	63.1	223	36.9	605	100.0	0	0.0	216	35.7	199	32.9	190	31.4	0	0.0	605		205

GPA & LSAT Scores

	Full Time	Part Time	Total
# of apps	843	0	843
# admits	545	0	545
# of matrics	217	0	217
75% GPA	3.31	0.00	
25% GPA	2.72	0.00	
75% LSAT	153	0	
25% LSAT	148	0	

Tuition & Fees

	Resident	Non-resident
Full-Time	$18,350	$18,350
Part-Time	$0	$0

Living Expenses

Estimated living expenses for Singles

Living on campus	Living off campus	Living at home
N/A	$11,949	$5,914

Grants/Scholarships

	Full-time		Part-time		Total	
	#	%	#	%	#	%
Total # of Students						
Total # receiving grants	137	22.6	0	0.0	137	22.6
Less than 1/2 tuition	62	10.2	0	0.0	62	10.2
Half to full tuition	19	3.1	0	0.0	19	3.1
Full tuition	28	4.6	0	0.0	28	4.6
More than full tuition	28	4.6	0	0.0	28	4.6
Median Grant Amount	$10,000		$0			

Informational & Library Resources

# of volumes & volume equivalents	247,324	# of professional staff	7
# of titles	33,985	Hours per week with professional staff	61
# of active serial subscriptions	2,762	Hours per week without professional staff	46
Study seating capacity inside the library	474	# of student computer work stations for entire law school	54
Square feet of law library	42,500	# of additional networked connections	170
Square feet of law school (excl. Library)	72,900	Require Laptop Computer?	N

Employment

	Total	%
Employment status known	202	95.3
Employment status unknown	10	4.7
Employed	183	90.6
Pursuing graduate degrees	9	4.5
Unemployed seeking employment	3	1.5
Unemployed not seeking employment	7	3.5
Type of Employment		
# employed in law firms	118	64.5
# employed in business & industry	16	8.7
# employed in government	27	14.8
# employed in public interest	2	1.1
# employed as judicial clerks	18	9.8
# employed in academia	0	0.0
Geographic Location		
# employed in state	94	51.4
# employed in foreign countries	0	0.0
# of states where employed	16	

J.D. Attrition (from Prior Year)

	Academic	Other	TOTALS	
	#	#	#	%
1st Year	1	12	13	6.3%
2nd Year	2	5	7	3.5%
3rd Year	1	0	1	0.5%
4th Year	0	0	0	0.0%

Bar Passage Rates

Jurisdiction	Alabama		
Exam	Sum 97	Win 98	Total
# from school taking bar for the first time	110	8	118
School's pass rate for all first-time takers	90%	63%	88%
State's pass rate for all first-time takers	80%	68%	76%

SAN DIEGO, UNIVERSITY OF

5998 Alcala Park
San Diego, CA 92110-2492
(619)260-4527
http://www.acusd.edu/~usdlaw

ABA Approved Since 1961

The Basics

Type of School: Private   Term: Semester

Application deadline: 02/01

Application fee: $40

Financial Aid deadline: 03/01

Can first year start other than Fall? No

Student faculty ratio: 17.2 to 1

Does the University offer:
- housing restricted to law students? No
- graduate student housing for which law students are eligible? Yes

Faculty & Administrators

	Total		Men		Women		Minorities	
	Fall	Spr	Fall	Spr	Fall	Spr	Fall	Spr
Full-time	43	44	34	35	9	9	5	5
Other Full-Time	8	8	1	1	7	7	1	1
Deans, librarians, & others who teach > 1/2	3	3	2	2	1	1	1	1
Part-time	29	28	22	26	7	2	2	1
Total	83	83	59	64	24	19	9	8
Deans, librarians, & others who teach < 1/2	8	8	1	1	7	7	0	0

Curriculum

	Full time	Part time
Typical first-year section size	80	80
Is there typically a "small section" of the first year class, other than Legal Writing, taught by full-time faculty?	Yes	Yes
If yes, typical size offered last year	40	40
# of classroom course titles beyond 1st year curriculum	84	46
# of upper division courses, excluding seminars, with an enrollment:		
Under 25	52	23
25 - 49	39	16
50 - 74	12	7
75 - 99	12	6
100 +	0	0
# of seminars	22	11
# of seminar positions available	695	
# of seminar positions filled	451	120
# of positions available in simulation courses	761	
# of simulation positions filled	608	111
# of positions available in faculty supervised clinical courses	120	
# of fac. sup. clin. positions filled	88	20
# involved in field placements	123	10
# involved in law journals	59	22
# in moot court or trial competitions	104	6
# of credit hrs required to graduate	85	

J.D. Enrollment & Ethnicity

	Men		Women		Fl-Time		Pt-Time		1st Yr		2nd Yr		3rd Yr		4th Yr		Total		JD Degrees Awarded
	#	%	#	%	#	%	#	%	#	%	#	%	#	%	#	%	#	%	
African-American	7	1.2	10	2.4	13	1.8	4	1.5	11	3.3	5	1.6	1	0.3	0	0.0	17	1.7	7
American Indian	11	1.9	7	1.7	13	1.8	5	1.9	4	1.2	5	1.6	8	2.6	1	3.3	18	1.8	3
Asian American	58	10.2	69	16.9	95	13.4	32	11.9	42	12.6	43	14.0	38	12.3	4	13.3	127	13.0	34
Mexican American	27	4.7	12	2.9	28	3.9	11	4.1	21	6.3	12	3.9	5	1.6	1	3.3	39	4.0	18
Puerto Rican	0	0.0	2	0.5	2	0.3	0	0.0	1	0.3	1	0.3	0	0.0	0	0.0	2	0.2	0
Hispanic American	19	3.3	10	2.4	21	3.0	8	3.0	8	2.4	9	2.9	12	3.9	0	0.0	29	3.0	0
Total Minorities	122	21.4	110	26.9	172	24.2	60	22.3	87	26.0	75	24.4	64	20.7	6	20.0	232	23.7	62
Foreign Nationals	2	0.4	3	0.7	4	0.6	1	0.4	3	0.9	0	0.0	2	0.6	0	0.0	5	0.5	4
Caucasian	447	78.3	296	72.4	535	75.2	208	77.3	244	73.1	232	75.6	243	78.6	24	80.0	743	75.8	243
Total	571	58.3	409	41.7	711	72.6	269	27.4	334	34.1	307	31.3	309	31.5	30	3.1	980		309

GPA & LSAT Scores

	Full Time	Part Time	Total
# of apps	2,458	237	2,695
# admits	1,106	190	1,296
# of matrics	251	99	350
75% GPA	3.35	3.45	
25% GPA	2.86	2.86	
75% LSAT	160	156	
25% LSAT	156	153	

Tuition & Fees

	Resident	Non-resident
Full-Time	$20,980	$20,980
Part-Time	$14,890	$14,890

Living Expenses

Estimated living expenses for Singles		
Living on campus	Living off campus	Living at home
$12,538	$12,538	$6,940

Grants/Scholarships

	Full-time		Part-time		Total	
	#	%	#	%	#	%
Total # of Students	711		269		980	
Total # receiving grants	235	33.1	72	26.8	307	31.3
Less than 1/2 tuition	43	6.0	45	16.7	88	9.0
Half to full tuition	145	20.4	22	8.2	167	17.0
Full tuition	25	3.5	5	1.9	30	3.1
More than full tuition	22	3.1	0	0.0	22	2.2
Median Grant Amount	$0		$0			

Informational & Library Resources

# of volumes & volume equivalents	439,042	# of professional staff	11
# of titles	192,069	Hours per week with professional staff	70
# of active serial subscriptions	5,405	Hours per week without professional staff	38
Study seating capacity inside the library	600	# of student computer work stations for entire law school	37
Square feet of law library	53,800	# of additional networked connections	83
Square feet of law school (excl. Library)	62,040	Require Laptop Computer?	N

Employment

	Total	%
Employment status known	271	88.9
Employment status unknown	34	11.1
Employed	235	86.7
Pursuing graduate degrees	19	7.0
Unemployed seeking employment	14	5.2
Unemployed not seeking employment	3	1.1
Type of Employment		
# employed in law firms	152	64.7
# employed in business & industry	28	11.9
# employed in government	39	16.6
# employed in public interest	5	2.1
# employed as judicial clerks	6	2.6
# employed in academia	0	0.0
Geographic Location		
# employed in state	202	86.0
# employed in foreign countries	0	0.0
# of states where employed	13	

J.D. Attrition (from Prior Year)

	Academic	Other	TOTALS	
	#	#	#	%
1st Year	21	20	41	13%
2nd Year	3	12	15	5.1%
3rd Year	0	5	5	1.6%
4th Year	0	0	0	0.0%

Bar Passage Rates

Jurisdiction	California		
Exam	Sum 97	Win 98	Total
# from school taking bar for the first time	237	31	268
School's pass rate for all first-time takers	85%	65%	82%
State's pass rate for all first-time takers	75%	57%	71%

SAN FRANCISCO, UNIVERSITY OF

2130 Fulton Street
San Francisco, CA 94117-1080
(415)422-6586
http://www.law.usfca.edu

ABA Approved Since 1935

The Basics

Type of School: Private   Term: Semester

Application deadline: 04/01

Application fee: $40

Financial Aid deadline: 02/15

Can first year start other than Fall? No

Student faculty ratio: 20.9 to 1

Does the University offer:
- housing restricted to law students? No
- graduate student housing for which law students are eligible? Yes

Faculty & Administrators

	Total		Men		Women		Minorities	
	Fall	Spr	Fall	Spr	Fall	Spr	Fall	Spr
Full-time	24	23	16	16	8	7	5	6
Other Full-Time	1	0	0	0	1	0	0	0
Deans, librarians, & others who teach > 1/2	2	2	2	2	0	0	0	0
Part-time	38	42	25	29	13	12	9	6
Total	65	67	43	47	22	19	14	12
Deans, librarians, & others who teach < 1/2	0	0	0	0	0	0	0	0

Curriculum

	Full time	Part time
Typical first-year section size	87	50
Is there typically a "small section" of the first year class, other than Legal Writing, taught by full-time faculty?	No	No
If yes, typical size offered last year	N/A	N/A
# of classroom course titles beyond 1st year curriculum	50	44
# of upper division courses, excluding seminars, with an enrollment:		
Under 25	20	14
25 - 49	15	14
50 - 74	6	9
75 - 99	0	4
100 +	0	1
# of seminars	9	2
# of seminar positions available	269	
# of seminar positions filled	196	44
# of positions available in simulation courses	288	
# of simulation positions filled	88	135
# of positions available in faculty supervised clinical courses	119	
# of fac. sup. clin. positions filled	98	9
# involved in field placements	107	9
# involved in law journals	63	5
# in moot court or trial competitions	66	6
# of credit hrs required to graduate	86	

J.D. Enrollment & Ethnicity

	Men		Women		Fl-Time		Pt-Time		1st Yr		2nd Yr		3rd Yr		4th Yr		Total		JD Degrees Awarded
	#	%	#	%	#	%	#	%	#	%	#	%	#	%	#	%	#	%	
African-American	9	3.1	18	5.0	16	3.1	11	8.7	11	4.6	11	6.0	5	2.6	0	0.0	27	4.2	5
American Indian	1	0.3	3	0.8	3	0.6	1	0.8	1	0.4	1	0.5	1	0.5	1	3.7	4	0.6	2
Asian American	31	10.8	49	13.6	62	12.0	18	14.2	29	12.0	19	10.4	28	14.4	4	14.8	80	12.4	40
Mexican American	0	0.0	0	0.0	0	0.0	0	0.0	0	0.0	0	0.0	0	0.0	0	0.0	0	0.0	2
Puerto Rican	0	0.0	0	0.0	0	0.0	0	0.0	0	0.0	0	0.0	0	0.0	0	0.0	0	0.0	0
Hispanic American	21	7.3	23	6.4	35	6.8	9	7.1	18	7.5	14	7.7	11	5.7	1	3.7	44	6.8	12
Total Minorities	62	21.7	93	25.9	116	22.4	39	30.7	59	24.5	45	24.6	45	23.2	6	22.2	155	24.0	61
Foreign Nationals	1	0.3	3	0.8	4	0.8	0	0.0	2	0.8	1	0.5	1	0.5	0	0.0	4	0.6	1
Caucasian	223	78.0	263	73.3	398	76.8	88	69.3	180	74.7	137	74.9	148	76.3	21	77.8	486	75.3	141
Total	286	44.3	359	55.7	518	80.3	127	19.7	241	37.4	183	28.4	194	30.1	27	4.2	645		203

GPA & LSAT Scores

	Full Time	Part Time	Total
# of apps	2,023	219	2,242
# admits	845	142	987
# of matrics	186	62	248
75% GPA	3.45	3.39	
25% GPA	3.03	2.76	
75% LSAT	159	159	
25% LSAT	154	151	

Tuition & Fees

	Resident	Non-resident
Full-Time	$21,008	$21,008
Part-Time	$15,040	$15,040

Living Expenses

Estimated living expenses for Singles		
Living on campus	Living off campus	Living at home
$11,260	$12,850	$5,800

Employment

	Total	%
Employment status known	198	90.0
Employment status unknown	22	10.0
Employed	164	82.8
Pursuing graduate degrees	4	2.0
Unemployed seeking employment	24	12.1
Unemployed not seeking employment	6	3.0
Type of Employment		
# employed in law firms	101	61.6
# employed in business & industry	20	12.2
# employed in government	21	12.8
# employed in public interest	4	2.4
# employed as judicial clerks	6	3.7
# employed in academia	2	1.2
Geographic Location		
# employed in state	150	91.5
# employed in foreign countries	2	1.2
# of states where employed	6	

Grants/Scholarships

	Full-time		Part-time		Total	
	#	%	#	%	#	%
Total # of Students	518		127		645	
Total # receiving grants	277	53.5	52	40.9	329	51.0
Less than 1/2 tuition	263	50.8	37	29.1	300	46.5
Half to full tuition	14	2.7	14	11.0	28	4.3
Full tuition	0	0.0	0	0.0	0	0.0
More than full tuition	0	0.0	1	0.8	1	0.2
Median Grant Amount	$5,000		$3,000			

Informational & Library Resources

# of volumes & volume equivalents	288,678	# of professional staff	6
# of titles	28,724	Hours per week with professional staff	64
# of active serial subscriptions	2,558	Hours per week without professional staff	36
Study seating capacity inside the library	304	# of student computer work stations for entire law school	61
Square feet of law library	21,708	# of additional networked connections	4
Square feet of law school (excl. Library)	30,792	Require Laptop Computer?	N

J.D. Attrition (from Prior Year)

	Academic	Other	TOTALS	
	#	#	#	%
1st Year	23	8	31	14%
2nd Year	4	14	18	9.1%
3rd Year	2	1	3	1.5%
4th Year	0	0	0	0.0%

Bar Passage Rates

Jurisdiction	California		
Exam	Sum 97	Win 98	Total
# from school taking bar for the first time	197	27	224
School's pass rate for all first-time takers	90%	85%	89%
State's pass rate for all first-time takers	75%	57%	71%

SANTA CLARA UNIVERSITY

500 El Camino Real
Santa Clara, CA 95053
(408)554-4767
http://www.scu.edu/law

ABA Approved Since 1937

The Basics

Type of School: Private   Term: Semester
Application deadline: 03/01
Application fee: $40
Financial Aid deadline: 02/01
Can first year start other than Fall? No
Student faculty ratio: 19.5 to 1
Does the University offer:
- housing restricted to law students? Yes
- graduate student housing for which law students are eligible? Yes

Faculty & Administrators

	Total		Men		Women		Minorities	
	Fall	Spr	Fall	Spr	Fall	Spr	Fall	Spr
Full-time	35	37	23	25	12	12	8	7
Other Full-Time	8	8	2	2	6	6	0	0
Deans, librarians, & others who teach > 1/2	1	1	0	0	1	1	0	0
Part-time	25	20	15	15	10	5	3	3
Total	69	66	40	42	29	24	11	10
Deans, librarians, & others who teach < 1/2	4	4	2	2	2	2	2	2

Curriculum

	Full time	Part time
Typical first-year section size	74	61
Is there typically a "small section" of the first year class, other than Legal Writing, taught by full-time faculty?	Yes	No
If yes, typical size offered last year	37	N/A
# of classroom course titles beyond 1st year curriculum	137	137
# of upper division courses, excluding seminars, with an enrollment:		
Under 25	90	90
25 - 49	39	39
50 - 74	13	13
75 - 99	16	16
100 +	8	8
# of seminars	35	35
# of seminar positions available	1,110	
# of seminar positions filled	530	530
# of positions available in simulation courses	306	
# of simulation positions filled	241	241
# of positions available in faculty supervised clinical courses	136	
# of fac. sup. clin. positions filled	63	63
# involved in field placements	235	235
# involved in law journals	71	71
# in moot court or trial competitions	92	92
# of credit hrs required to graduate	86	

J.D. Enrollment & Ethnicity

	Men		Women		Fl-Time		Pt-Time		1st Yr		2nd Yr		3rd Yr		4th Yr		Total		JD Degrees Awarded
	#	%	#	%	#	%	#	%	#	%	#	%	#	%	#	%	#	%	
African-American	14	3.0	19	4.2	21	3.3	12	4.2	14	4.9	5	1.9	11	3.8	3	3.6	33	3.6	15
American Indian	2	0.4	3	0.7	1	0.2	4	1.4	1	0.4	3	1.1	0	0.0	1	1.2	5	0.5	4
Asian American	77	16.5	97	21.6	120	19.1	54	18.8	62	21.8	40	15.2	59	20.6	13	15.7	174	19.0	58
Mexican American	0	0.0	0	0.0	0	0.0	0	0.0	0	0.0	0	0.0	0	0.0	0	0.0	0	0.0	0
Puerto Rican	0	0.0	0	0.0	0	0.0	0	0.0	0	0.0	0	0.0	0	0.0	0	0.0	0	0.0	0
Hispanic American	36	7.7	31	6.9	50	7.9	17	5.9	17	6.0	22	8.4	22	7.7	6	7.2	67	7.3	18
Total Minorities	129	27.6	150	33.4	192	30.5	87	30.2	94	33.1	70	26.6	92	32.1	23	27.7	279	30.4	95
Foreign Nationals	0	0.0	0	0.0	0	0.0	0	0.0	0	0.0	0	0.0	0	0.0	0	0.0	0	0.0	0
Caucasian	339	72.4	299	66.6	437	69.5	201	69.8	190	66.9	193	73.4	197	68.6	58	69.9	638	69.6	197
Total	468	51.0	449	49.0	629	68.6	288	31.4	284	31.0	263	28.7	287	31.3	83	9.1	917		292

GPA & LSAT Scores

	Full Time	Part Time	Total
# of apps	2,315	215	2,530
# admits	1,176	105	1,281
# of matrics	224	69	293
75% GPA	3.49	3.32	
25% GPA	2.96	2.85	
75% LSAT	158	160	
25% LSAT	153	153	

Tuition & Fees

	Resident	Non-resident
Full-Time	$20,782	$20,782
Part-Time	$14,360	$14,360

Living Expenses

Estimated living expenses for Singles		
Living on campus	Living off campus	Living at home
$15,734	$15,734	N/A

Grants/Scholarships

	Full-time		Part-time		Total	
	#	%	#	%	#	%
Total # of Students	629		288		917	
Total # receiving grants	256	40.7	34	11.8	290	31.6
Less than 1/2 tuition	190	30.2	24	8.3	214	23.3
Half to full tuition	58	9.2	6	2.1	64	7.0
Full tuition	8	1.3	4	1.4	12	1.3
More than full tuition	0	0.0	0	0.0	0	0.0
Median Grant Amount	$10,000		$7,500			

Informational & Library Resources

# of volumes & volume equivalents	275,160	# of professional staff	7
# of titles	111,349	Hours per week with professional staff	76
# of active serial subscriptions	3,590	Hours per week without professional staff	29
Study seating capacity inside the library	452	# of student computer work stations for entire law school	57
Square feet of law library	39,554	# of additional networked connections	564
Square feet of law school (excl. Library)	61,718	Require Laptop Computer?	N

Employment

	Total	%
Employment status known	237	90.8
Employment status unknown	24	9.2
Employed	219	92.4
Pursuing graduate degrees	4	1.7
Unemployed seeking employment	6	2.5
Unemployed not seeking employment	8	3.4
Type of Employment		
# employed in law firms	127	58.0
# employed in business & industry	51	23.3
# employed in government	15	6.8
# employed in public interest	6	2.7
# employed as judicial clerks	8	3.7
# employed in academia	12	5.5
Geographic Location		
# employed in state	198	90.4
# employed in foreign countries	1	0.5
# of states where employed	12	

J.D. Attrition (from Prior Year)

	Academic	Other	TOTALS	
	#	#	#	%
1st Year	28	22	50	17%
2nd Year	4	5	9	2.9%
3rd Year	1	0	1	0.4%
4th Year	0	0	0	0.0%

Bar Passage Rates

Jurisdiction	California		
Exam	Sum 97	Win 98	Total
# from school taking bar for the first time	213	25	238
School's pass rate for all first-time takers	84%	60%	81%
State's pass rate for all first-time takers	75%	57%	71%

SEATTLE UNIVERSITY

950 Broadway Plaza
Tacoma, WA 98402
(253)591-2273
http://www.law.seattleu.edu

ABA Approved Since 1994

The Basics

Type of School: Private   Term: Semester
Application deadline: 04/01
Application fee: $50
Financial Aid deadline: 04/01
Can first year start other than Fall? Yes
Student faculty ratio: 22.3 to 1
Does the University offer:
- housing restricted to law students? No
- graduate student housing for which law students are eligible? No

Faculty & Administrators

	Total		Men		Women		Minorities	
	Fall	Spr	Fall	Spr	Fall	Spr	Fall	Spr
Full-time	29	26	19	18	10	8	4	4
Other Full-Time	6	6	2	2	4	4	1	1
Deans, librarians, & others who teach > 1/2	0	0	0	0	0	0	0	0
Part-time	26	35	17	27	9	8	4	3
Total	61	67	38	47	23	20	9	8
Deans, librarians, & others who teach < 1/2	2	2	1	1	1	1	0	0

Curriculum

	Full time	Part time
Typical first-year section size	68	54
Is there typically a "small section" of the first year class, other than Legal Writing, taught by full-time faculty?	No	No
If yes, typical size offered last year	N/A	N/A
# of classroom course titles beyond 1st year curriculum	87	42
# of upper division courses, excluding seminars, with an enrollment:		
Under 25	57	14
25 - 49	23	16
50 - 74	16	7
75 - 99	6	2
100 +	3	3
# of seminars	7	4
# of seminar positions available	229	
# of seminar positions filled	130	73
# of positions available in simulation courses	727	
# of simulation positions filled	298	235
# of positions available in faculty supervised clinical courses	192	
# of fac. sup. clin. positions filled	121	17
# involved in field placements	42	7
# involved in law journals	55	5
# in moot court or trial competitions	20	1
# of credit hrs required to graduate	90	

J.D. Enrollment & Ethnicity

	Men		Women		Fl-Time		Pt-Time		1st Yr		2nd Yr		3rd Yr		4th Yr		Total		JD Degrees Awarded
	#	%	#	%	#	%	#	%	#	%	#	%	#	%	#	%	#	%	
African-American	12	3.2	39	8.4	34	5.2	17	9.0	26	8.4	14	6.1	10	3.8	1	2.8	51	6.1	11
American Indian	7	1.9	8	1.7	10	1.5	5	2.7	5	1.6	3	1.3	5	1.9	2	5.6	15	1.8	10
Asian American	33	8.8	52	11.2	72	11.0	13	6.9	33	10.7	27	11.8	25	9.4	0	0.0	85	10.1	21
Mexican American	5	1.3	13	2.8	17	2.6	1	0.5	10	3.2	4	1.7	4	1.5	0	0.0	18	2.1	3
Puerto Rican	1	0.3	1	0.2	2	0.3	0	0.0	0	0.0	1	0.4	1	0.4	0	0.0	2	0.2	0
Hispanic American	9	2.4	4	0.9	7	1.1	6	3.2	5	1.6	7	3.1	0	0.0	1	2.8	13	1.5	3
Total Minorities	67	17.8	117	25.3	142	21.8	42	22.3	79	25.6	56	24.5	45	16.9	4	11.1	184	21.9	48
Foreign Nationals	0	0.0	0	0.0	0	0.0	0	0.0	0	0.0	0	0.0	0	0.0	0	0.0	0	0.0	0
Caucasian	310	82.2	346	74.7	510	78.2	146	77.7	230	74.4	172	75.1	222	83.5	32	88.9	656	78.1	196
Total	377	44.9	463	55.1	652	77.6	188	22.4	309	36.8	229	27.3	266	31.7	36	4.3	840		244

GPA & LSAT Scores

	Full Time	Part Time	Total
# of apps	945	113	1,058
# admits	726	80	806
# of matrics	234	69	303
75% GPA	3.50	3.37	
25% GPA	3.04	2.68	
75% LSAT	157	156	
25% LSAT	150	146	

Tuition & Fees

	Resident	Non-resident
Full-Time	$17,926	$17,926
Part-Time	$14,932	$14,932

Living Expenses

Estimated living expenses for Singles		
Living on campus	Living off campus	Living at home
N/A	$11,559	$7,050

Employment

	Total	%
Employment status known	254	89.1
Employment status unknown	31	10.9
Employed	219	86.2
Pursuing graduate degrees	4	1.6
Unemployed seeking employment	25	9.8
Unemployed not seeking employment	6	2.4
Type of Employment		
# employed in law firms	121	55.3
# employed in business & industry	38	17.4
# employed in government	34	15.5
# employed in public interest	6	2.7
# employed as judicial clerks	8	3.7
# employed in academia	3	1.4
Geographic Location		
# employed in state	194	88.6
# employed in foreign countries	3	1.4
# of states where employed	14	

Grants/Scholarships

	Full-time		Part-time		Total	
	#	%	#	%	#	%
Total # of Students	652		188		840	
Total # receiving grants	235	36.0	53	28.2	288	34.3
Less than 1/2 tuition	200	30.7	50	26.6	250	29.8
Half to full tuition	35	5.4	3	1.6	38	4.5
Full tuition	0	0.0	0	0.0	0	0.0
More than full tuition	0	0.0	0	0.0	0	0.0
Median Grant Amount	$5,047		$3,770			

Informational & Library Resources

# of volumes & volume equivalents	321,920	# of professional staff	7
# of titles	50,378	Hours per week with professional staff	49
# of active serial subscriptions	4,350	Hours per week without professional staff	70
Study seating capacity inside the library	589	# of student computer work stations for entire law school	89
Square feet of law library	40,397	# of additional networked connections	10
Square feet of law school (excl. Library)	59,290	Require Laptop Computer?	N

J.D. Attrition (from Prior Year)

	Academic	Other	TOTALS	
	#	#	#	%
1st Year	4	22	26	10%
2nd Year	3	1	4	1.5%
3rd Year	0	2	2	0.6%
4th Year	0	0	0	0.0%

Bar Passage Rates

Jurisdiction	Washington		
Exam	Sum 97	Win 98	Total
# from school taking bar for the first time	204	40	244
School's pass rate for all first-time takers	79%	83%	80%
State's pass rate for all first-time takers	73%	83%	76%

SETON HALL UNIVERSITY

One Newark Center
Newark, NJ 07102
(973)642-8500
http://www.shu.edu/law

ABA Approved Since 1951

The Basics

Type of School: Private   Term: Semester

Application deadline: 04/01

Application fee: $50

Financial Aid deadline: 04/15

Can first year start other than Fall? No

Student faculty ratio: 24.5 to 1

Does the University offer:
- housing restricted to law students? No
- graduate student housing for which law students are eligible? No

Faculty & Administrators

	Total		Men		Women		Minorities	
	Fall	Spr	Fall	Spr	Fall	Spr	Fall	Spr
Full-time	37	36	22	21	15	15	7	8
Other Full-Time	1	2	1	1	0	1	0	0
Deans, librarians, & others who teach > 1/2	5	5	3	3	2	2	0	0
Part-time	97	101	73	80	24	20	7	6
Total	140	144	99	105	41	38	14	14
Deans, librarians, & others who teach < 1/2	0	0	0	0	0	0	0	0

Curriculum

	Full time	Part time
Typical first-year section size	80	80
Is there typically a "small section" of the first year class, other than Legal Writing, taught by full-time faculty?	No	No
If yes, typical size offered last year	N/A	N/A
# of classroom course titles beyond 1st year curriculum	107	84
# of upper division courses, excluding seminars, with an enrollment:		
Under 25	45	36
25 - 49	35	16
50 - 74	15	8
75 - 99	12	6
100 +	0	0
# of seminars	50	42
# of seminar positions available	1,533	
# of seminar positions filled	796	570
# of positions available in simulation courses	1,366	
# of simulation positions filled	241	191
# of positions available in faculty supervised clinical courses	118	
# of fac. sup. clin. positions filled	114	14
# involved in field placements	85	5
# involved in law journals	114	12
# in moot court or trial competitions	148	26
# of credit hrs required to graduate	85	

J.D. Enrollment & Ethnicity

	Men		Women		Fl-Time		Pt-Time		1st Yr		2nd Yr		3rd Yr		4th Yr		Total		JD Degrees Awarded
	#	%	#	%	#	%	#	%	#	%	#	%	#	%	#	%	#	%	
African-American	17	2.5	29	5.8	31	3.5	15	4.7	18	4.7	15	4.1	10	2.8	3	3.3	46	3.9	25
American Indian	2	0.3	2	0.4	3	0.3	1	0.3	2	0.5	0	0.0	2	0.6	0	0.0	4	0.3	2
Asian American	37	5.3	28	5.6	50	5.7	15	4.7	20	5.2	23	6.3	20	5.6	2	2.2	65	5.4	24
Mexican American	1	0.1	0	0.0	1	0.1	0	0.0	0	0.0	1	0.3	0	0.0	0	0.0	1	0.1	0
Puerto Rican	11	1.6	8	1.6	11	1.3	8	2.5	9	2.4	3	0.8	5	1.4	2	2.2	19	1.6	6
Hispanic American	23	3.3	31	6.2	38	4.3	16	5.0	24	6.3	14	3.9	11	3.1	5	5.6	54	4.5	15
Total Minorities	91	13.2	98	19.5	134	15.3	55	17.4	73	19.2	56	15.4	48	13.3	12	13.3	189	15.8	72
Foreign Nationals	0	0.0	0	0.0	0	0.0	0	0.0	0	0.0	0	0.0	0	0.0	0	0.0	0	0.0	0
Caucasian	601	86.8	404	80.5	743	84.7	262	82.6	308	80.8	307	84.6	312	86.7	78	86.7	1005	84.2	330
Total	692	58.0	502	42.0	877	73.5	317	26.5	381	31.9	363	30.4	360	30.2	90	7.5	1194		402

GPA & LSAT Scores

	Full Time	Part Time	Total
# of apps	1,706	410	2,116
# admits	838	132	970
# of matrics	299	82	381
75% GPA	3.41	3.28	
25% GPA	2.83	2.55	
75% LSAT	157	157	
25% LSAT	151	150	

Tuition & Fees

	Resident	Non-resident
Full-Time	$19,734	$19,734
Part-Time	$0	$14,050

Living Expenses

Estimated living expenses for Singles

Living on campus	Living off campus	Living at home
N/A	$15,370	$9,895

Grants/Scholarships

	Full-time		Part-time		Total	
	#	%	#	%	#	%
Total # of Students	877		317		1194	
Total # receiving grants	655	74.7	93	29.3	748	62.6
Less than 1/2 tuition	575	65.6	72	22.7	647	54.2
Half to full tuition	75	8.6	20	6.3	95	8.0
Full tuition	5	0.6	1	0.3	6	0.5
More than full tuition	0	0.0	0	0.0	0	0.0
Median Grant Amount	$1,800		$500			

Informational & Library Resources

# of volumes & volume equivalents	385,614	# of professional staff	10
# of titles	65,163	Hours per week with professional staff	74
# of active serial subscriptions	3,462	Hours per week without professional staff	45
Study seating capacity inside the library	600	# of student computer work stations for entire law school	175
Square feet of law library	55,250	# of additional networked connections	200
Square feet of law school (excl. Library)	154,750	Require Laptop Computer?	N

Employment

	Total	%
Employment status known	342	96.1
Employment status unknown	14	3.9
Employed	323	94.4
Pursuing graduate degrees	2	0.6
Unemployed seeking employment	15	4.4
Unemployed not seeking employment	2	0.6
Type of Employment		
# employed in law firms	115	35.6
# employed in business & industry	75	23.2
# employed in government	23	7.1
# employed in public interest	2	0.6
# employed as judicial clerks	106	32.8
# employed in academia	0	0.0
Geographic Location		
# employed in state	240	74.3
# employed in foreign countries	1	0.3
# of states where employed	15	

J.D. Attrition (from Prior Year)

	Academic	Other	TOTALS	
	#	#	#	%
1st Year	0	16	16	4.2%
2nd Year	14	11	25	7.0%
3rd Year	0	0	0	0.0%
4th Year	0	0	0	0.0%

Bar Passage Rates

Jurisdiction	New Jersey			New York		
Exam	Sum 97	Win 98	Total	Sum 97	Win 98	Total
# from school taking bar for the first time	316	25	341	194	14	208
School's pass rate for all first-time takers	81%	56%	79%	80%	43%	77%
State's pass rate for all first-time takers	77%	0%	77%	78%	65%	76%

SOUTH CAROLINA, UNIVERSITY OF

Main and Greene Streets
Columbia, SC 29208
(803)777-6857
http://www.law.sc.edu

ABA Approved Since 1925

The Basics

Type of School: Public Term: Semester
Application deadline: 02/15
Application fee: $25
Financial Aid deadline: 04/01
Can first year start other than Fall? No
Student faculty ratio: 22.8 to 1
Does the University offer:
- housing restricted to law students? No
- graduate student housing for which law students are eligible? No

Faculty & Administrators

	Total		Men		Women		Minorities	
	Fall	Spr	Fall	Spr	Fall	Spr	Fall	Spr
Full-time	31	32	27	29	4	3	0	0
Other Full-Time	0	0	0	0	0	0	0	0
Deans, librarians, & others who teach > 1/2	3	3	3	3	0	0	0	0
Part-time	0	0	0	0	0	0	0	0
Total	34	35	30	32	4	3	0	0
Deans, librarians, & others who teach < 1/2	1	1	1	1	0	0	0	0

Curriculum

	Full time	Part time
Typical first-year section size	80	0
Is there typically a "small section" of the first year class, other than Legal Writing, taught by full-time faculty?	No	No
If yes, typical size offered last year	N/A	N/A
# of classroom course titles beyond 1st year curriculum	108	0
# of upper division courses, excluding seminars, with an enrollment:		
Under 25	40	0
25 - 49	32	0
50 - 74	14	0
75 - 99	22	0
100 +	3	0
# of seminars	13	0
# of seminar positions available	260	
# of seminar positions filled	175	0
# of positions available in simulation courses	368	
# of simulation positions filled	281	0
# of positions available in faculty supervised clinical courses	62	
# of fac. sup. clin. positions filled	57	0
# involved in field placements	25	0
# involved in law journals	158	0
# in moot court or trial competitions	23	0
# of credit hrs required to graduate	90	

J.D. Enrollment & Ethnicity

	Men		Women		Fl-Time		Pt-Time		1st Yr		2nd Yr		3rd Yr		4th Yr		Total		JD Degrees Awarded
	#	%	#	%	#	%	#	%	#	%	#	%	#	%	#	%	#	%	
African-American	23	5.3	41	13.2	64	8.6	0	0.0	25	10.8	18	7.4	21	7.7	0	0.0	64	8.6	15
American Indian	1	0.2	0	0.0	1	0.1	0	0.0	0	0.0	0	0.0	1	0.4	0	0.0	1	0.1	0
Asian American	3	0.7	5	1.6	8	1.1	0	0.0	2	0.9	3	1.2	3	1.1	0	0.0	8	1.1	2
Mexican American	0	0.0	0	0.0	0	0.0	0	0.0	0	0.0	0	0.0	0	0.0	0	0.0	0	0.0	0
Puerto Rican	0	0.0	0	0.0	0	0.0	0	0.0	0	0.0	0	0.0	0	0.0	0	0.0	0	0.0	0
Hispanic American	1	0.2	1	0.3	2	0.3	0	0.0	1	0.4	1	0.4	0	0.0	0	0.0	2	0.3	3
Total Minorities	28	6.4	47	15.2	75	10.1	0	0.0	28	12.1	22	9.0	25	9.2	0	0.0	75	10.1	20
Foreign Nationals	2	0.5	1	0.3	3	0.4	0	0.0	2	0.9	0	0.0	1	0.4	0	0.0	3	0.4	0
Caucasian	406	93.1	262	84.5	668	89.5	0	0.0	201	87.0	222	91.0	245	90.4	0	0.0	668	89.5	222
Total	436	58.4	310	41.6	746	100.0	0	0.0	231	31.0	244	32.7	271	36.3	0	0.0	746		242

GPA & LSAT Scores

	Full Time	Part Time	Total
# of apps	1,199	0	1,199
# admits	421	0	421
# of matrics	228	0	228
75% GPA	3.54	0.00	
25% GPA	2.86	0.00	
75% LSAT	160	0	
25% LSAT	152	0	

Tuition & Fees

	Resident	Non-resident
Full-Time	$7,328	$14,986
Part-Time	$0	$0

Living Expenses

Estimated living expenses for Singles		
Living on campus	Living off campus	Living at home
$11,009	$11,009	$6,696

Grants/Scholarships

	Full-time		Part-time		Total	
	#	%	#	%	#	%
Total # of Students	746		0		746	
Total # receiving grants	223	29.9	0	0.0	223	29.9
Less than 1/2 tuition	199	26.7	0	0.0	199	26.7
Half to full tuition	6	0.8	0	0.0	6	0.8
Full tuition	6	0.8	0	0.0	6	0.8
More than full tuition	12	1.6	0	0.0	12	1.6
Median Grant Amount	$1,000		$0			

Informational & Library Resources

# of volumes & volume equivalents	431,101	# of professional staff	9
# of titles	71,435	Hours per week with professional staff	49
# of active serial subscriptions	3,166	Hours per week without professional staff	62
Study seating capacity inside the library	642	# of student computer work stations for entire law school	103
Square feet of law library	55,040	# of additional networked connections	0
Square feet of law school (excl. Library)	80,045	Require Laptop Computer?	N

Employment

	Total	%
Employment status known	229	97.4
Employment status unknown	6	2.6
Employed	211	92.1
Pursuing graduate degrees	4	1.7
Unemployed seeking employment	13	5.7
Unemployed not seeking employment	1	0.4
Type of Employment		
# employed in law firms	108	51.2
# employed in business & industry	23	10.9
# employed in government	38	18.0
# employed in public interest	3	1.4
# employed as judicial clerks	39	18.5
# employed in academia	0	0.0
Geographic Location		
# employed in state	171	81.0
# employed in foreign countries	1	0.5
# of states where employed	14	

J.D. Attrition (from Prior Year)

	Academic	Other	TOTALS	
	#	#	#	%
1st Year	1	5	6	2.5%
2nd Year	0	8	8	3.1%
3rd Year	0	0	0	0.0%
4th Year	0	0	0	0.0%

Bar Passage Rates

Jurisdiction	South Carolina		
Exam	Sum 97	Win 98	Total
# from school taking bar for the first time	215	22	237
School's pass rate for all first-time takers	87%	77%	86%
State's pass rate for all first-time takers	86%	75%	84%

SOUTH DAKOTA, UNIVERSITY OF

414 E. Clark Street
Vermillion, SD 57069-2390
(605)677-5443
http://www.usd.edu/law

ABA Approved Since 1923

The Basics

Type of School: Public Term: Semester
Application deadline: 03/01 (Preferred)
Application fee: $15
Financial Aid deadline: 05/01
Can first year start other than Fall? No
Student faculty ratio: 14.4 to 1
Does the University offer:
- housing restricted to law students? No
- graduate student housing for which law students are eligible? Yes

Faculty & Administrators

	Total		Men		Women		Minorities	
	Fall	Spr	Fall	Spr	Fall	Spr	Fall	Spr
Full-time	12	12	10	10	2	2	1	1
Other Full-Time	2	2	1	1	1	1	0	0
Deans, librarians, & others who teach > 1/2	1	1	1	1	0	0	0	0
Part-time	2	1	2	1	0	0	0	0
Total	17	16	14	13	3	3	1	1
Deans, librarians, & others who teach < 1/2	2	2	1	1	1	1	0	0

Curriculum

	Full time	Part time
Typical first-year section size	88	0
Is there typically a "small section" of the first year class, other than Legal Writing, taught by full-time faculty?	No	No
If yes, typical size offered last year	N/A	N/A
# of classroom course titles beyond 1st year curriculum	46	0
# of upper division courses, excluding seminars, with an enrollment:		
Under 25	34	0
25 - 49	13	0
50 - 74	6	0
75 - 99	0	0
100 +	0	0
# of seminars	1	0
# of seminar positions available	12	
# of seminar positions filled	12	0
# of positions available in simulation courses	118	
# of simulation positions filled	118	0
# of positions available in faculty supervised clinical courses	0	
# of fac. sup. clin. positions filled	0	0
# involved in field placements	25	0
# involved in law journals	27	0
# in moot court or trial competitions	34	0
# of credit hrs required to graduate	90	

J.D. Enrollment & Ethnicity

	Men		Women		Fl-Time		Pt-Time		1st Yr		2nd Yr		3rd Yr		4th Yr		Total		JD Degrees Awarded
	#	%	#	%	#	%	#	%	#	%	#	%	#	%	#	%	#	%	
African-American	3	2.5	0	0.0	3	1.4	0	0.0	0	0.0	1	1.2	2	3.0	0	0.0	3	1.4	1
American Indian	2	1.6	3	3.5	5	2.4	0	0.0	1	1.6	2	2.5	2	3.0	0	0.0	5	2.4	0
Asian American	1	0.8	2	2.3	3	1.4	0	0.0	1	1.6	0	0.0	2	3.0	0	0.0	3	1.4	0
Mexican American	0	0.0	0	0.0	0	0.0	0	0.0	0	0.0	0	0.0	0	0.0	0	0.0	0	0.0	0
Puerto Rican	0	0.0	0	0.0	0	0.0	0	0.0	0	0.0	0	0.0	0	0.0	0	0.0	0	0.0	0
Hispanic American	0	0.0	0	0.0	0	0.0	0	0.0	0	0.0	0	0.0	0	0.0	0	0.0	0	0.0	0
Total Minorities	6	4.9	5	5.8	11	5.3	0	0.0	2	3.3	3	3.7	6	9.1	0	0.0	11	5.3	1
Foreign Nationals	0	0.0	0	0.0	0	0.0	0	0.0	0	0.0	0	0.0	0	0.0	0	0.0	0	0.0	0
Caucasian	116	95.1	81	94.2	197	94.7	0	0.0	59	96.7	78	96.3	60	90.9	0	0.0	197	94.7	62
Total	122	58.7	86	41.3	208	100.0	0	0.0	61	29.3	81	38.9	66	31.7	0	0.0	208		63

GPA & LSAT Scores

	Full Time	Part Time	Total
# of apps	224	0	224
# admits	129	0	129
# of matrics	62	0	62
75% GPA	3.54	0.00	
25% GPA	3.01	0.00	
75% LSAT	156	0	
25% LSAT	146	0	

Tuition & Fees

	Resident	Non-resident
Full-Time	$4,960	$10,434
Part-Time	$0	$0

Living Expenses

Estimated living expenses for Singles

Living on campus	Living off campus	Living at home
$8,100	$11,270	$7,640

Grants/Scholarships

	Full-time		Part-time		Total	
	#	%	#	%	#	%
Total # of Students	208		0		208	
Total # receiving grants	156	75.0	0	0.0	156	75.0
Less than 1/2 tuition	124	59.6	0	0.0	124	59.6
Half to full tuition	7	3.4	0	0.0	7	3.4
Full tuition	8	3.8	0	0.0	8	3.8
More than full tuition	17	8.2	0	0.0	17	8.2
Median Grant Amount	$1,000		$0			

Informational & Library Resources

# of volumes & volume equivalents	182,522	# of professional staff	6
# of titles	37,840	Hours per week with professional staff	53
# of active serial subscriptions	2,104	Hours per week without professional staff	43
Study seating capacity inside the library	227	# of student computer work stations for entire law school	36
Square feet of law library	25,650	# of additional networked connections	8
Square feet of law school (excl. Library)	34,582	Require Laptop Computer?	N

Employment

	Total	%
Employment status known	75	100.0
Employment status unknown	0	0.0
Employed	64	85.3
Pursuing graduate degrees	4	5.3
Unemployed seeking employment	7	9.3
Unemployed not seeking employment	0	0.0
Type of Employment		
# employed in law firms	29	45.3
# employed in business & industry	7	10.9
# employed in government	9	14.1
# employed in public interest	0	0.0
# employed as judicial clerks	17	26.6
# employed in academia	2	3.1
Geographic Location		
# employed in state	36	56.2
# employed in foreign countries	1	1.6
# of states where employed	15	

J.D. Attrition (from Prior Year)

	Academic	Other	TOTALS	
	#	#	#	%
1st Year	0	8	8	9.1%
2nd Year	0	0	0	0.0%
3rd Year	0	0	0	0.0%
4th Year	0	0	0	0.0%

Bar Passage Rates

Jurisdiction	South Dakota		
Exam	Sum 97	Win 98	Total
# from school taking bar for the first time	53	6	59
School's pass rate for all first-time takers	92%	83%	92%
State's pass rate for all first-time takers	90%	82%	89%

SOUTH TEXAS COLLEGE OF LAW

affiliated with Texas A&M University
1303 San Jacinto Street
Houston, TX 77002-7000
(713)659-8040
http://www.stcl.edu

ABA Approved Since 1959

The Basics

Type of School: Private Term: Semester
Application deadline: 10/01
Application fee: $40
Financial Aid deadline: Rolling
Can first year start other than Fall? Yes
Student faculty ratio: 20.3 to 1
Does the University offer:
- housing restricted to law students? No
- graduate student housing for which law students are eligible? No

Faculty & Administrators

	Total		Men		Women		Minorities	
	Fall	Spr	Fall	Spr	Fall	Spr	Fall	Spr
Full-time	44	40	30	28	14	12	6	6
Other Full-Time	0	0	0	0	0	0	0	0
Deans, librarians, & others who teach > 1/2	2	2	1	1	1	1	0	0
Part-time	32	38	25	31	7	7	2	1
Total	78	80	56	60	22	20	8	7
Deans, librarians, & others who teach < 1/2	6	4	5	3	1	1	0	0

Curriculum

	Full time	Part time
Typical first-year section size	90	60
Is there typically a "small section" of the first year class, other than Legal Writing, taught by full-time faculty?	No	No
If yes, typical size offered last year	N/A	N/A
# of classroom course titles beyond 1st year curriculum	60	54
# of upper division courses, excluding seminars, with an enrollment:		
Under 25	31	32
25 - 49	30	19
50 - 74	19	9
75 - 99	20	12
100 +	0	0
# of seminars	7	18
# of seminar positions available	500	
# of seminar positions filled	103	282
# of positions available in simulation courses	682	
# of simulation positions filled	426	256
# of positions available in faculty supervised clinical courses	80	
# of fac. sup. clin. positions filled	53	0
# involved in field placements	91	0
# involved in law journals	150	0
# in moot court or trial competitions	76	0
# of credit hrs required to graduate	90	

J.D. Enrollment & Ethnicity

	Men		Women		Fl-Time		Pt-Time		1st Yr		2nd Yr		3rd Yr		4th Yr		Total		JD Degrees Awarded
	#	%	#	%	#	%	#	%	#	%	#	%	#	%	#	%	#	%	
African-American	21	3.1	32	6.1	27	3.4	26	6.5	26	4.4	15	4.6	10	4.0	2	5.0	53	4.4	22
American Indian	7	1.0	4	0.8	9	1.1	2	0.5	7	1.2	2	0.6	2	0.8	0	0.0	11	0.9	3
Asian American	25	3.7	37	7.0	41	5.1	21	5.2	33	5.6	17	5.2	11	4.4	1	2.5	62	5.1	26
Mexican American	40	5.9	26	4.9	53	6.6	13	3.2	37	6.3	13	4.0	15	6.0	1	2.5	66	5.5	6
Puerto Rican	2	0.3	4	0.8	4	0.5	2	0.5	2	0.3	3	0.9	1	0.4	0	0.0	6	0.5	0
Hispanic American	26	3.8	28	5.3	41	5.1	13	3.2	27	4.6	15	4.6	11	4.4	1	2.5	54	4.5	9
Total Minorities	121	17.8	131	24.9	175	21.8	77	19.2	132	22.4	65	19.9	50	19.8	5	12.5	252	20.9	66
Foreign Nationals	0	0.0	1	0.2	1	0.1	0	0.0	1	0.2	0	0.0	0	0.0	0	0.0	1	0.1	0
Caucasian	559	82.2	394	74.9	628	78.1	325	80.8	455	77.4	261	80.1	202	80.2	35	87.5	953	79.0	259
Total	680	56.4	526	43.6	804	66.7	402	33.3	588	48.8	326	27.0	252	20.9	40	3.3	1206		325

SOUTH TEXAS COLLEGE OF LAW

GPA & LSAT Scores

	Full Time	Part Time	Total
# of apps	1,361	295	1,656
# admits	829	196	1,025
# of matrics	320	145	465
75% GPA	3.14	3.29	
25% GPA	2.67	2.67	
75% LSAT	153	152	
25% LSAT	146	146	

Tuition & Fees

	Resident	Non-resident
Full-Time	$15,450	$15,450
Part-Time	$10,500	$10,500

Living Expenses

Estimated living expenses for Singles		
Living on campus	Living off campus	Living at home
N/A	$12,372	$8,604

Employment

	Total	%
Employment status known	238	73.2
Employment status unknown	87	26.8
Employed	184	77.3
Pursuing graduate degrees	4	1.7
Unemployed seeking employment	46	19.3
Unemployed not seeking employment	4	1.7
Type of Employment		
# employed in law firms	131	71.2
# employed in business & industry	25	13.6
# employed in government	17	9.2
# employed in public interest	1	0.5
# employed as judicial clerks	5	2.7
# employed in academia	3	1.6
Geographic Location		
# employed in state	167	90.8
# employed in foreign countries	2	1.1
# of states where employed	8	

Grants/Scholarships

	Full-time		Part-time		Total	
	#	%	#	%	#	%
Total # of Students	804		402		1206	
Total # receiving grants	299	37.2	114	28.4	413	34.2
Less than 1/2 tuition	297	36.9	114	28.4	411	34.1
Half to full tuition	2	0.2	0	0.0	2	0.2
Full tuition	0	0.0	0	0.0	0	0.0
More than full tuition	0	0.0	0	0.0	0	0.0
Median Grant Amount	$1,163		$1,189			

Informational & Library Resources

# of volumes & volume equivalents	357,491	# of professional staff	8
# of titles	58,177	Hours per week with professional staff	83
# of active serial subscriptions	4,142	Hours per week without professional staff	20
Study seating capacity inside the library	564	# of student computer work stations for entire law school	90
Square feet of law library	43,767	# of additional networked connections	12
Square feet of law school (excl. Library)	101,984	Require Laptop Computer?	N

J.D. Attrition (from Prior Year)

	Academic	Other	TOTALS	
	#	#	#	%
1st Year	46	35	81	13%
2nd Year	8	4	12	3.6%
3rd Year	0	0	0	0.0%
4th Year	0	0	0	0.0%

Bar Passage Rates

Jurisdiction	Texas		
Exam	Sum 97	Win 98	Total
# from school taking bar for the first time	205	101	306
School's pass rate for all first-time takers	88%	73%	83%
State's pass rate for all first-time takers	83%	73%	81%

SOUTHERN CALIFORNIA, UNIVERSITY OF

University Park
Los Angeles, CA 90089-0071
(213)740-7331
http://www.usc.edu/dept/law

ABA Approved Since 1924

The Basics

Type of School: Private   Term: Semester

Application deadline: 02/01

Application fee: $60

Financial Aid deadline: 02/15

Can first year start other than Fall? No

Student faculty ratio: 15.7 to 1

Does the University offer:
- housing restricted to law students? Yes
- graduate student housing for which law students are eligible? Yes

Faculty & Administrators

	Total		Men		Women		Minorities	
	Fall	Spr	Fall	Spr	Fall	Spr	Fall	Spr
Full-time	33	26	21	16	12	10	3	1
Other Full-Time	2	2	0	0	2	2	0	0
Deans, librarians, & others who teach > 1/2	3	3	3	3	0	0	0	0
Part-time	21	28	18	23	3	5	3	10
Total	59	59	42	42	17	17	6	11
Deans, librarians, & others who teach < 1/2	4	3	2	1	2	2	0	0

Curriculum

	Full time	Part time
Typical first-year section size	70	0
Is there typically a "small section" of the first year class, other than Legal Writing, taught by full-time faculty?	No	No
If yes, typical size offered last year	N/A	N/A
# of classroom course titles beyond 1st year curriculum	101	0
# of upper division courses, excluding seminars, with an enrollment:		
Under 25	54	0
25 - 49	27	0
50 - 74	5	0
75 - 99	2	0
100 +	5	0
# of seminars	8	0
# of seminar positions available	141	
# of seminar positions filled	112	0
# of positions available in simulation courses	338	
# of simulation positions filled	295	0
# of positions available in faculty supervised clinical courses	90	
# of fac. sup. clin. positions filled	77	0
# involved in field placements	130	0
# involved in law journals	133	0
# in moot court or trial competitions	19	0
# of credit hrs required to graduate	88	

J.D. Enrollment & Ethnicity

	Men		Women		Fl-Time		Pt-Time		1st Yr		2nd Yr		3rd Yr		4th Yr		Total		JD Degrees Awarded
	#	%	#	%	#	%	#	%	#	%	#	%	#	%	#	%	#	%	
African-American	26	7.7	47	16.6	73	11.8	0	0.0	30	14.4	22	10.9	21	9.9	0	0.0	73	11.8	28
American Indian	1	0.3	1	0.4	2	0.3	0	0.0	0	0.0	0	0.0	2	0.9	0	0.0	2	0.3	0
Asian American	46	13.6	44	15.5	90	14.5	0	0.0	34	16.3	27	13.4	29	13.7	0	0.0	90	14.5	26
Mexican American	34	10.1	30	10.6	64	10.3	0	0.0	22	10.6	24	11.9	18	8.5	0	0.0	64	10.3	24
Puerto Rican	0	0.0	0	0.0	0	0.0	0	0.0	0	0.0	0	0.0	0	0.0	0	0.0	0	0.0	0
Hispanic American	8	2.4	11	3.9	19	3.1	0	0.0	6	2.9	6	3.0	7	3.3	0	0.0	19	3.1	9
Total Minorities	115	34.0	133	47.0	248	39.9	0	0.0	92	44.2	79	39.3	77	36.3	0	0.0	248	39.9	87
Foreign Nationals	2	0.6	0	0.0	2	0.3	0	0.0	1	0.5	0	0.0	1	0.5	0	0.0	2	0.3	0
Caucasian	221	65.4	150	53.0	371	59.7	0	0.0	115	55.3	122	60.7	134	63.2	0	0.0	371	59.7	118
Total	338	54.4	283	45.6	621	100.0	0	0.0	208	33.5	201	32.4	212	34.1	0	0.0	621		205

GPA & LSAT Scores

	Full Time	Part Time	Total
# of apps	3,524	0	3,524
# admits	850	0	850
# of matrics	208	0	208
75% GPA	3.65	0.00	
25% GPA	3.30	0.00	
75% LSAT	165	0	
25% LSAT	159	0	

Tuition & Fees

	Resident	Non-resident
Full-Time	$25,052	$25,052
Part-Time	$0	$0

Living Expenses

Estimated living expenses for Singles		
Living on campus	Living off campus	Living at home
$11,344	$12,024	$5,984

Employment

	Total	%
Employment status known	202	95.7
Employment status unknown	9	4.3
Employed	190	94.1
Pursuing graduate degrees	2	1.0
Unemployed seeking employment	3	1.5
Unemployed not seeking employment	7	3.5
Type of Employment		
# employed in law firms	131	68.9
# employed in business & industry	26	13.7
# employed in government	10	5.3
# employed in public interest	5	2.6
# employed as judicial clerks	18	9.5
# employed in academia	0	0.0
Geographic Location		
# employed in state	151	79.5
# employed in foreign countries	3	1.6
# of states where employed	18	

Grants/Scholarships

	Full-time		Part-time		Total	
	#	%	#	%	#	%
Total # of Students	621		0		621	
Total # receiving grants	323	52.0	0	0.0	323	52.0
Less than 1/2 tuition	251	40.4	0	0.0	251	40.4
Half to full tuition	46	7.4	0	0.0	46	7.4
Full tuition	23	3.7	0	0.0	23	3.7
More than full tuition	3	0.5	0	0.0	3	0.5
Median Grant Amount	$7,500		$0			

Informational & Library Resources

# of volumes & volume equivalents	360,112	# of professional staff	8
# of titles	152,942	Hours per week with professional staff	52
# of active serial subscriptions	4,197	Hours per week without professional staff	49
Study seating capacity inside the library	298	# of student computer work stations for entire law school	97
Square feet of law library	40,000	# of additional networked connections	68
Square feet of law school (excl. Library)	121,447	Require Laptop Computer?	N

J.D. Attrition (from Prior Year)

	Academic	Other	TOTALS	
	#	#	#	%
1st Year	0	3	3	1.5%
2nd Year	0	3	3	1.5%
3rd Year	0	0	0	0.0%
4th Year	0	0	0	0.0%

Bar Passage Rates

Jurisdiction	California		
Exam	Sum 97	Win 98	Total
# from school taking bar for the first time	172	4	176
School's pass rate for all first-time takers	89%	50%	88%
State's pass rate for all first-time takers	75%	57%	71%

SOUTHERN ILLINOIS UNIVERSITY-CARBONDALE

Lesar Law Building
Carbondale, IL 62901-6804
(618)536-7711
http://www.siu.edu/~lawsch

ABA Approved Since 1974

The Basics

Type of School: Public   Term: Semester

Application deadline: 03/01

Application fee: $25

Financial Aid deadline: 04/01

Can first year start other than Fall? No

Student faculty ratio: 14.4 to 1

Does the University offer:
- housing restricted to law students? No
- graduate student housing for which law students are eligible? Yes

Faculty & Administrators

	Total		Men		Women		Minorities	
	Fall	Spr	Fall	Spr	Fall	Spr	Fall	Spr
Full-time	22	23	14	15	8	8	1	1
Other Full-Time	2	2	1	1	1	1	0	0
Deans, librarians, & others who teach > 1/2	7	5	3	1	4	4	0	0
Part-time	5	6	3	3	2	3	0	0
Total	36	36	21	20	15	16	1	1
Deans, librarians, & others who teach < 1/2	2	2	2	2	0	0	0	0

Curriculum

	Full time	Part time
Typical first-year section size	71	0
Is there typically a "small section" of the first year class, other than Legal Writing, taught by full-time faculty?	No	No
If yes, typical size offered last year	N/A	N/A
# of classroom course titles beyond 1st year curriculum	60	0
# of upper division courses, excluding seminars, with an enrollment:		
Under 25	41	0
25 - 49	27	0
50 - 74	13	0
75 - 99	1	0
100 +	0	0
# of seminars	8	0
# of seminar positions available	96	
# of seminar positions filled	86	0
# of positions available in simulation courses	366	
# of simulation positions filled	282	0
# of positions available in faculty supervised clinical courses	72	
# of fac. sup. clin. positions filled	39	0
# involved in field placements	69	0
# involved in law journals	58	0
# in moot court or trial competitions	47	0
# of credit hrs required to graduate	90	

J.D. Enrollment & Ethnicity

	Men		Women		Fl-Time		Pt-Time		1st Yr		2nd Yr		3rd Yr		4th Yr		Total		JD Degrees Awarded
	#	%	#	%	#	%	#	%	#	%	#	%	#	%	#	%	#	%	
African-American	10	4.1	12	8.8	22	5.9	0	0.0	6	4.2	4	3.6	12	9.4	0	0.0	22	5.8	6
American Indian	2	0.8	1	0.7	3	0.8	0	0.0	0	0.0	0	0.0	3	2.4	0	0.0	3	0.8	1
Asian American	9	3.7	7	5.1	16	4.3	0	0.0	5	3.5	4	3.6	7	5.5	0	0.0	16	4.2	12
Mexican American	1	0.4	2	1.5	3	0.8	0	0.0	2	1.4	0	0.0	1	0.8	0	0.0	3	0.8	2
Puerto Rican	0	0.0	0	0.0	0	0.0	0	0.0	0	0.0	0	0.0	0	0.0	0	0.0	0	0.0	2
Hispanic American	4	1.6	1	0.7	5	1.3	0	0.0	2	1.4	1	0.9	2	1.6	0	0.0	5	1.3	2
Total Minorities	26	10.6	23	16.9	49	13.0	0	0.0	15	10.6	9	8.0	25	19.7	0	0.0	49	12.9	25
Foreign Nationals	2	0.8	0	0.0	2	0.5	0	0.0	2	1.4	0	0.0	0	0.0	0	0.0	2	0.5	0
Caucasian	217	88.6	113	83.1	325	86.4	5	100.0	125	88.0	103	92.0	102	80.3	0	0.0	330	86.6	88
Total	245	64.3	136	35.7	376	98.7	5	1.3	142	37.3	112	29.4	127	33.3	0	0.0	381		113

SOUTHERN ILLINOIS UNIVERSITY-CARBONDALE

GPA & LSAT Scores

	Full Time	Part Time	Total
# of apps	737	0	737
# admits	425	0	425
# of matrics	145	0	145
75% GPA	3.38	0.00	
25% GPA	2.67	0.00	
75% LSAT	155	0	
25% LSAT	150	0	

Tuition & Fees

	Resident	Non-resident
Full-Time	$5,652	$14,892
Part-Time	$0	$0

Living Expenses

Estimated living expenses for Singles		
Living on campus	Living off campus	Living at home
$8,226	$8,226	$4,246

Grants/Scholarships

	Full-time		Part-time		Total	
	#	%	#	%	#	%
Total # of Students	376		5		381	
Total # receiving grants	123	32.7	0	0.0	123	32.3
Less than 1/2 tuition	82	21.8	0	0.0	82	21.5
Half to full tuition	32	8.5	0	0.0	32	8.4
Full tuition	0	0.0	0	0.0	0	0.0
More than full tuition	9	2.4	0	0.0	9	2.4
Median Grant Amount	$1,000		$0			

Informational & Library Resources

# of volumes & volume equivalents	343,429	# of professional staff	7
# of titles	67,427	Hours per week with professional staff	52
# of active serial subscriptions	4,059	Hours per week without professional staff	34
Study seating capacity inside the library	364	# of student computer work stations for entire law school	49
Square feet of law library	34,613	# of additional networked connections	0
Square feet of law school (excl. Library)	36,833	Require Laptop Computer?	N

Employment

	Total	%
Employment status known	86	73.5
Employment status unknown	31	26.5
Employed	81	94.2
Pursuing graduate degrees	1	1.2
Unemployed seeking employment	3	3.5
Unemployed not seeking employment	1	1.2
Type of Employment		
# employed in law firms	45	55.6
# employed in business & industry	11	13.6
# employed in government	17	21.0
# employed in public interest	2	2.5
# employed as judicial clerks	3	3.7
# employed in academia	3	3.7
Geographic Location		
# employed in state	64	79.0
# employed in foreign countries	0	0.0
# of states where employed	8	

J.D. Attrition (from Prior Year)

	Academic	Other	TOTALS	
	#	#	#	%
1st Year	0	4	4	3.3%
2nd Year	3	10	13	11%
3rd Year	0	0	0	0.0%
4th Year	0	0	0	0.0%

Bar Passage Rates

Jurisdiction	Illinois		
Exam	Sum 97	Win 98	Total
# from school taking bar for the first time	80	14	94
School's pass rate for all first-time takers	79%	57%	76%
State's pass rate for all first-time takers	87%	80%	85%

SOUTHERN METHODIST UNIVERSITY

P.O. Box 750116
Dallas, TX 75275-0116
(214)768-2618
http://www.smu.edu/~law

ABA Approved Since 1927

The Basics

Type of School: Private   Term: Semester
Application deadline: 02/01
Application fee: $50
Financial Aid deadline: 05/01
Can first year start other than Fall? No
Student faculty ratio: 17.2 to 1
Does the University offer:
- housing restricted to law students? No
- graduate student housing for which law students are eligible? Yes

Faculty & Administrators

	Total		Men		Women		Minorities	
	Fall	Spr	Fall	Spr	Fall	Spr	Fall	Spr
Full-time	36	28	27	21	9	7	5	4
Other Full-Time	0	0	0	0	0	0	0	0
Deans, librarians, & others who teach > 1/2	0	0	0	0	0	0	0	0
Part-time	61	70	43	56	18	14	3	3
Total	97	98	70	77	27	21	8	7
Deans, librarians, & others who teach < 1/2	7	7	5	5	2	2	1	1

Curriculum

	Full time	Part time
Typical first-year section size	80	0
Is there typically a "small section" of the first year class, other than Legal Writing, taught by full-time faculty?	No	No
If yes, typical size offered last year	N/A	N/A
# of classroom course titles beyond 1st year curriculum	116	0
# of upper division courses, excluding seminars, with an enrollment:		
Under 25	61	0
25 - 49	43	0
50 - 74	21	0
75 - 99	12	0
100 +	2	0
# of seminars	16	0
# of seminar positions available	320	
# of seminar positions filled	315	0
# of positions available in simulation courses	445	
# of simulation positions filled	429	0
# of positions available in faculty supervised clinical courses	92	
# of fac. sup. clin. positions filled	92	0
# involved in field placements	63	0
# involved in law journals	133	0
# in moot court or trial competitions	36	0
# of credit hrs required to graduate	90	

J.D. Enrollment & Ethnicity

	Men		Women		Fl-Time		Pt-Time		1st Yr		2nd Yr		3rd Yr		4th Yr		Total		JD Degrees Awarded
	#	%	#	%	#	%	#	%	#	%	#	%	#	%	#	%	#	%	
African-American	14	3.4	20	5.9	32	4.4	2	11.1	7	2.9	3	1.3	24	8.7	0	0.0	34	4.5	22
American Indian	2	0.5	4	1.2	4	0.5	2	11.1	1	0.4	1	0.4	4	1.5	0	0.0	6	0.8	2
Asian American	18	4.4	13	3.8	30	4.1	1	5.6	10	4.2	9	3.8	12	4.4	0	0.0	31	4.1	13
Mexican American	26	6.3	19	5.6	45	6.1	0	0.0	10	4.2	13	5.5	22	8.0	0	0.0	45	6.0	21
Puerto Rican	0	0.0	0	0.0	0	0.0	0	0.0	0	0.0	0	0.0	0	0.0	0	0.0	0	0.0	0
Hispanic American	0	0.0	0	0.0	0	0.0	0	0.0	0	0.0	0	0.0	0	0.0	0	0.0	0	0.0	0
Total Minorities	60	14.6	56	16.4	111	15.1	5	27.8	28	11.7	26	11.0	62	22.5	0	0.0	116	15.4	58
Foreign Nationals	2	0.5	3	0.9	5	0.7	0	0.0	1	0.4	2	0.8	2	0.7	0	0.0	5	0.7	0
Caucasian	348	84.9	282	82.7	617	84.2	13	72.2	211	87.9	208	88.1	211	76.7	0	0.0	630	83.9	213
Total	410	54.6	341	45.4	733	97.6	18	2.4	240	32.0	236	31.4	275	36.6	0	0.0	751		271

GPA & LSAT Scores

	Full Time	Part Time	Total
# of apps	1,637	30	1,667
# admits	712	4	716
# of matrics	233	0	233
75% GPA	3.49	0.00	
25% GPA	2.94	0.00	
75% LSAT	160	0	
25% LSAT	154	0	

Tuition & Fees

	Resident	Non-resident
Full-Time	$20,514	$20,514
Part-Time	$14,920	$14,920

Living Expenses

Estimated living expenses for Singles		
Living on campus	Living off campus	Living at home
$9,459	$7,380	$4,380

Employment

	Total	%
Employment status known	220	99.5
Employment status unknown	1	0.5
Employed	202	91.8
Pursuing graduate degrees	8	3.6
Unemployed seeking employment	6	2.7
Unemployed not seeking employment	4	1.8
Type of Employment		
# employed in law firms	131	64.9
# employed in business & industry	22	10.9
# employed in government	26	12.9
# employed in public interest	3	1.5
# employed as judicial clerks	11	5.4
# employed in academia	0	0.0
Geographic Location		
# employed in state	154	76.2
# employed in foreign countries	1	0.5
# of states where employed	17	

Grants/Scholarships

	Full-time		Part-time		Total	
	#	%	#	%	#	%
Total # of Students	733		18		751	
Total # receiving grants	312	42.6	0	0.0	312	41.5
Less than 1/2 tuition	203	27.7	0	0.0	203	27.0
Half to full tuition	89	12.1	0	0.0	89	11.9
Full tuition	3	0.4	0	0.0	3	0.4
More than full tuition	17	2.3	0	0.0	17	2.3
Median Grant Amount	$6,000		$0			

Informational & Library Resources

# of volumes & volume equivalents	511,488	# of professional staff	7
# of titles	180,232	Hours per week with professional staff	60
# of active serial subscriptions	5,184	Hours per week without professional staff	42
Study seating capacity inside the library	716	# of student computer work stations for entire law school	93
Square feet of law library	100,000	# of additional networked connections	13
Square feet of law school (excl. Library)	87,000	Require Laptop Computer?	N

J.D. Attrition (from Prior Year)

	Academic	Other	TOTALS	
	#	#	#	%
1st Year	3	12	15	6.3%
2nd Year	3	1	4	1.6%
3rd Year	0	0	0	0.0%
4th Year	0	0	0	0.0%

Bar Passage Rates

Jurisdiction	Texas		
Exam	Sum 97	Win 98	Total
# from school taking bar for the first time	177	10	187
School's pass rate for all first-time takers	85%	80%	85%
State's pass rate for all first-time takers	83%	73%	81%

SOUTHERN UNIVERSITY

P. O. Box 9294
Baton Rouge, LA 70813
(225)771-2552
website is currently under construction

ABA Approved Since 1953

The Basics

Type of School: Public   Term: Semester
Application deadline: 03/31
Application fee: $0
Financial Aid deadline: 04/15
Can first year start other than Fall? No
Student faculty ratio: 11.7 to 1
Does the University offer:
- housing restricted to law students? No
- graduate student housing for which law students are eligible? No

Faculty & Administrators

	Total		Men		Women		Minorities	
	Fall	Spr	Fall	Spr	Fall	Spr	Fall	Spr
Full-time	24	24	14	14	10	10	14	14
Other Full-Time	0	0	0	0	0	0	0	0
Deans, librarians, & others who teach > 1/2	3	3	3	3	0	0	3	3
Part-time	7	0	6	0	1	0	5	0
Total	34	27	23	17	11	10	22	17
Deans, librarians, & others who teach < 1/2	0	0	0	0	0	0	0	0

Curriculum

	Full time	Part time
Typical first-year section size	40	0
Is there typically a "small section" of the first year class, other than Legal Writing, taught by full-time faculty?	No	No
If yes, typical size offered last year	N/A	N/A
# of classroom course titles beyond 1st year curriculum	58	0
# of upper division courses, excluding seminars, with an enrollment:		
Under 25	34	0
25 - 49	40	0
50 - 74	8	0
75 - 99	0	0
100 +	0	0
# of seminars	12	0
# of seminar positions available	250	
# of seminar positions filled	197	0
# of positions available in simulation courses	160	
# of simulation positions filled	125	0
# of positions available in faculty supervised clinical courses	78	
# of fac. sup. clin. positions filled	78	0
# involved in field placements	14	0
# involved in law journals	19	0
# in moot court or trial competitions	64	0
# of credit hrs required to graduate	96	

J.D. Enrollment & Ethnicity

	Men		Women		Fl-Time		Pt-Time		1st Yr		2nd Yr		3rd Yr		4th Yr		Total		JD Degrees Awarded
	#	%	#	%	#	%	#	%	#	%	#	%	#	%	#	%	#	%	
African-American	86	54.8	120	77.9	206	66.2	0	0.0	80	67.8	63	67.7	63	63.0	0	0.0	206	66.2	72
American Indian	0	0.0	0	0.0	0	0.0	0	0.0	0	0.0	0	0.0	0	0.0	0	0.0	0	0.0	0
Asian American	0	0.0	0	0.0	0	0.0	0	0.0	0	0.0	0	0.0	0	0.0	0	0.0	0	0.0	0
Mexican American	0	0.0	0	0.0	0	0.0	0	0.0	0	0.0	0	0.0	0	0.0	0	0.0	0	0.0	0
Puerto Rican	0	0.0	0	0.0	0	0.0	0	0.0	0	0.0	0	0.0	0	0.0	0	0.0	0	0.0	0
Hispanic American	0	0.0	0	0.0	0	0.0	0	0.0	0	0.0	0	0.0	0	0.0	0	0.0	0	0.0	0
Total Minorities	86	54.8	120	77.9	206	66.2	0	0.0	80	67.8	63	67.7	63	63.0	0	0.0	206	66.2	72
Foreign Nationals	0	0.0	0	0.0	0	0.0	0	0.0	0	0.0	0	0.0	0	0.0	0	0.0	0	0.0	0
Caucasian	71	45.2	34	22.1	105	33.8	0	0.0	38	32.2	30	32.3	37	37.0	0	0.0	105	33.8	30
Total	157	50.5	154	49.5	311	100.0	0	0.0	118	37.9	93	29.9	100	32.2	0	0.0	311		102

GPA & LSAT Scores

	Full Time	Part Time	Total
# of apps	762	0	762
# admits	207	0	207
# of matrics	118	0	118
75% GPA	3.11	0.00	
25% GPA	2.40	0.00	
75% LSAT	146	0	
25% LSAT	141	0	

Tuition & Fees

	Resident	Non-resident
Full-Time	$3,128	$7,728
Part-Time	$0	$0

Living Expenses

Estimated living expenses for Singles		
Living on campus	Living off campus	Living at home
$8,572	$10,016	$10,016

Grants/Scholarships

	Full-time		Part-time		Total	
	#	%	#	%	#	%
Total # of Students	311		0		311	
Total # receiving grants	50	16.1	0	0.0	50	16.1
Less than 1/2 tuition	0	0.0	0	0.0	0	0.0
Half to full tuition	6	1.9	0	0.0	6	1.9
Full tuition	0	0.0	0	0.0	0	0.0
More than full tuition	44	14.1	0	0.0	44	14.1
Median Grant Amount	$4,000		$0			

Informational & Library Resources

# of volumes & volume equivalents	400,270	# of professional staff	7
# of titles	57,922	Hours per week with professional staff	86
# of active serial subscriptions	4,365	Hours per week without professional staff	8
Study seating capacity inside the library	284	# of student computer work stations for entire law school	52
Square feet of law library	28,940	# of additional networked connections	0
Square feet of law school (excl. Library)	50,768	Require Laptop Computer?	N

Employment

	Total	%
Employment status known	75	79.8
Employment status unknown	19	20.2
Employed	61	81.3
Pursuing graduate degrees	5	6.7
Unemployed seeking employment	9	12.0
Unemployed not seeking employment	0	0.0
Type of Employment		
# employed in law firms	33	54.1
# employed in business & industry	0	0.0
# employed in government	16	26.2
# employed in public interest	0	0.0
# employed as judicial clerks	10	16.4
# employed in academia	2	3.3
Geographic Location		
# employed in state	50	82.0
# employed in foreign countries	1	1.6
# of states where employed	4	

J.D. Attrition (from Prior Year)

	Academic	Other	TOTALS	
	#	#	#	%
1st Year	10	9	19	16%
2nd Year	1	3	4	4.0%
3rd Year	0	0	0	0.0%
4th Year	0	0	0	0.0%

Bar Passage Rates

Jurisdiction	Louisiana		
Exam	Sum 97	Win 98	Total
# from school taking bar for the first time	76	5	81
School's pass rate for all first-time takers	38%	0%	36%
State's pass rate for all first-time takers	62%	54%	61%

SOUTHWESTERN UNIVERSITY

675 South Westmoreland Avenue
Los Angeles, CA 90005-3992
(213)738-6717
http://www.swlaw.edu

ABA Approved Since 1970

The Basics

Type of School: Private Term: Semester
Application deadline: 06/30
Application fee: $50
Financial Aid deadline: 06/01
Can first year start other than Fall? No
Student faculty ratio: 18.1 to 1
Does the University offer:
- housing restricted to law students? No
- graduate student housing for which law students are eligible? No

Faculty & Administrators

	Total		Men		Women		Minorities	
	Fall	Spr	Fall	Spr	Fall	Spr	Fall	Spr
Full-time	37	37	27	27	10	10	4	4
Other Full-Time	4	4	2	2	2	2	1	1
Deans, librarians, & others who teach > 1/2	2	2	1	1	1	1	1	1
Part-time	16	17	13	14	3	3	6	2
Total	59	60	43	44	16	16	12	8
Deans, librarians, & others who teach < 1/2	1	1	1	1	0	0	0	0

Curriculum

	Full time	Part time
Typical first-year section size	76	63
Is there typically a "small section" of the first year class, other than Legal Writing, taught by full-time faculty?	No	No
If yes, typical size offered last year	N/A	N/A
# of classroom course titles beyond 1st year curriculum	71	50
# of upper division courses, excluding seminars, with an enrollment:		
Under 25	30	21
25 - 49	23	12
50 - 74	7	15
75 - 99	10	3
100 +	4	0
# of seminars	14	6
# of seminar positions available	400	
# of seminar positions filled	232	80
# of positions available in simulation courses	645	
# of simulation positions filled	345	157
# of positions available in faculty supervised clinical courses	0	
# of fac. sup. clin. positions filled	0	0
# involved in field placements	258	47
# involved in law journals	86	14
# in moot court or trial competitions	71	17
# of credit hrs required to graduate	87	

J.D. Enrollment & Ethnicity

	Men		Women		Fl-Time		Pt-Time		1st Yr		2nd Yr		3rd Yr		4th Yr		Total		JD Degrees Awarded
	#	%	#	%	#	%	#	%	#	%	#	%	#	%	#	%	#	%	
African-American	34	7.7	30	6.5	31	5.0	33	11.5	23	7.1	15	6.8	18	6.6	8	9.4	64	7.1	16
American Indian	5	1.1	3	0.6	7	1.1	1	0.3	4	1.2	1	0.5	3	1.1	0	0.0	8	0.9	2
Asian American	78	17.8	89	19.2	123	20.0	44	15.4	56	17.4	36	16.3	61	22.3	14	16.5	167	18.5	46
Mexican American	26	5.9	22	4.8	31	5.0	17	5.9	16	5.0	13	5.9	12	4.4	7	8.2	48	5.3	17
Puerto Rican	2	0.5	2	0.4	4	0.6	0	0.0	2	0.6	1	0.5	1	0.4	0	0.0	4	0.4	0
Hispanic American	20	4.6	24	5.2	30	4.9	14	4.9	14	4.3	12	5.4	15	5.5	3	3.5	44	4.9	12
Total Minorities	165	37.6	170	36.7	226	36.7	109	38.1	115	35.7	78	35.3	110	40.1	32	37.6	335	37.1	93
Foreign Nationals	3	0.7	5	1.1	8	1.3	0	0.0	2	0.6	3	1.4	3	1.1	0	0.0	8	0.9	1
Caucasian	271	61.7	288	62.2	382	62.0	177	61.9	205	63.7	140	63.3	161	58.8	53	62.4	559	62.0	228
Total	439	48.7	463	51.3	616	68.3	286	31.7	322	35.7	221	24.5	274	30.4	85	9.4	902		322

GPA & LSAT Scores

	Full Time	Part Time	Total
# of apps	1,773	367	2,140
# admits	885	133	1,018
# of matrics	255	82	337
75% GPA	3.20	3.22	
25% GPA	2.69	2.61	
75% LSAT	153	153	
25% LSAT	149	148	

Tuition & Fees

	Resident	Non-resident
Full-Time	$21,040	$21,040
Part-Time	$13,362	$13,362

Living Expenses

Estimated living expenses for Singles		
Living on campus	Living off campus	Living at home
N/A	$11,430	$5,040

Employment

	Total	%
Employment status known	325	91.3
Employment status unknown	31	8.7
Employed	266	81.8
Pursuing graduate degrees	1	0.3
Unemployed seeking employment	52	16.0
Unemployed not seeking employment	6	1.8
Type of Employment		
# employed in law firms	148	55.6
# employed in business & industry	69	25.9
# employed in government	27	10.2
# employed in public interest	4	1.5
# employed as judicial clerks	6	2.3
# employed in academia	3	1.1
Geographic Location		
# employed in state	248	93.2
# employed in foreign countries	1	0.4
# of states where employed	11	

Grants/Scholarships

	Full-time		Part-time		Total	
	#	%	#	%	#	%
Total # of Students	616		286		902	
Total # receiving grants	60	9.7	30	10.5	90	10.0
Less than 1/2 tuition	20	3.2	10	3.5	30	3.3
Half to full tuition	29	4.7	14	4.9	43	4.8
Full tuition	11	1.8	6	2.1	17	1.9
More than full tuition	0	0.0	0	0.0	0	0.0
Median Grant Amount	$5,520		$5,910			

Informational & Library Resources

# of volumes & volume equivalents	394,089	# of professional staff	10
# of titles	103,902	Hours per week with professional staff	85
# of active serial subscriptions	4,559	Hours per week without professional staff	18
Study seating capacity inside the library	610	# of student computer work stations for entire law school	97
Square feet of law library	83,000	# of additional networked connections	95
Square feet of law school (excl. Library)	108,971	Require Laptop Computer?	N

J.D. Attrition (from Prior Year)

	Academic	Other	TOTALS	
	#	#	#	%
1st Year	62	17	79	24%
2nd Year	31	6	37	13%
3rd Year	3	1	4	1.2%
4th Year	0	0	0	0.0%

Bar Passage Rates

Jurisdiction	California		
Exam	Sum 97	Win 98	Total
# from school taking bar for the first time	292	56	348
School's pass rate for all first-time takers	67%	52%	65%
State's pass rate for all first-time takers	75%	57%	71%

ST. JOHN'S UNIVERSITY

8000 Utopia Parkway
Jamaica, NY 11439
(718)990-6600
http://www.stjohns.edu

ABA Approved Since 1937

The Basics

Type of School: Private Term: Semester
Application deadline: 03/01
Application fee: $50
Financial Aid deadline: 04/01
Can first year start other than Fall? Yes
Student faculty ratio: 18.9 to 1
Does the University offer:
- housing restricted to law students? No
- graduate student housing for which law students are eligible? Yes

Faculty & Administrators

	Total		Men		Women		Minorities	
	Fall	Spr	Fall	Spr	Fall	Spr	Fall	Spr
Full-time	41	38	30	29	11	9	2	2
Other Full-Time	1	1	1	1	0	0	0	0
Deans, librarians, & others who teach > 1/2	2	2	0	0	2	2	0	0
Part-time	27	45	22	36	5	9	5	8
Total	71	86	53	66	18	20	7	10
Deans, librarians, & others who teach < 1/2	2	2	2	2	0	0	1	1

Curriculum

	Full time	Part time
Typical first-year section size	69	69
Is there typically a "small section" of the first year class, other than Legal Writing, taught by full-time faculty?	No	No
If yes, typical size offered last year	N/A	N/A
# of classroom course titles beyond 1st year curriculum	72	52
# of upper division courses, excluding seminars, with an enrollment:		
Under 25	41	19
25 - 49	25	10
50 - 74	10	9
75 - 99	16	5
100 +	12	1
# of seminars	27	17
# of seminar positions available	1,150	
# of seminar positions filled	580	466
# of positions available in simulation courses	860	
# of simulation positions filled	565	181
# of positions available in faculty supervised clinical courses	629	
# of fac. sup. clin. positions filled	392	20
# involved in field placements	375	20
# involved in law journals	161	26
# in moot court or trial competitions	290	22
# of credit hrs required to graduate	85	

J.D. Enrollment & Ethnicity

	Men		Women		Fl-Time		Pt-Time		1st Yr		2nd Yr		3rd Yr		4th Yr		Total		JD Degrees Awarded
	#	%	#	%	#	%	#	%	#	%	#	%	#	%	#	%	#	%	
African-American	37	6.3	34	8.0	40	5.4	31	11.2	20	7.7	22	7.4	23	5.8	6	10.0	71	7.0	26
American Indian	1	0.2	2	0.5	1	0.1	2	0.7	0	0.0	2	0.7	1	0.3	0	0.0	3	0.3	2
Asian American	34	5.7	33	7.8	56	7.6	11	4.0	10	3.8	31	10.5	24	6.0	2	3.3	67	6.6	23
Mexican American	6	1.0	7	1.7	10	1.4	3	1.1	7	2.7	5	1.7	1	0.3	0	0.0	13	1.3	0
Puerto Rican	15	2.5	16	3.8	20	2.7	11	4.0	10	3.8	9	3.0	10	2.5	2	3.3	31	3.1	14
Hispanic American	20	3.4	13	3.1	21	2.8	12	4.3	4	1.5	8	2.7	16	4.0	5	8.3	33	3.2	20
Total Minorities	113	19.1	105	24.8	148	20.0	70	25.4	51	19.6	77	26.0	75	18.8	15	25.0	218	21.5	85
Foreign Nationals	6	1.0	12	2.8	13	1.8	5	1.8	11	4.2	5	1.7	2	0.5	0	0.0	18	1.8	2
Caucasian	473	79.9	307	72.4	579	78.2	201	72.8	198	76.2	214	72.3	323	80.8	45	75.0	780	76.8	233
Total	592	58.3	424	41.7	740	72.8	276	27.2	260	25.6	296	29.1	400	39.4	60	5.9	1016		320

GPA & LSAT Scores

	Full Time	Part Time	Total
# of apps	1,932	456	2,388
# admits	1,017	156	1,173
# of matrics	246	65	311
75% GPA	3.46	3.36	
25% GPA	2.85	2.85	
75% LSAT	158	156	
25% LSAT	151	149	

Tuition & Fees

	Resident	Non-resident
Full-Time	$22,000	$22,000
Part-Time	$16,500	$16,500

Living Expenses

Estimated living expenses for Singles		
Living on campus	Living off campus	Living at home
$8,550	$14,990	$8,240

Employment

	Total	%
Employment status known	334	84.3
Employment status unknown	62	15.7
Employed	284	85.0
Pursuing graduate degrees	2	0.6
Unemployed seeking employment	23	6.9
Unemployed not seeking employment	25	7.5
Type of Employment		
# employed in law firms	169	59.5
# employed in business & industry	37	13.0
# employed in government	44	15.5
# employed in public interest	4	1.4
# employed as judicial clerks	19	6.7
# employed in academia	4	1.4
Geographic Location		
# employed in state	255	89.8
# employed in foreign countries	2	0.7
# of states where employed	14	

Grants/Scholarships

	Full-time		Part-time		Total	
	#	%	#	%	#	%
Total # of Students	740		276		1016	
Total # receiving grants	272	36.8	85	30.8	357	35.1
Less than 1/2 tuition	229	30.9	62	22.5	291	28.6
Half to full tuition	15	2.0	12	4.3	27	2.7
Full tuition	21	2.8	7	2.5	28	2.8
More than full tuition	7	0.9	4	1.4	11	1.1
Median Grant Amount	$5,000		$3,000			

Informational & Library Resources

# of volumes & volume equivalents	435,953	# of professional staff	7
# of titles	61,869	Hours per week with professional staff	76
# of active serial subscriptions	2,573	Hours per week without professional staff	34
Study seating capacity inside the library	601	# of student computer work stations for entire law school	72
Square feet of law library	56,000	# of additional networked connections	62
Square feet of law school (excl. Library)	96,100	Require Laptop Computer?	N

J.D. Attrition (from Prior Year)

	Academic	Other	TOTALS	
	#	#	#	%
1st Year	3	29	32	12%
2nd Year	5	11	16	3.9%
3rd Year	0	2	2	0.7%
4th Year	0	1	1	1.3%

Bar Passage Rates

Jurisdiction	New York			Connecticut		
Exam	Sum 97	Win 98	Total	Sum 97	Win 98	Total
# from school taking bar for the first time	330	21	351	40	4	44
School's pass rate for all first-time takers	86%	71%	85%	85%	50%	82%
State's pass rate for all first-time takers	78%	65%	76%	85%	81%	84%

ST. LOUIS UNIVERSITY

3700 Lindell Blvd.
St. Louis, MO 63108
(314)977-2766
http://lawlib.slu.edu

ABA Approved Since 1924

The Basics

Type of School: Private Term: Semester

Application deadline: 03/01

Application fee: $40

Financial Aid deadline: Rolling

Can first year start other than Fall? No

Student faculty ratio: 22.9 to 1

Does the University offer:
- housing restricted to law students? No
- graduate student housing for which law students are eligible? No

Faculty & Administrators

	Total		Men		Women		Minorities	
	Fall	Spr	Fall	Spr	Fall	Spr	Fall	Spr
Full-time	26	31	21	25	5	6	4	4
Other Full-Time	4	4	1	1	3	3	0	0
Deans, librarians, & others who teach > 1/2	2	1	1	1	1	0	0	0
Part-time	19	28	15	18	4	10	0	0
Total	51	64	38	45	13	19	4	4
Deans, librarians, & others who teach < 1/2	1	1	1	1	0	0	0	0

Curriculum

	Full time	Part time
Typical first-year section size	90	65
Is there typically a "small section" of the first year class, other than Legal Writing, taught by full-time faculty?	No	No
If yes, typical size offered last year	N/A	N/A
# of classroom course titles beyond 1st year curriculum	90	33
# of upper division courses, excluding seminars, with an enrollment:		
Under 25	23	8
25 - 49	20	3
50 - 74	11	3
75 - 99	5	2
100 +	6	2
# of seminars	25	13
# of seminar positions available	456	
# of seminar positions filled	255	107
# of positions available in simulation courses	548	
# of simulation positions filled	248	41
# of positions available in faculty supervised clinical courses	100	
# of fac. sup. clin. positions filled	78	17
# involved in field placements	68	8
# involved in law journals	109	12
# in moot court or trial competitions	187	28
# of credit hrs required to graduate	88	

J.D. Enrollment & Ethnicity

	Men		Women		Fl-Time		Pt-Time		1st Yr		2nd Yr		3rd Yr		4th Yr		Total		JD Degrees Awarded
	#	%	#	%	#	%	#	%	#	%	#	%	#	%	#	%	#	%	
African-American	28	6.6	35	9.4	33	6.0	30	11.9	15	6.2	16	7.0	20	8.0	12	15.2	63	7.9	15
American Indian	3	0.7	3	0.8	5	0.9	1	0.4	0	0.0	2	0.9	3	1.2	1	1.3	6	0.8	0
Asian American	19	4.5	11	2.9	22	4.0	8	3.2	6	2.5	9	4.0	11	4.4	4	5.1	30	3.8	13
Mexican American	2	0.5	2	0.5	4	0.7	0	0.0	0	0.0	2	0.9	2	0.8	0	0.0	4	0.5	0
Puerto Rican	0	0.0	0	0.0	0	0.0	0	0.0	0	0.0	0	0.0	0	0.0	0	0.0	0	0.0	1
Hispanic American	7	1.6	8	2.1	10	1.8	5	2.0	4	1.6	5	2.2	5	2.0	1	1.3	15	1.9	1
Total Minorities	59	13.8	59	15.8	74	13.6	44	17.4	25	10.3	34	15.0	41	16.4	18	22.8	118	14.8	30
Foreign Nationals	3	0.7	1	0.3	4	0.7	0	0.0	4	1.6	0	0.0	0	0.0	0	0.0	4	0.5	0
Caucasian	364	85.4	313	83.9	468	85.7	209	82.6	214	88.1	193	85.0	209	83.6	61	77.2	677	84.7	187
Total	426	53.3	373	46.7	546	68.3	253	31.7	243	30.4	227	28.4	250	31.3	79	9.9	799		217

GPA & LSAT Scores

	Full Time	Part Time	Total
# of apps	828	167	995
# admits	517	96	613
# of matrics	180	68	248
75% GPA	3.60	3.41	
25% GPA	3.00	2.77	
75% LSAT	157	156	
25% LSAT	150	148	

Tuition & Fees

	Resident	Non-resident
Full-Time	$19,170	$19,170
Part-Time	$14,360	$14,360

Living Expenses

Estimated living expenses for Singles		
Living on campus	Living off campus	Living at home
$10,140	$10,980	$9,740

Employment

	Total	%
Employment status known	208	94.1
Employment status unknown	13	5.9
Employed	192	92.3
Pursuing graduate degrees	3	1.4
Unemployed seeking employment	9	4.3
Unemployed not seeking employment	4	1.9
Type of Employment		
# employed in law firms	107	55.7
# employed in business & industry	31	16.1
# employed in government	28	14.6
# employed in public interest	2	1.0
# employed as judicial clerks	17	8.9
# employed in academia	4	2.1
Geographic Location		
# employed in state	143	74.5
# employed in foreign countries	1	0.5
# of states where employed	19	

Grants/Scholarships

	Full-time		Part-time		Total	
	#	%	#	%	#	%
Total # of Students	546		253		799	
Total # receiving grants	337	61.7	75	29.6	412	51.6
Less than 1/2 tuition	263	48.2	71	28.1	334	41.8
Half to full tuition	74	13.6	4	1.6	78	9.8
Full tuition	0	0.0	0	0.0	0	0.0
More than full tuition	0	0.0	0	0.0	0	0.0
Median Grant Amount	$5,600		$3,000			

Informational & Library Resources

# of volumes & volume equivalents	530,941	# of professional staff	8
# of titles	194,195	Hours per week with professional staff	85
# of active serial subscriptions	6,315	Hours per week without professional staff	19
Study seating capacity inside the library	465	# of student computer work stations for entire law school	41
Square feet of law library	51,223	# of additional networked connections	0
Square feet of law school (excl. Library)	93,234	Require Laptop Computer?	N

J.D. Attrition (from Prior Year)

	Academic	Other	TOTALS	
	#	#	#	%
1st Year	14	13	27	11%
2nd Year	5	4	9	3.9%
3rd Year	0	3	3	1.2%
4th Year	0	0	0	0.0%

Bar Passage Rates

Jurisdiction	Missouri		
Exam	Sum 97	Win 98	Total
# from school taking bar for the first time	147	36	183
School's pass rate for all first-time takers	81%	78%	80%
State's pass rate for all first-time takers	86%	81%	85%

ST. MARY'S UNIVERSITY

One Camino Santa Maria
San Antonio, TX 78228-8602
(210)436-3424
http://www.stmarylaw.edu

ABA Approved Since 1948

The Basics

Type of School: Private   Term: Semester

Application deadline: 03/01

Application fee: $45

Financial Aid deadline: 04/01

Can first year start other than Fall? No

Student faculty ratio: 22.2 to 1

Does the University offer:
- housing restricted to law students? No
- graduate student housing for which law students are eligible? Yes

Faculty & Administrators

	Total		Men		Women		Minorities	
	Fall	Spr	Fall	Spr	Fall	Spr	Fall	Spr
Full-time	29	28	21	20	8	8	5	6
Other Full-Time	0	0	0	0	0	0	0	0
Deans, librarians, & others who teach > 1/2	2	1	1	0	1	1	1	0
Part-time	29	0	20	0	9	0	3	0
Total	60	29	42	20	18	9	9	6
Deans, librarians, & others who teach < 1/2	0	0	0	0	0	0	0	0

Curriculum

	Full time	Part time
Typical first-year section size	88	0
Is there typically a "small section" of the first year class, other than Legal Writing, taught by full-time faculty?	No	No
If yes, typical size offered last year	N/A	N/A
# of classroom course titles beyond 1st year curriculum	134	0
# of upper division courses, excluding seminars, with an enrollment:		
Under 25	65	0
25 - 49	28	0
50 - 74	23	0
75 - 99	18	0
100 +	0	0
# of seminars	16	0
# of seminar positions available	200	
# of seminar positions filled	200	0
# of positions available in simulation courses	128	
# of simulation positions filled	96	0
# of positions available in faculty supervised clinical courses	44	
# of fac. sup. clin. positions filled	44	0
# involved in field placements	39	0
# involved in law journals	52	0
# in moot court or trial competitions	67	0
# of credit hrs required to graduate	90	

J.D. Enrollment & Ethnicity

	Men		Women		Fl-Time		Pt-Time		1st Yr		2nd Yr		3rd Yr		4th Yr		Total		JD Degrees Awarded
	#	%	#	%	#	%	#	%	#	%	#	%	#	%	#	%	#	%	
African-American	11	2.7	31	8.4	42	5.4	0	0.0	14	5.3	12	4.8	16	6.3	0	0.0	42	5.4	10
American Indian	1	0.2	2	0.5	3	0.4	0	0.0	2	0.8	1	0.4	0	0.0	0	0.0	3	0.4	5
Asian American	9	2.2	14	3.8	23	3.0	0	0.0	5	1.9	6	2.4	12	4.7	0	0.0	23	3.0	10
Mexican American	112	27.7	113	30.6	225	29.1	0	0.0	90	33.8	70	27.9	65	25.4	0	0.0	225	29.1	59
Puerto Rican	4	1.0	3	0.8	7	0.9	0	0.0	2	0.8	2	0.8	3	1.2	0	0.0	7	0.9	1
Hispanic American	12	3.0	15	4.1	27	3.5	0	0.0	8	3.0	11	4.4	8	3.1	0	0.0	27	3.5	3
Total Minorities	149	36.9	178	48.2	327	42.3	0	0.0	121	45.5	102	40.6	104	40.6	0	0.0	327	42.3	88
Foreign Nationals	0	0.0	0	0.0	0	0.0	0	0.0	0	0.0	0	0.0	0	0.0	0	0.0	0	0.0	0
Caucasian	255	63.1	191	51.8	446	57.7	0	0.0	145	54.5	149	59.4	152	59.4	0	0.0	446	57.7	156
Total	404	52.3	369	47.7	773	100.0	0	0.0	266	34.4	251	32.5	256	33.1	0	0.0	773		244

GPA & LSAT Scores

	Full Time	Part Time	Total
# of apps	1,094	0	1,094
# admits	665	0	665
# of matrics	269	0	269
75% GPA	3.12	0.00	
25% GPA	2.61	0.00	
75% LSAT	152	0	
25% LSAT	146	0	

Tuition & Fees

	Resident	Non-resident
Full-Time	$15,560	$15,560
Part-Time	$0	$0

Living Expenses

Estimated living expenses for Singles		
Living on campus	Living off campus	Living at home
$9,608	$12,296	$12,296

Grants/Scholarships

	Full-time		Part-time		Total	
	#	%	#	%	#	%
Total # of Students	773		0		773	
Total # receiving grants	258	33.4	0	0.0	258	33.4
Less than 1/2 tuition	245	31.7	0	0.0	245	31.7
Half to full tuition	12	1.6	0	0.0	12	1.6
Full tuition	0	0.0	0	0.0	0	0.0
More than full tuition	1	0.1	0	0.0	1	0.1
Median Grant Amount	$800		$0			

Informational & Library Resources

# of volumes & volume equivalents	331,735	# of professional staff	9
# of titles	34,182	Hours per week with professional staff	87
# of active serial subscriptions	3,175	Hours per week without professional staff	23
Study seating capacity inside the library	446	# of student computer work stations for entire law school	94
Square feet of law library	65,000	# of additional networked connections	124
Square feet of law school (excl. Library)	87,207	Require Laptop Computer?	N

Employment

	Total	%
Employment status known	213	89.5
Employment status unknown	25	10.5
Employed	192	90.1
Pursuing graduate degrees	7	3.3
Unemployed seeking employment	13	6.1
Unemployed not seeking employment	1	0.5
Type of Employment		
# employed in law firms	126	65.6
# employed in business & industry	17	8.9
# employed in government	28	14.6
# employed in public interest	4	2.1
# employed as judicial clerks	13	6.8
# employed in academia	2	1.0
Geographic Location		
# employed in state	167	87.0
# employed in foreign countries	0	0.0
# of states where employed	17	

J.D. Attrition (from Prior Year)

	Academic	Other	TOTALS	
	#	#	#	%
1st Year	4	13	17	6.4%
2nd Year	0	16	16	6.7%
3rd Year	0	0	0	0.0%
4th Year	0	0	0	0.0%

Bar Passage Rates

Jurisdiction	Texas		
Exam	Sum 97	Win 98	Total
# from school taking bar for the first time	147	67	214
School's pass rate for all first-time takers	76%	82%	78%
State's pass rate for all first-time takers	83%	73%	81%

ST. THOMAS UNIVERSITY

16400 N.W. 32 Avenue
Miami, FL 33054
(305)623-2320
http://www.stu.edu

ABA Approved Since 1988

The Basics

Type of School: Private | Term: Semester

Application deadline: 04/30

Application fee: $40

Financial Aid deadline: 05/01

Can first year start other than Fall? No

Student faculty ratio: 25.4 to 1

Does the University offer:
- housing restricted to law students? Yes
- graduate student housing for which law students are eligible? No

Faculty & Administrators

	Total		Men		Women		Minorities	
	Fall	Spr	Fall	Spr	Fall	Spr	Fall	Spr
Full-time	16	16	11	11	5	5	5	5
Other Full-Time	2	2	0	0	2	2	1	1
Deans, librarians, & others who teach > 1/2	4	4	4	4	0	0	0	0
Part-time	19	24	13	18	6	6	3	4
Total	41	46	28	33	13	13	9	10
Deans, librarians, & others who teach < 1/2	2	2	2	2	0	0	0	0

Curriculum

	Full time	Part time
Typical first-year section size	65	0
Is there typically a "small section" of the first year class, other than Legal Writing, taught by full-time faculty?	No	No
If yes, typical size offered last year	N/A	N/A
# of classroom course titles beyond 1st year curriculum	90	0
# of upper division courses, excluding seminars, with an enrollment:		
Under 25	46	0
25 - 49	22	0
50 - 74	21	0
75 - 99	1	0
100 +	0	0
# of seminars	11	0
# of seminar positions available	176	
# of seminar positions filled	166	0
# of positions available in simulation courses	288	
# of simulation positions filled	285	0
# of positions available in faculty supervised clinical courses	124	
# of fac. sup. clin. positions filled	61	0
# involved in field placements	45	0
# involved in law journals	36	0
# in moot court or trial competitions	76	0
# of credit hrs required to graduate	90	

J.D. Enrollment & Ethnicity

	Men		Women		Fl-Time		Pt-Time		1st Yr		2nd Yr		3rd Yr		4th Yr		Total		JD Degrees Awarded
	#	%	#	%	#	%	#	%	#	%	#	%	#	%	#	%	#	%	
African-American	20	6.8	32	16.6	52	10.7	0	0.0	20	11.8	13	8.8	19	11.1	0	0.0	52	10.7	23
American Indian	2	0.7	4	2.1	6	1.2	0	0.0	3	1.8	2	1.4	1	0.6	0	0.0	6	1.2	2
Asian American	9	3.1	4	2.1	13	2.7	0	0.0	6	3.6	3	2.0	4	2.3	0	0.0	13	2.7	1
Mexican American	5	1.7	2	1.0	7	1.4	0	0.0	4	2.4	1	0.7	2	1.2	0	0.0	7	1.4	0
Puerto Rican	3	1.0	6	3.1	9	1.8	0	0.0	1	0.6	1	0.7	7	4.1	0	0.0	9	1.8	5
Hispanic American	67	22.8	47	24.4	114	23.4	0	0.0	45	26.6	37	25.2	32	18.7	0	0.0	114	23.4	18
Total Minorities	106	36.1	95	49.2	201	41.3	0	0.0	79	46.7	57	38.8	65	38.0	0	0.0	201	41.3	49
Foreign Nationals	1	0.3	2	1.0	3	0.6	0	0.0	3	1.8	0	0.0	0	0.0	0	0.0	3	0.6	1
Caucasian	187	63.6	96	49.7	283	58.1	0	0.0	87	51.5	90	61.2	106	62.0	0	0.0	283	58.1	113
Total	294	60.4	193	39.6	487	100.0	0	0.0	169	34.7	147	30.2	171	35.1	0	0.0	487		163

GPA & LSAT Scores

	Full Time	Part Time	Total
# of apps	1,836	0	1,836
# admits	1,308	0	1,308
# of matrics	190	0	190
75% GPA	3.23	0.00	
25% GPA	2.55	0.00	
75% LSAT	151	0	
25% LSAT	146	0	

Tuition & Fees

	Resident	Non-resident
Full-Time	$19,974	$19,974
Part-Time	$0	$0

Living Expenses

Estimated living expenses for Singles		
Living on campus	Living off campus	Living at home
$12,065	$13,265	N/A

Grants/Scholarships

	Full-time		Part-time		Total	
	#	%	#	%	#	%
Total # of Students	487		0		487	
Total # receiving grants	147	30.2	0	0.0	147	30.2
Less than 1/2 tuition	104	21.4	0	0.0	104	21.4
Half to full tuition	41	8.4	0	0.0	41	8.4
Full tuition	0	0.0	0	0.0	0	0.0
More than full tuition	2	0.4	0	0.0	2	0.4
Median Grant Amount	$6,882		$0			

Informational & Library Resources

# of volumes & volume equivalents	281,019	# of professional staff	7
# of titles	42,857	Hours per week with professional staff	96
# of active serial subscriptions	2,175	Hours per week without professional staff	9
Study seating capacity inside the library	313	# of student computer work stations for entire law school	51
Square feet of law library	25,116	# of additional networked connections	0
Square feet of law school (excl. Library)	42,884	Require Laptop Computer?	N

Employment

	Total	%
Employment status known	119	85.6
Employment status unknown	20	14.4
Employed	101	84.9
Pursuing graduate degrees	7	5.9
Unemployed seeking employment	5	4.2
Unemployed not seeking employment	6	5.0
Type of Employment		
# employed in law firms	54	53.5
# employed in business & industry	12	11.9
# employed in government	33	32.7
# employed in public interest	1	1.0
# employed as judicial clerks	0	0.0
# employed in academia	1	1.0
Geographic Location		
# employed in state	88	87.1
# employed in foreign countries	0	0.0
# of states where employed	15	

J.D. Attrition (from Prior Year)

	Academic	Other	TOTALS	
	#	#	#	%
1st Year	15	33	48	25%
2nd Year	1	2	3	1.7%
3rd Year	1	0	1	0.6%
4th Year	0	0	0	0.0%

Bar Passage Rates

Jurisdiction	Florida		
Exam	Sum 97	Win 98	Total
# from school taking bar for the first time	119	18	137
School's pass rate for all first-time takers	79%	61%	77%
State's pass rate for all first-time takers	84%	82%	83%

STANFORD UNIVERSITY

Crown Quadrangle
Stanford, CA 94305-8610
(650)723-4985
http://www-leland.stanford.edu/group/law

ABA Approved Since 1923

The Basics

Type of School: Private   Term: Semester
Application deadline: 02/01
Application fee: $65
Financial Aid deadline: 03/15
Can first year start other than Fall? No
Student faculty ratio: 13.4 to 1
Does the University offer:
- housing restricted to law students? No
- graduate student housing for which law students are eligible? Yes

Faculty & Administrators

	Total		Men		Women		Minorities	
	Fall	Spr	Fall	Spr	Fall	Spr	Fall	Spr
Full-time	34	32	25	24	9	8	6	6
Other Full-Time	0	0	0	0	0	0	0	0
Deans, librarians, & others who teach > 1/2	2	2	2	2	0	0	0	0
Part-time	28	61	16	39	12	22	3	5
Total	64	95	43	65	21	30	9	11
Deans, librarians, & others who teach < 1/2	1	1	1	1	0	0	0	0

Curriculum

	Full time	Part time
Typical first-year section size	60	0
Is there typically a "small section" of the first year class, other than Legal Writing, taught by full-time faculty?	Yes	No
If yes, typical size offered last year	30	N/A
# of classroom course titles beyond 1st year curriculum	19	0
# of upper division courses, excluding seminars, with an enrollment:		
Under 25	21	0
25 - 49	38	0
50 - 74	22	0
75 - 99	6	0
100 +	5	0
# of seminars	44	0
# of seminar positions available	776	
# of seminar positions filled	587	0
# of positions available in simulation courses	449	
# of simulation positions filled	352	0
# of positions available in faculty supervised clinical courses	0	
# of fac. sup. clin. positions filled	81	0
# involved in field placements	29	0
# involved in law journals	400	0
# in moot court or trial competitions	44	0
# of credit hrs required to graduate	86	

J.D. Enrollment & Ethnicity

	Men		Women		Fl-Time		Pt-Time		1st Yr		2nd Yr		3rd Yr		4th Yr		Total		JD Degrees Awarded
	#	%	#	%	#	%	#	%	#	%	#	%	#	%	#	%	#	%	
African-American	23	7.5	22	9.4	45	8.3	0	0.0	17	9.4	12	6.6	16	8.9	0	0.0	45	8.3	18
American Indian	8	2.6	6	2.6	14	2.6	0	0.0	2	1.1	6	3.3	6	3.3	0	0.0	14	2.6	2
Asian American	23	7.5	23	9.8	46	8.5	0	0.0	19	10.6	14	7.7	13	7.2	0	0.0	46	8.5	12
Mexican American	26	8.5	29	12.3	55	10.2	0	0.0	25	13.9	15	8.3	15	8.3	0	0.0	55	10.2	21
Puerto Rican	4	1.3	1	0.4	5	0.9	0	0.0	0	0.0	2	1.1	3	1.7	0	0.0	5	0.9	2
Hispanic American	2	0.7	2	0.9	4	0.7	0	0.0	1	0.6	1	0.6	2	1.1	0	0.0	4	0.7	0
Total Minorities	86	28.1	83	35.3	169	31.2	0	0.0	64	35.6	50	27.6	55	30.6	0	0.0	169	31.2	55
Foreign Nationals	9	2.9	7	3.0	16	3.0	0	0.0	6	3.3	6	3.3	4	2.2	0	0.0	16	3.0	10
Caucasian	211	69.0	145	61.7	356	65.8	0	0.0	110	61.1	125	69.1	121	67.2	0	0.0	356	65.8	124
Total	306	56.6	235	43.4	541	100.0	0	0.0	180	33.3	181	33.5	180	33.3	0	0.0	541		189

GPA & LSAT Scores

	Full Time	Part Time	Total
# of apps	3,947	0	3,947
# admits	426	0	426
# of matrics	180	0	180
75% GPA	3.91	0.00	
25% GPA	3.55	0.00	
75% LSAT	170	0	
25% LSAT	164	0	

Tuition & Fees

	Resident	Non-resident
Full-Time	$25,190	$25,190
Part-Time	$0	$0

Living Expenses

Estimated living expenses for Singles

Living on campus	Living off campus	Living at home
$11,472	$16,707	N/A

Employment

	Total	%
Employment status known	182	98.9
Employment status unknown	2	1.1
Employed	175	96.2
Pursuing graduate degrees	3	1.6
Unemployed seeking employment	3	1.6
Unemployed not seeking employment	1	0.5
Type of Employment		
# employed in law firms	98	56.0
# employed in business & industry	14	8.0
# employed in government	5	2.9
# employed in public interest	7	4.0
# employed as judicial clerks	50	28.6
# employed in academia	1	0.6
Geographic Location		
# employed in state	100	57.1
# employed in foreign countries	2	1.1
# of states where employed	25	

Grants/Scholarships

	Full-time		Part-time		Total	
	#	%	#	%	#	%
Total # of Students	541		0		541	
Total # receiving grants	220	40.7	0	0.0	220	40.7
Less than 1/2 tuition	144	26.6	0	0.0	144	26.6
Half to full tuition	65	12.0	0	0.0	65	12.0
Full tuition	11	2.0	0	0.0	11	2.0
More than full tuition	0	0.0	0	0.0	0	0.0
Median Grant Amount	$9,702		$0			

Informational & Library Resources

# of volumes & volume equivalents	473,855	# of professional staff	7
# of titles	174,776	Hours per week with professional staff	56
# of active serial subscriptions	7,401	Hours per week without professional staff	40
Study seating capacity inside the library	555	# of student computer work stations for entire law school	102
Square feet of law library	56,617	# of additional networked connections	0
Square feet of law school (excl. Library)	96,513	Require Laptop Computer?	N

J.D. Attrition (from Prior Year)

	Academic	Other	TOTALS	
	#	#	#	%
1st Year	0	0	0	0.0%
2nd Year	0	0	0	0.0%
3rd Year	0	0	0	0.0%
4th Year	0	0	0	0.0%

Bar Passage Rates

Jurisdiction	California		
Exam	Sum 97	Win 98	Total
# from school taking bar for the first time	104	10	114
School's pass rate for all first-time takers	91%	90%	91%
State's pass rate for all first-time takers	75%	57%	71%

STATE UNIVERSITY OF NEW YORK AT BUFFALO

319 O'Brian Hall
North Campus
Buffalo, NY 14260
(716)645-2053
http://www.buffalo.edu/law/js.html

ABA Approved Since 1936

The Basics

Type of School: Public   Term: Semester

Application deadline: 02/15

Application fee: $50

Financial Aid deadline: 03/19

Can first year start other than Fall? No

Student faculty ratio: 16.1 to 1

Does the University offer:

- housing restricted to law students? No
- graduate student housing for which law students are eligible? Yes

Faculty & Administrators

	Total		Men		Women		Minorities	
	Fall	Spr	Fall	Spr	Fall	Spr	Fall	Spr
Full-time	34	36	23	24	11	12	4	5
Other Full-Time	5	5	3	3	2	2	0	0
Deans, librarians, & others who teach > 1/2	5	5	2	2	3	3	1	1
Part-time	43	78	30	53	13	25	2	5
Total	87	124	58	82	29	42	7	11
Deans, librarians, & others who teach < 1/2	0	0	0	0	0	0	0	0

Curriculum

	Full time	Part time
Typical first-year section size	100	0
Is there typically a "small section" of the first year class, other than Legal Writing, taught by full-time faculty?	Yes	No
If yes, typical size offered last year	30	N/A
# of classroom course titles beyond 1st year curriculum	146	0
# of upper division courses, excluding seminars, with an enrollment:		
Under 25	84	0
25 - 49	44	0
50 - 74	11	0
75 - 99	6	0
100 +	1	0
# of seminars	35	0
# of seminar positions available	537	
# of seminar positions filled	344	0
# of positions available in simulation courses	207	
# of simulation positions filled	207	0
# of positions available in faculty supervised clinical courses	111	
# of fac. sup. clin. positions filled	111	0
# involved in field placements	84	0
# involved in law journals	221	0
# in moot court or trial competitions	62	0
# of credit hrs required to graduate	87	

J.D. Enrollment & Ethnicity

	Men		Women		Fl-Time		Pt-Time		1st Yr		2nd Yr		3rd Yr		4th Yr		Total		JD Degrees Awarded
	#	%	#	%	#	%	#	%	#	%	#	%	#	%	#	%	#	%	
African-American	17	4.9	29	9.3	46	7.0	0	0.0	17	7.7	15	7.4	14	6.0	0	0.0	46	7.0	19
American Indian	2	0.6	4	1.3	6	0.9	0	0.0	3	1.4	2	1.0	1	0.4	0	0.0	6	0.9	2
Asian American	17	4.9	17	5.4	34	5.2	0	0.0	9	4.1	14	6.9	11	4.7	0	0.0	34	5.2	9
Mexican American	0	0.0	0	0.0	0	0.0	0	0.0	0	0.0	0	0.0	0	0.0	0	0.0	0	0.0	0
Puerto Rican	3	0.9	7	2.2	10	1.5	0	0.0	2	0.9	2	1.0	6	2.6	0	0.0	10	1.5	2
Hispanic American	15	4.4	8	2.6	23	3.5	0	0.0	5	2.3	9	4.4	9	3.9	0	0.0	23	3.5	6
Total Minorities	54	15.7	65	20.8	119	18.1	0	0.0	36	16.3	42	20.7	41	17.6	0	0.0	119	18.1	38
Foreign Nationals	0	0.0	0	0.0	0	0.0	0	0.0	0	0.0	0	0.0	0	0.0	0	0.0	0	0.0	0
Caucasian	290	84.3	248	79.2	538	81.9	0	0.0	185	83.7	161	79.3	192	82.4	0	0.0	538	81.9	230
Total	344	52.4	313	47.6	657	100.0	0	0.0	221	33.6	203	30.9	233	35.5	0	0.0	657		268

STATE UNIVERSITY OF NEW YORK AT BUFFALO

GPA & LSAT Scores

	Full Time	Part Time	Total
# of apps	885	0	885
# admits	492	0	492
# of matrics	221	0	221
75% GPA	3.49	0.00	
25% GPA	2.93	0.00	
75% LSAT	157	0	
25% LSAT	150	0	

Tuition & Fees

	Resident	Non-resident
Full-Time	$8,292	$13,442
Part-Time	$0	$0

Living Expenses

Estimated living expenses for Singles		
Living on campus	Living off campus	Living at home
$10,771	$10,771	$10,771

Employment

	Total	%
Employment status known	248	98.4
Employment status unknown	4	1.6
Employed	218	87.9
Pursuing graduate degrees	11	4.4
Unemployed seeking employment	6	2.4
Unemployed not seeking employment	13	5.2
Type of Employment		
# employed in law firms	101	46.3
# employed in business & industry	41	18.8
# employed in government	39	17.9
# employed in public interest	14	6.4
# employed as judicial clerks	16	7.3
# employed in academia	7	3.2
Geographic Location		
# employed in state	185	84.9
# employed in foreign countries	1	0.5
# of states where employed	18	

Grants/Scholarships

	Full-time		Part-time		Total	
	#	%	#	%	#	%
Total # of Students	657		0		657	
Total # receiving grants	296	45.1	0	0.0	296	45.1
Less than 1/2 tuition	239	36.4	0	0.0	239	36.4
Half to full tuition	9	1.4	0	0.0	9	1.4
Full tuition	25	3.8	0	0.0	25	3.8
More than full tuition	23	3.5	0	0.0	23	3.5
Median Grant Amount	$2,500		$0			

Informational & Library Resources

# of volumes & volume equivalents	517,227	# of professional staff	9
# of titles	104,640	Hours per week with professional staff	74
# of active serial subscriptions	6,769	Hours per week without professional staff	19
Study seating capacity inside the library	508	# of student computer work stations for entire law school	102
Square feet of law library	52,385	# of additional networked connections	42
Square feet of law school (excl. Library)	68,217	Require Laptop Computer?	N

J.D. Attrition (from Prior Year)

	Academic	Other	TOTALS	
	#	#	#	%
1st Year	0	8	8	3.7%
2nd Year	0	8	8	3.9%
3rd Year	0	3	3	1.0%
4th Year	0	0	0	0.0%

Bar Passage Rates

Jurisdiction	New York		
Exam	Sum 97	Win 98	Total
# from school taking bar for the first time	209	45	254
School's pass rate for all first-time takers	73%	62%	71%
State's pass rate for all first-time takers	78%	65%	76%

STETSON UNIVERSITY

1401 61st Street South
St. Petersburg, FL 33707
(727)562-7800
http://www.law.stetson.edu

ABA Approved Since 1930

The Basics

Type of School: Private   Term: Semester

Application deadline: 02/15

Application fee: $50

Financial Aid deadline: 03/01

Can first year start other than Fall? Yes

Student faculty ratio: 17.2 to 1

Does the University offer:

- housing restricted to law students? Yes
- graduate student housing for which law students are eligible? No

Faculty & Administrators

	Total		Men		Women		Minorities	
	Fall	Spr	Fall	Spr	Fall	Spr	Fall	Spr
Full-time	32	32	22	23	10	9	4	4
Other Full-Time	0	0	0	0	0	0	0	0
Deans, librarians, & others who teach > 1/2	3	3	2	2	1	1	0	0
Part-time	23	24	18	22	5	2	0	2
Total	58	59	42	47	16	12	4	6
Deans, librarians, & others who teach < 1/2	2	2	1	1	1	1	1	1

Curriculum

	Full time	Part time
Typical first-year section size	68	0
Is there typically a "small section" of the first year class, other than Legal Writing, taught by full-time faculty?	No	No
If yes, typical size offered last year	N/A	N/A
# of classroom course titles beyond 1st year curriculum	139	0
# of upper division courses, excluding seminars, with an enrollment:		
Under 25	115	0
25 - 49	37	0
50 - 74	22	0
75 - 99	2	0
100 +	0	0
# of seminars	12	0
# of seminar positions available	240	
# of seminar positions filled	177	0
# of positions available in simulation courses	540	
# of simulation positions filled	446	0
# of positions available in faculty supervised clinical courses	208	
# of fac. sup. clin. positions filled	138	0
# involved in field placements	234	0
# involved in law journals	66	0
# in moot court or trial competitions	67	0
# of credit hrs required to graduate	88	

J.D. Enrollment & Ethnicity

	Men		Women		Fl-Time		Pt-Time		1st Yr		2nd Yr		3rd Yr		4th Yr		Total		JD Degrees Awarded
	#	%	#	%	#	%	#	%	#	%	#	%	#	%	#	%	#	%	
African-American	22	7.3	27	7.5	49	7.4	0	0.0	22	7.8	14	7.4	13	6.8	0	0.0	49	7.4	11
American Indian	0	0.0	6	1.7	6	0.9	0	0.0	3	1.1	2	1.1	1	0.5	0	0.0	6	0.9	3
Asian American	4	1.3	6	1.7	10	1.5	0	0.0	4	1.4	3	1.6	3	1.6	0	0.0	10	1.5	6
Mexican American	0	0.0	0	0.0	0	0.0	0	0.0	0	0.0	0	0.0	0	0.0	0	0.0	0	0.0	1
Puerto Rican	6	2.0	7	1.9	13	2.0	0	0.0	3	1.1	7	3.7	3	1.6	0	0.0	13	2.0	0
Hispanic American	16	5.3	24	6.6	40	6.1	0	0.0	18	6.4	10	5.3	12	6.3	0	0.0	40	6.0	20
Total Minorities	48	16.0	70	19.3	118	17.9	0	0.0	50	17.7	36	19.1	32	16.7	0	0.0	118	17.8	41
Foreign Nationals	10	3.3	10	2.8	20	3.0	0	0.0	12	4.3	4	2.1	4	2.1	0	0.0	20	3.0	7
Caucasian	242	80.7	282	77.9	523	79.1	1	100.0	220	78.0	148	78.7	156	81.3	0	0.0	524	79.2	211
Total	300	45.3	362	54.7	661	99.8	1	0.2	282	42.6	188	28.4	192	29.0	0	0.0	662		259

GPA & LSAT Scores

	Full Time	Part Time	Total
# of apps	1,716	0	1,716
# admits	802	0	802
# of matrics	291	0	291
75% GPA	3.40	0.00	
25% GPA	2.91	0.00	
75% LSAT	154	0	
25% LSAT	146	0	

Tuition & Fees

	Resident	Non-resident
Full-Time	$19,890	$19,890
Part-Time	$0	$0

Living Expenses

Estimated living expenses for Singles		
Living on campus	Living off campus	Living at home
$10,790	$12,570	$6,270

Grants/Scholarships

	Full-time		Part-time		Total	
	#	%	#	%	#	%
Total # of Students	661		1		662	
Total # receiving grants	119	18.0	0	0.0	119	18.0
Less than 1/2 tuition	67	10.1	0	0.0	67	10.1
Half to full tuition	19	2.9	0	0.0	19	2.9
Full tuition	33	5.0	0	0.0	33	5.0
More than full tuition	0	0.0	0	0.0	0	0.0
Median Grant Amount	$10,490		$0			

Informational & Library Resources

# of volumes & volume equivalents	351,490	# of professional staff	8
# of titles	101,080	Hours per week with professional staff	71
# of active serial subscriptions	5,426	Hours per week without professional staff	32
Study seating capacity inside the library	487	# of student computer work stations for entire law school	90
Square feet of law library	45,200	# of additional networked connections	983
Square feet of law school (excl. Library)	112,300	Require Laptop Computer?	Y

Employment

	Total	%
Employment status known	218	92.8
Employment status unknown	17	7.2
Employed	185	84.9
Pursuing graduate degrees	13	6.0
Unemployed seeking employment	20	9.2
Unemployed not seeking employment	0	0.0
Type of Employment		
# employed in law firms	98	53.0
# employed in business & industry	19	10.3
# employed in government	54	29.2
# employed in public interest	1	0.5
# employed as judicial clerks	13	7.0
# employed in academia	0	0.0
Geographic Location		
# employed in state	161	87.0
# employed in foreign countries	1	0.5
# of states where employed	18	

J.D. Attrition (from Prior Year)

	Academic	Other	TOTALS	
	#	#	#	%
1st Year	4	7	11	5.0%
2nd Year	3	7	10	6.2%
3rd Year	0	1	1	0.4%
4th Year	0	0	0	0.0%

Bar Passage Rates

Jurisdiction	Florida		
Exam	Sum 97	Win 98	Total
# from school taking bar for the first time	151	106	257
School's pass rate for all first-time takers	88%	84%	86%
State's pass rate for all first-time takers	84%	82%	83%

SUFFOLK UNIVERSITY

41 Temple Street
Boston, MA 02114-4280
(617)573-8155
http://www.suffolk.edu/law

ABA Approved Since 1953

The Basics

Type of School: Private | Term: Semester

Application deadline: 03/01

Application fee: $50

Financial Aid deadline: 04/01

Can first year start other than Fall? No

Student faculty ratio: 23.4 to 1

Does the University offer:

- housing restricted to law students? No
- graduate student housing for which law students are eligible? No

Curriculum

	Full time	Part time
Typical first-year section size	94	100
Is there typically a "small section" of the first year class, other than Legal Writing, taught by full-time faculty?	Yes	No
If yes, typical size offered last year	45	N/A
# of classroom course titles beyond 1st year curriculum	114	140
# of upper division courses, excluding seminars, with an enrollment:		
Under 25	32	37
25 - 49	31	35
50 - 74	8	12
75 - 99	13	10
100 +	7	0
# of seminars	31	33
# of seminar positions available	1,140	
# of seminar positions filled	563	491
# of positions available in simulation courses	564	
# of simulation positions filled	305	218
# of positions available in faculty supervised clinical courses	106	
# of fac. sup. clin. positions filled	88	18
# involved in field placements	128	29
# involved in law journals	96	28
# in moot court or trial competitions	191	48
# of credit hrs required to graduate	84	

Faculty & Administrators

	Total		Men		Women		Minorities	
	Fall	Spr	Fall	Spr	Fall	Spr	Fall	Spr
Full-time	53	51	44	43	9	8	4	4
Other Full-Time	13	13	7	7	6	6	1	1
Deans, librarians, & others who teach > 1/2	7	7	3	3	4	4	0	0
Part-time	61	80	43	58	18	22	5	6
Total	134	151	97	111	37	40	10	11
Deans, librarians, & others who teach < 1/2	5	5	4	4	1	1	0	0

J.D. Enrollment & Ethnicity

	Men		Women		Fl-Time		Pt-Time		1st Yr		2nd Yr		3rd Yr		4th Yr		Total		JD Degrees Awarded
	#	%	#	%	#	%	#	%	#	%	#	%	#	%	#	%	#	%	
African-American	13	1.5	43	5.0	29	2.9	27	3.6	28	4.9	17	3.4	6	1.2	5	2.6	56	3.2	25
American Indian	0	0.0	3	0.4	2	0.2	1	0.1	1	0.2	1	0.2	1	0.2	0	0.0	3	0.2	4
Asian American	25	2.8	43	5.0	46	4.6	22	2.9	28	4.9	22	4.5	13	2.6	5	2.6	68	3.9	11
Mexican American	0	0.0	0	0.0	0	0.0	0	0.0	0	0.0	0	0.0	0	0.0	0	0.0	0	0.0	0
Puerto Rican	0	0.0	0	0.0	0	0.0	0	0.0	0	0.0	0	0.0	0	0.0	0	0.0	0	0.0	0
Hispanic American	21	2.4	25	2.9	27	2.7	19	2.5	16	2.8	15	3.0	8	1.6	7	3.6	46	2.6	15
Total Minorities	59	6.6	114	13.4	104	10.5	69	9.2	73	12.9	55	11.2	28	5.7	17	8.9	173	9.9	55
Foreign Nationals	0	0.0	0	0.0	0	0.0	0	0.0	0	0.0	0	0.0	0	0.0	0	0.0	0	0.0	0
Caucasian	833	93.4	739	86.6	887	89.5	685	90.8	495	87.1	438	88.8	464	94.3	175	91.1	1572	90.1	446
Total	892	51.1	853	48.9	991	56.8	754	43.2	568	32.6	493	28.3	492	28.2	192	11.0	1745		501

GPA & LSAT Scores

	Full Time	Part Time	Total
# of apps	1,420	454	1,874
# admits	1,073	321	1,394
# of matrics	370	203	573
75% GPA	3.35	3.35	
25% GPA	2.81	2.65	
75% LSAT	153	156	
25% LSAT	146	146	

Tuition & Fees

	Resident	Non-resident
Full-Time	$20,330	$20,330
Part-Time	$15,248	$15,248

Living Expenses

Estimated living expenses for Singles		
Living on campus	Living off campus	Living at home
N/A	$15,018	$8,053

Grants/Scholarships

	Full-time		Part-time		Total	
	#	%	#	%	#	%
Total # of Students	991		754		1745	
Total # receiving grants	380	38.3	172	22.8	552	31.6
Less than 1/2 tuition	370	37.3	160	21.2	530	30.4
Half to full tuition	10	1.0	11	1.5	21	1.2
Full tuition	0	0.0	1	0.1	1	0.1
More than full tuition	0	0.0	0	0.0	0	0.0
Median Grant Amount	$3,000		$1,500			

Informational & Library Resources

# of volumes & volume equivalents	316,303	# of professional staff	12
# of titles	112,755	Hours per week with professional staff	78
# of active serial subscriptions	5,850	Hours per week without professional staff	25
Study seating capacity inside the library	602	# of student computer work stations for entire law school	78
Square feet of law library	35,524	# of additional networked connections	14
Square feet of law school (excl. Library)	57,292	Require Laptop Computer?	N

Employment

	Total	%
Employment status known	394	82.4
Employment status unknown	84	17.6
Employed	356	90.4
Pursuing graduate degrees	3	0.8
Unemployed seeking employment	32	8.1
Unemployed not seeking employment	3	0.8
Type of Employment		
# employed in law firms	150	42.1
# employed in business & industry	105	29.5
# employed in government	57	16.0
# employed in public interest	4	1.1
# employed as judicial clerks	30	8.4
# employed in academia	9	2.5
Geographic Location		
# employed in state	294	82.6
# employed in foreign countries	1	0.3
# of states where employed	20	

J.D. Attrition (from Prior Year)

	Academic	Other	TOTALS	
	#	#	#	%
1st Year	12	4	16	3.0%
2nd Year	4	33	37	7.2%
3rd Year	1	13	14	2.7%
4th Year	0	3	3	1.8%

Bar Passage Rates

Jurisdiction	Massachusetts		
Exam	Sum 97	Win 98	Total
# from school taking bar for the first time	387	44	431
School's pass rate for all first-time takers	82%	84%	82%
State's pass rate for all first-time takers	84%	72%	82%

SYRACUSE UNIVERSITY

College of Law
Syracuse, NY 13244-1030
(315)443-2524
http://www.law.syr.edu

ABA Approved Since 1923

The Basics

Type of School: Private   Term: Semester
Application deadline: 04/01
Application fee: $50
Financial Aid deadline: 03/01
Can first year start other than Fall? No
Student faculty ratio: 17.8 to 1
Does the University offer:
- housing restricted to law students? Yes
- graduate student housing for which law students are eligible? Yes

Faculty & Administrators

	Total		Men		Women		Minorities	
	Fall	Spr	Fall	Spr	Fall	Spr	Fall	Spr
Full-time	35	34	21	19	14	15	6	4
Other Full-Time	2	2	1	1	1	1	0	0
Deans, librarians, & others who teach > 1/2	2	2	0	0	2	2	0	0
Part-time	22	24	21	20	1	4	1	1
Total	61	62	43	40	18	22	7	5
Deans, librarians, & others who teach < 1/2	2	2	1	1	1	1	0	0

Curriculum

	Full time	Part time
Typical first-year section size	90	0
Is there typically a "small section" of the first year class, other than Legal Writing, taught by full-time faculty?	Yes	No
If yes, typical size offered last year	50	N/A
# of classroom course titles beyond 1st year curriculum	166	0
# of upper division courses, excluding seminars, with an enrollment:		
Under 25	105	0
25 - 49	31	0
50 - 74	10	0
75 - 99	7	0
100 +	6	0
# of seminars	7	0
# of seminar positions available	112	
# of seminar positions filled	57	0
# of positions available in simulation courses	416	
# of simulation positions filled	331	0
# of positions available in faculty supervised clinical courses	69	
# of fac. sup. clin. positions filled	62	0
# involved in field placements	86	0
# involved in law journals	180	0
# in moot court or trial competitions	140	0
# of credit hrs required to graduate	87	

J.D. Enrollment & Ethnicity

	Men		Women		Fl-Time		Pt-Time		1st Yr		2nd Yr		3rd Yr		4th Yr		Total		JD Degrees Awarded
	#	%	#	%	#	%	#	%	#	%	#	%	#	%	#	%	#	%	
African-American	18	4.5	39	11.2	57	7.7	0	0.0	25	8.7	14	5.7	18	8.3	0	0.0	57	7.6	14
American Indian	2	0.5	0	0.0	2	0.3	0	0.0	1	0.3	1	0.4	0	0.0	0	0.0	2	0.3	0
Asian American	37	9.2	25	7.2	62	8.4	0	0.0	21	7.3	20	8.1	21	9.7	0	0.0	62	8.3	22
Mexican American	0	0.0	0	0.0	0	0.0	0	0.0	0	0.0	0	0.0	0	0.0	0	0.0	0	0.0	0
Puerto Rican	2	0.5	6	1.7	8	1.1	0	0.0	1	0.3	5	2.0	2	0.9	0	0.0	8	1.1	0
Hispanic American	13	3.2	13	3.7	26	3.5	0	0.0	7	2.4	6	2.4	13	6.0	0	0.0	26	3.5	10
Total Minorities	72	17.8	83	23.9	155	21.1	0	0.0	55	19.2	46	18.6	54	24.9	0	0.0	155	20.6	46
Foreign Nationals	20	5.0	6	1.7	26	3.5	0	0.0	8	2.8	12	4.9	6	2.8	0	0.0	26	3.5	4
Caucasian	312	77.2	258	74.4	555	75.4	15	100.0	224	78.0	189	76.5	157	72.4	0	0.0	570	75.9	206
Total	404	53.8	347	46.2	736	98.0	15	2.0	287	38.2	247	32.9	217	28.9	0	0.0	751		256

GPA & LSAT Scores

	Full Time	Part Time	Total
# of apps	1,675	24	1,699
# admits	1,012	10	1,022
# of matrics	284	4	288
75% GPA	3.40	3.38	
25% GPA	2.95	3.23	
75% LSAT	154	155	
25% LSAT	147	152	

Tuition & Fees

	Resident	Non-resident
Full-Time	$22,364	$22,364
Part-Time	$19,309	$19,309

Living Expenses

Estimated living expenses for Singles		
Living on campus	Living off campus	Living at home
$12,520	$12,520	$12,520

Employment

	Total	%
Employment status known	236	98.3
Employment status unknown	4	1.7
Employed	220	93.2
Pursuing graduate degrees	4	1.7
Unemployed seeking employment	9	3.8
Unemployed not seeking employment	3	1.3
Type of Employment		
# employed in law firms	141	64.1
# employed in business & industry	36	16.4
# employed in government	19	8.6
# employed in public interest	5	2.3
# employed as judicial clerks	14	6.4
# employed in academia	5	2.3
Geographic Location		
# employed in state	109	49.5
# employed in foreign countries	3	1.4
# of states where employed	27	

Grants/Scholarships

	Full-time		Part-time		Total	
	#	%	#	%	#	%
Total # of Students	736		15		751	
Total # receiving grants	425	57.7	4	26.7	429	57.1
Less than 1/2 tuition	378	51.4	4	26.7	382	50.9
Half to full tuition	26	3.5	0	0.0	26	3.5
Full tuition	17	2.3	0	0.0	17	2.3
More than full tuition	4	0.5	0	0.0	4	0.5
Median Grant Amount	$7,950		$1,000			

Informational & Library Resources

# of volumes & volume equivalents	377,386	# of professional staff	9
# of titles	70,937	Hours per week with professional staff	45
# of active serial subscriptions	6,042	Hours per week without professional staff	60
Study seating capacity inside the library	476	# of student computer work stations for entire law school	137
Square feet of law library	36,546	# of additional networked connections	0
Square feet of law school (excl. Library)	98,409	Require Laptop Computer?	N

J.D. Attrition (from Prior Year)

	Academic	Other	TOTALS	
	#	#	#	%
1st Year	0	2	2	0.8%
2nd Year	1	12	13	5.8%
3rd Year	0	5	5	1.9%
4th Year	0	0	0	0.0%

Bar Passage Rates

Jurisdiction	New York		
Exam	Sum 97	Win 98	Total
# from school taking bar for the first time	125	22	147
School's pass rate for all first-time takers	81%	59%	78%
State's pass rate for all first-time takers	78%	65%	76%

TEMPLE UNIVERSITY

1719 North Broad Street
Philadelphia, PA 19122
(215)204-7861
http://www.temple.edu/lawschool

ABA Approved Since 1933

The Basics

Type of School: Public   Term: Semester
Application deadline: 03/01
Application fee: $50
Financial Aid deadline: 03/01
Can first year start other than Fall? No
Student faculty ratio: 18.6 to 1
Does the University offer:
- housing restricted to law students? No
- graduate student housing for which law students are eligible? Yes

Faculty & Administrators

	Total		Men		Women		Minorities	
	Fall	Spr	Fall	Spr	Fall	Spr	Fall	Spr
Full-time	43	41	32	29	11	12	9	10
Other Full-Time	4	4	1	1	3	3	0	0
Deans, librarians, & others who teach > 1/2	5	5	4	4	1	1	1	1
Part-time	71	97	42	68	29	29	7	11
Total	123	147	79	102	44	45	17	22
Deans, librarians, & others who teach < 1/2	9	9	4	4	5	5	1	1

Curriculum

	Full time	Part time
Typical first-year section size	70	85
Is there typically a "small section" of the first year class, other than Legal Writing, taught by full-time faculty?	No	No
If yes, typical size offered last year	N/A	N/A
# of classroom course titles beyond 1st year curriculum	136	59
# of upper division courses, excluding seminars, with an enrollment:		
Under 25	95	37
25 - 49	39	21
50 - 74	7	6
75 - 99	10	1
100 +	2	0
# of seminars	45	8
# of seminar positions available	743	
# of seminar positions filled	438	149
# of positions available in simulation courses	786	
# of simulation positions filled	563	191
# of positions available in faculty supervised clinical courses	10	
# of fac. sup. clin. positions filled	6	0
# involved in field placements	261	22
# involved in law journals	157	17
# in moot court or trial competitions	64	1
# of credit hrs required to graduate	86	

J.D. Enrollment & Ethnicity

	Men		Women		Fl-Time		Pt-Time		1st Yr		2nd Yr		3rd Yr		4th Yr		Total		JD Degrees Awarded
	#	%	#	%	#	%	#	%	#	%	#	%	#	%	#	%	#	%	
African-American	40	7.1	90	16.6	92	12.1	38	11.0	34	9.9	35	9.8	50	15.9	11	12.4	130	11.8	43
American Indian	3	0.5	3	0.6	3	0.4	3	0.9	1	0.3	1	0.3	2	0.6	2	2.2	6	0.5	3
Asian American	39	6.9	41	7.6	67	8.8	13	3.8	21	6.1	32	8.9	25	7.9	2	2.2	80	7.2	20
Mexican American	4	0.7	5	0.9	8	1.1	1	0.3	2	0.6	2	0.6	5	1.6	0	0.0	9	0.8	4
Puerto Rican	8	1.4	9	1.7	12	1.6	5	1.4	6	1.8	4	1.1	4	1.3	3	3.4	17	1.5	8
Hispanic American	11	2.0	6	1.1	13	1.7	4	1.2	8	2.3	7	2.0	2	0.6	0	0.0	17	1.5	6
Total Minorities	105	18.7	154	28.5	195	25.7	64	18.5	72	21.1	81	22.6	88	27.9	18	20.2	259	23.5	84
Foreign Nationals	6	1.1	8	1.5	12	1.6	2	0.6	4	1.2	10	2.8	0	0.0	0	0.0	14	1.3	0
Caucasian	452	80.3	379	70.1	551	72.7	280	80.9	266	77.8	267	74.6	227	72.1	71	79.8	831	75.3	237
Total	563	51.0	541	49.0	758	68.7	346	31.3	342	31.0	358	32.4	315	28.5	89	8.1	1104		321

GPA & LSAT Scores

	Full Time	Part Time	Total
# of apps	2,354	340	2,694
# admits	915	137	1,052
# of matrics	248	97	345
75% GPA	3.52	3.35	
25% GPA	3.02	2.80	
75% LSAT	157	155	
25% LSAT	150	150	

Tuition & Fees

	Resident	Non-resident
Full-Time	$9,236	$15,942
Part-Time	$7,450	$12,816

Living Expenses

Estimated living expenses for Singles		
Living on campus	Living off campus	Living at home
$13,382	$13,382	$11,433

Grants/Scholarships

	Full-time		Part-time		Total	
	#	%	#	%	#	%
Total # of Students	758		346		1104	
Total # receiving grants	358	47.2	42	12.1	400	36.2
Less than 1/2 tuition	272	35.9	37	10.7	309	28.0
Half to full tuition	47	6.2	4	1.2	51	4.6
Full tuition	39	5.1	1	0.3	40	3.6
More than full tuition	0	0.0	0	0.0	0	0.0
Median Grant Amount	$2,835		$1,390			

Informational & Library Resources

# of volumes & volume equivalents	497,574	# of professional staff	10
# of titles	87,874	Hours per week with professional staff	78
# of active serial subscriptions	2,620	Hours per week without professional staff	18
Study seating capacity inside the library	644	# of student computer work stations for entire law school	114
Square feet of law library	45,462	# of additional networked connections	152
Square feet of law school (excl. Library)	69,407	Require Laptop Computer?	N

Employment

	Total	%
Employment status known	366	97.1
Employment status unknown	11	2.9
Employed	334	91.3
Pursuing graduate degrees	5	1.4
Unemployed seeking employment	20	5.5
Unemployed not seeking employment	7	1.9
Type of Employment		
# employed in law firms	154	46.1
# employed in business & industry	72	21.6
# employed in government	37	11.1
# employed in public interest	31	9.3
# employed as judicial clerks	39	11.7
# employed in academia	1	0.3
Geographic Location		
# employed in state	201	60.2
# employed in foreign countries	4	1.2
# of states where employed	20	

J.D. Attrition (from Prior Year)

	Academic	Other	TOTALS	
	#	#	#	%
1st Year	7	7	14	3.8%
2nd Year	1	10	11	3.4%
3rd Year	0	5	5	1.5%
4th Year	0	0	0	0.0%

Bar Passage Rates

Jurisdiction	Pennsylvania		
Exam	Sum 97	Win 98	Total
# from school taking bar for the first time	254	29	283
School's pass rate for all first-time takers	70%	55%	68%
State's pass rate for all first-time takers	81%	73%	79%

TENNESSEE, UNIVERSITY OF

1505 W. Cumberland Ave.
Knoxville, TN 37996-1810
(423)974-4241
http://www.law.utk.edu

ABA Approved Since 1925

The Basics

Type of School: Public   Term: Semester

Application deadline: 02/01

Application fee: $15

Financial Aid deadline: 02/14

Can first year start other than Fall? No

Student faculty ratio: 15.1 to 1

Does the University offer:
- housing restricted to law students? No
- graduate student housing for which law students are eligible? Yes

Faculty & Administrators

	Total		Men		Women		Minorities	
	Fall	Spr	Fall	Spr	Fall	Spr	Fall	Spr
Full-time	27	26	18	18	9	8	2	2
Other Full-Time	0	0	0	0	0	0	0	0
Deans, librarians, & others who teach > 1/2	3	3	3	3	0	0	0	0
Part-time	23	32	18	23	5	9	0	0
Total	53	61	39	44	14	17	2	2
Deans, librarians, & others who teach < 1/2	1	1	1	1	0	0	0	0

Curriculum

	Full time	Part time
Typical first-year section size	57	0
Is there typically a "small section" of the first year class, other than Legal Writing, taught by full-time faculty?	No	No
If yes, typical size offered last year	N/A	N/A
# of classroom course titles beyond 1st year curriculum	65	0
# of upper division courses, excluding seminars, with an enrollment:		
Under 25	54	0
25 - 49	32	0
50 - 74	6	0
75 - 99	6	0
100 +	0	0
# of seminars	8	0
# of seminar positions available	128	
# of seminar positions filled	112	0
# of positions available in simulation courses	430	
# of simulation positions filled	388	0
# of positions available in faculty supervised clinical courses	104	
# of fac. sup. clin. positions filled	99	0
# involved in field placements	4	0
# involved in law journals	77	0
# in moot court or trial competitions	70	0
# of credit hrs required to graduate	89	

J.D. Enrollment & Ethnicity

	Men		Women		Fl-Time		Pt-Time		1st Yr		2nd Yr		3rd Yr		4th Yr		Total		JD Degrees Awarded
	#	%	#	%	#	%	#	%	#	%	#	%	#	%	#	%	#	%	
African-American	15	5.5	32	14.7	47	9.6	0	0.0	15	9.6	16	9.5	16	9.7	0	0.0	47	9.6	12
American Indian	2	0.7	2	0.9	4	0.8	0	0.0	0	0.0	1	0.6	3	1.8	0	0.0	4	0.8	1
Asian American	3	1.1	2	0.9	5	1.0	0	0.0	3	1.9	1	0.6	1	0.6	0	0.0	5	1.0	0
Mexican American	0	0.0	0	0.0	0	0.0	0	0.0	0	0.0	0	0.0	0	0.0	0	0.0	0	0.0	0
Puerto Rican	0	0.0	0	0.0	0	0.0	0	0.0	0	0.0	0	0.0	0	0.0	0	0.0	0	0.0	0
Hispanic American	0	0.0	0	0.0	0	0.0	0	0.0	0	0.0	0	0.0	0	0.0	0	0.0	0	0.0	1
Total Minorities	20	7.4	36	16.5	56	11.5	0	0.0	18	11.5	18	10.7	20	12.1	0	0.0	56	11.5	14
Foreign Nationals	0	0.0	1	0.5	1	0.2	0	0.0	1	0.6	0	0.0	0	0.0	0	0.0	1	0.2	0
Caucasian	251	92.6	181	83.0	432	88.3	0	0.0	137	87.8	150	89.3	145	87.9	0	0.0	432	88.3	139
Total	271	55.4	218	44.6	489	100.0	0	0.0	156	31.9	168	34.4	165	33.7	0	0.0	489		153

GPA & LSAT Scores

	Full Time	Part Time	Total
# of apps	1,096	0	1,096
# admits	394	0	394
# of matrics	159	0	159
75% GPA	3.70	0.00	
25% GPA	3.20	0.00	
75% LSAT	160	0	
25% LSAT	153	0	

Tuition & Fees

	Resident	Non-resident
Full-Time	$4,502	$11,424
Part-Time	$0	$0

Living Expenses

Estimated living expenses for Singles		
Living on campus	Living off campus	Living at home
$10,927	$10,927	$7,511

Grants/Scholarships

	Full-time		Part-time		Total	
	#	%	#	%	#	%
Total # of Students	489		0		489	
Total # receiving grants	120	24.5	0	0.0	120	24.5
Less than 1/2 tuition	32	6.5	0	0.0	32	6.5
Half to full tuition	23	4.7	0	0.0	23	4.7
Full tuition	23	4.7	0	0.0	23	4.7
More than full tuition	42	8.6	0	0.0	42	8.6
Median Grant Amount	$4,400		$0			

Informational & Library Resources

# of volumes & volume equivalents	452,892	# of professional staff	7
# of titles	91,837	Hours per week with professional staff	71
# of active serial subscriptions	6,277	Hours per week without professional staff	41
Study seating capacity inside the library	455	# of student computer work stations for entire law school	82
Square feet of law library	57,400	# of additional networked connections	9
Square feet of law school (excl. Library)	46,987	Require Laptop Computer?	N

Employment

	Total	%
Employment status known	129	98.5
Employment status unknown	2	1.5
Employed	120	93.0
Pursuing graduate degrees	6	4.7
Unemployed seeking employment	2	1.6
Unemployed not seeking employment	1	0.8
Type of Employment		
# employed in law firms	81	67.5
# employed in business & industry	7	5.8
# employed in government	14	11.7
# employed in public interest	1	0.8
# employed as judicial clerks	14	11.7
# employed in academia	3	2.5
Geographic Location		
# employed in state	95	79.2
# employed in foreign countries	0	0.0
# of states where employed	10	

J.D. Attrition (from Prior Year)

	Academic	Other	TOTALS	
	#	#	#	%
1st Year	0	11	11	6.1%
2nd Year	0	4	4	2.6%
3rd Year	0	2	2	1.3%
4th Year	0	0	0	0.0%

Bar Passage Rates

Jurisdiction	Tennessee		
Exam	Sum 97	Win 98	Total
# from school taking bar for the first time	96	11	107
School's pass rate for all first-time takers	88%	82%	87%
State's pass rate for all first-time takers	81%	76%	80%

TEXAS AT AUSTIN, UNIVERSITY OF

727 E. Dean Keeton Street
Austin, TX 78705
(512)232-1120
http://www.utexas.edu/law

ABA Approved Since 1923

The Basics

Type of School: Public Term: Semester
Application deadline: 02/01
Application fee: $65
Financial Aid deadline: 03/31
Can first year start other than Fall? No
Student faculty ratio: 18.3 to 1
Does the University offer:
- housing restricted to law students? No
- graduate student housing for which law students are eligible? No

Faculty & Administrators

	Total		Men		Women		Minorities	
	Fall	Spr	Fall	Spr	Fall	Spr	Fall	Spr
Full-time	61	66	47	52	14	14	5	5
Other Full-Time	0	0	0	0	0	0	0	0
Deans, librarians, & others who teach > 1/2	5	4	3	2	2	2	1	0
Part-time	54	56	40	46	14	10	9	8
Total	120	126	90	100	30	26	15	13
Deans, librarians, & others who teach < 1/2	0	0	0	0	0	0	0	0

Curriculum

	Full time	Part time
Typical first-year section size	114	0
Is there typically a "small section" of the first year class, other than Legal Writing, taught by full-time faculty?	Yes	No
If yes, typical size offered last year	33	N/A
# of classroom course titles beyond 1st year curriculum	139	0
# of upper division courses, excluding seminars, with an enrollment:		
Under 25	146	0
25 - 49	49	0
50 - 74	31	0
75 - 99	12	0
100 +	16	0
# of seminars	59	0
# of seminar positions available	772	
# of seminar positions filled	647	0
# of positions available in simulation courses	612	
# of simulation positions filled	501	0
# of positions available in faculty supervised clinical courses	302	
# of fac. sup. clin. positions filled	224	0
# involved in field placements	64	0
# involved in law journals	432	0
# in moot court or trial competitions	678	0
# of credit hrs required to graduate	86	

J.D. Enrollment & Ethnicity

	Men		Women		Fl-Time		Pt-Time		1st Yr		2nd Yr		3rd Yr		4th Yr		Total		JD Degrees Awarded
	#	%	#	%	#	%	#	%	#	%	#	%	#	%	#	%	#	%	
African-American	11	1.5	32	5.2	43	3.1	0	0.0	8	1.7	6	1.3	29	5.9	0	0.0	43	3.1	35
American Indian	6	0.8	6	1.0	12	0.9	0	0.0	5	1.1	1	0.2	6	1.2	0	0.0	12	0.9	2
Asian American	45	6.0	47	7.6	92	6.7	0	0.0	31	6.7	33	7.3	28	5.7	0	0.0	92	6.7	28
Mexican American	66	8.8	57	9.2	123	9.0	0	0.0	40	8.6	30	6.7	53	10.7	0	0.0	123	9.0	66
Puerto Rican	0	0.0	0	0.0	0	0.0	0	0.0	0	0.0	0	0.0	0	0.0	0	0.0	0	0.0	0
Hispanic American	0	0.0	0	0.0	0	0.0	0	0.0	0	0.0	0	0.0	0	0.0	0	0.0	0	0.0	0
Total Minorities	128	17.0	142	22.9	270	19.7	0	0.0	84	18.0	70	15.6	116	23.4	0	0.0	270	19.7	131
Foreign Nationals	2	0.3	2	0.3	4	0.3	0	0.0	2	0.4	2	0.4	0	0.0	0	0.0	4	0.3	0
Caucasian	624	82.8	476	76.8	1100	80.1	0	0.0	345	74.0	376	83.7	379	76.6	0	0.0	1100	80.1	363
Total	754	54.9	620	45.1	1374	100.0	0	0.0	466	33.9	449	32.7	495	36.0	0	0.0	1374		494

GPA & LSAT Scores

	Full Time	Part Time	Total
# of apps	3,184	0	3,184
# admits	1,188	0	1,188
# of matrics	468	0	468
75% GPA	3.77	0.00	
25% GPA	3.40	0.00	
75% LSAT	164	0	
25% LSAT	158	0	

Tuition & Fees

	Resident	Non-resident
Full-Time	$7,234	$15,064
Part-Time	$0	$0

Living Expenses

Estimated living expenses for Singles

Living on campus	Living off campus	Living at home
$9,264	$10,492	N/A

Grants/Scholarships

	Full-time		Part-time		Total	
	#	%	#	%	#	%
Total # of Students	1374		0		1374	
Total # receiving grants	1248	90.8	0	0.0	1248	90.8
Less than 1/2 tuition	1059	77.1	0	0.0	1059	77.1
Half to full tuition	69	5.0	0	0.0	69	5.0
Full tuition	70	5.1	0	0.0	70	5.1
More than full tuition	50	3.6	0	0.0	50	3.6
Median Grant Amount	$1,050		$0			

Informational & Library Resources

# of volumes & volume equivalents	936,323	# of professional staff	17
# of titles	275,494	Hours per week with professional staff	80
# of active serial subscriptions	10,151	Hours per week without professional staff	22
Study seating capacity inside the library	1,361	# of student computer work stations for entire law school	155
Square feet of law library	173,500	# of additional networked connections	0
Square feet of law school (excl. Library)	94,553	Require Laptop Computer?	N

Employment

	Total	%
Employment status known	540	99.6
Employment status unknown	2	0.4
Employed	489	90.6
Pursuing graduate degrees	14	2.6
Unemployed seeking employment	19	3.5
Unemployed not seeking employment	18	3.3
Type of Employment		
# employed in law firms	318	65.0
# employed in business & industry	64	13.1
# employed in government	32	6.5
# employed in public interest	8	1.6
# employed as judicial clerks	50	10.2
# employed in academia	1	0.2
Geographic Location		
# employed in state	355	72.6
# employed in foreign countries	2	0.4
# of states where employed	28	

J.D. Attrition (from Prior Year)

	Academic	Other	TOTALS	
	#	#	#	%
1st Year	4	17	21	4.6%
2nd Year	0	8	8	1.6%
3rd Year	0	1	1	0.2%
4th Year	0	0	0	0.0%

Bar Passage Rates

Jurisdiction	Texas		
Exam	Sum 97	Win 98	Total
# from school taking bar for the first time	388	41	429
School's pass rate for all first-time takers	91%	71%	89%
State's pass rate for all first-time takers	83%	73%	81%

TEXAS SOUTHERN UNIVERSITY

Thurgood Marshall School of Law
3100 Cleburne
Houston, TX 77004-3216
(713)313-1075
http://www.tsulaw.edu

ABA Approved Since 1949

The Basics

Type of School: Public — Term: Semester
Application deadline: 04/01
Application fee: $40
Financial Aid deadline: 05/01
Can first year start other than Fall? No
Student faculty ratio: 20.3 to 1
Does the University offer:
- housing restricted to law students? Yes
- graduate student housing for which law students are eligible? No

Faculty & Administrators

	Total		Men		Women		Minorities	
	Fall	Spr	Fall	Spr	Fall	Spr	Fall	Spr
Full-time	26	25	21	20	5	5	21	20
Other Full-Time	5	5	2	2	3	3	0	0
Deans, librarians, & others who teach > 1/2	2	2	2	2	0	0	3	3
Part-time	7	0	5	0	2	0	5	0
Total	40	32	30	24	10	8	29	23
Deans, librarians, & others who teach < 1/2	1	1	0	0	1	1	1	1

Curriculum

	Full time	Part time
Typical first-year section size	305	0
Is there typically a "small section" of the first year class, other than Legal Writing, taught by full-time faculty?	No	No
If yes, typical size offered last year	N/A	N/A
# of classroom course titles beyond 1st year curriculum	45	0
# of upper division courses, excluding seminars, with an enrollment:		
Under 25	42	0
25 - 49	12	0
50 - 74	5	0
75 - 99	23	0
100 +	4	0
# of seminars	21	0
# of seminar positions available	21	
# of seminar positions filled	21	0
# of positions available in simulation courses	10	
# of simulation positions filled	10	0
# of positions available in faculty supervised clinical courses	8	
# of fac. sup. clin. positions filled	8	0
# involved in field placements	25	0
# involved in law journals	25	0
# in moot court or trial competitions	20	0
# of credit hrs required to graduate	90	

J.D. Enrollment & Ethnicity

	Men		Women		Fl-Time		Pt-Time		1st Yr		2nd Yr		3rd Yr		4th Yr		Total		JD Degrees Awarded
	#	%	#	%	#	%	#	%	#	%	#	%	#	%	#	%	#	%	
African-American	155	47.0	211	71.3	366	58.5	0	0.0	162	58.9	111	56.3	93	57.8	0	0.0	366	58.5	74
American Indian	1	0.3	1	0.3	2	0.3	0	0.0	0	0.0	2	1.0	0	0.0	0	0.0	2	0.3	0
Asian American	14	4.2	15	5.1	29	4.6	0	0.0	8	2.9	9	4.6	12	7.5	0	0.0	29	4.6	11
Mexican American	91	27.6	42	14.2	133	21.2	0	0.0	61	22.2	47	23.9	25	15.5	0	0.0	133	21.2	37
Puerto Rican	0	0.0	0	0.0	0	0.0	0	0.0	0	0.0	0	0.0	0	0.0	0	0.0	0	0.0	2
Hispanic American	0	0.0	0	0.0	0	0.0	0	0.0	0	0.0	0	0.0	0	0.0	0	0.0	0	0.0	7
Total Minorities	261	79.1	269	90.9	530	84.7	0	0.0	231	84.0	169	85.8	130	80.7	0	0.0	530	84.7	131
Foreign Nationals	9	2.7	1	0.3	10	1.6	0	0.0	2	0.7	0	0.0	8	5.0	0	0.0	10	1.6	0
Caucasian	60	18.2	26	8.8	86	13.7	0	0.0	42	15.3	28	14.2	16	9.9	0	0.0	86	13.7	29
Total	330	52.7	296	47.3	626	100.0	0	0.0	275	43.9	197	31.5	161	25.7	0	0.0	626		160

GPA & LSAT Scores

	Full Time	Part Time	Total
# of apps	937	0	937
# admits	511	0	511
# of matrics	290	0	290
75% GPA	3.00	0.00	
25% GPA	2.37	0.00	
75% LSAT	144	0	
25% LSAT	139	0	

Tuition & Fees

	Resident	Non-resident
Full-Time	$5,404	$9,274
Part-Time	$0	$0

Living Expenses

Estimated living expenses for Singles

Living on campus	Living off campus	Living at home
N/A	$9,872	$5,850

Grants/Scholarships

	Full-time		Part-time		Total	
	#	%	#	%	#	%
Total # of Students	626		0		626	
Total # receiving grants	388	62.0	0	0.0	388	62.0
Less than 1/2 tuition	380	60.7	0	0.0	380	60.7
Half to full tuition	6	1.0	0	0.0	6	1.0
Full tuition	1	0.2	0	0.0	1	0.2
More than full tuition	1	0.2	0	0.0	1	0.2
Median Grant Amount	$1,550		$0			

Informational & Library Resources

# of volumes & volume equivalents	386,673	# of professional staff	3
# of titles	70,549	Hours per week with professional staff	61
# of active serial subscriptions	2,448	Hours per week without professional staff	47
Study seating capacity inside the library	348	# of student computer work stations for entire law school	42
Square feet of law library	47,883	# of additional networked connections	0
Square feet of law school (excl. Library)	49,326	Require Laptop Computer?	N

Employment

	Total	%
Employment status known	93	84.5
Employment status unknown	17	15.5
Employed	37	39.8
Pursuing graduate degrees	4	4.3
Unemployed seeking employment	40	43.0
Unemployed not seeking employment	12	12.9
Type of Employment		
# employed in law firms	15	40.5
# employed in business & industry	7	18.9
# employed in government	8	21.6
# employed in public interest	0	0.0
# employed as judicial clerks	3	8.1
# employed in academia	0	0.0
Geographic Location		
# employed in state	30	81.1
# employed in foreign countries	0	0.0
# of states where employed	6	

J.D. Attrition (from Prior Year)

	Academic	Other	TOTALS	
	#	#	#	%
1st Year	71	12	83	30%
2nd Year	2	7	9	5.5%
3rd Year	0	4	4	2.5%
4th Year	0	0	0	0.0%

Bar Passage Rates

Jurisdiction	Texas		
Exam	Sum 97	Win 98	Total
# from school taking bar for the first time	94	39	133
School's pass rate for all first-time takers	65%	144%	88%
State's pass rate for all first-time takers	83%	73%	81%

TEXAS TECH UNIVERSITY

1802 Hartford
Lubbock, TX 79409-0004
(806)742-3791
http://www.law.ttu.edu

ABA Approved Since 1969

The Basics

Type of School: Public　　Term: Semester
Application deadline: 02/01
Application fee: $50
Financial Aid deadline: 03/01
Can first year start other than Fall? Yes
Student faculty ratio: 27.0 to 1
Does the University offer:
- housing restricted to law students? No
- graduate student housing for which law students are eligible? No

Faculty & Administrators

	Total		Men		Women		Minorities	
	Fall	Spr	Fall	Spr	Fall	Spr	Fall	Spr
Full-time	19	19	14	14	5	5	2	2
Other Full-Time	4	4	0	0	4	4	0	0
Deans, librarians, & others who teach > 1/2	6	6	3	3	3	3	0	0
Part-time	12	12	10	10	2	2	1	2
Total	41	41	27	27	14	14	3	4
Deans, librarians, & others who teach < 1/2	0	0	0	0	0	0	0	0

Curriculum

	Full time	Part time
Typical first-year section size	75	0
Is there typically a "small section" of the first year class, other than Legal Writing, taught by full-time faculty?	No	No
If yes, typical size offered last year	N/A	N/A
# of classroom course titles beyond 1st year curriculum	77	0
# of upper division courses, excluding seminars, with an enrollment:		
Under 25	5	0
25 - 49	28	0
50 - 74	13	0
75 - 99	5	0
100 +	8	0
# of seminars	18	0
# of seminar positions available	410	
# of seminar positions filled	308	0
# of positions available in simulation courses	134	
# of simulation positions filled	130	0
# of positions available in faculty supervised clinical courses	48	
# of fac. sup. clin. positions filled	52	0
# involved in field placements	81	0
# involved in law journals	69	0
# in moot court or trial competitions	150	0
# of credit hrs required to graduate	90	

J.D. Enrollment & Ethnicity

	Men		Women		Fl-Time		Pt-Time		1st Yr		2nd Yr		3rd Yr		4th Yr		Total		JD Degrees Awarded
	#	%	#	%	#	%	#	%	#	%	#	%	#	%	#	%	#	%	
African-American	5	1.4	6	2.3	11	1.8	0	0.0	5	2.3	1	0.5	5	2.4	0	0.0	11	1.8	5
American Indian	1	0.3	3	1.1	4	0.6	0	0.0	1	0.5	1	0.5	2	1.0	0	0.0	4	0.6	6
Asian American	1	0.3	3	1.1	4	0.6	0	0.0	2	0.9	2	1.0	0	0.0	0	0.0	4	0.6	4
Mexican American	37	10.5	26	9.9	63	10.2	0	0.0	27	12.6	15	7.8	21	10.0	0	0.0	63	10.2	18
Puerto Rican	0	0.0	0	0.0	0	0.0	0	0.0	0	0.0	0	0.0	0	0.0	0	0.0	0	0.0	0
Hispanic American	0	0.0	0	0.0	0	0.0	0	0.0	0	0.0	0	0.0	0	0.0	0	0.0	0	0.0	0
Total Minorities	44	12.5	38	14.4	82	13.3	0	0.0	35	16.4	19	9.9	28	13.3	0	0.0	82	13.3	33
Foreign Nationals	12	3.4	5	1.9	17	2.8	0	0.0	12	5.6	3	1.6	2	1.0	0	0.0	17	2.8	1
Caucasian	297	84.1	220	83.7	517	83.9	0	0.0	167	78.0	170	88.5	180	85.7	0	0.0	517	83.9	181
Total	353	57.3	263	42.7	616	100.0	0	0.0	214	34.7	192	31.2	210	34.1	0	0.0	616		215

GPA & LSAT Scores

	Full Time	Part Time	Total
# of apps	1,049	0	1,049
# admits	510	0	510
# of matrics	217	0	217
75% GPA	3.59	0.00	
25% GPA	3.12	0.00	
75% LSAT	158	0	
25% LSAT	151	0	

Tuition & Fees

	Resident	Non-resident
Full-Time	$6,621	$11,691
Part-Time	$0	$0

Living Expenses

Estimated living expenses for Singles		
Living on campus	Living off campus	Living at home
$9,488	$9,488	N/A

Grants/Scholarships

	Full-time		Part-time		Total	
	#	%	#	%	#	%
Total # of Students	616		0		616	
Total # receiving grants	274	44.5	0	0.0	274	44.5
Less than 1/2 tuition	146	23.7	0	0.0	146	23.7
Half to full tuition	15	2.4	0	0.0	15	2.4
Full tuition	0	0.0	0	0.0	0	0.0
More than full tuition	113	18.3	0	0.0	113	18.3
Median Grant Amount	$3,000		$0			

Informational & Library Resources

# of volumes & volume equivalents	267,843	# of professional staff	5
# of titles	56,332	Hours per week with professional staff	40
# of active serial subscriptions	2,368	Hours per week without professional staff	53
Study seating capacity inside the library	380	# of student computer work stations for entire law school	250
Square feet of law library	49,302	# of additional networked connections	0
Square feet of law school (excl. Library)	40,436	Require Laptop Computer?	N

Employment

	Total	%
Employment status known	163	84.5
Employment status unknown	30	15.5
Employed	142	87.1
Pursuing graduate degrees	0	0.0
Unemployed seeking employment	21	12.9
Unemployed not seeking employment	0	0.0
Type of Employment		
# employed in law firms	118	83.1
# employed in business & industry	2	1.4
# employed in government	13	9.2
# employed in public interest	0	0.0
# employed as judicial clerks	9	6.3
# employed in academia	0	0.0
Geographic Location		
# employed in state	139	97.9
# employed in foreign countries	0	0.0
# of states where employed	3	

J.D. Attrition (from Prior Year)

	Academic	Other	TOTALS	
	#	#	#	%
1st Year	8	6	14	6.9%
2nd Year	0	3	3	1.4%
3rd Year	0	3	3	1.4%
4th Year	0	0	0	0.0%

Bar Passage Rates

Jurisdiction	Texas			New Mexico		
Exam	Sum 97	Win 98	Total	Sum 97	Win 98	Total
# from school taking bar for the first time	136	18	154	0	0	0
School's pass rate for all first-time takers	92%	83%	91%			
State's pass rate for all first-time takers	83%	73%	81%	94%	92%	93%

TEXAS WESLEYAN UNIVERSITY (Provisional)

1515 Commerce Street
Fort Worth, TX 76102
(817)212-4100
http://www.law.txwes.edu

ABA Approved Since 1994

The Basics

Type of School: Private   Term: Semester
Application deadline: 03/15 (Preferred)
Application fee: $50
Financial Aid deadline: 04/15 (Preferred)
Can first year start other than Fall? No
Student faculty ratio: 21.3 to 1
Does the University offer:
- housing restricted to law students? No
- graduate student housing for which law students are eligible? Yes

Faculty & Administrators

	Total		Men		Women		Minorities	
	Fall	Spr	Fall	Spr	Fall	Spr	Fall	Spr
Full-time	19	19	15	15	4	4	3	3
Other Full-Time	0	0	0	0	0	0	0	0
Deans, librarians, & others who teach > 1/2	4	4	3	3	1	1	0	0
Part-time	32	30	16	16	16	14	1	2
Total	55	53	34	34	21	19	4	5
Deans, librarians, & others who teach < 1/2	1	1	1	1	0	0	0	0

Curriculum

	Full time	Part time
Typical first-year section size	65	68
Is there typically a "small section" of the first year class, other than Legal Writing, taught by full-time faculty?	Yes	Yes
If yes, typical size offered last year	33	33
# of classroom course titles beyond 1st year curriculum	42	43
# of upper division courses, excluding seminars, with an enrollment:		
Under 25	22	19
25 - 49	16	22
50 - 74	11	6
75 - 99	1	2
100 +	0	0
# of seminars	4	4
# of seminar positions available	132	
# of seminar positions filled	59	49
# of positions available in simulation courses	279	
# of simulation positions filled	133	98
# of positions available in faculty supervised clinical courses	16	
# of fac. sup. clin. positions filled	8	8
# involved in field placements	31	12
# involved in law journals	36	25
# in moot court or trial competitions	44	3
# of credit hrs required to graduate	88	

J.D. Enrollment & Ethnicity

	Men		Women		Fl-Time		Pt-Time		1st Yr		2nd Yr		3rd Yr		4th Yr		Total		JD Degrees Awarded
	#	%	#	%	#	%	#	%	#	%	#	%	#	%	#	%	#	%	
African-American	10	2.9	16	6.9	13	4.2	13	4.8	9	5.1	5	3.6	6	3.4	6	7.1	26	4.5	13
American Indian	6	1.7	4	1.7	4	1.3	6	2.2	2	1.1	5	3.6	3	1.7	0	0.0	10	1.7	2
Asian American	10	2.9	5	2.2	11	3.6	4	1.5	4	2.3	3	2.1	7	4.0	1	1.2	15	2.6	1
Mexican American	17	4.9	12	5.2	15	4.9	14	5.2	8	4.5	13	9.3	6	3.4	2	2.4	29	5.0	9
Puerto Rican	0	0.0	1	0.4	1	0.3	0	0.0	1	0.6	0	0.0	0	0.0	0	0.0	1	0.2	0
Hispanic American	10	2.9	8	3.5	10	3.2	8	3.0	5	2.8	0	0.0	9	5.1	4	4.7	18	3.1	9
Total Minorities	53	15.3	46	19.9	54	17.5	45	16.7	29	16.4	26	18.6	31	17.7	13	15.3	99	17.2	34
Foreign Nationals	0	0.0	0	0.0	0	0.0	0	0.0	0	0.0	0	0.0	0	0.0	0	0.0	0	0.0	0
Caucasian	293	84.7	185	80.1	254	82.5	224	83.3	148	83.6	114	81.4	144	82.3	72	84.7	478	82.8	145
Total	346	60.0	231	40.0	308	53.4	269	46.6	177	30.7	140	24.3	175	30.3	85	14.7	577		179

TEXAS WESLEYAN UNIVERSITY (Provisional)

GPA & LSAT Scores

	Full Time	Part Time	Total
# of apps	622	179	801
# admits	335	103	438
# of matrics	124	71	195
75% GPA	3.19	3.26	
25% GPA	2.66	2.75	
75% LSAT	153	154	
25% LSAT	145	146	

Tuition & Fees

	Resident	Non-resident
Full-Time	$13,000	$13,000
Part-Time	$9,400	$9,400

Living Expenses

Estimated living expenses for Singles		
Living on campus	Living off campus	Living at home
$7,141	$9,106	$6,339

Grants/Scholarships

	Full-time		Part-time		Total	
	#	%	#	%	#	%
Total # of Students	308		269		577	
Total # receiving grants	218	70.8	107	39.8	325	56.3
Less than 1/2 tuition	214	69.5	107	39.8	321	55.6
Half to full tuition	0	0.0	0	0.0	0	0.0
Full tuition	1	0.3	0	0.0	1	0.2
More than full tuition	3	1.0	0	0.0	3	0.5
Median Grant Amount	$1,800		$1,400			

Informational & Library Resources

# of volumes & volume equivalents	157,125	# of professional staff	7
# of titles	21,674	Hours per week with professional staff	89
# of active serial subscriptions	3,471	Hours per week without professional staff	23
Study seating capacity inside the library	254	# of student computer work stations for entire law school	30
Square feet of law library	14,222	# of additional networked connections	0
Square feet of law school (excl. Library)	60,264	Require Laptop Computer?	N

Employment

	Total	%
Employment status known	141	91.6
Employment status unknown	13	8.4
Employed	113	80.1
Pursuing graduate degrees	2	1.4
Unemployed seeking employment	10	7.1
Unemployed not seeking employment	16	11.3
Type of Employment		
# employed in law firms	47	41.6
# employed in business & industry	40	35.4
# employed in government	10	8.8
# employed in public interest	4	3.5
# employed as judicial clerks	7	6.2
# employed in academia	5	4.4
Geographic Location		
# employed in state	107	94.7
# employed in foreign countries	2	1.8
# of states where employed	4	

J.D. Attrition (from Prior Year)

	Academic	Other	TOTALS	
	#	#	#	%
1st Year	31	43	74	37%
2nd Year	9	0	9	4.6%
3rd Year	0	2	2	1.0%
4th Year	2	0	2	3.1%

Bar Passage Rates

Jurisdiction	Texas		
Exam	Sum 97	Win 98	Total
# from school taking bar for the first time	89	52	141
School's pass rate for all first-time takers	54%	54%	54%
State's pass rate for all first-time takers	83%	73%	81%

THOMAS JEFFERSON SCHOOL OF LAW (Provisional)

2121 San Diego Avenue
San Diego, CA 92110
(619)297-9700
http://www.jeffersonlaw.edu

ABA Approved Since 1996

The Basics

Type of School: Private   Term: Semester

Application deadline: Rolling

Application fee: $35

Financial Aid deadline: 04/23

Can first year start other than Fall? Yes

Student faculty ratio: 18.4 to 1

Does the University offer:
- housing restricted to law students? No
- graduate student housing for which law students are eligible? No

Faculty & Administrators

	Total		Men		Women		Minorities	
	Fall	Spr	Fall	Spr	Fall	Spr	Fall	Spr
Full-time	22	20	12	12	10	8	2	2
Other Full-Time	0	0	0	0	0	0	0	0
Deans, librarians, & others who teach > 1/2	1	1	0	0	1	1	0	0
Part-time	23	20	17	16	6	4	1	2
Total	46	41	29	28	17	13	3	4
Deans, librarians, & others who teach < 1/2	2	2	1	1	1	1	0	0

Curriculum

	Full time	Part time
Typical first-year section size	45	45
Is there typically a "small section" of the first year class, other than Legal Writing, taught by full-time faculty?	No	No
If yes, typical size offered last year	N/A	N/A
# of classroom course titles beyond 1st year curriculum	47	52
# of upper division courses, excluding seminars, with an enrollment:		
Under 25	34	27
25 - 49	10	16
50 - 74	7	6
75 - 99	0	0
100 +	0	0
# of seminars	5	8
# of seminar positions available	195	
# of seminar positions filled	36	71
# of positions available in simulation courses	423	
# of simulation positions filled	165	209
# of positions available in faculty supervised clinical courses	0	
# of fac. sup. clin. positions filled	0	0
# involved in field placements	44	21
# involved in law journals	30	24
# in moot court or trial competitions	22	9
# of credit hrs required to graduate	88	

J.D. Enrollment & Ethnicity

	Men		Women		Fl-Time		Pt-Time		1st Yr		2nd Yr		3rd Yr		4th Yr		Total		JD Degrees Awarded
	#	%	#	%	#	%	#	%	#	%	#	%	#	%	#	%	#	%	
African-American	9	2.6	13	6.1	13	3.9	9	3.9	13	4.1	6	4.8	3	3.3	0	0.0	22	3.9	1
American Indian	4	1.1	2	0.9	5	1.5	1	0.4	3	0.9	1	0.8	2	2.2	0	0.0	6	1.1	0
Asian American	28	8.0	14	6.6	22	6.6	20	8.7	28	8.8	7	5.6	4	4.3	3	11.1	42	7.5	7
Mexican American	14	4.0	13	6.1	5	1.5	22	9.6	16	5.0	5	4.0	5	5.4	1	3.7	27	4.8	7
Puerto Rican	1	0.3	2	0.9	2	0.6	1	0.4	2	0.6	0	0.0	1	1.1	0	0.0	3	0.5	1
Hispanic American	8	2.3	12	5.6	13	3.9	7	3.0	12	3.8	5	4.0	3	3.3	0	0.0	20	3.6	4
Total Minorities	64	18.3	56	26.3	60	18.0	60	26.1	74	23.2	24	19.2	18	19.6	4	14.8	120	21.3	20
Foreign Nationals	0	0.0	1	0.5	0	0.0	1	0.4	0	0.0	0	0.0	0	0.0	1	3.7	1	0.2	0
Caucasian	286	81.7	156	73.2	273	82.0	169	73.5	245	76.8	101	80.8	74	80.4	22	81.5	442	78.5	110
Total	350	62.2	213	37.8	333	59.1	230	40.9	319	56.7	125	22.2	92	16.3	27	4.8	563		130

THOMAS JEFFERSON SCHOOL OF LAW (Provisional)

GPA & LSAT Scores

	Full Time	Part Time	Total
# of apps	1,254	144	1,398
# admits	898	95	993
# of matrics	174	61	235
75% GPA	3.12	3.19	
25% GPA	2.45	2.50	
75% LSAT	155	153	
25% LSAT	145	145	

Tuition & Fees

	Resident	Non-resident
Full-Time	$18,880	$18,880
Part-Time	$11,680	$11,680

Living Expenses

Estimated living expenses for Singles		
Living on campus	Living off campus	Living at home
N/A	$13,525	$8,935

Employment

	Total	%
Employment status known	112	64.4
Employment status unknown	62	35.6
Employed	83	74.1
Pursuing graduate degrees	2	1.8
Unemployed seeking employment	11	9.8
Unemployed not seeking employment	16	14.3
Type of Employment		
# employed in law firms	43	51.8
# employed in business & industry	22	26.5
# employed in government	11	13.3
# employed in public interest	2	2.4
# employed as judicial clerks	1	1.2
# employed in academia	2	2.4
Geographic Location		
# employed in state	66	79.5
# employed in foreign countries	1	1.2
# of states where employed	8	

Grants/Scholarships

	Full-time		Part-time		Total	
	#	%	#	%	#	%
Total # of Students	333		230		563	
Total # receiving grants	115	34.5	112	48.7	227	40.3
Less than 1/2 tuition	101	30.3	98	42.6	199	35.3
Half to full tuition	11	3.3	10	4.3	21	3.7
Full tuition	3	0.9	4	1.7	7	1.2
More than full tuition	0	0.0	0	0.0	0	0.0
Median Grant Amount	$4,061		$2,831			

Informational & Library Resources

# of volumes & volume equivalents	121,180	# of professional staff	9
# of titles	16,796	Hours per week with professional staff	81
# of active serial subscriptions	4,102	Hours per week without professional staff	14
Study seating capacity inside the library	283	# of student computer work stations for entire law school	37
Square feet of law library	17,588	# of additional networked connections	2
Square feet of law school (excl. Library)	49,412	Require Laptop Computer?	N

J.D. Attrition (from Prior Year)

	Academic	Other	TOTALS	
	#	#	#	%
1st Year	54	40	94	32%
2nd Year	4	11	15	14%
3rd Year	2	3	5	4.3%
4th Year	0	2	2	3.3%

Bar Passage Rates

Jurisdiction	California		
Exam	Sum 97	Win 98	Total
# from school taking bar for the first time	61	56	117
School's pass rate for all first-time takers	46%	39%	43%
State's pass rate for all first-time takers	75%	57%	71%

THOMAS M. COOLEY LAW SCHOOL

217 South Capitol Avenue
P.O. Box 13038
Lansing, MI 48901
(517)371-5140
http://www.cooley.edu

ABA Approved Since 1975

The Basics

Type of School: Private Term: Semester
Application deadline: Rolling
Application fee: $50
Financial Aid deadline: Rolling
Can first year start other than Fall? No
Student faculty ratio: 21.8 to 1
Does the University offer:
- housing restricted to law students? No
- graduate student housing for which law students are eligible? No

Faculty & Administrators

	Total		Men		Women		Minorities	
	Fall	Spr	Fall	Spr	Fall	Spr	Fall	Spr
Full-time	48	46	35	34	13	12	4	5
Other Full-Time	3	3	0	0	3	3	0	0
Deans, librarians, & others who teach > 1/2	0	0	0	0	0	0	0	0
Part-time	90	77	62	53	28	24	4	4
Total	141	126	97	87	44	39	8	9
Deans, librarians, & others who teach < 1/2	7	7	4	4	3	3	0	0

Curriculum

	Full time	Part time
Typical first-year section size	0	54
Is there typically a "small section" of the first year class, other than Legal Writing, taught by full-time faculty?	No	No
If yes, typical size offered last year	N/A	N/A
# of classroom course titles beyond 1st year curriculum	0	87
# of upper division courses, excluding seminars, with an enrollment:		
Under 25	0	215
25 - 49	0	49
50 - 74	0	23
75 - 99	0	21
100 +	0	11
# of seminars	0	141
# of seminar positions available	2,427	
# of seminar positions filled	0	1,846
# of positions available in simulation courses	1,258	
# of simulation positions filled	0	1,002
# of positions available in faculty supervised clinical courses	74	
# of fac. sup. clin. positions filled	0	71
# involved in field placements	0	239
# involved in law journals	0	147
# in moot court or trial competitions	0	96
# of credit hrs required to graduate	90	

J.D. Enrollment & Ethnicity

	Men		Women		Fl-Time		Pt-Time		1st Yr		2nd Yr		3rd Yr		4th Yr		Total		JD Degrees Awarded
	#	%	#	%	#	%	#	%	#	%	#	%	#	%	#	%	#	%	
African-American	120	12.6	156	21.1	73	18.0	203	15.8	203	21.8	50	12.0	23	6.6	0	0.0	276	16.3	30
American Indian	9	0.9	10	1.4	4	1.0	15	1.2	13	1.4	3	0.7	3	0.9	0	0.0	19	1.1	3
Asian American	36	3.8	31	4.2	17	4.2	50	3.9	49	5.3	8	1.9	10	2.9	0	0.0	67	4.0	5
Mexican American	26	2.7	13	1.8	10	2.5	29	2.3	30	3.2	7	1.7	2	0.6	0	0.0	39	2.3	3
Puerto Rican	4	0.4	6	0.8	3	0.7	7	0.5	8	0.9	1	0.2	1	0.3	0	0.0	10	0.6	0
Hispanic American	14	1.5	17	2.3	10	2.5	21	1.6	21	2.3	5	1.2	5	1.4	0	0.0	31	1.8	4
Total Minorities	209	21.9	233	31.5	117	28.8	325	25.3	324	34.8	74	17.8	44	12.7	0	0.0	442	26.1	45
Foreign Nationals	22	2.3	17	2.3	18	4.4	21	1.6	25	2.7	8	1.9	6	1.7	0	0.0	39	2.3	6
Caucasian	723	75.8	489	66.2	271	66.7	941	73.1	583	62.6	333	80.2	296	85.5	0	0.0	1212	71.6	344
Total	954	56.3	739	43.7	406	24.0	1287	76.0	932	55.1	415	24.5	346	20.4	0	0.0	1693		395

GPA & LSAT Scores

	Full Time	Part Time	Total
# of apps	1,335	1,566	2,901
# admits	1,137	1,276	2,413
# of matrics	386	493	879
75% GPA	3.20	3.20	
25% GPA	2.66	2.63	
75% LSAT	145	147	
25% LSAT	139	139	

Tuition & Fees

	Resident	Non-resident
Full-Time	$16,015	$16,015
Part-Time	$12,820	$12,820

Living Expenses

Estimated living expenses for Singles		
Living on campus	Living off campus	Living at home
N/A	$11,103	$5,743

Employment

	Total	%
Employment status known	297	76.9
Employment status unknown	89	23.1
Employed	248	83.5
Pursuing graduate degrees	12	4.0
Unemployed seeking employment	37	12.5
Unemployed not seeking employment	0	0.0
Type of Employment		
# employed in law firms	146	58.9
# employed in business & industry	31	12.5
# employed in government	38	15.3
# employed in public interest	12	4.8
# employed as judicial clerks	18	7.3
# employed in academia	3	1.2
Geographic Location		
# employed in state	107	43.1
# employed in foreign countries	0	0.0
# of states where employed	32	

Grants/Scholarships

	Full-time		Part-time		Total	
	#	%	#	%	#	%
Total # of Students	406		1287		1693	
Total # receiving grants	92	22.7	286	22.2	378	22.3
Less than 1/2 tuition	66	16.3	212	16.5	278	16.4
Half to full tuition	17	4.2	64	5.0	81	4.8
Full tuition	9	2.2	10	0.8	19	1.1
More than full tuition	0	0.0	0	0.0	0	0.0
Median Grant Amount	$2,163		$824			

Informational & Library Resources

# of volumes & volume equivalents	395,151	# of professional staff	8
# of titles	75,868	Hours per week with professional staff	80
# of active serial subscriptions	5,229	Hours per week without professional staff	40
Study seating capacity inside the library	530	# of student computer work stations for entire law school	69
Square feet of law library	65,000	# of additional networked connections	0
Square feet of law school (excl. Library)	149,924	Require Laptop Computer?	N

J.D. Attrition (from Prior Year)

	Academic	Other	TOTALS	
	#	#	#	%
1st Year	92	156	248	34%
2nd Year	63	162	225	44%
3rd Year	1	2	3	0.9%
4th Year	0	0	0	0.0%

Bar Passage Rates

Jurisdiction	Michigan			Florida		
Exam	Sum 97	Win 98	Total	Sum 97	Win 98	Total
# from school taking bar for the first time	64	99	163	18	31	49
School's pass rate for all first-time takers	84%	85%	85%	83%	74%	78%
State's pass rate for all first-time takers	89%	79%	86%	84%	82%	83%

TOLEDO, UNIVERSITY OF

2801 West Bancroft
Toledo, OH 43606
(419)530-2882
http://www.utoledo.edu/law

ABA Approved Since 1939

The Basics

Type of School: Public   Term: Semester

Application deadline: 03/15

Application fee: $30

Financial Aid deadline: 04/01

Can first year start other than Fall? No

Student faculty ratio: 16.6 to 1

Does the University offer:
- housing restricted to law students? No
- graduate student housing for which law students are eligible? No

Faculty & Administrators

	Total		Men		Women		Minorities	
	Fall	Spr	Fall	Spr	Fall	Spr	Fall	Spr
Full-time	26	27	17	18	9	9	3	3
Other Full-Time	3	3	0	0	3	3	0	0
Deans, librarians, & others who teach > 1/2	1	1	1	1	0	0	0	0
Part-time	11	12	7	7	4	4	0	0
Total	41	43	25	26	16	16	3	3
Deans, librarians, & others who teach < 1/2	2	2	2	2	0	0	0	0

Curriculum

	Full time	Part time
Typical first-year section size	55	42
Is there typically a "small section" of the first year class, other than Legal Writing, taught by full-time faculty?	No	No
If yes, typical size offered last year	N/A	N/A
# of classroom course titles beyond 1st year curriculum	51	46
# of upper division courses, excluding seminars, with an enrollment:		
Under 25	41	16
25 - 49	11	13
50 - 74	6	6
75 - 99	5	1
100 +	0	0
# of seminars	8	3
# of seminar positions available	170	
# of seminar positions filled	73	30
# of positions available in simulation courses	174	
# of simulation positions filled	151	29
# of positions available in faculty supervised clinical courses	110	
# of fac. sup. clin. positions filled	87	13
# involved in field placements	15	1
# involved in law journals	51	7
# in moot court or trial competitions	36	2
# of credit hrs required to graduate	89	

J.D. Enrollment & Ethnicity

	Men		Women		Fl-Time		Pt-Time		1st Yr		2nd Yr		3rd Yr		4th Yr		Total		JD Degrees Awarded
	#	%	#	%	#	%	#	%	#	%	#	%	#	%	#	%	#	%	
African-American	17	5.7	7	2.8	18	4.0	6	6.3	13	6.0	5	3.4	4	2.5	2	7.7	24	4.4	8
American Indian	5	1.7	1	0.4	4	0.9	2	2.1	2	0.9	2	1.3	1	0.6	1	3.8	6	1.1	0
Asian American	2	0.7	6	2.4	7	1.5	1	1.1	1	0.5	4	2.7	2	1.3	1	3.8	8	1.5	2
Mexican American	3	1.0	1	0.4	3	0.7	1	1.1	2	0.9	2	1.3	0	0.0	0	0.0	4	0.7	2
Puerto Rican	0	0.0	1	0.4	1	0.2	0	0.0	0	0.0	1	0.7	0	0.0	0	0.0	1	0.2	2
Hispanic American	2	0.7	1	0.4	3	0.7	0	0.0	1	0.5	0	0.0	2	1.3	0	0.0	3	0.5	2
Total Minorities	29	9.7	17	6.8	36	7.9	10	10.5	19	8.8	14	9.4	9	5.7	4	15.4	46	8.4	16
Foreign Nationals	0	0.0	0	0.0	0	0.0	0	0.0	0	0.0	0	0.0	0	0.0	0	0.0	0	0.0	0
Caucasian	271	90.3	233	93.2	419	92.1	85	89.5	197	91.2	135	90.6	150	94.3	22	84.6	504	91.6	144
Total	300	54.5	250	45.5	455	82.7	95	17.3	216	39.3	149	27.1	159	28.9	26	4.7	550		160

GPA & LSAT Scores

	Full Time	Part Time	Total
# of apps	515	80	595
# admits	346	50	396
# of matrics	130	36	166
75% GPA	3.34	3.36	
25% GPA	2.69	2.81	
75% LSAT	156	154	
25% LSAT	146	146	

Tuition & Fees

	Resident	Non-resident
Full-Time	$7,350	$14,173
Part-Time	$6,125	$11,811

Living Expenses

Estimated living expenses for Singles		
Living on campus	Living off campus	Living at home
N/A	$6,039	$2,625

Grants/Scholarships

	Full-time		Part-time		Total	
	#	%	#	%	#	%
Total # of Students	455		95		550	
Total # receiving grants	132	29.0	20	21.1	152	27.6
Less than 1/2 tuition	44	9.7	20	21.1	64	11.6
Half to full tuition	2	0.4	0	0.0	2	0.4
Full tuition	61	13.4	0	0.0	61	11.1
More than full tuition	25	5.5	0	0.0	25	4.5
Median Grant Amount	$7,350		$2,000			

Informational & Library Resources

# of volumes & volume equivalents	310,904	# of professional staff	5
# of titles	45,344	Hours per week with professional staff	76
# of active serial subscriptions	3,196	Hours per week without professional staff	37
Study seating capacity inside the library	489	# of student computer work stations for entire law school	88
Square feet of law library	41,900	# of additional networked connections	48
Square feet of law school (excl. Library)	59,972	Require Laptop Computer?	N

Employment

	Total	%
Employment status known	166	82.2
Employment status unknown	36	17.8
Employed	154	92.8
Pursuing graduate degrees	3	1.8
Unemployed seeking employment	6	3.6
Unemployed not seeking employment	3	1.8
Type of Employment		
# employed in law firms	76	49.4
# employed in business & industry	34	22.1
# employed in government	30	19.5
# employed in public interest	2	1.3
# employed as judicial clerks	9	5.8
# employed in academia	3	1.9
Geographic Location		
# employed in state	91	59.1
# employed in foreign countries	1	0.6
# of states where employed	12	

J.D. Attrition (from Prior Year)

	Academic	Other	TOTALS	
	#	#	#	%
1st Year	11	28	39	20%
2nd Year	0	9	9	4.7%
3rd Year	1	2	3	1.9%
4th Year	0	0	0	0.0%

Bar Passage Rates

Jurisdiction	Ohio			Michigan		
Exam	Sum 97	Win 98	Total	Sum 97	Win 98	Total
# from school taking bar for the first time	92	31	123	42	16	58
School's pass rate for all first-time takers	67%	74%	69%	74%	75%	74%
State's pass rate for all first-time takers	79%	75%	78%	89%	79%	86%

TOURO COLLEGE

Jacob D. Fuchsberg Law Center
300 Nassau Road
Huntington, NY 11743
(516)421-2244
http://www.tourolaw.edu

ABA Approved Since 1983

The Basics

Type of School: Private   Term: Semester

Application deadline: 05/01

Application fee: $50

Financial Aid deadline: 04/15

Can first year start other than Fall? No

Student faculty ratio: 16.3 to 1

Does the University offer:
- housing restricted to law students? Yes
- graduate student housing for which law students are eligible? No

Faculty & Administrators

	Total		Men		Women		Minorities	
	Fall	Spr	Fall	Spr	Fall	Spr	Fall	Spr
Full-time	31	30	21	20	10	10	2	2
Other Full-Time	1	1	1	1	0	0	0	0
Deans, librarians, & others who teach > 1/2	3	3	1	1	2	2	0	0
Part-time	12	15	10	11	2	4	0	0
Total	47	49	33	33	14	16	2	2
Deans, librarians, & others who teach < 1/2	1	1	1	1	0	0	0	0

Curriculum

	Full time	Part time
Typical first-year section size	80	52
Is there typically a "small section" of the first year class, other than Legal Writing, taught by full-time faculty?	Yes	Yes
If yes, typical size offered last year	52	44
# of classroom course titles beyond 1st year curriculum	51	39
# of upper division courses, excluding seminars, with an enrollment:		
Under 25	37	18
25 - 49	21	9
50 - 74	9	6
75 - 99	4	6
100 +	1	0
# of seminars	8	5
# of seminar positions available	260	
# of seminar positions filled	145	99
# of positions available in simulation courses	360	
# of simulation positions filled	182	130
# of positions available in faculty supervised clinical courses	167	
# of fac. sup. clin. positions filled	128	24
# involved in field placements	84	11
# involved in law journals	44	24
# in moot court or trial competitions	21	6
# of credit hrs required to graduate	87	

J.D. Enrollment & Ethnicity

	Men		Women		Fl-Time		Pt-Time		1st Yr		2nd Yr		3rd Yr		4th Yr		Total		JD Degrees Awarded
	#	%	#	%	#	%	#	%	#	%	#	%	#	%	#	%	#	%	
African-American	27	7.2	62	18.8	40	11.5	49	13.6	31	13.4	28	13.9	19	9.3	11	15.7	89	12.6	29
American Indian	0	0.0	1	0.3	0	0.0	1	0.3	0	0.0	0	0.0	0	0.0	1	1.4	1	0.1	0
Asian American	16	4.2	22	6.7	28	8.0	10	2.8	13	5.6	13	6.5	10	4.9	2	2.9	38	5.4	14
Mexican American	0	0.0	0	0.0	0	0.0	0	0.0	0	0.0	0	0.0	0	0.0	0	0.0	0	0.0	0
Puerto Rican	0	0.0	0	0.0	0	0.0	0	0.0	0	0.0	0	0.0	0	0.0	0	0.0	0	0.0	0
Hispanic American	17	4.5	26	7.9	16	4.6	27	7.5	13	5.6	9	4.5	13	6.3	8	11.4	43	6.1	9
Total Minorities	60	15.9	111	33.6	84	24.1	87	24.2	57	24.7	50	24.9	42	20.5	22	31.4	171	24.2	52
Foreign Nationals	0	0.0	0	0.0	0	0.0	0	0.0	0	0.0	0	0.0	0	0.0	0	0.0	0	0.0	0
Caucasian	317	84.1	219	66.4	264	75.9	272	75.8	174	75.3	151	75.1	163	79.5	48	68.6	536	75.8	179
Total	377	53.3	330	46.7	348	49.2	359	50.8	231	32.7	201	28.4	205	29.0	70	9.9	707		231

GPA & LSAT Scores

	Full Time	Part Time	Total
# of apps	1,160	456	1,616
# admits	618	181	799
# of matrics	141	102	243
75% GPA	3.20	3.31	
25% GPA	2.73	2.69	
75% LSAT	151	153	
25% LSAT	144	144	

Tuition & Fees

	Resident	Non-resident
Full-Time	$20,370	$20,370
Part-Time	$15,900	$15,900

Living Expenses

Estimated living expenses for Singles		
Living on campus	Living off campus	Living at home
$16,003	$16,003	$8,433

Employment

	Total	%
Employment status known	209	86.0
Employment status unknown	34	14.0
Employed	168	80.4
Pursuing graduate degrees	2	1.0
Unemployed seeking employment	37	17.7
Unemployed not seeking employment	2	1.0
Type of Employment		
# employed in law firms	94	56.0
# employed in business & industry	29	17.3
# employed in government	30	17.9
# employed in public interest	8	4.8
# employed as judicial clerks	2	1.2
# employed in academia	3	1.8
Geographic Location		
# employed in state	151	89.9
# employed in foreign countries	3	1.8
# of states where employed	7	

Grants/Scholarships

	Full-time		Part-time		Total	
	#	%	#	%	#	%
Total # of Students	348		359		707	
Total # receiving grants	178	51.1	113	31.5	291	41.2
Less than 1/2 tuition	143	41.1	92	25.6	235	33.2
Half to full tuition	25	7.2	18	5.0	43	6.1
Full tuition	5	1.4	3	0.8	8	1.1
More than full tuition	5	1.4	0	0.0	5	0.7
Median Grant Amount	$3,500		$3,500			

Informational & Library Resources

# of volumes & volume equivalents	372,717	# of professional staff	7
# of titles	57,914	Hours per week with professional staff	76
# of active serial subscriptions	3,411	Hours per week without professional staff	10
Study seating capacity inside the library	380	# of student computer work stations for entire law school	37
Square feet of law library	27,950	# of additional networked connections	24
Square feet of law school (excl. Library)	93,050	Require Laptop Computer?	N

J.D. Attrition (from Prior Year)

	Academic	Other	TOTALS	
	#	#	#	%
1st Year	10	32	42	19%
2nd Year	5	5	10	5.2%
3rd Year	0	0	0	0.0%
4th Year	0	0	0	0.0%

Bar Passage Rates

Jurisdiction	New York		
Exam	Sum 97	Win 98	Total
# from school taking bar for the first time	190	49	239
School's pass rate for all first-time takers	64%	43%	59%
State's pass rate for all first-time takers	78%	65%	76%

TULANE UNIVERSITY

6329 Freret Street
New Orleans, LA 70118-6231
(504)865-5939
http://www.law.tulane.edu

ABA Approved Since 1925

The Basics

Type of School: Private   Term: Semester

Application deadline: 05/01

Application fee: $45

Financial Aid deadline: 02/15

Can first year start other than Fall? No

Student faculty ratio: 20.6 to 1

Does the University offer:

- housing restricted to law students? No
- graduate student housing for which law students are eligible? No

Faculty & Administrators

	Total		Men		Women		Minorities	
	Fall	Spr	Fall	Spr	Fall	Spr	Fall	Spr
Full-time	38	37	30	28	8	9	3	3
Other Full-Time	7	7	2	2	5	5	0	0
Deans, librarians, & others who teach > 1/2	1	1	1	1	0	0	0	0
Part-time	61	61	42	50	18	9	2	2
Total	107	106	75	81	31	23	5	5
Deans, librarians, & others who teach < 1/2	6	6	4	4	2	2	0	0

Curriculum

	Full time	Part time
Typical first-year section size	93	0
Is there typically a "small section" of the first year class, other than Legal Writing, taught by full-time faculty?	Yes	No
If yes, typical size offered last year	38	N/A
# of classroom course titles beyond 1st year curriculum	190	0
# of upper division courses, excluding seminars, with an enrollment:		
Under 25	77	0
25 - 49	65	0
50 - 74	27	0
75 - 99	9	0
100 +	11	0
# of seminars	21	0
# of seminar positions available	528	
# of seminar positions filled	494	0
# of positions available in simulation courses	331	
# of simulation positions filled	329	0
# of positions available in faculty supervised clinical courses	127	
# of fac. sup. clin. positions filled	116	0
# involved in field placements	30	0
# involved in law journals	248	0
# in moot court or trial competitions	69	0
# of credit hrs required to graduate	88	

J.D. Enrollment & Ethnicity

	Men		Women		Fl-Time		Pt-Time		1st Yr		2nd Yr		3rd Yr		4th Yr		Total		JD Degrees Awarded
	#	%	#	%	#	%	#	%	#	%	#	%	#	%	#	%	#	%	
African-American	24	4.8	48	10.9	72	7.7	0	0.0	26	7.5	27	9.2	19	6.3	0	0.0	72	7.6	31
American Indian	1	0.2	2	0.5	3	0.3	0	0.0	1	0.3	0	0.0	2	0.7	0	0.0	3	0.3	3
Asian American	20	4.0	24	5.4	43	4.6	1	50.0	13	3.8	19	6.4	12	4.0	0	0.0	44	4.7	19
Mexican American	3	0.6	3	0.7	6	0.6	0	0.0	0	0.0	2	0.7	4	1.3	0	0.0	6	0.6	3
Puerto Rican	6	1.2	8	1.8	13	1.4	1	50.0	8	2.3	2	0.7	4	1.3	0	0.0	14	1.5	3
Hispanic American	13	2.6	22	5.0	35	3.7	0	0.0	6	1.7	17	5.8	12	4.0	0	0.0	35	3.7	8
Total Minorities	67	13.3	107	24.3	172	18.3	2	100.0	54	15.7	67	22.7	53	17.5	0	0.0	174	18.5	67
Foreign Nationals	3	0.6	9	2.0	12	1.3	0	0.0	2	0.6	7	2.4	3	1.0	0	0.0	12	1.3	6
Caucasian	432	86.1	325	73.7	757	80.4	0	0.0	289	83.8	221	74.9	247	81.5	0	0.0	757	80.3	276
Total	502	53.2	441	46.8	941	99.8	2	0.2	345	36.6	295	31.3	303	32.1	0	0.0	943		349

GPA & LSAT Scores

	Full Time	Part Time	Total
# of apps	2,266	1	2,267
# admits	1,193	1	1,194
# of matrics	347	0	347
75% GPA	3.53	0.00	
25% GPA	3.01	0.00	
75% LSAT	161	0	
25% LSAT	155	0	

Tuition & Fees

	Resident	Non-resident
Full-Time	$23,588	$23,588
Part-Time	$0	$0

Living Expenses

Estimated living expenses for Singles		
Living on campus	Living off campus	Living at home
$11,540	$11,540	$6,310

Grants/Scholarships

	Full-time		Part-time		Total	
	#	%	#	%	#	%
Total # of Students						
Total # receiving grants	408	43.4	0	0.0	408	43.3
Less than 1/2 tuition	248	26.4	0	0.0	248	26.3
Half to full tuition	147	15.6	0	0.0	147	15.6
Full tuition	7	0.7	0	0.0	7	0.7
More than full tuition	6	0.6	0	0.0	6	0.6
Median Grant Amount	$9,000		$0			

Informational & Library Resources

# of volumes & volume equivalents	491,091	# of professional staff	19
# of titles	207,984	Hours per week with professional staff	69
# of active serial subscriptions	4,669	Hours per week without professional staff	44
Study seating capacity inside the library	557	# of student computer work stations for entire law school	113
Square feet of law library	52,000	# of additional networked connections	32
Square feet of law school (excl. Library)	72,760	Require Laptop Computer?	N

Employment

	Total	%
Employment status known	322	99.1
Employment status unknown	3	0.9
Employed	292	90.7
Pursuing graduate degrees	6	1.9
Unemployed seeking employment	17	5.3
Unemployed not seeking employment	7	2.2
Type of Employment		
# employed in law firms	183	62.7
# employed in business & industry	36	12.3
# employed in government	23	7.9
# employed in public interest	6	2.1
# employed as judicial clerks	34	11.6
# employed in academia	1	0.3
Geographic Location		
# employed in state	93	31.8
# employed in foreign countries	6	2.1
# of states where employed	31	

J.D. Attrition (from Prior Year)

	Academic	Other	TOTALS	
	#	#	#	%
1st Year	3	24	27	8.9%
2nd Year	5	3	8	2.5%
3rd Year	0	0	0	0.0%
4th Year	0	0	0	0.0%

Bar Passage Rates

Jurisdiction	Louisiana			New York		
Exam	Sum 97	Win 98	Total	Sum 97	Win 98	Total
# from school taking bar for the first time	99	25	124	49	3	52
School's pass rate for all first-time takers	72%	68%	71%	82%	100%	83%
State's pass rate for all first-time takers	62%	54%	61%	78%	65%	76%

TULSA, UNIVERSITY OF

3120 East Fourth Place
Tulsa, OK 74104
(918)631-2401
http://www.utulsa.edu/law

ABA Approved Since 1950

The Basics

Type of School: Private   Term: Semester
Application deadline: 08/15
Application fee: $0
Financial Aid deadline: Rolling
Can first year start other than Fall? Yes
Student faculty ratio: 16.7 to 1
Does the University offer:
- housing restricted to law students? No
- graduate student housing for which law students are eligible? Yes

Faculty & Administrators

	Total		Men		Women		Minorities	
	Fall	Spr	Fall	Spr	Fall	Spr	Fall	Spr
Full-time	27	26	16	15	11	11	6	7
Other Full-Time	0	0	0	0	0	0	0	0
Deans, librarians, & others who teach > 1/2	6	6	4	4	2	2	1	1
Part-time	28	32	21	22	7	10	0	1
Total	61	64	41	41	20	23	7	9
Deans, librarians, & others who teach < 1/2	1	1	1	1	0	0	0	0

Curriculum

	Full time	Part time
Typical first-year section size	66	66
Is there typically a "small section" of the first year class, other than Legal Writing, taught by full-time faculty?	Yes	Yes
If yes, typical size offered last year	30	30
# of classroom course titles beyond 1st year curriculum	87	36
# of upper division courses, excluding seminars, with an enrollment:		
Under 25	107	28
25 - 49	29	14
50 - 74	9	3
75 - 99	2	0
100 +	0	0
# of seminars	7	3
# of seminar positions available	166	
# of seminar positions filled	87	36
# of positions available in simulation courses	472	
# of simulation positions filled	279	112
# of positions available in faculty supervised clinical courses	40	
# of fac. sup. clin. positions filled	31	9
# involved in field placements	62	5
# involved in law journals	115	5
# in moot court or trial competitions	190	30
# of credit hrs required to graduate	88	

J.D. Enrollment & Ethnicity

	Men		Women		Fl-Time		Pt-Time		1st Yr		2nd Yr		3rd Yr		4th Yr		Total		JD Degrees Awarded
	#	%	#	%	#	%	#	%	#	%	#	%	#	%	#	%	#	%	
African-American	9	2.7	10	3.9	13	2.8	6	4.8	9	5.1	8	4.0	2	1.1	0	0.0	19	3.3	3
American Indian	25	7.6	26	10.2	34	7.4	17	13.7	15	8.5	15	7.5	16	9.0	5	16.7	51	8.7	10
Asian American	12	3.6	5	2.0	15	3.3	2	1.6	9	5.1	4	2.0	4	2.2	0	0.0	17	2.9	6
Mexican American	14	4.3	7	2.8	17	3.7	4	3.2	9	5.1	5	2.5	7	3.9	0	0.0	21	3.6	1
Puerto Rican	0	0.0	0	0.0	0	0.0	0	0.0	0	0.0	0	0.0	0	0.0	0	0.0	0	0.0	0
Hispanic American	0	0.0	0	0.0	0	0.0	0	0.0	0	0.0	0	0.0	0	0.0	0	0.0	0	0.0	0
Total Minorities	60	18.2	48	18.9	79	17.2	29	23.4	42	23.9	32	16.1	29	16.3	5	16.7	108	18.5	20
Foreign Nationals	1	0.3	5	2.0	5	1.1	1	0.8	1	0.6	4	2.0	1	0.6	0	0.0	6	1.0	0
Caucasian	268	81.5	201	79.1	375	81.7	94	75.8	133	75.6	162	81.4	149	83.7	25	83.3	469	80.4	154
Total	329	56.4	254	43.6	459	78.7	124	21.3	176	30.2	199	34.1	178	30.5	30	5.1	583		174

GPA & LSAT Scores

	Full Time	Part Time	Total
# of apps	711	81	792
# admits	473	51	524
# of matrics	171	30	201
75% GPA	3.20	3.33	
25% GPA	2.61	2.62	
75% LSAT	153	154	
25% LSAT	144	145	

Tuition & Fees

	Resident	Non-resident
Full-Time	$16,064	$16,064
Part-Time	$10,864	$10,864

Living Expenses

Estimated living expenses for Singles		
Living on campus	Living off campus	Living at home
$8,400	$8,710	$5,810

Grants/Scholarships

	Full-time		Part-time		Total	
	#	%	#	%	#	%
Total # of Students	459		124		583	
Total # receiving grants	167	36.4	39	31.5	206	35.3
Less than 1/2 tuition	111	24.2	25	20.2	136	23.3
Half to full tuition	39	8.5	9	7.3	48	8.2
Full tuition	17	3.7	5	4.0	22	3.8
More than full tuition	0	0.0	0	0.0	0	0.0
Median Grant Amount	$4,000		$2,200			

Informational & Library Resources

# of volumes & volume equivalents	270,325	# of professional staff	8
# of titles	49,965	Hours per week with professional staff	61
# of active serial subscriptions	3,842	Hours per week without professional staff	46
Study seating capacity inside the library	446	# of student computer work stations for entire law school	68
Square feet of law library	32,849	# of additional networked connections	0
Square feet of law school (excl. Library)	46,520	Require Laptop Computer?	N

Employment

	Total	%
Employment status known	193	99.0
Employment status unknown	2	1.0
Employed	161	83.4
Pursuing graduate degrees	6	3.1
Unemployed seeking employment	24	12.4
Unemployed not seeking employment	2	1.0
Type of Employment		
# employed in law firms	97	60.2
# employed in business & industry	33	20.5
# employed in government	24	14.9
# employed in public interest	1	0.6
# employed as judicial clerks	5	3.1
# employed in academia	1	0.6
Geographic Location		
# employed in state	92	57.1
# employed in foreign countries	2	1.2
# of states where employed	26	

J.D. Attrition (from Prior Year)

	Academic	Other	TOTALS	
	#	#	#	%
1st Year	0	3	3	1.6%
2nd Year	10	2	12	6.1%
3rd Year	0	0	0	0.0%
4th Year	0	0	0	0.0%

Bar Passage Rates

Jurisdiction	Oklahoma		
Exam	Sum 97	Win 98	Total
# from school taking bar for the first time	61	26	87
School's pass rate for all first-time takers	79%	92%	83%
State's pass rate for all first-time takers	81%	87%	82%

UTAH, UNIVERSITY OF

332 South 1400 East Front
Salt Lake City, UT 84112-0730
(801)581-6833
http://info.law.utah.edu

ABA Approved Since 1927

The Basics

Type of School: Public   Term: Semester

Application deadline: 02/01

Application fee: $40

Financial Aid deadline: 02/15

Can first year start other than Fall? No

Student faculty ratio: 14.5 to 1

Does the University offer:
- housing restricted to law students? No
- graduate student housing for which law students are eligible? Yes

Faculty & Administrators

	Total		Men		Women		Minorities	
	Fall	Spr	Fall	Spr	Fall	Spr	Fall	Spr
Full-time	20	20	16	16	4	4	5	4
Other Full-Time	2	2	1	1	1	1	0	0
Deans, librarians, & others who teach > 1/2	4	4	2	2	2	2	0	0
Part-time	7	21	5	15	2	6	0	0
Total	33	47	24	34	9	13	5	4
Deans, librarians, & others who teach < 1/2	7	7	3	3	4	4	0	0

Curriculum

	Full time	Part time
Typical first-year section size	40	0
Is there typically a "small section" of the first year class, other than Legal Writing, taught by full-time faculty?	No	No
If yes, typical size offered last year	N/A	N/A
# of classroom course titles beyond 1st year curriculum	103	0
# of upper division courses, excluding seminars, with an enrollment:		
Under 25	55	0
25 - 49	17	0
50 - 74	5	0
75 - 99	0	0
100 +	0	0
# of seminars	15	0
# of seminar positions available	225	
# of seminar positions filled	157	0
# of positions available in simulation courses	311	
# of simulation positions filled	311	0
# of positions available in faculty supervised clinical courses	0	
# of fac. sup. clin. positions filled	124	0
# involved in field placements	0	0
# involved in law journals	75	0
# in moot court or trial competitions	192	0
# of credit hrs required to graduate	88	

J.D. Enrollment & Ethnicity

	Men		Women		Fl-Time		Pt-Time		1st Yr		2nd Yr		3rd Yr		4th Yr		Total		JD Degrees Awarded
	#	%	#	%	#	%	#	%	#	%	#	%	#	%	#	%	#	%	
African-American	5	2.2	0	0.0	5	1.4	0	0.0	2	1.7	3	2.4	0	0.0	0	0.0	5	1.4	0
American Indian	0	0.0	3	2.4	3	0.9	0	0.0	1	0.8	0	0.0	2	1.9	0	0.0	3	0.9	2
Asian American	8	3.6	6	4.8	14	4.0	0	0.0	5	4.2	5	4.0	4	3.8	0	0.0	14	4.0	10
Mexican American	5	2.2	3	2.4	8	2.3	0	0.0	1	0.8	5	4.0	2	1.9	0	0.0	8	2.3	0
Puerto Rican	0	0.0	1	0.8	1	0.3	0	0.0	0	0.0	1	0.8	0	0.0	0	0.0	1	0.3	0
Hispanic American	6	2.7	9	7.1	15	4.3	0	0.0	4	3.4	7	5.6	4	3.8	0	0.0	15	4.3	2
Total Minorities	24	10.8	22	17.5	46	13.2	0	0.0	13	10.9	21	16.8	12	11.4	0	0.0	46	13.2	14
Foreign Nationals	1	0.4	0	0.0	1	0.3	0	0.0	1	0.8	0	0.0	0	0.0	0	0.0	1	0.3	0
Caucasian	198	88.8	104	82.5	302	86.5	0	0.0	105	88.2	104	83.2	93	88.6	0	0.0	302	86.5	112
Total	223	63.9	126	36.1	349	100.0	0	0.0	119	34.1	125	35.8	105	30.1	0	0.0	349		126

GPA & LSAT Scores

	Full Time	Part Time	Total
# of apps	742	0	742
# admits	302	0	302
# of matrics	123	0	123
75% GPA	3.76	0.00	
25% GPA	3.19	0.00	
75% LSAT	162	0	
25% LSAT	155	0	

Tuition & Fees

	Resident	Non-resident
Full-Time	$4,607	$10,249
Part-Time	$0	$0

Living Expenses

Estimated living expenses for Singles		
Living on campus	Living off campus	Living at home
$10,041	$10,041	$8,370

Grants/Scholarships

	Full-time		Part-time		Total	
	#	%	#	%	#	%
Total # of Students	349		0		349	
Total # receiving grants	129	37.0	0	0.0	129	37.0
Less than 1/2 tuition	87	24.9	0	0.0	87	24.9
Half to full tuition	15	4.3	0	0.0	15	4.3
Full tuition	3	0.9	0	0.0	3	0.9
More than full tuition	24	6.9	0	0.0	24	6.9
Median Grant Amount	$3,039		$0			

Informational & Library Resources

# of volumes & volume equivalents	299,544	# of professional staff	7
# of titles	102,772	Hours per week with professional staff	58
# of active serial subscriptions	4,596	Hours per week without professional staff	42
Study seating capacity inside the library	356	# of student computer work stations for entire law school	61
Square feet of law library	38,895	# of additional networked connections	661
Square feet of law school (excl. Library)	53,982	Require Laptop Computer?	N

Employment

	Total	%
Employment status known	124	96.9
Employment status unknown	4	3.1
Employed	118	95.2
Pursuing graduate degrees	3	2.4
Unemployed seeking employment	0	0.0
Unemployed not seeking employment	3	2.4
Type of Employment		
# employed in law firms	57	48.3
# employed in business & industry	19	16.1
# employed in government	11	9.3
# employed in public interest	6	5.1
# employed as judicial clerks	20	16.9
# employed in academia	3	2.5
Geographic Location		
# employed in state	82	69.5
# employed in foreign countries	0	0.0
# of states where employed	13	

J.D. Attrition (from Prior Year)

	Academic	Other	TOTALS	
	#	#	#	%
1st Year	0	6	6	4.8%
2nd Year	0	4	4	4.0%
3rd Year	0	0	0	0.0%
4th Year	0	0	0	0.0%

Bar Passage Rates

Jurisdiction	Utah		
Exam	Sum 97	Win 98	Total
# from school taking bar for the first time	71	14	85
School's pass rate for all first-time takers	90%	93%	91%
State's pass rate for all first-time takers	93%	92%	93%

VALPARAISO UNIVERSITY

Valparaiso, IN 46383
(219)465-7829
http://www.valpo.edu/law/

ABA Approved Since 1929

The Basics

Type of School: Private Term: Semester

Application deadline: 04/15

Application fee: $30

Financial Aid deadline: 03/01

Can first year start other than Fall? No

Student faculty ratio: 18.6 to 1

Does the University offer:
- housing restricted to law students? No
- graduate student housing for which law students are eligible? No

Faculty & Administrators

	Total		Men		Women		Minorities	
	Fall	Spr	Fall	Spr	Fall	Spr	Fall	Spr
Full-time	18	16	12	12	6	4	2	2
Other Full-Time	3	3	2	2	1	1	0	0
Deans, librarians, & others who teach > 1/2	2	2	1	1	1	1	0	0
Part-time	15	21	6	13	9	8	0	0
Total	38	42	21	28	17	14	2	2
Deans, librarians, & others who teach < 1/2	6	6	3	3	3	3	0	0

Curriculum

	Full time	Part time
Typical first-year section size	65	65
Is there typically a "small section" of the first year class, other than Legal Writing, taught by full-time faculty?	Yes	Yes
If yes, typical size offered last year	45	45
# of classroom course titles beyond 1st year curriculum	90	90
# of upper division courses, excluding seminars, with an enrollment:		
Under 25	71	71
25 - 49	19	19
50 - 74	6	6
75 - 99	5	5
100 +	1	1
# of seminars	10	10
# of seminar positions available	125	
# of seminar positions filled	112	5
# of positions available in simulation courses	867	
# of simulation positions filled	694	29
# of positions available in faculty supervised clinical courses	86	
# of fac. sup. clin. positions filled	79	0
# involved in field placements	61	2
# involved in law journals	39	0
# in moot court or trial competitions	52	2
# of credit hrs required to graduate	90	

J.D. Enrollment & Ethnicity

	Men		Women		Fl-Time		Pt-Time		1st Yr		2nd Yr		3rd Yr		4th Yr		Total		JD Degrees Awarded
	#	%	#	%	#	%	#	%	#	%	#	%	#	%	#	%	#	%	
African-American	18	8.0	16	8.2	27	7.4	7	13.2	9	5.3	15	12.5	10	7.7	0	0.0	34	8.1	15
American Indian	2	0.9	1	0.5	3	0.8	0	0.0	1	0.6	1	0.8	1	0.8	0	0.0	3	0.7	2
Asian American	4	1.8	4	2.1	7	1.9	1	1.9	4	2.4	1	0.8	3	2.3	0	0.0	8	1.9	2
Mexican American	5	2.2	4	2.1	7	1.9	2	3.8	2	1.2	5	4.2	2	1.5	0	0.0	9	2.1	2
Puerto Rican	2	0.9	1	0.5	3	0.8	0	0.0	1	0.6	0	0.0	2	1.5	0	0.0	3	0.7	2
Hispanic American	1	0.4	1	0.5	1	0.3	1	1.9	2	1.2	0	0.0	0	0.0	0	0.0	2	0.5	0
Total Minorities	32	14.2	27	13.8	48	13.1	11	20.8	19	11.2	22	18.3	18	13.8	0	0.0	59	14.0	23
Foreign Nationals	1	0.4	4	2.1	4	1.1	1	1.9	3	1.8	1	0.8	1	0.8	0	0.0	5	1.2	0
Caucasian	192	85.3	164	84.1	315	85.8	41	77.4	148	87.1	97	80.8	111	85.4	0	0.0	356	84.8	108
Total	225	53.6	195	46.4	367	87.4	53	12.6	170	40.5	120	28.6	130	31.0	0	0.0	420		131

GPA & LSAT Scores

	Full Time	Part Time	Total
# of apps	642	50	692
# admits	462	32	494
# of matrics	143	23	166
75% GPA	3.55	3.11	
25% GPA	2.92	2.45	
75% LSAT	157	151	
25% LSAT	148	143	

Tuition & Fees

	Resident	Non-resident
Full-Time	$17,580	$17,580
Part-Time	$13,450	$13,450

Living Expenses

Estimated living expenses for Singles		
Living on campus	Living off campus	Living at home
$4,880	$7,350	$2,250

Grants/Scholarships

	Full-time		Part-time		Total	
	#	%	#	%	#	%
Total # of Students	367		53		420	
Total # receiving grants	158	43.1	7	13.2	165	39.3
Less than 1/2 tuition	49	13.4	7	13.2	56	13.3
Half to full tuition	35	9.5	0	0.0	35	8.3
Full tuition	34	9.3	0	0.0	34	8.1
More than full tuition	40	10.9	0	0.0	40	9.5
Median Grant Amount	$8,550		$2,000			

Informational & Library Resources

# of volumes & volume equivalents	275,392	# of professional staff	6
# of titles	96,077	Hours per week with professional staff	65
# of active serial subscriptions	3,258	Hours per week without professional staff	48
Study seating capacity inside the library	347	# of student computer work stations for entire law school	58
Square feet of law library	29,370	# of additional networked connections	150
Square feet of law school (excl. Library)	49,825	Require Laptop Computer?	N

Employment

	Total	%
Employment status known	143	99.3
Employment status unknown	1	0.7
Employed	140	97.9
Pursuing graduate degrees	0	0.0
Unemployed seeking employment	2	1.4
Unemployed not seeking employment	1	0.7
Type of Employment		
# employed in law firms	72	51.4
# employed in business & industry	19	13.6
# employed in government	27	19.3
# employed in public interest	8	5.7
# employed as judicial clerks	13	9.3
# employed in academia	1	0.7
Geographic Location		
# employed in state	59	42.1
# employed in foreign countries	1	0.7
# of states where employed	17	

J.D. Attrition (from Prior Year)

	Academic	Other	TOTALS	
	#	#	#	%
1st Year	0	8	8	5.8%
2nd Year	6	23	29	21%
3rd Year	2	0	2	1.6%
4th Year	0	0	0	0.0%

Bar Passage Rates

Jurisdiction	Indiana			Illinois		
Exam	Sum 97	Win 98	Total	Sum 97	Win 98	Total
# from school taking bar for the first time	55	12	67	34	2	36
School's pass rate for all first-time takers	91%	100%	93%	88%	50%	86%
State's pass rate for all first-time takers	93%	92%	93%	87%	80%	85%

VANDERBILT UNIVERSITY

21st Avenue South
Nashville, TN 37240
(615)322-2615
http://www.vanderbilt.edu/law

ABA Approved Since 1925

The Basics

Type of School: Private Term: Semester

Application deadline: 03/01

Application fee: $50

Financial Aid deadline: 03/01

Can first year start other than Fall? No

Student faculty ratio: 15.9 to 1

Does the University offer:

- housing restricted to law students? No
- graduate student housing for which law students are eligible? Yes

Faculty & Administrators

	Total		Men		Women		Minorities	
	Fall	Spr	Fall	Spr	Fall	Spr	Fall	Spr
Full-time	29	29	23	23	6	6	3	1
Other Full-Time	0	0	0	0	0	0	0	0
Deans, librarians, & others who teach > 1/2	4	4	3	3	1	1	1	1
Part-time	19	21	10	13	9	8	2	0
Total	52	54	36	39	16	15	6	2
Deans, librarians, & others who teach < 1/2	0	0	0	0	0	0	0	0

Curriculum

	Full time	Part time
Typical first-year section size	94	0
Is there typically a "small section" of the first year class, other than Legal Writing, taught by full-time faculty?	No	No
If yes, typical size offered last year	N/A	N/A
# of classroom course titles beyond 1st year curriculum	97	0
# of upper division courses, excluding seminars, with an enrollment:		
Under 25	39	0
25 - 49	24	0
50 - 74	8	0
75 - 99	5	0
100 +	7	0
# of seminars	15	0
# of seminar positions available	244	
# of seminar positions filled	192	0
# of positions available in simulation courses	136	
# of simulation positions filled	118	0
# of positions available in faculty supervised clinical courses	64	
# of fac. sup. clin. positions filled	58	0
# involved in field placements	0	0
# involved in law journals	120	0
# in moot court or trial competitions	125	0
# of credit hrs required to graduate	88	

J.D. Enrollment & Ethnicity

	Men		Women		Fl-Time		Pt-Time		1st Yr		2nd Yr		3rd Yr		4th Yr		Total		JD Degrees Awarded
	#	%	#	%	#	%	#	%	#	%	#	%	#	%	#	%	#	%	
African-American	21	6.6	42	18.1	63	11.5	0	0.0	29	15.3	21	11.4	13	7.4	0	0.0	63	11.5	17
American Indian	0	0.0	0	0.0	0	0.0	0	0.0	0	0.0	0	0.0	0	0.0	0	0.0	0	0.0	1
Asian American	10	3.2	19	8.2	29	5.3	0	0.0	9	4.8	5	2.7	15	8.6	0	0.0	29	5.3	8
Mexican American	3	0.9	1	0.4	4	0.7	0	0.0	1	0.5	2	1.1	1	0.6	0	0.0	4	0.7	0
Puerto Rican	2	0.6	0	0.0	2	0.4	0	0.0	1	0.5	0	0.0	1	0.6	0	0.0	2	0.4	0
Hispanic American	1	0.3	4	1.7	5	0.9	0	0.0	2	1.1	2	1.1	1	0.6	0	0.0	5	0.9	2
Total Minorities	37	11.7	66	28.4	103	18.8	0	0.0	42	22.2	30	16.3	31	17.7	0	0.0	103	18.8	28
Foreign Nationals	21	6.6	12	5.2	33	6.0	0	0.0	13	6.9	8	4.3	12	6.9	0	0.0	33	6.0	1
Caucasian	258	81.6	154	66.4	412	75.2	0	0.0	134	70.9	146	79.3	132	75.4	0	0.0	412	75.2	152
Total	316	57.7	232	42.3	548	100.0	0	0.0	189	34.5	184	33.6	175	31.9	0	0.0	548		181

GPA & LSAT Scores

	Full Time	Part Time	Total
# of apps	2,222	0	2,222
# admits	718	0	718
# of matrics	190	0	190
75% GPA	3.81	0.00	
25% GPA	3.41	0.00	
75% LSAT	164	0	
25% LSAT	157	0	

Tuition & Fees

	Resident	Non-resident
Full-Time	$23,010	$23,010
Part-Time	$0	$0

Living Expenses

Estimated living expenses for Singles		
Living on campus	Living off campus	Living at home
$13,870	$13,870	$13,870

Grants/Scholarships

	Full-time		Part-time		Total	
	#	%	#	%	#	%
Total # of Students	548		0		548	
Total # receiving grants	297	54.2	0	0.0	297	54.2
Less than 1/2 tuition	250	45.6	0	0.0	250	45.6
Half to full tuition	35	6.4	0	0.0	35	6.4
Full tuition	10	1.8	0	0.0	10	1.8
More than full tuition	2	0.4	0	0.0	2	0.4
Median Grant Amount	$8,322		$0			

Informational & Library Resources

# of volumes & volume equivalents	521,151	# of professional staff	9
# of titles	109,917	Hours per week with professional staff	60
# of active serial subscriptions	6,127	Hours per week without professional staff	51
Study seating capacity inside the library	402	# of student computer work stations for entire law school	57
Square feet of law library	38,010	# of additional networked connections	41
Square feet of law school (excl. Library)	55,688	Require Laptop Computer?	N

Employment

	Total	%
Employment status known	184	100.0
Employment status unknown	0	0.0
Employed	175	95.1
Pursuing graduate degrees	6	3.3
Unemployed seeking employment	2	1.1
Unemployed not seeking employment	1	0.5
Type of Employment		
# employed in law firms	117	66.9
# employed in business & industry	10	5.7
# employed in government	16	9.1
# employed in public interest	8	4.6
# employed as judicial clerks	24	13.7
# employed in academia	0	0.0
Geographic Location		
# employed in state	46	26.3
# employed in foreign countries	2	1.1
# of states where employed	30	

J.D. Attrition (from Prior Year)

	Academic	Other	TOTALS	
	#	#	#	%
1st Year	0	1	1	0.5%
2nd Year	0	3	3	1.6%
3rd Year	0	0	0	0.0%
4th Year	0	0	0	0.0%

Bar Passage Rates

Jurisdiction	Tennessee		
Exam	Sum 97	Win 98	Total
# from school taking bar for the first time	46	6	52
School's pass rate for all first-time takers	93%	83%	92%
State's pass rate for all first-time takers	81%	76%	80%

VERMONT LAW SCHOOL

Chelsea Street
P.O. Box 96
South Royalton, VT 05068-0096
(802)763-8303
http://www.vermontlaw.edu

ABA Approved Since 1975

The Basics

Type of School: Private Term: Semester
Application deadline: 02/01
Application fee: $50
Financial Aid deadline: 03/01
Can first year start other than Fall? No
Student faculty ratio: 15.5 to 1
Does the University offer:
- housing restricted to law students? No
- graduate student housing for which law students are eligible? No

Faculty & Administrators

	Total		Men		Women		Minorities	
	Fall	Spr	Fall	Spr	Fall	Spr	Fall	Spr
Full-time	26	23	13	13	13	10	1	1
Other Full-Time	6	5	1	1	5	4	0	0
Deans, librarians, & others who teach > 1/2	5	5	4	4	1	1	1	1
Part-time	12	19	10	17	2	2	0	0
Total	49	52	28	35	21	17	2	2
Deans, librarians, & others who teach < 1/2	1	1	1	1	0	0	0	0

Curriculum

	Full time	Part time
Typical first-year section size	80	0
Is there typically a "small section" of the first year class, other than Legal Writing, taught by full-time faculty?	Yes	No
If yes, typical size offered last year	40	N/A
# of classroom course titles beyond 1st year curriculum	107	0
# of upper division courses, excluding seminars, with an enrollment:		
Under 25	52	0
25 - 49	20	0
50 - 74	11	0
75 - 99	3	0
100 +	0	0
# of seminars	21	0
# of seminar positions available	380	
# of seminar positions filled	302	0
# of positions available in simulation courses	212	
# of simulation positions filled	176	0
# of positions available in faculty supervised clinical courses	42	
# of fac. sup. clin. positions filled	30	0
# involved in field placements	123	0
# involved in law journals	61	0
# in moot court or trial competitions	155	0
# of credit hrs required to graduate	84	

J.D. Enrollment & Ethnicity

	Men		Women		Fl-Time		Pt-Time		1st Yr		2nd Yr		3rd Yr		4th Yr		Total		JD Degrees Awarded
	#	%	#	%	#	%	#	%	#	%	#	%	#	%	#	%	#	%	
African-American	0	0.0	4	1.7	4	0.8	0	0.0	3	1.5	1	0.7	0	0.0	0	0.0	4	0.8	3
American Indian	3	1.2	2	0.9	5	1.0	0	0.0	2	1.0	0	0.0	3	1.9	0	0.0	5	1.0	1
Asian American	7	2.8	7	3.0	14	2.9	0	0.0	6	3.1	5	3.7	3	1.9	0	0.0	14	2.9	2
Mexican American	1	0.4	2	0.9	3	0.6	0	0.0	1	0.5	0	0.0	2	1.3	0	0.0	3	0.6	1
Puerto Rican	1	0.4	1	0.4	2	0.4	0	0.0	0	0.0	2	1.5	0	0.0	0	0.0	2	0.4	0
Hispanic American	8	3.2	4	1.7	12	2.5	0	0.0	9	4.6	0	0.0	3	1.9	0	0.0	12	2.5	0
Total Minorities	20	7.9	20	8.6	40	8.2	0	0.0	21	10.8	8	6.0	11	7.0	0	0.0	40	8.2	7
Foreign Nationals	1	0.4	5	2.2	6	1.2	0	0.0	2	1.0	2	1.5	2	1.3	0	0.0	6	1.2	0
Caucasian	232	91.7	207	89.2	439	90.5	0	0.0	171	88.1	124	92.5	144	91.7	0	0.0	439	90.5	137
Total	253	52.2	232	47.8	485	100.0	0	0.0	194	40.0	134	27.6	157	32.4	0	0.0	485		144

GPA & LSAT Scores

	Full Time	Part Time	Total
# of apps	894	0	894
# admits	649	0	649
# of matrics	192	0	192
75% GPA	3.30	0.00	
25% GPA	2.70	0.00	
75% LSAT	156	0	
25% LSAT	148	0	

Tuition & Fees

	Resident	Non-resident
Full-Time	$19,490	$19,490
Part-Time	$0	$0

Living Expenses

Estimated living expenses for Singles		
Living on campus	Living off campus	Living at home
N/A	$12,626	N/A

Employment

	Total	%
Employment status known	147	98.7
Employment status unknown	2	1.3
Employed	125	85.0
Pursuing graduate degrees	5	3.4
Unemployed seeking employment	13	8.8
Unemployed not seeking employment	4	2.7
Type of Employment		
# employed in law firms	47	37.6
# employed in business & industry	30	24.0
# employed in government	20	16.0
# employed in public interest	14	11.2
# employed as judicial clerks	11	8.8
# employed in academia	2	1.6
Geographic Location		
# employed in state	22	17.6
# employed in foreign countries	0	0.0
# of states where employed	35	

Grants/Scholarships

	Full-time		Part-time		Total	
	#	%	#	%	#	%
Total # of Students						
Total # receiving grants	187	38.6	0	0.0	187	38.6
Less than 1/2 tuition	178	36.7	0	0.0	178	36.7
Half to full tuition	8	1.6	0	0.0	8	1.6
Full tuition	1	0.2	0	0.0	1	0.2
More than full tuition	0	0.0	0	0.0	0	0.0
Median Grant Amount	$4,925		$0			

Informational & Library Resources

# of volumes & volume equivalents	221,376	# of professional staff	6
# of titles	34,216	Hours per week with professional staff	48
# of active serial subscriptions	2,458	Hours per week without professional staff	62
Study seating capacity inside the library	414	# of student computer work stations for entire law school	42
Square feet of law library	35,143	# of additional networked connections	48
Square feet of law school (excl. Library)	95,652	Require Laptop Computer?	N

J.D. Attrition (from Prior Year)

	Academic	Other	TOTALS	
	#	#	#	%
1st Year	0	17	17	12%
2nd Year	0	1	1	0.6%
3rd Year	0	0	0	0.0%
4th Year	0	0	0	0.0%

Bar Passage Rates

Jurisdiction	New York			Vermont		
Exam	Sum 97	Win 98	Total	Sum 97	Win 98	Total
# from school taking bar for the first time	27	0	27	19	0	19
School's pass rate for all first-time takers	85%		85%	79%		79%
State's pass rate for all first-time takers	78%	65%	76%	80%	86%	82%

VILLANOVA UNIVERSITY

299 North Spring Mill Road
Villanova, PA 19085-1682
(610)519-7000
http://www.law.vill.edu/vls

ABA Approved Since 1954

The Basics

Type of School: Private Term: Semester
Application deadline: 03/01
Application fee: $75
Financial Aid deadline: Rolling
Can first year start other than Fall? No
Student faculty ratio: 21.3 to 1
Does the University offer:
- housing restricted to law students? No
- graduate student housing for which law students are eligible? No

Faculty & Administrators

	Total		Men		Women		Minorities	
	Fall	Spr	Fall	Spr	Fall	Spr	Fall	Spr
Full-time	27	27	20	21	7	6	3	3
Other Full-Time	6	6	2	2	4	4	1	1
Deans, librarians, & others who teach > 1/2	7	6	6	5	1	1	1	1
Part-time	24	27	16	20	8	7	1	0
Total	64	66	44	48	20	18	6	5
Deans, librarians, & others who teach < 1/2	0	0	0	0	0	0	0	0

Curriculum

	Full time	Part time
Typical first-year section size	100	0
Is there typically a "small section" of the first year class, other than Legal Writing, taught by full-time faculty?	Yes	No
If yes, typical size offered last year	30	N/A
# of classroom course titles beyond 1st year curriculum	121	0
# of upper division courses, excluding seminars, with an enrollment:		
Under 25	68	0
25 - 49	20	0
50 - 74	10	0
75 - 99	7	0
100 +	13	0
# of seminars	15	0
# of seminar positions available	209	
# of seminar positions filled	156	0
# of positions available in simulation courses	682	
# of simulation positions filled	542	0
# of positions available in faculty supervised clinical courses	114	
# of fac. sup. clin. positions filled	82	0
# involved in field placements	81	0
# involved in law journals	134	0
# in moot court or trial competitions	183	0
# of credit hrs required to graduate	87	

J.D. Enrollment & Ethnicity

	Men		Women		Fl-Time		Pt-Time		1st Yr		2nd Yr		3rd Yr		4th Yr		Total		JD Degrees Awarded
	#	%	#	%	#	%	#	%	#	%	#	%	#	%	#	%	#	%	
African-American	9	2.4	16	5.1	25	3.6	0	0.0	6	2.6	13	5.7	6	2.6	0	0.0	25	3.6	10
American Indian	1	0.3	2	0.6	3	0.4	0	0.0	0	0.0	1	0.4	2	0.9	0	0.0	3	0.4	1
Asian American	23	6.1	27	8.6	50	7.3	0	0.0	12	5.2	22	9.6	16	7.0	0	0.0	50	7.3	11
Mexican American	0	0.0	0	0.0	0	0.0	0	0.0	0	0.0	0	0.0	0	0.0	0	0.0	0	0.0	0
Puerto Rican	0	0.0	0	0.0	0	0.0	0	0.0	0	0.0	0	0.0	0	0.0	0	0.0	0	0.0	0
Hispanic American	15	4.0	11	3.5	26	3.8	0	0.0	9	3.9	12	5.2	5	2.2	0	0.0	26	3.8	6
Total Minorities	48	12.8	56	17.8	104	15.1	0	0.0	27	11.6	48	20.9	29	12.8	0	0.0	104	15.1	28
Foreign Nationals	0	0.0	0	0.0	0	0.0	0	0.0	0	0.0	0	0.0	0	0.0	0	0.0	0	0.0	0
Caucasian	327	87.2	258	82.2	585	84.9	0	0.0	205	88.4	182	79.1	198	87.2	0	0.0	585	84.9	191
Total	375	54.4	314	45.6	689	100.0	0	0.0	232	33.7	230	33.4	227	32.9	0	0.0	689		219

GPA & LSAT Scores

	Full Time	Part Time	Total
# of apps	1,245	0	1,245
# admits	780	0	780
# of matrics	232	0	232
75% GPA	3.51	0.00	
25% GPA	3.03	0.00	
75% LSAT	158	0	
25% LSAT	153	0	

Tuition & Fees

	Resident	Non-resident
Full-Time	$19,490	$19,490
Part-Time	$0	$0

Living Expenses

Estimated living expenses for Singles		
Living on campus	Living off campus	Living at home
$12,050	$14,045	$5,485

Employment

	Total	%
Employment status known	207	93.2
Employment status unknown	15	6.8
Employed	181	87.4
Pursuing graduate degrees	5	2.4
Unemployed seeking employment	21	10.1
Unemployed not seeking employment	0	0.0
Type of Employment		
# employed in law firms	94	51.9
# employed in business & industry	32	17.7
# employed in government	15	8.3
# employed in public interest	0	0.0
# employed as judicial clerks	40	22.1
# employed in academia	0	0.0
Geographic Location		
# employed in state	122	67.4
# employed in foreign countries	0	0.0
# of states where employed	12	

Grants/Scholarships

	Full-time		Part-time		Total	
	#	%	#	%	#	%
Total # of Students	689		0		689	
Total # receiving grants	52	7.5	0	0.0	52	7.5
Less than 1/2 tuition	27	3.9	0	0.0	27	3.9
Half to full tuition	22	3.2	0	0.0	22	3.2
Full tuition	3	0.4	0	0.0	3	0.4
More than full tuition	0	0.0	0	0.0	0	0.0
Median Grant Amount	$5,000		$0			

Informational & Library Resources

# of volumes & volume equivalents	436,083	# of professional staff	8
# of titles	131,761	Hours per week with professional staff	72
# of active serial subscriptions	3,173	Hours per week without professional staff	38
Study seating capacity inside the library	368	# of student computer work stations for entire law school	150
Square feet of law library	31,056	# of additional networked connections	64
Square feet of law school (excl. Library)	42,898	Require Laptop Computer?	N

J.D. Attrition (from Prior Year)

	Academic	Other	TOTALS	
	#	#	#	%
1st Year	0	3	3	1.3%
2nd Year	1	7	8	3.5%
3rd Year	0	0	0	0.0%
4th Year	0	0	0	0.0%

Bar Passage Rates

Jurisdiction	Pennsylvania		
Exam	Sum 97	Win 98	Total
# from school taking bar for the first time	166	8	174
School's pass rate for all first-time takers	80%	75%	79%
State's pass rate for all first-time takers	81%	73%	79%

VIRGINIA, UNIVERSITY OF

580 Massie Road
Charlottesville, VA 22903-1789
(804)924-7354
http://www.law.virginia.edu/index.htm

ABA Approved Since 1923

The Basics

Type of School: Public   Term: Semester

Application deadline: 01/15

Application fee: $65

Financial Aid deadline: 02/28

Can first year start other than Fall? No

Student faculty ratio: 15.3 to 1

Does the University offer:
- housing restricted to law students? No
- graduate student housing for which law students are eligible? Yes

Faculty & Administrators

	Total		Men		Women		Minorities	
	Fall	Spr	Fall	Spr	Fall	Spr	Fall	Spr
Full-time	63	60	50	48	13	12	4	4
Other Full-Time	0	0	0	0	0	0	0	0
Deans, librarians, & others who teach > 1/2	0	0	0	0	0	0	0	0
Part-time	44	47	35	37	9	10	0	2
Total	107	107	85	85	22	22	4	6
Deans, librarians, & others who teach < 1/2	1	1	1	1	0	0	0	0

Curriculum

	Full time	Part time
Typical first-year section size	64	0
Is there typically a "small section" of the first year class, other than Legal Writing, taught by full-time faculty?	Yes	No
If yes, typical size offered last year	30	N/A
# of classroom course titles beyond 1st year curriculum	153	0
# of upper division courses, excluding seminars, with an enrollment:		
Under 25	68	0
25 - 49	25	0
50 - 74	13	0
75 - 99	15	0
100 +	23	0
# of seminars	58	0
# of seminar positions available	935	
# of seminar positions filled	771	0
# of positions available in simulation courses	632	
# of simulation positions filled	548	0
# of positions available in faculty supervised clinical courses	32	
# of fac. sup. clin. positions filled	28	0
# involved in field placements	73	0
# involved in law journals	496	0
# in moot court or trial competitions	322	0
# of credit hrs required to graduate	86	

J.D. Enrollment & Ethnicity

	Men		Women		Fl-Time		Pt-Time		1st Yr		2nd Yr		3rd Yr		4th Yr		Total		JD Degrees Awarded
	#	%	#	%	#	%	#	%	#	%	#	%	#	%	#	%	#	%	
African-American	37	5.3	37	9.0	74	6.7	0	0.0	22	6.2	32	8.6	20	5.3	0	0.0	74	6.7	36
American Indian	5	0.7	1	0.2	6	0.5	0	0.0	3	0.8	2	0.5	1	0.3	0	0.0	6	0.5	1
Asian American	24	3.4	27	6.6	51	4.6	0	0.0	21	5.9	19	5.1	11	2.9	0	0.0	51	4.6	17
Mexican American	0	0.0	0	0.0	0	0.0	0	0.0	0	0.0	0	0.0	0	0.0	0	0.0	0	0.0	0
Puerto Rican	0	0.0	0	0.0	0	0.0	0	0.0	0	0.0	0	0.0	0	0.0	0	0.0	0	0.0	0
Hispanic American	6	0.9	7	1.7	13	1.2	0	0.0	6	1.7	2	0.5	5	1.3	0	0.0	13	1.2	2
Total Minorities	72	10.3	72	17.6	144	13.0	0	0.0	52	14.6	55	14.7	37	9.8	0	0.0	144	13.0	56
Foreign Nationals	0	0.0	0	0.0	0	0.0	0	0.0	0	0.0	0	0.0	0	0.0	0	0.0	0	0.0	0
Caucasian	624	89.7	337	82.4	961	87.0	0	0.0	304	85.4	318	85.3	339	90.2	0	0.0	961	87.0	325
Total	696	63.0	409	37.0	1105	100.0	0	0.0	356	32.2	373	33.8	376	34.0	0	0.0	1105		381

GPA & LSAT Scores

	Full Time	Part Time	Total
# of apps	3,443	0	3,443
# admits	957	0	957
# of matrics	358	0	358
75% GPA	3.78	0.00	
25% GPA	3.51	0.00	
75% LSAT	168	0	
25% LSAT	163	0	

Tuition & Fees

	Resident	Non-resident
Full-Time	$14,606	$20,706
Part-Time	$0	$0

Living Expenses

Estimated living expenses for Singles		
Living on campus	Living off campus	Living at home
$11,060	$11,060	$11,060

Grants/Scholarships

	Full-time		Part-time		Total	
	#	%	#	%	#	%
Total # of Students	1105		0		1105	
Total # receiving grants	344	31.1	0	0.0	344	31.1
Less than 1/2 tuition	253	22.9	0	0.0	253	22.9
Half to full tuition	73	6.6	0	0.0	73	6.6
Full tuition	4	0.4	0	0.0	4	0.4
More than full tuition	14	1.3	0	0.0	14	1.3
Median Grant Amount	$6,400		$0			

Informational & Library Resources

# of volumes & volume equivalents	788,674	# of professional staff	12
# of titles	235,049	Hours per week with professional staff	69
# of active serial subscriptions	12,999	Hours per week without professional staff	41
Study seating capacity inside the library	768	# of student computer work stations for entire law school	123
Square feet of law library	88,370	# of additional networked connections	84
Square feet of law school (excl. Library)	172,112	Require Laptop Computer?	Y

Employment

	Total	%
Employment status known	376	96.2
Employment status unknown	15	3.8
Employed	370	98.4
Pursuing graduate degrees	3	0.8
Unemployed seeking employment	3	0.8
Unemployed not seeking employment	0	0.0
Type of Employment		
# employed in law firms	256	69.2
# employed in business & industry	23	6.2
# employed in government	14	3.8
# employed in public interest	3	0.8
# employed as judicial clerks	74	20.0
# employed in academia	0	0.0
Geographic Location		
# employed in state	60	16.2
# employed in foreign countries	1	0.3
# of states where employed	34	

J.D. Attrition (from Prior Year)

	Academic	Other	TOTALS	
	#	#	#	%
1st Year	1	5	6	1.7%
2nd Year	1	4	5	1.4%
3rd Year	1	0	1	0.3%
4th Year	0	0	0	0.0%

Bar Passage Rates

Jurisdiction	Virginia			New York		
Exam	Sum 97	Win 98	Total	Sum 97	Win 98	Total
# from school taking bar for the first time	102	9	111	78	9	87
School's pass rate for all first-time takers	88%	89%	88%	87%	100%	89%
State's pass rate for all first-time takers	76%	68%	75%	78%	65%	76%

WAKE FOREST UNIVERSITY

P.O. Box 7206
Reynolda Station
Winston-Salem, NC 27109-7206
(336)758-5435
http://www.wfu.edu

ABA Approved Since 1935

The Basics

Type of School: Private   Term: Semester
Application deadline: 03/15
Application fee: $60
Financial Aid deadline: 05/01
Can first year start other than Fall? No
Student faculty ratio: 15.5 to 1
Does the University offer:
- housing restricted to law students? No
- graduate student housing for which law students are eligible? No

Faculty & Administrators

	Total		Men		Women		Minorities	
	Fall	Spr	Fall	Spr	Fall	Spr	Fall	Spr
Full-time	25	27	18	19	7	8	2	2
Other Full-Time	4	4	0	0	4	4	1	1
Deans, librarians, & others who teach > 1/2	4	4	3	3	1	1	0	0
Part-time	19	14	17	11	2	3	1	1
Total	52	49	38	33	14	16	4	4
Deans, librarians, & others who teach < 1/2	2	2	1	1	1	1	0	0

Curriculum

	Full time	Part time
Typical first-year section size	40	0
Is there typically a "small section" of the first year class, other than Legal Writing, taught by full-time faculty?	Yes	No
If yes, typical size offered last year	40	N/A
# of classroom course titles beyond 1st year curriculum	77	0
# of upper division courses, excluding seminars, with an enrollment:		
Under 25	55	0
25 - 49	27	0
50 - 74	10	0
75 - 99	5	0
100 +	0	0
# of seminars	15	0
# of seminar positions available	361	
# of seminar positions filled	233	0
# of positions available in simulation courses	510	
# of simulation positions filled	454	0
# of positions available in faculty supervised clinical courses	71	
# of fac. sup. clin. positions filled	51	0
# involved in field placements	7	0
# involved in law journals	62	0
# in moot court or trial competitions	44	0
# of credit hrs required to graduate	89	

J.D. Enrollment & Ethnicity

	Men		Women		Fl-Time		Pt-Time		1st Yr		2nd Yr		3rd Yr		4th Yr		Total		JD Degrees Awarded
	#	%	#	%	#	%	#	%	#	%	#	%	#	%	#	%	#	%	
African-American	9	3.2	13	7.1	22	4.8	0	0.0	3	1.9	9	6.0	10	6.3	0	0.0	22	4.7	11
American Indian	1	0.4	2	1.1	3	0.7	0	0.0	0	0.0	1	0.7	2	1.3	0	0.0	3	0.6	0
Asian American	5	1.8	5	2.7	10	2.2	0	0.0	5	3.1	3	2.0	2	1.3	0	0.0	10	2.1	2
Mexican American	0	0.0	0	0.0	0	0.0	0	0.0	0	0.0	0	0.0	0	0.0	0	0.0	0	0.0	0
Puerto Rican	0	0.0	0	0.0	0	0.0	0	0.0	0	0.0	0	0.0	0	0.0	0	0.0	0	0.0	0
Hispanic American	1	0.4	1	0.5	2	0.4	0	0.0	1	0.6	1	0.7	0	0.0	0	0.0	2	0.4	1
Total Minorities	16	5.6	21	11.4	37	8.0	0	0.0	9	5.6	14	9.4	14	8.8	0	0.0	37	7.9	14
Foreign Nationals	2	0.7	0	0.0	2	0.4	0	0.0	1	0.6	1	0.7	0	0.0	0	0.0	2	0.4	1
Caucasian	267	93.7	163	88.6	421	91.5	9	100.0	150	93.8	134	89.9	146	91.3	0	0.0	430	91.7	130
Total	285	60.8	184	39.2	460	98.1	9	1.9	160	34.1	149	31.8	160	34.1	0	0.0	469		145

GPA & LSAT Scores

	Full Time	Part Time	Total
# of apps	1,219	0	1,219
# admits	554	0	554
# of matrics	160	0	160
75% GPA	3.57	0.00	
25% GPA	3.04	0.00	
75% LSAT	162	0	
25% LSAT	156	0	

Tuition & Fees

	Resident	Non-resident
Full-Time	$20,450	$20,450
Part-Time	$0	$0

Living Expenses

Estimated living expenses for Singles		
Living on campus	Living off campus	Living at home
N/A	$11,500	N/A

Grants/Scholarships

	Full-time		Part-time		Total	
	#	%	#	%	#	%
Total # of Students	460		9		469	
Total # receiving grants	120	26.1	0	0.0	120	25.6
Less than 1/2 tuition	65	14.1	0	0.0	65	13.9
Half to full tuition	33	7.2	0	0.0	33	7.0
Full tuition	16	3.5	0	0.0	16	3.4
More than full tuition	6	1.3	0	0.0	6	1.3
Median Grant Amount	$11,526		$0			

Informational & Library Resources

# of volumes & volume equivalents	330,757	# of professional staff	6
# of titles	74,654	Hours per week with professional staff	57
# of active serial subscriptions	5,849	Hours per week without professional staff	52
Study seating capacity inside the library	552	# of student computer work stations for entire law school	99
Square feet of law library	43,000	# of additional networked connections	493
Square feet of law school (excl. Library)	41,573	Require Laptop Computer?	N

Employment

	Total	%
Employment status known	149	96.1
Employment status unknown	6	3.9
Employed	142	95.3
Pursuing graduate degrees	0	0.0
Unemployed seeking employment	4	2.7
Unemployed not seeking employment	3	2.0
Type of Employment		
# employed in law firms	94	66.2
# employed in business & industry	15	10.6
# employed in government	15	10.6
# employed in public interest	2	1.4
# employed as judicial clerks	16	11.3
# employed in academia	0	0.0
Geographic Location		
# employed in state	90	63.4
# employed in foreign countries	0	0.0
# of states where employed	21	

J.D. Attrition (from Prior Year)

	Academic	Other	TOTALS	
	#	#	#	%
1st Year	3	5	8	4.9%
2nd Year	0	9	9	5.6%
3rd Year	0	0	0	0.0%
4th Year	0	0	0	0.0%

Bar Passage Rates

Jurisdiction	North Carolina		
Exam	Sum 97	Win 98	Total
# from school taking bar for the first time	105	6	111
School's pass rate for all first-time takers	91%	100%	92%
State's pass rate for all first-time takers	85%	73%	82%

WASHBURN UNIVERSITY

1700 College Avenue
Topeka, KS 66621
(785)231-1010
http://www.washburnlaw.wuacc.edu/school

ABA Approved Since 1923

The Basics

Type of School: Public   Term: Semester
Application deadline: 03/15 (Preferred)
Application fee: $30
Financial Aid deadline: 03/15
Can first year start other than Fall? Yes
Student faculty ratio: 16.5 to 1
Does the University offer:
- housing restricted to law students? No
- graduate student housing for which law students are eligible? Yes

Faculty & Administrators

	Total		Men		Women		Minorities	
	Fall	Spr	Fall	Spr	Fall	Spr	Fall	Spr
Full-time	22	20	15	13	7	7	6	5
Other Full-Time	1	1	0	0	1	1	0	0
Deans, librarians, & others who teach > 1/2	0	0	0	0	0	0	0	0
Part-time	16	27	13	22	3	5	0	0
Total	39	48	28	35	11	13	6	5
Deans, librarians, & others who teach < 1/2	3	3	3	3	0	0	1	1

Curriculum

	Full time	Part time
Typical first-year section size	75	0
Is there typically a "small section" of the first year class, other than Legal Writing, taught by full-time faculty?	Yes	No
If yes, typical size offered last year	25	N/A
# of classroom course titles beyond 1st year curriculum	79	0
# of upper division courses, excluding seminars, with an enrollment:		
Under 25	31	0
25 - 49	24	0
50 - 74	16	0
75 - 99	6	0
100 +	0	0
# of seminars	23	0
# of seminar positions available	612	
# of seminar positions filled	453	0
# of positions available in simulation courses	235	
# of simulation positions filled	154	0
# of positions available in faculty supervised clinical courses	85	
# of fac. sup. clin. positions filled	59	0
# involved in field placements	18	0
# involved in law journals	63	0
# in moot court or trial competitions	88	0
# of credit hrs required to graduate	90	

J.D. Enrollment & Ethnicity

	Men		Women		Fl-Time		Pt-Time		1st Yr		2nd Yr		3rd Yr		4th Yr		Total		JD Degrees Awarded
	#	%	#	%	#	%	#	%	#	%	#	%	#	%	#	%	#	%	
African-American	8	3.2	9	4.8	17	3.9	0	0.0	6	3.9	5	3.9	6	3.9	0	0.0	17	3.9	5
American Indian	0	0.0	3	1.6	3	0.7	0	0.0	2	1.3	0	0.0	1	0.7	0	0.0	3	0.7	3
Asian American	5	2.0	5	2.7	10	2.3	0	0.0	4	2.6	3	2.4	3	2.0	0	0.0	10	2.3	6
Mexican American	2	0.8	5	2.7	7	1.6	0	0.0	4	2.6	2	1.6	1	0.7	0	0.0	7	1.6	0
Puerto Rican	0	0.0	1	0.5	1	0.2	0	0.0	0	0.0	1	0.8	0	0.0	0	0.0	1	0.2	0
Hispanic American	2	0.8	8	4.3	10	2.3	0	0.0	3	1.9	4	3.1	3	2.0	0	0.0	10	2.3	3
Total Minorities	17	6.9	31	16.5	48	11.0	0	0.0	19	12.3	15	11.8	14	9.2	0	0.0	48	11.0	17
Foreign Nationals	7	2.8	3	1.6	10	2.3	0	0.0	5	3.2	3	2.4	2	1.3	0	0.0	10	2.3	5
Caucasian	223	90.3	154	81.9	377	86.7	0	0.0	131	84.5	109	85.8	137	89.5	0	0.0	377	86.7	122
Total	247	56.8	188	43.2	435	100.0	0	0.0	155	35.6	127	29.2	153	35.2	0	0.0	435		144

GPA & LSAT Scores

	Full Time	Part Time	Total
# of apps	500	0	500
# admits	340	0	340
# of matrics	158	0	158
75% GPA	3.49	0.00	
25% GPA	2.85	0.00	
75% LSAT	153	0	
25% LSAT	146	0	

Tuition & Fees

	Resident	Non-resident
Full-Time	$6,732	$10,064
Part-Time	$0	$0

Living Expenses

Estimated living expenses for Singles		
Living on campus	Living off campus	Living at home
$11,704	$11,704	$11,704

Grants/Scholarships

	Full-time		Part-time		Total	
	#	%	#	%	#	%
Total # of Students	435		0		435	
Total # receiving grants	153	35.2	0	0.0	153	35.2
Less than 1/2 tuition	109	25.1	0	0.0	109	25.1
Half to full tuition	13	3.0	0	0.0	13	3.0
Full tuition	25	5.7	0	0.0	25	5.7
More than full tuition	6	1.4	0	0.0	6	1.4
Median Grant Amount	$2,000		$0			

Informational & Library Resources

# of volumes & volume equivalents	311,932	# of professional staff	7
# of titles	201,799	Hours per week with professional staff	87
# of active serial subscriptions	3,797	Hours per week without professional staff	12
Study seating capacity inside the library	346	# of student computer work stations for entire law school	78
Square feet of law library	41,270	# of additional networked connections	0
Square feet of law school (excl. Library)	45,928	Require Laptop Computer?	N

Employment

	Total	%
Employment status known	124	95.4
Employment status unknown	6	4.6
Employed	110	88.7
Pursuing graduate degrees	2	1.6
Unemployed seeking employment	8	6.5
Unemployed not seeking employment	4	3.2
Type of Employment		
# employed in law firms	42	38.2
# employed in business & industry	13	11.8
# employed in government	39	35.5
# employed in public interest	8	7.3
# employed as judicial clerks	7	6.4
# employed in academia	1	0.9
Geographic Location		
# employed in state	68	61.8
# employed in foreign countries	1	0.9
# of states where employed	14	

J.D. Attrition (from Prior Year)

	Academic	Other	TOTALS	
	#	#	#	%
1st Year	4	6	10	7.1%
2nd Year	3	3	6	4.3%
3rd Year	0	2	2	1.2%
4th Year	0	0	0	0.0%

Bar Passage Rates

Jurisdiction	Kansas		
Exam	Sum 97	Win 98	Total
# from school taking bar for the first time	73	30	103
School's pass rate for all first-time takers	88%	80%	85%
State's pass rate for all first-time takers	87%	87%	87%

WASHINGTON AND LEE UNIVERSITY

Sydney Lewis Hall
Lexington, VA 24450-0303
(540)463-8400
http://www.wlu.edu

ABA Approved Since 1923

The Basics

Type of School: Private — Term: Semester
Application deadline: 02/01
Application fee: $40
Financial Aid deadline: 02/15
Can first year start other than Fall? No
Student faculty ratio: 11.5 to 1
Does the University offer:
- housing restricted to law students? Yes
- graduate student housing for which law students are eligible? Yes

Curriculum

	Full time	Part time
Typical first-year section size	63	0
Is there typically a "small section" of the first year class, other than Legal Writing, taught by full-time faculty?	Yes	No
If yes, typical size offered last year	21	N/A
# of classroom course titles beyond 1st year curriculum	76	0
# of upper division courses, excluding seminars, with an enrollment:		
Under 25	36	0
25 - 49	20	0
50 - 74	10	0
75 - 99	1	0
100 +	0	0
# of seminars	21	0
# of seminar positions available	329	
# of seminar positions filled	227	0
# of positions available in simulation courses	303	
# of simulation positions filled	245	0
# of positions available in faculty supervised clinical courses	46	
# of fac. sup. clin. positions filled	46	0
# involved in field placements	32	0
# involved in law journals	97	0
# in moot court or trial competitions	136	0
# of credit hrs required to graduate	85	

Faculty & Administrators

	Total		Men		Women		Minorities	
	Fall	Spr	Fall	Spr	Fall	Spr	Fall	Spr
Full-time	29	30	25	24	4	6	5	4
Other Full-Time	1	1	0	0	1	1	0	0
Deans, librarians, & others who teach > 1/2	3	3	1	1	2	2	0	0
Part-time	4	11	4	11	0	0	0	0
Total	37	45	30	36	7	9	5	4
Deans, librarians, & others who teach < 1/2	0	0	0	0	0	0	0	0

J.D. Enrollment & Ethnicity

	Men		Women		Fl-Time		Pt-Time		1st Yr		2nd Yr		3rd Yr		4th Yr		Total		JD Degrees Awarded
	#	%	#	%	#	%	#	%	#	%	#	%	#	%	#	%	#	%	
African-American	8	3.7	6	4.1	14	3.8	0	0.0	7	5.8	1	0.8	6	5.0	0	0.0	14	3.8	8
American Indian	2	0.9	1	0.7	3	0.8	0	0.0	2	1.7	1	0.8	0	0.0	0	0.0	3	0.8	2
Asian American	2	0.9	10	6.8	12	3.3	0	0.0	3	2.5	3	2.4	6	5.0	0	0.0	12	3.3	3
Mexican American	1	0.5	0	0.0	1	0.3	0	0.0	0	0.0	1	0.8	0	0.0	0	0.0	1	0.3	0
Puerto Rican	0	0.0	0	0.0	0	0.0	0	0.0	0	0.0	0	0.0	0	0.0	0	0.0	0	0.0	0
Hispanic American	1	0.5	0	0.0	1	0.3	0	0.0	1	0.8	0	0.0	0	0.0	0	0.0	1	0.3	2
Total Minorities	14	6.4	17	11.6	31	8.5	0	0.0	13	10.7	6	4.8	12	9.9	0	0.0	31	8.5	15
Foreign Nationals	1	0.5	1	0.7	2	0.5	0	0.0	2	1.7	0	0.0	0	0.0	0	0.0	2	0.5	0
Caucasian	204	93.2	129	87.8	333	91.0	0	0.0	106	87.6	118	95.2	109	90.1	0	0.0	333	91.0	102
Total	219	59.8	147	40.2	366	100.0	0	0.0	121	33.1	124	33.9	121	33.1	0	0.0	366		117

GPA & LSAT Scores

	Full Time	Part Time	Total
# of apps	1,267	0	1,267
# admits	463	0	463
# of matrics	122	0	122
75% GPA	3.75	0.00	
25% GPA	3.05	0.00	
75% LSAT	166	0	
25% LSAT	161	0	

Tuition & Fees

	Resident	Non-resident
Full-Time	$17,711	$17,711
Part-Time	$0	$0

Living Expenses

Estimated living expenses for Singles

Living on campus	Living off campus	Living at home
$10,460	$10,460	$750

Employment

	Total	%
Employment status known	115	97.5
Employment status unknown	3	2.5
Employed	108	93.9
Pursuing graduate degrees	2	1.7
Unemployed seeking employment	4	3.5
Unemployed not seeking employment	1	0.9
Type of Employment		
# employed in law firms	57	52.8
# employed in business & industry	10	9.3
# employed in government	9	8.3
# employed in public interest	1	0.9
# employed as judicial clerks	28	25.9
# employed in academia	3	2.8
Geographic Location		
# employed in state	30	27.8
# employed in foreign countries	0	0.0
# of states where employed	23	

Grants/Scholarships

	Full-time		Part-time		Total	
	#	%	#	%	#	%
Total # of Students	366		0		366	
Total # receiving grants	234	63.9	0	0.0	234	63.9
Less than 1/2 tuition	117	32.0	0	0.0	117	32.0
Half to full tuition	112	30.6	0	0.0	112	30.6
Full tuition	2	0.5	0	0.0	2	0.5
More than full tuition	3	0.8	0	0.0	3	0.8
Median Grant Amount	$8,600		$0			

Informational & Library Resources

# of volumes & volume equivalents	360,850	# of professional staff	7
# of titles	138,912	Hours per week with professional staff	60
# of active serial subscriptions	4,553	Hours per week without professional staff	108
Study seating capacity inside the library	551	# of student computer work stations for entire law school	92
Square feet of law library	56,650	# of additional networked connections	0
Square feet of law school (excl. Library)	46,648	Require Laptop Computer?	N

J.D. Attrition (from Prior Year)

	Academic	Other	TOTALS	
	#	#	#	%
1st Year	0	3	3	2.3%
2nd Year	0	5	5	4.2%
3rd Year	0	1	1	0.8%
4th Year	0	0	0	0.0%

Bar Passage Rates

Jurisdiction	Virginia			Maryland		
Exam	Sum 97	Win 98	Total	Sum 97	Win 98	Total
# from school taking bar for the first time	34	2	36	11	2	13
School's pass rate for all first-time takers	94%	50%	92%	82%	100%	85%
State's pass rate for all first-time takers	76%	68%	75%	69%	83%	72%

WASHINGTON UNIVERSITY

1 Brookings Drive
Campus Box 1120
St. Louis, MO 63130-4899
(314)935-6400
http://www.wulaw.wustl.edu

ABA Approved Since 1923

The Basics

Type of School: Private   Term: Semester
Application deadline: 03/01
Application fee: $50
Financial Aid deadline: 03/01
Can first year start other than Fall? No
Student faculty ratio: 16.6 to 1
Does the University offer:
- housing restricted to law students? No
- graduate student housing for which law students are eligible? Yes

Faculty & Administrators

	Total		Men		Women		Minorities	
	Fall	Spr	Fall	Spr	Fall	Spr	Fall	Spr
Full-time	31	30	19	17	12	13	3	3
Other Full-Time	3	4	0	0	3	4	0	0
Deans, librarians, & others who teach > 1/2	4	4	1	1	3	3	0	0
Part-time	34	40	27	31	6	8	4	4
Total	72	78	47	49	24	28	7	7
Deans, librarians, & others who teach < 1/2	1	1	1	1	0	0	0	0

Curriculum

	Full time	Part time
Typical first-year section size	66	0
Is there typically a "small section" of the first year class, other than Legal Writing, taught by full-time faculty?	No	No
If yes, typical size offered last year	N/A	N/A
# of classroom course titles beyond 1st year curriculum	91	0
# of upper division courses, excluding seminars, with an enrollment:		
Under 25	64	0
25 - 49	22	0
50 - 74	12	0
75 - 99	9	0
100 +	3	0
# of seminars	13	0
# of seminar positions available	246	
# of seminar positions filled	234	0
# of positions available in simulation courses	504	
# of simulation positions filled	494	0
# of positions available in faculty supervised clinical courses	40	
# of fac. sup. clin. positions filled	40	0
# involved in field placements	93	0
# involved in law journals	137	0
# in moot court or trial competitions	221	0
# of credit hrs required to graduate	85	

J.D. Enrollment & Ethnicity

	Men		Women		Fl-Time		Pt-Time		1st Yr		2nd Yr		3rd Yr		4th Yr		Total		JD Degrees Awarded
	#	%	#	%	#	%	#	%	#	%	#	%	#	%	#	%	#	%	
African-American	15	4.5	34	11.9	48	7.8	1	10.0	17	8.0	17	8.3	15	7.3	0	0.0	49	7.9	25
American Indian	6	1.8	5	1.8	11	1.8	0	0.0	2	0.9	6	2.9	3	1.5	0	0.0	11	1.8	2
Asian American	21	6.2	34	11.9	54	8.8	1	10.0	22	10.4	15	7.3	18	8.8	0	0.0	55	8.8	22
Mexican American	2	0.6	2	0.7	4	0.7	0	0.0	0	0.0	3	1.5	1	0.5	0	0.0	4	0.6	1
Puerto Rican	0	0.0	0	0.0	0	0.0	0	0.0	0	0.0	0	0.0	0	0.0	0	0.0	0	0.0	1
Hispanic American	4	1.2	7	2.5	11	1.8	0	0.0	3	1.4	5	2.4	3	1.5	0	0.0	11	1.8	1
Total Minorities	48	14.2	82	28.8	128	20.9	2	20.0	44	20.8	46	22.4	40	19.5	0	0.0	130	20.9	52
Foreign Nationals	3	0.9	0	0.0	2	0.3	1	10.0	1	0.5	0	0.0	2	1.0	0	0.0	3	0.5	0
Caucasian	286	84.9	203	71.2	482	78.8	7	70.0	167	78.8	159	77.6	163	79.5	0	0.0	489	78.6	160
Total	337	54.2	285	45.8	612	98.4	10	1.6	212	34.1	205	33.0	205	33.0	0	0.0	622		212

GPA & LSAT Scores

	Full Time	Part Time	Total
# of apps	1,640	0	1,640
# admits	885	0	885
# of matrics	213	0	213
75% GPA	3.58	0.00	
25% GPA	3.12	0.00	
75% LSAT	163	0	
25% LSAT	155	0	

Tuition & Fees

	Resident	Non-resident
Full-Time	$23,120	$23,120
Part-Time	$0	$0

Living Expenses

Estimated living expenses for Singles

Living on campus	Living off campus	Living at home
N/A	$13,204	$7,378

Employment

	Total	%
Employment status known	198	96.1
Employment status unknown	8	3.9
Employed	191	96.5
Pursuing graduate degrees	1	0.5
Unemployed seeking employment	2	1.0
Unemployed not seeking employment	4	2.0
Type of Employment		
# employed in law firms	114	59.7
# employed in business & industry	18	9.4
# employed in government	29	15.2
# employed in public interest	9	4.7
# employed as judicial clerks	15	7.9
# employed in academia	1	0.5
Geographic Location		
# employed in state	85	44.5
# employed in foreign countries	1	0.5
# of states where employed	23	

Grants/Scholarships

	Full-time		Part-time		Total	
	#	%	#	%	#	%
Total # of Students	612		10		622	
Total # receiving grants	353	57.7	0	0.0	353	56.8
Less than 1/2 tuition	274	44.8	0	0.0	274	44.1
Half to full tuition	38	6.2	0	0.0	38	6.1
Full tuition	31	5.1	0	0.0	31	5.0
More than full tuition	10	1.6	0	0.0	10	1.6
Median Grant Amount	$10,000		$0			

Informational & Library Resources

# of volumes & volume equivalents	584,197	# of professional staff	4
# of titles	109,823	Hours per week with professional staff	55
# of active serial subscriptions	6,496	Hours per week without professional staff	65
Study seating capacity inside the library	517	# of student computer work stations for entire law school	54
Square feet of law library	64,229	# of additional networked connections	700
Square feet of law school (excl. Library)	50,863	Require Laptop Computer?	N

J.D. Attrition (from Prior Year)

	Academic	Other	TOTALS	
	#	#	#	%
1st Year	2	13	15	7.6%
2nd Year	0	2	2	1.0%
3rd Year	0	0	0	0.0%
4th Year	0	0	0	0.0%

Bar Passage Rates

Jurisdiction	Missouri			Illinois		
Exam	Sum 97	Win 98	Total	Sum 97	Win 98	Total
# from school taking bar for the first time	85	5	90	40	34	74
School's pass rate for all first-time takers	88%	100%	89%	83%	91%	86%
State's pass rate for all first-time takers	86%	81%	85%	87%	80%	85%

WASHINGTON, UNIVERSITY OF

1100 NE Campus Parkway
Seattle, WA 98105-6617
(206)543-4551
http:/www2.law.washington.edu

ABA Approved Since 1924

The Basics

Type of School: Public
Term: Quarter
Application deadline: 01/15
Application fee: $50
Financial Aid deadline: 02/28
Can first year start other than Fall? Yes
Student faculty ratio: 11.4 to 1
Does the University offer:
- housing restricted to law students? No
- graduate student housing for which law students are eligible? No

Curriculum

	Full time	Part time
Typical first-year section size	105	0
Is there typically a "small section" of the first year class, other than Legal Writing, taught by full-time faculty?	Yes	No
If yes, typical size offered last year	23	N/A
# of classroom course titles beyond 1st year curriculum	75	0
# of upper division courses, excluding seminars, with an enrollment:		
Under 25	51	0
25 - 49	22	0
50 - 74	14	0
75 - 99	5	0
100 +	2	0
# of seminars	12	0
# of seminar positions available	135	
# of seminar positions filled	112	0
# of positions available in simulation courses	193	
# of simulation positions filled	176	0
# of positions available in faculty supervised clinical courses	96	
# of fac. sup. clin. positions filled	76	0
# involved in field placements	202	0
# involved in law journals	86	0
# in moot court or trial competitions	119	0
# of credit hrs required to graduate	135	

Faculty & Administrators

	Total		Men		Women		Minorities	
	Fall	Spr	Fall	Spr	Fall	Spr	Fall	Spr
Full-time	39	40	21	23	18	17	3	4
Other Full-Time	0	0	0	0	0	0	0	0
Deans, librarians, & others who teach > 1/2	2	2	1	1	1	1	0	0
Part-time	14	36	10	19	4	17	1	4
Total	55	78	32	43	23	35	4	8
Deans, librarians, & others who teach < 1/2	1	1	1	1	0	0	0	0

J.D. Enrollment & Ethnicity

	Men		Women		Fl-Time		Pt-Time		1st Yr		2nd Yr		3rd Yr		4th Yr		Total		JD Degrees Awarded
	#	%	#	%	#	%	#	%	#	%	#	%	#	%	#	%	#	%	
African-American	9	3.9	8	3.1	17	3.5	0	0.0	9	5.2	3	2.1	5	2.9	0	0.0	17	3.5	5
American Indian	3	1.3	6	2.3	9	1.8	0	0.0	0	0.0	4	2.8	5	2.9	0	0.0	9	1.8	6
Asian American	14	6.1	40	15.4	54	11.1	0	0.0	19	10.9	24	16.7	11	6.4	0	0.0	54	11.0	14
Mexican American	12	5.2	16	6.2	28	5.7	0	0.0	6	3.4	10	6.9	12	7.0	0	0.0	28	5.7	12
Puerto Rican	0	0.0	0	0.0	0	0.0	0	0.0	0	0.0	0	0.0	0	0.0	0	0.0	0	0.0	0
Hispanic American	7	3.1	14	5.4	21	4.3	0	0.0	7	4.0	5	3.5	9	5.3	0	0.0	21	4.3	4
Total Minorities	45	19.7	84	32.3	129	26.4	0	0.0	41	23.6	46	31.9	42	24.6	0	0.0	129	26.4	41
Foreign Nationals	2	0.9	3	1.2	5	1.0	0	0.0	4	2.3	0	0.0	1	0.6	0	0.0	5	1.0	1
Caucasian	182	79.5	173	66.5	354	72.5	1	100.0	129	74.1	98	68.1	128	74.9	0	0.0	355	72.6	119
Total	229	46.8	260	53.2	488	99.8	1	0.2	174	35.6	144	29.4	171	35.0	0	0.0	489		161

GPA & LSAT Scores

	Full Time	Part Time	Total
# of apps	1,717	0	1,717
# admits	493	0	493
# of matrics	173	0	173
75% GPA	3.72	0.00	
25% GPA	3.38	0.00	
75% LSAT	166	0	
25% LSAT	158	0	

Tuition & Fees

	Resident	Non-resident
Full-Time	$5,763	$14,169
Part-Time	$0	$0

Living Expenses

Estimated living expenses for Singles		
Living on campus	Living off campus	Living at home
$11,400	$11,400	$5,800

Grants/Scholarships

	Full-time		Part-time		Total	
	#	%	#	%	#	%
Total # of Students	488		1		489	
Total # receiving grants	222	45.5	1	100.0	223	45.6
Less than 1/2 tuition	99	20.3	1	100.0	100	20.4
Half to full tuition	48	9.8	0	0.0	48	9.8
Full tuition	10	2.0	0	0.0	10	2.0
More than full tuition	65	13.3	0	0.0	65	13.3
Median Grant Amount	$1,600		$1,200			

Informational & Library Resources

# of volumes & volume equivalents	518,686	# of professional staff	14
# of titles	116,798	Hours per week with professional staff	60
# of active serial subscriptions	7,866	Hours per week without professional staff	29
Study seating capacity inside the library	372	# of student computer work stations for entire law school	22
Square feet of law library	48,950	# of additional networked connections	0
Square feet of law school (excl. Library)	40,440	Require Laptop Computer?	N

Employment

	Total	%
Employment status known	171	95.5
Employment status unknown	8	4.5
Employed	146	85.4
Pursuing graduate degrees	11	6.4
Unemployed seeking employment	13	7.6
Unemployed not seeking employment	1	0.6
Type of Employment		
# employed in law firms	74	50.7
# employed in business & industry	23	15.8
# employed in government	21	14.4
# employed in public interest	11	7.5
# employed as judicial clerks	15	10.3
# employed in academia	2	1.4
Geographic Location		
# employed in state	105	71.9
# employed in foreign countries	4	2.7
# of states where employed	17	

J.D. Attrition (from Prior Year)

	Academic	Other	TOTALS	
	#	#	#	%
1st Year	0	0	0	0.0%
2nd Year	0	0	0	0.0%
3rd Year	0	0	0	0.0%
4th Year	0	0	0	0.0%

Bar Passage Rates

Jurisdiction	Washington		
Exam	Sum 97	Win 98	Total
# from school taking bar for the first time	132	11	143
School's pass rate for all first-time takers	86%	91%	86%
State's pass rate for all first-time takers	73%	83%	76%

WAYNE STATE UNIVERSITY

468 Ferry Mall
Detroit, MI 48202
(313)577-3933
http://www.law.wayne.edu/

ABA Approved Since 1936

The Basics

Type of School: Public Term: Semester
Application deadline: 03/15
Application fee: $20
Financial Aid deadline: 04/30
Can first year start other than Fall? No
Student faculty ratio: 21.2 to 1
Does the University offer:
- housing restricted to law students? No
- graduate student housing for which law students are eligible? Yes

Faculty & Administrators

	Total		Men		Women		Minorities	
	Fall	Spr	Fall	Spr	Fall	Spr	Fall	Spr
Full-time	26	22	20	18	6	4	3	2
Other Full-Time	3	3	0	0	3	3	1	1
Deans, librarians, & others who teach > 1/2	3	3	1	1	2	2	0	0
Part-time	27	29	20	26	7	3	0	2
Total	59	57	41	45	18	12	4	5
Deans, librarians, & others who teach < 1/2	1	1	0	0	1	1	0	0

Curriculum

	Full time	Part time
Typical first-year section size	97	59
Is there typically a "small section" of the first year class, other than Legal Writing, taught by full-time faculty?	No	No
If yes, typical size offered last year	N/A	N/A
# of classroom course titles beyond 1st year curriculum	49	30
# of upper division courses, excluding seminars, with an enrollment:		
Under 25	25	23
25 - 49	14	13
50 - 74	7	2
75 - 99	4	4
100 +	3	1
# of seminars	11	5
# of seminar positions available	303	
# of seminar positions filled	157	40
# of positions available in simulation courses	360	
# of simulation positions filled	132	213
# of positions available in faculty supervised clinical courses	0	
# of fac. sup. clin. positions filled	0	0
# involved in field placements	90	10
# involved in law journals	47	8
# in moot court or trial competitions	148	20
# of credit hrs required to graduate	86	

J.D. Enrollment & Ethnicity

	Men		Women		Fl-Time		Pt-Time		1st Yr		2nd Yr		3rd Yr		4th Yr		Total		JD Degrees Awarded
	#	%	#	%	#	%	#	%	#	%	#	%	#	%	#	%	#	%	
African-American	27	6.8	51	15.2	41	7.9	37	16.8	22	8.6	26	11.3	22	11.2	8	15.4	78	10.6	19
American Indian	2	0.5	0	0.0	1	0.2	1	0.5	0	0.0	0	0.0	2	1.0	0	0.0	2	0.3	1
Asian American	12	3.0	8	2.4	13	2.5	7	3.2	9	3.5	6	2.6	3	1.5	2	3.8	20	2.7	4
Mexican American	1	0.3	4	1.2	4	0.8	1	0.5	3	1.2	0	0.0	2	1.0	0	0.0	5	0.7	3
Puerto Rican	2	0.5	4	1.2	5	1.0	1	0.5	3	1.2	3	1.3	0	0.0	0	0.0	6	0.8	0
Hispanic American	2	0.5	3	0.9	4	0.8	1	0.5	1	0.4	2	0.9	1	0.5	1	1.9	5	0.7	3
Total Minorities	46	11.5	70	20.8	68	13.2	48	21.8	38	14.8	37	16.0	30	15.2	11	21.2	116	15.8	30
Foreign Nationals	0	0.0	0	0.0	0	0.0	0	0.0	0	0.0	0	0.0	0	0.0	0	0.0	0	0.0	0
Caucasian	354	88.5	266	79.2	448	86.8	172	78.2	218	85.2	194	84.0	167	84.8	41	78.8	620	84.2	180
Total	400	54.3	336	45.7	516	70.1	220	29.9	256	34.8	231	31.4	197	26.8	52	7.1	736		210

GPA & LSAT Scores

	Full Time	Part Time	Total
# of apps	707	275	982
# admits	413	96	509
# of matrics	197	64	261
75% GPA	3.46	3.36	
25% GPA	3.06	2.86	
75% LSAT	157	158	
25% LSAT	151	150	

Tuition & Fees

	Resident	Non-resident
Full-Time	$7,194	$14,782
Part-Time	$5,178	$10,598

Living Expenses

Estimated living expenses for Singles		
Living on campus	Living off campus	Living at home
$15,020	$15,020	$9,870

Grants/Scholarships

	Full-time		Part-time		Total	
	#	%	#	%	#	%
Total # of Students	516		220		736	
Total # receiving grants	323	62.6	0	0.0	323	43.9
Less than 1/2 tuition	0	0.0	0	0.0	0	0.0
Half to full tuition	0	0.0	0	0.0	0	0.0
Full tuition	323	62.6	0	0.0	323	43.9
More than full tuition	0	0.0	0	0.0	0	0.0
Median Grant Amount	$1,600		$0			

Informational & Library Resources

# of volumes & volume equivalents	558,524	# of professional staff	4
# of titles	230,276	Hours per week with professional staff	69
# of active serial subscriptions	4,771	Hours per week without professional staff	28
Study seating capacity inside the library	506	# of student computer work stations for entire law school	44
Square feet of law library	28,257	# of additional networked connections	0
Square feet of law school (excl. Library)	41,942	Require Laptop Computer?	N

Employment

	Total	%
Employment status known	185	90.7
Employment status unknown	19	9.3
Employed	172	93.0
Pursuing graduate degrees	1	0.5
Unemployed seeking employment	12	6.5
Unemployed not seeking employment	0	0.0
Type of Employment		
# employed in law firms	92	53.5
# employed in business & industry	32	18.6
# employed in government	26	15.1
# employed in public interest	5	2.9
# employed as judicial clerks	12	7.0
# employed in academia	4	2.3
Geographic Location		
# employed in state	162	94.2
# employed in foreign countries	0	0.0
# of states where employed	5	

J.D. Attrition (from Prior Year)

	Academic	Other	TOTALS	
	#	#	#	%
1st Year	17	23	40	16%
2nd Year	2	7	9	4.2%
3rd Year	2	1	3	1.4%
4th Year	0	0	0	0.0%

Bar Passage Rates

Jurisdiction	Michigan		
Exam	Sum 97	Win 98	Total
# from school taking bar for the first time	199	32	231
School's pass rate for all first-time takers	95%	94%	95%
State's pass rate for all first-time takers	89%	79%	86%

WEST VIRGINIA UNIVERSITY

P.O. Box 6130
Morgantown, WV 26506-6130
(304)293-3199
http://www.wvu.edu/~law

ABA Approved Since 1923

The Basics

Type of School: Public | Term: Semester

Application deadline: 03/01

Application fee: $45

Financial Aid deadline: 03/01

Can first year start other than Fall? No

Student faculty ratio: 16.4 to 1

Does the University offer:
- housing restricted to law students? No
- graduate student housing for which law students are eligible? Yes

Faculty & Administrators

	Total		Men		Women		Minorities	
	Fall	Spr	Fall	Spr	Fall	Spr	Fall	Spr
Full-time	22	21	15	14	7	7	2	2
Other Full-Time	0	0	0	0	0	0	0	0
Deans, librarians, & others who teach > 1/2	2	2	1	1	1	1	0	0
Part-time	18	12	14	7	4	5	0	0
Total	42	35	30	22	12	13	2	2
Deans, librarians, & others who teach < 1/2	1	1	1	1	0	0	0	0

Curriculum

	Full time	Part time
Typical first-year section size	75	0
Is there typically a "small section" of the first year class, other than Legal Writing, taught by full-time faculty?	No	No
If yes, typical size offered last year	N/A	N/A
# of classroom course titles beyond 1st year curriculum	64	0
# of upper division courses, excluding seminars, with an enrollment:		
Under 25	32	0
25 - 49	20	0
50 - 74	13	0
75 - 99	6	0
100 +	1	0
# of seminars	11	0
# of seminar positions available	170	
# of seminar positions filled	148	0
# of positions available in simulation courses	328	
# of simulation positions filled	311	0
# of positions available in faculty supervised clinical courses	30	
# of fac. sup. clin. positions filled	30	0
# involved in field placements	0	0
# involved in law journals	46	0
# in moot court or trial competitions	110	0
# of credit hrs required to graduate	93	

J.D. Enrollment & Ethnicity

	Men		Women		Fl-Time		Pt-Time		1st Yr		2nd Yr		3rd Yr		4th Yr		Total		JD Degrees Awarded
	#	%	#	%	#	%	#	%	#	%	#	%	#	%	#	%	#	%	
African-American	4	1.7	8	3.9	12	2.8	0	0.0	7	4.7	1	0.7	4	2.7	0	0.0	12	2.7	2
American Indian	1	0.4	1	0.5	2	0.5	0	0.0	2	1.3	0	0.0	0	0.0	0	0.0	2	0.5	1
Asian American	4	1.7	5	2.4	9	2.1	0	0.0	4	2.7	3	2.1	2	1.3	0	0.0	9	2.1	0
Mexican American	0	0.0	0	0.0	0	0.0	0	0.0	0	0.0	0	0.0	0	0.0	0	0.0	0	0.0	0
Puerto Rican	0	0.0	0	0.0	0	0.0	0	0.0	0	0.0	0	0.0	0	0.0	0	0.0	0	0.0	0
Hispanic American	3	1.3	1	0.5	4	0.9	0	0.0	2	1.3	2	1.4	0	0.0	0	0.0	4	0.9	1
Total Minorities	12	5.2	15	7.2	27	6.4	0	0.0	15	10.1	6	4.3	6	4.0	0	0.0	27	6.2	4
Foreign Nationals	0	0.0	0	0.0	0	0.0	0	0.0	0	0.0	0	0.0	0	0.0	0	0.0	0	0.0	0
Caucasian	220	94.8	192	92.8	396	93.6	16	100.0	134	89.9	135	95.7	143	96.0	0	0.0	412	93.8	130
Total	232	52.8	207	47.2	423	96.4	16	3.6	149	33.9	141	32.1	149	33.9	0	0.0	439		134

GPA & LSAT Scores

	Full Time	Part Time	Total
# of apps	503	7	510
# admits	245	7	252
# of matrics	142	7	149
75% GPA	3.62	0.00	
25% GPA	2.96	0.00	
75% LSAT	156	0	
25% LSAT	150	0	

Tuition & Fees

	Resident	Non-resident
Full-Time	$5,296	$12,568
Part-Time	$0	$0

Living Expenses

Estimated living expenses for Singles		
Living on campus	Living off campus	Living at home
$8,440	$10,439	$5,374

Grants/Scholarships

	Full-time		Part-time		Total	
	#	%	#	%	#	%
Total # of Students	423		16		439	
Total # receiving grants	90	21.3	0	0.0	90	20.5
Less than 1/2 tuition	63	14.9	0	0.0	63	14.4
Half to full tuition	5	1.2	0	0.0	5	1.1
Full tuition	10	2.4	0	0.0	10	2.3
More than full tuition	12	2.8	0	0.0	12	2.7
Median Grant Amount	$3,271		$0			

Informational & Library Resources

# of volumes & volume equivalents	255,023	# of professional staff	4
# of titles	44,181	Hours per week with professional staff	40
# of active serial subscriptions	2,989	Hours per week without professional staff	56
Study seating capacity inside the library	274	# of student computer work stations for entire law school	51
Square feet of law library	32,476	# of additional networked connections	30
Square feet of law school (excl. Library)	99,490	Require Laptop Computer?	N

Employment

	Total	%
Employment status known	131	94.2
Employment status unknown	8	5.8
Employed	123	93.9
Pursuing graduate degrees	4	3.1
Unemployed seeking employment	4	3.1
Unemployed not seeking employment	0	0.0
Type of Employment		
# employed in law firms	83	67.5
# employed in business & industry	5	4.1
# employed in government	21	17.1
# employed in public interest	4	3.3
# employed as judicial clerks	10	8.1
# employed in academia	0	0.0
Geographic Location		
# employed in state	99	80.5
# employed in foreign countries	1	0.8
# of states where employed	12	

J.D. Attrition (from Prior Year)

	Academic	Other	TOTALS	
	#	#	#	%
1st Year	6	7	13	8.7%
2nd Year	0	2	2	1.4%
3rd Year	3	0	3	2.1%
4th Year	0	0	0	0.0%

Bar Passage Rates

Jurisdiction	West Virginia		
Exam	Sum 97	Win 98	Total
# from school taking bar for the first time	127	27	154
School's pass rate for all first-time takers	81%	67%	79%
State's pass rate for all first-time takers	85%	67%	84%

WESTERN NEW ENGLAND COLLEGE

1215 Wilbraham Road
Springfield, MA 01119
(413)782-1412
http://www.law.wnec.edu

ABA Approved Since 1974

The Basics

Type of School: Private Term: Semester
Application deadline: Rolling
Application fee: $45
Financial Aid deadline: 04/01
Can first year start other than Fall? No
Student faculty ratio: 16.9 to 1
Does the University offer:
- housing restricted to law students? No
- graduate student housing for which law students are eligible? No

Faculty & Administrators

	Total		Men		Women		Minorities	
	Fall	Spr	Fall	Spr	Fall	Spr	Fall	Spr
Full-time	25	25	19	19	6	6	1	1
Other Full-Time	5	5	0	0	5	5	1	1
Deans, librarians, & others who teach > 1/2	1	1	1	1	0	0	0	0
Part-time	24	24	11	15	12	9	2	1
Total	55	55	31	35	23	20	4	3
Deans, librarians, & others who teach < 1/2	1	1	1	1	0	0	0	0

Curriculum

	Full time	Part time
Typical first-year section size	64	57
Is there typically a "small section" of the first year class, other than Legal Writing, taught by full-time faculty?	No	No
If yes, typical size offered last year	N/A	N/A
# of classroom course titles beyond 1st year curriculum	73	75
# of upper division courses, excluding seminars, with an enrollment:		
Under 25	26	26
25 - 49	16	17
50 - 74	5	10
75 - 99	4	0
100 +	0	0
# of seminars	3	0
# of seminar positions available	90	
# of seminar positions filled	53	3
# of positions available in simulation courses	410	
# of simulation positions filled	254	87
# of positions available in faculty supervised clinical courses	20	
# of fac. sup. clin. positions filled	19	1
# involved in field placements	44	6
# involved in law journals	30	7
# in moot court or trial competitions	12	5
# of credit hrs required to graduate	88	

J.D. Enrollment & Ethnicity

	Men		Women		Fl-Time		Pt-Time		1st Yr		2nd Yr		3rd Yr		4th Yr		Total		JD Degrees Awarded
	#	%	#	%	#	%	#	%	#	%	#	%	#	%	#	%	#	%	
African-American	15	5.1	13	4.4	17	4.8	11	4.8	13	7.1	9	5.0	3	1.8	3	5.8	28	4.8	7
American Indian	2	0.7	2	0.7	3	0.8	1	0.4	4	2.2	0	0.0	0	0.0	0	0.0	4	0.7	0
Asian American	10	3.4	3	1.0	9	2.5	4	1.7	5	2.7	2	1.1	5	2.9	1	1.9	13	2.2	3
Mexican American	0	0.0	0	0.0	0	0.0	0	0.0	0	0.0	0	0.0	0	0.0	0	0.0	0	0.0	0
Puerto Rican	0	0.0	0	0.0	0	0.0	0	0.0	0	0.0	0	0.0	0	0.0	0	0.0	0	0.0	0
Hispanic American	11	3.8	11	3.7	13	3.6	9	3.9	10	5.4	5	2.8	4	2.4	3	5.8	22	3.8	7
Total Minorities	38	13.0	29	9.9	42	11.8	25	10.9	32	17.4	16	8.9	12	7.1	7	13.5	67	11.4	17
Foreign Nationals	0	0.0	0	0.0	0	0.0	0	0.0	0	0.0	0	0.0	0	0.0	0	0.0	0	0.0	0
Caucasian	254	87.0	265	90.1	315	88.2	204	89.1	152	82.6	164	91.1	158	92.9	45	86.5	519	88.6	174
Total	292	49.8	294	50.2	357	60.9	229	39.1	184	31.4	180	30.7	170	29.0	52	8.9	586		191

GPA & LSAT Scores

	Full Time	Part Time	Total
# of apps	799	163	962
# admits	555	113	668
# of matrics	124	60	184
75% GPA	3.36	3.31	
25% GPA	2.78	2.61	
75% LSAT	151	151	
25% LSAT	142	140	

Tuition & Fees

	Resident	Non-resident
Full-Time	$18,394	$18,394
Part-Time	$13,570	$13,570

Living Expenses

Estimated living expenses for Singles		
Living on campus	Living off campus	Living at home
N/A	$11,143	$6,008

Grants/Scholarships

	Full-time		Part-time		Total	
	#	%	#	%	#	%
Total # of Students	357		229		586	
Total # receiving grants	116	32.5	54	23.6	170	29.0
Less than 1/2 tuition	101	28.3	51	22.3	152	25.9
Half to full tuition	7	2.0	3	1.3	10	1.7
Full tuition	8	2.2	0	0.0	8	1.4
More than full tuition	0	0.0	0	0.0	0	0.0
Median Grant Amount	$2,000		$1,500			

Informational & Library Resources

# of volumes & volume equivalents	350,275	# of professional staff	6
# of titles	42,929	Hours per week with professional staff	69
# of active serial subscriptions	4,681	Hours per week without professional staff	34
Study seating capacity inside the library	397	# of student computer work stations for entire law school	48
Square feet of law library	30,151	# of additional networked connections	0
Square feet of law school (excl. Library)	54,627	Require Laptop Computer?	N

Employment

	Total	%
Employment status known	210	96.3
Employment status unknown	8	3.7
Employed	185	88.1
Pursuing graduate degrees	2	1.0
Unemployed seeking employment	18	8.6
Unemployed not seeking employment	5	2.4
Type of Employment		
# employed in law firms	72	38.9
# employed in business & industry	48	25.9
# employed in government	41	22.2
# employed in public interest	3	1.6
# employed as judicial clerks	17	9.2
# employed in academia	4	2.2
Geographic Location		
# employed in state	74	40.0
# employed in foreign countries	1	0.5
# of states where employed	22	

J.D. Attrition (from Prior Year)

	Academic	Other	TOTALS	
	#	#	#	%
1st Year	11	24	35	17%
2nd Year	0	4	4	2.3%
3rd Year	0	0	0	0.0%
4th Year	0	0	0	0.0%

Bar Passage Rates

Jurisdiction	Massachusetts			Connecticut		
Exam	Sum 97	Win 98	Total	Sum 97	Win 98	Total
# from school taking bar for the first time	96	18	114	52	21	73
School's pass rate for all first-time takers	67%	83%	69%	81%	86%	82%
State's pass rate for all first-time takers	84%	72%	82%	85%	81%	84%

WESTERN STATE UNIVERSITY (Provisional)

1111 North State College Blvd.
Fullerton, CA 92831-3014
(714)738-1000
http://www.wsulaw.edu

ABA Approved Since 1998

The Basics

Type of School: Private   Term: Semester
Application deadline: 05/31
Application fee: $35
Financial Aid deadline: 04/16
Can first year start other than Fall? Yes
Student faculty ratio: 23.3 to 1
Does the University offer:
- housing restricted to law students? No
- graduate student housing for which law students are eligible? No

Faculty & Administrators

	Total		Men		Women		Minorities	
	Fall	Spr	Fall	Spr	Fall	Spr	Fall	Spr
Full-time	20	20	11	11	9	9	6	6
Other Full-Time	0	0	0	0	0	0	0	0
Deans, librarians, & others who teach > 1/2	3	3	2	2	1	1	0	0
Part-time	30	25	21	19	9	6	2	2
Total	53	48	34	32	19	16	8	8
Deans, librarians, & others who teach < 1/2	1	1	1	1	0	0	0	0

Curriculum

	Full time	Part time
Typical first-year section size	36	36
Is there typically a "small section" of the first year class, other than Legal Writing, taught by full-time faculty?	No	No
If yes, typical size offered last year	N/A	N/A
# of classroom course titles beyond 1st year curriculum	37	48
# of upper division courses, excluding seminars, with an enrollment:		
Under 25	26	54
25 - 49	16	44
50 - 74	7	16
75 - 99	0	3
100 +	0	0
# of seminars	7	1
# of seminar positions available	200	
# of seminar positions filled	118	12
# of positions available in simulation courses	725	
# of simulation positions filled	198	407
# of positions available in faculty supervised clinical courses	0	
# of fac. sup. clin. positions filled	0	0
# involved in field placements	72	62
# involved in law journals	21	16
# in moot court or trial competitions	6	7
# of credit hrs required to graduate	88	

J.D. Enrollment & Ethnicity

	Men		Women		Fl-Time		Pt-Time		1st Yr		2nd Yr		3rd Yr		4th Yr		Total		JD Degrees Awarded
	#	%	#	%	#	%	#	%	#	%	#	%	#	%	#	%	#	%	
African-American	29	6.9	21	6.8	12	5.2	38	7.6	12	7.6	11	9.6	14	5.9	13	5.9	50	6.8	13
American Indian	3	0.7	3	1.0	1	0.4	5	1.0	1	0.6	1	0.9	2	0.8	2	0.9	6	0.8	1
Asian American	55	13.1	47	15.2	43	18.6	59	11.8	18	11.5	5	4.3	43	18.2	36	16.2	102	14.0	30
Mexican American	38	9.0	34	11.0	23	10.0	49	9.8	12	7.6	13	11.3	25	10.6	22	9.9	72	9.9	1
Puerto Rican	0	0.0	1	0.3	1	0.4	0	0.0	1	0.6	0	0.0	0	0.0	0	0.0	1	0.1	0
Hispanic American	10	2.4	3	1.0	5	2.2	8	1.6	7	4.5	0	0.0	2	0.8	4	1.8	13	1.8	26
Total Minorities	135	32.1	109	35.3	85	36.8	159	31.9	51	32.5	30	26.1	86	36.4	77	34.7	244	33.4	71
Foreign Nationals	10	2.4	8	2.6	6	2.6	12	2.4	14	8.9	4	3.5	0	0.0	0	0.0	18	2.5	0
Caucasian	276	65.6	192	62.1	140	60.6	328	65.7	92	58.6	81	70.4	150	63.6	145	65.3	468	64.1	162
Total	421	57.7	309	42.3	231	31.6	499	68.4	157	21.5	115	15.8	236	32.3	222	30.4	730		233

GPA & LSAT Scores

	Full Time	Part Time	Total
# of apps	365	335	700
# admits	207	179	386
# of matrics	79	94	173
75% GPA	3.17	3.13	
25% GPA	2.45	2.49	
75% LSAT	151	151	
25% LSAT	143	142	

Tuition & Fees

	Resident	Non-resident
Full-Time	$18,900	$18,900
Part-Time	$12,600	$12,600

Living Expenses

Estimated living expenses for Singles		
Living on campus	Living off campus	Living at home
N/A	$15,266	$8,462

Grants/Scholarships

	Full-time		Part-time		Total	
	#	%	#	%	#	%
Total # of Students	231		499		730	
Total # receiving grants	130	56.3	195	39.1	325	44.5
Less than 1/2 tuition	111	48.1	175	35.1	286	39.2
Half to full tuition	17	7.4	18	3.6	35	4.8
Full tuition	2	0.9	2	0.4	4	0.5
More than full tuition	0	0.0	0	0.0	0	0.0
Median Grant Amount	$4,826		$3,486			

Informational & Library Resources

# of volumes & volume equivalents	148,506	# of professional staff	8
# of titles	15,250	Hours per week with professional staff	100
# of active serial subscriptions	2,834	Hours per week without professional staff	16
Study seating capacity inside the library	340	# of student computer work stations for entire law school	60
Square feet of law library	27,176	# of additional networked connections	312
Square feet of law school (excl. Library)	53,450	Require Laptop Computer?	N

Employment

	Total	%
Employment status known	246	84.5
Employment status unknown	45	15.5
Employed	220	89.4
Pursuing graduate degrees	3	1.2
Unemployed seeking employment	10	4.1
Unemployed not seeking employment	13	5.3
Type of Employment		
# employed in law firms	127	57.7
# employed in business & industry	48	21.8
# employed in government	24	10.9
# employed in public interest	8	3.6
# employed as judicial clerks	1	0.5
# employed in academia	5	2.3
Geographic Location		
# employed in state	219	99.5
# employed in foreign countries	0	0.0
# of states where employed	2	

J.D. Attrition (from Prior Year)

	Academic	Other	TOTALS	
	#	#	#	%
1st Year	13	17	30	17%
2nd Year	38	54	92	43%
3rd Year	10	14	24	8.2%
4th Year	4	17	21	***%

Bar Passage Rates

Jurisdiction	California		
Exam	Sum 97	Win 98	Total
# from school taking bar for the first time	136	121	257
School's pass rate for all first-time takers	50%	46%	48%
State's pass rate for all first-time takers	75%	57%	71%

WHITTIER COLLEGE

3333 Harbor Boulevard
Costa Mesa, CA 92626
(714)444-4141
http://www.whittier.edu

ABA Approved Since 1978

The Basics

Type of School: Private — Term: Semester

Application deadline: 03/15

Application fee: $50

Financial Aid deadline: 04/15

Can first year start other than Fall? Yes

Student faculty ratio: 17.4 to 1

Does the University offer:
- housing restricted to law students? No
- graduate student housing for which law students are eligible? No

Faculty & Administrators

	Total		Men		Women		Minorities	
	Fall	Spr	Fall	Spr	Fall	Spr	Fall	Spr
Full-time	27	27	16	16	11	11	3	3
Other Full-Time	0	0	0	0	0	0	0	0
Deans, librarians, & others who teach > 1/2	0	0	0	0	0	0	0	0
Part-time	25	17	16	13	9	4	1	2
Total	52	44	32	29	20	15	4	5
Deans, librarians, & others who teach < 1/2	3	3	3	3	0	0	0	0

Curriculum

	Full time	Part time
Typical first-year section size	85	74
Is there typically a "small section" of the first year class, other than Legal Writing, taught by full-time faculty?	Yes	Yes
If yes, typical size offered last year	42	37
# of classroom course titles beyond 1st year curriculum	47	21
# of upper division courses, excluding seminars, with an enrollment:		
Under 25	28	15
25 - 49	15	9
50 - 74	8	5
75 - 99	7	0
100 +	0	0
# of seminars	8	0
# of seminar positions available	160	
# of seminar positions filled	67	19
# of positions available in simulation courses	640	
# of simulation positions filled	400	179
# of positions available in faculty supervised clinical courses	0	
# of fac. sup. clin. positions filled	0	0
# involved in field placements	87	54
# involved in law journals	38	23
# in moot court or trial competitions	52	23
# of credit hrs required to graduate	87	

J.D. Enrollment & Ethnicity

	Men		Women		Fl-Time		Pt-Time		1st Yr		2nd Yr		3rd Yr		4th Yr		Total		JD Degrees Awarded
	#	%	#	%	#	%	#	%	#	%	#	%	#	%	#	%	#	%	
African-American	17	5.0	24	7.6	22	5.6	19	7.3	11	5.0	12	5.6	12	7.1	6	12.0	41	6.3	4
American Indian	6	1.8	3	1.0	6	1.5	3	1.2	5	2.3	2	0.9	2	1.2	0	0.0	9	1.4	0
Asian American	47	13.9	46	14.6	59	15.1	34	13.1	33	15.1	41	19.2	12	7.1	7	14.0	93	14.3	22
Mexican American	31	9.2	26	8.3	36	9.2	21	8.1	23	10.5	10	4.7	21	12.5	3	6.0	57	8.8	12
Puerto Rican	0	0.0	1	0.3	1	0.3	0	0.0	0	0.0	1	0.5	0	0.0	0	0.0	1	0.2	0
Hispanic American	19	5.6	18	5.7	23	5.9	14	5.4	6	2.7	16	7.5	11	6.5	4	8.0	37	5.7	7
Total Minorities	120	35.6	118	37.6	147	37.5	91	35.1	78	35.6	82	38.3	58	34.5	20	40.0	238	36.6	45
Foreign Nationals	0	0.0	0	0.0	0	0.0	0	0.0	0	0.0	0	0.0	0	0.0	0	0.0	0	0.0	0
Caucasian	217	64.4	196	62.4	245	62.5	168	64.9	141	64.4	132	61.7	110	65.5	30	60.0	413	63.4	107
Total	337	51.8	314	48.2	392	60.2	259	39.8	219	33.6	214	32.9	168	25.8	50	7.7	651		152

GPA & LSAT Scores

	Full Time	Part Time	Total
# of apps	1,170	286	1,456
# admits	708	154	862
# of matrics	152	80	232
75% GPA	3.24	3.25	
25% GPA	2.68	2.62	
75% LSAT	153	152	
25% LSAT	146	146	

Tuition & Fees

	Resident	Non-resident
Full-Time	$21,064	$21,064
Part-Time	$12,652	$12,652

Living Expenses

Estimated living expenses for Singles		
Living on campus	Living off campus	Living at home
N/A	$15,219	N/A

Employment

	Total	%
Employment status known	173	92.0
Employment status unknown	15	8.0
Employed	129	74.6
Pursuing graduate degrees	5	2.9
Unemployed seeking employment	21	12.1
Unemployed not seeking employment	18	10.4
Type of Employment		
# employed in law firms	82	63.6
# employed in business & industry	20	15.5
# employed in government	17	13.2
# employed in public interest	3	2.3
# employed as judicial clerks	3	2.3
# employed in academia	4	3.1
Geographic Location		
# employed in state	104	80.6
# employed in foreign countries	0	0.0
# of states where employed	11	

Grants/Scholarships

	Full-time		Part-time		Total	
	#	%	#	%	#	%
Total # of Students	392		259		651	
Total # receiving grants	163	41.6	53	20.5	216	33.2
Less than 1/2 tuition	136	34.7	51	19.7	187	28.7
Half to full tuition	15	3.8	1	0.4	16	2.5
Full tuition	12	3.1	1	0.4	13	2.0
More than full tuition	0	0.0	0	0.0	0	0.0
Median Grant Amount	$5,000		$4,000			

Informational & Library Resources

# of volumes & volume equivalents	306,459	# of professional staff	6
# of titles	117,832	Hours per week with professional staff	81
# of active serial subscriptions	4,971	Hours per week without professional staff	21
Study seating capacity inside the library	386	# of student computer work stations for entire law school	68
Square feet of law library	45,000	# of additional networked connections	225
Square feet of law school (excl. Library)	82,182	Require Laptop Computer?	N

J.D. Attrition (from Prior Year)

	Academic	Other	TOTALS	
	#	#	#	%
1st Year	38	22	60	24%
2nd Year	6	5	11	6.1%
3rd Year	0	0	0	0.0%
4th Year	0	0	0	0.0%

Bar Passage Rates

Jurisdiction	California		
Exam	Sum 97	Win 98	Total
# from school taking bar for the first time	137	23	160
School's pass rate for all first-time takers	68%	74%	69%
State's pass rate for all first-time takers	75%	57%	71%

WIDENER UNIVERSITY

4601 Concord Pike
P.O. Box 7474
Wilmington, DE 19803-0474
(302)477-2100
http://www.widener.edu/law/law.html

ABA Approved Since 1975

The Basics

Type of School: Private — Term: Semester
Application deadline: 05/15
Application fee: $60
Financial Aid deadline: 04/15
Can first year start other than Fall? No
Student faculty ratio: 27.6 to 1
Does the University offer:
- housing restricted to law students? Yes
- graduate student housing for which law students are eligible? Yes

Faculty & Administrators

	Total		Men		Women		Minorities	
	Fall	Spr	Fall	Spr	Fall	Spr	Fall	Spr
Full-time	28	27	17	16	11	11	0	0
Other Full-Time	7	7	2	2	5	5	1	1
Deans, librarians, & others who teach > 1/2	10	10	6	6	4	4	1	1
Part-time	41	37	29	23	12	14	2	1
Total	86	81	54	47	32	34	4	3
Deans, librarians, & others who teach < 1/2	0	0	0	0	0	0	0	0

Curriculum

	Full time	Part time
Typical first-year section size	104	63
Is there typically a "small section" of the first year class, other than Legal Writing, taught by full-time faculty?	Yes	Yes
If yes, typical size offered last year	53	45
# of classroom course titles beyond 1st year curriculum	66	101
# of upper division courses, excluding seminars, with an enrollment:		
Under 25	48	55
25 - 49	30	27
50 - 74	15	11
75 - 99	13	3
100 +	3	2
# of seminars	9	13
# of seminar positions available	440	
# of seminar positions filled	121	261
# of positions available in simulation courses	760	
# of simulation positions filled	380	380
# of positions available in faculty supervised clinical courses	80	
# of fac. sup. clin. positions filled	60	20
# involved in field placements	135	50
# involved in law journals	245	50
# in moot court or trial competitions	115	30
# of credit hrs required to graduate	87	

J.D. Enrollment & Ethnicity

	Men		Women		Fl-Time		Pt-Time		1st Yr		2nd Yr		3rd Yr		4th Yr		Total		JD Degrees Awarded
	#	%	#	%	#	%	#	%	#	%	#	%	#	%	#	%	#	%	
African-American	15	2.6	27	5.4	18	2.8	24	5.6	21	6.4	13	3.8	6	1.9	2	2.2	42	3.9	16
American Indian	2	0.3	1	0.2	2	0.3	1	0.2	0	0.0	0	0.0	2	0.6	1	1.1	3	0.3	1
Asian American	9	1.6	10	2.0	9	1.4	10	2.3	7	2.1	6	1.8	3	0.9	3	3.3	19	1.8	5
Mexican American	0	0.0	1	0.2	1	0.2	0	0.0	0	0.0	1	0.3	0	0.0	0	0.0	1	0.1	0
Puerto Rican	2	0.3	1	0.2	1	0.2	2	0.5	0	0.0	1	0.3	2	0.6	0	0.0	3	0.3	0
Hispanic American	3	0.5	2	0.4	3	0.5	2	0.5	3	0.9	1	0.3	1	0.3	0	0.0	5	0.5	2
Total Minorities	31	5.4	42	8.5	34	5.3	39	9.1	31	9.5	22	6.5	14	4.4	6	6.5	73	6.8	24
Foreign Nationals	0	0.0	0	0.0	0	0.0	0	0.0	0	0.0	0	0.0	0	0.0	0	0.0	0	0.0	0
Caucasian	547	94.6	454	91.5	611	94.7	390	90.9	295	90.5	318	93.5	302	95.6	86	93.5	1001	93.2	308
Total	578	53.8	496	46.2	645	60.1	429	39.9	326	30.4	340	31.7	316	29.4	92	8.6	1074		332

GPA & LSAT Scores

	Full Time	Part Time	Total
# of apps	945	322	1,267
# admits	681	213	894
# of matrics	206	124	330
75% GPA	3.22	3.23	
25% GPA	2.64	2.47	
75% LSAT	149	152	
25% LSAT	145	145	

Tuition & Fees

	Resident	Non-resident
Full-Time	$18,550	$18,550
Part-Time	$13,930	$13,930

Living Expenses

Estimated living expenses for Singles

Living on campus	Living off campus	Living at home
$11,970	$11,970	$8,070

Grants/Scholarships

	Full-time		Part-time		Total	
	#	%	#	%	#	%
Total # of Students	645		429		1074	
Total # receiving grants	134	20.8	58	13.5	192	17.9
Less than 1/2 tuition	94	14.6	26	6.1	120	11.2
Half to full tuition	21	3.3	23	5.4	44	4.1
Full tuition	19	2.9	9	2.1	28	2.6
More than full tuition	0	0.0	0	0.0	0	0.0
Median Grant Amount	$6,128		$6,738			

Informational & Library Resources

# of volumes & volume equivalents	396,579	# of professional staff	10
# of titles	77,086	Hours per week with professional staff	77
# of active serial subscriptions	5,420	Hours per week without professional staff	30
Study seating capacity inside the library	443	# of student computer work stations for entire law school	95
Square feet of law library	36,198	# of additional networked connections	0
Square feet of law school (excl. Library)	166,265	Require Laptop Computer?	N

Employment

	Total	%
Employment status known	351	93.6
Employment status unknown	24	6.4
Employed	284	80.9
Pursuing graduate degrees	8	2.3
Unemployed seeking employment	51	14.5
Unemployed not seeking employment	8	2.3
Type of Employment		
# employed in law firms	99	34.9
# employed in business & industry	57	20.1
# employed in government	28	9.9
# employed in public interest	3	1.1
# employed as judicial clerks	46	16.2
# employed in academia	0	0.0
Geographic Location		
# employed in state	65	22.9
# employed in foreign countries	0	0.0
# of states where employed	11	

J.D. Attrition (from Prior Year)

	Academic	Other	TOTALS	
	#	#	#	%
1st Year	31	17	48	13%
2nd Year	12	27	39	10%
3rd Year	0	2	2	0.6%
4th Year	1	0	1	1.0%

Bar Passage Rates

Jurisdiction	Pennsylvania			New Jersey		
Exam	Sum 97	Win 98	Total	Sum 97	Win 98	Total
# from school taking bar for the first time	199	60	259	210	35	245
School's pass rate for all first-time takers	76%	70%	75%	76%	71%	75%
State's pass rate for all first-time takers	81%	73%	79%	77%	0%	77%

WIDENER UNIVERSITY-HARRISBURG

3800 Vartan Way
P.O. Box 69382
Harrisburg, PA 17106-9382
(717)541-3900
http://www.widener.edu/law/law.html

ABA Approved Since 1989

The Basics

Type of School: Private   Term: Semester

Application deadline: 05/15

Application fee: $60

Financial Aid deadline: 04/15

Can first year start other than Fall? No

Student faculty ratio: 16.6 to 1

Does the University offer:
- housing restricted to law students? No
- graduate student housing for which law students are eligible? No

Faculty & Administrators

	Total		Men		Women		Minorities	
	Fall	Spr	Fall	Spr	Fall	Spr	Fall	Spr
Full-time	17	14	11	9	6	5	1	1
Other Full-Time	3	3	1	1	2	2	0	0
Deans, librarians, & others who teach > 1/2	2	2	2	2	0	0	0	0
Part-time	7	10	4	8	3	2	0	0
Total	29	29	18	20	11	9	1	1
Deans, librarians, & others who teach < 1/2	0	0	0	0	0	0	0	0

Curriculum

	Full time	Part time
Typical first-year section size	88	58
Is there typically a "small section" of the first year class, other than Legal Writing, taught by full-time faculty?	No	No
If yes, typical size offered last year	N/A	N/A
# of classroom course titles beyond 1st year curriculum	36	55
# of upper division courses, excluding seminars, with an enrollment:		
Under 25	32	30
25 - 49	8	17
50 - 74	4	4
75 - 99	7	0
100 +	0	0
# of seminars	3	7
# of seminar positions available	200	
# of seminar positions filled	39	77
# of positions available in simulation courses	250	
# of simulation positions filled	149	82
# of positions available in faculty supervised clinical courses	75	
# of fac. sup. clin. positions filled	66	7
# involved in field placements	34	8
# involved in law journals	90	12
# in moot court or trial competitions	55	5
# of credit hrs required to graduate	87	

J.D. Enrollment & Ethnicity

	Men		Women		Fl-Time		Pt-Time		1st Yr		2nd Yr		3rd Yr		4th Yr		Total		JD Degrees Awarded
	#	%	#	%	#	%	#	%	#	%	#	%	#	%	#	%	#	%	
African-American	2	0.9	5	3.0	3	1.3	4	2.6	1	0.7	3	3.2	2	1.6	1	3.7	7	1.8	2
American Indian	0	0.0	1	0.6	1	0.4	0	0.0	1	0.7	0	0.0	0	0.0	0	0.0	1	0.3	0
Asian American	5	2.2	3	1.8	6	2.5	2	1.3	3	2.1	2	2.1	3	2.4	0	0.0	8	2.0	1
Mexican American	2	0.9	0	0.0	1	0.4	1	0.6	1	0.7	1	1.1	0	0.0	0	0.0	2	0.5	0
Puerto Rican	2	0.9	2	1.2	2	0.8	2	1.3	3	2.1	1	1.1	0	0.0	0	0.0	4	1.0	2
Hispanic American	0	0.0	1	0.6	0	0.0	1	0.6	1	0.7	0	0.0	0	0.0	0	0.0	1	0.3	0
Total Minorities	11	4.8	12	7.3	13	5.5	10	6.5	10	6.9	7	7.4	5	4.0	1	3.7	23	5.9	5
Foreign Nationals	0	0.0	0	0.0	0	0.0	0	0.0	0	0.0	0	0.0	0	0.0	0	0.0	0	0.0	0
Caucasian	217	95.2	152	92.7	225	94.5	144	93.5	134	93.1	88	92.6	121	96.0	26	96.3	369	94.1	163
Total	228	58.2	164	41.8	238	60.7	154	39.3	144	36.7	95	24.2	126	32.1	27	6.9	392		168

GPA & LSAT Scores

	Full Time	Part Time	Total
# of apps	461	130	591
# admits	258	83	341
# of matrics	86	62	148
75% GPA	3.37	3.31	
25% GPA	2.62	2.53	
75% LSAT	151	155	
25% LSAT	144	145	

Tuition & Fees

	Resident	Non-resident
Full-Time	$18,550	$18,550
Part-Time	$13,930	$13,930

Living Expenses

Estimated living expenses for Singles		
Living on campus	Living off campus	Living at home
N/A	$11,970	$8,070

Grants/Scholarships

	Full-time		Part-time		Total	
	#	%	#	%	#	%
Total # of Students	238		154		392	
Total # receiving grants	49	20.6	27	17.5	76	19.4
Less than 1/2 tuition	34	14.3	9	5.8	43	11.0
Half to full tuition	8	3.4	16	10.4	24	6.1
Full tuition	7	2.9	2	1.3	9	2.3
More than full tuition	0	0.0	0	0.0	0	0.0
Median Grant Amount	$6,685		$5,817			

Informational & Library Resources

# of volumes & volume equivalents	179,115	# of professional staff	5
# of titles	22,806	Hours per week with professional staff	77
# of active serial subscriptions	3,558	Hours per week without professional staff	27
Study seating capacity inside the library	358	# of student computer work stations for entire law school	48
Square feet of law library	20,241	# of additional networked connections	0
Square feet of law school (excl. Library)	69,638	Require Laptop Computer?	N

Employment

	Total	%
Employment status known	161	92.0
Employment status unknown	14	8.0
Employed	130	80.7
Pursuing graduate degrees	1	0.6
Unemployed seeking employment	23	14.3
Unemployed not seeking employment	7	4.3
Type of Employment		
# employed in law firms	37	28.5
# employed in business & industry	20	15.4
# employed in government	36	27.7
# employed in public interest	4	3.1
# employed as judicial clerks	23	17.7
# employed in academia	1	0.8
Geographic Location		
# employed in state	81	62.3
# employed in foreign countries	0	0.0
# of states where employed	14	

J.D. Attrition (from Prior Year)

	Academic	Other	TOTALS	
	#	#	#	%
1st Year	6	38	44	35%
2nd Year	3	2	5	3.8%
3rd Year	0	2	2	1.2%
4th Year	0	0	0	0.0%

Bar Passage Rates

Jurisdiction	Pennsylvania			New Jersey		
Exam	Sum 97	Win 98	Total	Sum 97	Win 98	Total
# from school taking bar for the first time	109	24	133	44	8	52
School's pass rate for all first-time takers	81%	83%	81%	84%	38%	77%
State's pass rate for all first-time takers	81%	73%	79%	77%	0%	77%

WILLAMETTE UNIVERSITY

245 Winter St. SE
Salem, OR 97301-3922
(503)370-6282
http://www.willamette.edu

ABA Approved Since 1938

The Basics

Type of School: Private   Term: Semester

Application deadline: 04/01

Application fee: $50

Financial Aid deadline: 04/01

Can first year start other than Fall? No

Student faculty ratio: 18.7 to 1

Does the University offer:

- housing restricted to law students? No
- graduate student housing for which law students are eligible? Yes

Faculty & Administrators

	Total		Men		Women		Minorities	
	Fall	Spr	Fall	Spr	Fall	Spr	Fall	Spr
Full-time	18	17	13	12	5	5	1	1
Other Full-Time	5	5	2	2	3	3	0	0
Deans, librarians, & others who teach > 1/2	0	1	0	0	0	1	0	0
Part-time	11	14	6	9	5	5	0	1
Total	34	37	21	23	13	14	1	2
Deans, librarians, & others who teach < 1/2	3	3	3	3	0	0	0	0

Curriculum

	Full time	Part time
Typical first-year section size	100	0
Is there typically a "small section" of the first year class, other than Legal Writing, taught by full-time faculty?	Yes	No
If yes, typical size offered last year	25	N/A
# of classroom course titles beyond 1st year curriculum	66	0
# of upper division courses, excluding seminars, with an enrollment:		
Under 25	33	0
25 - 49	22	0
50 - 74	12	0
75 - 99	0	0
100 +	1	0
# of seminars	12	0
# of seminar positions available	180	
# of seminar positions filled	138	0
# of positions available in simulation courses	224	
# of simulation positions filled	175	0
# of positions available in faculty supervised clinical courses	32	
# of fac. sup. clin. positions filled	20	0
# involved in field placements	23	0
# involved in law journals	50	0
# in moot court or trial competitions	105	0
# of credit hrs required to graduate	88	

J.D. Enrollment & Ethnicity

	Men		Women		Fl-Time		Pt-Time		1st Yr		2nd Yr		3rd Yr		4th Yr		Total		JD Degrees Awarded
	#	%	#	%	#	%	#	%	#	%	#	%	#	%	#	%	#	%	
African-American	2	0.9	3	1.7	5	1.2	0	0.0	3	1.9	0	0.0	2	1.7	0	0.0	5	1.2	4
American Indian	3	1.3	2	1.1	5	1.2	0	0.0	3	1.9	1	0.7	1	0.8	0	0.0	5	1.2	2
Asian American	13	5.7	18	10.0	30	7.5	1	16.7	18	11.7	5	3.7	8	6.8	0	0.0	31	7.6	6
Mexican American	1	0.4	3	1.7	4	1.0	0	0.0	2	1.3	1	0.7	1	0.8	0	0.0	4	1.0	3
Puerto Rican	0	0.0	0	0.0	0	0.0	0	0.0	0	0.0	0	0.0	0	0.0	0	0.0	0	0.0	0
Hispanic American	3	1.3	1	0.6	4	1.0	0	0.0	0	0.0	2	1.5	2	1.7	0	0.0	4	1.0	1
Total Minorities	22	9.7	27	15.0	48	12.0	1	16.7	26	16.9	9	6.7	14	11.9	0	0.0	49	12.0	16
Foreign Nationals	4	1.8	1	0.6	5	1.2	0	0.0	1	0.6	2	1.5	2	1.7	0	0.0	5	1.2	2
Caucasian	201	88.5	152	84.4	348	86.8	5	83.3	127	82.5	124	91.9	102	86.4	0	0.0	353	86.7	106
Total	227	55.8	180	44.2	401	98.5	6	1.5	154	37.8	135	33.2	118	29.0	0	0.0	407		124

GPA & LSAT Scores

	Full Time	Part Time	Total
# of apps	671	1	672
# admits	497	1	498
# of matrics	152	1	153
75% GPA	3.33	0.00	
25% GPA	2.78	0.00	
75% LSAT	157	0	
25% LSAT	150	0	

Tuition & Fees

	Resident	Non-resident
Full-Time	$17,780	$17,780
Part-Time	$0	$0

Living Expenses

Estimated living expenses for Singles		
Living on campus	Living off campus	Living at home
$11,000	$11,000	$6,530

Grants/Scholarships

	Full-time		Part-time		Total	
	#	%	#	%	#	%
Total # of Students	401		6		407	
Total # receiving grants	171	42.6	0	0.0	171	42.0
Less than 1/2 tuition	121	30.2	0	0.0	121	29.7
Half to full tuition	47	11.7	0	0.0	47	11.5
Full tuition	3	0.7	0	0.0	3	0.7
More than full tuition	0	0.0	0	0.0	0	0.0
Median Grant Amount	$8,000		$0			

Informational & Library Resources

# of volumes & volume equivalents	280,077	# of professional staff	5
# of titles	40,957	Hours per week with professional staff	69
# of active serial subscriptions	4,243	Hours per week without professional staff	44
Study seating capacity inside the library	398	# of student computer work stations for entire law school	44
Square feet of law library	38,552	# of additional networked connections	16
Square feet of law school (excl. Library)	73,497	Require Laptop Computer?	N

J.D. Attrition (from Prior Year)

	Academic	Other	TOTALS	
	#	#	#	%
1st Year	5	16	21	13%
2nd Year	1	3	4	3.3%
3rd Year	0	0	0	0.0%
4th Year	0	0	0	0.0%

Employment

	Total	%
Employment status known	170	97.7
Employment status unknown	4	2.3
Employed	140	82.4
Pursuing graduate degrees	3	1.8
Unemployed seeking employment	24	14.1
Unemployed not seeking employment	3	1.8
Type of Employment		
# employed in law firms	81	57.9
# employed in business & industry	24	17.1
# employed in government	22	15.7
# employed in public interest	3	2.1
# employed as judicial clerks	3	2.1
# employed in academia	3	2.1
Geographic Location		
# employed in state	80	57.1
# employed in foreign countries	2	1.4
# of states where employed	16	

Bar Passage Rates

Jurisdiction	Oregon			Washington		
Exam	Sum 97	Win 98	Total	Sum 97	Win 98	Total
# from school taking bar for the first time	97	5	102	36	9	45
School's pass rate for all first-time takers	65%	60%	65%	78%	78%	78%
State's pass rate for all first-time takers	74%	68%	72%	73%	83%	76%

WILLIAM AND MARY SCHOOL OF LAW

Marshall-Wythe School of Law
P.O. Box 8795
Williamsburg, VA 23187-8795
(757)221-3800
http://www.wm.edu/law

ABA Approved Since 1932

The Basics

Type of School: Public   Term: Semester

Application deadline: 03/01

Application fee: $40

Financial Aid deadline: 02/15

Can first year start other than Fall? No

Student faculty ratio: 18.3 to 1

Does the University offer:

- housing restricted to law students? No
- graduate student housing for which law students are eligible? Yes

Faculty & Administrators

	Total		Men		Women		Minorities	
	Fall	Spr	Fall	Spr	Fall	Spr	Fall	Spr
Full-time	24	22	19	16	5	6	3	4
Other Full-Time	0	0	0	0	0	0	0	0
Deans, librarians, & others who teach > 1/2	4	4	3	3	1	1	0	0
Part-time	27	32	17	21	10	11	2	4
Total	55	58	39	40	16	18	5	8
Deans, librarians, & others who teach < 1/2	1	2	1	2	0	0	0	0

Curriculum

	Full time	Part time
Typical first-year section size	70	0
Is there typically a "small section" of the first year class, other than Legal Writing, taught by full-time faculty?	Yes	No
If yes, typical size offered last year	58	N/A
# of classroom course titles beyond 1st year curriculum	90	0
# of upper division courses, excluding seminars, with an enrollment:		
Under 25	30	0
25 - 49	19	0
50 - 74	12	0
75 - 99	5	0
100 +	2	0
# of seminars	17	0
# of seminar positions available	271	
# of seminar positions filled	246	0
# of positions available in simulation courses	816	
# of simulation positions filled	804	0
# of positions available in faculty supervised clinical courses	37	
# of fac. sup. clin. positions filled	30	0
# involved in field placements	81	0
# involved in law journals	247	0
# in moot court or trial competitions	33	0
# of credit hrs required to graduate	90	

J.D. Enrollment & Ethnicity

	Men		Women		Fl-Time		Pt-Time		1st Yr		2nd Yr		3rd Yr		4th Yr		Total		JD Degrees Awarded
	#	%	#	%	#	%	#	%	#	%	#	%	#	%	#	%	#	%	
African-American	28	9.6	45	19.1	73	13.8	0	0.0	20	11.8	22	12.4	31	17.1	0	0.0	73	13.8	22
American Indian	3	1.0	1	0.4	4	0.8	0	0.0	3	1.8	0	0.0	1	0.6	0	0.0	4	0.8	2
Asian American	7	2.4	11	4.7	18	3.4	0	0.0	6	3.5	5	2.8	7	3.9	0	0.0	18	3.4	6
Mexican American	0	0.0	0	0.0	0	0.0	0	0.0	0	0.0	0	0.0	0	0.0	0	0.0	0	0.0	0
Puerto Rican	0	0.0	0	0.0	0	0.0	0	0.0	0	0.0	0	0.0	0	0.0	0	0.0	0	0.0	0
Hispanic American	5	1.7	1	0.4	6	1.1	0	0.0	2	1.2	1	0.6	3	1.7	0	0.0	6	1.1	3
Total Minorities	43	14.7	58	24.7	101	19.1	0	0.0	31	18.2	28	15.8	42	23.2	0	0.0	101	19.1	33
Foreign Nationals	9	3.1	2	0.9	11	2.1	0	0.0	4	2.4	5	2.8	2	1.1	0	0.0	11	2.1	2
Caucasian	241	82.3	175	74.5	416	78.8	0	0.0	135	79.4	144	81.4	137	75.7	0	0.0	416	78.8	136
Total	293	55.5	235	44.5	528	100.0	0	0.0	170	32.2	177	33.5	181	34.3	0	0.0	528		171

GPA & LSAT Scores

	Full Time	Part Time	Total
# of apps	2,176	0	2,176
# admits	732	0	732
# of matrics	175	0	175
75% GPA	3.53	0.00	
25% GPA	3.03	0.00	
75% LSAT	164	0	
25% LSAT	159	0	

Tuition & Fees

	Resident	Non-resident
Full-Time	$8,494	$17,940
Part-Time	$0	$0

Living Expenses

Estimated living expenses for Singles		
Living on campus	Living off campus	Living at home
$12,830	$12,830	$12,830

Grants/Scholarships

	Full-time		Part-time		Total	
	#	%	#	%	#	%
Total # of Students	528		0		528	
Total # receiving grants	225	42.6	0	0.0	225	42.6
Less than 1/2 tuition	170	32.2	0	0.0	170	32.2
Half to full tuition	55	10.4	0	0.0	55	10.4
Full tuition	0	0.0	0	0.0	0	0.0
More than full tuition	0	0.0	0	0.0	0	0.0
Median Grant Amount	$2,000		$0			

Informational & Library Resources

# of volumes & volume equivalents	345,914	# of professional staff	7
# of titles	61,574	Hours per week with professional staff	64
# of active serial subscriptions	5,242	Hours per week without professional staff	73
Study seating capacity inside the library	428	# of student computer work stations for entire law school	72
Square feet of law library	36,522	# of additional networked connections	25
Square feet of law school (excl. Library)	31,738	Require Laptop Computer?	N

Employment

	Total	%
Employment status known	165	98.8
Employment status unknown	2	1.2
Employed	147	89.1
Pursuing graduate degrees	11	6.7
Unemployed seeking employment	3	1.8
Unemployed not seeking employment	4	2.4
Type of Employment		
# employed in law firms	77	52.4
# employed in business & industry	14	9.5
# employed in government	27	18.4
# employed in public interest	4	2.7
# employed as judicial clerks	25	17.0
# employed in academia	0	0.0
Geographic Location		
# employed in state	47	32.0
# employed in foreign countries	4	2.7
# of states where employed	26	

J.D. Attrition (from Prior Year)

	Academic	Other	TOTALS	
	#	#	#	%
1st Year	1	3	4	2.4%
2nd Year	0	5	5	2.7%
3rd Year	0	0	0	0.0%
4th Year	0	0	0	0.0%

Bar Passage Rates

Jurisdiction	Virginia			New York		
Exam	Sum 97	Win 98	Total	Sum 97	Win 98	Total
# from school taking bar for the first time	73	4	77	16	4	20
School's pass rate for all first-time takers	86%	0%	82%	94%	75%	90%
State's pass rate for all first-time takers	76%	68%	75%	78%	65%	76%

WILLIAM MITCHELL COLLEGE OF LAW

875 Summit Avenue
St. Paul, MN 55105-3076
(612)227-9171
http://www.wmitchell.edu

ABA Approved Since 1938

The Basics

Type of School: Private Term: Semester
Application deadline: 07/01
Application fee: $45
Financial Aid deadline: 03/15
Can first year start other than Fall? Yes
Student faculty ratio: 23.5 to 1
Does the University offer:
- housing restricted to law students? No
- graduate student housing for which law students are eligible? No

Faculty & Administrators

	Total		Men		Women		Minorities	
	Fall	Spr	Fall	Spr	Fall	Spr	Fall	Spr
Full-time	29	29	19	21	10	8	2	2
Other Full-Time	0	0	0	0	0	0	0	0
Deans, librarians, & others who teach > 1/2	1	1	0	0	1	1	0	0
Part-time	81	78	52	48	28	30	10	7
Total	111	108	71	69	39	39	12	9
Deans, librarians, & others who teach < 1/2	2	2	2	2	0	0	0	0

Curriculum

	Full time	Part time
Typical first-year section size	66	59
Is there typically a "small section" of the first year class, other than Legal Writing, taught by full-time faculty?	No	No
If yes, typical size offered last year	N/A	N/A
# of classroom course titles beyond 1st year curriculum	63	58
# of upper division courses, excluding seminars, with an enrollment:		
Under 25	50	35
25 - 49	37	39
50 - 74	9	10
75 - 99	8	4
100 +	0	0
# of seminars	9	5
# of seminar positions available	275	
# of seminar positions filled	156	101
# of positions available in simulation courses	803	
# of simulation positions filled	456	278
# of positions available in faculty supervised clinical courses	26	
# of fac. sup. clin. positions filled	13	12
# involved in field placements	183	39
# involved in law journals	36	28
# in moot court or trial competitions	64	26
# of credit hrs required to graduate	86	

J.D. Enrollment & Ethnicity

	Men		Women		Fl-Time		Pt-Time		1st Yr		2nd Yr		3rd Yr		4th Yr		Total		JD Degrees Awarded
	#	%	#	%	#	%	#	%	#	%	#	%	#	%	#	%	#	%	
African-American	19	3.6	11	2.3	10	2.1	20	3.8	10	3.5	11	3.8	6	2.2	3	2.1	30	3.0	15
American Indian	5	1.0	9	1.9	7	1.5	7	1.3	3	1.0	3	1.0	5	1.8	3	2.1	14	1.4	3
Asian American	17	3.3	16	3.4	16	3.4	17	3.2	7	2.4	9	3.1	12	4.3	5	3.5	33	3.3	13
Mexican American	4	0.8	5	1.0	5	1.1	4	0.8	2	0.7	4	1.4	2	0.7	1	0.7	9	0.9	2
Puerto Rican	2	0.4	0	0.0	1	0.2	1	0.2	1	0.3	0	0.0	0	0.0	1	0.7	2	0.2	1
Hispanic American	4	0.8	6	1.3	6	1.3	4	0.8	3	1.0	3	1.0	1	0.4	3	2.1	10	1.0	3
Total Minorities	51	9.8	47	9.9	45	9.6	53	10.1	26	9.1	30	10.4	26	9.3	16	11.2	98	9.8	37
Foreign Nationals	11	2.1	6	1.3	9	1.9	8	1.5	1	0.3	14	4.8	1	0.4	1	0.7	17	1.7	0
Caucasian	459	88.1	424	88.9	417	88.5	466	88.4	260	90.6	245	84.8	252	90.3	126	88.1	883	88.5	256
Total	521	52.2	477	47.8	471	47.2	527	52.8	287	28.8	289	29.0	279	28.0	143	14.3	998		293

GPA & LSAT Scores

	Full Time	Part Time	Total
# of apps	954	0	954
# admits	668	0	668
# of matrics	171	119	290
75% GPA	3.44	3.45	
25% GPA	2.90	2.71	
75% LSAT	155	156	
25% LSAT	147	148	

Tuition & Fees

	Resident	Non-resident
Full-Time	$17,260	$17,260
Part-Time	$12,540	$0

Living Expenses

Estimated living expenses for Singles		
Living on campus	Living off campus	Living at home
N/A	$11,414	$5,464

Employment

	Total	%
Employment status known	277	90.8
Employment status unknown	28	9.2
Employed	259	93.5
Pursuing graduate degrees	1	0.4
Unemployed seeking employment	16	5.8
Unemployed not seeking employment	1	0.4
Type of Employment		
# employed in law firms	104	40.2
# employed in business & industry	73	28.2
# employed in government	36	13.9
# employed in public interest	7	2.7
# employed as judicial clerks	37	14.3
# employed in academia	2	0.8
Geographic Location		
# employed in state	239	92.3
# employed in foreign countries	0	0.0
# of states where employed	14	

Grants/Scholarships

	Full-time		Part-time		Total	
	#	%	#	%	#	%
Total # of Students	471		527		998	
Total # receiving grants	289	61.4	241	45.7	530	53.1
Less than 1/2 tuition	233	49.5	192	36.4	425	42.6
Half to full tuition	32	6.8	35	6.6	67	6.7
Full tuition	22	4.7	13	2.5	35	3.5
More than full tuition	2	0.4	1	0.2	3	0.3
Median Grant Amount	$4,215		$3,350			

Informational & Library Resources

# of volumes & volume equivalents	286,036	# of professional staff	7
# of titles	96,973	Hours per week with professional staff	85
# of active serial subscriptions	4,360	Hours per week without professional staff	21
Study seating capacity inside the library	674	# of student computer work stations for entire law school	84
Square feet of law library	58,000	# of additional networked connections	0
Square feet of law school (excl. Library)	142,000	Require Laptop Computer?	N

J.D. Attrition (from Prior Year)

	Academic	Other	TOTALS	
	#	#	#	%
1st Year	0	20	20	6.1%
2nd Year	17	20	37	14%
3rd Year	0	0	0	0.0%
4th Year	0	2	2	1.6%

Bar Passage Rates

Jurisdiction	Minnesota			Wisconsin		
Exam	Sum 97	Win 98	Total	Sum 97	Win 98	Total
# from school taking bar for the first time	205	61	266	6	6	12
School's pass rate for all first-time takers	91%	69%	86%	83%	67%	75%
State's pass rate for all first-time takers	93%	77%	90%	86%	86%	86%

WISCONSIN, UNIVERSITY OF

975 Bascom Mall
Madison, WI 53706-1399
(608)262-2240
http://www.wisc.edu

ABA Approved Since 1923

The Basics

Type of School: Public   Term: Semester
Application deadline: 02/01
Application fee: $45
Financial Aid deadline: 03/01
Can first year start other than Fall? No
Student faculty ratio: 18.1 to 1
Does the University offer:
- housing restricted to law students? No
- graduate student housing for which law students are eligible? Yes

Faculty & Administrators

	Total		Men		Women		Minorities	
	Fall	Spr	Fall	Spr	Fall	Spr	Fall	Spr
Full-time	36	35	24	23	12	12	4	4
Other Full-Time	7	7	5	5	2	2	2	2
Deans, librarians, & others who teach > 1/2	6	6	6	6	0	0	0	0
Part-time	46	0	29	0	17	0	4	0
Total	95	48	64	34	31	14	10	6
Deans, librarians, & others who teach < 1/2	0	0	0	0	0	0	0	0

Curriculum

	Full time	Part time
Typical first-year section size	116	0
Is there typically a "small section" of the first year class, other than Legal Writing, taught by full-time faculty?	Yes	No
If yes, typical size offered last year	20	N/A
# of classroom course titles beyond 1st year curriculum	166	0
# of upper division courses, excluding seminars, with an enrollment:		
Under 25	57	0
25 - 49	38	0
50 - 74	13	0
75 - 99	3	0
100 +	4	0
# of seminars	51	0
# of seminar positions available	672	
# of seminar positions filled	672	0
# of positions available in simulation courses	226	
# of simulation positions filled	226	0
# of positions available in faculty supervised clinical courses	178	
# of fac. sup. clin. positions filled	178	0
# involved in field placements	130	0
# involved in law journals	357	0
# in moot court or trial competitions	138	0
# of credit hrs required to graduate	90	

J.D. Enrollment & Ethnicity

	Men		Women		Fl-Time		Pt-Time		1st Yr		2nd Yr		3rd Yr		4th Yr		Total		JD Degrees Awarded
	#	%	#	%	#	%	#	%	#	%	#	%	#	%	#	%	#	%	
African-American	35	8.2	38	10.0	68	9.0	5	10.4	23	7.8	17	7.3	33	11.8	0	0.0	73	9.1	28
American Indian	7	1.6	16	4.2	23	3.0	0	0.0	7	2.4	6	2.6	10	3.6	0	0.0	23	2.9	6
Asian American	17	4.0	22	5.8	38	5.0	1	2.1	21	7.2	9	3.9	9	3.2	0	0.0	39	4.8	2
Mexican American	0	0.0	0	0.0	0	0.0	0	0.0	0	0.0	0	0.0	0	0.0	0	0.0	0	0.0	0
Puerto Rican	0	0.0	0	0.0	0	0.0	0	0.0	0	0.0	0	0.0	0	0.0	0	0.0	0	0.0	0
Hispanic American	27	6.3	23	6.1	47	6.2	3	6.3	17	5.8	10	4.3	23	8.2	0	0.0	50	6.2	20
Total Minorities	86	20.2	99	26.1	176	23.2	9	18.8	68	23.2	42	18.1	75	26.8	0	0.0	185	23.0	56
Foreign Nationals	0	0.0	0	0.0	0	0.0	0	0.0	0	0.0	0	0.0	0	0.0	0	0.0	0	0.0	0
Caucasian	340	79.8	280	73.9	581	76.8	39	81.3	225	76.8	190	81.9	205	73.2	0	0.0	620	77.0	214
Total	426	52.9	379	47.1	757	94.0	48	6.0	293	36.4	232	28.8	280	34.8	0	0.0	805		270

GPA & LSAT Scores

	Full Time	Part Time	Total
# of apps	1,506	0	1,506
# admits	725	0	725
# of matrics	273	8	281
75% GPA	3.66	3.56	
25% GPA	3.25	2.64	
75% LSAT	160	162	
25% LSAT	154	154	

Tuition & Fees

	Resident	Non-resident
Full-Time	$6,206	$16,382
Part-Time	$5,170	$13,590

Living Expenses

Estimated living expenses for Singles

Living on campus	Living off campus	Living at home
$9,950	$9,950	$5,670

Employment

	Total	%
Employment status known	246	93.2
Employment status unknown	18	6.8
Employed	231	93.9
Pursuing graduate degrees	6	2.4
Unemployed seeking employment	9	3.7
Unemployed not seeking employment	0	0.0
Type of Employment		
# employed in law firms	133	57.6
# employed in business & industry	30	13.0
# employed in government	43	18.6
# employed in public interest	5	2.2
# employed as judicial clerks	19	8.2
# employed in academia	1	0.4
Geographic Location		
# employed in state	161	69.7
# employed in foreign countries	1	0.4
# of states where employed	20	

Grants/Scholarships

	Full-time		Part-time		Total	
	#	%	#	%	#	%
Total # of Students	757		48		805	
Total # receiving grants	121	16.0	0	0.0	121	15.0
Less than 1/2 tuition	0	0.0	0	0.0	0	0.0
Half to full tuition	56	7.4	0	0.0	56	7.0
Full tuition	0	0.0	0	0.0	0	0.0
More than full tuition	65	8.6	0	0.0	65	8.1
Median Grant Amount	$10,250		$0			

Informational & Library Resources

# of volumes & volume equivalents	480,846	# of professional staff	14
# of titles	241,456	Hours per week with professional staff	73
# of active serial subscriptions	4,876	Hours per week without professional staff	31
Study seating capacity inside the library	565	# of student computer work stations for entire law school	50
Square feet of law library	54,773	# of additional networked connections	0
Square feet of law school (excl. Library)	62,385	Require Laptop Computer?	N

J.D. Attrition (from Prior Year)

	Academic	Other	TOTALS	
	#	#	#	%
1st Year	0	9	9	3.6%
2nd Year	0	13	13	4.3%
3rd Year	2	9	11	4.1%
4th Year	0	0	0	0.0%

Bar Passage Rates

Jurisdiction	Wisconsin	Illinois		
Exam		Sum 97	Win 98	Total
# from school taking bar for the first time	All graduates were admitted to the Wisconsin bar via the diploma privilege.	27	6	33
School's pass rate for all first-time takers		89%	100%	91%
State's pass rate for all first-time takers		87%	80%	85%

WYOMING, UNIVERSITY OF

P.O. Box 3035
Laramie, WY 82071
(307)766-6416
http://www.uwyo.edu/law/law.htm

ABA Approved Since 1923

The Basics

Type of School: Public   Term: Semester
Application deadline: 03/15
Application fee: $35
Financial Aid deadline: 02/15
Can first year start other than Fall? No
Student faculty ratio: 14.9 to 1
Does the University offer:
- housing restricted to law students? No
- graduate student housing for which law students are eligible? Yes

Faculty & Administrators

	Total		Men		Women		Minorities	
	Fall	Spr	Fall	Spr	Fall	Spr	Fall	Spr
Full-time	13	14	7	8	6	6	0	0
Other Full-Time	0	0	0	0	0	0	0	0
Deans, librarians, & others who teach > 1/2	1	1	1	1	0	0	0	0
Part-time	3	5	1	3	2	2	0	0
Total	17	20	9	12	8	8	0	0
Deans, librarians, & others who teach < 1/2	3	3	1	1	2	2	0	0

Curriculum

	Full time	Part time
Typical first-year section size	80	0
Is there typically a "small section" of the first year class, other than Legal Writing, taught by full-time faculty?	No	No
If yes, typical size offered last year	N/A	N/A
# of classroom course titles beyond 1st year curriculum	52	0
# of upper division courses, excluding seminars, with an enrollment:		
Under 25	38	0
25 - 49	7	0
50 - 74	8	0
75 - 99	1	0
100 +	0	0
# of seminars	5	0
# of seminar positions available	50	
# of seminar positions filled	30	0
# of positions available in simulation courses	88	
# of simulation positions filled	76	0
# of positions available in faculty supervised clinical courses	64	
# of fac. sup. clin. positions filled	57	0
# involved in field placements	41	0
# involved in law journals	30	0
# in moot court or trial competitions	12	0
# of credit hrs required to graduate	88	

J.D. Enrollment & Ethnicity

	Men		Women		Fl-Time		Pt-Time		1st Yr		2nd Yr		3rd Yr		4th Yr		Total		JD Degrees Awarded
	#	%	#	%	#	%	#	%	#	%	#	%	#	%	#	%	#	%	
African-American	1	0.7	0	0.0	1	0.4	0	0.0	0	0.0	0	0.0	1	1.5	0	0.0	1	0.4	0
American Indian	0	0.0	0	0.0	0	0.0	0	0.0	0	0.0	0	0.0	0	0.0	0	0.0	0	0.0	0
Asian American	1	0.7	1	1.1	2	0.9	0	0.0	2	2.4	0	0.0	0	0.0	0	0.0	2	0.9	0
Mexican American	3	2.2	4	4.4	7	3.1	0	0.0	4	4.7	1	1.4	2	3.0	0	0.0	7	3.1	1
Puerto Rican	0	0.0	0	0.0	0	0.0	0	0.0	0	0.0	0	0.0	0	0.0	0	0.0	0	0.0	0
Hispanic American	0	0.0	0	0.0	0	0.0	0	0.0	0	0.0	0	0.0	0	0.0	0	0.0	0	0.0	0
Total Minorities	5	3.7	5	5.6	10	4.5	0	0.0	6	7.1	1	1.4	3	4.5	0	0.0	10	4.5	1
Foreign Nationals	0	0.0	0	0.0	0	0.0	0	0.0	0	0.0	0	0.0	0	0.0	0	0.0	0	0.0	0
Caucasian	129	96.3	85	94.4	214	95.5	0	0.0	79	92.9	71	98.6	64	95.5	0	0.0	214	95.5	60
Total	134	59.8	90	40.2	224	100.0	0	0.0	85	37.9	72	32.1	67	29.9	0	0.0	224		61

GPA & LSAT Scores

	Full Time	Part Time	Total
# of apps	376	0	376
# admits	263	0	263
# of matrics	86	0	86
75% GPA	3.56	0.00	
25% GPA	3.03	0.00	
75% LSAT	157	0	
25% LSAT	148	0	

Tuition & Fees

	Resident	Non-resident
Full-Time	$4,234	$9,322
Part-Time	$0	$0

Living Expenses

Estimated living expenses for Singles

Living on campus	Living off campus	Living at home
$7,112	$7,112	$3,712

Grants/Scholarships

	Full-time		Part-time		Total	
	#	%	#	%	#	%
Total # of Students	224		0		224	
Total # receiving grants	62	27.7	0	0.0	62	27.7
Less than 1/2 tuition	53	23.7	0	0.0	53	23.7
Half to full tuition	3	1.3	0	0.0	3	1.3
Full tuition	3	1.3	0	0.0	3	1.3
More than full tuition	3	1.3	0	0.0	3	1.3
Median Grant Amount	$1,780		$0			

Informational & Library Resources

# of volumes & volume equivalents	206,120	# of professional staff	3
# of titles	20,294	Hours per week with professional staff	62
# of active serial subscriptions	2,380	Hours per week without professional staff	45
Study seating capacity inside the library	248	# of student computer work stations for entire law school	16
Square fcet of law library	30,000	# of additional networked connections	22
Square feet of law school (excl. Library)	30,060	Require Laptop Computer?	N

Employment

	Total	%
Employment status known	64	94.1
Employment status unknown	4	5.9
Employed	54	84.4
Pursuing graduate degrees	0	0.0
Unemployed seeking employment	9	14.1
Unemployed not seeking employment	1	1.6
Type of Employment		
# employed in law firms	26	48.1
# employed in business & industry	2	3.7
# employed in government	14	25.9
# employed in public interest	2	3.7
# employed as judicial clerks	9	16.7
# employed in academia	1	1.9
Geographic Location		
# employed in state	37	68.5
# employed in foreign countries	1	1.9
# of states where employed	10	

J.D. Attrition (from Prior Year)

	Academic	Other	TOTALS	
	#	#	#	%
1st Year	1	9	10	12%
2nd Year	1	1	2	2.8%
3rd Year	0	0	0	0.0%
4th Year	0	0	0	0.0%

Bar Passage Rates

Jurisdiction	Wyoming		
Exam	Sum 97	Win 98	Total
# from school taking bar for the first time	48	0	48
School's pass rate for all first-time takers	85%		85%
State's pass rate for all first-time takers	78%	69%	74%

YALE UNIVERSITY

P.O. Box 208215
New Haven, CT 06520-8215
(203)432-1660
http://www.yale.edu/lawweb/lawschool

ABA Approved Since 1923

The Basics

Type of School: Private   Term: Semester

Application deadline: 02/15

Application fee: $65

Financial Aid deadline: 03/15

Can first year start other than Fall? No

Student faculty ratio: 12.3 to 1

Does the University offer:
- housing restricted to law students? Yes
- graduate student housing for which law students are eligible? Yes

Faculty & Administrators

	Total		Men		Women		Minorities	
	Fall	Spr	Fall	Spr	Fall	Spr	Fall	Spr
Full-time	41	34	33	29	8	5	5	3
Other Full-Time	1	1	1	1	0	0	0	0
Deans, librarians, & others who teach > 1/2	2	3	2	2	0	1	0	0
Part-time	24	18	13	13	11	5	3	0
Total	68	56	49	45	19	11	8	3
Deans, librarians, & others who teach < 1/2	0	0	0	0	0	0	0	0

Curriculum

	Full time	Part time
Typical first-year section size	85	0
Is there typically a "small section" of the first year class, other than Legal Writing, taught by full-time faculty?	Yes	No
If yes, typical size offered last year	17	N/A
# of classroom course titles beyond 1st year curriculum	163	0
# of upper division courses, excluding seminars, with an enrollment:		
Under 25	54	0
25 - 49	19	0
50 - 74	8	0
75 - 99	7	0
100 +	5	0
# of seminars	58	0
# of seminar positions available	1,160	
# of seminar positions filled	725	0
# of positions available in simulation courses	175	
# of simulation positions filled	94	0
# of positions available in faculty supervised clinical courses	180	
# of fac. sup. clin. positions filled	165	0
# involved in field placements	41	0
# involved in law journals	563	0
# in moot court or trial competitions	81	0
# of credit hrs required to graduate	82	

J.D. Enrollment & Ethnicity

	Men		Women		Fl-Time		Pt-Time		1st Yr		2nd Yr		3rd Yr		4th Yr		Total		JD Degrees Awarded
	#	%	#	%	#	%	#	%	#	%	#	%	#	%	#	%	#	%	
African-American	27	7.9	31	12.3	58	9.8	0	0.0	24	13.0	18	8.9	16	7.8	0	0.0	58	9.8	20
American Indian	1	0.3	1	0.4	2	0.3	0	0.0	1	0.5	0	0.0	1	0.5	0	0.0	2	0.3	0
Asian American	47	13.8	37	14.7	84	14.2	0	0.0	28	15.1	26	12.8	30	14.6	0	0.0	84	14.2	23
Mexican American	12	3.5	7	2.8	19	3.2	0	0.0	7	3.8	5	2.5	7	3.4	0	0.0	19	3.2	1
Puerto Rican	4	1.2	4	1.6	8	1.3	0	0.0	2	1.1	4	2.0	2	1.0	0	0.0	8	1.3	1
Hispanic American	6	1.8	8	3.2	14	2.4	0	0.0	3	1.6	6	3.0	5	2.4	0	0.0	14	2.4	5
Total Minorities	97	28.4	88	34.9	185	31.2	0	0.0	65	35.1	59	29.1	61	29.8	0	0.0	185	31.2	50
Foreign Nationals	6	1.8	5	2.0	11	1.9	0	0.0	2	1.1	3	1.5	6	2.9	0	0.0	11	1.9	1
Caucasian	238	69.8	159	63.1	397	66.9	0	0.0	118	63.8	141	69.5	138	67.3	0	0.0	397	66.9	127
Total	341	57.5	252	42.5	593	100.0	0	0.0	185	31.2	203	34.2	205	34.6	0	0.0	593		178

GPA & LSAT Scores

	Full Time	Part Time	Total
# of apps	3,195	0	3,195
# admits	225	0	225
# of matrics	185	0	185
75% GPA	3.97	0.00	
25% GPA	3.75	0.00	
75% LSAT	175	0	
25% LSAT	168	0	

Tuition & Fees

	Resident	Non-resident
Full-Time	$25,550	$25,550
Part-Time	$0	$0

Living Expenses

Estimated living expenses for Singles		
Living on campus	Living off campus	Living at home
$11,320	$11,320	N/A

Employment

	Total	%
Employment status known	202	99.0
Employment status unknown	2	1.0
Employed	198	98.0
Pursuing graduate degrees	4	2.0
Unemployed seeking employment	0	0.0
Unemployed not seeking employment	0	0.0
Type of Employment		
# employed in law firms	80	40.4
# employed in business & industry	10	5.1
# employed in government	4	2.0
# employed in public interest	8	4.0
# employed as judicial clerks	95	48.0
# employed in academia	1	0.5
Geographic Location		
# employed in state	12	6.1
# employed in foreign countries	7	3.5
# of states where employed	36	

Grants/Scholarships

	Full-time		Part-time		Total	
	#	%	#	%	#	%
Total # of Students	593		0		593	
Total # receiving grants	266	44.9	0	0.0	266	44.9
Less than 1/2 tuition	172	29.0	0	0.0	172	29.0
Half to full tuition	78	13.2	0	0.0	78	13.2
Full tuition	12	2.0	0	0.0	12	2.0
More than full tuition	4	0.7	0	0.0	4	0.7
Median Grant Amount	$7,334		$0			

Informational & Library Resources

# of volumes & volume equivalents	1,002,151	# of professional staff	18
# of titles	252,433	Hours per week with professional staff	89
# of active serial subscriptions	9,504	Hours per week without professional staff	79
Study seating capacity inside the library	135	# of student computer work stations for entire law school	46
Square feet of law library	40,000	# of additional networked connections	200
Square feet of law school (excl. Library)	72,692	Require Laptop Computer?	N

J.D. Attrition (from Prior Year)

	Academic	Other	TOTALS	
	#	#	#	%
1st Year	0	0	0	0.0%
2nd Year	0	0	0	0.0%
3rd Year	0	0	0	0.0%
4th Year	0	0	0	0.0%

Bar Passage Rates

Jurisdiction	New York		
Exam	Sum 97	Win 98	Total
# from school taking bar for the first time	96	13	109
School's pass rate for all first-time takers	98%	100%	98%
State's pass rate for all first-time takers	78%	65%	76%

YESHIVA UNIVERSITY

Benjamin N. Cardozo School of Law
55 Fifth Avenue
New York, NY 10003
(212)790-0200
http://www.yu.edu/cardozo

ABA Approved Since 1978

The Basics

Type of School: Private   Term: Semester
Application deadline: 04/01
Application fee: $60
Financial Aid deadline: 04/15
Can first year start other than Fall? Yes
Student faculty ratio: 17.2 to 1
Does the University offer:
- housing restricted to law students? Yes
- graduate student housing for which law students are eligible? No

Faculty & Administrators

	Total		Men		Women		Minorities	
	Fall	Spr	Fall	Spr	Fall	Spr	Fall	Spr
Full-time	43	42	30	29	13	13	2	2
Other Full-Time	0	0	0	0	0	0	0	0
Deans, librarians, & others who teach > 1/2	3	3	1	1	2	2	1	1
Part-time	53	58	31	41	22	17	2	2
Total	99	103	62	71	37	32	5	5
Deans, librarians, & others who teach < 1/2	1	1	1	1	0	0	0	0

Curriculum

	Full time	Part time
Typical first-year section size	50	0
Is there typically a "small section" of the first year class, other than Legal Writing, taught by full-time faculty?	No	No
If yes, typical size offered last year	N/A	N/A
# of classroom course titles beyond 1st year curriculum	139	0
# of upper division courses, excluding seminars, with an enrollment:		
Under 25	62	0
25 - 49	35	0
50 - 74	22	0
75 - 99	9	0
100 +	9	0
# of seminars	44	0
# of seminar positions available	805	
# of seminar positions filled	437	0
# of positions available in simulation courses	657	
# of simulation positions filled	476	0
# of positions available in faculty supervised clinical courses	134	
# of fac. sup. clin. positions filled	120	0
# involved in field placements	170	0
# involved in law journals	217	0
# in moot court or trial competitions	58	0
# of credit hrs required to graduate	84	

J.D. Enrollment & Ethnicity

	Men		Women		Fl-Time		Pt-Time		1st Yr		2nd Yr		3rd Yr		4th Yr		Total		JD Degrees Awarded
	#	%	#	%	#	%	#	%	#	%	#	%	#	%	#	%	#	%	
African-American	21	4.5	29	6.8	50	5.6	0	0.0	15	5.4	16	5.1	19	6.4	0	0.0	50	5.6	17
American Indian	1	0.2	3	0.7	4	0.5	0	0.0	2	0.7	1	0.3	1	0.3	0	0.0	4	0.5	1
Asian American	32	6.9	50	11.7	82	9.2	0	0.0	17	6.1	41	13.1	24	8.1	0	0.0	82	9.2	27
Mexican American	0	0.0	0	0.0	0	0.0	0	0.0	0	0.0	0	0.0	0	0.0	0	0.0	0	0.0	0
Puerto Rican	8	1.7	4	0.9	12	1.4	0	0.0	2	0.7	5	1.6	5	1.7	0	0.0	12	1.4	0
Hispanic American	18	3.9	16	3.8	34	3.8	0	0.0	6	2.1	17	5.4	11	3.7	0	0.0	34	3.8	14
Total Minorities	80	17.3	102	23.9	182	20.5	0	0.0	42	15.0	80	25.6	60	20.3	0	0.0	182	20.5	59
Foreign Nationals	14	3.0	13	3.1	27	3.0	0	0.0	8	2.9	11	3.5	8	2.7	0	0.0	27	3.0	2
Caucasian	368	79.7	311	73.0	679	76.5	0	0.0	230	82.1	221	70.8	228	77.0	0	0.0	679	76.5	285
Total	462	52.0	426	48.0	888	100.0	0	0.0	280	31.5	312	35.1	296	33.3	0	0.0	888		346

GPA & LSAT Scores

	Full Time	Part Time	Total
# of apps	2,380	0	2,380
# admits	1,054	0	1,054
# of matrics	330	0	330
75% GPA	3.57	0.00	
25% GPA	3.03	0.00	
75% LSAT	159	0	
25% LSAT	154	0	

Tuition & Fees

	Resident	Non-resident
Full-Time	$22,030	$22,030
Part-Time	$0	$0

Living Expenses

Estimated living expenses for Singles		
Living on campus	Living off campus	Living at home
N/A	$19,093	$8,293

Grants/Scholarships

	Full-time		Part-time		Total	
	#	%	#	%	#	%
Total # of Students	888		0		888	
Total # receiving grants	570	64.2	0	0.0	570	64.2
Less than 1/2 tuition	483	54.4	0	0.0	483	54.4
Half to full tuition	84	9.5	0	0.0	84	9.5
Full tuition	3	0.3	0	0.0	3	0.3
More than full tuition	0	0.0	0	0.0	0	0.0
Median Grant Amount	$5,000		$0			

Informational & Library Resources

# of volumes & volume equivalents	427,383	# of professional staff	7
# of titles	67,520	Hours per week with professional staff	62
# of active serial subscriptions	6,005	Hours per week without professional staff	26
Study seating capacity inside the library	472	# of student computer work stations for entire law school	104
Square feet of law library	37,012	# of additional networked connections	0
Square feet of law school (excl. Library)	84,988	Require Laptop Computer?	N

Employment

	Total	%
Employment status known	281	82.4
Employment status unknown	60	17.6
Employed	259	92.2
Pursuing graduate degrees	7	2.5
Unemployed seeking employment	5	1.8
Unemployed not seeking employment	10	3.6
Type of Employment		
# employed in law firms	166	64.1
# employed in business & industry	34	13.1
# employed in government	36	13.9
# employed in public interest	4	1.5
# employed as judicial clerks	17	6.6
# employed in academia	2	0.8
Geographic Location		
# employed in state	201	77.6
# employed in foreign countries	1	0.4
# of states where employed	18	

J.D. Attrition (from Prior Year)

	Academic	Other	TOTALS	
	#	#	#	%
1st Year	4	10	14	5.2%
2nd Year	1	2	3	1.1%
3rd Year	0	0	0	0.0%
4th Year	0	0	0	0.0%

Bar Passage Rates

Jurisdiction	New York		
Exam	Sum 97	Win 98	Total
# from school taking bar for the first time	272	35	307
School's pass rate for all first-time takers	76%	71%	76%
State's pass rate for all first-time takers	78%	65%	76%

Chapter Thirteen

Unapproved Law Schools

Below is a list of non ABA approved law schools as of October 1, 1998. A law school in the United States that is not approved by the ABA has either not applied for approval or does not satisfy the requirements of the ABA Standards for Approval of Law Schools. The list below is not comprehensive; but it is the most current data on record at the Office of the Consultant on Legal Education. You may wish to contact the bar admission authorities in the state(s) in which you intend to practice for more information on whether graduation from a law school that is not approved will qualify you to take the bar examination in that state. For your convenience, chapter seven contains contact information for state bar examiners.

ALABAMA

Birmingham School of Law
923 Frank Nelson Building
Birmingham, AL 35203

Miles Law School
P.O. Box 3800
Birmingham, AL 35208

Jones School of Law
Faulkner University
5345 Atlanta Highway
Montgomery, AL 36193-4601

CALIFORNIA

American College of Law
1717 S. State College Blvd.
Suite 100
Anaheim, CA 92806

Cal Northern
School of Law
2525 Dominic Drive, Suite F
Chico, CA 95928

California Pacific
School of Law
1600 Truxtun Avenue,
Suite 100
Bakersfield, CA 93301

Empire College School of Law
3033 Cleveland Avenue
Suite 102
Santa Rosa, CA 95403

Glendale College of Law
220 North Glendale Avenue
Glendale, CA 91206

John F. Kennedy University
School of Law
547 Ygnacio Valley Road
Walnut Creek, CA 94596

Lincoln University
3000 S. Robertson Blvd.
Los Angeles, California 90034

New College of California
School of Law
50 Fell Street
San Francisco, CA 94102

Pacific Coast University
College of Law
440 Redondo Avenue #203
Long Beach, CA 90814

San Francisco Law School
20 Haight Street
San Francisco, CA 94102

Santa Barbara College of Law
911 Tremonto Road
Santa Barbara, CA 93101

Simon Greenleaf School of Law
3855 E. La Palma Avenue
Anaheim, CA 92801

Southern California
Institute of Law
Santa Barbara Campus:
1525 State Street, #202
Santa Barbara, CA 93101

University of La Verne
College of Law
21300 Oxnard Street
Woodland Hills, CA 91367

University of La Verne
College of Law
1950 Third Street
La Verne, CA 91750

University of West
Los Angeles
School of Law
1155 West Arbor Vitae Street
Inglewood, CA 90301-2902

Ventura College of Law
4475 Market Street
Ventura, CA 93001

FLORIDA

Florida Coastal School of Law
7555 Beach Blvd.
Jacksonville, FL 32216

University of Orlando
School of Law
6441 East Colonial Drive
Orlando, FL 32807

GEORGIA

John Marshall Law School
805 Peachtree Street, N.E.
Atlanta, GA 30308

KANSAS

President's College Law School
123 South Market Street
Wichita, KS 67202

MASSACHUSETTS

Massachusetts School of Law
Woodland Park
500 Federal Street
Andover, MA 01810

Southern New England
School of Law
874 Purchase Street
New Bedford, MA 02740-6232

NEVADA

William S. Boyd
School of Law -- UNLV
4505 Maryland Parkway
Box 451003
Las Vegas, NV 89154

PUERTO RICO

Eugenio Maria De Hostos
School of Law
GPO Box 1900
Mayaguez, PR 00681

TENNESSEE

Nashville School of Law
2934 Sidco Drive
Nashville, TN 37204

VIRGINIA

Appalachian Regional
Law School
702 Park Avenue
Norton, VA 24273

Chapter Fourteen

Legal Education Statistics

Law School Attendance Figures, Fall 1998

		Full Time	Part Time	Total
First Year	Total	36,144	6,660	42,804
	Women	17,222	3,097	20,319
Second Year	Total	33,808	5,075	38,883
	Women	15,691	2,311	18,002
Third Year	Total	34,569	4,889	39,458
	Women	15,609	2,157	17,766
Fourth Year	Total	0	4,482	4,482
	Women	0	1,865	1,865
J.D. Total	Total	104,521	21,106	125,627
	Women	48,522	9,430	57,952
Post J.D.	Total	2,951	2,224	5,175
	Women	1,105	873	1,978
Other	Total	666	365	1,031
	Women	315	184	499
Grand Total	Total	108,138	23,695	131,833
	Women	49,942	10,487	60,429

Professional Degrees Conferred, 1998

		Full Time	Part Time	Total
J.D. / LL.B.	Total	34,490	4,965	39,455
	Women	15,532	2,130	17,662
LL.M.	Total	2,333	613	2,946
	Women	810	222	1,032
M.C.L. / M.C.J.	Total	155	1	156
	Women	48	0	48
S.J.D. / J.S.D.	Total	51	0	51
	Women	22	0	22
Other	Total	245	146	391
	Women	81	68	149
Total	Total	37,274	5,725	42,999
	Women	16,493	2,420	18,913

Teachers in Law Schools, Fall 1998

	Women	Minorities	Total
Full-Time	1,608	736	5,491
Part-Time	1,541	482	5,347
Deans & Administrators	2,002	536	3,080
Librarians	955	213	1,442

Legal Education and Bar Admission Statistics, 1963 - 1999

Academic Year	Number of Schools	First Year Enrollment	First Year Women Enrollment	Total J.D. Enrollment	Total J.D. Women Enrollment	Total [1] Overall Enrollment	Total LSAT Administrations	J.D. or LL.B. Awarded	Admissions to the Bar
1998 - 99	181	42,804	20,319	125,627	57,952	131,833	NA	39,455	NA
1997 - 98	178[2]	42,186	19,409	125,886	56,915	131,801	103,990	40,114	56,184
1996 - 97	179	43,245	19,402	128,623	57,123	134,949	105,313	39,920	56,629
1995 - 96	178	43,676	19,462	129,397	56,961	135,595	114,756	39,271	56,613
1994 - 95	177[3]	44,298	19,312	128,989	55,808	134,784	128,553	39,710	57,875
1993 - 94	176	43,644	19,059	127,802	55,134	133,339	132,028	40,213	51,152
1992 - 93	176	42,793	18,325	128,212	54,644	133,783	140,054	39,425	57,117
!991 - 92	176	44,050	18,773	129,580	55,110	135,157	145,567	38,800	54,577
1990 - 91	175	44,104	18,592	127,261	54,097	132,433	152,685	36,385	43,286[5]
1989 - 90	75	43,826	18,722	124,471	53,113	129,698	138,865	35,520	47,174
1988 - 89	174	42,860	18,395	120,694	50,932	125,870	137,088	35,701	46,528
1987 - 88	175	41,055	17,506	117,997	48,920	123,198	115,988	35,478	39,918
1986 - 87	175[4]	40,195	14,491	117,813	47,920	123,277	101,235	36,121	40,247[5]
1985 - 86	175[4]	40,796	16,510	118,700	47,486	124,092	91,848	36,829	42,450[5]
1984 - 85	174	40,747	16,236	119,847	46,897	125,698	95,563	36,687	42,630
1983 - 84	173	41,159	16,049	121,201	46,361	127,195	105,076	36,389	41,684
1982 - 83	172	42,034	16,136	121,791	45,539	127,828	112,125	34,846	42,905
1981 - 82	172	42,521	15,811	120,879	43,245	127,312	119,291	35,598	42,382
1980 - 81	171	42,296	15,272	119,501	40,834	125,397	108,022	35,059	41,997
1979 - 80	169	40,717	13,490	117,297	37,534	122,860	113,145	34,590	42,756
1978 - 79	167	40,479	13,324	116,150	35,775	121,606	115,284	33,317	39,068
1977 - 78	163	39,676	11,928	113,080	31,650	118,557	127,760	33,640	37,302
1976 - 77	163	39,996	11,354	112,401	29,343	117,451	128,135	32,597	35,741
1975 - 76	163	39,038	10,472	111,047	26,020	116,991	133,316	29,961	34,930
1974 - 75	157	38,074	9,006	105,708	21,283	110,713	133,546	28,729	30,707
1973 - 74	151	37,018	7,464	101,675	16,303	106,102	135,397	27,756	30,879
1972 - 73	149	35,131	5,508	98,042	11,878	101,707	121,262	22,342	25,086
1971 - 72	147	36,171	4,326	91,225	8,567	94,468	119,694	17,006	20,485
1970 - 71	146	34,289	3,542	78,018	6,682	82,041	107,479	17,183	17,922
1969 - 70	144	29,128	2,103	64,416	4,485	68,386	74,092	16,733	19,123
1968 - 69	138	23,652	1,742	59,498	3,554	62,779	59,050	16,077	17,764
1967 - 68	136	24,267	1,179	61,084	2,769	64,406	49,756	14,738	16,007
1966 - 67	135	24,077	1,059	59,236	2,520	62,556	47,110	13,115	14,644
1965 - 66	136	24,167	1,064	56,510	2,374	59,744	44,905	11,507	13,109
1964 - 65	135[6]	22,753	986	51,079	2,056	54,265	39,406	10,491	12,023
1963 - 64	135	20,776	877	46,666	1,739	49,552	37,598	9,638	10,788

NOTES: Enrollment is in American Bar Association-approved schools as of October 1. The LSAT test year begins in June and ends in February of the following year. J.D. or LL.B. degrees are those awarded by approved schools for the academic year ending in the first year stated. Total new admissions to the bar include those admitted by office study, diploma privilege, and examination and study at an unapproved law school. The great bulk of those admitted were graduated from approved schools.

[1] Total overall enrollment includes post-J.D. and other.

[2] The District of Columbia School of Law is not included in this figure.

[3] Roger Williams not included.

[4] This number includes Oral Roberts University, Coburn School of Law, which terminated its program effective June 1, 1986. However, the Council advised it to retain degree-ranting authority for those former students who completed satisfactorily 30 additional hours in ABA-approved law schools by Sept, 1, 1988.

[5] Data was not complete for these years, thus figure is lower than prior years.

[6] Stanford enrollment not included.

Survey of Minority Group Students Enrolled in J.D. Programs in Approved Law Schools, 1971 to Present

Enrollment Comparison: Fall 1998 vs. Fall 1997
By Rick L. Morgan, Data Specialist, ABA

The following observations resulted from a comparison of Fall 1998 enrollment and Fall 1997 enrollment. First, it should be noted that there were three schools added to the list of ABA approved law schools: University of the District of Columbia, Chapman University, and Western State University. There are currently 181 ABA approved law schools.

Total J.D. enrollment in Fall 1998 was 125,627. This represents a decrease of 259 students from Fall 1997 when J.D. enrollment was 125,886. Total law school enrollment for Fall 1998 was 131,833. Even with the addition of three schools, total law school enrollment was down by 161 students from Fall 1997 (131,994). The entering class for the Fall 1998 semester (42,804) increased, however by 1.5% (618) from Fall 1997 (42,186).

Although men represent a slight majority of the 1998 entering class (53%), their enrollment decreased from 22,777 in 1997 to 22,485 in 1998. In comparison, women entering law school increased this year by 910 new students; 20,319 women enrolled in 1998, while only 19,409 enrolled in 1997. Examining the percentages of these statistics, we find that first year male enrollment decreased 1% from 1997 to 1998, while first year female enrollment increased 5%. The entering class was comprised of 47% women in 1998, whereas women only represented 46% of the entering class in 1997. Total J.D. enrollment of women increased by 1,037 students; in 1997, 45.2% (56,915) of students enrolled in a J.D. program were women, as opposed to 46.1% (57,952) in 1998.

1998 Minority J.D. enrollment (25,266) increased 2.4% (581) over minority J.D. enrollment from 1997 (24,685). This year, first year minority students (9,076) increased 6.9% (583) from last year, 8,493.

Minorities constituted 20.1% of total J.D. students this year. In 1997, minority enrollment represented 19.6%. Minority students accounted for 21.2% of the total entering class in 1998. In 1997, minorities represented 20.1% of the entering class.

Please note that the minority enrollment charts on pages 451 through 454 do not include students from the three Puerto Rican schools. J.D. Enrollment for the law schools in Puerto Rico was 1,804 for Fall 1998.

Total Minority Enrollment

Academic Year	No. of Schools Reporting	1st Year	2nd Year	3rd Year	4th Year	Total
1998-99	178/181	9,076	7,635	7,761	794	25,266
1997-98	175/178	8,493	7,740	7,705	747	24,685
1996-97	176/179	8,722	8,009	7,869	679	25,279
1995-96	175/178	9,119	8,402	7,411	622	25,554
1994-95	174/177	9,249	7,633	7,124	605	24,611
1993-94	173/176	8,595	7,244	6,409	551	22,799
1992-93	173/176	8,070	6,682	6,032	482	21,266
1991-92	173/176	7,575	6,155	5,255	425	19,410
1990-91	172/175	6,933	5,325	4,676	396	17,330
1989-90	172/175	6,172	4,890	4,264	394	15,720
1988-89	171/174	5,565	4,408	3,911	411	14,295
1987-88	171/175	5,130	3,994	3,717	409	13,250
1986-87	171/175	4,738	3,839	3,648	325	12,550
1985-86	172/175	4,534	3,810	3,625	388	12,357
1984-85	171/174	4,429	3,725	3,432	331	11,917
1983-84	170/173	4,393	3,691	3,424	358	11,866
1982-83	169/172	4,421	3,624	3,217	349	11,611
1981-82	169/172	4,314	3,401	3,118	301	11,134
1980-81	168/171	4,124	3,215	2,976	260	10,575
1979-80	166/169	3,825	3,150	2,755	283	10,013
1978-79	164/167	3,801	2,925	2,902	324	9,952
1977-78	160/163	3,574	2,991	2,690	325	9,580
1976-77	160/163	3,698	2,892	2,641	358	9,589
1975-76	160/163	3,417	2,689	2,407	190	8,712
1974-75	154/157	3,373	2,630	2,173	196	8,372
1973-74	147/151	3,277	2,313	1,816	195	7,601
1972-73	144/149	2,947	2,041	1,619	123	6,730
1971-72	142/147	2,682	1,707	1,099	80	5,568

American Indian or Alaska Native Enrollment

Academic Year	No. of Schools Reporting	1st Year	2nd Year	3rd Year	4th Year	Total
1998-99	178/181	361	307	351	45	1,064
1997-98	175/178	355	348	355	27	1,085
1996-97	176/179	391	397	310	18	1,116
1995-96	175/178	436	338	294	17	1,085
1994-95	174/177	377	283	290	12	962
1993-94	173/176	336	280	243	14	873
1992-93	173/176	313	243	206	14	776
1991-92	173/176	286	219	176	11	692
1990-91	172/175	224	185	129	16	554
1989-90	172/175	220	147	143	17	527
1988-89	171/174	177	165	149	8	499
1987-88	171/175	189	144	148	11	492
1986-87	171/175	176	155	148	9	488
1985-86	172/174	183	146	124	10	463
1984-85	171/174	173	135	111	10	429
1983-84	170/173	169	126	134	12	441
1982-83	169/172	154	134	110	8	406
1981-82	169/172	160	112	125	5	402
1980-81	168/171	163	138	107	7	415
1979-80	166/169	171	110	100	11	392
1978-79	164/167	145	110	124	11	390
1977-78	160/163	137	130	90	6	363
1976-77	160/163	133	87	75	6	301
1975-76	160/163	118	88	84	5	295
1974-75	154/157	110	90	65	0	265
1973-74	147/151	110	65	44	3	222
1972-73	144/149	79	48	4	42	173
1971-72	142/147	74	46	18	2	140

Asian or Pacific Islander Enrollment

Academic Year	No. of Schools Reporting	1st Year	2nd Year	3rd Year	4th Year	Total
1998-99	178/181	2,762	2,403	2,497	215	7,877
1997-98	175/178	2,562	2,463	2,394	180	7,599
1996-97	176/179	2,695	2,451	2,380	180	7,706
1995-96	175/178	2,773	2,572	2,225	149	7,719
1994-95	174/177	2,740	2,247	2,087	122	7,196
1993-94	173/176	2,432	2,101	1,789	136	6,458
1992-93	173/176	2,235	1,873	1,618	97	5,823
1991-92	173/176	2,019	1,621	1,306	82	5,028
1990-91	172/175	1,753	1,343	1,134	76	4,306
1989-90	172/175	1,501	1,151	946	78	3,676
1988-89	171/174	1,282	954	825	72	3,133
1987-88	171/175	1,064	804	724	64	2,656
1986-87	171/175	929	685	650	39	2,303
1985-86	172/175	799	678	622	54	2,153
1984-85	171/174	766	610	600	50	2,026
1983-84	170/173	711	610	578	63	1,962
1982-83	169/172	731	593	562	61	1,947
1981-82	169/172	650	579	486	40	1,755
1980-81	168/171	641	485	473	42	1,641
1979-80	166/169	577	487	452	31	1,547
1978-79	164/167	557	435	398	34	1,424
1977-78	160/163	509	409	423	41	1,382
1976-77	160/163	484	439	378	23	1,324
1975-76	160/163	436	343	287	33	1,099
1974-75	154/157	432	322	288	21	1,063
1973-74	147/151	332	297	202	19	850
1972-73	144/149	299	218	144	20	681
1971-72	142/147	259	142	72	7	480

Black American Enrollment

Academic Year	No. of Schools Reporting	1st Year	2nd Year	3rd Year	4th Year	Total
1998-99	178/181	3,478	2,728	2,754	311	9,271
1997-98	175/178	3,126	2,752	2,887	367	9,132
1996-97	176/179	3,223	3,013	2,991	315	9,542
1995-96	175/178	3,474	3,161	2,855	289	9,542
1994-95	174/177	3,600	3,000	2,771	310	9,681
1993-94	173/176	3,455	2,846	2,573	282	9,156
1992-93	173/176	3,303	2,603	2,465	267	8,638
1991-92	173/176	3,169	2,556	2,196	228	8,149
1990-91	172/175	2,982	2,222	2,023	205	7,432
1989-90	172/175	2,628	2,128	1,816	219	6,791
1988-89	171/174	2,463	1,913	1,728	217	6,321
1987-88	171/175	2,339	1,761	1,690	238	6,028
1986-87	171/175	2,159	1,800	1,735	200	5,894
1985-86	172/175	1,800	1,838	1,791	240	6,052
1984-85	171/174	1,735	1,878	1,686	177	5,955
1983-84	170/173	1,735	1,813	1,711	196	5,967
1982-83	169/172	2,217	1,827	1,623	185	5,852
1981-82	169/172	2,238	1,793	1,596	162	5,789
1980-81	168/171	2,144	1,684	1,531	146	5,506
1979-80	166/169	2,002	1,647	1,438	170	5,257
1978-79	164/167	2,021	1,565	1,572	192	5,350
1977-78	160/163	1,945	1,648	1,508	203	5,304
1976-77	160/163	2,128	1,654	1,488	233	5,303
1975-76	160/163	2,045	1,511	1,452	119	5,127
1974-75	154/157	1,934	1,587	1,329	145	4,995
1973-74	147/151	2,066	1,443	1,207	101	4,817
1972-73	144/149	1,919	1,324	1,106	74	4,423
1971-72	142/147	1,781	1,147	761	55	3,744

Mexican American Enrollment

Academic Year	No. of Schools Reporting	1st Year	2nd Year	3rd Year	4th Year	Total
1998-99	178/181	885	734	764	68	2,451
1997-98	175/178	859	766	777	50	2,452
1996-97	176/179	861	768	751	49	2,429
1995-96	175/178	896	820	743	36	2,495
1994-95	174/177	902	739	719	42	2,402
1993-94	173/176	838	698	639	28	2,203
1992-93	173/176	807	744	683	24	2,258
1991-92	173/176	770	644	584	29	2,027
1990-91	172/175	768	624	527	31	1,950
1989-90	172/175	640	531	469	23	1,663
1988-89	171/174	656	510	458	33	1,657
1987-88	171/175	610	528	472	34	1,644
1986-87	171/176	564	486	431	31	1,512
1985-86	172/175	609	503	500	23	1,635
1984-85	171/174	607	538	486	30	1,661
1983-84	170/173	642	558	511	33	1,744
1982-83	169/172	628	573	491	47	1,739
1981-82	169/172	665	490	542	59	1,756
1980-81	168/171	659	501	498	32	1,690
1979-80	166/169	642	517	471	40	1,670
1978-79	164/167	606	471	510	62	1,649
1977-78	160/163	588	519	421	36	1,564
1976-77	160/163	591	465	463	69	1,588
1975-76	160/163	535	480	407	21	1,443
1974-75	154/157	568	439	338	17	1,362
1973-74	147/151	539	386	271	63	1,259
1972-73	144/149	480	337	238	17	1,072
1971-72	142/147	440	262	170	11	883

Puerto Rican Enrollment

Academic Year	No. of Schools Reporting	1st Year	2nd Year	3rd Year	4th Year	Total
1998-99	178/181	206	205	196	25	632
1997-98	175/178	224	198	188	26	636
1996-97	176/179	206	213	238	29	686
1995-96	175/178	236	238	214	17	705
1994-95	174/177	263	244	186	25	718
1993-94	173/176	275	195	177	17	664
1992-93	173/176	202	193	177	15	587
1991-92	173/176	208	177	140	14	539
1990-91	172/175	183	153	158	12	506
1989-90	172/175	171	150	156	6	483
1988-89	171/174	168	156	141	13	478
1987-88	171/175	178	134	140	7	459
1986-87	171/175	183	152	130	6	471
1985-86	172/175	171	126	108	7	412
1984-85	171/174	132	137	123	15	407
1983-84	170/173	166	152	120	12	450
1982-83	169/172	171	130	105	12	418
1981-82	169/172	149	120	116	11	396
1980-81	168-171	158	135	141	8	442
1979-80	166/169	172	153	107	9	441
1978-79	164/167	184	126	104	9	423
1977-78	160/163	138	92	106	14	350
1976-77	160/163	118	95	105	17	335
1975-76	160/163	113	121	96	3	333
1974-75	154/157	119	91	59	3	272
1973-74	147/151	96	47	32	5	180
1972-73	144/149	73	40	25	5	143
1971-72	142/147	49	25	18	2	94

Other Hispanic American Enrollment

Academic Year	No. of Schools Reporting	1st Year	2nd Year	3rd Year	4th Year	Total
1998-99	178/181	1,384	1,258	1,199	130	3,971
1997-98	175/178	1,367	1,213	1,104	97	3,781
1996-97	176/179	1,346	1,167	1,199	88	3,880
1995-96	175/178	1,304	1,273	1,079	114	3,770
1994-95	174/177	1,367	1,120	1,071	94	3,652
1993-94	173/176	1,259	1,124	988	74	3,445
1992-93	173/176	1,210	966	883	65	3,124
1991-92	173/176	1,123	938	853	61	2.975
1990-91	172/175	1,023	798	705	56	2,582
1989-90	172/175	1,019	783	734	51	2,587
1988-89	171/174	819	710	610	68	2,207
1987-88	171/175	750	623	543	55	1,971
1986-87	171/175	727	561	554	40	1,882
1985-86	172/175	589	516	477	50	1,632
1984-85	171/174	537	427	426	49	1,439
1983-84	170/173	458	432	370	42	1,302
1982-83	169/172	520	367	326	36	1,249
1981-82	169/172	452	307	254	24	1,037
1980-81	168/171	359	272	226	25	882
1979-80	166/169	261	236	187	22	706
1978-79	164/167	288	218	194	16	716
1977-78	160/163	257	193	142	25	617
1976-77	160/163	244	152	132	10	538
1975-76	160/163	170	146	81	9	406
1974-75	154/157	187	101	94	10	392
1973-74	147/151	128	70	59	4	261
1972-73	144/149	96	72	60	3	231
1971-72	142/147	79	62	35	3	179

Chapter Fifteen

Post J.D. Programs

Standard 307 of the ABA Standards for Approval of Law Schools states that an ABA approved law school may not establish a degree program in addition to its J.D. degree program without obtaining the Council's acquiescence. An ABA approved law school may not establish a degree program in addition to its J.D. degree program unless the school is fully approved, and the quality of its J.D. degree program meets the requirements of the Standards, and the additional degree program may not detract from a law school's ability to maintain a sound J.D. degree program.

For additional information about post-J.D. programs you should visit the Section's website at **http://www.abanet.org/legaled.** However, for specific information about post-J.D. programs you should contact the school(s) directly. In addition, if you have not obtained a J.D. from an ABA approved law school you may wish to contact the bar admission authorities in the state(s) in which you intend to practice for more information on whether graduation from a post-J.D. type of program will qualify you to take the bar examination in that state. For your convenience, chapter seven contains contact information for state bar examiners. Please note, however, that it is the ABA Section of Legal Education and Admissions to the Bar Council's position that no graduate degree in law is or should be a substitute for the first professional degree in law (J.D.) and should not serve as the same basis as the J.D. degree for bar admissions purposes.

Please note, that the Section is currently reviewing the information on this list. For updates or corrections to this book, please visit the Section's website: **http://www.abanet.org/legaled**.

POST J.D. PROGRAMS BY SCHOOL

Alabama, University of
Taxation, LL.M.
Comparative Law (For International Lawyers), LL.M.
General, LL.M.

Albany Law School
Legal Studies, M.S. (July 1998)

American University
International Legal Studies, LL.M.
Law and Government, LL.M. (February 1998)

Arizona, University of
International Trade Law, LL.M. (February 1993)

Arkansas, Fayetteville
Agriculture Law, LL.M.

Baltimore, University of
Taxation, LL.M.

Boston University
Taxation, LL.M.
Banking, LL.M. (February 1984)
American Law, LL.M. (February 1994)

Brigham Young University
Comparative Law For Foreign Lawyers, LL.M.

California-Berkeley, University of
General, LL.M.
General, J.S.D.

California-Davis, University of
United States Law (For Foreign Lawyers), LL.M. (February 1997)

California-Los Angeles, University of
As Approved, LL.M. (For Non-US Students)

California Western
Comparative Law, LL.M./M.C.L. (February 1998)

Capital University
Taxation, LL.M. (June 1986)
Business And Taxation, LL.M. (June 1988)

Case Western Reserve University
Taxation, LL.M. (August 1992)
U.S. Legal Studies, LL.M. (August 1992)

Chicago, University of
General, LL.M.
General, M.COMP
General, D.COMP
General, J.S.D.

Cleveland State University
General, LL.M.

Columbia University
General, LL.M.
General, J.S.D.

Connecticut, University of
U.S. Legal Studies, LL.M. (August 1994)
Insurance Law, LL.M. (July 1998)

Cornell University
General, LL.M.
General, J.S.D.

Denver, University of
Taxation, LL.M.
Natural Resources, LL.M. (June 1997)
American and Comparative Law, LL.M.

DePaul University
Taxation, LL.M. (August 1987)
Health Law, LL.M. (August 1987)

Duke University
Research, S.J.D.
U.S. Law for International Students, LL.M.

Emory University
General, LL.M.

Florida, University of
Taxation, LL.M.
Comparative Law, LL.M. (June 1994)

Fordham University
Banking Corporations and Finance Law, LL.M.
International Business and Trade Law, LL.M.

Franklin Pierce Law Center
Intellectual Property, LL.M. (August 1989)
Masters In Education Law, (August 1998)

George Washington University
General, LL.M.
Environmental Law, LL.M.
Government and Procurement Law, LL.M.
International and Comparative law, LL.M.
Intellectual Property, LL.M.
Various, S.J.D.
Litigation & Dispute Resolution, LL.M. (June 1997)

Georgetown University
As Approved, S.J.D.
General, LL.M.
Advocacy, LL.M.
International and Comparative Law, LL.M.
Labor & Employment, LL.M.
Securities and Fin. Reg., LL.M.
Taxation, LL.M.
Common Law Studies, LL.M.

Georgia, University of
General, LL.M.

Golden Gate University
American Legal Studies, LL.M. (February 1998)
Environment, LL.M. (February 1998)
International Legal Studies, LL.M.
International Legal Studies, S.J.D.
Taxation, LL.M.

Hamline University
Foreign Lawyers, LL.M.

Harvard University
General, LL.M.
General, S.J.D.

Hofstra University
International Law, LL.M. (July 1998)

Houston, University of
International Economic Law, LL.M.
Energy Environment and Natural Resources, LL.M.
Health Law, LL.M. (July 1998)
Intellectual Property, LL.M. (July 1998)
Tax Law, LL.M.
Foreign Lawyer Program, LL.M.

Howard University
American Jurisprudence, LL.M.

Illinois Institute of Technology
Taxation, LL.M.
International and Comparative Law, LL.M.
Financial Services Law, LL.M.

Illinois, University of
General, J.S.D.
General, LL.M.

Indiana University - Bloomington
As Approved, LL.M.
Comparative Law, M.C.L.
Research, S.J.D.

Iowa, University of
International and Comparative Law, LL.M.

John Marshall Law School
Taxation, LL.M.
Information Technology Law, LL.M.
Information Technology Law, M.S.L. (December 1997)
Intellectual Property, LL.M.
International Business and Trade Law, LL. M. (December 1997)
Comparative Legal Studies, LL.M.
Real Estate, LL.M.
Employee Benefits, LL.M. (July 1998)

Judge Advocate General's
Military Law, LL.M. (August 1988)

Lewis And Clark College
Environmental / Natural Resources, LL.M. (August 1987)

Louisiana State University
As Approved, LL.M.
As Approved, M.C.L.

Loyola University-Chicago
Health Law, LL.M. (August 1987)
Child Law, LL.M. (June 1995)
Health Law, S.J.D. (June 1995)
Health Law, M.J.
Child Law, M.J.

McGeorge School of Law
Taxation, LL.M.
Business and Taxation, LL.M.
Transnational Business Practice, LL.M.

Miami, University of
Taxation, LL.M.
Estate Planning, LL.M.
Ocean and Coastal Law, LL.M.
International Law, LL.M.
Inter-American Law, LL.M.
Real Property & Land Development, LL.M.
Comparative Law, LL.M.
General (For Foreign Law Graduates), LL.M.

Michigan, University of
As Approved, M.C.L.
As Approved, LL.M.
As Approved, S.J.D.

Minnesota, University of
American Law (For Foreign Lawyers), LL.M.

Missouri-Columbia, University of
Dispute Resolution, LL.M. (February 1998)

Missouri-Kansas City, University of
General, LL.M.
Taxation, LL.M.
Urban Affairs, LL.M.

New York University
As Approved, J.S.D.
Corporate Law, LL.M.
International Legal Studies, LL.M.
Taxation, LL.M.
Trade Regulation, LL.M.
General Studies, LL.M.
International Taxation, LL.M.
Comparative Jurisprudence, M.C.J.
Labor Law, LL.M.

Northwestern University
Research, S.J.D.
Research, LL.M.

Notre Dame, University of
International and Comparative Law, LL.M.
International Human Rights, LL.M.
International Human Rights, S.J.D. (June 1992)

Pace University
Comparative Legal Studies, LL.M. (December 1998)
Environmental Law, LL.M.
Environmental Law, S.J.D. (December 1994)

Pennsylvania State University
Comparative Law, LL.M.

Pennsylvania, University of
As Approved, LL.CM.
As Approved, LL.M.
As Approved, S.J.D.

Pepperdine University
Dispute Resolution-ADR, M.D.R.

Pittsburgh, University of
International and Comparative Law, LL.M. (February 1995)

Puerto Rico, University of
International Law, LL.M. (December 1998)

Regent University
International Taxation, LL.M. (July 1998)

Samford University
Comparative Law, M.C.L. (June 1994)

San Diego, University of
Taxation, LL.M.
General, LL.M.
Comparative Law, LL.M.

San Francisco, University of
International Transactions and Comparative Law, LL.M.

Seton Hall University
Health Law, LL.M.
Southern Methodist University
General, LL.M.
Comparative and International Law, LL.M.
Doctor of Science of Law, S.J.D.
Taxation, LL.M.

St. John's University
Bankruptcy Law, LL.M. (February 1999)

St. Louis University
Health law, LL.M.
American Law For Foreign Lawyers, LL.M.

St. Mary's University
International and Comparative Law, LL.M.
American Legal Studies, LL.M.

Stanford University
As Approved, J.S.D.
As Approved, J.S.M.

State University of New York at Buffalo
Criminal Law, LL.M. (December 1998)

Stetson University
International Law and Business, LL.M.

Temple University
American Law for Foreign Lawyers in China, LL.M. (December 1998)
General, LL.M.
Taxation, LL.M.
American Common Law Legal System & Transnational Law, LL.M. (December 1994)
Law & Humanities, Clinical Legal, LL.M.

Texas, University of
General, LL.M.

Touro College
American Legal Studies, LL.M. (August 1993)
Professional Studies in Law, M.P.S.L. (February 1998)

Tulane University
General, LL.M.
Admiralty, LL.M.
Energy & Environment, LL.M.
Comparative Law, M.C.L.
Comparative Law & Latin American Studies, M.C.L.
General, S.J.D.

Utah, University of
Environmental and Natural Resources, LL.M.

Valparaiso University
Program for Foreign Lawyers, LL.M. (February 1998)

Vermont Law School
Environmental Law, LL.M. (February 1999)
Environmental Law And Policy, M.S.E.L.

Villanova University
Taxation, LL.M.

Virginia, University of
General, LL.M.
General, S.J.D.
Judicial Process, LL.M.

Wake Forest University
American Law, LL.M. (December 1994)

Washington University
Taxation, LL.M. (June 1995)
Research, J.S.D.
Urban Studies, LL.M.
Master of Laws for International, LL.M.

Washington, University of
Asian & Comparative Law, LL.M.
Law & Marine Affairs, LL.M.
International Environmental Law, LL.M.
Sustainable International Development, LL.M.
Taxation, LL.M.
Asian & Comparative Law, Ph.D.

Wayne State University
General, LL.M.
Corporate and Finance, LL.M.
Labor Law, LL.M.
Taxation, LL.M.

Widener University
Corporate Law & Finance, LL.M.
Health Law, LL.M.
Health Law, M.J. (July 1998)
Health Law, S.J.D. (July 1998)
Health Law, D.L. (July 1998)

William and Mary, College of
American Legal System, LL.M.

William Mitchell
Taxation, LL.M.

Wisconsin, University of
As Approved, LL.M.
As Approved, S.J.D.
As Approved, M.L.I.

Yale University
General, LL.M.
General, J.S.D.

Yeshiva University
General, LL.M. (February 1998)
Intellectual Property, LL.M. (February 1998)

GRADUATE DEGREES DEFINED

DEGREE	DEFINITION
LL.M.	Master of Laws
S.J.D.	Doctor of Juridical Science
J.S.D.	Doctor of the Science of Law
J.S.D.	Doctor of Jurisprudence
J.S.D.	Doctor of Juridical Science
J.S.M.	Master of the Science of Law
D.C.L.	Doctor of Comparative Law
M.C.L.	Master of Comparative Law
LL.C.M.	Master of Comparative Law
M.C.J.	Master of Comparative Jurisprudence
M.L.S.	Master of Library Science
M.A.L.S.	Master of American Legal Studies
M.L.I.	Master of Arts or of Science in Legal Institutions

POST J.D. PROGRAMS BY CATEGORY

Admiralty
Tulane University, LL.M.

Agriculture Law
University of Arkansas - Fayetteville, LL.M.

American Jurisprudence
Howard University, M.C.J.

American Legal System/American Legal Studies
Golden Gate University, LL.M. (February 1994)
Touro College, LL.M. (August 1993)
St. Mary's University, LL.M.
William and Mary, College of, LL.M.

American Law/American & Comparative Law
Boston University, LL.M. (June 1994)
Denver, University of, LL.M.
Minnesota, University of, LL.M.
Pace University LL.M. (December 1998)
Temple University (Common), LL.M. (December 1994)
Wake Forest, LL.M. (December 1994)

As Approved
Georgetown University, S.J.D.
Indiana University - Bloomington, LL.M.
Louisiana State University, LL.M.
Louisiana State University, M.C.L.
Michigan, University of, LL.M.
Michigan, University of, M.C.L.
Michigan, University of, S.J.D.
New York University, J.S.D.
Pennsylvania, University of, LL.M.
Pennsylvania, University of, M.C.L.
Pennsylvania, University of, S.J.D.
Southern Methodist University, S.J.D.
Stanford University, J.S.D.
Stanford University, J.S.M.
Wisconsin, University of, LL.M.
Wisconsin, University of, S.J.D.
Wisconsin, University of, M.L.I.

Asian and Comparative Law
Washington, University of, LL.M.
Washington, University of, Ph.D.

Banking, Corporate, and Finance Law/Financial Services
Fordham University, LL.M.
IIT- Chicago Kent, LL.M. (August 1988)

Banking Law Studies
Boston University, LL.M. (February 1984)

Bankruptcy Law
St. John's University, LL.M. (February 1999)

Business and Taxation
McGeorge - University of the Pacific, LL.M.
Capital University, LL.M. (June 1988)

Child Law
Loyola - Chicago, LL.M. (June 1995)
Loyola - Chicago, M.J. (June 1995)

Clinical Legal Education
Temple University, LL.M.

Comparative Law/Comparative Legal Studies/Comparative Jurisprudence
Alabama, University of, LL.M.
California Western, LL.M../M.C.L.
Florida, University of, LL.M. (June 1994)
Indiana University - Bloomington, M.C.L.
John Marshall, LL.M.
Miami, University of, LL.M.
New York University, M.C.J.
Pennsylvania State University, LL.M.
Samford, M.C.L. (June 1994)
San Diego, University of, M.C.L
Tulane University, M.C.L.

Corporate Law and Finance/Corporate & Finance Law
New York University, LL.M.
Wayne State University, LL.M.
Widener University, LL.M.

Criminal Law
State University of New York at Buffalo, LL.M. (December 1998)

Dispute Resolution
Missouri-Columbia, University of, LL.M. (February 1998)

Education Law
Franklin Pierce, Masters (July 1998)

Energy, Environment/ Natural Resources
Denver, University of, LL.M.
George Washington University, LL.M.
Golden Gate University, LL.M. (February 1998)
Houston, University of, LL.M.
Lewis and Clark, LL.M.
Pace University, LL.M.
Pace University, S.J.D. (December 1994)
Tulane University, LL.M.
Utah, University of, LL.M.
Vermont, LL.M. (February 1999)
Vermont, M.S.E.L.

Employee Benefits
John Marshall, LL.M. (July 1998)
Estate Planning
Miami, University of, LL.M.

General
Alabama, University of, LL.M.
California - Berkeley, University of , LL.M.
California - Berkeley, University of , J.S.D.
Chicago, University of, D.C.L.
Chicago, University of, LL.M.
Chicago, University of, M.C.L.
Chicago, University of, S.J.D.
Cleveland State University, LL.M.
Columbia University, LL.M.
Columbia University, J.S.D.
Cornell University, LL.M.
Cornell University, S.J.D.
Emory University, LL.M.
Georgetown University, LL.M.
George Washington University, LL.M.
Georgia, University of, LL.M.
Illinois, University of, LL.M.
Illinois, University of, J.S.D.
Missouri - Kansas City, University of, LL.M.
New York University, LL.M.
San Diego, University of, LL.M.
Southern Methodist, LL.M.
Temple University, LL.M.
Texas, University of, LL.M.
Tulane University, LL.M.
Tulane University, S.J.D.
Virginia, University of, LL.M.
Virginia, University of, S.J.D.
Wayne State University, LL.M.
Yale University, LL.M.
Yale University, J.S.D.
Yeshiva, LL.M. (February 1998)

Health Law
DePaul University, LL.M. (August 1987)
Houston, University of, LL.M. (July 1998)
Loyola - Chicago, M.J.
Loyola - Chicago, LL.M. (August 1987)
Loyola - Chicago S.J.D. (June 1995)
Saint Louis University, LL.M. (August 1989)
Seton Hall, LL.M.
Widener University, LL.M.
Widener University, M.J. (July 1998)
Widener University, S.J.D. (July 1998)
Widener University, D.L. (July 1998)

Information Technology Law
John Marshall, LL.M. (December 1997)
John Marshall, M.S.L. (December 1997)

Insurance Law
Connecticut, University of, LL.M. (July 1998)

Intellectual Property
Franklin Pierce, LL.M. (August 1989)
George Washington University, LL.M.
Houston, University of, LL.M. (July 1998)
John Marshall, LL.M.
Yeshiva, LL.M. (February 1998)

International/International and Comparative Law/Comparative and International Law/International Legal Studies
American University, LL.M.
Georgetown University, LL.M.
George Washington University, LL.M.
Golden Gate, LL.M.
Golden Gate, S.J.D.
Hofstra University, LL.M. (July 1998)
John Marshall, LL.M. (December 1997)
IIT - Chicago Kent, LL.M.
Iowa, University of, LL.M.
Miami, University of, LL.M.
New York University, LL.M.
Notre Dame, University of, LL.M.
Puerto Rico, University of, LL.M. (December 1998)
Pittsburgh, University of, LL.M. (February 1995)
Southern Methodist University, LL.M.
Stetson University, LL.M.
St. Mary's, LL.M.

International Business and Trade Law/Transnational Business Practice
Arizona, University of, LL.M. (February 1993)
Fordham University, LL.M.
John Marshall Law School, LL.M.
McGeorge - University of the Pacific, LL.M.
San Francisco, University of, LL.M.

International Economic Law
Houston, University of, LL.M.
International Environmental Law
Washington, University of, LL.M.

International Human Rights
Notre Dame, University of, LL.M.
Notre Dame, University of, S.J.D. (June 1992)

International Taxation
Regent University, LL.M. (July 1998)

Inter-American
Miami, University of, LL.M.

Judicial Process
Virginia, University of, LL.M.

Labor Law/Employment Law
Georgetown University, LL.M.
New York University, LL.M.
Wayne State University, LL.M.

Law and Government
American University, LL.M. (February 1998)

Law and Marine Affairs
Washington, University of, LL.M.

Legal Studies
Albany Law School, M.S. (July 1998)
Connecticut, University of , LL.M.

Litigation/Trial Advocacy/Advocacy
Georgetown University, LL.M. (Clinical Fellows)
George Washington University, LL.M. (June 1997)

Military Law
Judge Advocate General's, LL.M. (August 1988)

Ocean and Coastal Law
Miami, University of, LL.M.

Professional Studies in Law
Touro College, M.P.S.L.

Real Estate
John Marshall, LL.M.

Real Property Land Development& Finance Law
Miami, University of, LL.M.

Research
Duke University, S.J.D.
Indiana University-Bloomington, S.J.D.
Northwestern University, LL.M.
Northwestern University, S.J.D.
Washington University, J.S.D.

Securities Regulation
Georgetown University, LL.M.

Sustainable International Development
Washington, University of, LL.M. (June 1992)

Taxation
Alabama, University of, LL.M.
Baltimore, University of, LL.M
Boston University, LL.M.
Case Western Reserve, LL.M. (August 1992)
Capital University, LL.M. (June 1986)
Denver, University of, LL.M.
DePaul University, LL.M. (August 1987)
Florida, University of, LL.M.
Georgetown University, LL.M.
Golden Gate University, LL.M.
Houston , University of, LL.M.
IIT - Chicago Kent, LL.M.
John Marshall, LL.M.
McGeorge - University of the Pacific, LL.M.
Miami, University of, LL.M.
Missouri - Kansas City, University of, LL.M.
New York University, LL.M.
San Diego, University of, LL.M.
Southern Methodist University, LL.M.
Temple University, LL.M.
Villanova University, LL.M.
Washington University, LL.M.
Washington, University of, LL.M. (June 1995)
Wayne State University, LL.M.
William Mitchell, LL.M.

Trade Regulation
New York University, LL.M.

Urban Affairs
Missouri - Kansas City, University of, LL.M.
Urban Studies
Washington University, LL.M. (June 1992)

Programs for Foreign lawyers or international students, include. "U.S. Comparative Law"; "U.S. Legal Studies"
Brigham Young University, LL.M.
California - Davis, University of, LL.M. (February 1997)
California - Los Angeles, University of, LL.M.
California Western, LL.M./M.C.L. (February 1998)
Case Western Reserve, LL.M. (August 1992)
Duke University, LL.M.
Georgetown University, LL.M.
Hamline, LL.M.
Houston, University of, LL.M..
Miami, University of, LL.M.
Pace University, LL.M. (December 1998)
Saint Louis University, LL.M. (August 1989)
Temple University in China, LL.M. (December 1998)
Valparaiso University, LL.M. (February 1998)
Wake Forest, LL.M.
Washington University, LL.M.

Chapter Sixteen

Selected Statements

What follows are several statements as adopted by the Council of the Section of Legal Education and Admissions to the Bar of the American Bar Association. To order a copy of the ABA Standards for Approval of Law Schools call (800) 285-2221. The cost is $12.00 plus shipping and handling. The information is also available on the Section's website at **http://www.abanet.org/legaled.**

Standard 101. BASIC REQUIREMENTS FOR APPROVAL.
A law school approved by the Association or seeking approval by the Association shall demonstrate that its program is consistent with sound legal education principles. It does so by establishing that it is being operated in compliance with the Standards.

Standard 211. EQUAL OPPORTUNITY EFFORT.
Consistent with sound legal education policy and the Standards, a law school shall demonstrate, or have carried out and maintained, by concrete action, a commitment to providing full opportunities for the study of law and entry into the profession by qualified members of groups, notably racial and ethnic minorities, which have been victims of discrimination in various forms. This commitment typically includes a special concern for determining the potential of these applicants through the admission process, special recruitment efforts, and a program that assists in meeting the unusual financial needs of many of these students, but a law school is not obligated to apply standards for the award of financial assistance different from those applied to other students.

Standard 212. INDIVIDUALS WITH DISABILITIES.
A law school may not discriminate against individuals with disabilities in its program of legal education. A law school shall provide full opportunities for the study of law and entry into the profession by qualified disabled individuals. A law school may not discriminate on the basis of disability in the hiring, promotion, and retention of otherwise qualified faculty and staff.

Standard 213. CAREER SERVICES.
A law school should provide adequate staff, space, and resources, in view of the size and program of the school, to maintain an active career counseling service to assist its students and graduates to make sound career choices and obtain employment.

Standard 301. OBJECTIVES.
(a) A law school shall maintain an educational program that is designed to qualify its graduates for admission to the bar and to prepare them to participate effectively in the legal profession.

(b) The educational program of a law school shall be designed to prepare the students to deal with both current and anticipated legal problems.

(c) A law school may offer an educational program designed to emphasize certain aspects of the law or the legal profession.

Standard 302. CURRICULUM.
(a) A law school shall offer to all students:

(1) instruction in those subjects generally regarded as the core of the law school curriculum;

(2) an educational program designed to provide its graduates with basic competence in legal analysis and reasoning, legal research, problem solving, and oral and written communication;

(3) at least one rigorous writing experience; and

(4) adequate opportunities for instruction in professional skills.

(b) A law school shall require of all students in the J.D. degree program instruction in the history, goals, structure, duties, values, and responsibilities of the legal profession and its members, including instruction in the Model Rules of Professional Conduct of the American Bar Association. A law school should involve members of the bench and bar in this instruction.

(c) The educational program of a law school shall provide students with adequate opportunities for study in seminars or by directed research and in small classes.

(d) A law school shall offer live-client or other real-life practice experiences. This might be accomplished through clinics or externships. A law school need not offer this experience to all students.

(e) A law school should encourage its students to participate in pro bono activities and provide opportunities for them to do so.

(f) A law school may offer a bar examination preparation course, but may not grant credit for the course or require it as a condition for graduation.

Standard 303. SCHOLASTIC ACHIEVEMENT; EVALUATION.
(a) A law school shall have and adhere to sound standards of scholastic achievement, including clearly defined standards for good standing, advancement, and graduation.

(b) The scholastic achievements of students shall be evaluated from the beginning of the students' studies.

(c) A law school shall not continue the enrollment of a student whose inability to do satisfactory work is sufficiently manifest so that the student's continuation in school would inculcate false hopes, constitute economic exploitation, or detrimentally affect the education of other students.

Standard 306. PARTICIPATION IN STUDIES OR ACTIVITIES IN A FOREIGN COUNTRY.
A law school may grant credit for student participation in studies or activities in a foreign country only if the studies or activities are approved in accordance with the Rules, Criteria, and Procedures as adopted by the Council.

Standard 401. QUALIFICATIONS.
(a) A law school shall have a faculty that possesses a high degree of competence, as demonstrated by its education, classroom teaching ability, experience in teaching or practice, and scholarly research and writing.

(b) A law school shall take reasonable steps to ensure the teaching effectiveness of its faculty.

Standard 501. ADMISSIONS.
(a) A law school's admission policies shall be consistent with the objectives of its educational program and the resources available for implementing those objectives.

(b) A law school shall not admit applicants who do not appear capable of satisfactorily completing its educational program and being admitted to the bar.

Interpretation 501-1:
A law school may not permit financial considerations detrimentally to affect its admission and retention policies and their administration. A law school may face a conflict of interest whenever the exercise of sound judgment in the application of admission policies or academic standards and retention policies might reduce enrollment below the level necessary to support the program.

Standard 502. EDUCATIONAL REQUIREMENTS.
(a) A law school shall require for admission to its J.D. degree program a bachelor's degree, or successful completion of three-fourths of the work acceptable for a bachelor's degree, from an institution that is accredited by a regional accrediting agency recognized by the Department of Education.

(b) In an extraordinary case, a law school may admit to its J.D. degree program an applicant who does not possess the educational requirements of subsection (a) if the applicant's experience, ability, and other characteristics clearly show an aptitude for the study of law. The admitting officer shall sign and place in the admittee's file a statement of the considerations that led to the decision to admit the applicant.

Interpretation 502-1:
Before an admitted student registers, or within a reasonable time thereafter, a law school shall have on file the student's official transcript showing receipt of a bachelors degree, if any, and all academic work undertaken. "Official transcript" means a transcript certified by the issuing school to the admitting school or delivered to the admitting school in a sealed envelope with seal intact. A copy supplied by the Law School Data Assembly Service is not an official transcript, even though it is adequate for preliminary determination of admission.

Standard 503. ADMISSION TEST.
A law school shall require all applicants to take an acceptable test for the purpose of assessing the applicants' capability of satisfactorily completing its education program. A law school that is not using the Law School Admission Test sponsored by the Law School Admission Council shall establish that it is using an acceptable test.

Standard 504. CHARACTER AND FITNESS.
A law school shall advise each applicant to secure information regarding the character and other qualifications for admission to the bar in the state in which the applicant intends to practice. The law school may, to the extent it deems appropriate, adopt such tests, questionnaires, or required references as the proper admission authorities may find useful and relevant, in determining the character and fitness of the applicants to the law school. If a law school considers an applicant's character qualifications, it shall exercise care that the consideration is not used as a reason to deny admission to a qualified applicant because of political, social, or economic views which might be considered unorthodox.

Standard 505. PREVIOUSLY DISQUALIFIED APPLICANT.
A law school may admit or readmit a student who has been previously disqualified for academic reasons upon an affirmative showing that the student possesses the requisite ability and that the prior disqualification does not indicate a lack of capacity to complete the course of study at the admitting school. In the case of admission to a law school other than the disqualifying school, this showing shall be made either by a letter from the disqualifying school, or if two or more years have elapsed since that disqualification, by the nature of interim work, activity, or studies indicating a stronger potential for law study. In each case, the admitting officer shall sign and place in the admittee's file a statement of the considerations that led to the decision to admit or readmit the applicant.

Interpretation 505-1:
The two year period begins on the date of the decision to disqualify the student for academic reasons. A review, appeal, or request for reconsideration of that decision is in the nature of post-decision remedies.

Interpretation 505-2:
A student who enrolled in a pre-admission program but was not granted admission is not a student who was disqualified for academic reasons under this Standard.

Standard 506. APPLICANTS FROM STATE-ACCREDITED LAW SCHOOLS.
(a) A law school may admit a student with advanced standing and allow credit for studies at a state-accredited law school if:

(1) the studies were "in residence" as provided in Standard 304, or qualify for credit under Standard 305; and

(2) the content of the studies was such that credit therefor would have been granted towards satisfaction of degree requirements at the admitting school.

(b) Advanced standing and credit hours granted for study at a state-accredited law school may not exceed one-third of the total required by an admitting school for its J.D. degree.

Standard 507. APPLICANTS FROM FOREIGN LAW SCHOOLS.
(a) A law school may admit a student with advanced standing and allow credit for studies at a law school outside the United States if:

(1) the studies were "in residence" as provided in Standard 304, or qualify for credit under Standard 305;

(2) the content of the studies was such that credit therefor would have been granted towards satisfaction of degree requirements at the admitting school; and

(3) the admitting school is satisfied that the quality of the educational program at the foreign law school was at least equal to that required by an approved school.

(b) Advanced standing and credit hours granted for foreign study may not exceed one-third of the total required by an admitting school for its J.D. degree.

Interpretation 507-1:
This Standard applies only to graduates of foreign law schools or students enrolled in a first degree granting law program in a foreign educational institution.

Standard 508. ENROLLMENT OF NON-DEGREE CANDIDATES.
Without requiring compliance with its admission standards and procedures, a law school may enroll individuals in a particular course or limited number of courses, as auditors, non-degree candidates, or candidates for a degree other than a law degree, provided that such enrollment does not adversely affect the quality of the course or the law school program.

Standard 509. BASIC CONSUMER INFORMATION.
A law school shall publish basic consumer information. The information shall be published in a fair and accurate manner reflective of actual practice.

Interpretation 509-1:
The following categories of consumer information are considered basic:

(1) admission data;

(2) tuition, fees, living costs, financial aid, and refunds;

(3) enrollment data and graduation rates;

(4) composition and number of faculty and administrators;

(5) curricular offerings;

(6) library resources;

(7) physical facilities; and

(8) placement rates and bar passage data.

Interpretation 509-2:
To comply with its obligation to publish basic consumer information under the first sentence of this Standard, a law school may either provide the information to a publication designated by the Council or publish the information in its own publication. If the school chooses to meet this obligation through its own publication, the basic consumer information shall be published in a manner comparable to that used in the Council-designated publication, and the school shall provide the publication to all of its applicants.

Interpretation 509-3:
All law schools shall have and make publicly available a student tuition and fee refund policy. This policy shall contain a complete statement of all student tuition and fees and a schedule for the refund of student tuition and fees.

Standard 510. STUDENT LOAN PROGRAMS.
A law school shall take reasonable steps to minimize student loan defaults, including provision of debt counseling at both the inception of a student's loan obligations and prior to graduation.

Interpretation 510-1:
The student loan default rates of a law school's graduates, including any results of financial or compliance audits and reviews, shall be considered in assessing the extent to which a law school complies with this Standard.

Interpretation 510-2:
The law school's obligation shall be satisfied if the university, of which the law school is a part, provides to law students the reasonable steps described in this Standard.

Standard 601. GENERAL PROVISIONS.
(a) A law school shall maintain a law library that is an active and responsive force in the educational life of the law school. A law library's effective support of the school's teaching, research and service programs requires a direct, continuing, and informed relationship with the faculty, students, and administration of the law school.

(b) A law library shall have sufficient financial resources to support the law school's teaching, research, and service programs. These resources shall be supplied on a consistent basis.

Standard 701. GENERAL REQUIREMENTS.
A law school shall have physical facilities and technological capacities that are adequate both for its current program of legal education and for growth anticipated in the immediate future.

Standard 703. RESEARCH AND STUDY SPACE.
A law school shall provide, on site, sufficient quiet study and research seating for its students and faculty. A law school should provide suitable group study rooms.

Rule 26. Release of Information Concerning Applications for Provisional or Full Approval of Law Schools.
In the case of schools seeking provisional or full approval, the staff persons of the American Bar Association may state:

(a) Whether or not a specific school has submitted an application to the American Bar Association for provisional approval.

(b) The procedural steps for consideration of an application, including:

(i) consideration of an application by the Accreditation Committee;

(ii) action by the Council upon the Accreditation Committee's recommendation and an explanation that action of the Council may not follow that of the recommendation made by the Accreditation Committee; and

(iii) action by the House of Delegates.

(c) After notification of the Accreditation Committee's action or the Council action, as the case may be, to the school, the staff may release the status of the school to the public, with the explanation of the procedural steps for consideration of an application as outlined in subparagraph (b) of this Rule.

Pass/Fail Grading

At its August, 1970 meeting the Council of the Section of Legal Education and Admissions to the Bar decided to endorse the following statement issued earlier by the Law School Admission Council on the impact of pass/fail grading by undergraduate colleges upon the law school admission process. This statement has also been endorsed by the Executive Committee of the Association of American Law Schools.

The adoption by an increasing number of colleges and universities of pass/fail or similar grading systems for some or all of their students' work has implications for the law school admissions process. When a student with a transcript bearing such grades seeks to enter law school, law school admissions committees will be deprived of data that have served them well in the past in making the admissions decision. In the belief that college and university faculties and administrations who are considering conversion of a conventional grading system to a pass/fail or some variant system may be interested in the possible effect of such grading systems upon their graduates who seek admission to law school, the Law School Admission Council issues this statement.

The Law School Admission Test (LSAT) was developed more than twenty years ago in response to an expressed need of law schools for additional data upon which to base their admissions decisions. Validity studies conducted over the years demonstrate that the LSAT score contributes significantly to the prediction of an applicant's grades in law school and thus aids in the making of the admissions decision. These studies show that the LSAT score and the undergraduate grade-point average are the two best quantitative predictors, and that when they are used together they are better than either used separately. College grades represent both academic competence and achievement; the LSAT score largely indicates academic competence—the kind relevant to the study of law. The academic achievement of an applicant to law school indicates the extent of his preparation and motivation for the study of law. It is apparent, then, that college grades make a significant contribution to prediction of law school grades that is not supplied by the LSAT score.

Where an applicant for admission to law school submits a transcript in which all or virtually all of his grades are on pass/fail basis, and submits no other indication of his level of achievement in college, the admissions committee can make little specific use of his college work in predicting his law school grades. This means that this prediction must be based on the LSAT score, even though the committee would much prefer not to place sole reliance on the test scores in making this prediction. Even when such a transcript is supplemented by a narrative evaluation of the applicant by several of his teachers and deans, the committee can make only limited use of the college work in predicting performance in law school. Like interviews, these evaluations give the committee some help in making the admissions judgment, but they are largely helpful in deciding which risks to take and which to reject.

Where the applicant for admission to law school submits a transcript containing some conventional grades and some pass/fail grades, the admissions committee can develop a grade-point average for that portion of the student's college work bearing the conventional grades. However, many admissions officers will not feel justified in assigning to that average the conventional weight.

They may well assume that the student chose to receive a conventional grade in those courses in which he gauged his probabilities for a premium grade to be good. This indicates that his grade-point average so developed will overstate his academic competence and achievement as compared with the average of a student whose grades are all conventional. Furthermore, the committee may reasonably assume that the applicant did not make the same effort in the courses graded on a pass/fail basis as he did in those graded on the conventional basis. In short, a grade-point average based only upon the limited part of a student's work in which conventional grades were assigned seems to overstate in a compound way the student's general academic ability and achievement. Therefore, it is understandable that many admissions officers are already discounting such a grade-point average, and discounting it more if there is a large proportion of pass/fail grades.

The Council recognizes that the increased use of the pass/fail grading system—or some variant thereof—will mean that law school admissions committees and officers will place an increased reliance upon the LSAT score, a greater reliance than either the Council or law school admissions committee would like. The Council recognizes that there are many educational considerations to be taken into account by the faculty and administration in determining the appropriate grading system for that college or university. The Council, of course, respects the authority and judgment of the college and university faculty and administration in making that decision. The Law School Admission Council offers this statement concerning the effect of pass/fail grades upon the proper evaluation of a college graduate's application for admission to law school only in the hope that it may be useful to college faculties and administrations in determining what grading system to use.

Correspondence Study

The American Bar Association expressly disapproves of correspondence law courses as a means of preparation for bar examination and for practice. Before one pursues a correspondence law course, it is suggested that he first familiarize himself with the rules and regulations of the state in which he intends to practice and inquire whether correspondence law courses are acceptable under the applicable rules and regulations of the state and any governmental agency with which one expects to secure employment. Correspondence law school graduates may take the bar examinations only in California and even there only under special conditions.

Postponement of Graduation

WHEREAS, most state supreme courts require graduation from an ABA approved law school as a requisite for bar admissions in order to assure the public that persons representing them in legal matters have received a quality legal education, and

WHEREAS, some individuals begin and complete substantially all of their legal education at unapproved law schools, which law schools have been inspected for possible ABA provisional approval but are found not to meet the ABA Standards during the time of such attendance; and these individuals may then delay their formal graduation until after the law school received ABA provisional approval, and

WHEREAS, some law schools receiving ABA provisional approval have permitted students to delay their graduation until such approval was received by the school and have then awarded degrees dated subsequent to receipt of ABA provisional approval to such students,

THEREFORE, the Council of the Section of Legal Education and Admissions to the Bar hereby adopts a policy disapproving this practice, and requests that all provisionally approved law schools, all other schools seeking provisional approval, all law school site team members and all state bar admitting authorities be notified of this policy.

Law School Admission Fees

The American Bar Association Section of Legal Education and Admissions to the Bar condemns the practice of requiring persons seeking admission to a law school to pay a fee, in addition to the regular application fee, to be placed on a list of persons who will be admitted if additional places become available, commonly known as a "waiting list."

Rating of Law Schools

No rating of law schools beyond the simple statement of their accreditation status is attempted or advocated by the official organizations in legal education. Qualities that make one kind of school good for one student may not be as important to another. The American Bar Association and its Section of Legal Education and Admissions to the Bar have issued disclaimers of any law school rating system. Prospective law students should consider a variety of factors in making their choice among schools.

Propriety of Examination by Public Authority before Admission to Practice

A half century ago the American Bar Association adopted standards for legal education, the second of which is as follows:

> "The American Bar Association is of the opinion that graduation from a law school should not confer the right of admission to the bar, and that every candidate should be subject to an examination by public authority to determine his fitness."

The criticism of bar examinations, which is daily becoming more prevalent, makes it most appropriate for the Council of the Section of Legal Education and Admissions to the Bar and the Board of Managers of the National Conference of Bar Examiners to state their opinion on the matter of the so-called Diploma Privilege.

It is the position of the Council and Board that the above-quoted standard, adopted in 1921, is as valid today—perhaps more so with the mobility of law graduates—as it was at the time and that every applicant for admission to the bar should be subject to examination by public authority.

Very great progress has taken place in the caliber of legal

education in the fifty years intervening since 1921. In part the improvement in legal education has been the result of experimentation in teaching techniques. Not all such experiments have proved successful. Public authority should not dictate teaching techniques but it should make sure that all applicants have the training necessary to adequately serve the public upon their admission.

Not only are law schools quite properly experimenting in teaching techniques but they are experimenting in curriculum content. Again, public authority should not dictate curriculum content but by examination should determine that the content of the applicant's education is such that upon admission he will be able to adequately serve the public. In one of the jurisdictions where graduates of certain law schools are admitted without examination, the Court found it necessary to a certain extent to dictate the curriculum content of those schools—an unfortunate limitation on the educational freedom of these schools.

Bar examinations themselves serve additional functions. They encourage law graduates to study subjects not taken in law school. They require the applicant to review all he has learned in law school with a result that he is made to realize the interrelation of the various divisions of the law—to view the separate subject courses which he took in law school as a related whole. This the curriculum of most law schools does not achieve. Also, it is the first time many of the applicants will have been examined by persons other than those who taught them, a valuable experience in preparation for appearing before a completely strange judge.

To reiterate, it is the position of the Council and the Board of Managers that there must be examination by public authority. This is not to say that public authority must not be very careful in its examination procedure to make sure that it is fulfilling its responsibilities. It should continually strive to make its methods of examination more effective so that the results will be the nondiscriminatory admission of none not qualified and the exclusion of none qualified, even though this requires the use of innovative examining techniques and constant consideration of the ever changing needs of our society. The necessity to train lawyers to represent all members of society is a continual challenge to teachers of law and legal education. To test this properly the examining authority can perform effectively and satisfactorily only if it makes responsive changes in its techniques.

Period of Time for Completion of Requirements to Obtain J. D. Degree

The normal maximum period for a full-time law student to complete requirements for a J.D. degree is five years. The normal maximum completion time for a part-time law student to complete requirements for a J.D. degree is six years.

Encouragement of Increased Emphasis on Pro-Bono Activities

Law Schools should make law students aware of the special needs of those persons often under-represented in legal matters, including minorities, the poor, elderly and handicapped members of society, facilitate student services to these groups and should instill a sense in their students of the profession's obligation to provide legal services to those who are unable to afford them.

Student Tuition and Fee Refund Policy

It is the policy of the Council that all law schools approved by the American Bar Association have and make publicly available an equitable student tuition and fee refund policy. This policy shall contain a complete statement of all student tuition and fees and a schedule for the equitable refund of student tuition and fees.

Policy on Timely Grading of Law School Examinations

The Council of the Section of Legal Education and Admissions to the Bar reports that as a result of the expressed concern of the Law Student Division concerning timely grading of examinations, the Consultant on Legal Education to the American Bar Association has conducted a survey of grading practices at all law schools approved by the American Bar Association. The Law Student Division proposal and resultant survey has promoted thoughtful discussion among the deans and faculties of ABA approved law schools. The Council urges that all law schools continue adoption and maintenance of timely grading practices of law school examinations. The Council is aware that on occasion, a faculty member may not honor their professional obligation in this regard. The Council urges enforcement by each school of its own adopted policies, and urges completion of the grading and notice provision to the students not later than 30 days following the last examination of the term.

Law School Policy Encouraging Faculty to Engage in Reasonable Post-Examination Review With Students

It is recommended that a law school have a policy encouraging faculty members to engage in reasonable post examination review with students, preferably individual review upon request. Absent good cause, students should also have a right to reasonably review their examination papers. This does not mean that faculty members are obligated to review examinations individually with all students in every course. A reasonable policy may take into account the workload of individual teachers, the number of examinations in the course, the academic needs of the particular students requesting review, and the availability of review in courses throughout the school. Faculty members may choose to carry out such a policy using alternative means, including engaging in individual review of examinations upon student's request, by holding a general review concerning the examination open to all students, or by providing an outline or exemplar of good examination answers. (June, 1990)

Student Complaints

It is the policy of the Council that each law school approved by the American Bar Association should communicate in written form to its students the manner in which it receives and responds to student complaints.

Chapter Seventeen
School Directory and Miscellaneous

As of the publication date of this book, a total of 182 institutions are approved by the American Bar Association: 181 confer the first degree in law (the J.D. degree); the other ABA approved school is the U.S. Army Judge Advocate General's School, which offers an officer's resident graduate course, a specialized program beyond the first degree in law. One of the 181 ABA approved law schools (Widener) also has a branch campus. Five of the 181 law schools are provisionally approved: Chapman University School of Law, Texas Wesleyan University School of Law, Thomas Jefferson School of Law, University of the District of Columbia School of Law, and the Western State University College of Law. Of the 181 ABA approved law schools 77 are considered public institutions and 104 are considered private. Moreover, 79 have a part-time program.

AKRON, UNIVERSITY OF
C. Blake McDowell Law Center
Akron, OH 44325-2901
800-4akron-u

ALABAMA, UNIVERSITY OF
P.O. Box 870382
Tuscaloosa, AL 35487
(205)348-5117

ALBANY LAW SCHOOL
80 New Scotland Avenue
Albany, NY 12208
(518)445-2311

AMERICAN UNIVERSITY
Washington College of Law
4801 Massachusetts Ave, NW
Washington, DC 20016
(202)274-4000

ARIZONA STATE UNIVERSITY
P.O. Box 877906
Tempe, AZ 85287-7906
(602)965-6181

ARIZONA, UNIVERSITY OF
James E. Rogers Law Center
P.O. Box 210176
Tucson, AZ 85721-0176
(520)621-1373

ARKANSAS, FAYETTEVILLE, UNIVERSITY OF
Waterman Hall
Leflar Law Center
Fayetteville, AR 72701-1201
(501)575-5601

ARKANSAS, LITTLE ROCK, UNIVERSITY OF
1201 McAlmont Street
Little Rock, AR 72202-5142
(501)324-9434

BALTIMORE, UNIVERSITY OF
1420 North Charles Street
Baltimore, MD 21201
(410)837-4458

BAYLOR UNIVERSITY
P.O. Box 97288
1400 S. 5th Street
Waco, TX 76798-7288
254.710.1911

BOSTON COLLEGE
885 Centre Street
Newton Centre, MA 02159
(617)552-4340

BOSTON UNIVERSITY
765 Commonwealth Ave
Boston, MA 02215
(617)353-3112

BRIGHAM YOUNG UNIVERSITY
J. Reuben Clark Law School
Provo, UT 84602
(801)378-4274

BROOKLYN LAW SCHOOL
250 Joralemon Street
Brooklyn, NY 11201
(718)625-2200

CALIFORNIA WESTERN SCHOOL OF LAW
225 Cedar Street
San Diego, CA 92101-3046
(619)239-0391

CALIFORNIA-BERKELEY, UNIVERSITY OF
221 Boalt Hall
Berkeley, CA 94720
(510)642-1741

CALIFORNIA-DAVIS, UNIVERSITY OF
400 Mrak Hall Drive
Davis, CA 95616-5201
(530)752-0243

CALIFORNIA-HASTINGS, UNIVERSITY OF
Hastings College of the Law
200 McAllister Street
San Francisco, CA 94102
(415)565-4600

CALIFORNIA-LOS ANGELES, UNIVERSITY OF
405 Hilgard Avenue
Los Angeles, CA 90095
(310)825-4841

CAMPBELL UNIVERSITY
Norman Adrian Wiggins School of
P.O. Box 158
Buies Creek, NC 27506
(910)893-1750

CAPITAL UNIVERSITY
303 East Broad Street
Columbus, OH 43215
(614)236-6500

CASE WESTERN RESERVE UNIVERSITY
Franklin Thomas Backus School of
Gund Hall
Cleveland, OH 44106-7148
(216)368-6350

CATHOLIC UNIVERSITY OF AMERICA
Columbus School of Law
Washington, DC 20064
(319)319-5140

CHAPMAN UNIVERSITY
1240 South State College Blvd.
Suite 200
Anaheim, CA 92806
(714)517-0300

CHICAGO, UNIVERSITY OF
1111 East 60th Street
Chicago, IL 60637
(773)702-9494

CINCINNATI, UNIVERSITY OF
P.O. Box 210040
Cincinnati, OH 45221-0040
(513)556-6805

CITY UNIVERSITY OF NEW YORK
65-21 Main Street
Flushing, NY 11367
(718)340-4200

CLEVELAND STATE UNIVERSITY
Cleveland-Marshall College of
1801 Euclid Avenue
Cleveland, OH 44115-2223
(216)687-2344

COLORADO, UNIVERSITY OF
Campus Box 401
Boulder, CO 80309-0401
(303)492-7203

COLUMBIA UNIVERSITY
435 West 116th Street
New York, NY 10027
(212)854-2640

CONNECTICUT, UNIVERSITY OF
55 Elizabeth Street
Hartford, CT 06105-2296
(860)570-5127

CORNELL LAW SCHOOL
Myron Taylor Hall
Ithaca, NY 14853-4901
(607)255-3527

CREIGHTON UNIVERSITY
2500 California Plaza
Omaha, NE 68178
(402)280-2872

DAYTON, UNIVERSITY OF
300 College Park Ave.
Dayton, OH 45469-2772
(937)229-3211

DENVER, UNIVERSITY OF
7039 East 18th Street
Denver, CO 80220
(303)871-6000

DEPAUL UNIVERSITY
25 East Jackson Boulevard
Chicago, IL 60604-2287
(312)362-8701

DETROIT COLLEGE
AT MICHIGAN STATE UNIV.
368 Law College Bldg.
East Lansing, MI 48824-1300
(517)432-6800

DETROIT MERCY,
UNIVERSITY OF
651 E. Jefferson
Detroit, MI 48226
(313)596-0200

DISTRICT OF COLUMBIA,
UNIVERSITY OF
David A. Clarke School of Law
4200 Connecticut Ave., NW
Washington, DC 20008
(202)274-7400

DRAKE UNIVERSITY
2507 University Avenue
Des Moines, IA 50311
(515)271-2824

DUKE UNIVERSITY
P.O. Box 90362
Science Drive and Toweview Road
Durham, NC 27708-0362
(919)613-7000

DUQUESNE UNIVERSITY
900 Locust Street
Pittsburgh, PA 15282
(412)396-6280

EMORY UNIVERSITY
Gambrell Hall
1301 Clifton Road
Atlanta, GA 30322-2770
(404)727-6816

FLORIDA STATE UNIVERSITY
425 W. Jefferson Street
Tallahassee, FL 32306-1601
(850)644-3400

FLORIDA, UNIVERSITY OF
P.O. Box 117620
Gainesville, FL 32611
(352)392-9238

FORDHAM UNIVERSITY
140 West 62nd Street
New York, NY 10023-7485
(212)636-6875

FRANKLIN PIERCE LAW
CENTER
2 White Street
Concord, NH 03301
(603)228-1541

GEORGE MASON UNIVERSITY
3401 North Fairfax Drive
Arlington, VA 22201-4498
(703)993-8000

GEORGE WASHINGTON
UNIVERSITY
2000 H Street, N.W.
Washington, DC 20052
(202)994-7230

GEORGETOWN UNIVERSITY
600 New Jersey Avenue N.W.
Washington, DC 20001
(202)662-9000

GEORGIA STATE UNIVERSITY
P.O. Box 4037
Atlanta, GA 30302-4037
(404)651-2096

GEORGIA, UNIVERSITY OF
Herty Drive
Athens, GA 30602
(706)542-7140

GOLDEN GATE UNIVERSITY
536 Mission Street
San Francisco, CA 94105-2968
(415)442-6600

GONZAGA UNIVERSITY
P.O. Box 3528
Spokane, WA 99220-3528
(509)328-4220

HAMLINE UNIVERSITY
1536 Hewitt Avenue
St. Paul, MN 55104
(651)523-2941

HARVARD UNIVERSITY
Harvard Law School
Cambridge, MA 02138
(617)495-1000

HAWAII, UNIVERSITY OF
William S. Richardson School of
2515 Dole Street
Honolulu, HI 96822
(808)956-8636

HOFSTRA UNIVERSITY
121 Hofstra University
Hempstead, NY 11549-1210
(516)463-5858

HOUSTON, UNIVERSITY OF
4800 Calhoun
Entrance 19
Houston, TX 77004-6371
(713)743-2100

HOWARD UNIVERSITY
2900 Van Ness Street
Washington, DC 20008
(202)806-8021

IDAHO, UNIVERSITY OF
6th & Rayburn
Moscow, ID 83844-2321
(208)885-4977

ILLINOIS INSTITUTE OF
TECHNOLOGY
Chicago-Kent College of Law
565 West Adams Street
Chicago, IL 60661
(312)906-5000

ILLINOIS, UNIVERSITY OF
504 East Pennsylvania Avenue
Champaign, IL 61820
(217)333-0931

INDIANA UNIVERSITY -
BLOOMINGTON
211 S. Indiana Avenue
Bloomington, IN 47405
(812)855-7995

INDIANA UNIVERSITY -
INDIANAPOLIS
735 West New York Street
Indianapolis, IN 46202-5194
(317)274-8523

INTER AMERICAN UNIVERSITY
OF PUERTO RICO
P.O. Box 70351
San Juan, PR 00936-8351
(787)751-1912

IOWA, UNIVERSITY OF
Melrose and Byington
Iowa City, IA 52242-1113
(319)335-9034

JOHN MARSHALL
LAW SCHOOL
315 S. Plymouth Ct.
Chicago, IL 60604
(312)427-2737

JUDGE ADVOCATE
GENERAL'S SCHOOL
600 Massie Road
Charlottesville, VA 22903
(804)972-6300

KANSAS, UNIVERSITY OF
Green Hall
Lawrence, KS 66045
(785)864-4550

KENTUCKY, UNIVERSITY OF
209 Law Building
Lexington, KY 40506-0048
(606)257-1678

LEWIS AND CLARK COLLEGE
Northwestern School of Law
10015 S.W. Terwilliger Blvd.
Portland, OR 97219-7799
(503)768-6600

LOUISIANA STATE UNIVERSITY
Paul M. Hebert Law Center
210 Law Center
Baton Rouge, LA 70803
(504)388-8491

LOUISVILLE, UNIVERSITY OF
Louis D. Brandeis School of Law
Louisville, KY 40292
(502)852-6879

LOYOLA MARYMOUNT UNIVERSITY-LOS ANGELES
919 South Albany Street
Los Angeles, CA 90015
(213)736-1000

LOYOLA UNIVERSITY-CHICAGO
One East Pearson Street
Chicago, IL 60611
(312)915-7120

LOYOLA UNIVERSITY-NEW ORLEANS
7214 St. Charles Avenue
New Orleans, LA 70118
(504)861-5550

MAINE, UNIVERSITY OF
246 Deering Avenue
Portland, ME 04102
(207)780-4355

MARQUETTE UNIVERSITY
Sensenbrenner Hall
P.O. Box 1881
Milwaukee, WI 53201-1881
(414)288-7090

MARYLAND, UNIVERSITY OF
500 West Baltimore Street
Baltimore, MD 21201-1786
(410)706-3492

MCGEORGE SCHOOL OF LAW
University of the Pacific
5200 Fifth Avenue
Sacramento, CA 95817
(916)739-7105

MEMPHIS, UNIVERSITY OF
Cecil C. Humphreys School of Law
Campus Box 526513
Memphis, TN 39152-6513
(901)678-2421

MERCER UNIVERSITY
Walter F. George School of Law
1021 Georgia Avenue
Macon, GA 31207
(912)752-2601

MIAMI, UNIVERSITY OF
P.O. Box 248087
Coral Gables, FL 33124
(305)284-2394

MICHIGAN, UNIVERSITY OF
Hutchins Hall
625 South State Street
Ann Arbor, MI 48109-1215
(734)764-1358

MINNESOTA, UNIVERSITY OF
229 - 19th Ave S.
Minneapolis, MN 55455
(612)625-1000

MISSISSIPPI COLLEGE
151 East Griffith Street
Jackson, MS 39201
(601)925-7105

MISSISSIPPI, UNIVERSITY OF
Office of the Dean
Law Center
University, MS 38677
(601)232-6900

MISSOURI-COLUMBIA, UNIVERSITY OF
203 Hulston Hall
University of Missouri-Columbia
Columbia, MO 65211
(573)882-6487

MISSOURI-KANSAS CITY, UNIVERSITY OF
5100 Rockhill Road
Kansas City, MO 64110
(816)235-1644

MONTANA, UNIVERSITY OF
School of Law
Missoula, MT 59812
(406)243-4311

NEBRASKA, UNIVERSITY OF
P.O. Box 830902
Lincoln, NE 68583-0902
(402)472-2161

NEW ENGLAND SCHOOL OF LAW
154 Stuart Street
Boston, MA 02116
(617)451-0010

NEW MEXICO, UNIVERSITY OF
1117 Stanford, N.E.
Albuquerque, NM 87131-1431
(505)277-2146

NEW YORK LAW SCHOOL
57 Worth Street
New York, NY 10013-2960
(212)431-2100

NEW YORK UNIVERSITY
40 Washington Square South
New York, NY 10012
(212)998-6100

NORTH CAROLINA CENTRAL UNIVERSITY
1512 South Alston Avenue
Durham, NC 27707
(919)560-6333

NORTH CAROLINA, UNIVERSITY OF
Campus Box 3380
Van Hecke-Wettach Hall
Chapel Hill, NC 27599-3380
(919)962-5106

NORTH DAKOTA, UNIVERSITY OF
Centennial Drive
P.O. Box 9003
Grand Forks, ND 58202
(701)777-2104

NORTHEASTERN UNIVERSITY
400 Huntington Avenue
Boston, MA 02115
(617)373-5149

NORTHERN ILLINOIS UNIVERSITY
College of Law
DeKalb, IL 60115
(815)753-1420

NORTHERN KENTUCKY UNIVERSITY
Salmon P. Chase College of Law
Nunn Drive
Highland Heights, KY 41099
(606)572-5340

NORTHWESTERN UNIVERSITY
357 East Chicago Avenue
Chicago, IL 60611
(312)503-8462

NOTRE DAME, UNIVERSITY OF
P.O. Box R
Notre Dame, IN 46556
(219)631-6627

NOVA SOUTHEASTERN UNIVERSITY
Shepard Broad Law Center
3305 College Avenue
Fort Lauderdale, FL 33314-7721
(954)262-6100

OHIO NORTHERN UNIVERSITY
Pettit College of Law
525 S. Main Street
Ada, OH 45810-1599
(419)772-2205

OHIO STATE UNIVERSITY
55 W. 12th Avenue
Columbus, OH 43210
(614)292-2631

OKLAHOMA CITY UNIVERSITY
2501 North Blackwelder
Oklahoma City, OK 73106
(405)521-5354

OKLAHOMA, UNIVERSITY OF
300 Timberdell Road
Norman, OK 73019-5081
(405)325-4699

OREGON, UNIVERSITY OF
1221 University of Oregon
Eugene, OR 97403-1221
(541)346-3852

PACE UNIVERSITY
78 North Broadway
White Plains, NY 10603
(914)422-4210

PENNSYLVANIA STATE UNIVERSITY
The Dickinson School of Law
150 S. College Street
Carlisle, PA 17013-2899
(717)240-5000

PENNSYLVANIA, UNIVERSITY OF
3400 Chestnut Street
Philadelphia, PA 19104-6204
(215)898-7483

PEPPERDINE UNIVERSITY
24255 Pacific Coast Highway
Malibu, CA 90263
(310)456-4611

PITTSBURGH, UNIVERSITY OF
3900 Forbes Avenue
Pittsburgh, PA 15260
(412)648-1400

PONTIFICAL CATHOLIC UNIVERSITY OF P.R.
2250 Las Americas Avenue Suite
Ponce, PR 00717-0777
(787)841-2000

PUERTO RICO, UNIVERSITY OF
P.O. Box 23349
San Juan, PR 00931-3349
(787)764-2680

QUINNIPIAC COLLEGE
275 Mount Carmel Avenue
Hamden, CT 06518-1950
(203)287-3400

REGENT UNIVERSITY
1000 Regent University Drive
Virginia Beach, VA 23464
(757)226-4040

RICHMOND, UNIVERSITY OF
T.C. Williams School of Law
Richmond, VA 23173
(804)289-8740

ROGER WILLIAMS UNIVERSITY
Ralph R. Papitto School of Law
Ten Metacom Avenue
Bristol, RI 02809
(401)254-4500

RUTGERS UNIVERSITY-CAMDEN
217 North Fifth Street
Camden, NJ 08102-1203
(609)225-6102

RUTGERS UNIVERSITY-NEWARK
15 Washington Street
Newark, NJ 07102-3192
(973)353-5561

SAMFORD UNIVERSITY
800 Lakeshore Drive
Birmingham, AL 35229
(205)870-2400

SAN DIEGO, UNIVERSITY OF
5998 Alcala Park
San Diego, CA 92110-2492
(619)260-4527

SAN FRANCISCO, UNIVERSITY OF
2130 Fulton Street
San Francisco, CA 94117-1080
(415)422-6586

SANTA CLARA UNIVERSITY
500 El Camino Real
Santa Clara, CA 95053
(408)554-4767

SEATTLE UNIVERSITY
950 Broadway Plaza
Tacoma, WA 98402
(253)591-2273

SETON HALL UNIVERSITY
One Newark Center
Newark, NJ 07102
(973)642-8500

SOUTH CAROLINA, UNIVERSITY OF
Main and Greene Streets
Columbia, SC 29208
(803)777-6857

SOUTH DAKOTA, UNIVERSITY OF
414 E. Clark Street
Vermillion, SD 57069-2390
(605)677-5443

SOUTH TEXAS COLLEGE OF LAW
affiliated with Texas A&M
1303 San Jacinto Street
Houston, TX 77002-7000
(713)659-8040

SOUTHERN CALIFORNIA, UNIVERSITY OF
University Park
Los Angeles, CA 90089-0071
(213)740-7331

SOUTHERN ILLINOIS UNIVERSITY-CARBONDALE
Lesar Law Building
Carbondale, IL 62901-6804
(618)536-7711

SOUTHERN METHODIST UNIVERSITY
P.O. Box 750116
Dallas, TX 75275-0116
(214)768-2618

SOUTHERN UNIVERSITY
P. O. Box 9294
Baton Rouge, LA 70813
(225)771-2552

SOUTHWESTERN UNIVERSITY
675 South Westmoreland Avenue
Los Angeles, CA 90005-3992
(213)738-6717

ST. JOHN'S UNIVERSITY
8000 Utopia Parkway
Jamaica, NY 11439
(718)990-6600

ST. LOUIS UNIVERSITY
3700 Lindell Blvd.
St. Louis, MO 63108
(314)977-2766

ST. MARY'S UNIVERSITY
One Camino Santa Maria
San Antonio, TX 78228-8602
(210)436-3424

ST. THOMAS UNIVERSITY
16400 N.W. 32 Avenue
Miami, FL 33054
(305)623-2320

STANFORD UNIVERSITY
Crown Quadrangle
Stanford, CA 94305-8610
(650)723-4985

STATE UNIVERSITY OF NEW YORK AT BUFFALO
319 O'Brian Hall
North Campus
Buffalo, NY 14260
(716)645-2053

STETSON UNIVERSITY
1401 61st Street South
St. Petersburg, FL 33707
(727)562-7800

SUFFOLK UNIVERSITY
41 Temple Street
Boston, MA 02114-4280
(617)573-8155

SYRACUSE UNIVERSITY
College of Law
Syracuse, NY 13244-1030
(315)443-2524

TEMPLE UNIVERSITY
1719 North Broad Street
Philadelphia, PA 19122
(215)204-7861

TENNESSEE, UNIVERSITY OF
1505 W. Cumberland Ave.
Knoxville, TN 37996-1810
(423)974-4241

TEXAS, UNIVERSITY OF
727 E. Dean Keeton Street
Austin, TX 78705
(512)232-1120

TEXAS SOUTHERN UNIVERSITY
Thurgood Marshall School of Law
3100 Cleburne
Houston, TX 77004-3216
(713)313-1075

TEXAS TECH UNIVERSITY
1802 Hartford
Lubbock, TX 79409-0004
(806)742-3791

TEXAS WESLEYAN UNIVERSITY
1515 Commerce Street
Fort Worth, TX 76102
(817)212-4100

THOMAS JEFFERSON SCHOOL OF LAW
2121 San Diego Avenue
San Diego, CA 92110
(619)297-9700

THOMAS M. COOLEY LAW SCHOOL
217 South Capitol Avenue
P.O. Box 13038
Lansing, MI 48901
(517)371-5140

TOLEDO, UNIVERSITY OF
2801 West Bancroft
Toledo, OH 43606
(419)530-2882

TOURO COLLEGE
Jacob D. Fuchsberg Law Center
300 Nassau Road
Huntington, NY 11743
(516)421-2244

TULANE UNIVERSITY
6329 Freret Street
New Orleans, LA 70118-6231
(504)865-5939

TULSA, UNIVERSITY OF
3120 East Fourth Place
Tulsa, OK 74104
(918)631-2401

UTAH, UNIVERSITY OF
332 South 1400 East Front
Salt Lake City, UT 84112-0730
(801)581-6833

VALPARAISO UNIVERSITY
Valparaiso, IN 46383
(219)465-7829

VANDERBILT UNIVERSITY
21st Avenue South
Nashville, TN 37240
(615)322-2615

VERMONT LAW SCHOOL
Chelsea Street
P.O. Box 96
South Royalton, VT 05068-0096
(802)763-8303

VILLANOVA UNIVERSITY
299 North Spring Mill Road
Villanova, PA 19085-1682
(610)519-7000

VIRGINIA, UNIVERSITY OF
580 Massie Road
Charlottesville, VA 22903-1789
(804)924-7354

WAKE FOREST UNIVERSITY
P.O. Box 7206
Reynolda Station
Winston-Salem, NC 27109-7206
(336)758-5435

WASHBURN UNIVERSITY
1700 College Avenue
Topeka, KS 66621
(785)231-1010

WASHINGTON AND LEE UNIVERSITY
Sydney Lewis Hall
Lexington, VA 24450-0303
(540)463-8400

WASHINGTON UNIVERSITY
1 Brookings Drive
Campus Box 1120
St. Louis, MO 63130-4899
(314)935-6400

WASHINGTON, UNIVERSITY OF
1100 NE Campus Parkway
Seattle, WA 98105-6617
(206)543-4551

WAYNE STATE UNIVERSITY
468 Ferry Mall
Detroit, MI 48202
(313)577-3933

WEST VIRGINIA UNIVERSITY
P.O. Box 6130
Morgantown, WV 26506-6130
(304)293-3199

WESTERN NEW ENGLAND COLLEGE
1215 Wilbraham Road
Springfield, MA 01119
(413)782-1412

WESTERN STATE UNIVERSITY
1111 North State College Blvd.
Fullerton, CA 92831-3014
(714)738-1000

WHITTIER COLLEGE
3333 Harbor Boulevard
Costa Mesa, CA 92626
(714)444-4141

WIDENER UNIVERSITY
4601 Concord Pike
P.O. Box 7474
Wilmington, DE 19803-0474
(302)477-2100

WIDENER UNIVERSITY-HARRISBURG
3800 Vartan Way
P.O. Box 69382
Harrisburg, PA 17106-9382
(717)541-3900

WILLAMETTE UNIVERSITY
245 Winter St. SE
Salem, OR 97301-3922
(503)370-6282

WILLIAM AND MARY SCHOOL OF LAW
Marshall-Wythe School of Law
P.O. Box 8795
Williamsburg, VA 23187-8795
(757)221-3800

WILLIAM MITCHELL COLLEGE OF LAW
875 Summit Avenue
St. Paul, MN 55105-3076
(612)227-9171

WISCONSIN, UNIVERSITY OF
975 Bascom Mall
Madison, WI 53706-1399
(608)262-2240

WYOMING, UNIVERSITY OF
P.O. Box 3035
Laramie, WY 82071
(307)766-6416

YALE UNIVERSITY
P.O. Box 208215
New Haven, CT 06520-8215
(203)432-1660

YESHIVA UNIVERSITY
Benjamin N. Cardozo School of
55 Fifth Avenue
New York, NY 10003
(212)790-0200

The list below contains those schools that reported on their 1998 Annual Questionnaire that they enroll a significant number of students on a part-time basis. For the purpose of this list, any school reporting 30 or more part-time students was included. Please note, however, that many of these schools only do this in limited circumstances. Also, please note that many schools without a part-time program may permit an individual to take a lighter load in special circumstances. For specific information, please contact the school(s) directly.

AKRON, UNIVERSITY OF
C. Blake McDowell Law Center
ALBANY LAW SCHOOL
of Union University
AMERICAN UNIVERSITY
Washington College of Law
ARKANSAS, LITTLE ROCK, UNIVERSITY OF
School of Law
BALTIMORE, UNIVERSITY OF
School of Law
BROOKLYN
Law School
CALIFORNIA WESTERN
School of Law
CAPITAL UNIVERSITY
Law School
CATHOLIC UNIVERSITY OF AMERICA
Columbus School of Law
CHAPMAN UNIVERSITY
School of Law
CLEVELAND STATE UNIVERSITY
Cleveland-Marshall College of Law
CONNECTICUT, UNIVERSITY OF
School of Law
DENVER, UNIVERSITY OF
College of Law
DEPAUL UNIVERSITY
College of Law
DETROIT COLLEGE OF LAW
At Michigan State University
DETROIT MERCY, UNIVERSITY OF
School of Law
DUQUESNE UNIVERSITY
School of Law
FORDHAM UNIVERSITY
School of Law
GEORGE MASON UNIVERSITY
School of Law
GEORGE WASHINGTON UNIVERSITY
Law School
GEORGETOWN UNIVERSITY
Law Center
GEORGIA STATE UNIVERSITY
College of Law
GOLDEN GATE UNIVERSITY
School of Law
HOUSTON, UNIVERSITY OF
Law Center
ILLINOIS INSTITUTE OF TECHNOLOGY
Chicago-Kent College of Law
INDIANA UNIVERSITY - INDIANAPOLIS
School of Law
INTER AMERICAN UNIVERSITY OF PUERTO RICO
School of Law
JOHN MARSHALL
Law School
LEWIS AND CLARK COLLEGE
Northwestern School of Law
LOUISVILLE, UNIVERSITY OF
Louis D. Brandeis School of Law
LOYOLA MARYMOUNT UNIVERSITY-LOS ANGELES
Law School
LOYOLA UNIVERSITY-CHICAGO
School of Law
LOYOLA UNIVERSITY-NEW ORLEANS
School of Law
MARQUETTE UNIVERSITY
Law School
MARYLAND, UNIVERSITY OF
School of Law
MCGEORGE SCHOOL OF LAW
University of the Pacific
MEMPHIS, UNIVERSITY OF
Cecil C. Humphreys School of Law

MIAMI, UNIVERSITY OF
School of Law
MISSOURI-KANSAS CITY, UNIVERSITY OF
School of Law
NEW ENGLAND
School of Law
NEW YORK
Law School
NORTH CAROLINA CENTRAL UNIVERSITY
School of Law
NORTHERN KENTUCKY UNIVERSITY
Salmon P. Chase College of Law
NOVA SOUTHEASTERN UNIVERSITY
Shepard Broad Law Center
OKLAHOMA CITY UNIVERSITY
Law Center
PACE UNIVERSITY
School of Law
PONTIFICAL CATHOLIC UNIVERSITY OF P.R.
School of Law
PUERTO RICO, UNIVERSITY OF
School of Law
QUINNIPIAC COLLEGE
School of Law
REGENT UNIVERSITY
School of Law
ROGER WILLIAMS UNIVERSITY
Ralph R. Papitto School of Law
RUTGERS UNIVERSITY-CAMDEN
School of Law
RUTGERS UNIVERSITY-NEWARK
School of Law
SAN DIEGO, UNIVERSITY OF
School of Law
SAN FRANCISCO, UNIVERSITY OF
School of Law
SANTA CLARA UNIVERSITY
School of Law
SEATTLE UNIVERSITY
School of Law
SETON HALL UNIVERSITY
School of Law
SOUTH TEXAS COLLEGE OF LAW
affiliated with Texas A&M University
SOUTHWESTERN UNIVERSITY
School of Law
ST. JOHN'S UNIVERSITY
School of Law
ST. LOUIS UNIVERSITY
School of Law
SUFFOLK UNIVERSITY
Law School
TEMPLE UNIVERSITY
School of Law
TEXAS WESLEYAN UNIVERSITY
School of Law
THOMAS JEFFERSON
School of Law
THOMAS M. COOLEY
Law School
TOLEDO, UNIVERSITY OF
College of Law
TOURO COLLEGE
Jacob D. Fuchsberg Law Center
TULSA, UNIVERSITY OF
College of Law
VALPARAISO UNIVERSITY
School of Law
WAYNE STATE UNIVERSITY
Law School
WESTERN NEW ENGLAND
College of Law
WESTERN STATE UNIVERSITY
College of Law
WHITTIER COLLEGE
School of Law
WIDENER UNIVERSITY
School of Law
WIDENER UNIVERSITY-HARRISBURG
School of Law
WILLIAM MITCHELL
College of Law
WISCONSIN, UNIVERSITY OF
Law School

The list below contains those schools that reported on their 1998 Annual Questionnaire that they enroll students at times ***in addition*** *to the fall. Please note, however, that many of these schools only do this in limited circumstances. For specific information, please contact the school(s) directly.*

BAYLOR UNIVERSITY
School of Law
CALIFORNIA WESTERN
School of Law
CITY UNIVERSITY OF NEW YORK
School of Law at Queens College
DRAKE UNIVERSITY
Law School
FLORIDA, UNIVERSITY OF
College of Law
FRANKLIN PIERCE
Law Center
GOLDEN GATE UNIVERSITY
School of Law
HOUSTON, UNIVERSITY OF
Law Center
INDIANA UNIVERSITY - BLOOMINGTON
School of Law
INDIANA UNIVERSITY - INDIANAPOLIS
School of Law
IOWA, UNIVERSITY OF
College of Law
JOHN MARSHALL
Law School
KANSAS, UNIVERSITY OF
School of Law
LOYOLA UNIVERSITY-CHICAGO
School of Law
MICHIGAN, UNIVERSITY OF
School of Law
MISSISSIPPI, UNIVERSITY OF
School of Law
PONTIFICAL CATHOLIC UNIVERSITY OF P.R.
School of Law
QUINNIPIAC COLLEGE
School of Law
RICHMOND, UNIVERSITY OF
T.C. Williams School of Law
SEATTLE UNIVERSITY
School of Law
SOUTH TEXAS COLLEGE OF LAW
affiliated with Texas A&M University
ST. JOHN'S UNIVERSITY
School of Law
STETSON UNIVERSITY
College of Law
TEXAS TECH UNIVERSITY
School of Law
THOMAS JEFFERSON
School of Law
TULSA, UNIVERSITY OF
College of Law
WASHBURN UNIVERSITY
School of Law
WASHINGTON, UNIVERSITY OF
School of Law
WESTERN STATE UNIVERSITY
College of Law
WHITTIER COLLEGE
School of Law
WILLIAM MITCHELL
College of Law
YESHIVA UNIVERSITY
Benjamin N. Cardozo School of Law

Other Organizations

Association of American Law Schools (AALS)

Founded in 1900, the nonprofit AALS has grown to 162 member law schools. The purpose of the Association is "the improvement of the legal profession through legal education." To carry out this mission, the AALS serves as the learned society for law teachers. It facilitates excellence in legal education through the establishment and enforcement of membership requirements for its members and by providing workshops, conferences, a quarterly newsletter and other publications, including the AALS Directory of Law Teachers, to law teachers and law schools. In addition, the AALS is legal education's principal representative to the federal government and to other national higher education organizations and learned societies.

Association of American Law Schools
1201 Connecticut Avenue, NW
Suite 800
Washington, DC 20036-2605
(202) 296-8851
http://www.aals.org

National Conference of Bar Examiners (NCBE)

The nonprofit NCBE was formed in 1931. Its mission is to "work with other institutions to develop, maintain, and apply reasonable and uniform standards of education and character for eligibility for admission to the practice of law." NCBE assists bar authorities in the various jurisdictions by providing uniform, high quality standardized examinations for testing applicants for admission to the practice of law, disseminating information concerning admission standards and practices and conducting educational programs for members and staffs of bar authorities. NCBE also provides character and fitness investigative services to the various bar authorities. NCBE tests include the Multistate Bar Examination (MBE), the Multistate Essay Examination (MEE), the Multistate Performance Test (MPT), and the Multistate Professional Responsibility Examination (MPRE). In conjunction with the ABA, NCBE publishes the Comprehensive Guide to Bar Admission Requirements containing bar admission requirements in all U.S. jurisdictions.

National Conference of Bar Examiners
Suite 1025
333 North Michigan Avenue
Chicago, Illinois 60601-4001
(312) 641-0963
Fax: (312) 641-2052
TDD: (312) 641-0709
http://www.ncbex.org

Law School Admission Council (LSAC)

LSAC is a nonprofit corporation whose members are 194 U.S. and Canadian law schools. It is best known as the sponsor of the Law School Admission Test (LSAT). Its other services include the Law School Data Assembly Service, which summarizes applicants' prior academic work and distributes that information to the law schools to which each candidate applies; Law School Forums--recruitment fairs, free-of-charge to applicants, held in seven American cities each year; and a host of outreach programs targeted to minorities underrepresented in the legal profession. For additional information about LSAC, please see chapter four or visit their website.

Law School Admission Council
Box 2000
Newtown, PA 18940-0998
(215) 968-1001
http://www.LSAC.org

National Association for Law Placement (NALP)

Since its founding in 1971, the National Association for Law Placement (NALP) has served the legal community as a nonprofit organization dedicated to meeting the needs of the participants in the legal employment process. NALP provides information, coordination and standards that pertain to the hiring of law students and attorneys, and fosters fair and informed decision-making in legal career planning, recruiting and employment.

Virtually all of the ABA accredited law schools and approximately 850 legal employers, including most of the largest law firms, corporations, public interest and government agencies are NALP members.

NALP is widely respected for its ability to provide essential research data on legal recruiting and employment. NALP's research spans more than two decades and is extensively referenced throughout the legal community. Additionally, NALP publishes definitive print and electronic resources designed to support clear and accurate communication between and education of all participants in the legal hiring process.

National Association for Law Placement
1666 Connecticut Avenue, Suite 325
Washington, DC 20009-1039
(202) 667-1666
http://www.nalp.org

Chapter Eighteen

Websites

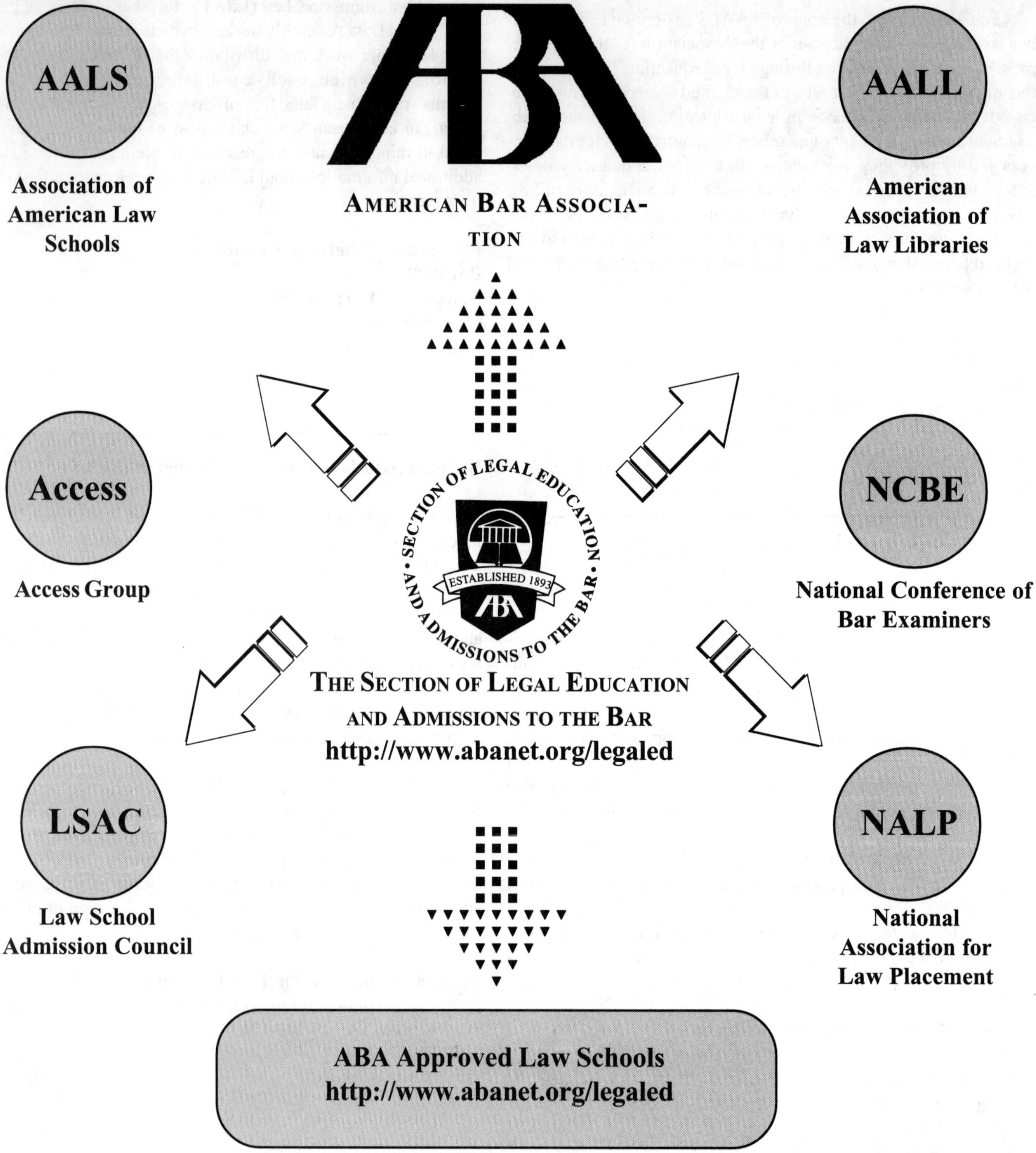

2000 Edition

Give Us Your Thoughts

In an effort to improve future editions of this book, the ABA is actively seeking constructive criticism. Please take the time to complete this questionnaire, and return to Kurt Snyder, Office of the Consultant on Legal Education, 550 West North Street, Suite 349, Indianapolis, IN 46202. Thank You!

Name:____

Phone:__________________________, E-mail:____________________________

Gender:_________, Race:_________, Age:_________

Where did you earn your undergraduate degree?____________________________

What law school will you attend?___________________________________

Please rate the following. One is the lowest and five is the highest.

For example,

NOT Very Helpful	Slightly Helpful	Helpful	More Than Helpful	Very Helpful
1	2	3	4	5

Introduction:

1 2 3 4 5

Chapter One, ABA's Role in the Accreditation Process:

1 2 3 4 5

Chapter Two, Pro Bono Publico:

1 2 3 4 5

Chapter Three, Prelaw Preparation:

1 2 3 4 5

Chapter Four, Admissions Process:

1 2 3 4 5

Chapter Five, Finance & Debt Management:

1 2 3 4 5

Continued on Next Page

Cut on Dotted Line

Chapter Six, Career Outlook:

1 2 3 4 5

Chapter Seven, Bar Admissions:

1 2 3 4 5

Chapter Eight, Values of the Profession:

1 2 3 4 5

Chapter Ten, About the Data:

1 2 3 4 5

Chapter Eleven, Comparison Charts:

1 2 3 4 5

Chapter Twelve, School Profile, two page spread:

1 2 3 4 5

Chapter Fourteen, Legal Education Statistics:

1 2 3 4 5

Chapter Sixteen, Selected Statements:

1 2 3 4 5

How would you rate the value of this book?

1 2 3 4 5

How did you hear about this book?

___

How can we make the book better, especially on the schools' two page spread?

___

___

___

___

___

General Comments:

___

___

___

___

___

Cut on Dotted Line